Religion
for a New
Generation

D1141920

Religion

for a New

Generation

Second Edition

Edited by

Jacob Needleman

A. K. Bierman

James A. Gould

Macmillan Publishing Co., Inc.
New York

Macmillan Publishing Co., Inc.
866 Third Avenue, New York, New York 10022

Collier Macmillan Canada, Ltd.

Library of Congress Cataloging in Publication Data

Needleman, Jacob, comp.
  Religion for a new generation.

  Includes bibliographies.
    1. Religion—Addresses, essays, lectures. I. Bier-
man, Arthur Kalmer, (date)   joint comp. II. Gould,
James A., (date)   joint comp. III. Title.
BL50.N39 1977   200'.8   76-10540
ISBN 0-02-385990-3

Printing:1 2 3 4 5 6 7 8   Year:7 8 9 0 1 2 3

Preface to the Second Edition

The success of the first edition of this text has confirmed our vision of its aims. And the gratifying number of criticisms and suggestions we have received from all parts of the country has challenged us to produce an extensively revised book that reflects the ever-widening interest in religion throughout the contemporary world.

We say "interest in religion," but that phrase hardly does justice to the hunger that nearly everyone feels for a new understanding of the realities of religion. Not only has there been no abatement in the stream of new religious writings, but whole areas of thought which have hitherto been considered separate from the current "spiritual revolution" have begun to bring themselves into relationship with it. It is as though a deeply felt question, asked by our young people, has finally called forth a mature response from the intellectual community of America. The older generation has begun to speak to the new generation. At the same time, there has appeared among the latter an appreciation of the issues and formulations that have guided the religious thought of those who have gone before them.

While retaining the aims of our first edition, the present text therefore seeks to move further in two directions: (1) indicating the newly envisioned relevance of religious questions in heretofore "secular" areas of concern and (2) presenting traditional material and issues which now have new life in them as a direct result of the "spiritual revolution." An example of the first concern is our inclusion of a section devoted to the problem of money and the meaning of life. The second direction is highlighted by Chapter Six, which presents the classical arguments for the existence of God, an area which we intentionally omitted in the first edition because in the minds of many people these formulations had grown threadbare and cliché-ridden.

Even more than in our first edition, the aim of this book is to *introduce* religion. It is meant not only for students who have never taken an academic course in the subject and who are considering it as a major course of study, but also—if we may say so—for any student in any academic setting who thinks of his college years as a time to begin thinking seriously and carefully about the most important questions that can ever concern a human being.

J. N.

A. K. B.

J. A. G.

Contents

Three

Religion and the Current Crisis

The Crisis of Community

Fulfillment, Work, and Money

Four
HUMANITY IN SEARCH OF VIRTUE

Five

MYSTICISM AND SPIRITUAL DISCIPLINE

Six

THE EXISTENCE OF GOD

Seven

THE INTERPRETATION OF DEATH

One

The Spiritual Revolution Takes Root

Introduction

The "spiritual revolution," as it has been called, began as a distinct phenomenon in San Francisco in the early 1960s. Zen Buddhism had already become
respectable throughout the Western world, owing in large measure to the
writings of D. T. Suzuki. On a popular level, the writers of the Beat generation
had fastened on certain dramatic aspects of Zen and other Eastern religions
and used them in their outcry against the value system of contemporary
America. Against this very mixed intellectual background, there arose among
the young a fascination with and then a dependence on psychedelic drugs, along
with a profound reaction against the Vietnam war, technology, and almost
every other aspect of modern society, from food to sexual mores to social
injustice and organized religion.

Suddenly, God was no longer "dead." Now free to ask simple, fundamental questions of life, the younger generation groped for metaphysical
answers within systems of thought as disconnected as possible from the religion
of their parents. But however awkward, naive, or impatient this groping, it
was nevertheless answered by the arrival in America, particularly in California,
of numerous other Eastern teachings and spiritual leaders. In addition to
providing what the younger generation felt it wanted from religion, these
teachings also tapped into the widespread interest in the occult that has always
existed among us in this country. The result was that Eastern religious ideas
now began to enter into the stream of American thought with unprecedented
speed.

A sure sign that this movement is more than a youthful fad is the fact that
lately many scientists—the chief representatives of modern culture—have

begun to look to the teachings of Eastern and Western mystics for a new vision of the cosmos. Speaking to this development, the opening essay by **Jacob Needleman** sounds a warning about the way powerful new spiritual ideas and methods are often adopted in order to mask rather than face our ignorance about ourselves. The suggestion is offered that awakening to one's illusions is always as painful as it is precious and is easily squandered by the haste to "know" without really *knowing*.

The next selections offer a spectrum of responses to the spiritual revolution by four thoughtful Christians. **Aelred Graham** sees the influence of the Oriental religions as a possible ally in Christianity's struggle to speak to the present "postsecular" world, where both conventional religion and scientific materialism are being cast aside by men and women who are religious in a new way. Supporting this claim, **Bede Griffiths** explains how a study of the philosophy and meditational practices of the Hindu tradition can reawaken the discipline of contemplative experience in a Christianity that has neglected its own practical techniques of self-knowledge.

Arguing against the possible interaction between Christianity and Eastern religions, **Jean Daniélou** vigorously denounces any cultivation of the interior life which even slightly compromises the idea that obedience to Christ is the sole means of human salvation. His is an extraordinarily bold statement of commitment to the uniqueness of Christianity among the world religions, and one which is bound to provoke serious debate.

The problem of the occult is dealt with by **Richard Woods**, who provides the historical background for the Church's hostility to magic and occultism and places the whole issue in terms of mankind's desire for an impossible security in a world which is actually "the realm of death." Speaking from this point of view, he outlines the dangers both of occultism and of a narrow refusal by the Church to understand the human need which lies at its root.

In the concluding selection, by the British psychiatrist **A. C. Robin Skynner**, we are confronted with one of the most urgent and subtle problems in the contemporary spiritual drama: In the personal crises of life, does one turn to therapy or religion? This issue has loomed large in recent years as many psychiatrists have begun to adopt the ideas and methods of Eastern religions and as many spiritual leaders from the East and West have adapted certain aspects of the traditional teachings to conform with the language of modern psychology. What is the line that separates psychotherapy from the spiritual path?

J. N.

Modern Man Between Two Dreams

Jacob Needleman

Jacob Needleman (1934–   ) teaches philosophy and comparative religion at San Francisco State University. His most recent book, *A Sense of the Cosmos*, is a study of contemporary efforts to relate modern science to traditional teachings of Eastern and Western traditions. He is also author of *The New Religions* and is general editor of the Dutton Metaphysical Library.

For several centuries Western civilization has operated under the assumption that man can understand the universe without understanding himself. But having turned the available energy of our minds toward the external world, we now find ourselves more perplexed and anxious than ever in front of a reality that simply will not yield to our hopes and desires. Our technological achievements are great, but we see they have not brought understanding.

Now—fitfully, and with great uncertainty—it seems we are being called back from the impulse to believe we can stride into nature with our mind pointed outward like an unsheathed sword. Both within and outside of the sciences a new sense of the unknown has appeared. The unknown is ourselves.

New teachings about man and his place in the cosmos are entering our culture from the Orient and the ancient worlds. These teachings from India, Tibet, China, and the Middle East; these ideas from the priests of Pharaonic Egypt and from the alchemists and mystics of antiquity now exist among us like the whisperings of another reality. And the discoveries of science about the organic interconnection of all things from the atomic nucleus to the unfathomed psyche of man to the inconceivable entities of cosmic space, in a like manner invite us to something greater than the search for additional facts and explanations.

How will we respond to this invitation from the unknown? That is the question I wish to open in this book. I do not think it is a simple question, nor that the answer will necessarily be comforting. We may find that while something is now possible for us that has not been possible since the onset of the scientific revolution, something as well is demanded of us which is equally unprecedented. Some new effort within ourselves, some change of attitude so revolutionary and so uncompromising that it may very simply prove to be beyond us.

More and more one hears it said that the new religions from the East, with their "technologies of inwardness" and their encompassing metaphysical doctrines, are precisely what our epoch needs in order to humanize the thrust of modern

Source: Jacob Needleman, *A Sense of the Cosmos* (New York, 1975), pp. 1–9. Copyright © 1975 by Jacob Needleman. Reprinted by permission of Doubleday & Company, Inc.

science. The so-called "antiscience" movement among many of our young people is in part an expression of this feeling. The claim is that through the psychological development offered by the Eastern religions modern man can transform those moral and psychological flaws which have made his use of scientific discoveries so destructive. The goal of mastering ourselves to the extent that we have "mastered" nature now seems a real possibility to an increasing number of people.

But perhaps we are only dreaming. What is required of us personally, privately, if we are not simply to replace a dream of outer progress with a dream of inner progress?

There is an oft-repeated saying of the ancient Greeks: "Whom the gods wish to destroy they first make mad." But have we understood this saying? What does it mean to be driven mad by the "gods"? The medieval alchemists said it more clearly: "Mother Nature sings a lullaby before she slays."

The lullaby of scientific progress, the dream of manipulating nature to suit our egoistic purposes, is ended. An increasing number of us, both scientists and nonscientists, pause rather longer and more quietly in front of the numerous breakthroughs in the sciences. And we are rather more sensitive to the ripple of new emotion that passes through us in front of the unknown. *In front of the unknown:* that means, when explanations break down and for a moment I am suspended between dreams. It is a moment of relative awakening.

But what is the new song that is now being heard by so many of us? Is it only another lullaby?

The premise of this book is that Western civilization as a whole now finds itself between dreams. In the true meaning of the word, it is a time of *crisis*—with all that implies of both extraordinary danger and opportunity. For there is nothing to guarantee that we will be able to remain long enough or deeply enough in front of the unknown, a psychological state which the great traditional *paths* have always recognized as sacred. In that fleeting state between dreams, which is called "despair" in some Western teachings and "self-questioning" in Eastern traditions, a man is said to be able to receive the truth, both about nature and his own possible role in the universal order. Throughout the ages, the hidden psychological methods of the ancient traditions have operated to guide people in that state between dreams, where a man can begin the long and difficult work of self-investigation leading to transformation.

Science and the New Mysticism

Recently, I received a letter from a young physics professor asking me to advise him about changing his career in the direction of the study of spiritual traditions. "The most technologically advanced society in the world," he wrote, "is now the site of a rebirth of spiritual practice." In this development, he envisioned the possibility of a "humanization of science and technology and a transformation of religion." There followed five closely typed pages in which he carefully outlined all the issues involved and the themes he wished to explore. The Eastern religions, he said, had showed him that spiritual tradition itself can be viewed as a science and a technology, a kind of "internal science, in which the materials and apparatus are simply oneself." He went on to speak of the need to develop a deeper understanding of the symbolic modes of communication found in ancient traditions and he then put the question of whether modern science itself could be transformed into a spiritual path, what the Hindu tradition calls a "sadhana." He cited our contemporary visionary critics of modern science who urge "the return of science to its origins in Hermetic philosophy and alchemy or who foresee a new Pythagorean science." He proposed the creation of a discipline leading to a more direct and personal experience of scientific knowledge through which modern men could attain to a new consciousness of meaning in nature and human life.

Then, at the end of this long, carefully formulated letter, he added a hastily composed note in his own handwriting: "I am searching for something for myself. I love science and I don't want to give it up. But it is not enough. I am searching for knowledge that is enough."

While reading the letter, I was mentally formulating replies to the various points he made. But the concluding words, which he had probably added just before putting the letter in an envelope, stopped me. At the last minute, he had dared to expose his real hope and it jolted me like the sudden appearance of another level of truth. It caused me to remember something that the writing of this book has brought me to again and again: *The real unknown is always an emotional unknown.* It is not merely a question of new, exciting facts about nature, or comprehensive new paradigms of explanation; nor is it a matter of new religions. The real question of the moment between dreams is whether we can bear the vibration of this new feeling of the unknown which carries with it the taste of a different quality of intelligence, but which at the same time utterly exposes all our illusions about ourselves. *We awaken to darkness.* This phrase has often come back to me during the writing of this book—along with the question: Do I fear the darkness more than I love the awakening?

Weeks went by before I mailed a reply to the letter. I tried to be academically proper and to give him information about careers in the fields of comparative religion and philosophy. But above all I wanted to respond to what he showed me at the end of his letter. I found myself settling for a few awkward words in a postscript:

Dear Dr. A——: Could it be that we are all looking in a wrong way for a knowledge greater than what science has offered? I wonder how you see this. Like you, I am surrounded by new religions, fragments of ancient spiritual traditions and new psychological methods for producing changes within ourselves. Like you, I hear people calling for a new synthesis of science and religion and I find myself dreaming of the transformation of human nature spoken of in the great teachings of the past. But, for myself, I begin to see how fragile and impermanent this wish for new knowledge actually is. I'm sure this is true of most of us, for there is very little in the conditions of modern life to support this wish and to help it ripen into a merciless self-interrogation. Is there, do you think, a way of approaching the truths of both modern science and the ancient traditions that fully takes into account this weakness in ourselves and all that is connected with it of impatience, fear and self-suggestibility?

Months went by during which I forgot about Dr. A. Then one morning I received another letter from him, informing me that he and a group of colleagues had organized a society called The New Pythagoreans. Their aim, he said, was to establish a community of scientists and spiritual leaders "to rekindle the vision of Pythagoras who brought to ancient Greece and to the Western world its first great fusion of spiritual discipline and the mathematical science of nature." Their project had already attracted the attention of several teachers from the Orient who were now living in America—a well-known swami, a Buddhist and a Sufi[1] master. Their membership included physicists, biologists, a famous astronomer, a psychiatrist, a neurologist and representatives from the fields of philosophy, history and anthropology. Most with extremely solid names. Would I be interested in joining?

Attached to the letter was a brief, scholarly essay by the historian who had been named as one of the group's charter members. In it he outlined the background and subsequent influence of Pythagoreanism throughout the centuries, laying particular stress on the body of writings known as the *Hermetica*, which appeared in Egypt under the Roman Empire several hundred years after the birth of Christ. I had long been intrigued by the Hermetic tradition, though I had never thought of connecting it unequivocally with the origins of modern science. As in the reputed teachings of Pythagoras in ancient Greece, the Hermetic writings develop a concept of man as a mirror of the cosmic order, a microcosm. And throughout these ancient texts there are also hints of a personal discipline which is said to enable a man to experience in himself the laws of a divinely ordered universe. The natural world is spoken of as the "book of God"; and the fully developed human being is understood to be the integration of all the purposes and energies of cosmic nature.

I had always surmised that the Hermetic teachings had once offered themselves as more than a mere system of belief, and that connected with them there had perhaps once been a key to the primordial science of awakening. But I had always assumed that this key was lost long ago, and that in more recent centuries all attempts to revive practical Hermeticism were mainly self-deceptions.

Not so, according to the article. The Hermetic tradition, so I read, had not died out after the Middle Ages (during which period it concealed itself under the symbolism of alchemy). In the fifteenth century the original Hermetic texts were translated for the first time into Latin and gradually entered the broad mainstream of European thought. "Eventually displacing the world view of Christianity, the teachings of the Hermeticists about the universe and the nature of man formed the basis of the scientific revolution. Modern science is actually the child of Western esotericism." The essay went on to list some of the ideas which were transmitted to Renaissance man through the Hermeticists: for example, the idea of an infinite universe and the idea of the human body as a great mechanism. Even the modern conception of the experimental method was traced back to the Hermetic teaching that "man has the power to know through direct experience all the secrets of the cosmos which are hidden in the microcosm."

All this struck an extremely responsive chord in me. The idea of the New Pythagoreans was that early on in the scientific era the exploration of nature became wrongly separated from the quest for self-knowledge. And this point corresponded almost exactly with one of the central issues of the present book—which at that time I had almost completed. As the reader will see, this book is directly concerned with

---

[1] Sufism, the esoteric or inner teachings of the Islamic tradition.

the way certain ideas, which are meant to help men discover the truth for themselves, become instead mere tranquilizers or even forms of psychological poison.

Yet although the program of the New Pythagoreans interested me very much, although it seemed a logical expression of the present hunger for a new kind of knowledge, something caused me to back away. It was not an intellectual judgment on my part, just as I cannot justify solely through intellectual reasons my hesitancy in front of most current attempts to correct the inadequacies of modern science through the enthusiastic adoption of new metaphysical ideas or spiritual techniques.

It is the same feeling—the impulse of plunging into a new dream—that I personally associate with that extraordinary period of transition between the Middle Ages and the modern, scientific era. I am not a professional historian, but it seems to me that then, as now, in the period we call "The Renaissance," Western man found himself between two dreams: behind him the dream of a Christianized world, before him the dream of the conquest of nature. In that period between dreams, something new entered into the life of man. Yet not all new things are automatically beneficial.

The expression of the teachings of Jesus which we call "medieval Christianity" was breaking down. The scholastic theologians had systematized Christianity to such a point that little remained in it to call man into the state of total self-questioning. The passions, needs and aspirations of human beings could not be contained by scholastic thought; and the universe of Christian theology could no longer serve as the mansion within which general human life could proceed in all its vibration and color. At the same time, the extraordinary interaction of forces—spirituality, political power, the accumulation and abandonment of wealth and property—that had nourished the creative development of the monasteries was now dissolving. As for the organized Church, it won its battles too well. For centuries it had been a vital force precisely because it had constantly to rediscover its role in the interface between monastic asceticism on the one hand and the worldly claims of the secular state on the other. The life-giving interplay of these three forces—monastery, Church and state—came to an end as the Church both absorbed the monasteries into its organizational structure and also allowed itself to become too much of a secular power. Organized Christianity ceased to be an influence that could touch all sides of human existence—the life of the body, the emotions of family and social life and the aspirations of the mind.

Against this background, new ideas about man and the universe began to enter into the bloodstream of Western civilization. The result—at least, the result which we are concerned with here—was modern science.

Where did these ideas come from? And were they intentionally fed into the vortex of European life in the same way and from the same *kind* of source that had originally transmitted the teachings of Jesus into the life of the Western world? Or did these new ideas exert the mixed sort of influence they have eventually had because Western man could not bear to remain in the state between dreams?

I hope the above does not give a wrong impression. I do not claim to know where new, awakening ideas come from or how they need to be transmitted so as to serve as a positive influence on the life of a civilization. I do say, however, that this is a crucial question. And that it is not being spoken about very much at the present moment when so many people are turning to teachings that challenge the world view of science. We are so accustomed to believe that great truths need only to be put before us and they will have a beneficent effect. But I wonder if there is not something exceedingly naive in this assumption, some naive estimation of our un-aided ability to *be* what we know, some failure to realize how swift and subtle is the passage from seeing the darkness to dreaming of light.

In any event, the great traditions make no such easy assumption about man's ability to digest the truth. From one point of view, in fact, sacred tradition can even be defined as the science of transmitting truth by degrees so that it can enter cor-rectly and harmoniously into the human psyche. To this end, a tradition both with-holds and reveals at the same time. Transmission of truth is always understood in this way. There is always a "secret." Because there is always that in man, in our-selves, which seeks only to believe and explain and to manipulate, rather than under-stand. We are calling that part of ourselves "the dreamer," but it has many names in the traditions, chief among which is "the ego." We shall have much occasion to speak of this in the following chapters as we explore the fate that overtakes living ideas when they fall into the hands of the dreamer.

There is always a secret, an unknown, because there are always these two sides of human nature which the traditions tell us must be kept separate and distinct. Each requires a different "food" in order to live and serve its purpose. Therefore, the great traditions speak to the ego in one way and to the other part of ourselves, which we have not yet named, in another way. At the same time, an authentic tradition offers itself as a guide by which to help a man distinguish these two sides of himself so that he may recognize which part of himself is active from moment to moment and so that he may see how he wrongly gives to one part that which be-longs to the other. I am speaking here about ideas which a teacher formulates differently according to the state of consciousness of those to whom he is speaking.

This book is therefore an effort to see modern science as an aspect of ourselves —much as a person would study his own mind, his own life, in order to learn precisely what sort of help he needs amid the colossal breakdown of his world view, and in order that he might become sensitive to that help in its real and not illusory forms.

Contemplative Christianity

Aelred Graham

Aelred Graham (1907–   ) is a Benedictine monk of Ampleforth Abbey, England. A lifelong Catholic, he has been deeply interested in the teachings of the Eastern religions and in the possibility of a vitalizing exchange between Christianity and Buddhism. His other works include *Zen Catholicism*, *Conversations Christian and Buddhist*, and *The End of Religion*.

"At the present moment there are two things about the Christian religion which must be obvious to every percipient person," observed Matthew Arnold in the reign of Queen Victoria. "One, that men cannot do without it; the other that they cannot do with it as it is." That was a century ago. Today even the most unperceptive churchman may concede that there is something wrong with Christianity as it is. But now we are obliged to go further and admit that there are plenty of people who can do without it altogether. This was true of the Victorian age, as Arnold would doubtless have agreed; for our contemporaries it has become a truism. Apart from the hundreds of millions in Asia who have always done without it, Christianity as a religion for the western world has begun to present itself as but one option among many.

The means hardly exist for examining this situation statistically. Head counting, in terms of baptisms, communicants and attendance at church, gives little indication of what is really going on inside people's minds. Many of the Christian churches, by virtue of their holdings in real estate, constitute enormous vested interests—for which self-perservation takes high priority. Church officials, with few exceptions, see themselves as committed upholders of an historic tradition, not as concerned expositors of religious truth in the light of all the available evidence. However inevitable this state of affairs may be, given that signs of stability are commonly looked for in religion as elsewhere, it helps to explain why in a changing and revolutionary world, the Church's message, while still resolutely proclaimed, is increasingly losing its appeal.

At its beginnings Christianity had about it a sense of urgency; it was a life and death affair; it really mattered whether you believed or not. Even when the early apocalyptic expectations of some brave new world remained unfulfilled, and the Son of Man did not appear on the clouds of heaven, the Church had sufficient vitality to overcome the widespread disappointment. Faith in the risen Christ and the belief that each person now held within him- or herself the seeds of eternal life

Source: Aelred Graham, *Contemplative Christianity* (New York, 1974), pp. 1–3, 19–22, 31–35. Copyright © 1974 by Aelred Graham. Reprinted by permission of The Seabury Press, Inc., and A. R. Mowbray & Co. Ltd.

more than compensated for the as yet unrealised promise of a new world order. Besides, Christians, despite persecution, were able to adjust to the world as it actually existed. The Gospel stories, so it was believed, portrayed not fables and legends, but events that had taken place at a known place and time. The saving death and resurrection of Jesus, unlike such seemingly corresponding pagan myths as those of Orpheus, Osiris and Attis, could be attested by witnesses. Belief in them was so important as to be worth dying for. The kind of rational thought that had sapped the credibility of the Greek and Roman gods was now turned to the service of the Church. Men like Justin, Clement of Alexandria and Origen, by treating the unpalatable passages in the Old Testament as allegories, and universalising the person and message of Jesus, in Platonic and Stoic terms, made Christianity intellectually respectable.

Religion as a Form of Knowledge

Gnosticism—that is, Christian belief as a form of esoteric knowledge—came to be officially repudiated by the Church, in favour of a faith based on trust and the acceptance of ecclesiastical authority. But the deviations of the gnostics, with respect to the Incarnation, could not hide from the more thoughtful the fact that genuine religion has at its root a personal experience, an existential rebirth that cleanses the mind. The Pauline epistles (e.g., 2 Corinthians 4.6, Philippians 1.9) and the Fourth Gospel (e.g., John 8.28, 17.3) were there to show that the religion of Jesus demanded more than blind faith; it was in fact a form of *gnosis*, however liable to misunderstanding the word itself might be. The initiated, that is, baptised, Christian had a *knowledge* that outsiders apparently did not have. What that knowledge was, or more precisely, how it can be reinterpreted in terms of today, it is largely the purpose of the present essay to explore.

St. John's gospel presents Jesus as the manifestation of ultimate truth, the truth which God is. The majority of persons interested in Jesus, however, have shown little concern to investigate questions of ultimate truth. The role of the Church, understandably enough, has been to articulate statements about him which can be considered "true," and to devise forms of worship and a code of conduct appropriate to what is believed. To preserve intact, as an unchanging deposit, "the faith which was once for all delivered to the saints," was the chief objective of the early ecclesiastical councils. Right belief, signified by a declared adherence to approved verbal formulas, eventually became the test of whether or not you were a Christian.

. . .

From Criticism to Free Religious Choice

An honest admission of the facts by churchmen is indispensable if attempts at Christian renewal are to carry conviction. It is hard not to agree, in general terms, with the verdict of F. C. Happold who has written so much, wisely and well, in support of genuine Christianity:

If one surveys the part secularism and humanism have played since the Renaissance, one cannot but feel that it has been a beneficent one. It has been, not the Christian Church, but the scientists and humanists who have led the advance in the march towards toleration and free enquiry and towards social justice and a better life for the common man. In spite of its saints, mystics, and martyrs, the history of the Christian Church is a sorry one. It is far too much the story of intolerance, persecution and bigotry, of inquisitions, torture and burnings, of "images" of God which had little resemblance to the loving Father or our Lord Jesus Christ, or to the inner Christ of St. Paul. One can sympathize with the couplet in Martin Skinner's satirical poem:

> And God in welcome smiled from Buddha's face,
> Though Calvin in Geneva preached of grace.[1]

Two further continuing events were to frustrate the efforts of those who still strove to present the case for Christianity in the form of dogmatic pronouncements. The first was the development of a critical approach to history, particularly as this applied to the contents of the Bible. The second was the all-pervasive effects of scientific technology and the theories of the structure of the universe on which that technology was based. Close study of the biblical material revealed that there was comparatively little to be found in the Old Testament that could be regarded as historically reliable, or even ethically edifying. Today Jewish and Christian scholars claim that these writings retain their importance, not as accurate records of what actually happened, but on account of their theological meaning. Whether that meaning emerges in every case from an impartial study of the text, or has been imposed upon it in virtue of scholarly or religious preconceptions, is a question that is still under review.

As for the New Testament, it soon became apparent that the gospels were based on earlier written sources and that their authors were not eyewitnesses of the events they record. Our present texts could not have been composed earlier than a generation, perhaps two generations, after the lifetime of Jesus. The Pauline epistles, besides being earlier than the gospels, were not originally written for general publication; their purpose was to convey to various local churches St. Paul's understanding of the significance of the crucifixion and resurrection of Jesus, in whose Galilean and Judean ministry Paul had curiously little interest. In the light of these and other related findings, the conclusion was hard to escape that the Jesus of history, as distinct from the Christ of faith, may have been very different from the picture of him presented by popular piety.

If Christianity is to survive the challenge of a scientific age, it can hardly do so by basing its claims on memories of the past or expectations for the future. Variations on the theme of the quest for the historical Jesus, or exercises in a recently devised "theology of hope," may illustrate how far Catholic thought has sunk from the days when its exponents could have talked on equal terms with a Plato or Aristotle. Understandably the official Church cannot initiate the task of re-thinking her message from its foundations, lest she appear to be modifying the belief system adhered to by the unreflecting Christian majority. What Church authority can do, however—and, happily, appears to be doing—is to recognise the problems and how urgent is the need for their informed discussion.

[1] F. G. Happold, *Religious Faith and Twentieth-Century Man*, Penguin Books, 1966, p. 29.

Christian sociologists tell us that today's is not a secularist but rather a post-secularist world. The average man and woman is not less religious than in past ages; he or she is religious with a difference. The questions now are not: What has been revealed? What is the content of "the faith once delivered to the saints"? But—does it matter? And assuming that it does, what does it mean? Considered within its conceptual framework, every religion may be regarded as the basic symbol system of its respective adherents. Conversely, a person's basic symbol system is for all practical purposes his or her religion. Thus a multiplicity of religious choices present themselves. Besides a fragmented Christianity (for which "ecumenism" is another name), Judaism in its various forms, Hinduism, Buddhism, Sufism and other accepted claimants, we have agnosticism, secular humanism, nature worship, Marxism and psycho-analysis, to name but a few of the refuges in which people seek a solution to life's problems—or salvation, to use the old-fashioned language of religion.

Such a conclusion need not prove as daunting to a Christian's will to believe as it might appear. What is implied may turn out to be no more than a call to look a little deeper, to open the mind to a wider perspective. Over thirty years ago the Hindu scholar Sarvepalli Radhakrishnan observed: "The indifference to organised religions is the product not so much of growing secularism as of deepening spirituality. Scrupulous sensitiveness in our search for truth is making it difficult for us to accept doubtful authority or half-heard traditions. If genuine religious belief has become for many a phenomenon of the past, it is because religions confound eternal truth with temporal facts, metaphysics with history. They have become largely a traffic with the past."[2] These words, besides suggesting a clue to much that is to follow here, seem as pertinent today as when they were first written.

. . .

Of greater consequence than the Church's internal debates is the Christian's attitude to the two revolutions—one of thought, the other of action—which are going on in the world at the present time. Together they could combine to clarify, at least by negation, the goal of the religious quest. The first revolution results from the long-term impact of the work of Marx and Freud. For Marx, whose effects may be the more enduring, religion was the product of a defective understanding that prevented people from coming to grips with the evils of their society. For Freud, religion was an illusion or projection that impaired self-knowledge and rendered people incapable of dealing with their own problems. It would be idle to pretend that a measure of truth does not underlie these judgements. The second revolution, that of action, which is largely Marxian inspired, may yet bring about the nuclear holocaust. It is the egalitarian movement towards the classless society, from three worlds to only one: which is a part of Christianity's message, however strongly it may be resisted by Christians both corporately and individually.

As is to be expected, these prospects are much more readily faced by the younger generation than by their elders. A characteristic of many young Catholics in their attitude towards the institutional Church is not scepticism or hostility, merely boredom and apathy. What she has to offer is *déjà vu*; they have heard it all before. There are few signs of anticlericalism; what is called for is a different kind of clergy.

[2] S. Radhakrishnan, *Eastern Religions and Western Thought*, Oxford University Press, 1940, pp. 58–59.

Not authority figures with a sense of status, but simple Christians who are open and available and ready to serve. The time may be approaching when priests in their ministerial capacity will become rather like doctors and lawyers—not taking the initiative but ready to answer calls for their professional services: to celebrate the Eucharist or administer the sacraments. Their leadership will be in response to demands and opportunities; its success will depend on such obvious factors as knowledge, energy, tact, and above all on their capacity to be wisely compassionate. Always, especially with the young, they will be teachers, but again, more by what they are than what they say. How agreeably the Church would be transformed, and how much closer to the spirit of the Gospel, if her leaders would take to heart the 2,500 year-old wisdom of the Chinese sage, the legendary Lao Tzu: "As for the best leaders, the people do not notice their existence. The next best, the people honour and praise. The next, the people fear; and the next, the people hate. If you have no faith people will have no faith in you, and you must resort to oaths. When the best leader's work is done the people say: We did it ourselves."

Our eyes should be on the young: for they are the teachable ones, as they are often unconscious teachers themselves. Many of them already have an understanding that this is one world. Often the young people of Europe and America are nearer to the youth of Africa and Asia than to their own parents and teachers. They are in no need of being told that if there is only one God there can be only one human community. Not that they have any desire to see what are obvious cultural differences swamped by an international "great Church." Community living must first be practised on a small scale, so arranged as to allow each of its members at times to be alone, fulfilling a person's twofold need: to belong and to be on one's own. The interest now is in loosely structured communities, as open and free as possible, their few necessary rules being reached on a basis of mutual agreement, with honesty and truth and loving-kindness as their ideals. In this context, but perhaps only here, wisdom requires that we should all be conformists; for then we shall be conforming to "that perfect law, which is the law of freedom" (James 1.25).

The importance of the religions originating in India is becoming increasingly widely recognised in the West—though probably more so in America and on the European continent than in England, where our native insularity leaves us in the grip of theological inertia. The still weighty influence of the Anglican establishment combined with an unenterprising Roman Catholicism may largely account for this state of affairs. Serious students as well as hippies take themselves off to India, Nepal and points further east while the Christian clergy look on, defensive or vaguely anxious. The Churches are now so insecure that they have an understandable reluctance to expose themselves to what might prove a radical challenge to accepted modes of thought. Courses on comparative religion available in the universities, instead of being handled by representative insiders, are not seldom offered by the religiously indifferent or by conventional Christians, for whom the study of Hinduism and Buddhism is clearly a subordinate interest. When books on these subjects attract attention, it is usually ill-informed or nervously hostile. Even the *Times Literary Supplement,* to say nothing of the Catholic journals, apparently cannot find reviewers able to evaluate such work unpolemically, with sympathy and sufficient knowledge.

Yet many convinced Christians are now learning the techniques of yoga or practising meditation in a form derived from Zen Buddhism. They have discovered, with Rudolph Otto, what is no longer open to dispute, that "a lofty and advanced theism and not a 'heathenish polytheism' is the basis upon which the mystic speculation of India rises." Numbers of the younger generation, while dedicating their lives wholeheartedly to Christ in monasteries and convents and less structured religious communities, are finding that the traditional round of public worship and private prayer are somehow not enough to generate the degree of alert responsiveness demanded by their own religion in today's world. Can these innovations, and more important, the philosophy which underlies them, be assimilated by Christianity without changing its very nature? Here the answer may prove of greater consequence than reaching finality in many of the current discussions within the Church. For these are generally focused on ways and means of making human society more genuinely Christian; whereas those who turn to eastern religions are often seeking to resolve a more basic problem: whether Christianity itself, at least as it is commonly proclaimed, provides adequate answers to the fundamental religious questions. Widespread clerical ignorance of what attracts so many young people to the religions of the East could have serious results: chief among them being either the abandonment of religion altogether, or the delusion that Christians can only find elsewhere what is actually latent within their own tradition.

Eastern Religious Experience

Bede Griffiths

A(lan) Bede Griffiths (1906–   ) is a Benedictine monk at the Kurisumala Ashram, Vaghamon, India. This ashram belongs to the Syrian Rite of the Roman Catholic Church and Syriac is used in prayers at the monastery. Among his major works are *The Golden String* (an autobiography), *Christ in India: Essays Toward a Hindu-Christian Dialogue*, and *Vedanta and Christian Faith*.

About five centuries before the birth of Christ the Eastern world awoke to a profound experience of God, or rather of an absolute, infinite, transcendent Reality,

Source: Bede Griffiths, "Eastern Religious Experience," *Monastic Studies*, no. 9 (Autumn 1972), pp. 153–160. Reprinted by permission of the Mount Saviour Monastry, Pine City, N.Y. 14871, publishers.

which was known variously as Brahman or Atman or Nirvana or Tao, which was destined to shape the religious life of the East for all succeeding centuries. In its depth and intensity this experience can only be compared to the experience of God in Israel, which took place at about the same time, and was destined to shape the religious life not only of Israel but also of Christianity and Islam. These two religious traditions, the Oriental and the Semitic, have often appeared to be in violent opposition with one another, but a deeper study reveals that they are essentially complementary, and it is one of the principal tasks of the Church at the present time to come to an understanding of this oriental tradition and to integrate its religious insights into its own tradition.

In order to deal adequately with this subject it would be necessary to study the experience of God, or the Absolute, not only in Hinduism but also in Buddhism and Taoism, but as there is a basic similarity in this experience and the time at our disposal is strictly limited, we will confine our attention to Hinduism, and within Hinduism to the classical system of Yoga, in which the nature of this experience and the method by which it can be realised has been reduced to a fine art. It may be added that this system of Yoga is basically the same in Buddhism and in Taoism, so that what is said of Hinduism will have its bearing on the whole oriental tradition.

The Hindu experience of God which took shape in the Upanishads was essentially the discovery that beneath all the external forms of nature there is one, absolute, infinite, transcendent Reality, which was known as the Brahman. At the same time it was discovered that beneath all the phenomena of human consciousness, beyond not only sense but also thought, there is the one, absolute transcendent Self, the Atman; and this Self, the ground of all consciousness, it was declared, is one with the Brahman, the ground of Being. This is expressed in the great saying of the Upanishads: Thou art That—Thou, the Self in its transcendent ground, art one with That, the transcendent ground of the universe. Now this affirmation is not a matter of philosophical speculation, but of religious experience. The Self is known not by abstraction or by any philosophical method but by direct experience beyond sense and reason in the ground or center of the soul. The soul knows itself by direct intuition in its own ground as one with the ground of all being, and this experience of Being in pure consciousness is one of absolute bliss.

Such in its barest outline is the original Hindu experience of God as *saccidananda*, Being–Knowledge–Bliss, which underlies all subsequent Hindu religion. It is, one may say, an experience of God, the one transcendent Reality, in his immanence in nature and the soul. Now this experience was the result of certain ascetic practices on the part of the "seers" or rishis, who withdrew into solitude to meditate in the forest, and in the course of time a whole science of the art of meditation was developed which came to be known as Yoga. The word Yoga is derived from the same root as the English "yoke" and its essential meaning is to "unite." Yoga was seen as the art of "unification" of human nature, first of the human being in himself, then, as the deeper meaning of this was realised, of the human being with the divine, and finally of the human being with the cosmos—of the microcosm within the macrocosm. Ultimately Yoga is seen as an attempt to restore man to his original state of Paradise, in which man is found in harmony with himself, with nature and with God.

In its earlier stages this unification was seen in terms of a break with our present "fallen" state of subjection to the body and the material world. There has to be a "death" to the present state of "sin" and "ignorance" and a rebirth to a new state, in which man transcends the limitations of this world and attains immortality. In the Yoga system of Patanjali this is conceived in terms of the separation of Purusha, who is pure Spirit, or Consciousness, from Prakriti, the principle of change and becoming, which underlies the whole world of nature. The end of Yoga is defined as *citta vritti nirodha*, the "cessation of the movements of the mind." The purpose of Yoga is thus to break the movement of thought which is derived from "nature" and to bring the mind to rest, so that the soul may discover its own depth of spiritual awareness. The first movement of Yoga is therefore toward a separation of the mind from the body and the senses, so that it rests in pure tranquillity in its own spiritual depth, liberated from the body and the world of change and decay.

There is a tendency in all oriental thought to rest content with this kind of separation from the world and to seek a state of pure transcendence in which the soul remains untouched by matter or time in absolute self-awareness. But this tendency has throughout history been corrected by another movement of thought, which seeks to relate man positively both to nature and to God. The decisive moment in this respect for Hinduism came with the Bhagavad Gita. The fundamental purpose of the Gita is to teach that man can reach the supreme state not only by an ascetic withdrawal from the world but also by the path of "works," or Karma Yoga. If the householder, living his life in the world, offers all the actions of his life as a "sacrifice," not seeking the "fruit" of works but surrendering it to God, then he can reach the same state of perfection as the ascetic who renounces the world. The essence of this state is "detachment." It consists not so much in a withdrawal from the body and the senses as from the "ego." It is the ego with its appetites and passions and desires, attached to its own will and seeking its own selfish interests, which is the real enemy of the soul. When this attachment to the ego has been withdrawn and the soul surrendered to God, then it reaches perfect tranquillity and is "established in wisdom" and is one with Brahman.

The ideal of the Gita is therefore not renunciation of action in order to reach a state of pure contemplation, but rather the acceptance of one's duty in a spirit of detachment, offering every action to God as a sacrifice. By this, it is held, the soul is no longer subject to "nature," but is subject to the higher Self, the Atman, and acts freely and spontaneously from this inner principle of Being. But in the Bhagavad Gita this inner principle, this Self, is seen not merely as the ground of Being and of Consciousness, but as a personal being, as God. It is at this point that a genuine theism begins to emerge in Hinduism. The Supreme Self, the Brahman, is recognised as the "highest Person," the Lord, who sustains the universe and rules it by his providence. He is an object of love and worship and he himself declares that he "loves" his worshippers. Thus whereas in the Yoga of Patanjali the personal God is of little importance and is conceived merely as a means to Self-realisation, in the Bhagavad Gita he takes the highest place and devotion to him (bhakti) is held to be the supreme way to enlightenment and salvation.

In this new perspective of Bhakti Yoga the goal of life is no longer separation from the world and the flesh, but surrender to the will of a personal God. The perfect yogi is not one who is absorbed in solitary contemplation and has passed beyond the limits of this world, but one who has reached personal fulfilment in relation to others. He is "fearless and pure in heart, steadfast in the exercise of wisdom, open-handed and restrained, performing sacrifice, intent on studying Holy Writ, ascetic and upright, hurting none, truthful, free from anger, renouncing all, at peace, averse to calumny, compassionate to all beings, free from greed, gentle, modest, never fickle, patient, enduring, pure, not treacherous nor arrogant."

There is finally in the Gita another element which further transforms the conception of Yoga, that is the idea of grace. Whereas Yoga had originally been an ascetic discipline, leading through the control of the body and of the mind to a state of pure contemplation, in which human effort was practically everything and the action of God was negligible, now it is the grace of God which is of supreme importance. "Let him then do all manner of works," says Krishna, "putting his trust in Me; for by my grace he will attain to the eternal changeless state." In the course of time this idea of grace was to be consistently developed, until the total surrender of the soul to God, by which he does everything and the soul has only to surrender itself passively into his hands, became one of the main themes of Hindu spirituality.

Thus the idea of a personal God, whose providence extends over all the world, and who delivers souls from sin and ignorance by his grace so as to bring them to share in his own beatitude, enters into the main current of Hindu thought. At the same time this God is believed to manifest himself to the world by his "incarnation" in the form of Krishna, in order to restore "righteousness" or "dharma." It is true that neither Krishna nor Rama, who is considered to be another "incarnation" of God, is fully human. They are both legendary heroes of epic poems, and the emphasis is on their divine nature, which tends to swallow up the human. But once the idea of an "incarnation" of God, appearing in a human form, had entered, it was inevitable that the emphasis on human values would grow. This we can see in the development of Tantrism which took place in about the sixth century after Christ.

The basis of Tantrism is a sacramental view of the universe. Whereas in the early stages of Yoga the purpose had been to separate Purusha from Prakriti, Spirit from Nature, now it is Nature herself, the Shakti, or feminine Power of God, which is conceived as the agent of deliverance, and the body is the sphere of its activity. It must be remembered that even in the Yoga of Patanjali, asana and pranayama, the position of the body and the control of the breath, had always been essential elements in the practice of Yoga. But in Hatha Yoga, as it is called, this discipline of the body becomes all-important. It is through the body that deliverance is sought and the final goal is the transformation of the body, so that it becomes a spiritual or "diamond" body. Hatha Yoga is often considered merely as a system of physical exercises aiming at the health and discipline of the body, or else as a method of obtaining extraordinary "powers," such as levitation or walking over water or being able to be buried alive, all of which are variously attested. But in reality it has a much deeper purpose than this. Its aim is nothing less than the transformation of the body by the Spirit. In its most developed form, known as Kundalini Yoga, the divine power is conceived as coiled up like a serpent at the base of the spine. This power, or shakti, has to be led through the various "chakras," of psychic centers of the body, from the base of the spine to the top of the head. When this is achieved, then shakti, the feminine power of nature, is believed to unite with Siva, the masculine power of Spirit or Consciousness, and a total transformation of the human being takes place. This is not only a physical but also a psychological transformation, so that both body and soul are re-integrated in a new mode of existence, in which they participate in the divine life and consciousness.

When we come to ask what is the bearing of this oriental doctrine and practice on our Western life and thought, I do not think that it can be doubted that its implications are immense. Our Western methods of prayer and meditation, based on the teaching of the fathers, which have come down to us through the Rule of St. Benedict, have a deep supernatural foundation, but their natural basis, that is, the physical and psychological basis, is extremely weak. Scarcely any attention has been paid to the position of the body in prayer, which is of fundamental importance. The method of Yoga teaches one to sit in a position for prayer which is both "firm and pleasant." That is to say, it must be so firm that one is able to sit for three hours without moving, and yet without experiencing any inconvenience. This firm and steady position of the body must be accompanied by slow and regular breathing. This not only serves to stabilize the body, but also gives control over the mind. It produces a "harmony" of body and soul, which is the best possible disposition for prayer and meditation.

The science of Yoga not only teaches a minute control over the movements of the body, it also provides a profound psychological analysis of the movements of the mind. In the course of meditation it is necessary to trace the thoughts back to their original source. Every movement on the surface of the mind has to be controlled and led back to its original ground in the depths of the soul. This is akin to the Eastern Orthodox method of prayer, which seeks to "lead the thoughts from the head to the heart and keep them there"; and it must be said that this Eastern method of the "prayer of the heart" is the nearest approach in the West to the oriental way of prayer. But though the Christian analysis of moral motives and their control is perhaps deeper than any other, its analysis of mental processes is much less profound.

However, it is not in the sphere of physical or psychological analysis and control that the greatest value of oriental spirituality is to be found. It is in the penetration of the mind beyond the physical and psychological level to the ground of the Spirit, to the ultimate encounter with God, that the East has most to teach us. We have in the West a wonderful tradition of contemplative and mystical prayer, but it has been reached almost entirely by reliance on divine grace, and no precise method has been elaborated to enable the soul to reach this state. In the East every effort has been made from the earliest times to pass beyond the level of the senses and the reason and to reach the center or ground of the soul, where it is in direct contact with the ultimate source of Being. This is done by learning to still the mind, to allow all movements of the discursive mind to cease by concentrating the mind on a single point, so that it becomes totally recollected in itself. A great assistance in this is the use of *japa*, the repetition of the divine name, as in the prayer of Jesus, which has the effect both of quieting the discursive mind and focusing it on the transcendent Reality. When this stage is reached the soul is gathered into itself without distraction and is freed from all the impediments of the mind and the senses.

It is in this state of total recollection, both mind and body being in harmony and the spirit at rest in itself, that the soul is perfectly open to the action of God. At this point there is a transition from the natural to the supernatural order. Something intervenes which is not of this world. Whether it is the Chinese Tao, the Buddhist Nirvana, or the Hindu Atman, there is an experience of absolute transcendence, so much so that no words can express what then takes place. This is the point at which in Christian prayer the action of the Holy Spirit intervenes. All these techniques of Yoga, physical, psychological and spiritual, should be seen as a means of preparation for the free action of the Holy Spirit which has to take possession of the soul. According to the teaching of St. Thomas, in the state of contemplation it is the gifts of the Holy Spirit which take control. The soul is passive to the action of the Spirit, *patiens divina*, as he says. This is the state for which all oriental methods of prayer and meditation are a preparation. The soul has to become completely passive to the divine action, so that we can say: "I live no longer, it is Christ who lives in me."

Now this state of contemplation, understood in the sense that body and soul are brought under the control of the Holy Spirit, so that we act not of ourselves but by the action of the Spirit of Christ in us, is the end or goal of all monastic life, and in fact of all Christian life. But the monk is one who has dedicated his life to the realisation of this goal, so that nothing else is by comparison of any consideration. In our quest for this goal we have to join with our brothers in the oriental monastic tradition who are engaged in a similar quest. In the world today young people are everywhere seeking a new understanding and a new experience of God, the infinite Reality. Many of them are now going to Hindu ashrams and Buddhist monasteries, where they can learn methods of meditation and of control of mind and body, which they believe can lead them to this goal of "God-realisation." A Christian monastery should surely be a place where this "God-consciousness" can be found. But if this is to take place we need to learn all that the oriental tradition can teach us of methods of prayer and discipline and contemplation. We are living at a moment in history when the Church is for the first time beginning a serious encounter with this oriental tradition, a moment which may be as decisive in the history of the Church as the encounter with the Greek philosophical and spiritual tradition. But since the oriental tradition is essentially a mystical tradition, a tradition which seeks not an abstract, theoretical knowledge of God but a direct experience of the divine reality in the depths of the soul, it is surely in the monastic order, dedicated from its beginnings to the search for God, that this meeting with the oriental tradition should primarily take place. For this we need to open ourselves fully to what the Holy Spirit is saying to us through the religions of the East.

Christianity as the Transformation of Religions

Jean Daniélou

Jean Cardinal Daniélou (1905–   ) is professor of primitive Christianity at the Institute Catholique in Paris and is one of the leading Roman Catholic theologians of the twentieth century.

In making a study of the great non-Christian religions—Hinduism, Islamism, Buddhism—one finds at the same time a problem which cannot be avoided, that of the confrontation between these religions and Christianity. It is this decisive question that we should like to take up here. We do not intend to set forth Christianity as it is in itself, but to see how we can best represent to ourselves its relation to the other religions.

The existence of Hindu speculation on three divinities or on the symbolism of the cross, for example, raises for us the question of the possible relation of these doctrines to the Christian Trinity or to the cross of Jesus Christ. The good we derive from reading a certain Hindu or Moslem mystic makes us think carefully about the specific character of the Christian mystics and, at times, we might be tempted to say with Simone Weil: "In fact, the mystics of almost all religious traditions resemble one another, nearly to the point of identity" (*Letters to a Religious*, p. 49).

The two temptations which lie in wait here for the Christian, that of disdain and that of syncretism, are both dangerous and difficult to overcome. It is accordingly necessary to delineate the problem carefully and, while doing justice to the values of the pagan religions, to see how Christianity goes beyond them.

The first trait which characterizes Christianity is that it is faith in an event, that of the Incarnation and Resurrection of Christ. This event constitutes an intervention of God in history which radically changes the human condition and is an absolute novelty. Now this distinguishes Christianity completely from all the other religions. To reduce it, as René Guénon does, to merely one of the forms of the primitive tradition, is precisely to empty it of its original element. The great non-Christian religions affirm the existence of an eternal world opposed to the world of time. They know nothing about an intervention of the eternal in time which gives time consistency and transforms it into history.

This intervention constitutes a thenceforth irrevocable promotion, an irreversible acquisition, so that man shall nevermore be able to turn back. Nothing will be able to separate the union in Jesus Christ of the divine nature and human nature.

Source: Jean Daniélou, "The Transcendence of Christianity," Chap. 9 of *Introduction to the Great Religions* (Notre Dame, 1964), pp. 149–159. Reprinted by permission of Fides Publishers, Inc.

From that time forward, there is a past and a future in the complete sense of those words. The world becomes organized into a history of which the divine interventions form the decisive acts. From the Creation to the Resurrection of Jesus Christ, passing through the election of Abraham, the Christian Revelation is that of a sacred history, the history of the "*mirabilia Dei*," the "marvelous deeds of God." The Bible is the documentation of this history. And it is remarkable that, alone of all the sacred Books, that of the Christians is a history and not an exposition of doctrines.

This history does not consist merely of ancient events. The New Testament is continued among us in the sacraments of the Church. The Christian is someone who is aware of living at the heart of sacred history, in a world in which God never ceases to act, to intervene, to perform His admirable actions, those which are fulfilled in the conversion and sanctification of hearts. That is the real history, more real than that of empires or inventions, a history in which the incorruptible Body of Christ is fashioned mysteriously through the activity of supernatural charity.

This history appears as constituting a plan ordered to an end, which is the glorification of God and the sanctification of man. It is accomplished in Jesus Christ. In Him, Creation achieved its goal, the world became successful. In this sense, He is the "novissimus Adam," ever the newest man. It is a characteristic feature of the Christian view of the world that no new event shall ever bring us anything as important as Jesus Christ; thus, the concept of some religion of the future, with Christianity as but a stage leading to it, is excluded. One does not go beyond Jesus Christ.

Nevertheless, while the order of things instituted in Jesus Christ is the final one, it involves interior growth. The Incarnation started it. But it awaits its fulfilment. This fulfilment will be the Parousia, the last event in the history of salvation. It will be characterized by the reverberation throughout the entire cosmos of the Resurrection of Jesus Christ, which heretofore has produced its effects only in the world of souls. And so Christianity, even after the Incarnation, remains an eschatology. It is the expectation of an ultimate intervention by God taking up His work again in order to bring it to its final conclusion.

We have said that Christianity was faith in an intervention by God in the world, in Jesus Christ. Now we come to a second affirmation, namely, that only this action of God's can save man, that is, that there is no salvation outside of Jesus Christ. This is what is overlooked by a position, derived from a kind of syncretism, which believes that the mystiques of all religions "meet one another even to identity." The breadth of this view seduces certain minds, which contrast it with Christian intransigence. But, in affirming that the mystiques of all religions are similar, it is saying in effect that what saves is the ascetical effort at detachment and union with God, and not the efficacy of the Cross in Jesus Christ. Once again, we are faced with a radical opposition.

What we are saying here should not be misunderstood. In no way is it a question of deprecating the examples of interior life and of detachment which we find in non-Christian religions. China, along with the doctrines of Confucius, has brought us some admirable rules of wisdom for relations among men. India offers us the example of a people who have always seen in asceticism and contemplation the highest ideal. Nor can one read its masters, from the author of the Bhaghavad Gita to Aurobindo, without experiencing the feeling of the unreality of worldly goods and of the sovereign reality of the invisible world. It is understandable that, in our modern Western world, which is concerned only with harnessing the energies of the cosmos, and which has absorbed from Marxism the illusion that man can be transformed by changing his material living conditions, the wisdom of India attracts souls thirsting for silence and the interior life.

But the fact remains that this assumes that man is able to reach God by his own powers. Christianity must categorically deny this, for two reasons. The first is the reality of original sin. This consists in a separation between man and God, which man cannot abolish by himself. It is not enough, therefore, to say that man alienated himself by turning toward the exterior world, and that he has only to turn aside from the life of the body to discover the pure spirituality which is his very being. For Christianity, it is not the body which is the principle of sin, but the whole man, soul and body, is the captive of evil and God alone can liberate him from this captivity, through grace.

The second reason is that the Christian God is absolutely inaccessible. He alone can, therefore, introduce man to this participation in His nature which supernatural life is. For Hinduism, in fact, or neo-Platonism, the soul is divine by nature, and it only needs to move away from what is alien to it in order to find God by finding itself. But this concept assumes that there is no radical distinction between the uncreated God and the created spirit. The mystique of India presupposes a certain pantheism. On the other hand, the first article of Christian faith is the doctrine of the Creator-God, that is, the radical distinction between God and man. Accordingly, God alone is able to raise man to this participation in Him which is the supernatural life, the apex of which is the mystical life. It is inaccessible to any human asceticism.

The fundamental reversal of perspectives is clear. For syncretism, the saved are the interior souls, regardless of the religion to which they may belong. For Christianity, the saved are those who believe, regardless of their level of interior life. A little child, a worker weighed down by his labors, if they believe, are superior to the greatest ascetics. "We are not great religious personalities," as Guardini put it so well, "we are servants of the Word." Christ had already said that, while St. John the Baptist might be "the greatest among the sons of men, yet the least of the sons of the kingdom is greater than he." It is possible that there are in the world some great religious personalities outside Christianity; it may even happen that at a given time, the greatest religious personalities will be found outside Christianity. This is of no consequence. What does matter, is obedience to the words of Jesus Christ.

In this light, the difference between non-Christian mystiques and the Christian mystique appears. For the former, union with God is the goal of an asceticism through which the soul, stripping itself of what is alien to it, discovers its pure essence, which is God Himself. The emphasis will therefore be placed on ascetical techniques: exercises of recollection, unification of the soul, etc. It happens that Christian mystics make use of these methods. But they are always secondary, and they are never sufficient. The Christian God is, in fact, a living and transcendent God whom no technique could ever reach. He communicates Himself freely, when and as He wishes. The mystical experience is not conditioned upon any technique.

Thus, the grace of God strikes Paul enroute to Damascus, enters the soul of Marie of the Incarnation rolling casks on the Loire docks. It has no other source than the sovereign liberty of the divine love. It is not so much psychological exercises which dispose the soul to receive it as it is the religious attitudes which render the soul pleasing to God.

Up to now, we have stressed primarily Christianity's nature as a divine fact. But its transcendence is also apparent on the level of doctrines. This fact is disregarded by a third type of syncretism which believes it can find the main Christian dogmas, the Trinity, the Redemption, etc., in other religions. Thus, there are a number of comparisons the superficiality of which has been demonstrated many times and which no serious mind should retain, but which continue to be spread, sowing some uncertainty in the minds of many of our contemporaries, which dilutes the faith. It is astonishing that Simone Weil, otherwise gifted with a very sharp critical sense, should have yielded to this temptation. In her *Letter to a Religious*, she repeats a large share of these slogans.

Thus, she compares the words of Christ: "I am the true vine," to the role of the vine in the cult of Dionysos (p. 21). But it has been established that we are dealing here with two different themes: the Palestinian theme of the vine as the figure of the people of God (Isaias 5 : 1), and the Greek theme in which the vine symbolizes immortality, in connection with drunkenness. The maternity of the Virgin is compared to the mother goddesses of antiquity. Yet it is certain that the cult of the Virgin in Christianity stems from the historical role of Mary in the plan of salvation, and not from a sublimation of feminity, as in the religions of nature. The death of Christ on the Cross is compared to the crucifixion of the soul of the world in Plato's *Timeus* (p. 23). It is clear, however, that the role of the Cross in Christianity derives from the gibbet on which Jesus was sacrificed, which was in the form of a T. In no way does it come from the symbolism of the four dimensions which is found in various religions. The Christian Trinity is compared to the Greek triads (p. 27) and the Hindu triads (p. 33). But it is certain that, far from proceeding from a dialectical requirement, the Trinity constitutes a stumbling block as far as reason is concerned, for it is not a question of a primordial unity and its manifestations, but of Three Persons Who subsist eternally in the unity of one nature.

I cannot take more than a word here to indicate the essential contrast for each of these points. It has often happened that Christianity has utilized in its liturgy symbols borrowed from the religions of nature. Thus, in the third century A.D., Hippolyte of Rome gave the cross a cosmic symbolism. The language of the pagan mysteries was employed for the sacraments beginning in the fourth century. The catacomb paintings show us the vine as a symbol of immortality. And in our own time, Father Monchanin proposes to designate the Trinity by means of the sacred formula *saccidânanda*, which describes the Hindu triad. But those are secondary developments and cultural adaptations. Insofar as their origins are concerned, the Christian dogmas are a new revelation.

Does this mean that the natural religions have not attained certain truths concerning God? Such a statement would be inaccurate. St. Paul himself teaches that "since the creation of the world, the invisible perfections of God are known through visible things." The non-Christian religions have been able to grasp that which human reason left to itself is capable of discovering, that is, God's exterior, His existence and His perfections as they are manifest through His action in the world.

But there is something no reason has ever been able to suspect, a threshold no foot has ever crossed, a darkness where no one enters by stealth: it is the mystery of the inner life of God. The depths of the Trinity are absolutely inaccessible to man and only the Son of God has been able to introduce man thereto: "No one has ever seen God. But the only Son, who is in the bosom of the Father, he has made him known to us." We have reached the heart of what constitutes the irreducible originality of Christianity, namely, the fact that the Son of God, having come among us, has revealed to us these two truths, which are closely joined to one another: the presence of this mysterious life of love in God called the Trinity, and our own calling, in Him and through Him, to participate eternally in this life. It is summed up in one person, the person of Jesus Christ, God made man, in Whom can be found all that we must know. The religions of nature—and this is what is valuable about them—testify to man's movement toward God; Christianity is the movement of God Who, in Jesus Christ, comes to take man in order to lead him to Himself.

Thus, compared with Christianity, the pagan religions seem out of date and distorted. Still, they contain some worthwhile elements. Would not their disappearance then be an impoverishment? Simone Weil feared that it would: "If the other traditions disappear from the surface of the earth," she wrote, "it would be an irreparable loss. As it is, the missionaries have already caused too many to disappear." (p. 35.) Against this accusation, we must set forth the true concept of the Christian mission. Pius XII enunciated it thus in the encyclical *Divini Praecones;* "The Church has never treated the doctrines of the pagans with contempt and disdain; rather, she has freed them from all error, then completed them and crowned them with Christian wisdom."

This formula admirably sums up the attitude of Christianity. It does not treat the religious values of the pagan religions with disdain. But it first purifies them from all error, that is, it destroys the corruption—especially idolatry. This is why conversion will always be a rupture. Progress from paganism to Christianity is never accomplished through homogeneous evolution. Then, Christianity, through Christian wisdom, completes and fulfills the imperfect truths which exist in the pagan religions. It takes up the natural values of the religious man, it recovers them in order to consecrate them. Thus, we find early Christianity integrating the values of Greek philosophy after having purified them. Thus shall we be able to see in the future, Christianity assuming all the values contained in the asceticism of the Hindus or the wisdom of Confucius, after having purified them. The Christian mission, when it is what it is supposed to be, is not destruction, but liberation and transformation of the religious values of paganism. Christ did not come to destroy, but to fulfill.

Christ and the Powers

Richard Woods

Richard (John) Woods (1941–   ) entered the Order of Preachers (Domini-
cans) in 1962 and was ordained as a Roman Catholic priest in 1969. He is
author of *The Occult Revolution* and *The Devil* and is a contributor to numerous
journals. He lives and teaches in Chicago.

When the son of the late Episcopal Bishop James Pike took his life in February
of 1966, there began a series of incidents that not only profoundly reoriented the
controversial cleric's own life, but also thrust into the public eye the religious
dimension of the occult revolution. Contact with the dead has had many names—
necromancy, spiritualism, spiritism, and so on—and although regarded as a particularly baneful form of un-Christian practice, it has recently received new attention by theologians and scientists. (A comprehensive bibliography of writings in
this area can be found in an appendix to Bishop Pike's *The Other Side*.) It has also
become a matter of concern to young occultists, whose seances have produced
some uncommon experiences.

As Bishop Pike learned after he had "contacted" his son through the aid of
several mediums—or, rather, after his son had contacted him in that manner—
many Christians interpret quite literally the Bible's injunction against necromancy
as a prohibition forbidding seances and any other attempts to "reach" the departed
directly: "Do not have recourse to the spirits of the dead or to magicians; they
will defile you" (Lev. 19, 31); "If a man has recourse to the spirits of the dead or
to magicians, to prostitute himself by following after them, I shall set my face
against that man and outlaw him from his people" (Lev. 20, 6); and "Any man or
woman who is a necromancer must be put to death by stoning; their blood shall be
on their own heads" (Lev. 20, 27). Letters reviling him for exposing himself to the
power of Satan were directed to Pike by well-meaning people, and after his un-
timely death in the desert near Bethlehem, only three years later, there were many
who saw in the affair the punishing hand of God.

Most objections to spiritualist seances come from Christians who have no
doubts that the souls of the dead are either in heaven or hell. Their opposition is
not aimed against belief in the survival of the soul beyond death (something Bishop
Pike was skeptical about even after his son's death), but against the attempt to
communicate with them, which is seen as a diabolical trap.

Here the paradox of the Church's attitude towards occultism becomes manifest:
while professing belief in the communion of saints, and while affirming the real
existence of disembodied spirits, traditional Christianity refuses to accept the
possibility of a non-sinful approach to the souls of the dead other than prayers

Source: Richard Woods, *The Occult Revolution* (New York, 1971), pp. 192–194, 196–199, 201–203,
204–206, 210–213, 215. Copyright © 1971 by Herder and Herder, Inc. Reprinted by permission of The
Seabury Press, Inc.

offered on their behalf and to them. And even though the Church has at times acknowledged that the dead (such as saints) have appeared to men, the dread of seances and condemnation of conjurations has gone on unabated.

As we noted earlier, the official representatives of organized religion never took kindly to the attempts of their rivals—magicians, seers, and their company—to duplicate feats which they themselves performed or at least believed in. Understandably so, for magic and occult practices have always been—and been recognized as—counter-religious behavior. Occasionally, such conduct actually became anti-religious, especially as venal purveyors of magical arts sold their services to ambitious monarchs and pontiffs. The crime of simony, now defined as traffic in sacred offices, originated with Simon Magus, a Samaritan magician who wanted to buy the power of conferring the Holy Spirit and performing miracles (Acts 8, 9–24). It did not take too many centuries of wealth and power for the successors of Peter, as well as emperors and kings, not only to sell positions of authority but to hire magicians and astrologers. Some popes were magicians themselves. Aside from the corruption of Church dignitaries, there was also a traditional fear among pastors and spiritual theologians that feats of power such as miracles could be achieved by demonic influence and they remained wary of anything extraordinary. So thoroughly was the mass of the faithful convinced of the reality of miracles (as well as of demons and the whole magical panoply), that reports of phenomena surpassing the "natural" were officially discounted in canonization processes unless they could withstand a rigorous investigation by a trained clerical lawyer appropriately titled "the devil's advocate." This, however, was a later development and largely the result of popular credulity.

Today, as the occult arts and sciences bloom again in what appears to be the decaying remains of Western civilization, and seances compete with protest demonstrations and football games for the allegiance of the young, it seems at least "relevant" to explore some of the theological aspects from an historical as well as contemporary perspective. Most of our theological evaluations of occult phenomena are derived from medieval and Renaissance interpretations in any case.

· · ·

An Alternative View

In the Renaissance, the witchcraft trials, extensive legislation and inflammatory sermons, tracts and debates among experts amply testify to the continuing belief in and disfavor of the power of demons who lure men into damnation through magic and witchcraft. To be sure, there were clergymen who delved into the magical arts even then, but the official position was never in doubt. Not until the nineteenth century did the ban begin to weaken (except with the Swedenborgian movement which began a century before). In England especially, clergymen began paying greater heed to psychic research—in France, Mesmer and Charcot had begun the long trek that would lead to the discovery of hypnotism as well as psycho-therapy. Noted scientists and public figures such as Sir Arthur Conan Doyle, William James, and Henri Bergson became involved in psychic research as the century waned; Doyle in particular was a firm believer in spiritualism. In America, after the famous case of the Fox sisters of Hydesville, N.Y., there was also a veritable psychic revolution.

Throughout the northern hemisphere, scientists and philosophers were beginning to wonder if all the supernatural furor of the past thousand years was in fact based on natural, human powers, and even if contact with the departed was a possibility. However, the rise and vindication of psychiatric psychology and behavioralism soon eclipsed interest in psychic phenomena for their own sake and as avenues into the secret parts of the mind, for the Freudians had discovered the subconscious, which could be relied on to explain almost everything. Even Carl Jung, who of all the new psychologists was most open to a critical evaluation of the occult, found in it primarily a support for his theories of the collective unconscious and the archetypes.

In 1937, however, the Church of England approved a report which dealt with spiritualistic matters. It had been submitted at the request of the Archbishops of Canterbury and York, although they perhaps had no intention of making the findings known to the public. Nevertheless, in 1946, the report was "leaked," and many Anglican clergymen were soon openly claiming mediumistic abilities. On the Catholic side, Father Herbert Thurston, a Jesuit of the Bollandist school, was meanwhile studying poltergeist phenomena and cases of demonic seizure from a keenly analytic point of view. His *Ghosts and Poltergeists* remains a classic work on this subject.

Possibly the most comprehensive accounts of recent theological interest in the area of spiritualism and psychic phenomena are in Bishop Pike's *The Other Side* and *If This Be Heresy*. He very carefully distinguishes between the desire to "use" the dead for knowledge of the future and the desire to communicate with them across the unknown barrier between life and afterlife. He makes his own attitude as a theologian quite clear: "It would seem that many of those who for years have been mouthing the words 'I believe in . . . the Communion of Saints . . . the Resurrection of the Body; and the Life everlasting' and have been purporting to accept scriptural passages about these themes, including the communication of Jesus with his disciples, either do not really believe them or have never thought about their meaning at all. If the Church is to continue to make such affirmations, one would hope that more enlightened Church members will begin to take into account the rapid accumulation of scientific data which are supportive of them. If not, the Church may find itself in a very awkward position of being less believing with regard to some of its basic doctrinal tenets than secularists who have objectively examined factual evidence pointing to their truth."[1]

Today, as accounts of miracles, demonic possession, and other "supernatural" events are less and less well-received by Scripture scholars and theologians, the likelihood of "natural" explanations for the phenomena themselves is becoming stronger. ESP and mental powers such as psychokinesis and telepathy are no longer regarded by scientists as so much gobbledegook from the ages of superstition and religious frenzy. At the same time, and more to the point in the present context, supernaturalism itself is making something of a "comeback" in recent religious thought, as for instance in sociologist Peter Berger's *A Rumor of Angels*. As we have likewise already seen, the pentecostal movement, faith-healing, glossolalia,

[1] *The Other Side*, Garden City, N.Y., 1968, pages 291–292.

and xenoglossy are as much a part of parish life in the United States and Latin America as Holy Name societies and sodalities were a few years ago. (The identical phenomena appear in occult sects, as well, a fact which has yet to create any real friction between the "Jesus freaks" and "devil worshippers," perhaps because they are as yet unaware of the irony of it all.) From a pastoral viewpoint, a reassessment of supernaturalism is a theological imperative, especially if John Henry Newman's *consensus fidelium* argument is to have further meaning to the post-Vatican II world.

Perhaps the most impressive of recent developments in the contrapuntal progress of popular religion—if not the most profound—is the emergence in the midst of the counter culture of groups of young people derisively called "Jesus freaks." Their appearance was conceivably inevitable, but it was no less surprising when placards at demonstrations were discovered reading "Jesus Loves *You!*" or to be confronted (as I was) in midtown Chicago by twoscore and ten Children of God robed in sackcloth and wearing ashes in their hair, silently marching back from a pray-in during the Days of Rage.

. . .

On Eschatology

Georges Cuvier, the father of vertebrate paleontology, was startled to learn in the declining years of the eighteenth century that his native France had been alternately inundated and elevated in three successive periods of geological transformation, separated by thousands of years. Glacial ages have, in addition, repeatedly entombed the northern hemisphere under miles of ice, gouging canyons, valleys, and basins where rivers and lakes would one day be the left-overs of mighty glaciers. Continents have been raised and have sunk beneath the oceans, split apart and drifted away from the central land mass. Enormous meteors have collided with the earth, and if the theories of Immanuel Velikovsky are correct, even planets have narrowly missed destroying the world.

Mankind's memory is comparatively short. There is evidence that our ancestors walked the land more than two million years ago, and yet written records date back hardly farther than five thousand years. There are no accounts of the ice ages or of other disasters—unless, of course, the stories of the Deluge and similar catastrophes that figure in the folklore of almost every people are taken to be indicative of some proto-historical fact. Such cataclysms, according to myths and legends, nearly destroyed life on earth; had it not been for God's intervention, everything would have perished.

We believe today that the earth is quiet, that volcanoes are unpleasant anachronisms, and that earthquakes are unfortunate disasters. We are quite sure that the upheavals that created the mountains are over, and that the huge earth will continue to absorb our insignificant waste forever if need be. How often do we think that we could be living in the interstices between glacial periods or that a totally devastating geological "accident" such as the reversal of the poles (which happened some millions of years ago) might reoccur? If we do have such paranoid thoughts, we see a psychiatrist or at least hope that God will intervene and save us.

It seems likely that the religious experience of salvation from greater or lesser global catastrophes (what could be more ultimate?) formed the eschatological element of the world's great faiths. In the Judaeo-Christian tradition, such a view of history—God's miraculous interventions and his ultimate eschatological triumph —is central to the proclamation of the Gospel. The immediacy of Christ's return became an article of faith for the early Christians, and even after a thousand years the belief had not died out completely. We still proclaim in our creeds that Jesus "will come again in glory to judge the living and the dead," and from the proclamations of the counter-cultural evangelists today it seems clear that another thousand years has not eroded completely the vision of the Last Judgment and the end of time.

Such a view of things is difficult to reconcile with a workaday attitude towards life, much less a "scientific" view of the world such as Bultmann cherishes. It is consequently not surprising that the rebellious and innovative Jesus freaks and Process People have eschewed both to a great extent—becoming "religious" in the old sense of the word (as in "religious order") and literal in their interpretation of Scripture. To be sure, their Sunday school and catechism classes admirably prepared them for that, but it took a major breakdown in the cultural system to bring it forth.

. . .

Many of those to whom *Hair* was a living reality—the radically disaffiliated youngsters who had dropped out of society by the thousands to seek samadhi in "the Haight" or the communes of Taos—eventually adopted the magical attitude foreshadowed by the Tarot magician dominating center stage. For occultism is an escape from the crushing depersonalization of contemporary life; it reaffirms the worth of the individual, promising him knowledge kept secret for aeons and power over his destiny and the lives of others. Magic is, in the final analysis, an ideology, a whole way of life fraught with religious dynamism. Like religion itself, magic (as Malinowski insists) is "not merely a doctrine or a philosophy, not merely an intellectual body of opinion, but a special mode of behavior, a pragmatic attitude built up of reason, feeling and will alike."[2] Richard Cavendish finds in magic "a titanic attempt to exalt the stature of man, to put man in the place which religious thought reserves for God."[3]

Hence the terrible anger of the prophets against sorcery, which they—and the Judaeo-Christian tradition—identified with idolatry. For the magician to attempt to know the future or to dictate the course of events was to usurp the providence of God, to make himself into a god—that is, into an idol. Even the ancient prophets of Israel seem to have realized that sorcery was baneful not merely because it poached on the preserves of a wrathfully jealous Lord, being a form of perverse worship, but because in that liturgical inversion the cultists themselves fell prey to the deadening power of the no-gods:

They have mouths but speak not;
They have eyes but see not;
They have ears but hear not,

---

[2] *Magic, Science and Religion*, pages 24–25.
[3] *The Black Arts*, New York, 1968, page 1.

nor is there breath in their mouths.
Their makers shall become like them,
so shall everyone who trusts in them.
    (Psalm 135, 15–18)

Demonic possession need not be dramatic and horrible to be real, and there is reason to be wary of the psychological influence which a reliance on occultism can exercise over the young in particular. The demonic, Rollo May writes, "is any natural function which has the power to take over the whole person."[4] Like Jung and the members of the Process Church, May finds that belief in demons outside the person are projections of our inner experience, which shuns direct responsibility for the anger, passion, and hatred that are a part of man's psychological endowment along with the powers of love, zeal, and creativity. When one element of the personality permanently dominates the whole, psychosis—demonic possession—results. The pressures of contemporary life impel many towards severe anxiety, and one way to escape is to allow the magical tendencies of the personality to take over, particularly because the demonic in man is "the enemy of technology."[5] Hence the radical opposition of contemporary occultism to the technocratic way of life; the drive of the human psyche to be in tune with the world of nature has been superseded by the claims of an automated, cybernetic, technological life dominated by the punch-clock. That is why it should not have been surprising when some Canadian students destroyed a computer; violence is the demonic run amok.

If, then, occultism can be seen as a counter-cultural folk religion based on magic in conscious and unconscious reaction against the technocratic domination of the modern world and in the absence of religious support from the organized churches, there is some cause to be concerned about the welfare of the new occultists. For deprived of the balancing influences of authentic tradition and the conflicting political interests of various groups (pluralism, in other words), the new sectaries run a grave risk of being trapped in ideological postures of extreme reaction and ritualism. Values uncritically accepted as absolute easily harden into creeds, which combined with organizational structure and behavioral patterns create monolithic institutions. The acceptance of both the beliefs of the cults and the discipline imposed on prospective converts necessitates a certain conformity to expectations of what the ideal image of the members should be. And this type of image, institution, and ideology is the manifest presence of the demonic in society, whether cultural or counter-cultural.

. . .

Perhaps the greatest danger in occultism is the sophistication with which technological man can approach it. Freed, he assumes, from the claims of superstition and supernaturalism, he is at first fascinated and then mystified by the answers of the ouija board or the Tarot deck. It all makes sense, somehow—astrology, crystalgazing, palmistry . . . Is it only when we begin to encounter teenagers on the brink of hysteria because of an ouija board's prediction of immanent death or read of

---

[4] *Love and Will*, New York, 1969, page 123.
[5] Ibid., page 127.

the ritual murders of Hollywood personalities or find the mutilated remains of sacrificial animals that we begin to explore our fears?

The literature of occultism grows daily, most of it merely sensational. But occasionally, we are struck by accounts of events that chill the blood—and this is the felt presence of the spirit of death.

The psychopathological transfer of occult eschatological fears to an innocent victim was emblematically recreated in the grotesque and tragic story of Bernadette Hasler, a seventeen-year-old Swiss girl tortured and beaten to death by a sect of religious fanatics in 1966. Bernadette had become the target for the maniacal persecutions of a defrocked German priest and his mistress, their febrile imaginations having been inflamed by the pseudomystical "revelations" of a Carmelite nun, Sister Stella, who was convinced that an apocalyptic disaster was about to befall the world. Bernadette, the daughter of a Swiss farmer on whose property the cult had established itself—a normal, cheerful girl—was singled out for punishment because of her imputed dealings with the devil. Systematically, the girl was abused and degraded physically and mentally until she half-believed and actually confessed to the fabrications. She was then beaten mercilessly, sometimes twice daily, until after months of such torture, and by then a pitiable lunatic, she died following an unusually severe thrashing at the hands of six of the "righteous" cultists. For their crime of inhuman cruelty, the main perpetrators of the cult were sentenced to ten years in prison, the lesser accomplices to four years or less.

Such incidents are not rare, despite the peculiar ugliness of the Hasler murder. The Tate–La Bianca killings at the hands of Charles Manson's "witches" revealed a similar pattern of eschatological fears, messianic delusions, sexual sadism, and cultic organization. In all, at least eleven persons died as a result of Manson's megalomaniacal pontifications, during the course of which he announced (and perhaps believed) that he was—simultaneously—Jesus Christ and Satan. Yet Manson was declared sane. Was he possessed? From a technical viewpoint, it is not likely; that he was in the power of a "demonic" force, completely under the sway of his own diseased self-image and the weird ideology that he espoused, cannot easily be discounted.

The Last Archon

We live in the realm of death. Despite the mounting birth rate in the world, we are mocked by the casualty lists from Asian conflicts and the Mideast. Earthquakes and storms bear off many thousands each year, while disease and hunger kill hundreds of thousands more. Accident and age kill; there are homicide and suicide. The "exploding population," the dearth of food and the means of its distribution portend famine for literally millions of people; the assault on the environment by unrestrained technological hubris also spawns death in the air we breathe and the water we drink. And, indeed, every man—every living thing—must in the proper time die his death. Man is, in his totality, his fallenness, as Heidegger says, a "being towards death." Death seems to be the ultimate reality of the universe.

Every religion and every philosophy of man is an attempt either to overcome death or to find meaning in it. Faith in the revelation of Jesus means that there is one and only life-assuring belief—"I have come that you might have life and have it more abundantly." For a Christian, all other claims and the works of man's hand and mind are only a mockery of the human longing for everlasting life. "He who strives to secure his life shall lose it." Therefore, every false allegiance and service is idolatrous, unwitting homage to the very power and sting of death.

In the thought of Paul, especially as interpreted by Schlier and Stringfellow, all the principalities and powers are acolytes of death; they promise but cannot achieve the gift of life. Our struggle against them must begin with ourselves. Self-love is the enemy of the self-less obedience of faith, which manifests itself primarily in loving service to our fellow men. But if we make our self-image the god of our idolatry through insecurity, self-seeking, ambition, jealousy, lust, envy— in short, as long as we direct our energies selfwards, we can never effectively break through the enslaving control of institutions and ideologies and least of all enable others to do so. We have already lost.

Insofar as astrology, palmistry, witchcraft, and other occultist beliefs answer a need for security and order amid a chaotic world, the freeing message of the Gospel will fall on deaf ears. We must learn that our only security comes from our loving trust in the Father, who alone can save. Every other form of security (or salvation, actually) is not only deceptive but idolatrous, for it attributes to creatures —no matter how powerful—what belongs to the Creator alone.

Real faith means not only enduring chaos, absurdity, and uncertainty in this world, ruled as it is by principalities and powers still warring against us, but doing so willingly, affirming our reliance on God alone, celebrating our debility and weakness as the opportunity for God to work through us and in us. We must affirm life as it is—an intense struggle of life against death, but we celebrate knowing that in Christ the definitive victory has been inaugurated and is now being carried to completion in his Holy Spirit.

The response of faith to the occult revolution is not some sort of counter-revolutionary strategem—witch hunts and persecutions, whether physical or psychological, have been revealed by history to be a heightening of the power of death in the world. Institutionalized religion easily becomes a principality when its own existence is threatened.

Rather, a vital Christian witness alone can counteract the power of death in the world. Mere presence is sufficient; the Church has as its principal task merely to be the Church. Thus we can avoid the tragic error of categorizing modern occultism as the work of Satan, for like all worldly phenomena it is a mixture of helpful and injurious elements. For many, occultism provides a refuge from the struggles within the Church itself, and it also serves to remind us of what the Church should be.

. . .

James A. Pike was for many a living symbol of the contemporary Christian's pilgrimage towards an ever deeper understanding of the ultimate mystery of life. Yet he was able to remain faithful to his Church while wandering the labyrinth of occult theories, claims, and experiences. His example may prevent others from plunging over the edge of the unknown in their quest. Time will tell.

The Relationship of Psychotherapy to Sacred Tradition

A. C. Robin Skynner

Robin Skynner is Senior Tutor in Psychotherapy at the Institute of Psychiatry, Great Britain's principal psychiatric training center. Dr. Skynner pioneered the development of family therapy in England and has published numerous articles in this and related areas. He is the author of *Systems of Family and Marital Psychotherapy*. Throughout his career, he has pursued the question of the relationship between spiritual experience and the therapeutic process.

Now what does a psychotherapist do? I don't mean *how* does he do it but rather *what* does he expect reliably to achieve, in the way for example that carpenters take it for granted that, given adequate wood, they can make a table that will not fall apart, or plumbers expect water to flow from taps they have installed. Such astonishing misconceptions surround this area, in my experience, that a few simple facts are necessary if we are to communicate at all. In England psychoanalysis has never been taken very seriously, either by the general public or by the medical profession, least of all by orthodox psychiatry, where it has never enjoyed (or suffered from) the power and influence it until recently possessed in America. At the same time, it is true that some of its effects are almost as pervasive as they have been here —the idealization of infancy and the child/mother relationship, the cult of the individual, the belief in indulgence and self-expression, the devaluation of the role of the father and of authority, structure, and discipline in family and social life generally.

This is not to say that psychiatrists are not assumed to see right through people and to be secretly analyzing them at parties when they are, in fact, only trying to attract the attention of the waiter, like everybody else. But I fancy that this overvaluation, even in the United States, is always accompanied by the other side of the coin, a complete disbelief that a psychotherapist can do anything at all except listen to rich old ladies and pocket their savings. Certainly I am constantly made aware, especially by acquaintances following one or another of the traditional paths, that although they accept that we might be able to relieve discomfort by drugs and soothing falsehoods, we could not possibly achieve much in the way of reliably facilitating change in those who come to see us. This is nonsense, of course, as untrue as the obverse assumption that we can change the world.

Because psychotherapy means so many things, I am going to stick to one or two brief examples, which can sometimes convey more than generalizations. Not

Source: Lecture reprinted by permission of the author.

long ago I found in my letter rack three Christmas cards from ex-patients. One would be rather worried if one received many such messages, for in the better therapeutic results people are too busy leading full lives and enjoying real relationships to maintain contact with the therapist, even though some warmth and gratitude usually remain. Typically they say, if you bump into them in the street, "I've been meaning to write for years, but I never seem to get around to it." But one does get a few communications, especially a brief note with a Christmas card after a year or two, and of course it is very pleasant to hear how things are going.

The first was from a business executive who throughout his life was childish, violent, and destructive in any close relationship with a woman, accompanied by bouts of alcoholism. He had left therapy at a point where the drinking was under control and he had sustained a relationship with a woman long enough to plan to marry her. In his card he said things were going very well. And the goal of marriage, which was his main hope, was evidently achieved, for he signed his card from his wife as well as himself.

The second card was from Australia, from a doctor's wife whose profoundly disturbed relationship with her mother had led to an inability to love her daughter and to sexual frigidity after the child arrived, as well as to chronic depression and other marital problems. After confirming that improvements in those areas had been maintained, she concluded: "I think leaving the group has been awfully good for me, as I have had to fend for myself and with the three years I'd had with you all— although it's been tough—the 'end' result is a very happy one. I feel alive and indestructable! I think of you all often and very fondly."

The third was from a couple living abroad in Europe, who had flown across for a few sessions because of a pathological sexual jealousy on the wife's part, really at a psychotic level and based on her fantasy, but fed nevertheless by the husband's weakness and nervous secretiveness. The task with them was to help the husband maintain his identity against his wife's implacable, devouring possessiveness, and it seems that something had, in fact, improved, even though the form the message took was another manifestation of the problem. Clipped to the Christmas card, which was signed by them both, was a blank piece of paper saying "very much improved" followed by the husband's initials.(Her delusions included the idea that he was constantly sending secret messages!)

I will add a fourth which arrived two months earlier and which I found when I put the cards away. This was from a young married woman lacking any secure sense of identity and so unable to control her intense negative feelings that I had found it difficult to be in the same room with her, and would not have taken her on for therapy myself had she not been so persistent in seeking it. As so often happens with such cases, she worked hard and did unusually well over her year of attendance, sending a card some months later from Los Angeles, to which she had returned. I will quote this in more detail, because it conveys so well what the psychotherapeutic process meant to her: "I guess the most important thing to say is that what I gained from being with you all is extremely supportive during a period of enormous adjustment. I truly carry you all around with me—and am able to accept the ups and downs with much more equanimity and lack of self-doubt than before. It is possible now to be more open and honest, without being consumed and defeated by self-doubt. I think I will never lead a conventional life, but I am better able now to contain reality and not be so frightened and disturbed by it (I think this a reference to her bisexuality), even to enjoy its good side. I send you all much love and all best wishes for continued progress and support—the same which enabled me to take hold of my own life and not feel so helpless in doing so."

All these people, you will notice, had failed to develop an adequate sense of identity (In Erikson's sense), having failed to internalize in their early family environments adequate "models" of behavior and relationship which could subsequently serve as reliable guides to action. Change appeared to take place through increased awareness of the existing, inappropriate "models," accompanied by learning of new ones from the therapist or other group members—a kind of second, corrective family experience. This is made very clear by the note from the last patient mentioned, when she says "I truly carry you all around with me . . . ."

Now none of these people displayed during their therapy any real interest in the deeper meaning of their life on this planet, orbiting our sun within its galaxy in this universe, at this time in its history. Usually I am given early on a clear indication from those patients who will later seek out a spiritual path. They are in some way more open and vulnerable, more aware of themselves as part of mankind, part of the universe, "leaves on a tree." They are more troubled about and interested in the meaning of their existence as a whole rather than the meaning of what happened to them yesterday or in their childhood, or in the hopes and fears of what will happen to them tomorrow. They behave as if they have at some time been given a view from higher up the mountain, which they dimly remember and which leads them thereafter to seek again what they once glimpsed. Such patients are more widely interested and more interesting to treat, not least because they are more directly challenging both to me as a person and to my practice as a psychotherapist. To work with them is a shared endeavor in which I am more in question and receive more myself in consequence.

At some point, often late in therapy, they usually express their impression that I am holding something back from them, that I have another kind of understanding which is implicit in all I do and say but not directly communicated. (This never happens with the other patients.) At this point I may become more explicit, although always in the context of the therapy, which remains my central concern, and within the context also of what they already understand. Some, previously members of established churches, may eventually return again to their faith with a more mature relationship to it, often after an earlier period in the therapy when they have rejected religion, or rather rejected the childish, magical attitude toward it with which they came. Others find their way to the eastern teachings which have emerged in England, as here—two, for example, without any suggestion from me, went to a Tibetan Buddhist monastery in Scotland.

This is not to say that other patients, or at least those whose treatment is successful, do not develop a deeper sense of themselves as part of something larger. Such a loss of egocentricity is, as Alfred Adler insisted, an inevitable accompaniment of any improvement, perhaps the most fundamental change of all. But there has always been for me a clear distinction between these patients and those who forget that they have once perceived this other meaning of life, who behave as if they are in some way "children of God."

Now why is it that these two kinds of enquiry are confused at all? Perhaps we could look first at features that *appear* similar between them, which might lead to some confusion. First, there is in both psychotherapy and tradition the idea that man's perception is clouded and distorted—that he does not see things as they are but as he wants to see them. In the spiritual teachings there are the ideas of samsara, the false world of appearances, the shadows in Plato's cave; in psychotherapy we have the defenses of denial, projection, idealization, and withdrawal into fantasy.

Second, in both man is seen as being divided. His problems and sufferings are believed to stem from this fragmentation, this failure to become whole and to take responsibility for himself.

Third, self-knowledge, whereby he can find the lost parts of himself and become whole again, is seen as the key to the rediscovery of his integrity, so that he may become no longer divided into "I" and "not-I"—identifying himself with some parts of his being and rejecting others which then become projected and perceived in negative fashion in those around him.

Fourth, this rediscovery and reacceptance is in both processes expected to be painful, but regarded as bitter medicine that can ultimately heal and lead to growth. In individual and group psychotherapy, in encounter techniques, in the Synanon "haircut" and in the challenging confrontations of family and marital therapy, we find a systematic exposure of associations of thought, or of spontaneous emotional responses, or of actions, in a situation where, although it is supportive and containing, escape is prevented and the truth has sooner or later to be acknowledged. In the "confession of sins," in the acceptance of whatever internal manifestations arise during the stillness of meditation, in the openness to the inner voice of conscience which is sought during the concentration of prayer, similar processes appear to be occurring. The unconscious is made conscious, the self is expanded as denial and projection are reduced and dissociated parts return; the lost sheep is found, the prodigal returns and is welcomed. Following from this, in both tradition and in psychotherapy a clearer perception of the world and a greater capacity to understand, accept, and relate to others can be seen to follow from this greater self-acceptance and objectivity.

Fifth, both see man as possessing hidden resources which cannot become available without this greater self-knowledge and integration, even though the scale of this hidden potential is differently perceived in different schools of psychotherapy and, of course, even more so as between psychotherapy generally and the spiritual traditions.

Sixth, as a corollary, much of man's suffering and pain is in both regarded as unnecessary, a product of ignorance and blindness, of confusion and complexity resulting from the inner division and the deceit and subterfuge necessary to preserve some illusion of coherence: intellectualization, fantasy, Jung's "persona," the "ego" in the ordinary sense, Horney's "ideal image," and what Krishnamurti calls "thought." It is expected, therefore (and it is the case), that negative feelings, suffering, and pain (or at least those which serve no useful purpose) gradually diminish and disappear in the course both of competent psychotherapy and the following of a sacred tradition.

And finally, seventh, both require that the searcher shall be in personal, regular contact with a teacher, guide, guru, analyst, or leader who has already been through the same experiences; has seen, understood, and accepted at least some aspects of himself; has escaped from some of his own fragmentation, delusions, and distorted perceptions; and so can, through being able to perceive the searcher more objectively, help him in turn to become more objective about himself.

There is, as we see, much *apparent* overlap, and I think we may be forgiven if we experience some confusion, at least initially, between these different kinds of exploration. My personal experience leads me to believe, however, that these two paths lie, if not in opposite *directions*, at least in quite different *dimensions*, and that we need to look for a much more subtle relationship between them. The fable of the two brothers, the golden thread and the black dog, and the idea of the third brother arising from the relation between them, hints at this. Having looked at some similarities between these two paths, let us now summarize some of the differences, which I believe are not only greater, but incommensurately greater.

First, all sacred traditions begin from the idea of an ordered, intelligent universe, where the idea of *hierarchy* is central and where each level is related to others in reciprocal dependence. Man appears very low down on this scale of being, although he has a definite place and serves purposes beyond himself, necessary to the total structure.

Second, in the sacred traditions man is perceived as having a choice of two purposes he may serve in this grand design—God or Caesar; the ordinary world of appearances or a more real world behind it; his natural appetites and desires or an inner voice or conscience which comes into conflict with these; the black dog, perhaps, or the golden thread. The traditions tell us that we all serve nature, in our ordinary state of development, as unconsciously as the grass feeds the cow and its manure in turn feeds the grass again; and that our illusion of power and freedom, and our fantasies about ourselves and mankind, ensure that we do this just as the beast of burden walking endlessly in a circle to drive the primitive pump is kept at its job by the pole attached to its back and the blindfold which prevents it from seeing its true plight. But the traditions tell us that it is also possible, in the scheme of things, for some men to awaken to the situation and to perceive another possibility, another task they can fulfil, another influence which, if they can submit to it, will free them in some measure from the blindness and slavery of their ordinary existence. Although they must still live on earth, a connection begins to be made with heaven. For the person who is awakened to this other realm, a higher energy, a more subtle intelligence becomes available and begins to change the whole purpose and meaning of ordinary life, although the latter continues as before and may show little change of a kind discernible to those still circling the treadmill and absorbed in their dreams. Caesar must still be served, but the service of God transforms this totally and causes life to become an endlessly rich source of knowledge and experience to feed the new life growing like a child within the person called to this new service.

Now this kind of idea is not part of ordinary psychology, whether "scientific" or "humanistic." Although the latter might recognize and show more serious interest in some of the *experiences* previously called "religious" or "mystical," man is still perceived as being at the center of things; his ordinary desires, ambitions, hopes, and plans, whether selfish or altruistic, are taken at face value and used as a basis for action, for planning utopias and eupsychias. There is no concept of the second purpose to which man can give himself, and because of this, no real questioning whether the first could be illusory. Ordinary psychology then becomes another elaboration of the delusion itself, providing more blindfolds, another ring through the nose, more "hope" to keep us turning the treadmill.

Third, and following on from this, the possibility of recognizing and beginning to understand the significance of the sacred traditions begins from a disillusionment with ordinary life, with one's ordinary self, with ordinary knowledge. Only after the blindfold is removed and we see that we are going in a circle all the time have we the hope of choosing another direction. We have to see that life is not going anywhere in the way we formerly imagined, that it never has and never will. Having faced this, we may realize that no escape is possible from the repetition of our ordinary level without help from another. Coming to disbelieve in our ordinary thought and emotion, and so becoming still enough and open enough to reach a deeper and more fundamental part of ourselves where another energy, a different possibility of consciousness exists, a connection may be made since we are for a moment available for it. Thus we have to begin from the point of failure, to relinquish our valuation of our ordinary selves and to let this be replaced gradually by something which at first does not seem to be ourselves at all. Having awakened, we have to die in order to be reborn.

Now does not ordinary psychology rather lead to an *increase* of our ordinary self, more efficient, more fruitful, more enjoyable and less conflicted perhaps, but still the same thing writ larger, the same ambitions fulfilled instead of unfulfilled, the same desires satisfied instead of frustrated. Ordinary psychology surely seeks to *improve* the self, according to the ideas *of* the ordinary self; it scarcely seeks to destroy it.

Fourth, sacred traditions are by definition, if they are anything at all, a manifestation of the higher level about which they tell us, a point at which the levels actually touch each other. And perhaps because they can only touch *within* man himself, they have been transmitted by a chain of individuals who actually manifest, with part of their being (rather than simply know about), the possibility with which these traditions are concerned. From this follow two further differences between the paths. One is the idea that the traditions have always existed, from the beginning of recorded time, and are simply spread into the world from the human chain that transmits them, the influence widening or contracting from one period to another and the means of expression being adapted to the prevailing forms of thought and current ordinary knowledge, although always conveying the same essential truth. If anything, the understanding *deteriorates* as it spreads wider from the teachers, like ripples on a pond. This is totally different from ordinary psychology, where knowledge is seen as a progressive development beginning perhaps from Mesmer and the nineteenth-century hypnotists, and leading through the pioneering work of Janet, Freud, Adler, and Jung to the achievements of the present day. For ordinary psychology, the present time is one of unusual enlightenment and progress; for the sacred traditions, it is more likely to be seen as a dark age.

A fifth difference, which also follows from what was just said, concerns the relation between teacher and pupil. The ordinary psychotherapist would certainly recognize a difference in authority between himself and his patient based on age, experience, knowledge, and skill, but this would be expected to change in the course of treatment. As the patient matures, the "transference" is hopefully dissipated and, while some regard and gratitude may remain, persistent dependency and acceptance of the analyst's authority are taken correctly to indicate incomplete treatment. In the sacred traditions, by contrast, the teacher is in some part of his being an actual manifestation of a higher level, and so a sharply hierarchical pupil/ teacher relationship is not only appropriate but, since the human chain continues presumably all the way up the mountain, the authority of the guide, or of the next man above on the rope, may appropriately continue indefinitely.[1]

I will mention other differences more briefly. The most important concerns their differing view of consciousness. Following what one might call an "archaeological" concept of consciousness, our ordinary western psychology tends to assume that we already possess the light of consciousness but that some parts of ourselves have been buried and need to be found and brought into this light again, after which they will remain at least potentially accessible. The light is assumed to be burning already, at least while we are out of bed and moving about, and its brightness and continuity are not very much questioned. By contrast, the great traditions maintain explicitly or implicitly the idea that man's consciousness is much more limited, fluctuating, and illusory than he usually realizes, and that an extraordinary amount of persistent effort is needed even to maintain it more steadily, let alone increase it. For the traditions, consciousness is more like the light powered by a dynamo, driven by the wheel of a bicycle, where we have to pedal constantly if it is to remain alight and pedal harder to make it brighter. It is true, of course, that the idea that attention and consciousness require effort and work, as well as the idea of finer levels of energy generated by the effort of more sustained attention, and the further idea that the two can lead automatically to the reintegration of dissociated psychic elements, are all present in the ideas of Janet, the Frenchman who in so many ways anticipated Freud. But then Janet was a religious man, and his eclipse by Freud was no doubt another consequence of the attitudes current in this epoch.

If we are to accept these differences as valid, it seems to me that they lead us to a view of psychotherapy and of sacred tradition as different dimensions at right angles to each other, with fundamental aims that cannot in their nature coincide at all. Psychotherapy is about ordinary life, the development of man along the horizontal line of time from birth to death. Just as the physician is concerned with countering threats to life and obstacles to physical growth, and remedying deficiencies and deviations in the development of the body, so the function of the psychotherapist (which developed originally, and is still based most firmly, within the role of the physician) can be seen as averting threats to psychological stability, relieving obstacles and inhibitions in the process of growth from the dependency of the child to the relative responsibility and autonomy of the adult. To do so the psychotherapist seeks to supply those experiences which have been lacking in the patient's history, particularly those which were missing or distorted in the early family environment.

---

[1] I am less sure about this difference than about the others. Although essentially true, I think analogous developmental processes must nevertheless occur in both kinds of change.

The sacred traditions begin from the horizontal line of time, but are concerned with a quite different, vertical line of development: man's increasing awareness of, connection with, and service to the chain of reciprocal transformation and exchange between levels of excellence which the cosmic design appears to need some (but not all or even most) of mankind to fulfill. There is an analogy here with the physical sphere, where man is obliged to move about on the horizontal, two-dimensional surface of the earth if he is to survive at all, but is not obliged to fly and exist in the three-dimensional atmosphere, although he can do so if he wishes and may find that this has consequences for his ordinary existence.

If these two endeavors are in fact quite distinct, then forms of psychotherapy which confuse them could be much more harmful to the possibility of spiritual development than those that do not recognize the existence of the traditions at all. Thus I believe that the ideas offered by such people as Maslow, Fromm, Rogers, and many leaders of the Encounter movement may as easily hinder as help people toward a recognition of their actual position. It is true that these approaches may indeed stimulate a desire for the kind of understanding that only the traditions can supply, and I am grateful for the way in which they have all personally assisted me. But because they mix the levels, they stand in danger of offering a half-truth sufficiently like the real thing to satisfy this deeper hunger without leading to anything more real and perhaps even increasing the attachment to the ordinary self. Jung, too, although so much admired by people of a religious persuasion, in contrast to that terrible Sigmund Freud, seems to me to offer a particularly subtle temptation, precisely because of the depth and quality of his personal understanding, together with his fundamental confusion of psychology and sacred tradition, psyche and spirit.

This is why, when I cannot find a good eclectic psychotherapist (in the sense of someone who seeks to *integrate* the best of the different schools), I tend to refer patients to competent Freudian analysts, provided they are agnostic rather than militantly atheistic and demonstrate by the quality of their lives that they are decent and responsible people. For I find that the better Freudians at least have their feet on the ground rather than their heads in the clouds, a good beginning if one wishes to travel reliably along the surface of the earth. Being concerned first and foremost with the development of ordinary competence in making a living, forming responsible relationships, enjoying sexuality and other natural appetites, raising a family and generally coping adequately with life, they help to establish a firm base from which an interest in deeper meaning can develop.

The differences now seem clear enough, and it is hard to see how we could ever confuse these two different kinds of development. At this point we can all feel satisfied. Followers of sacred traditions could reassure themselves that, after all, they did not really need to have that analysis which seemed so much to improve the life of their neighbor. The psychotherapist could also feel relieved, finally satisfied that people who follow a traditional path are not really living in the real world and are best left to their delusions. I could comfort myself that I have answered in some measure the question Professor Needleman set us in his introductory talk. Had I been wiser, I would have arranged matters so that I could stop here and be well on my way home before the cracks appear and the whole edifice falls to pieces.

But if we go on, I fear that the simplicity disappears. Even though I believe that what I have said is correct as far as it goes, we begin to see that the important issue for us is the relationship which exists at the meeting point of these two dimensions: that cross, within each man, of the line of time and the line of eternity, level or scale. In approaching this, I find I have to reconcile a number of facts, or at least a number of observations which I can no longer doubt.

The first is that many who follow a sacred tradition change profoundly as regards their ordinary life adjustment, whereby many of the problems that might otherwise take them to a psychotherapist simply melt away, like ice in the sun, disappearing without any systematic attempt to change under the influence of some subtler, finer influence which begins to permeate and alter the whole organism.

Second, I have noticed that others who follow such traditions appear to become more closed, narrow and intolerant both of others and of their own hidden aspects. Of those I see professionally, this group is the most intractable and untreatable of all, for the knowledge derived from a religious tradition has been put to the service of perceptual defense, of complacency, of narcissistic self-satisfaction, of comfort and security.

Third, the difficulties of working with such individuals are only equalled by those encountered with people who have misused the ideas and techniques of psychotherapy in a similar fashion. Excepting only the group that I have just mentioned, no patients are as difficult to treat as psychoanalysts, particularly those who believe they have had a "full analysis" (what a marvellous expression!) already.

· And fourth, others in psychotherapy, particularly those in psychotherapy groups, and almost routinely those at a certain stage in large groups run in the way we attempt it in London—and I think also in encounter groups in the early stages, before they become a new game—can reach a point of simple openness, awareness of themselves as part of mankind and of the universe, and of direct communion with others, more intensely than many following a traditional teaching, at least as far as one can judge from the statements and external behavior of each. It does not last, of course, and cannot be pursued systematically, but in the psychotherapeutic experience it is often there, sometimes in an awe-inspiring fashion, and we have to make a place for this in our ideas.

For some time after writing this I was uncomfortable with it and could take it no further, till I saw that I had assumed, for want of any real question to myself, that I might belong to the first or fourth groups but that the second and third were made up of other people. But a moment's reflection showed that I was a member of all four, and that the principal obstacles to my own development were precisely those that stemmed from the misuse of such professional or religious understanding as I possessed, in order to preserve and enhance my ordinary image of myself. And this, I see, applies to us all; it is in the nature of things.

Whether in my ordinary life or in my search for its hidden significance, I am most alive, closest to the source and meaning of my existence, when I am open to my immediate experience, receptive to what it can teach me and vulnerable to its power to change my being. In this moment, when I am sure of nothing, I am yet most deeply confident of the possibility of understanding. My actions spring most truly from myself, yet I have no idea beforehand what I will manifest. Like water welling up from a spring, I am new every moment, appearing miraculously from some source hidden deep within the ground of my being.

The next instant I have lost this movement, this freedom, this life constantly renewed, and am once again trying to be right, to be good, to know, to change, to be normal, to be successful—or alternatively to be bad, rebellious, a tragic failure, a pathetic victim—but one way or another always seeking to preserve some experience like a butterfly gassed in a bottle and pinned to a board, losing in the process everything that made me wish to capture it in the first place. Seeking security, certainty, and beliefs to buoy me up, I cling to my experience in order to preserve it, but find myself holding only the dead residue of a living process that has already changed and moved elsewhere. Small wonder that I find my life colorless, dull, flat, and boring, needing ever-increasing artificial stimulation to restore me to some feeling of alertness.

Perceiving this, I realize that I must live nearer the source of this inner spring, somehow maintaining myself at the point where this "living water" gushes forth into the visible world. I may see that I am constantly carried by the current into the more superficial manifestations to which this energy gives rise as it flows away from the source, that it cannot be different while I remain passive, my attention captured and carried downstream by the flow. Once I see this, I may begin to swim against the current, struggling to remain closer to the source where my life is constantly renewed, no longer trying to hold on to things for fear of sinking, and realizing that the formlessness and endless change from which I shrink is a condition of real life itself.

If I can only *realize* my true situation and thereby loosen my attachment to the forms my life-energy takes as it moves further from its origin, I may find that I *remember* the source, and that this memory brings a desire to find it again. Now I find myself swimming against the current to regain it, from love and delight; the effort follows directly from my desire, just as my heart beats faster as I begin to run, and my running follows from my perception of the goal I wish to reach. I need only free myself from my hypnosis long enough to remember what I have lost.

Then I am in the middle, between the hidden source of my life in a higher realm and its manifestations in this world, and I must then struggle not to deny either. If I forget the source, I drift downstream toward increasing repetition; or if I forget the nature of the stream itself and its constant downward pull, then I begin to dream I am already at the source, rather than to experience it and swim toward it, and so I drift downstream again. Only when I realize my nature as a creature of two worlds do I discover the full potential of my life, which must be lived everlastingly between them.

Now this immediate experience of my living energy can be brought about by many kinds of events. Vivid and profound emotional experience can produce it, such as death of a loved one, the birth of a child, sometimes sexual love, great beauty, pain, an event on a world scale. Drugs such as LSD and mescaline can give a taste of such experience by their capacity to destroy defenses and release emotion, and so can psychotherapy, particularly perhaps encounter techniques and the gestalt approaches that seek to release the most primitive and childlike emotions.

But without deeper knowledge we drift downstream imagining we still love at this zenith, while the experience in fact becomes degraded, copied and repeated, fantasied. Then we need larger doses, stronger stimuli, bigger groups, new techniques, to startle us out of our dreams again. If this is in fact the case, it would at least explain why those undergoing analysis appear for a time more real and open, only to become more closed than others sometimes, when the analytic process is over, particularly if there is a professional vested interest in demonstrating a good result. Many will recognize exactly the same process among followers of the sacred traditions—a marvellous openness and simplicity in younger people just beginning, deteriorating gradually toward compacency, rigidity, and parroting of formulas in those who begin to "know" and in doing so, cease to live.

It is here, perhaps, that the place of the family and community as a "middle zone," and the need for ordinary effort and work, become vital factors. For our natural tendency to drift with the streaming of our life energy into increasingly dead and ritualized manifestation—or to put it another way, our predisposition to convert real experience into fantasy and then repeat it, so that our lives not only become B-movies but even the same old B-movie over and over again—is so great that we need the discipline of *effort* to convince us, through our constantly experienced inability to swim against *any* current, that we are always drifting. And for this we need also the discipline of a group of intimates who know us well and love us enough to make demands on us for ordinary effort, who remind us when we drift too far from our more real selves and begin to live in dreams and selfish fantasies, and who demand of us that we be not less than ordinary men and women, fulfilling our ordinary responsibilities. For if we are not at least this, how can we hope to be more? Here, I believe, psychotherapy has its proper place, above all in the facilitation of this function of the family and the outer discipline and support it provides, or the provision of substitute group experience where this is missing. Given this ground, the sacred traditions have some possibility to guide us back to the source of our lives.

Two

Is Religion
Religion?

Introduction

Among the important cultural changes that have occurred in the last hundred
years, we certainly must include the sweep of science. It has spawned a
pervasive technology; more and more aspects of the world have become
scientific subject matter, and, with its wholesale introduction into the school
curriculum, science has shaped the cognitive and emotional consciousness of
every person in the literate societies. This "scientific" consciousness naturally
affects other cultural institutions and aspects of life; it has had a particularly
massive impact on the church and religion.

Reason and revelation have struggled for centuries for authority over
people's minds. The rise of science as a method of gaining knowledge has
tipped the balance away from revelation and toward reason. The result has
been a growing inability to believe the statements in sacred texts and the
reports of mystics; this has weakened the cognitive authority of religion and
put it on the defensive.

Perhaps even more contributory to the declining status of religion has
been the tendency to make "religious phenomena" themselves a subject
matter for science. Religion is something to be "explained." Given that a
scientific attitude discredits the cognitive claims of religion, science-minded
persons find it difficult to see how anyone could have literally believed religious
statements to be true. They find it necessary to give an account, an explanation,
of how people could could have believed something so patently false or
nonsensical. Surely, religion must be a causally produced response to some
natural conditions. They are curious to identify these conditions and, in terms
of laws from some science, to find the causal links between these natural
conditions and the phenomenon of religion.

Notice that "science" is not something to be explained. Scientific claims are to be examined, evidence looked for, hypotheses tested, experiments undertaken, all with the purpose of either validating or invalidating a scientific claim. The chief interest in scientific statements is their truth or falsity; we are not generally interested in explaining their occurrence. The most we might do is try to appreciate how someone could have "discovered" his or her hypothesis or "created" it. Discovery and creation are honorific events; that which needs explanation is reduced to the level of such mundane events as fertilization, internal combustion, and heat transfer.

An anthology on religion that purports to cover the main facets of the study of religion has to include a chapter such as this one, which presents claims that religion can be explained away as not being religion at all but something else. None of the authors, with the possible exception of R. D. Laing, takes the cognitive claims of religion seriously. However, they do see that religion does perform some function—Marx finds that it has a function that is harmful, Dewey that it has a useful function. The assignment of a function to religion is one way of explaining its nature, origin, and continued existence. In the first selection in this chapter, **Sigmund Freud** sees religion as a form of wish-fulfillment; for him, the dogmas of religion are illusions, derived from deep, persistent wishes. Religion is not, therefore, something *sui generis* but an aspect of our psychological life. In terms of his science of psychology, Freud finds laws that connect one of the natural conditions of our life, insecurity, with the characteristic phenomena of religion. For Freud, then, religion is not religion but a psychological manifestation.

In the second selection, **Karl Marx** describes religion as an ideological weapon of the ruling class. Man under capitalism is alienated from himself and from reality; his conditions of earthly existence are miserable. The proletariat everywhere suffers. Religion is a means the ruling class uses to pacify the proletariat and to keep them from revolting. Religion "is the *opium* of the people." Once again, religion is not religion; it is an ideational form of social control and, as such, is simply political. Man will be emancipated from religion when religion is replaced by philosophy.

In the third selection, **Emile Durkheim** finds that religions universally maintain a two-worlds view, of a world of the sacred and a world of the profane. Religion purportedly transports people from the profane to the sacred world. Of course, this is metaphysical nonsense to Durkheim; there is only one world, the natural world, the world that science studies. To understand religion, we must understand how the notion that there is a sacred world ever came into being. Durkheim claims that it is a social phenomenon and tries to isolate the social conditions that make it possible for men to have experiences in which they project an ideal world beyond the mundane, natural one. "The formation of the ideal world is therefore not an irreducible fact which escapes science; it depends upon conditions which observation can touch; it is a natural product of social life." So, once again, religion is not religion, it is a manifestation of man's social existence.

In the fourth selection, **John Dewey** finds that religion cannot claim people's loyalty as long as it sets itself in competition with science. Religion has a valuable function to perform, and if it surrenders its claims to knowledge while emphasizing its moral function, it can continue to claim human beings' loyalty. For Dewey, religious faith is "the unification of the self through allegiance to inclusive ideal ends, which imagination presents to us and to which the human will responds as worthy of controlling our desires and choices." Once again, religion is not, or ought not to be, religion as traditionally conceived; for continuing effectiveness, religion must become a dramatic form of morals, reconceiving God as "the unity of all ideal ends arousing us to desire and actions."

The writers of the first section of this chapter reduce traditional religion out of existence. This topples one of the pillars on which many persons believe the hope, sense of purpose, and meaning of life rest. Is there any other pillar that can be substituted for religion?

Wang Tao-ming provides a vivid, deeply felt, sincere expression of how political commitment can replace religion as a support for a purposeful life. If the opium of religion is smoked to ashes, we await Marx's promised emancipation. But emancipation to do what? Wang found his mission in Mao Tse-tung's philosophical statements and moral and political injunctions.

R. D. Laing recognizes that religious experiences seem hopelessly invalid to people enmeshed in the framework that our social, interpersonal mind constructs. The mystic makes deviant claims—deviant, at least, to the "normal," scientific person, who consigns the mystic to madness, and hence to illness. Laing realizes that to many who consider themselves sane because they are able to adapt to the external world as defined by "human collectivities," religion is not religion, but madness. Laing's substitute for this dismissed religion is generated by taking up a different stand toward these deviant, nonnormal experiences. For Laing, there is no privileged standpoint from which to view reality; ontology is relative; this reduces the ontological authority of our "sane" egoic experiences and opens the way for viewing "madness" as a transcendental state in which the normal self is lost. This may not be a pathological manifestation of the need for a cure; instead, it may be seen as inner illumination to light our way in the present age of outer darkness, a mediation of divine powers. The substitute for the old, vanished religion of a "sane" theology is the transcendent vision of "madness" given new ontological and religious authority.

Dietrich Bonhoeffer's "last letters from a Nazi prison" before he was executed reveal that he tried honestly to face his doubts about traditional religion. "We are proceeding toward a time of no religion at all: men as they are now simply cannot be religious any more." Still, he does not wish to give up the task of forming a substitute. He asks "what is a religionless Christianity?" It has to be something that acknowledges that "Man has learnt to deal with himself in all questions of importance without recourse to the 'working hypothesis' called 'God'." Bonhoeffer acknowledges: "I'm only gradually working my way to the non-religious interpretation of biblical concepts; the job is far too big for me to finish just yet." The direction that he takes here is to conceive of God as a being who forsakes us rather than one who supports us. The religious man "is summoned to share in God's sufferings at the hands of a godless world. . . . He must therefore really live in the godless world, without attempting to gloss over or explain its ungodliness in some religious way or other. He must live a 'secular' life, and thereby share in God's sufferings.'' In short, the substitute for the old religion is to take on the tasks formerly assigned to God.

Edgar D. Mitchell reports ''feeling a deep dissatisfaction with the ability of philosophy and theology to give answers to my questions about the meaning of life and man's place in the universe . . . the physical sciences . . . seemed to be doing very little about replacing those notions with stronger, more valid ones.'' As he viewed the earth from his moonbound spaceship, he was conscious of the misery human beings were inflicting on each other. What is to be substituted for religion—and for philosophy and the empirical, rational sciences? Mitchell recounts and argues for the efficacy of paranormal psychic experiences: ''psychic abilities such as telepathy are another type of knowing —a subjective knowing, a nonrational, cognitive process largely overlooked by the scientific world.'' He advocates development of our psychic, inner abilities. ''The result will be an expansion of awareness and a step toward developing higher consciousness in the race.'' Travelers of inner space find that their ''maps of inner space'' provide useful guides to unfamiliar territory. They have been unanimous in declaring that selflessness and freedom from egoism are an aspect of higher consciousness and the key to direct knowledge. Thus, Mitchell would substitute this higher consciousness for religion because its moral results are those aimed at by all religions. It also yields for him an overview of the cosmos, as religion has claimed to do, what he calls ''cosmic consciousness.'' ''It is a state in which there is constant awareness of unity with the universe pervading all aspects of one's life.'' These powers are ours; they do not need an outside source such as God, as religion has often claimed; the higher consciousness is *our* substitute.

Rudolf Bultmann, like Bonhoeffer after him (as Bonhoeffer remarks), believes that the mythical view of the world and redemption is ''incredible to modern man, for he is convinced that the mythical view of the world is obsolete.'' These mythic robes have to be stripped away to reveal the underlying truth. If Christianity remains tied to the New Testament myths, it loses its hold on people whose education includes science and technology: it must be replaced; something must be substituted for it. But what is the substitute? A demythologized Christianity. Is it still Christianity when stripped of its literal expression in the sacred text? To demythologize is to take interpretative liberties; interpretation is the work of men and women, who may differ among themselves. Whose interpretation are we to follow? That there are two incompatible interpretations means that Christian ''truth'' is in the hands of finite, fallible humans.

Bultmann attempts to circumvent these difficulties by getting to the bottom of the nature of myth. The purpose of myths should be separated from the form and imagery of their expression. Thus, if in demythologizing, we are simply stripping away the imagery and form of expression but preserving the purpose, we have not done away with the message of Christianity. For Bultmann, this means, finally, that we have an existential substitute. ''The real purpose of myth is not to present an objective picture of the world as it is, but to express man's understanding of himself in the world in which he lives. Myth should be interpreted not cosmologically, but anthropologically, or better still, existentially.'' (Note Bonhoeffer's criticism of Bultmann's proposed ''liberal'' substitute in his May 5, 1944, letter.)

A. K. B.

Can Religion Be Explained?

Religion as a Psychological Weakness

Sigmund Freud

Sigmund Freud (1856–1939), the founder of psychoanalysis, was the most influential psychologist of modern times.

Wherein lies the peculiar value of religious ideas?

We have spoken of the hostility to culture, produced by the pressure it exercises and the instinctual renunciations that it demands. If one imagined its prohibitions removed, then one could choose any woman who took one's fancy as one's sexual object, one could kill without hesitation one's rival or whoever interfered with one in any other way, and one could seize what one wanted of another man's goods without asking his leave: how splendid, what a succession of delights, life would be! True, one soon finds the first difficulty: everyone else has exactly the same wishes, and will treat one with no more consideration than one will treat him. And so in reality there is only one single person who can be made unrestrictedly happy by abolishing thus the restrictions imposed by culture, and that is a tyrant or dictator who has monopolized all the means of power; and even he has every reason to want the others to keep at least one cultural commandment: thou shalt not kill.

But how ungrateful, how short-sighted after all to strive for the abolition of culture! What would then remain would be the state of nature, and that is far harder to endure. It is true that nature does not ask us to restrain our instincts, she lets us do as we like; but she has her peculiarly effective mode of restricting us: she destroys us, coldly, cruelly, callously, as it seems to us, and possibly just through what has caused our satisfaction. It was because of these very dangers with which nature threatens us that we united together and created culture, which, amongst other things, is supposed to make our communal existence possible. Indeed, it is the principal task of culture, its real *raison d'être*, to defend us against nature.

One must confess that in many ways it already does this tolerably well, and clearly as time goes on it will be much more successful. But no one is under the illu-

Source: Sigmund Freud, *The Future of an Illusion*, trans. by W. D. Rosbon-Scott (New York, 1955), pp. 21–32, 41–58, 95–102. Reprinted by permission of Liveright, Publishers, New York. Acknowledgement is also made to Sigmund Freud Copyrights Ltd., The Institute of Psycho-Analysis, and The Hogarth Press Ltd. for permission to quote from "The Future of an Illusion" in Volume XXI of *The Standard Edition of the Complete Psychological Works of Sigmund Freud*, revised and edited by James Strachey.

sion that nature has so far been vanquished; few dare to hope that she will ever be completely under man's subjection. There are the elements, which seem to mock at all human control: the earth, which quakes, is rent asunder, and buries man and all his works; the water, which in tumult floods and submerges all things; the storm, which drives all before it; there are the diseases, which we have only lately recognized as the attacks of other living creatures; and finally there is the painful riddle of death, for which no remedy at all has yet been found, nor probably ever will be. With these forces nature rises up before us, sublime, pitiless, inexorable; thus she brings again to mind our weakness and helplessness, of which we thought the work of civilization had rid us. It is one of the few noble and gratifying spectacles that men can offer, when in the face of an elemental catastrophe they awake from their muddle and confusion, forget all their internal difficulties and animosities, and remember the great common task, the preservation of mankind against the supremacy of nature.

For the individual, as for mankind in general, life is hard to endure. The culture in which he shares imposes on him some measure of privation, and other men occasion him a certain degree of suffering, either in spite of the laws of this culture or because of its imperfections. Add to this the evils that unvanquished nature—he calls it Fate—inflicts on him. One would expect a permanent condition of anxious suspense and a severe injury to his innate narcissism to be the result of this state of affairs. We know already how the individual reacts to the injuries that culture and other men inflict on him: he develops a corresponding degree of resistance against the institutions of this culture, of hostility towards it. But how does he defend himself against the supremacy of nature, of fate, which threatens him, as it threatens all?

Culture relieves him of this task: it performs it in the same way for everyone. (It is also noteworthy that pretty well all cultures are the same in this respect.) It does not cry a halt, as it were, in its task of defending man against nature; it merely pursues it by other methods. This is a complex business; man's seriously menaced self-esteem craves for consolation, life and the universe must be rid of their terrors, and incidentally man's curiosity, reinforced, it is true, by the strongest practical motives, demands an answer.

With the first step, which is the humanization of nature, much is already won. Nothing can be made of impersonal forces and fates; they remain eternally remote. But if the elements have passions that rage like those in our own souls, if death itself is not something spontaneous, but the violent act of an evil Will, if everywhere in nature we have about us beings who resemble those of our own environment, then indeed we can breathe freely, we can feel at home in face of the supernatural, and we can deal psychically with our frantic anxiety. We are perhaps still defenceless, but no longer helplessly paralysed; we can at least react; perhaps indeed we are not even defenceless, we can have recourse to the same methods against these violent supermen of the beyond that we make use of in our own community; we can try to exorcise them, to appease them, to bribe them, and so rob them of part of their power by thus influencing them. Such a substitution of psychology for natural science provides not merely immediate relief, it also points the way to a further mastery of the situation.

For there is nothing new in this situation. It has an infantile prototype, and is really only the continuation of this. For once before one has been in such a state of helplessness: as a little child in one's relationship to one's parents. For one had reason to fear them, especially the father, though at the same time one was sure of his protection against the dangers then known to one. And so it was natural to assimilate and combine the two situations. Here, too, as in dream-life, the wish came into its own. The sleeper is seized by a presentiment of death, which seeks to carry him to the grave. But the dream-work knows how to select a condition that will turn even this dreaded event into a wish-fulfilment: the dreamer sees himself in an ancient Etruscan grave, into which he has descended, happy in the satisfaction it has given to his archaeological interests. Similarly man makes the forces of nature not simply in the image of men with whom he can associate as his equals—that would not do justice to the overpowering impression they make on him—but he gives them the characteristics of the father, makes them into gods, thereby following not only an infantile, but also, as I have tried to show, a phylogenetic prototype.

In the course of time the first observations of law and order in natural phenomena are made, and therewith the forces of nature lose their human traits. But men's helplessness remains, and with it their father-longing and the gods. The gods retain their threefold task: they must exorcise the terrors of nature, they must reconcile one to the cruelty of fate, particularly as shown in death, and they must make amends for the sufferings and privations that the communal life of culture has imposed on man.

But within these there is a gradual shifting of the accent. It is observed that natural phenomena develop of themselves from inward necessity; without doubt the gods are the lords of nature: they have arranged it thus and now they can leave it to itself. Only occasionally, in the so-called miracles, do they intervene in its course, as if to protest that they have surrendered nothing of their original sphere of power. As far as the vicissitudes of fate are concerned, an unpleasant suspicion persists that the perplexity and helplessness of the human race cannot be remedied. This is where the gods are most apt to fail us; if they themselves make fate, then their ways must be deemed inscrutable. The most gifted people of the ancient world dimly surmised that above the gods stands Destiny and that the gods themselves have their destinies. And the more autonomous nature becomes and the more earnestly are all expectations concentrated on the third task assigned to them and the more does morality become their real domain. It now becomes the business of the gods to adjust the defects and evils of culture, to attend to the sufferings that men inflict on each other in their communal life, and to see that the laws of culture, which men obey so ill, are carried out. The laws of culture themselves are claimed to be of divine origin, they are elevated to a position above human society, and they are extended over nature and the universe.

And so a rich store of ideas is formed, born of the need to make tolerable the helplessness of man, and built out of the material offered by memories of the helplessness of his own childhood and the childhood of the human race. It is easy to see that these ideas protect man in two directions; against the dangers to nature and fate, and against the evils of human society itself. What it amounts of is this: life in this world serves a higher purpose; true, it is not easy to guess the nature of this purpose, but certainly a perfecting of human existence is implied. Probably the spiritual part of man, the soul, which in the course of time has so slowly and unwillingly detached itself from the body, is to be regarded as the object of this elevation and exaltation. Everything that takes place in this world expresses the intentions of an Intelligence, superior to us, which in the end, though its devious ways may be difficult to follow, orders everything for good, that is, to our advantage. Over each one of us watches a benevolent, and only apparently severe, Providence, which will not suffer us to become the plaything of the stark and pitiless forces of nature; death itself is not annihilation, not a return to inorganic lifelessness, but the beginning of a new kind of existence, which lies on the road of development to something higher. And to turn to the other side of the question, the moral laws that have formed our culture govern also the whole universe, only they are upheld with incomparably more force and consistency by a supreme judicial court. In the end all good is rewarded, all evil punished, if not actually in this life, then in the further existences that begin after death. And thus all the terrors, the sufferings, and the hardships of life are destined to be obliterated; the life after death, which continues our earthly existence as the invisible part of the spectrum adjoins the visible, brings all the perfection that perhaps we have missed here. And the superior wisdom that directs this issue, the supreme goodness that expresses itself thus, the justice that thus achieves its aim— these are the qualities of the divine beings who have fashioned us and the world in general; or rather of the one divine being into which in our culture all the gods of antiquity have been condensed. The race that first succeeded in thus concentrating the divine qualities was not a little proud of this advance. It had revealed the father nucleus which had always lain hidden behind every divine figure; fundamentally it was a return to the historical beginnings of the idea of God. Now that God was a single person, man's relations to him could recover the intimacy and intensity of the child's relation to the father. If one had done so much for the father, then surely one would be rewarded—at least the only beloved child, the chosen people, would be. More recently, pious America has laid claim to be "God's own country," and for one of the forms under which men worship the deity the claim certainly holds good.

The religious ideas that have just been summarized have of course gone through a long process of development, and have been held in various phases by various cultures. I have singled out one such phase of development, which more or less corresponds to the final form of our contemporary Christian culture in the west. It is easy to see that not all the parts of this whole tally equally well with each other, that not all the questions that press for an answer receive one, and that the contradiction of daily experience can only with difficulty be dismissed. But such as they are, these ideas—religious, in the broadest sense of the word—are prized as the most precious possession of culture, as the most valuable thing it has to offer its members; far more highly prized than all our devices for winning the treasures of the earth, for providing men with sustenance, or for preventing their diseases, and so forth; men suppose that life would be intolerable if they did not accord these ideas the value that is claimed for them. And now the question arises: what are these ideas in the light of psychology; whence do they derive the esteem in which they are held; and further, in all diffidence, what is their real worth?

. . .

Now to take up again the threads of our enquiry: what is the psychological significance of religious ideas and how can we classify them? The question is at first not at all easy to answer. Having rejected various formulas, I shall take my stand by this one: religion consists of certain dogmas, assertions about facts and conditions of external (or internal) reality, which tell one something that one has not oneself discovered and which claim that one should give them credence. As they give information about what are to us the most interesting and important things in life, they are particularly highly valued. He who knows nothing of them is ignorant indeed, and he who has assimilated them may consider himself enriched.

. . .

If we ask on what their claim to be believed is based, we receive three answers, which accord remarkably ill with one another. They deserve to be believed: firstly, because our primal ancestors already believed them; secondly, because we possess proofs, which have been handed down to us from this very period of antiquity; and thirdly, because it is forbidden to raise the question of their authenticity at all. Formerly this presumptuous act was visited with the very severest penalties, and even to-day society is unwilling to see anyone renew it.

This third point cannot but rouse our strongest suspicions. Such a prohibition can surely have only one motive: that society knows very well the uncertain basis of the claim it makes for its religious doctrines. If it were otherwise, the relevant material would certainly be placed most readily at the disposal of anyone who wished to gain conviction for himself. And so we proceed to test the other two arguments with a feeling of mistrust not easily allayed. We ought to believe because our forefathers believed. But these ancestors of ours were far more ignorant than we; they believed in things we could not possibly accept to-day; so the possibility occurs that religious doctrines may also be in this category. The proofs they have bequeathed to us are deposited in writings that themselves bear every trace of being untrustworthy. They are full of contradictions, revisions, and interpolations; where they speak of actual authentic proofs they are themselves of doubtful authenticity. It does not help much if divine revelation is asserted to be the origin of their text or only of their content, for this assertion is itself already a part of those doctrines whose authenticity is to be examined, and no statement can bear its own proof.

Thus we arrive at the singular conclusion that just what might be of the greatest significance for us in our cultural system, the information which should solve for us the riddles of the universe and reconcile us to the troubles of life, that just this has the weakest possible claim to authenticity. We should not be able to bring ourselves to accept anything of as little concern to us as the fact that whales bear young instead of laying eggs, if it were not capable of better proof than this.

This state of things is in itself a very remarkable psychological problem. Let no one think that the foregoing remarks on the impossibility of proving religious doctrines contain anything new. It has been felt at all times, assuredly even by the ancestors who bequeathed this legacy. Probably many of them nursed the same doubts as we, but the pressure imposed on them was too strong for them to have dared to utter them. And since then countless people have been tortured by the same doubts, which they would fain have suppressed because they held themselves in duty bound to believe, and since then many brilliant intellects have been wrecked upon this conflict and many characters have come to grief through the compromises by which they sought a way out.

. . .

One must now mention two attempts to evade the problem, which both convey the impression of frantic effort. One of them, high-handed in its nature, is old; the other is subtle and modern. The first is the *Credo quia absurdum* of the early Fathers. It would imply that religious doctrines are outside reason's jurisdiction; they stand above reason. Their truth must inwardly be felt: one does not need to comprehend them. But this *Credo* is only of interest as a voluntary confession; as a decree it has no binding force. Am I to be obliged to believe every absurdity? And if not, why just this one? There is no appeal beyond reason. And if the truth of religious doctrines is dependent on an inner experience which bears witness to that truth, what is one to make of the many people who do not have that rare experience? One may expect all men to use the gift of reason that they possess, but one cannot set up an obligation that shall apply to all on a basis that only exists for quite a few. Of what significance is it for other people that you have won from a state of ecstasy, which has deeply moved you, an imperturbable conviction of the real truth of the doctrines of religion?

The second attempt is that of the philosophy of "As If." It explains that in our mental activity we assume all manner of things, the groundlessness, indeed the absurdity, of which we fully realize. They are called "fictions," but from a variety of practical motives we are led to behave "as if" we believed in these fictions. This, it is argued, is the case with religious doctrines on account of their unequalled importance for the maintenance of human society. This argument is not far removed from the *Credo quia absurdum*. But I think that the claim of the philosophy of "As If" is such as only a philosopher could make. The man whose thinking is not influenced by the wiles of philosophy will never be able to accept it; with the confession of absurdity, of illogicality, there is no more to be said as far as he is concerned. He cannot be expected to forgo the guarantees he demands for all his usual activities just in the matter of his most important interests. I am reminded of one of my children who was distinguished at an early age by a peculiarly marked sense of reality. When the children were told a fairy tale, to which they listened with rapt attention, he would come forward and ask: Is that a true story? Having been told that it was not, he would turn away with an air of disdain. It is to be expected that men will soon behave in like manner towards the religious fairy tales, despite the advocacy of the philosophy of "As If."

But at present they still behave quite differently, and in past ages, in spite of their incontrovertible lack of authenticity, religious ideas have exercised the very strongest influence on makind. This is a fresh psychological problem. We must ask where the inherent strength of these doctrines lies and to what circumstance they owe their efficacy, independent, as it is, of the acknowledgement of the reason.

. . .

I think we have sufficiently paved the way for the answer to both these questions. It will be found if we fix our attention on the psychical origin of religious ideas. These, which profess to be dogmas, are not the residue of experience or the final result of reflection; they are illusions, fulfilments of the oldest, strongest and most insistent wishes of mankind; the secret of their strength is the strength of these wishes. We know already that the terrifying effect of infantile helplessness aroused the need for protection—protection through love—which the father relieved, and that the discovery that this helplessness would continue through the whole of life made it necessary to cling to the existence of a father—but this time a more powerful one. Thus the benevolent rule of divine providence allays our anxiety in face of life's dangers, the establishment of a moral world order ensures the fulfilment of the demands of justice, which within human culture have so often remained unfulfilled and the prolongation of earthly existence by a future life provides in addition the local and temporal setting for these wish-fulfilments. Answers to the questions that tempt human curiosity, such as the origin of the universe and the relation between the body and the soul, are developed in accordance with the underlying assumptions of this system; it betokens a tremendous relief for the individual psyche if it is released from the conflicts of childhood arising out of the father complex, which are never wholly overcome, and if these conflicts are afforded a universally accepted solution.

When I say that they are illusions, I must define the meaning of the word. An illusion is not the same as an error, it is indeed not necessarily an error. Aristotle's belief that vermin are evolved out of dung, to which ignorant people still cling, was an error; so was the belief of a former generation of doctors that *tabes dorsalis* was the result of sexual excess. It would be improper to call these errors illusions. On the other hand, it was an illusion on the part of Columbus that he had discovered a new sea-route to India. The part played by his wish in this error is very clear. One may describe as an illusion the statement of certain nationalists that the Indo-Germanic race is the only one capable of culture, or the belief, which only psycho-analysis destroyed, that the child is a being without sexuality. It is characteristic of the illusion that it is derived from men's wishes; in this respect it approaches the psychiatric delusion, but it is to be distinguished from this, quite apart from the more complicated structure of the latter. In the delusion we emphasize as essential the conflict with reality; the illusion need not be necessarily false, that is to say, unrealizable or incompatible with reality. For instance, a poor girl may have an illusion that a prince will come and fetch her home. It is possible; some such cases have occurred. That the Messiah will come and found a golden age is much less probable; according to one's personal attitude one will classify this belief as an illusion or as analogous to a delusion. Examples of illusions that have come true are not easy to discover, but the illusion of the alchemists that all metals can be turned into gold may prove to be one. The desire to have lots of gold, as much gold as possible, has been considerably damped by our modern insight into the nature of wealth, yet chemistry no longer considers a transmutation of metals into gold as impossible. Thus we call a belief an illusion when wish-fulfilment is a prominent factor in its motivation, while disregarding its relations to reality, just as the illusion itself does.

If after this survey we turn again to religious doctrines, we may reiterate that they are all illusions, they do not admit of proof, and no one can be compelled to consider them as true or to believe in them. Some of them are so improbable, so very incompatible with everything we have laboriously discovered about the reality of the world, that we may compare them—taking adequately into account the psychological differences—to delusions. Of the reality value of most of them we cannot judge; just as they cannot be proved, neither can they be refuted. We still know too little to approach them critically. The riddles of the universe only reveal themselves slowly to our enquiry, to many questions science can as yet give no answer; but scientific work is our only way to the knowledge of external reality.

. . .

It does not lie within the scope of this enquiry to estimate the value of religious doctrines as truth. It suffices that we have recognized them, psychologically considered, as illusions. But we need not conceal the fact that this discovery strongly influences our attitude to what must appear to many the most important of questions. We know approximately at what periods and by what sort of men religious doctrines were formed. If we now learn from what motives this happened, our attitude to the problem of religion will suffer an appreciable change. We say to ourselves: it would indeed be very nice if there were a God, who was both creator of the world and a benevolent providence, if there were a moral world order and a future life, but at the same time it is very odd that this is all just as we should wish it ourselves. And it would be still odder if our poor, ignorant, enslaved ancestors had succeeded in solving all these difficult riddles of the universe.

. . .

I know how difficult it is to avoid illusions. But I hold fast to one distinction. My illusions—apart from the fact that no penalty is imposed for not sharing them—are not, like the religious ones, incapable of correction, they have no delusional character. If experience should show—not to me, but to others after me who think as I do—that we are mistaken, then we shall give up our expectations. Take my endeavour for what it is. A psychologist, who does not deceive himself about the difficulty of finding his bearings in this world, strives to review the development of mankind in accord with what insight he has won from studying the mental processes of the individual during his development from childhood to manhood. In this connection the idea forces itself upon him that religion is comparable to a childhood neurosis, and he is optimistic enough to assume that mankind will overcome this neurotic phase, just as so many children grow out of their similar neuroses.

. . .

But science has shown us by numerous and significant successes that it is no illusion. Science has many open, and still more secret, enemies among those who cannot forgive it for having weakened religious belief and for threatening to overthrow it. People reproach it for the small amount it has taught us and the incomparably greater amount it has left in the dark. But then they forget how young it is, how difficult its beginnings, and how infinitesimally small the space of time since the human intellect has been strong enough for the tasks it sets it. Do we not all do wrong in that the periods of time which we make the basis of our judgements are of too short duration? We should take an example from the geologist. People complain of the unreliability of science, that she proclaims as a law to-day what the next generation will recognize to be an error and which will replace by a new law of equally short currency. But that is unjust and in part untrue. The transformation of scientific ideas is a process of development and progress, not of revolution. A law that was at first held to be universally valid proves to be a special case of a more comprehensive law, or else its scope is limited by another law not discovered until later; a rough approximation to the truth is replaced by one more carefully adjusted, which in turn awaits a further approach to perfection. In several spheres we have not yet surmounted a phase of investigation in which we test hypotheses that have soon to be rejected as inadequate; but in others we have already an assured and almost immutable core of knowledge. Finally an attempt has been made to discredit radically scientific endeavour on the ground that, bound as it is to the conditions of our own organization, it can yield nothing but subjective results, while the real nature of things outside us remains inaccessible to it. But this is to disregard several factors of decisive importance for the understanding of scientific work. Firstly, our organization, *i.e.* our mental apparatus, has been developed actually in the attempt to explore the outer world, and therefore it must have realized in its structure a certain measure of appropriateness; secondly, it itself is a constituent part of that world which we are to investigate, and readily admits of such investigation; thirdly, the task of science is fully circumscribed if we confine it to showing how the world must appear to us in consequence of the particular character of our organization; fourthly, the ultimate findings of science, just because of the way in which they are attained, are conditioned not only by our organization but also by that which has affected this organization; and, finally, the problem of the nature of the world irrespective of our perceptive mental apparatus is an empty abstraction without practical interest.

No, science is no illusion. But it would be an illusion to suppose that we could get anywhere else what it cannot give us.

The Opium of the People

Karl Marx

Karl Marx (1818–1883), collaborated with Friedrich Engels on *The Communist Manifesto* (1848) and is the author of *Das Kapital* (1867–1888). Marx is the most important single figure in the development of the philosophy of modern Communism. Marx rebelled against the Hegelian philosophy, saying "the most important task of the philosopher is not to know the world but to change it."

Contribution to the Critique of Hegel's Philosophy of Right

Introduction. For Germany, the *criticism of religion* has been largely completed; and the criticism of religion is the premise of all criticism.

The *profane* existence of error is compromised once its *celestial oratio pro aris*

Source: Karl Marx, *Early Writings*, trans. and ed. by T. B. Bottomore (New York, 1963), pp. 43–44, 52–53, 58–59. Copyright © 1963 by T. B. Bottomore. Reprinted by permission of McGraw-Hill Book Company and Sir Isaac Pitman and Sons Ltd.

et focis has been refuted. Man, who has found in the fantastic reality of heaven, where he sought a supernatural being, only his own reflection, will no longer be tempted to find only the *semblance* of himself—a non-human being—where he seeks and must seek his true reality.

The basis of irreligious criticism is this: *man makes religion*; religion does not make man. Religion is indeed man's self-consciousness and self-awareness so long as he has not found himself or has lost himself again. But *man* is not an abstract being, squatting outside the world. Man is *the human world*, the state, society. This state, this society, produce religion which is an *inverted world consciousness*, because they are an *inverted world*. Religion is the general theory of this world, its encyclo-pedic compendium, its logic in popular form, its spiritual *point d'honneur*, its en-thusiasm, its moral sanction, its solemn complement, its general basis of consolation and justification. It is *the fantastic realization* of the human being inasmuch as the *human being* possesses no true reality. The struggle against religion is, therefore, indirectly a struggle against *that world* whose spiritual *aroma* is religion.

Religious suffering is at the same time an *expression* of real suffering and a *protest* against real suffering. Religion is the sigh of the oppressed creature, the sentiment of a heartless world, and the soul of soulless conditions. It is the *opium* of the people.

The abolition of religion as the *illusory* happiness of men, is a demand for their *real* happiness. The call to abandon their illusions about their condition is a *call to abandon a condition which requires illusions*. The criticism of religion is, therefore, *the embryonic criticism of this vale of tears* of which religion is the *halo*.

Criticism has plucked the imaginary flowers from the chain, not in order that man shall bear the chain without caprice or consolation but so that he shall cast off the chain and pluck the living flower. The criticism of religion disillusions man so that he will think, act and fashion his reality as a man who has lost his illusions and regained his reason; so that he will revolve about himself as his own true sun. Religion is only the illusory sun about which man revolves so long as he does not revolve about himself.

It is the *task of history*, therefore, once the *other-world of truth* has vanished, to establish the *truth of this world*. The immediate *task of philosophy*, which is in the service of history, is to unmask human self-alienation in its *secular form* now that it has been unmasked in its *sacred form*. Thus the criticism of heaven is trans-formed into the criticism of earth, the *criticism of religion* into the *criticism of law*, and the *criticism of theology* into the *criticism of politics*.

The following exposition[1]—which is a contribution to this undertaking—does not deal directly with the original but with a copy, the German *philosophy* of the state and of right, for the simple reason that it deals with Germany.

. . .

It is clear that the arm of criticism cannot replace the criticism of arms. Ma-terial force can only be overthrown by material force; but theory itself becomes a material force when it has seized the masses. Theory is capable of seizing the masses

---

[1] Marx refers to his intentions to publish a critical study of Hegel's *Philosophy of Right*, to which this essay was an introduction. One of Marx's preliminary manuscripts for such a study has been published entitled "Aus der Kritik der Hegelschen Rechtsphilosophie. Kritik des Hegelschen Staats-rechts." (*MEGA* I11, pp. 403–553). The "Economic and Philosophical Manuscripts" is another version of this study; *see* Marx's comment. . . . [*Editor's note*].

when it demonstrates *ad hominem*, and it demonstrates *ad hominen* as soon as it be-comes radical. To be radical is to grasp things by the root. But for man the root is man himself. What proves beyond doubt the radicalism of German theory, and thus its practical energy, is that it begins from the resolute *positive* abolition of religion. The criticism of religion ends with the doctrine that *man is the supreme being for man.* It ends, therefore, with the *categorical imperative to overthrow all those conditions* in which man is an abased, enslaved, abandonded, contemptible being—conditions which can hardly be better described than in the exclamation of a Frenchman on the occasion of a proposed tax upon dogs: "Wretched dogs! They want to treat you like men!"

Even from the historical standpoint theoretical emancipation has a specific prac-tical importance for Germany. In fact Germany's *revolutionary* past is theoretical—it is the *Reformation*. In that period the revolution originated in the brain of a monk, today in the brain of the philosopher.

Luther, without question, overcame servitude through devotion but only by substituting servitude through *conviction*. He shattered the faith in authority by re-storing the authority of faith. He transformed the priests into laymen by turning laymen into priests. He liberated man from external religiosity by making religiosity the innermost essence of man. He liberated the body from its chains because he fettered the heart with chains.

But if Protestantism was not the solution it did at least pose the problem cor-rectly. It was no longer a question, thereafter, of the layman's struggle against the priest outside himself, but of his struggle against his *own internal priest*, against his own *priestly nature*. And if the Protestant metamorphosis of German laymen into priests emancipated the lay popes—the *princes* together with their clergy, the privi-leged and the philistines—the philosophical metamorphosis of the priestly Germans into men will emancipate the *people*. But just as emancipation will not be confined to princes, so the *secularization* of property will not be limited to the *confiscation of church property*, which was practised especially by hypocritical Prussia. At that time, the Peasant War, the most radical event in German history, came to grief because of theology.

Today, when theology itself has come to grief, the most unfree phenomenon in German history—our *status quo*—will be shattered by philosophy. . . .

. . .

Where is there, then, a *real* possibility of emancipation in Germany?

This is our reply. A class must be formed which has *radical chains*, a class in civil society which is not a class of civil society, a class which is the dissolution of all classes, a sphere of society which has a universal character because its sufferings are universal, and which does not claim a *particular redress* because the wrong which is done to it is not a *particular wrong* but *wrong in general*. There must be formed a sphere of society which claims no *traditional* status but only a human status, a sphere which is not opposed to particular consequences but is totally opposed to the as-sumptions of the German political system; a sphere, finally, which cannot emanci-pate itself without emancipating itself from all the other spheres of society, without, therefore, emancipating all these other spheres, which is, in short, a *total loss* of humanity and which can only redeem itself by a *total redemption of humanity*. This dissolution of society, as a particular class, is the *proletariat*.

The proletariat is only beginning to form itself in Germany, as a result of the industrial movement. For what constitutes the proletariat is not *naturally existing* poverty, but poverty *artificially produced*, is not the mass of people mechanically oppressed by the weight of society, but the mass resulting from the *disintegration* of society and above all from the disintegration of the middle class. Needless to say, however, the numbers of the proletariat are also increased by the victims of natural poverty and of Christian-Germanic serfdom.

When the proletariat announces the *dissolution of the existing social order*, it only declares the *secret of its* own existence, for it *is* the *effective* dissolution of this order. When the proletariat demands the *negation of private property* it only lays down as a *principle for society* what society has already made a principle *for the proletariat*, and what the *latter* already involuntarily embodies as the negative result of society. Thus the proletarian has the the the same right, in relation to the new world which is coming into being, as the *German king* has in relation to the existing world when he calls the people *his* people or a horse *his* horse. In calling the people his private property the king simply declares that the owner of private property is king.

Just as philosophy finds its *material* weapons in the proletariat, so the proletariat finds its *intellectual* weapons in philosophy. And once the lightning of thought has penetrated deeply into this virgin soil of the people, the *Germans* will emancipate themselves and become *men*.

Let us sum up these results. The emancipation of Germany is only possible *in practice* if one adopts the point of view of that theory according to which man is the highest being for man. Germany will not be able to emancipate itself from the *Middle Ages* unless it emancipates itself at the same time from the *partial* victories over the Middle Ages. In Germany *no* type of enslavement can be abolished unless *all* enslavement is destroyed. Germany, which likes to get to the bottom of things, can only make a revolution which upsets *the whole order* of things. The *emancipation of Germany* will be an *emancipation of man*. *Philosophy* is the *head* of this emancipation and the *proletariat* is its *heart*. Philosophy can only be realized by the abolition of the proletariat, and the proletariat can only be abolished by the realization of philosophy.

Religion as a Product of Social Need

Emile Durkheim

Emile Durkheim (1858–1917) was a pioneer in the field of sociology, strongly influenced by the positivistic social philosophy of Auguste Comte. His major works are *The Elementary Forms of Religious Life*, *Suicide*, and *Rules of Sociological Method*.

The Social Foundation of Religion

All known religious beliefs, whether simple or complex, present one common characteristic: they presuppose a classification of all the things, real and ideal, of which men think, into two classes or opposed groups, generally designated by two distinct terms which are translated well enough by the words *profane* and *sacred* (*profane, sacré*). This division of the world into two domains, the one containing all that is sacred, the other all that is profane, is the distinctive trait of religious thought; the beliefs, myths, dogmas and legends are either representations or systems of representations which express the nature of sacred things, the virtues and powers which are attributed to them, or their relations with each other and with profane things. But by sacred things one must not understand simply those personal beings which are called gods or spirits; a rock, a tree, a spring, a pebble, a piece of wood, a house, in a word, anything can be sacred. A rite can have this character; in fact, the rite does not exist which does not have it to a certain degree. There are words, expressions and formulae which can be pronounced only by the mouths of consecrated persons; there are gestures and movements which everybody cannot perform. If the Vedic sacrifice has had such an efficacy that, according to mythology, it was the creator of the gods, and not merely a means of winning their favor, it is because it possessed a virtue comparable to that of the most sacred beings. The circle of sacred objects cannot be determined, then, once for all. Its extent varies infinitely, according to the different religions. That is how Buddhism is a religion: in default of gods, it admits the existence of sacred things, namely, the four noble truths and the practices derived from them.

Up to the present we have confined ourselves to enumerating a certain number of sacred things as examples: we must now show by what general characteristics they are to be distinguished from profane things.

One might be tempted, first of all, to define them by the place they are generally assigned in the hierarchy of things. They are naturally considered superior in dignity

Source: Emile Durkheim, *The Elementary Forms of Religious Life*, trans. by J. Swain (New York, 1961), pp. 42–54. Copyright © 1915 by George Allen & Unwin Ltd. First Free Press Paperback edition 1963. Reprinted by permission of Macmillan Publishing Co., Inc., and George Allen & Unwin Ltd.

and power to profane things, and particularly to man, when he is only a man and has nothing sacred about him. One thinks of himself as occupying an inferior and dependent position in relation to them; and surely this conception is not without some truth. Only there is nothing in it which is really characteristic of the sacred. It is not enough that one thing be subordinated to another for the second to be sacred in regard to the first. Slaves are inferior to their masters, subjects to their king, soldiers to their leaders, the miser to his gold, the man ambitious for power to the hands which keep it from him; but if it is sometimes said of a man that he makes a religion of those beings or things whose eminent value and superiority to himself he thus recognizes, it is clear that in any case the word is taken in a metaphorical sense, and that there is nothing in these relations which is really religious.

On the other hand it must not be lost to view that there are sacred things of every degree, and that there are some in relation to which a man feels himself relatively at his ease. An amulet has a sacred character, yet the respect which it inspires is nothing exceptional. Even before his gods, a man is not always in such a marked state of inferiority; for it very frequently happens that he exercises a veritable physical constraint upon them to obtain what he desires. He beats the fetish with which he is not contented, but only to reconcile himself with it again, if in the end it shows itself more docile to the wishes of its adorer. To have rain, he throws stones into the spring or sacred lake where the god of rain is thought to reside; he believes that by this means he forces him to come out and show himself. Moreover, if it is true that man depends upon his gods, this dependence is reciprocal. The gods also have need of man; without offerings and sacrifices they would die. We shall even have occasion to show that this dependence of the gods upon their worshippers is maintained even in the most idealistic religions.

But if a purely hierarchic distinction is a criterion at once too general and too imprecise, there is nothing left with which to characterize the sacred in its relation to the profane except their heterogeneity. However, this heterogeniety is sufficient to characterize this classification of things and to distinguish it from all others, because it is very particular: *it is absolute.* In all the history of human thought there exists no other example of two categories of things so profoundly differentiated or so radically opposed to one another. The traditional opposition of good and bad is nothing beside this; for the good and the bad are only two opposed species of the same class, namely morals, just as sickness and health are two different aspects of the same order of facts, life, while the sacred and the profane have always and everywhere been conceived by the human mind as two distinct classes, as two worlds between which there is nothing in common. The forces which play in one are not simply those which are met with in the other, but a little stronger; they are of a different sort. In different religions, this opposition has been conceived in different ways. Here, to separate these two sorts of things, it has seemed sufficient to localize them in different parts of the physical universe; there, the first have been put into an ideal and transcendental world, while the material world is left in full possession

---

[1] The conception according to which the profane is opposed to the sacred, just as the irrational is to the rational, or the intelligible is to the mysterious, is only one of the forms under which this opposition is expressed. Science being once constituted, it has taken a profane character, especially in the eyes of the Christian religions; from that it appears as though it could not be applied to sacred things.

of the others. But howsoever much the forms of the contrast may vary,[1] the fact of the contrast is universal.

This is not equivalent to saying that a being can never pass from one of these worlds into the other: but the manner in which this passage is effected, when it does take place, puts into relief the essential duality of the two kingdoms. In fact, it implies a veritable metamorphosis. This is notably demonstrated by the initiation rites, such as they are practised by a multitude of peoples. This initiation is a long series of ceremonies with the object of introducing the young man into the religious life: for the first time, he leaves the purely profane world where he passed his first infancy, and enters into the world of sacred things. Now this change of state is thought of, not as a simple and regular development of pre-existent germs, but as a transformation *totius substantiae*—of the whole being. It is said that at this moment the young man dies, that the person that he was ceases to exist, and that another is instantly substituted for it. He is reborn under a new form. Appropriate ceremonies are felt to bring about this death and rebirth, which are not understood in a merely symbolic sense, but are taken literally.[1] Does this not prove that between the profane being which he was and the religious being which he becomes, there is a break of continuity?

This heterogeneity is even so complete that it frequently degenerates into a veritable antagonism. The two worlds are not only conceived of as separate, but as even hostile and jealous rivals of each other. Since men cannot fully belong to one except on condition of leaving the other completely, they are exhorted to withdraw themselves completely from the profane world, in order to lead an exclusively religious life. Hence comes the monasticism which is artificially organized outside of and apart from the natural environment in which the ordinary man leads the life of this world, in a different one, closed to the first, and nearly its contrary. Hence comes the mystic asceticism whose object is to root out from man all the attachment for the profane world that remains in him. From that come all the forms of religious suicide, the logical working-out of this asceticism; for the only manner of fully escaping the profane life is, after all, to forsake all life.

The opposition of these two classes manifests itself outwardly with a visible sign by which we can easily recognize this very special classification, wherever it exists. Since the idea of the sacred is always and everywhere separated from the idea of the profane in the thought of men, and since we picture a sort of logical chasm between the two, the mind irresistibly refuses to allow the two corresponding things to be confounded, or even to be merely put in contact with each other; for such a promiscuity, or even too direct a contiguity, would contradict too violently the dissociation of these ideas in the mind. The sacred thing is *par excellence* that which the profane should not touch, and cannot touch with impunity. To be sure, this interdiction cannot go so far as to make all communication between the two worlds impossible; for if the profane could in no way enter into relations with the sacred, this latter could be good for nothing. But, in addition to the fact that this establishment of relations is always a delicate operation in itself, demanding great precautions

---

[1] See Frazer, "On some ceremonies of the Central Australian tribes" in *Australian Association for the Advancement of Science*, 1901, pp. 313ff. This conception is also of an extreme generality. In India, the simple participation in the sacrificial act has the same effects; the sacrificer, by the mere act of entering within the circle of sacred things, changes his personality. (See Hubert and Mauss, "Essai sur la nature et la fonction du sacrifice" in the *Année Sociologique*, vol. 2, 1899, p. 101.)

and a more or less complicated initiation, it is quite impossible, unless the profane is to lose its specific characteristics and become sacred after a fashion and to a certain degree itself. The two classes cannot even approach each other and keep their own nature at the same time.

Thus we arrive at the first criterion of religious beliefs. Undoubtedly there are secondary species within these two fundamental classes which, in their turn, are more or less incompatible with each other. But the real characteristic of religious phenomena is that they always suppose a bipartite division of the whole universe, known and knowable, into two classes which embrace all that exists, but which radically exclude each other. Sacred things are those which the interdictions protect and isolate; profane things, those to which these interdictions are applied and which must remain at a distance from the first. Religious beliefs are the representations which express the nature of sacred things and the relations which they sustain, either with each other or with profane things. Finally, rites are the rules of conduct which prescribe how a man should comport himself in the presence of these sacred objects.

... We arrive at the following definition: *a religion is a unified system of beliefs and practices relative to sacred things, that is to say, things set apart and forbidden— beliefs and practices which unite into one single moral community called a Church, all those who adhere to them.* The second element which finds a place in our definition is no less essential than the first; for by showing that the idea of religion is inseparable from that of the Church, it makes it clear that religion should be an eminently collective thing. . . .

Our entire study rests upon the postulate that the unanimous sentiment of the believers of all times cannot be purely illusory.[1] Together with an apologist of the faith[2] we admit that these religious beliefs rest upon a specific experience whose demonstrative value is, in one sense, not one bit inferior to that of scientific experiments, though different from them. We, too, think that "a tree is known by its fruits,"[3] and that fertility is the best proof of "what the roots are worth." But from the fact that a "religious experience," if we choose to call it this, does exist and that it has a certain foundation—and, by the way, is there any experience which has none?—it does not follow that the reality which is its foundation conforms objectively to the idea which believers have of it. The very fact that the fashion in which it has been conceived has varied infinitely in different times is enough to prove that none of these conceptions express it adequately. If a scientist states it as an axiom that the sensations of heat and light which we feel correspond to some objective cause, he does not conclude that this is what it appears to the senses to be. Likewise, even if the impressions which the faithful feel are not imaginary, still they are in no way privileged intuitions; there is no reason for believing that they inform us better upon the nature of their object than do ordinary sensations upon the nature of bodies and their properties. In order to discover what this object consists of, we must submit them to an examination and elaboration analogous to that which has substituted for the sensuous idea of the world another which is scientific and conceptual.

[1] Durkheim refers here and subsequently to the details of his analysis of aboriginal religion in Australia—*Ed.*

[2] William James, *The Varieties of Religious Experience.*

[3] Quoted by James, op. cit., p. 20.

This is precisely what we have tried to do, and we have seen that this reality, which mythologies have represented under so many different forms, but which is the universal and eternal objective cause of these sensations *sui generis* out of which religious experience is made, is society. We have shown what moral forces it develops and how it awakens this sentiment of a refuge, of a shield and of a guardian support which attaches the believer to his cult. It is that which raises him outside himself; it is even that which made him. For that which makes a man is the totality of the intellectual property which constitutes civilization, and civilization is the work of society. This is explained by the preponderating role of the cult in all religions, whichever they may be. This is because society cannot make its influence felt unless it is in action, and it is not in action unless the individuals who compose it are assembled together and act in common. It is by common action that it takes consciousness of itself and realizes its position; it is before all else an active cooperation. The collective ideas and sentiments are even possible only owing to these exterior movements which symbolize them, as we have established. Then it is action which dominates the religious life, because of the mere fact that it is society which is its source.

In addition to all the reasons which have been given to justify this conception, a final one may be added here, which is the result of our whole work. As we have progressed, we have established the fact that the fundamental categories of thought, and consequently of science, are of religious origin. We have seen that the same is true for magic and consequently for the different processes which have issued from it. On the other hand, it has long been known that up until a relatively advanced moment of evolution, moral and legal rules have been indistinguishable from ritual prescriptions. In summing up, then, it may be said that nearly all the great social institutions have been born in religion. Now in order that these principal aspects of the collective life may have commenced by being only varied aspects of the religious life, it is obviously necessary that the religious life be the eminent form and, as it were, the concentrated expression of the whole collective life. If religion has given birth to all that is essential in society, it is because the idea of society is the soul of religion.

Religious forces are therefore human forces, moral forces. It is true that since collective sentiments can become conscious of themselves only by fixing themselves upon external objects, they have not been able to take form without adopting some of their characteristics from other things: they have thus acquired a sort of physical nature; in this way they have come to mix themselves with the life of the material world, and then have considered themselves capable of explaining what passes there. But when they are considered only from this point of view and in this role, only their most superficial aspect is seen. In reality, the essential elements of which these collective sentiments are made have been borrowed by the understanding. It ordinarily seems that they should have a human character only when they are conceived under human forms;[1] but even the most impersonal and the most anonymous are nothing else than objectified sentiments.

It is only by regarding religion from this angle that it is possible to see its real

---

[1] It is for this reason that Frazer and even Preuss set impersonal religious forces outside of, or at least on the threshold of religion, to attach them to magic.

significance. If we stick closely to appearances, rites often give the effect of purely manual operations: they are anointings, washings, meals. To consecrate something, it is put in contact with a source of religious energy, just as today a body is put in contact with a source of heat or electricity to warm or electrize it; the two processes employed are not essentially different. Thus understood, religious technique seems to be a sort of mystic mechanics. But these material maneuvers are only the external envelope under which the mental operations are hidden. Finally, there is no question of exercising a physical constraint upon blind, and incidentally, imaginary forces, but rather of reaching individual consciousnesses of giving them a direction and of disciplining them. It is sometimes said that inferior religions are materialistic. Such an expression is inexact. All religions, even the crudest, are in a sense spiritualistic: for the powers they put in play are before all spiritual, and also their principal object is to act upon the moral life. Thus it is seen that whatever has been done in the name of religion cannot have been done in vain: for it is necessarily the society that did it, and it is humanity that has reaped the fruits.

But, it is said, what society is it that has thus made the basis of religion? Is it the real society, such as it is and acts before our very eyes, with the legal and moral organization which it has laboriously fashioned during the course of history? This is full of defects and imperfections. In it, eveil goes beside the good, injustice often reigns supreme, and the truth is often obscured by error. How could anything so crudely organized inspire the sentiments of love, the ardent enthusiasm and the spirit of abnegation which all religions claim of their followers? These perfect beings which are gods could not have taken their traits from so mediocre, and sometimes even so base a reality.

But, on the other hand, does someone think of a perfect society, where justice and truth would be sovereign, and from which evil in all its forms would be banished for ever? No one would deny that this is in close relations with the religious sentiment; for, they would say, it is towards the realization of this that all religions strive. But that society is not an empirical fact, definite and observable; it is a fancy, a dream with which men have lightened their sufferings, but in which they have never really lived. It is merely an idea which comes to express our more or less obscure aspirations towards the good, the beautiful and the ideal. Now these aspirations have their roots in us; they come from the very depths of our being; then there is nothing outside of us which can account for them. Moreover, they are already religious in themselves; thus it would seem that the ideal society presupposes religion, far from being able to explain it.

But, in the first place, things are arbitrarily simplified when religion is seen only on its idealistic side: in its way, it is realistic. There is no physical or moral ugliness, there are no vices or evils which do not have a special divinity. There are gods of theft and trickery, of lust and war, of sickness and of death. Christianity itself, howsoever high the idea which it has made of the divinity may be, has been obliged to give the spirit of evil a place in its mythology. Satan is an essential piece of the Christian system; even if he is an impure being, he is not a profane one. The anti-god is a god, inferior and subordinated, it is true, but nevertheless endowed with extended powers; he is even the object of rites, at least of negative ones. Thus religion, far from ignoring the real society and making abstraction of it, is in its image; it reflects all its aspects, even the most vulgar and the most repulsive. All is to be found there, and if in the majority of cases we see the good victorious over evil, life over death, the powers of light over the powers of darkness, it is because reality is not otherwise. If the relation between these two contrary forces were reversed, life would be impossible; but, as a matter of fact, it maintains itself and even tends to develop.

But if, in the midst of these mythologies and theologies we see reality clearly appearing, it is none the less true that it is found there only in an enlarged, transformed and idealized form. In this respect, the most primitive religions do not differ from the most recent and the most refined. For example, we have seen how the Arunta place at the beginning of time a mythical society whose organization exactly reproduces that which still exists today; it includes the same clans and phratries, it is under the same matrimonial rules and it practises the same rites. But the personages who compose it are ideal beings, gifted with powers and virtues to which common mortals cannot pretend. Their nature is not only higher, but it is different, since it is at once animal and human. The evil powers there undergo a similar metamorphosis: evil itself is, as it were, made sublime and idealized. The question now raises itself of whence this idealization comes.

Some reply that men have a natural faculty for idealizing, that is to say, of substituting for the real world another different one, to which they transport themselves by thought. But that is merely changing the terms of the problem; it is not resolving it or even advancing it. This systematic idealization is an essential characteristic of religions. Explaining them by an innate power of idealization is simply replacing one word by another which is the equivalent of the first; it is as if they said that men have made religions because they have a religious nature. Animals know only one world, the one which they perceive by experience, internal as well as external. Men alone have the faculty of conceiving the ideal, of adding something to the real. Now where does this singular privilege come from? Before making it an initial fact or a mysterious virtue which escapes science, we must be sure that it does not depend upon empirically determinable conditions.

The explanation of religion which we have proposed has precisely this advantage, that it gives an answer to this question. For our definition of the sacred is that it is something added to and above the real; now the ideal answers to this same definition; we cannot explain one without explaining the other. In fact, we have seen that if collective life awakens religious thought on reaching a certain degree of intensity, it is because it brings about a state of effervescence which changes the conditions of psychic activity. Vital energies are over-excited, passions more active, sensations stronger; there are even some which are produced only at this moment. A man does not recognize himself; he feels himself transformed and consequently he transforms the environment which surronds him. In order to account for the very particular impressions which he recieves, he attributes to the things with which he is in most direct contact properties which they have not, exceptional powers and virtues which the objects of everyday experience do not possess. In a word, above the real world where his profane life passes he has placed another which, in one sense, does not exist except in thought, but to which he attributes a higher sort of dignity than to the first. Thus, from a double point of view it is an ideal world.

The formation of the ideal world is therefore not an irreducible fact which escapes science; it depends upon conditions which observation can touch; it is a natural product of social life. For a society to become conscious of itself and maintain at the necessary degree of intensity the sentiments which it thus attains, it must assemble and concentrate itself. Now this concentration brings about an exaltation of the mental life which takes form in a group of ideal conceptions where is portrayed the new life thus awakened; they correspond to this new set of psychical forces which is added to those which we have at our disposition for the daily tasks of existence. A society can neither create itself nor recreate itself without at the same time creating an ideal. This creation is not a sort of work of supererogation for it, by which it would complete itself, being already formed; it is the act by which it is periodically made and remade. Therefore when some oppose the ideal society to the real society, like two antagonists which would lead us in opposite directions, they materialize and oppose abstractions. The ideal society is not outside of the real society; it is a part of it. Far from being divided between them as between two poles which mutually repel each other, we cannot hold to one without holding to the other. For a society is not made up merely of the mass of individuals who compose it, the ground which they occupy, the things which they use and the movements which they perform, but above all is the idea which it forms of itself. It is undoubtedly true that it hesitates over the manner in which it ought to conceive itself; it feels itself drawn in divergent directions. But these conflicts which break forth are not between the ideal and reality, but between two different ideals, that of yesterday and that of today, that which has the authority of tradition and that which has the hope of the future. There is surely a place for investigating whence these ideals evolve; but whatever solution may be given to this problem, it still remains that all passes in the world of the ideal.

Thus the collective ideal which religion expresses is far from being due to a vague innate power of the individual, but it is rather at the school of collective life that the individual has learned to idealize. It is in assimilating the ideals elaborated by society that he has become capable of conceiving the ideal. It is society which, by leading him within its sphere of action, has made him acquire the need of raising himself above the world of experience and has at the same time furnished him with the means of conceiving another. For society has constructed this new world in constructing itself, since it is society which this expresses. Thus both with the individual and in the group, the faculty of idealizing has nothing mysterious about it. It is not a sort of luxury which a man could get along without, but a condition of his very existence. He could not be a social being, that is to say, he could not be man, if he had not acquired it. It is true that in incarnating themselves in individuals, collective ideals tend to individualize themselves. Each understands them after his own fashion and marks them with his own stamp; he suppresses certain elements and adds others. Thus the personal ideal disengages itself from the social ideal in proportion as the individual personality develops itself and becomes an autonomous source of action. But if we wish to understand this aptitude, so singular in appearance, of living outside of reality, it is enough to connect it with the social conditions upon which it depends.

Therefore it is necessary to avoid seeing in this theory of religion a simple restatement of historical materialism: that would be misunderstanding our thought to an extreme degree. In showing that religion is something essentially social, we do not mean to say that it confines itself to translating into another language the material forms of society and its immediate vital necessities. It is true that we take it as evident that social life depends upon its material foundation and bears its mark, just as the mental life of an individual depends upon his nervous system and in fact his whole organism. But collective consciousness is something more than a mere epiphenomenon of its morphological basis, just as individual consciousness is something more than a simple efflorescence of the nervous system. In order that the former may appear, a synthesis *sui generis* of particular consciousness is required. Now this synthesis has the effect of disengaging a whole world of sentiments, ideas and images which, once born, obey laws all their own. They attract each other, repel each other, unite, divide themselves and multiply, though these combinations are not commanded and necessitated by the condition of the underlying reality. The life thus brought into being even enjoys so great an independence that it sometimes indulges in manifestations with no purpose or utility of any sort, for the mere pleasure of affirming itself. We have shown that this is often precisely the case with ritual activity and mythological thought.

Religion as an Ethical Ideal

John Dewey

John Dewey (1859–1952) has had a greater influence on the world of practical affairs in the United States than any other professor of philosophy. This is not accidental, for in all his writings Dewey regards philosophy as a human activity whose value lies in its social impact. Greatly influenced by C. S. Pierce and William James, Dewey developed his own type of pragmatism that has become known as instrumentalism, and wielded his instrumentalism to create new approaches to and new insights into all branches of philosophy, psychology, and educational theory.

All religions . . . involve specific intellectual beliefs, and they attach—some greater, some less—importance to assent to these doctrines as true, true in the intellectual sense. They have literatures held especially sacred, containing historical material with which the validity of the religions is connected. They have developed a

Source: John Dewey, ''Faith and Its Object,'' in *A Common Faith* (New Haven, Conn., 1934). Copyright © 1934 by Yale University Press. Reprinted by permission.

doctrinal apparatus it is incumbent upon "believers" (with varying degrees of strictness in different religions) to accept. They also insist that there is some special and isolated channel of access to the truths they hold.

No one will deny, I suppose, that the present crisis in religion is intimately bound up with these claims. The skepticism and agnosticism that are rife and that from the standpoint of the religionist are fatal to the religious spirit are directly bound up with the intellectual contents, historical, cosmological, ethical, and theological, asserted to be indispensable in everything religious. There is no need for me here to go with any minuteness into the causes that have generated doubt and disbelief, uncertainty and rejection, as to these contents. It is enough to point out that all the beliefs and ideas in question, whether having to do with historical and literary matters, or with astronomy, geology and biology, or with the creation and structure of the world and man, are connected with the supernatural, and that this connection is the factor that has brought doubt upon them; the factor that from the standpoint of historic and institutional religions is sapping the religious life itself.

The obvious and simple facts of the case are that some views about the origin and constitution of the world and man, some views about the course of human history and personages and incidents in that history, have become so interwoven with religion as to be identified with it. On the other hand, the growth of knowledge and of its methods and tests has been such as to make acceptance of these beliefs increasingly onerous and even impossible for large numbers of cultivated men and women. With such persons, the result is that the more these ideas are used as the basis and justification of a religion, the more dubious that religion becomes.

Protestant denominations have largely abandoned the idea that particular ecclesiastic sources can authoritatively determine cosmic, historic and theological beliefs. The more liberal among them have at least mitigated the older belief that individual hardness and corruption of heart are the causes of intellectual rejection of the intellectual apparatus of the Christian religion. But these denominations have also, with exceptions numerically insignificant, retained a certain indispensable minimum of intellectual content. They ascribe peculiar religious force to certain literary documents and certain historic personages. Even when they have greatly reduced the bulk of intellectual content to be accepted, they have insisted at least upon theism and the immortality of the individual.

It is no part of my intention to rehearse in any detail the weighty facts that collectively go by the name of the conflict of science and religion—a conflict that is not done away with by calling it a conflict of science with theology, as long as even a minimum of intellectual assent is prescribed as essential. The impact of astronomy not merely upon the older cosmogony of religion but upon elements of creeds dealing with historic events—witness the idea of ascent into heaven—is familiar. Geological discoveries have displaced creation myths which once bulked large. Biology has revolutionized conceptions of soul and mind which once occupied a central place in religious beliefs and ideas, and this science has made a profound impression upon ideas of sin. redemption, and immortality. Anthropology, history and literary criticism have furnished a radically different version of the historic events and personages upon which Christian religions have built. Psychology is already opening to us natural explanations of phenomena so extraordinary that once their supernatural origin was, to so say, the natural explanation.

The significant bearing for my purpose of all this is that new methods of inquiry and reflection have become for the educated man today the final arbiter of all questions of fact, existence, and intellectual assent. Nothing less than a revolution in the "seat of intellectual authority" has taken place. This revolution, rather than any particular aspect of its impact upon this and that religious belief, is the central thing. In this revolution, every defeat is a stimulus to renewed inquiry; every victory won is the open door to more discoveries, and every discovery is a new seed planted in the soil of intelligence, from which grow fresh plants with new fruits. The mind of man is being habituated to a new method and ideal: There is but one sure road of access to truth—the road of patient, cooperative inquiry operating by means of observation, experiment, record and controlled reflection.

The scope of the change is well illustrated by the fact that whenever a particular outpost is surrendered it is usually met by the remark from a liberal theologian that the particular doctrine or supposed historic or literary tenet surrendered was never, after all, an intrinsic part of religious belief, and that without it the true nature of religion stands out more clearly than before. Equally significant is the growing gulf between fundamentalists and liberals in the churches. What is not realized—although perhaps it is more definitely seen by fundamentalists than by liberals—is that the issue does not concern this and that piecemeal *item* of belief, but centers in the question of the method by which any and every item of intellectual belief is to be arrived at and justified.

The positive lesson is that religious qualities and values if they are real at all are not bound up with any single item of intellectual assent, not even that of the existence of the God of theism; and that, under existing conditions, the religious function in experience can be emancipated only through surrender of the whole notion of special truths that are religious by their own nature, together with the idea of peculiar avenues of access to such truths. For were we to admit that there is but one method for ascertaining fact and truth—that conveyed by the word "scientific" in its most general and generous sense—no discovery in any branch of knowledge and inquiry could then disturb the faith that is religious. I should describe this faith as the unification of the self through allegiance to inclusive ideal ends, which imagination presents to us and to which the human will respond as worthy of controlling our desires and choices.

It is probably impossible to imagine the amount of intellectual energy that has been diverted from normal processes of arriving at intellectual conclusions because it has gone into rationalization of the doctrines entertained by historic religions. The set that has thus been given the general mind is much more harmful, to my mind, than are the consequences of any one particular item of belief, serious as have been those flowing from acceptance of some of them. The modern liberal version of the intellectual content of Christianity seems to the modern mind to be more rational than some of the earlier doctrines that have been reacted against. Such is not the case in fact. The theological philosophers of the Middle Ages had no greater difficulty in giving rational form to all the doctrines of the Roman church than has the liberal theologian of today in formulating and justifying intellectually the doctrines he entertains. This statement is as applicable to the doctrine of continuing miracles, penance, indulgences, saints and angels, etc., as to the trinity, incarnation, atonement, and the sacraments. The fundamental question, I repeat, is not of this and that article of intellectual belief but of intellectual habit, method and criterion.

One method of swerving aside the impact of changed knowledge and method upon the intellectual content of religion is the method of division of territory and jurisdiction into two parts. Formerly these were called the realm of nature and the realm of grace. They are now often known as those of revelation and natural knowledge. Modern religious liberalism has no definite names for them, save, perhaps, the division . . . between scientific and religious experience. The implication is that in one territory the supremacy of scientific knowledge must be acknowledged, while there is another region, not very precisely defined, of intimate personal experience wherein other methods and criteria hold sway.

This method of justifying the peculiar and legitimate claim of certain elements of belief is always open to the objection that a positive conclusion is drawn from a negative fact. Existing ignorance or backwardness is employed to assert the existence of a division in the nature of the subject-matter dealt with. Yet the gap may only reflect, at most, a limitation now existing but in the future to be done away with. The argument that because some province or aspect of experience has not yet been "invaded" by scientific methods, it is not subject to them, is as old as it is dangerous. Time and time again, in some particular reserved field, it has been invalidated. Psychology is still in its infancy. He is bold to the point of rashness who asserts that intimate personal experience will never come within the ken of natural knowledge.

It is more to the present point, however, to consider the region that is claimed by religionists as a special reserve. It is mystical experience. The difference, however, between mystic experience and the theory about it that is offered to us must be noted. The experience is a fact to be inquired into. The theory, like any theory, is an interpretation of the fact. The idea that by its very nature the experience is a veridical realization of the direct presence of God does not rest so much upon examination of the facts as it does upon importing into their interpretation a conception that is formed outside them. In its dependence upon a prior conception of the supernatural, which is the thing to be proved, it begs the question.

History exhibits many types of mystic experience, and each of these types is contemporaneously explained by the concepts that prevail in the culture and the circle in which the phenomena occur. There are mystic crises that arise, as among some North American Indian tribes, induced by fasting. They are accompanied by trances and semi-hysteria. Their purpose is to gain some special power, such perhaps as locating a person who is lost or finding objects that have been secreted. There is the mysticism of Hindoo practice now enjoying some vogue in Western countries. There is the mystic ecstasy of Neoplatonism with its complete abrogation of the self and absorption into an impersonal whole of Being. There is the mysticism of intense esthetic experience independent of any theological or metaphysical interpretation. There is the heretical mysticism of William Blake. There is the mysticism of sudden unreasoning fear in which the very foundations seem shaken beneath one—to mention but a few of the types that may be found.

What common element is there between, say, the Neoplatonic conception of a super-divine Being wholly apart from human needs and conditions and the medieval theory of an immediate union that is fostered through attention to the sacraments or through concentration upon the heart of Jesus? The contemporary emphasis of some Protestant theologians upon the sense of inner personal communion with God, found in religious experience, is almost as far away from medieval Christianity as it is from Neoplatonism or Yoga. Interpretations of the experience have not grown from the experience itself with the aid of such scientific resources as may be available. They have been imported by borrowing without criticism from ideas that are current in the surrounding culture.

The mystic states of the shaman and of some North American Indians are frankly techniques for gaining a special power—*the* power as it is conceived by some revivalist sects. There is no especial intellectual objectification accompanying the experience. The knowledge that is said to be gained is not that of Being but of particular secrets and occult modes of operation. The aim is not to gain knowledge of superior divine power, but to get advice, cures for the sick, prestige, etc. The conception that mystic experience is a normal mode of religious experience by which we may acquire knowledge of God and divine things is a nineteenth-century interpretation that has gained vogue in direct ratio to the decline of older methods of religious apologetics.

There is no reason for denying the existence of experiences that are called mystical. On the contrary, there is every reason to suppose that, in some degree of intensity, they occur so frequently that they may be regarded as normal manifestations that take place at certain rhythmic points in the movement of experience. The assumption that denial of a particular interpretation of their objective content proves that those who make the denial do not have the experience in question, so that if they had it they would be equally persuaded of its objective source in the presence of God, has no foundation in fact. As with every empirical phenomenon, the occurrence of the state called mystical is simply an occasion for inquiry into its mode of causation. There is no more reason for converting the experience itself into an immediate knowledge of its cause than in the case of an experience of lightning or any other natural occurrence.

My purpose, then, in this brief reference to mysticism is not to throw doubt upon the existence of particular experiences called mystical. Nor is it to propound any theory to account for them. I have referred to the matter merely as an illustration of the general tendency to mark off two distinct realms in one of which science has jurisdiction, while in the other, special modes of immediate knowledge of religious objects have authority. This dualism as it operates in contemporary interpretation of mystic experience in order to validate certain beliefs is but a reinstatement of the old dualism between the natural and the supernatural, in terms better adapted to the cultural conditions of the present time. Since it is the conception of the supernatural that science calls in question, the circular nature of this type of reasoning is obvious.

Apologists for a religion often point to the shift that goes on in scientific ideas and materials as evidence of the unreliability of science as a mode of knowledge. They often seem peculiarly elated by the great, almost revolutionary, change in fundamental physical conceptions that has taken place in science during the present generation. Even if the alleged unreliability were as great as they assume (or even greater), the question would remain: Have we any other recourse for knowledge? But in fact they miss the point. Science is not constituted by any particular body of subject-matter. It is constituted by a method, a method of changing beliefs by means of tested inquiry as well as of arriving at them. It is its glory, not its condemnation, that its subject-matter develops as the method is improved. There is no special subject-matter of belief that is sacrosanct. The identification of science with a particular set of beliefs and ideas is itself a holdover of ancient and still current dogmatic habits of thought which are opposed to science in its actuality and which science is undermining.

For scientific method is adverse not only to dogma but to doctrine as well, provided we take "doctrine" in its usual meaning—a body of definite beliefs that need only to be taught and learned as true. This negative attitude of science to doctrine does not indicate indifference to truth. It signifies supreme loyalty to the method by which truth is attained. The scientific-religious conflict ultimately is a conflict between allegiance to this method and allegiance to even an irreducible minimum of belief so fixed in advance that it can never be modified.

The method of intelligence is open and public. The doctrinal method is limited and private. This limitation persists even when knowledge of the truth that is religious is said to be arrived at by a special mode of experience, that termed "religious." For the latter is assumed to be a very special kind of experience. To be sure it is asserted to be open to all who obey certain conditions. Yet the mystic experience yields, as we have seen, various results in the way of belief to different persons, depending upon the surrounding culture of those who undergo it. As a method, it lacks the public character belonging to the method of intelligence. Moreover, when the experience in question does not yield consciousness of the presence of God, in the sense that is alleged to exist, the retort is always at hand that it is not a genuine religious experience. For by definition, only that experience *is* religious which arrives at this particular result. The argument is circular. The traditional position is that some hardness or corruption of heart prevents one from having the experience. Liberal religionists are now more humane. But their logic does not differ.

It is sometimes held that beliefs about religious matters are symbolic, like rites and ceremonies. This view may be an advance upon that which holds to their literal objective validity. But as usually put forward it suffers from an ambiguity. Of what are the beliefs symbols? Are they symbols of things experienced in other modes than those set apart as religious, so that the things symbolized have an independent standing? Or are they symbols in the sense of standing for some transcendental reality—transcendental because not being the subject-matter of experience generally? Even the fundamentalist admits a certain quality and degree of symbolism in the latter sense in objects of religious belief. For he holds that the objects of these beliefs are so far beyond finite human capacity that our beliefs must be couched in more or less metaphorical terms. The conception that faith is the best available substitute for knowledge in our present estate still attaches to the notion of the symbolic character of the materials of faith; unless by ascribing to them a symbolic nature we mean that these materials stand for something that is verifiable in general and public experience.

Were we to adopt the latter point of view, it would be evident not only that the intellectual articles of a creed must be understood to be symbolic of moral and other ideal values, but that the facts taken to be historic and used as concrete evidence of the intellectual articles are themselves symbolic. These articles of a creed present events and persons that have been made over by the idealizing imagination in the interest, at their best, of moral ideals. Historic personages in their divine attributes are materializations of the ends that enlist devotion and inspire endeavor. They are symbolic of the reality of ends moving us in many forms of experience. The ideal values that are thus symbolized also mark human experience in science and art and the various modes of human association: they mark almost everything in life that rises from the level of manipulation of conditions as they exist. It is admitted that the objects of religion are ideal in contrast with our present state. What would be lost if it were also admitted that they have authoritative claim upon conduct just because they are ideal? The assumption that these objects of religion exist already in some realm of Being seems to add nothing to their force, while it weakens their claim over us as ideals, in so far as it bases that claim upon matters that are intellectually dubious. The question narrows itself to this: Are the ideals that move us genuinely ideal or are they only in contrast with our present estate?

The import of the question extends far. It determines the meaning given to the word "God." On one score, the word can mean only a particular Being. On the other score, it denotes the unity of all ideal ends arousing us to desire and actions. Does the unification have a claim upon our attitude and conduct because it is already, apart from us, in realized existence, or because of its own inherent meaning and value? Suppose for the moment that the word "God" means the ideal ends that at a given time and place one acknowledges as having authority over his volition and emotion, the values to which one is supremely devoted, as far as these ends, through imagination, take on unity. If we make this supposition, the issue will stand out clearly in contrast with the doctrine of religions that "God" designates some kind of Being having prior and therefore non-ideal existence.

The word "non-ideal" is to be taken literally in regard to some religions that have historically existed, to all of them as far as they are neglectful of moral qualities in their divine beings. It does not apply in the same *literal* way to Judaism and Christianity. For they have asserted that the Supreme Being has moral and spiritual attributes. But it applies to them none the less in that these moral and spiritual characters are thought of as properties of a particular existence and are thought to be of religious value for us because of this embodiment in such an existence. Here, as far as I can see, is the ultimate issue as to the difference between *a* religion and the religious as a function of experience.

The idea that "God" represents a unification of ideal values that is essentially imaginative in origin when the imagination supervenes in conduct is attended with verbal difficulties owing to our frequent use of the word "imagination" to denote fantasy and doubtful reality. But the reality of ideal ends as ideals is vouched for by their undeniable power in action. An ideal is not an illusion because imagination is the organ through which it is apprehended. For *all* possibilities reach us through the imagination. In a definite sense the only meaning that can be assigned the term "imagination" is that things unrealized in fact come home to us and have power to stir us. The unification effected through imagination is not fanciful, for it is the reflex of the unification of practical and emotional attitudes. The unity signifies not a single Being, but the unity of loyalty and effort evoked by the fact that many ends are one in the power of their ideal, or imaginative, quality to stir and hold us.

We may well ask whether the power and significance in life of the traditional conceptions of God are not due to the ideal qualities referred to by them, the hypostatization of them into an existence being due to a conflux of tendencies in human nature that converts the object of desire into an antecedent reality . . . with beliefs that have prevailed in the cultures of the past. For in the older cultures the idea of the supernatural was "natural," in the sense in which "natural" signifies something customary and familiar. It seems more credible that religious persons have been supported and consoled by the reality with which ideal values appeal to them than that they have been upborne by sheer matter of fact existence. That, when once men are inured to the idea of the union of the ideal and the physical, the two should be so bound together in emotion that it is difficult to institute a separation, agrees with all we know of human psychology.

The benefits that will accrue, however, from making the separation are evident. The dislocation frees the religious values of experience once for all from matters that are continually becoming more dubious. With that release there comes emancipation from the necessity of resort to apologetics. The reality of ideal ends and values in their authority over us is an undoubted fact. The validity of justice, affection, and that intellectual correspondence of our ideas with realities that we call truth, is so assured in its hold upon humanity that it is unnecessary for the religious attitude to encumber itself with the apparatus of dogma and doctrine. Any other conception of the religious attitude, when it is adequately analysed, means that those who hold it care more for force than for ideal values—since all that an Existence can add is force to establish, to punish, and to reward. There are, indeed, some persons who frankly say that their own faith does not require any guarantee that moral values are backed up by physical force, but who hold that the masses are so backward that ideal values will not affect their conduct unless in the popular belief these values have the sanction of a power that can enforce them and can execute justice upon those who fail to comply.

There are some persons, deserving of more respect, who say: "We agree that the beginning must be made with the primacy of the ideal. But why stop at this point? Why not search with the utmost eagerness and vigor for all the evidence we can find, such as is supplied by history, by presence of design in nature, which may lead on to the belief that the ideal is already extant in a Personality having objective existence?"

One answer to the question is that we are involved by this search in all the problems of the existence of evil that have haunted theology in the past and that the most ingenious apologetics have not faced, much less met. If these apologists had not identified the existence of ideal goods with that of a Person supposed to originate and support them—a Being, moreover, to whom omnipotent power is attributed— the problem of the occurrence of evil would be gratuitous. The significance of ideal ends and meanings is, indeed, closely connected with the fact that there are in life all sorts of things that are evil to us because we would have them otherwise. Were existing conditions wholly good, the notion of possibilities to be realized would never emerge.

But the more basic answer is that while if the search is conducted upon a strictly empirical basis there is no reason why it should not take place, as a matter of fact it is always undertaken in the interest of the supernatural. Thus it diverts attention and energy from ideal values and from the exploration of actual conditions by means of which they may be promoted. History is testimony to this fact. Men have never fully used the powers they possess to advance the good in life, because they have waited upon some power external to themselves and to nature to do the work they are responsible for doing. Dependence upon an external power is the counterpart of surrender of human endeavor. Nor is emphasis on exercising our own powers for good an egoistical or a sentimentally optimistic recourse. It is not the first, for it does not isolate man, either individually or collectively, from nature. It is not the second, because it makes no assumption beyond that of the need and responsibility for human endeavor, and beyond the conviction that, if human desire and endeavor were enlisted on behalf of natural ends, conditions would be bettered. It involves no expectation of a millennium of good.

Belief in the supernatural as a necessary power for apprehension of the ideal and for practical attachment to it has for its counterpart a pessimistic belief in the corruption and impotency of natural means. That is axiomatic in Christian dogma. But this apparent pessimism has a way of suddenly changing into an exaggerated optimism. For according to the terms of the doctrine, if the faith in the supernatural is of the required order, regeneration at once takes place. Goodness, in all essentials, is thereby established; if not, there is proof that the established relation to the supernatural has been vitiated. This romantic optimism is one cause for the excessive attention to individual salvation characteristic of traditional Christianity. Belief in a sudden and complete transmutation through conversion and in the objective efficacy of prayer, is too easy a way out of difficulties. It leaves matters in general just about as they were before; that is, sufficiently bad so that there is additional support for the idea that only supernatural aid can better them. The position of natural intelligence is that there exists a *mixture* of good and evil, and that reconstruction in the direction of the good which is indicated by ideal ends, must take place, if at all, through continued cooperative effort. There is at least enough impulse toward justice, kindliness, and order so that if it were mobilized for action, not expecting abrupt and complete transformation to occur, the disorder, cruelty, and oppression that exist would be reduced.

The discussion has arrived at a point where a more fundamental objection to the position I am taking needs consideration. The misunderstanding upon which this objection rests should be pointed out. The view I have advanced is sometimes treated as if the identification of the divine with ideal ends left the ideal wholly without roots in existence and without support from existence. The objection implies that my view commits one to such a separation of the ideal and the existent that the ideal has no chance to find lodgment even as a seed that might grow and bear fuit. On the contrary, what I have been criticizing is the *identification* of the ideal with a particular Being, especially when that identification makes necessary the conclusion that this Being is outside of nature, and what I have tried to show is that the ideal itself has its roots in natural conditions; it emerges when the imagination idealizes existence by laying hold of the possibilities offered to thought and action. There are values, goods, actually realized upon a natural basis—the goods of human association, of art and knowledge. The idealizing imagination seizes upon the most precious things found in the climacteric moments of experience and projects them. We need no external criterion and guarantee for their goodness. They are had, they exist as good, and out of them we frame our ideal ends.

Moreover, the ends that result from our projection of experienced goods into objects of thought, desire and effort exist, only they exist *as* ends. Ends, purposes, exercise determining power in human conduct. The aims of philanthropists, of Florence Nightingale, of Howard, of Wilberforce, of Peabody, have not been ideal dreams. They have modified institutions. Aims, ideals, do not exist simply in "mind"; they exist in character, in personality and action. One might call the roll of artists, intellectual inquirers, parents, friends, citizens who are neighbors, to show that purposes exist in an *operative* way. What I have been objecting to, I repeat, is not the idea that ideals are linked with existence and that they themselves exist, through human embodiment, as forces, but the idea that their authority and value depend upon some prior complete embodiment—as if the efforts of human beings on behalf of justice, or knowledge or beauty, depended for their effectiveness and validity upon assurance that there already existed in some supernal region a place where criminals are humanely treated, where there is no serfdom or slavery, where all facts and truths are already discovered and possessed, and all beauty is eternally displayed in actualized form.

The aims and ideals that move us are generated through imagination. But they are not made out of imaginary stuff. They are made out of the hard stuff of the world of physical and social experience. The locomotive did not exist before Stevenson, nor the telegraph before the time of Morse. But the conditions for their existence were there in physical material and energies and in human capacity. Imagination seized hold upon the idea of a rearrangement of existing things that would evolve new objects. The same thing is true of a painter, a musician, a poet, a philanthropist, a moral prophet. The new vision does not arise out of nothing, but emerges through seeing, in terms of possibilities, that is, of imagination, old things in new relations, serving a new end which the new end aids in creating.

Moreover the process of creation is experimental and continuous. The artist, scientific man, or good citizen, depends upon what others have done before him and are doing around him. The sense of new values that become ends to be realized arises first in dim and uncertain form. As the values are dwelt upon and carried forward in action they grow in definiteness and coherence. Interaction between aim and existent conditions improves and tests the ideal; and conditions are at the same time modified. Ideals change as they are applied in existent conditions. The process endures and advances with the life of humanity. What one person and one group accomplish becomes the standing ground and starting point of those who succeed them. When the vital factors in this natural process are generally acknowledged in emotion, thought and action, the process will be both accelerated and purified through elimination of that irrelevant element that culminates in the idea of the supernatural. When the vital factors attain the religious force that has been drafted into supernatural religions, the resulting reinforcement will be incalculable.

These considerations may be applied to the idea of God, or, to avoid misleading conceptions, to the idea of the divine. This idea is, as I have said, one of ideal possibilities unified through imaginative realization and projection. But this idea of God, or of the divine, is also connected with all the natural forces and conditions— including man and human association—that promote the growth of the ideal and that further its realization. We are in the presence neither of ideals completely embodied in existence nor yet of ideals that are mere rootless ideals, fantasies, utopias. For there are forces in nature and society that generate and support the ideals. They are further unified by the action that gives them coherence and solidity. It is this *active* relation between ideal and actual to which I would give the name "God." I would not insist that the name *must* be given. There are those who hold that the associations of the term with the supernatural are so numerous and close that any use of the word "God" is sure to give rise to misconception and be taken as a concession to traditional ideas.

They may be correct in this view. But the facts to which I have referred are there and they need to be brought out with all possible clearness and force. There exist concretely and experimentally goods—the values of art in all its forms, of knowledge, of effort and of rest after striving, of education and fellowship, of friendship and love, of growth in mind and body. These goods are there and yet they are relatively embryonic. Many persons are shut out from generous participation in them; there are forces at work that threaten and sap existent goods as well as prevent their expansion. A clear and intense conception of a union of ideal ends with actual conditions is capable of arousing steady emotion. It may be fed by every experience, no matter what its material.

In a distracted age, the need for such an idea is urgent. It can unify interests and energies now dispersed; it can direct action and generate the heat of emotion and the light of intelligence. Whether one gives the name "God" to this union, operative in thought and action, is a matter for individual decision. But the *function* of such a working union of the ideal and actual seems to me to be identical with the force that has in fact been attached to the conception of God in all the religions that have a spiritual content; and a clear idea of that function seems to me urgently needed at the present time.

The sense of this union may, with some persons, be furthered by mystical experiences, using the term "mystical" in its broadest sense. That result depends largely upon temperament. But there is a marked difference between the union associated with mysticism and the union which I had in mind. There is nothing mystical about the latter; it is natural and moral. Nor is there anything mystical about the perception or consciousness of such union. Imagination of ideal ends pertinent to actual conditions represents the fruition of a disciplined mind. There is, indeed, even danger that resort to mystical experiences will be an escape, and that its result will be the passive feeling that the union of actual and ideal is already accomplished. But in fact this union is active and practical; it is a *uniting*, not something given.

One reason why personally I think it fitting to use the word "God" to denote that uniting of the ideal and actual which has been spoken of, lies in the fact that aggressive atheism seems to me to have something in common with traditional supernaturalism. I do not mean merely that the former is mainly so negative that it fails to give positive direction to thought, though that fact is pertinent. What I have in mind especially is the exclusive preoccupation of both militant atheism and supernaturalism with man in isolation. For in spite of supernaturalism's reference to something beyond nature, it conceives of this earth as the moral center of the universe and of man as the apex of the whole scheme of things. It regards the drama of sin and redemption enacted within the isolated and lonely soul of man as the one thing of ultimate importance. Apart from man, nature is held either accursed or negligible. Militant atheism is also affected by lack of natural piety. The ties binding man to nature that poets have always celebrated are passed over lightly. The attitude taken is often that of man living in an indifferent and hostile world and issuing blasts of defiance. A religious attitude, however, needs the sense of a connection of man, in the way of both dependence and support, with the enveloping world that the imagination feels is a universe. Use of the words "God" or "divine" to convey the union of actual with ideal may protect man from a sense of isolation and from consequent despair or defiance.

In any case, whatever the name, the meaning is selective. For it involves no miscellaneous worship of everything in general. It selects those factors in existence that generate and support our idea of good as an end to be striven for. It excludes a multitude of forces that at any time are irrelevant to this function. Nature produces whatever gives reinforcement and direction but also what occasions discord and confusion. The "divine" is thus a term of human choice and aspiration. A humanistic religion, if it excludes our relation to nature, is pale and thin, as it is presumptuous, when it takes humanity as an object of worship. Matthew Arnold's conception of a "power not ourselves" is too narrow in its reference to operative and sustaining conditions. While it is selective, it is too narrow in its basis of selection—righteousness. The conception thus needs to be widened in two ways. The powers that generate and support the good as experienced and as ideal, work *within* as well as without. There seems to be a reminiscence of an external Jehovah in Arnold's statement. And the powers work to enforce other values and ideals than righteousness. Arnold's sense of an opposition between Hellenism and Hebraism resulted in exclusion of beauty, truth, and friendship from the list of the consequences toward which powers work within and without.

In the relation between nature and human ends and endeavors, recent science has broken down the older dualism. It has been engaged in this task for three centuries. But as long as the conceptions of science were strictly mechanical (mechanical in the sense of assuming separate things acting upon one another purely externally by push and pull), religious apologists had a standing ground in pointing out the differences between man and physical nature. The differences could be used for arguing that something supernatural had intervened in the case of man. The recent acclaim, however, by apologists for religion of the surrender by science of the classic type of mechanicalism[1] seems ill-advised from their own point of view. For the change in the modern scientific view of nature simply brings man and nature nearer together. We are no longer compelled to choose between explaining away what is distinctive in man through reducing him to another form of a mechanical model and the doctrine that something literally supernatural marks him off from nature. The less mechanical—in its older sense—physical nature is found to be, the closer is man to nature.

In his fascinating book, *The Dawn of Conscience*, James Henry Breasted refers to Haeckel as saying that the question he would most wish to have answered is this: Is the universe friendly to man? The question is an ambiguous one. Friendly to man in what respect? With respect to ease and comfort, to material success, to egoistic ambitions? Or to his aspiration to inquire and discover, to invent and create, to build a more secure order for human existence? In whatever form the question be put, the answer cannot in all honesty be an unqualified and absolute one. Mr. Breasted's answer, as a historian, is that nature has been friendly to the emergence

---

[1] I use this term because science has not abandoned its beliefs in working mechanisms in giving up the idea that they are of the nature of a strictly mechanical contact of discrete things.

and development of conscience and character. Those who will have all or nothing cannot be satisfied with this answer. Emergence and growth are not enough for them. They want something more than growth accompanied by toil and pain. They want final achievement. Others who are less absolutist may be content to think that, morally speaking, growth is a higher value and ideal than is sheer attainment. They will remember also that growth has not been confined to conscience and character; that it extends also to discovery, learning and knowledge, to creation in the arts, to furtherance of ties that hold men together in mutual aid and affection. These persons at least will be satisfied with an intellectual view of the religious function that is based on continuing choice directed toward ideal ends.

For, I would remind readers in conclusion, it is the intellectual side of the religious attitude that I have been considering. I have suggested that the religious element in life has been hampered by conceptions of the supernatural that were imbedded in those cultures wherein man had little control over outer nature and little in the way of sure method inquiry and test. The crisis today as to the intellectual content of religious belief has been caused by the change in the intellectual climate due to the increase of our knowledge and our means of understanding. I have tried to show that this change is not fatal to the religious values in our common experience, however adverse its impact may be upon historic religions. Rather, provided that the methods and results of intelligence at work are frankly adopted, the change is liberating.

It clarifies our ideals, rendering them less subject to illusion and fantasy. It relieves us of the incubus of thinking of them as fixed, as without power of growth. It discloses that they develop in coherence and pertinency with increase of natural intelligence. The change gives aspiration for natural knowledge a definitely religious character, since growth in understanding of nature is seen to be organically related to the formation of ideal ends. The same change enables man to select those elements in natural conditions that may be organized to support and extend the sway of ideals. All purpose is selective, and all intelligent action includes deliberate choice. In the degree in which we cease to depend upon belief in the supernatural, selection is enlightened and choice can be made in behalf of ideals whose inherent relations to conditions and consequences are understood. Were the naturalistic foundations and bearings of religion grasped, the religious element in life would emerge from the throes of the crisis in religion. Religion would then be found to have its natural place in every aspect of human experience that is concerned with estimate of possibilities, with emotional stir by possibilities as yet unrealized, and with all action in behalf of their realization. All that is significant in human experience falls within this frame.

Is There a Substitute for Religion?

Political Ideology as Religion

Wang Tao-ming

Wang Tao-ming is a deputy political instructor in a unit of the Red Chinese People's Liberation Army.

To Remould My World Outlook with Mao Tse-tung's Thought

Under the guidance of the Party and with the help of my comrades, I have been studying and applying Chairman Mao's works in a practical way in order to remould my ideology and as a result I have made some progress in class consciousness and theoretical understanding of revolution in the last few years. Following are some of my experiences in remoulding my thinking by studying and applying Chairman Mao's "Three Good Old Articles" and other articles in a positive way.

There Is No "Born Red"

I did not understand the importance of ideological remoulding before enlisting and was just not interested in the idea. I thought, "Our generation studies in the schools run by the Party, reads the books published in the new society, receives the Party's education from childhood and grows up with the song *The East Is Red* on the lips and the Young Pioneer's tie around the neck. Our thinking has been revolutionary since childhood. Because I am of a poor peasant family and my father is a revolutionary cadre, I have absorbed no undesirable ideas and there is no need for me to undergo any remoulding. I am a 'born red' youth and a 'born' revolutionary successor. My taking the revolutionary road is not in question at all." So when my father told me to work hard on Chairman Mao's works and remould my

Source: Mao Tse-tung's Thought Is the Invincible Weapon (Peking: Foreign Languages Press, 1968).

thinking earnestly or I would commit errors and would degenerate, I thought what he said was exaggerated to scare me.

After enlisting, I heard the leadership speaking of ideological remoulding and again doubted the necessity of it. I thought to myself: I am determine to become a good fighter, I have the desire to improve myself ideologically and I am doing well in work, drill and production and have been often singled out for praise. What is there to be remoulded?

But some later happenings caused contradictions in my mind and I sensed there was something wrong. For instance, I thought the uniform of our Army was not "tastefully" designed and the toe-cap of the padded shoes was too large to be attractive. In spite of the coldness of winter, I would rather put on the rubber shoes than the "big toe-capped shoes" when going out on the street. But the officers and veterans of our unit seemed to be quite satisfied with the uniform and the padded shoes. The officers often told us what a scarcity of clothes and shoes there had been in the revolutionary war periods and reminded us never to forget the hard and difficult life of the old days and never to forget the people. Why did the officers and veterans like the things which I did not like? What lay at the root of this difference? It was from these trifles that I began to feel that there *was* something in my mind which needed remoulding. It seemed that it was not enough to rely on the little class consciousness I had acquired in the "sugar-pot of socialism" in my boyhood.

But it was only after Chairman Mao issued the call "Learn from Comrade Lei Feng"[1] that I really and truly realized the importance of ideological remoulding and began conscientiously to remould myself with Mao Tse-tung's thought. I came to see that the reason why Comrade Lei Feng could perform great deeds in every-day life and become a communist fighter lies basically in the fact that by studying and applying Chairman Mao's works in a vital way, he understood the significance of life, knew whom he should serve and formed the world outlook of serving the people whole-heartedly. I had also studied the "Three Good Old Articles" and done a few good things. But I was far from being devoted utterly to the people without any thought of self as Lei Feng had done. Nor had I paid enough attention to tying up everything I did with ideological remoulding as he had done, and had not conscientiously followed his advice: "Live to better the lives of others." In learning from Lei Feng, I understood that to be able to devote oneself utterly to the people it is imperative to dig out selfishness from one's mind by the roots. A revolutionary must fight not only with the class enemies in society, but also with the class enemy in his mind—selfishness. He must resist all kinds of non-proletarian ideas, build up revolutionary quality with the thought of Mao Tse-tung and permeate his thinking with Chairman Mao's teaching of serving the people whole-heartedly.

Later, using the form of a small-scale rectification movement, the company leadership organized us to study Chairman Mao's teachings on class and class

[1] Lei Feng was a squad leader in a transportation company of the P.L.A. stationed in Shenyang. He worked very hard on Chairman Mao's works and put special emphasis on applying what he had learnt. As a result he attained a high political consciousness, a firm proletarian stand and the noble quality of serving the people whole-heartedly. He received distinction three times for meritorious service and was cited as a model Communist Youth Leaguer. He joined the Party in November 1960 and died in August 1962 while performing his duty. Chairman Mao wrote the inscription "Learn from Comrade Lei Feng!"

struggle. In the course of this study I examined myself and realized that I was far from being immune from non-proletarian influences and the force of old habits. For instance, there were such sayings as "Once you master mathematics, physics and chemistry, you don't have to worry about your livelihood anywhere!" I had thought that there was some reality behind such catch-phrases. I absorbed quite a few bad influences in school and the old idea of seeking personal fame and furthering my own interests had also left its imprint on my mind. This shows that there does exist acute and complicated class struggle in socialist society. Confronting our generation are two kinds of teachers: the proletariat, our teacher by positive example, and the bourgeoisie, our teacher by negative example. Unless we arm ourselves consciously with proletarian thinking, we will surely be influenced by bourgeois thinking.

With these problems in mind I studied the following quotation in Chairman Mao's "On the Correct Handling of Contradictions Among the People":

> In the building of a socialist society, everybody needs remoulding . . . . It [the working class] must ceaselessly learn in the course of its work and overcome its shortcomings step by step, and must never stop doing so.

Chairman Mao says everybody needs remoulding. Young men like myself who have grown up under the Red Banner should of course be included. What were my shortcomings? From the many problems posed, I felt the first I should overcome was the idea that because I was "born red" there was no need for me to undergo any remoulding.

Can the young people in socialist society be "born red"? I realized that what I considered as a sound ideology is just a simple class feeling. This feeling is born out of the understanding that socialism brings happiness to us and out of our thankfulness to the Party and Chairman Mao. This simple class feeling enables us to embrace Mao Tse-tung's thought more readily. However, it is not yet the full understanding that socialism is by no means for the happiness of just some individuals but for the well-being of the entire proletariat and labouring people. If we do not raise it to the stage of conscious class awareness we cannot resist the assault of bourgeois ideology and will not be able to stand the test if circumstances require us to sacrifice our personal interests for the interests of the majority of the poeple. One should never rest content with his simple class feeling, but should raise to a conscious class awareness, to the height of Mao Tse-tung's thought. To achieve this, one has to study and apply Chairman Mao's works in a living way and remould his ideology. There is no such thing as being "born red," one must learn to be red. I am now in the prime of life. I must study Chairman Mao's works earnestly and give myself a correct answer to the question of what I live for and whom should I serve. I must consciously arm myself with Mao Tse-tung's thought and lay a good foundation for my following the revolutionary road all my life.

Remould Myself in Accordance with the Standards of the Communist New Man

Once the need for conscientious self-remoulding became clear, I began in real earnest to study and apply in a positive way Chairman Mao's "Three Good Old

Articles" and other works and, with Mao Tse-tung's thought as a weapon, to make a painstaking effort to change my old thinking and alter my world outlook. After pin-pointing the problems uppermost in my mind at the different times, I successively solved some over the past several years.

Personal Interest and the Needs of the Revolution. A lover of painting since childhood, I took a drawing board with me when I joined the army after graduating from the middle school attached to the College of Fine Arts. I was immediately attracted by the exciting life of the army. I congratulated myself on having found the richest source of inspiration for my artistic efforts and hoped to do some real painting. I suggested to the officers that I should paint the history of the regiment and received a highly encouraging reply. But just as I was about to start the pictures, I got instructions to go to another camp for further training. I felt disconcerted and asked whether I could be allowed to stay behind. Seeing my reluctance, the deputy political commissar of the regiment sent for me and told me of his personal experience. He had been a turner before he joined the revolution. Though highly skilled, a poverty-stricken worker like him could not make a living in the old society and he joined the revolution. He had hoped to do some technical work after joining the revolution. However, what the revolution most needed then was men to take up arms and destroy the enemy. He did what was required of him. "Had all of us thought only of our own inclinations and skills and not followed the need of the revolution," he said to me, "where would the victory be that we see today?" He concluded by asking me to study hard the "Three Good Old Articles." I studied these articles and thought to myself, "Comrade Bethune was a very good surgeon, yet he never cared about his personal fame and position. He always served the needs of the revolution and finally he gave his life for the Chinese revolution. Why cannot I subordinate my petty interest in painting to the needs of the revolution?"

This ideological knot untied, I went off happily to the training camp. But the old idea could not be suppressed once and for all and it returned from time to time. It needs repeated ideological struggle to subordinate entirely one's personal inclinations to the needs of the revolution. For instance, when I heard some schoolmates had done some good painting or had been sent to a college for further studies, I would waver. On these occasions, I would study "In Memory of Norman Bethune" and Chairman Mao's teachings on serving the people heart and soul, to replace personal preference with the needs of the revolution. Finally I came to see that in our country there is room enough for each to cultivate his own interests and tastes. But this does not mean that we should develop our interests and tastes regardless of the needs of the Party and the goal of serving the people; instead, we should acquire skills and techniques in order to serve the people. If we develop our interests and pursuits regardless of the needs of the revolution, we will become bourgeois individualists. This understanding enables me to bear situations like this with a calmness of mind and to do whatever my superiors want me to do and do it well. But I did not lay aside my brushes. I took an active part in preparing the blackboard newspaper in my company. I painted pictures to commend fine deeds of my comrades and copied slogans. From this I realized that when needed by the revolution, one's personal interests can play their fullest role and serve the revolution. When divorced from the needs of the revolution, one's personal interests can only serve oneself, or may even serve the enemy.

Planting the Trees and Enjoying the Shade. I used to think that I was born at a good time, the time of socialism. As an old adage goes, "The fathers plant the trees, the sons enjoy the cool shade," Our predecessors in the revolution had endured so much suffering, had conquered and taken over the country, to let later generations enjoy a happy life. That is why I would not wear any mended clothes at home and did not even want to wear a coat my mother had made out of an old one of my father's. Over a period of time after my enlisting, I felt that life in the army was not as good as at home.

One Sunday, I was sent with a letter to the regimental commander at his living quarters. As soon as I stepped in I saw him mending shoes there, first his children's and then his own, with his own tools. I thought to myself: The leading officers like the regimental commander risked their lives for the revolution. Their revolutionary spirit is just as good as in the old days. They lead a frugal and simple life, work hard and often drill with the fighters. They go to great pains to bring up the revolutionary young generation. When later I saw a picture of Chairman Mao in patched padded-trousers taken in northern Shensi, I was greatly moved. Gradually I came to see that my former ideas were very wrong. At my age, the revolutionary predecessors had already taken up the burden of revolution and were struggling and shedding blood for it. What they had in mind was the great cause of the liberation of the oppressed classes and the nation. What they have in mind now is how to carry the revolutionary cause of the proletariat through to the end. They still maintain the style of hard work and simple living, while I think of nothing but personal comforts.

Why did I think of only "enjoying the shade" and not "planting the trees"? With this question in mind, I studied Chairman Mao's works. He said:

> Because of their lack of political and social experience, quite a number of young people are unable to see the contrast between the old China and the new, and it is not easy for them thoroughly to comprehend the hardships our people went through in the struggle to free themselves from the oppression of the imperialists and Kuomintang reactionaries, or the long period of arduous work needed before a happy socialist society can be established.

These words had a great impact on me. I had forgotten that the happiness we enjoy today is the fruit of bloodshed and the sacrifices of many people and that our country is still "poor and blank"; I had forgotten my responsibility. This realization made me see that I had no reason whatsoever to indulge in comforts and relax my will to fight. I asked myself further—what is happiness? Different classes have different views on this question. The poletarian concept of happiness is struggle, revolution, work and serving the people. Comrades Norman Bethune, Chang Szu-teh and Lei Feng set the finest examples. I felt I ought to be like them and regard serving the people whole-heartedly as the greatest pleasure and the greatest happiness.

Since then I have endeavoured to turn myself in practice into such a person, one who puts the interests of the public and the collective before those of his own and who is the first to bear hardship, the last to enjoy comforts. Sometimes I wanted to send some money home by post. But when I found some other comrades' families needed it more urgently, I sent the money to them instead. At meals, I would first take food made of coarse grains. In the night marches, I would walk in front to find the road. For the good of the others, I preferred to risk more stumblings and falls myself. After repeated ideological struggle and tempering in practice, a change in feeling is gradually effected. I have come to see that a man can be really happy only when he understands thoroughly what is bitterness and what is happiness, only when he has come to a proletarian viewpoint on happiness, whereas those who are fettered by bourgeois individualism, who are obsessed by selfishness can never have their desires satisfied and can never be happy. We are indeed enjoying the happy life our predecessors in the revolution have won for us at the cost of bloodshed and sacrifice and we are indeed enjoying the "cool shade." But we must not be people who just make use of the shade. First of all we should become tree-planters so that people throughout the world may enjoy the cool shade of socialism and communism.

The Defence of the Country and the Making of Revolution. I enlisted in August 1962 when the Chiang Kai-shek reactionaries were trying to invade the mainland. I thought, "I am of a poor peasant family and the son of a revolutionary cadre. It is my unshirkable duty to enlist and defend our motherland and the happy life of the people. I will never allow these cannibals to ride roughshod over us again." Day in and day out I dreamed about fighting the enemy and was always asking when we would set out for the front. When it turned out that the Chiang Kai-shek reactionaries did not dare to come, I went to the commander of my unit and said, "I'll now go home since there is no war for the time being. But I'll come back as soon as the war starts." The commander asked me, "What did you enlist for?" I replied, "To defend the country." The commander persisted, "And what else?" I was at a loss. "What else could there be?" I said to myself. "Our predecessors in revolution have liberated the country and the task of our generation is to defend it. What else are we to do?" The commander seemed able to read my thought and said, "There are still many oppressed and exploited labouring people in the world. We must not only defend our motherland, but should also support the world revolution. We should not just safeguard the country our predecessors have gained for us, but must make it function as the bastion of the revolution. War is inevitable as long as imperialism exists. There will be plenty of chances to fight in your generation. And to fight well, it is very important for us to bear in mind always the oppressed and the not yet liberated people, to bear in mind always imperialism and the reactionaries in various countries. We must learn from Norman Bethune."

After this talk, I read the article "In Memory of Norman Bethune." Chairman Mao says:

> We must unite with the proletariat of all the capitalist countries . . . to liberate our nation and people and to liberate the other nations and peoples of the world.

He also enjoins us to learn from Comrade Norman Bethune, who selflessly adopted the cause of the Chinese people's liberation as his own, and to learn from him the spirit of internationalism and spirit of communism. From these teachings of Chairman Mao, I came to see that the cause of the liberation of the proletariat is internationalist from beginning to end.

Later the company leadership organized activity for the purposes of recalling the grievances the labouring people suffered in the past. I thought again and again, "Why did the landlords and capitalists dare to exploit and oppress the workers and peasants so ferociously in the old society?" I studied Chairman Mao's works and realized that the landlords and capitalists were protected by the Kuomintang reactionaries, who in turn were backed by U.S. imperialism. U.S. imperialism had backed the Chiang Kai-shek reactionaries in their killing of the Chinese people, and today it is slaughtering the people of Vietnam, aiding and abetting the reactionaries in various countries in their massacres. Why does it do that? The reason is that U.S. imperialism and the reactionaries of various countries all protect the interests of the landlords and the capitalists. Therefore, they work hand in glove to bully and exploit the people, and to prevent them from making revolution and seeking liberation. U.S. imperialism is the general root-cause of the sufferings of the people of the world. Till it is wiped out the people of the world will never gain final liberation and we can never consider our victory as consolidated. The task resting on the shoulders of our generation is not only to defend the socialist land of China, but also to support the revolution of the people of the world, to bring about communism. We must emulate Norman Bethune and become internationalist fighters.

With the idea of making revolution for the world's people strongly in my mind, I set higher demands on myself and plunge into my work with greater enthusiasm. In daily life, I struggle hard against any manifestation of selfishness in me and sometimes while I am eating my meal I will ask myself whether I really put others before myself. While practising bayonet fighting last year, some comrades thought this method of fighting amounted to very little in modern warfare. I organized my comrades to study Chairman Mao's teachings on people's war and built up our belief in the importance of bayonet fighting. We arrived at the conclusion that "we can defeat atom bombs by bayonet fighting." We are ready at any time to support the revolutionary struggles of the people of the world.

Sunshine and Rice Shoot. Last year, after my articles "On Bayonet Practice" and "How Our Squad Tackle Ideological Problems" were published in the newspaper, many officers and comrades wrote to encourage me. I was confronted with the problem of how to treat the honours that were bestowed on me. What was uppermost in my mind was that people might think me conceited. I weighed every word I spoke, lest I might make some blunder and cause people to think that the honours had gone to my head. But I was also aware that if I went on like this, I would become a timid and overcautious man. So I felt I must speak whatever was right and proper. Another thing I feared was that people might discover my shortcomings. At the end of last year, a commander wanted to see the bayonet practice between Squad Eight and Squad Three and asked me to take part in it. I was then reporting my experience in the corps and had not practised bayonet fighting for a long time. I did not want to go for fear that I might disgrace myself. But on second thoughts, I saw it was very wrong of me to think of that and finally went as I was required. The fact that I should have such wrong ideas at all made me repeatedly ask myself why I was always thinking of myself since I had received some honours. I found it was "fear," engendered by honours, the root of which was "selfishness." It was precisely when I did not fear to expose my own shortcomings that I was able to get help from the comrades and make progress. My fear of having my shortcomings discovered was essentially a reflection of my vanity. This manifestation of selfishness must be resolutely repudiated.

At the beginning of this year in the Great Hall of the People in the capital I made a report on how I had studied Chairman Mao's works. I put the ticket in my notebook. On returning, many comrades in my unit wanted to have a look at it. This drew my attention. When I had gone out to make my report in the past, I never kept any momento. Why did I keep the ticket this time? Was it not that I wanted the comrades to know that I had made a report in the Great Hall of the People? Yes, that was what was at the back of my mind. I therefore cut the printed half off the ticket and wrote on the remaining blank part "Wage a bayonet fight against my selfish thinking" to warn myself against allowing undesirable ideas to creep into my mind.

The above-mentioned event set me thinking for a long time. I realized that it is most essential to adopt a correct view on the achievements of my study and the honours bestowed on me by the Party if I am to be able to have a correct attitude towards them. When I first took up Chairman Mao's works, I did not know how to study them in order to resolve problems, how to apply what I had learnt and how to summarize my experience. It was the officers and comrades who helped me to learn all this. I was encouraged when I made some progress and criticized when I had shortcomings. Just like the tender seedlings which cannot grow without sunshine, I cannot make an iota of progress without learning from Mao Tse-tung's thought. In a bumper harvest, people often say how strong the plants are. When I have made some progress in study, people tend to see only my good points and give me encouragement. But I myself know very well that I am just a very tender seedling. It is entirely due to Mao Tse-tung's thought that I have been able to grow at all. Mao Tse-tung's thought is the unsetting red sun in my heart and I will forever consider myself a seedling which cannot do without the sunshine even for a single moment.

With this realization, I have been more conscientious in dealing with problems. For instance, when I go out on business and return late the cooks often want to prepare a special meal for me. But I insist on having just what is left. The cooks know that I like onions and often want to give me some. But I refuse to accept any. It is out of their concern for me that they want to do these things. But if I accept these favours, I will put myself in a privileged position and become different from the masses. Another example, when some comrades have made some progress and say that this is due to my help, I will strictly examine myself to see whether I have given too much prominence to my personal role in the work and will organize the core members to talk with these comrades so that they will not only tell their ideological problems to me but also to the leader of the Party group and other Party members. It will never do to overemphasize one's own role in work and seek to win personal fame.

Chairman Mao has said:

Even if we achieve gigantic successes in our work, there is no reason whatsoever to feel conceited and arrogant. Modesty helps one to go forward, whereas conceit makes one lag behind. This is a truth we must always bear in mind.

He has also said, "It is not hard for one to do a bit of good. What is hard is to do good all one's life and never do anything bad. . . ." He teaches us to engage in arduous struggle for decades on end. I think that I have made some progress in studying Chairman Mao's works. Nevertheless I should not try to live on what I have achieved for the rest of my life. The road of revolution and the road of life still stretch out a long way ahead. As long as I am alive, I will go on making revolution, remoulding myself, and studying and applying Chairman Mao's works in a living way. I'll follow Mao Tse-tung's thought and be a revolutionary all my life. To persons with heads full of bourgeois individualism, achievements and honours are signboards painted in golden letters, are "capital" with which to gain personal position and comfort and at that point they come to the dead end of progress. But proletarian fighters never rest content because of achievements and honours. In their view, achievements and honours are a kind of encouragement and stimulant, prompting them to achieve still greater successes for the Party, setting new tasks for them, and setting still higher demands for revolutionizing their ideology; they are the point of departure for new progress.

Using Mao Tse-Tung's Thought to Wage A "Bayonet Fight" Against Selfishness

I have come to understand that it is of paramount importance to use Mao Tse-tung's thought to struggle against the bourgeois thinking within oneself, if one is to study and apply well Chairman Mao's works and to plant Mao Tse-tung's thought firmly in the mind. He must study, apply Chairman Mao's works in struggle, remould himself and grow up in struggle. Only through repeated struggle, can he raise his understanding about Chairman Mao's works, strengthen his class feelings for them and gain real understanding of his teachings. Otherwise, he won't be able to learn much and he will have difficulty in consolidating what he has learnt. "Using Mao Tse-tung's thought to wage a 'bayonet fight' against selfishness!" has long been the motto of Squad Eight in ideological remoulding. According to my experience, there are six points we should pay attention to in this respect:

1. It is essential to memorize Chairman Mao's teachings, especially many of his basic concepts and important statements. Only when we have memorized them, can we think of what his precepts are when confronted with problems. When I first studied his works, I could not find any quotations, or could not find the right ones, to solve the problem, I had in mind and therefore could not deal with my problems in a proper way. Later as I often studied and applied his teachings, I have managed to learn quite a few by heart with the passage of time. Of course, we do not memorize these teachings just to remember them, but to apply them in action. Only when we have memorized his teachings, can we study and apply them at any time and become more conscientious in our thinking and action.

2. It is necessary to set up "models," examples for ideological remoulding, for ourselves. That is to say, we must have a clear-cut view of what sort of a person we want to train and temper ourselves into becoming, we must have a future "image" of ourselves in our mind. I began to have "models" after studying the "Three Good Old Articles." Later I learnt from Lei Feng and had another "model" who

handles correctly the relation between public and private affairs. After listening to Chen Chin-yuan's report, I had one more "model" who takes great care to make his comrades lifelong revolutionaries. Every time I learn from a hero or an advanced person, I will add one more standard for my ideological remoulding. I also have "models" in my own company: the company commander who has a high sense of responsibility and an eager desire to learn, the political instructor who is highly-principled and persists in the struggle against anything undesirable, and a comrade who was wronged but still works very hard. In fact everyone has certain "models" in his mind. Everyone is learning from and is modelling himself on one or several persons. We must consciously model ourselves on and learn from the revolutionaries who are armed with the thought of Mao Tse-tung. We must wage struggle against any bad concept, squeeze it out, and firmly establish the concept of a communist fighter in our mind.

3. It is important to be able to grasp the ideas flashing through one's mind. The things we have seen, heard and smelt are bound to give rise to some ideas in the mind. We must be good at grasping these ideas in our daily life to see whether they are correct and whether they correspond to Mao Tse-tung's thought. To be able to study Chairman Mao's works with certain problems in mind, one must be able to grasp these problems. For instance, I once this year went with some comrades to a certain unit to report our experience in studying and later held a discussion there with the activists on learning from Chairman Mao's works. At the beginning, everybody said something to praise us and I felt quite at home. But when the comrade in charge of our party asked for comments and criticism, my heart missed a beat and I hardly dared raise my head, fearing that I might be criticized. Immediately I sensed that it was a very bad idea and made a self-criticism at this very meeting.

4. Develop an "ideological film" every night. The ears, eyes, nose and other sense organs of a person are comparable to the diaphragm of a camera. The things reflected through these sense organs will leave their impressions in one's mind. When I lay in bed at night, I would recall the day's life to see what is on the "ideological film." I will keep what is good and eliminate what is bad in accordance with Chairman Mao's teachings. On the points I cannot see clearly, I would ask others to "magnify" them for me. If I had not done this conscientiously, some bad thinking would have formed and grown before I knew what was happening.

5. Hold every pass. At the beginning of this year, I once went out on business. When I came back I went to the political instructor to report my recent thinking. By the time I finished, it was past ten o'clock. The political instructor asked me to stay in the company headquarters for the night and already had had the bed made. My first reflection was that though I was a platoon leader, it would not matter if I stayed in the company headquarters for a night, since I had been away from my platoon for some time. But on second thoughts, I found this was only making an excuse for myself. If I got into such a habit, I would be treating myself as someone different from others and become divorced from the masses. Instead of excusing myself with "It doesn't matter!," I should set a high ideological standard for myself and not do anything, not even once, which is not beneficial to the revolutionization of my ideology. So I went back to the platoon that night. I came to understand that mistaken and bad patterns are often formed through one's doing the first wrong thing. We must hold the first pass so that there would not be an opening, a point

of breakthrough for the first mistaken, bad ideas. The occasion when a man finds excuses for himself is the time he lowers the standard of ideological revolutionization and takes the downward road ideologically. One should never permit oneself any excuse to explain away one's mistaken ideas.

On the other hand good ideas, good style of work are formed but by bit through tempering over long years. One should never refuse to do the first good thing and at the same time should never rest content with doing only one good thing. Good ideas cannot be developed and good style of work cannot be formed overnight. One must be good at "accumulating ideological sparks." When he has accumulated enough of such sparks, a leap will take place and there will be a qualitative change in his ideology.

6. It is important to have an unflinching revolutionary will. In order to make revolution and remould and temper ourselves into a new, communist generation, we must have an unflinching revolutionary will. When I was guided by such a will, I gave way to no undesirable thought or action, and I struggled hard under the direction of Mao Tse-tung's thought against any selfish thinking in my mind and "compelled" myself to do good deeds. I would then think more of Chairman Mao's teachings, the heroes and models and the example I should follow in the future. In my opinion this revolutionary will is an essential thing. Chairman Mao has said:

> We the Chinese nation have the spirit to fight the enemy to the last drop of our blood, the determination to recover our lost territory by our own efforts, and the ability to stand on our own feet in the family of nations.

We must have the spirit, determination and ability referred to by Chairman Mao, to fight to the very end in our own minds, in order to train ourselves to be staunch fighters for communism.

Madness as Religious Experience

R. D. Laing

R. D. Laing (1927–   ) is a British psychologist whose controversial theories have lately attracted world-wide attention. Among his books are *The Self and Others*, *The Divided Self*, and *Knots*.

Transcendental Experience

Certain *transcendental experiences* seem to me to be the original wellspring of all religions. Some psychotic people have transcendental experiences. Often (to the best of their recollection), they have never had such experiences before, and frequently they will never have them again. I am not saying, however, that psychotic experience necessarily contains this element more manifestly than sane experience.

We experience in different modes. We perceive external realities, we dream, imagine, have semi-conscious reveries. Some people have visions, hallucinations, experience faces transfigured, see auras and so on. Most people most of the time experience themselves and others in one or another way that I shall call *egoic*. That is, centrally or peripherally, they experience the world and themselves in terms of a consistent identity, a me-here over against a you-there, within a framework of certain ground structures of space and time shared with other members of their society.

This identity-anchored, space-and-time-bound experience has been studied philosophically by Kant and later, by the phenomenologists, e.g. Husserl, Merleau-Ponty. Its historical and ontological relativity should be fully realized by any contemporary student of the human scene. Its cultural, socioeconomic relativity has become a commonplace among anthropologists and a platitude to the Marxists and neo-Marxists. And yet, with the consensual and interpersonal confirmation it offers, it gives us a sense of ontological security, whose validity we *experience* as self-validating, although metaphysically–historically–ontologically–socioeconomically–culturally we know its apparent absolute validity as an illusion.

In fact all religious and all existential philosophies have agreed that such *egoic experience* is a preliminary illusion, a veil, a film of *maya*—a dream to Heraclitus, and to Lao Tzu, the fundamental illusion of all Buddhism, a state of sleep, of death, of socially accepted madness, a womb state to which one has to die, from which one has to be born.

The person going through ego-loss or transcendental experiences may or may not become in different ways confused. Then he might legitimately be regarded as

Source: R. D. Laing, *The Politics of Experience* (Harmondsworth, England, 1967), pp. 137–145. Copyright © 1967 by R. D. Laing. Reprinted by permission of Penguin Books Ltd.

mad. But to be mad is not necessarily to be ill, notwithstanding that in our culture the two categories have become confused. It is assumed that if a person is mad (whatever that means) then *ipso facto* he is ill (whatever that means). The experience that a person may be absorbed in, while to others he appears simply ill-mad, may be for him veritable manna from heaven. The person's whole life may be changed, but it is difficult not to doubt the validity of such vision. Also, not everyone comes back to us again.

Are these experiences simply the effulgence of a pathological process or of a particular alienation? I do not think they are.

In certain cases, a man blind from birth may have an operation performed which gives him his sight. The result—frequently misery, confusion, disorientation. The light that illumines the madman is an unearthly light. It is not always a distorted refraction of his mundane life situation. He may be irradiated by light from other worlds. It may burn him out.

This "other" world is not essentially a battlefield wherein psychological forces, derived or diverted, displaced or sublimated from their original object-cathexes, are engaged in an illusionary fight—although such forces may obscure these realities, just as they may obscure so-called external realities. When Ivan in *The Brothers Karamazov* says, "If God does not exist, everything is permissible," he is *not* saying, "If my super-ego, in projected form, can be abolished, I can do anything with a good conscience." He *is* saying, "If there is *only* my conscience, then there is no ultimate validity for my will."

Among physicians and priests there should be some who are guides, who can educt the person from this world and induct him to the other. To guide him in it and to lead him back again.

One enters the other world by breaking a shell: or through a door: through a partition: the curtains part or rise: a veil is lifted. Seven veils: seven seals, seven heavens.

The "ego" is the instrument for living in *this* world. If the "ego" is broken up or destroyed (by the insurmountable contradictions of certain life situations, by toxins, chemical changes, etc.), then the person may be exposed to other worlds, "real" in different ways from the more familiar territory of dreams, imagination, perception or fantasy.

The world that one enters, one's capacity to experience it, seem to be partly conditional on the state of one's "ego."

Our time has been distinguished, more than by anything else, by a drive to control the external world, and by an almost total forgetfulness of the internal world. If one estimates human evolution from the point of view of knowledge of the external world, then we are in many respects progressing.

If our estimate is from the point of view of the internal world and of oneness of internal and external, then the judgement must be very different.

Phenomenologically the terms "internal" and "external" have little validity. But in this whole realm one is reduced to mere verbal expedients—words are simply the finger pointing at the moon. One of the difficulties of talking in the present day of these matters is that the very existence of inner realities is now called in question.

By "inner" I mean our way of seeing the external world and all those realties that have no "external," "objective" presence—imagination, dreams, fantasies, trances, the realities of contemplative and meditative states, realities of which modern man, for the most part, has not the slightest direct awareness.

For example, nowhere in the Bible is there any argument about the *existence* of gods, demons, angels. People did not first "believe in" God: they experienced His presence, as was true of other spiritual agencies. The question was not whether God existed, but whether this particular God was the greatest god of all, or the only God; and what was the relation of the various spiritual agencies to each other. Today, there is a public debate, not as to the trustworthiness of God, the particular place in the spiritual hierarchy of different spirits, etc., but whether God or such spirits *even* exist or ever have existed.

Sanity today appears to rest very largely on a capacity to adapt to the external world—the interpersonal world, and the realm of human collectivities.

As this external human world is almost completely and totally estranged from the inner, any personal direct awareness of the inner world already has grave risks.

But since society, without knowing it, is *starving* for the inner, the demands on people to evoke its presence in a "safe" way, in a way that need not be taken seriously, etc., is tremendous—while the ambivalence is equally intense. Small wonder that the list of artists, in say the last 150 years, who have become ship-wrecked on these reefs is so long—Hölderlin, John Clare, Rimbaud, Van Gogh, Nietzsche, Antonin Artaud. . . .

Those who survived have had exceptional qualities—a capacity for secrecy, slyness, cunning—a thoroughly realistic appraisal of the risks they run, not only from the spiritual realms they frequent, but from the hatred of their fellows for anyone engaged in this pursuit.

Let us *cure* them. The poet who mistakes a real woman for his Muse and acts accordingly. . . . The young man who sets off in a yacht in search of God. . . .

The outer divorced from any illumination from the inner is in a state of darkness. We are in an age of darkness. The state of outer darkness is a state of sin—i.e., alienation or estrangement from the *inner light*.[1] Certain actions lead to greater estrangement; certain others help one not to be so far removed. The former used to be called sinful.

The ways of losing one's way are legion. Madness is certainly not the least unambiguous. The countermadness of Kraepelinian psychiatry is the exact counter-part of "official" psychosis. Literally, and absolutely seriously, it is as *mad*, if by madness we mean any radical estrangement from the totality of what is the case. Remember Kierkegaard's objective madness.

As we experience the world, so we act. We conduct ourselves in the light of our view of what is the case and what is not the case. That is, each person is a more or less naïve ontologist. Each person has views of what is and what is not.

There is no doubt, it seems to me, that there have been profound changes in the experience of man in the last thousand years. In some ways this is more evident than changes in the patterns of his behavior. There is everything to suggest that man experienced God. Faith was never a matter of believing. He existed, but of trusting, in the presence that was experienced and known to exist as a self-validating datum. It seems likely that far more people in our time experience neither the

[1] M. Eliade, *The Two and the One* (London: Harvill Press, 1965), especially Chapter I.

presence of God, nor the presence of his absence, but the absence of his presence.

We require a history of phenomena, not simply more phenomena of history.

As it is, the secular psychotherapist is often in the role of the blind leading the half-blind.

The fountain has not played itself out, the frame still shines, the river still flows, the spring still bubbles forth, the light has not faded. But between *us* and It, there is a veil which is more like fifty feet of solid concrete. *Deus absconditus*. Or we have absconded.

Already everything in our time is directed to categorizing and segregating this reality from objective facts. This is precisely the concrete wall. Intellectually, emotionally, interpersonally, organizationally, intuitively, theoretically, we have to blast our way through the solid wall, even if at the risk of chaos, madness and death. For from *this* side of the wall, this is the risk. There are no assurances, no guarantees.

Many people are prepared to have faith in the sense of scientifically indefensible belief in an untested hypothesis. Few have trust enough to test it. Many people make-believe what they experience. Few are made to believe by their experience. Paul of Tarsus was picked up by the scruff of the neck, thrown to the ground and blinded for three days. This direct experience was self-validating.

We live in a secular world. To adapt to this world the child abdicates its esctasy. (*"L'enfant abdique son extase"*: Malarmé.) Having lost our experience of the spirit, we are expected to have faith. But this faith comes to be a belief in a reality which is not evident. There is a prophecy in Amos that a time will come when there will be a famine in the land, "not a famine for bread, nor a thirst for water, but of *hearing* the words of the Lord." That time has now come to pass. It is the present age.

From the alienated starting point of our pseudo-sanity, everything is equivocal. Our sanity is not "true" sanity. Their madness is not "true" madness. The madness of our patients is an artifact of the destruction wreaked on them by us and by them on themselves. Let no one suppose that we meet "true" madness any more than that we are truly sane. The madness that we encounter in "patients" is a gross travesty, a mockery, a grotesque caricature of what the natural healing of that estranged integration we call sanity might be. True sanity entails in one way or another the dissolution of the normal ego, that false self competently adjusted to our alienated social reality; the emergence of the "inner" archetypal mediators of divine power, and through this death a rebirth, and the eventual re-establishment of a new kind of ego-functioning, the ego now being the servant of the divine, no longer its betrayer.

Religionless Christianity

Dietrich Bonhoeffer

Dietrich Bonhoeffer (1906–1945) first achieved renown with the publication of *The Cost of Discipleship*, in which he protested against what he called the "cheap grace" purveyed by official religious institutions. Imprisoned by the Nazis for his involvment in a plot against Hitler, he came to understand the modern world as irreversibly non-religious and, in his letters from prison, called for the development of a "religionless Christianity," one no longer dependent on traditional concepts of God. He was executed at the concentration camp at Flossenburg just days before it was liberated by the Allies.

You would be surprised and, perhaps even worried, by my theological thoughts and the conclusions that they lead to; and this is where I miss you most of all, because I don't know anyone else with whom I could so well discuss them to have my thinking clarified. What is bothering me incessantly is the question what Christianity really is, or indeed who Christ really is, for us today. The time when people could be told everything by means of words, whether theological or pious, is over, and so is the time of inwardness and conscience—and that means the time of religion in general. We are moving towards a completely religionless time; people as they are now simply cannot be religious any more. Even those who honestly describe themselves as 'religious' do not in the least act up to it, and so they presumably mean something quite different by 'religious'.

Our whole nineteen-hundred-year-old Christian preaching and theology rest on the "religious *a priori*" of mankind. "Christianity" has always been a form—perhaps the true form—of "religion." But if one day it becomes clear that this *a priori* does not exist at all, but was a historically conditioned and transient form of human self-expression, and if therefore man becomes radically religionless—and I think that that is already more or less the case (else how is it, for example, that this war, in contrast to all previous ones, is not calling forth any "religious" reaction?) —what does that mean for "Christianity"? It means that the foundation is taken away from the whole of what has up to now been our "Christianity," and that there remain only a few "last survivors of the age of chivalry," or a few intellectually dishonest people, on whom we can descend as "religious." Are they to be the chosen few? Is it on this dubious group of people that we are to pounce in fervour, pique, or indignation, in order to sell them our goods? Are we to fall upon a few unfortunate people in their hour of need and exercise a sort of religious compulsion on them? If we don't want to do all that, if our final judgment must be that the western form of Christianity, too, was only a preliminary stage to a complete absence of religion, what kind of situation emerges for us, for the church? How can Christ

Source: Reprinted with permission of Macmillan Publishing Co., Inc. from *Letters and Papers from Prison* by Dietrich Bonhoeffer. Copyright © 1953, 1976, 1971 by SCM Press, Ltd.

become the Lord of the religionless as well? Are there religionless Christians? If religion is only a garment of Christianity—and even this garment has looked very different at different times—then what is a religionless Christianity?

Barth, who is the only one to have started along this line of thought, did not carry it to completion, but arrived at a positivism of revelation, which in the last analysis is essentially a restoration. For the religionless working man (or any other man) nothing decisive is gained here. The questions to be answered would surely be: What do a church, a community, a sermon, a liturgy, a Christian life mean in a religionless world? How do we speak of God—without religion, i.e. without the temporally conditioned presuppositions of metaphysics, inwardness, and so on? How do we speak (or perhaps we cannot now even "speak" as we used to) in a "secular" way about "God"? In what way are we "religionless-secular" Christians, in what way are we the ἐκ-κλησία, those who are called forth, not regarding ourselves from a religious point of view as specially favoured, but rather as belonging wholly to the world? In that case Christ is no longer an object of religion, but something quite different, really the Lord of the world. But what does that mean? What is the place of worship and prayer in a religionless situation? Does the secret discipline, or alternatively the difference (which I have suggested to you before) between penultimate and ultimate, take on a new importance here?

. . .

The Pauline question whether περιτομή [circumcision] is a condition of justification seems to me in present-day terms to be whether religion is a condition of salvation. Freedom from περιτομή is also freedom from religion. I often ask myself why a "Christian instinct" often draws me more to the religionless people than to the religious, by which I don't in the least mean with any evangelizing intention, but, I might almost say, "in brotherhood." While I'm often reluctant to mention God by name to religious people—because that name somehow seems to me here not to ring true, and I feel myself to be slightly dishonest (it's particularly bad when others start to talk in religious jargon; I then dry up almost completely and feel awkward and uncomfortable)—to people with no religion I can on occasion mention him by name quite calmly and as a matter of course. Religious people speak of God when human knowledge (perhaps simply because they are too lazy to think) has come to an end, or when human resources fail—in fact it is always the *deus ex machina* that they bring on to the scene, either for the apparent solution of insoluble problems, or as strength in human failure—always, that is to say, exploiting human weakness or human boundaries. Of necessity, that can go on only till people can by their own strength push these boundaries somewhat further out, so that God becomes superfluous as a *deus ex machina*. I've come to be doubtful of talking about any human boundaries (is even death, which people now hardly fear, and is sin, which they now hardly understand, still a genuine boundary today?). It always seems to me that we are trying anxiously in this way to reserve some space for God; I should like to speak of God not on the boundaries but at the centre, not in weaknesses but in strength; and therefore not in death and guilt but in man's life and goodness. As to the boundaries, it seems to me better to be silent and leave the insoluble unsolved. Belief in the resurrection is *not* the "solution" of the problem of death. God's "beyond" is not the beyond of our cognitive faculties. The transcendence of epistemological theory has nothing to do with the transcendence of God.

God is beyond in the midst of our life. The church stands, not at the boundaries where human powers give out, but in the middle of the village. That is how it is in the Old Testament, and in this sense we still read the New Testament far too little in the light of the Old.

.   .   .

A few more words about "religionlessness." I expect you remember Bultmann's essay on the "demythologizing" of the New Testament? My view of it today would be, not that he went "too far," as most people thought, but that he didn't go far enough. It's not only the "mythological" concepts, such as miracle, ascension, and so on (which are not in principle separable from the concepts of God, faith, etc.), but "religious" concepts generally, which are problematic. You can't, as Bultmann supposes, separate God and miracle, but you must be able to interpret and proclaim *both* in a "non-religious" sense. Bultmann's approach is fundamentally still a liberal one (i.e. abridging the gospel), whereas I'm trying to think theologically.

What does it mean to "interpet in a religious sense"? I think it means to speak on the one hand metaphysically, and on the other hand individualistically. Neither of these is relevant to the biblical message or to the man of today. Hasn't the individualistic question about personal salvation almost completely left us all? Aren't we really under the impression that there are more important things than that question (perhaps not more important than the *matter* itself, but more important than the *question!*)? I know it sounds pretty monstrous to say that. But, fundamentally, isn't this in fact biblical? Does the question about saving one's soul appear in the Old Testament at all? Aren't righteousness and the Kingdom of God on earth the focus of everything, and isn't it true that Rom. 3.24ff. is not an individualistic doctrine of salvation, but the culmination of the view that God alone is righteous? It is not with the beyond that we are concerned, but with this world as created and preserved, subjected to laws, reconciled, and restored. What is above this world is, in the gospel, intended to exist *for* this world; I mean that, not in the anthropocentric sense of liberal, mystic pietistic, ethical theology, but in the biblical sense of the creation and of the incarnation, crucifixion, and resurrection of Jesus Christ.

Barth was the first theologian to begin the criticism of religion, and that remains his really great merit; but he put in its place a positivist doctrine of revelation which says, in effect, "Like it or lump it": virgin birth, Trinity, or anything else; each is an equally significant and necessary part of the whole, which must simply be swallowed as a whole or not at all. That isn't biblical. There are degrees of knowledge and degrees of significance; that means that a secret discipline must be restored whereby the *mysteries* of the Christian faith are protected against profanation. The positivism of revelation makes it too easy for itself, by setting up, as it does in the last analysis, a law of faith, and so mutilates what is—by Christ's incarnation!—a gift for us. In the place of religion there now stands the church—that is in itself biblical—but the world is in some degree made to depend on itself and left to its own devices, and that's the mistake.

I'm thinking about how we can reinterpret in a "worldly" sense—in the sense of the Old Testament and of John 1.14—the concepts of repentance, faith, justification, rebirth, and sanctification. I shall be writing to you about it again.

.   .   .

Weizsäcker's book *The World-View of Physics* is still keeping me very busy. It has again brought home to me quite clearly how wrong it is to use God as a stop-gap for the incompleteness of our knowledge. If in fact the frontiers of knowledge are being pushed further and further back (and that is bound to be the case), then God is being pushed back with them, and is therefore continually in retreat. We are to find God in what we know, not in what we don't know; God wants us to realize his presence, not in unsolved problems but in those that are solved. That is true of the relationship between God and scientific knowledge, but it is also true of the wider human problems of death, suffering, and guilt. It is now possible to find, even for these questions, human answers that take no account whatever of God. In point of fact, people deal with these questions without God (it has always been so), and it is simply not true to say that only Christianity has the answers to them. As to the idea of "solving" problems, it may be that the Christian answers are just as unconvincing —or convincing—as any others. Here again, God is no stop-gap; he must be recognized at the centre of life, not when we are at the end of our resources; it is his will to be recognized in life, and not only when death comes; in health and vigour, and not only in suffering; in our activities, and not only in sin. The ground for this lies in the revelation of God in Jesus Christ. He is the centre of life, and he certainly didn't "come" to answer our unsolved problems. From the centre of life certain questions, and their answers, are seen to be wholly irrelevant (I'm thinking of the judgment pronounced on Job's friends). In Christ there are no "Christian problems."—Enough of this; I've just been disturbed again.

. . .

I wonder whether we have become too reasonable. When you've deliberately suppressed every desire for so long, it may have one of two bad results: either it burns you up inside, or it all gets so bottled up that one day there is a terrific explosion. It is, of course, conceivable that one may become completely selfless, and I know better than anyone else that that hasn't happened to me. Perhaps you will say that one oughtn't to suppress one's desires, and I expect you would be right.

. . .

The movement that began about the thirteenth century (I'm not going to get involved in any argument about the exact date) towards the autonomy of man (in which I should include the discovery of the laws by which the world lives and deals with itself in science, social and political matters, art, ethics, and religion) has in our time reached an undoubted completion. Man has learnt to deal with himself in all questions of importance without recourse to the "working hypothesis" called "God." In questions of science, art, and ethics this has become an understood thing at which one now hardly dares to tilt. But for the last hundred years or so it has also become increasingly true of religious questions; it is becoming evident that everything gets along without "God"—and, in fact, just as well as before. As in the scientific field, so in human affairs generally, "God" is being pushed more and more out of life, losing more and more ground.

Roman Catholic and Protestant historians agree that it is in this development that the great defection from God, from Christ, is to be seen; and the more they claim and play off God and Christ against it, the more the development considers itself to be anti-Christian. The world that has become conscious of itself and the laws that govern its own existence has grown self-confident in what seems to us to be an uncanny way. False developments and failures do not make the world doubt the necessity of the course that it is taking, or of its development; they are accepted with fortitude and detachment as part of the bargain, and even an event like the present war is no exception. Christian apologetic has taken the most varied forms of opposition to this self-assurance. Efforts are made to prove to a world thus come of age that it cannot live without the tutelage of "God." Even though there has been surrender on all secular problems, there still remain the so-called "ultimate questions"—death, guilt—to which only "God" can give an answer, and because of which we need God and the church and the pastor. So we live, in some degree, on these so-called ultimate questions of humanity. But what if one day they no longer exist as such, if they too can be answered "without God"? Of course, we now have the secularized offshoots of Christian theology, namely existentialist philosophy and the psychotherapists, who demonstrate to secure, contented, and happy mankind that it is really unhappy and desperate and simply unwilling to admit that it is in a predicament about which it knows nothing, and from which only they can rescue it. Wherever there is health, strength, security, simplicity, they scent luscious fruit to gnaw at or to lay their pernicious eggs in. They set themselves to drive people to inward despair, and then the game is in their hands. That is secularized methodism. And whom does it touch? A small number of intellectuals, of degenerates, of people who regard themselves as the most important thing in the world, and who therefore like to busy themselves with themselves. The ordinary man, who spends his everyday life at work and with his family, and of course with all kinds of diversions, is not affected. He has neither the time nor the inclination to concern himself with his existential despair, or to regard his perhaps modest share of happiness as a trial, a trouble, or a calamity.

The attack by Christian apologetic on the adulthood of the world I consider to be in the first place pointless, in the second place ignoble, and in the third place unchristian. Pointless, because it seems to me like an attempt to put a grown-up man back into adolescence, i.e. to make him dependent on things on which he is, in fact, no longer dependent, and thrusting him into problems that are, in fact, no longer problems to him. Ignoble, because it amounts to an attempt to exploit man's weakness for purposes that are alien to him and to which he has not freely assented. Unchristian, because it confuses Christ with one particular stage in man's religiousness, i.e. with a human law. More about this later.

But first, a little more about the historical position. The question is: Christ and the world that has come of age. The weakness of liberal theology was that it conceded to the world the right to determine Christ's place in the world; in the conflict between the church and the world it accepted the comparatively easy terms of peace that the world dictated. Its strength was that it did not try to put the clock back, and that it genuinely accepted the battle (Troeltsch), even though this ended with its defeat.

Defeat was followed by surrender, and by an attempt to make a completely fresh start based on the fundamentals of the Bible and the Reformation. Heim sought, along pietist and methodist lines, to convince the individual man that he was faced with the alternative "despair or Jesus." He gained "hearts." Althaus (carrying forward the modern and positive line with a strong confessional emphasis) tried to wring from the world a place for Lutheran teaching (ministry) and Lutheran worship, and otherwise left the world to its own devices. Tillich set out to interpret the evolution of the world (against its will) in a religious sense—to give it its shape through religion. That was very brave of him, but the world unseated him and went on by itself; he, too, sought to understand the world better than it understood itself; but it felt that it was completely misunderstood, and rejected the imputation. (Of course, the world *must* be understood better than it understands itself, but not "religiously" as the religious socialists wanted.)

Barth was the first to realize the mistake that all these attempts (which were all, in fact, still sailing, though unintentionally, in the channel of liberal theology) were making in leaving clear a space for religion in the world or against the world. He brought in against religion the God of Jesus Christ, "*pneuma* against *sarx*." That remains his greatest service (his *Epistle to the Romans*, second edition, in spite of all the neo-Kantian egg-shells). Through his later dogmatics, he enabled the church to effect this distinction, in principle, all along the line. It was not in ethics, as is often said, that he subsequently failed—his ethical observations, as far as they exist, are just as important as his dogmatic ones—; it was that in the non-religious interpretation of theological concepts he gave no concrete guidance, either in dogmatics or in ethics. There lies his limitation, and because of it his theology of revelation has become positivist, a "positivism of revelation," as I put it.

The Confessing Church has now largely forgotten all about the Barthian approach, and has lapsed from positivism into conservative restoration. The important thing about that church is that it carries on the great concepts of Christian theology; but it seems as if doing this is gradually just about exhausting it. It is true that there are in those concepts the elements of genuine prophecy (among them two things that you mention: the claim to truth, and mercy) and of genuine worship; and to that extent the Confessing Church gets only attention, hearing, and rejection. But both of them remain undeveloped and remote, because there is no interpretation of them. Those who, like e.g. Schütz or the Oxford Group or the Berneucheners, miss the "movement" and the "life," are dangerous reactionaries; they are reactionary because they go right back behind the approach of the theology of revelation and seek for "religious" renewal. They simply haven't understood the problem at all yet, and their talk is entirely beside the point. There is no future for them (though the Oxford Group would have the best chance if they were not so completely without biblical substance).

Bultmann seems to have somehow felt Barth's limitations, but he misconstrues them in the sense of liberal theology, and so goes off into the typical liberal process of reduction—the "mythological" elements of Christianity are dropped, and Christianity is reduced to its "essence."—My view is that the full content, including the "mythological" concepts, must be kept—the New Testmaent is not a mythological clothing of a universal truth; this mythology (resurrection etc.) is the thing itself— but the concepts must be interpreted in such a way as not to make religion a precondition of faith (cf. Paul and circumcision). Only in that way, I think, will liberal theology be overcome (and even Barth is still influenced by it, though negatively) and at the same time its question be genuinely taken up and answered (as is *not* the case in the Confessing Church's positivism of revelation!). Thus the world's coming of age is no longer an occasion for polemics and apologetics, but is now really better understood than it understands itself, namely on the basis of the gospel and in the light of Christ.

. . .

Now I will try to go on with the theological reflections that I broke off not long since. I had been saying that God is being increasingly pushed out of a world that has come of age, out of the spheres of our knowledge and life, and that since Kant he has been relegated to a realm beyond the world of experience. Theology has on the one hand resisted this development with apologetics, and has taken up arms—in vain—against Darwinism, etc. On the other hand, it has accommodated itself to the development by restricting God to the so-called ultimate questions as a *deus ex machina*; that means that he becomes the answer to life's problems, and the solution of its needs and conflicts. So if anyone has no such difficulties, or if he refuses to go into these things, to allow others to pity him, then either he cannot be open to God; or else he must be shown that he is, in fact, deeply involved in such problems, needs, and conflicts, without admitting or knowing it. If that can be done —and existentialist philosophy and psychotherapy have worked out some quite ingenious methods in that direction—then this man can now be claimed for God, and methodism can celebrate its triumph. But if he cannot be brought to see and admit that his happiness is really an evil, his health sickness, and his vigour despair, the theologian is at his wits' end. It's a case of having to do either with a hardened sinner of a particularly ugly type, or with a man of "bourgeois complacency," and the one is as far from salvation as the other.

You see, that is the attitude that I am contending against. When Jesus blessed sinners, they were real sinners, but Jesus did not make everyone a sinner first. He called them away from their sin, not into their sin. It is true that encounter with Jesus meant the reversal of all human values. So it was in the conversion of Paul, though in his case the encounter with Jesus preceded the realization of sin. It is true that Jesus cared about people on the fringe of human society, such as harlots and tax-collectors, but never about them alone, for he sought to care about man as such. Never did he question a man's health, vigour, or happiness, regarded in themselves, or regard them as evil fruits; else why should he heal the sick and restore strength to the weak? Jesus claims for himself and the Kingdom of God the whole of human life in all its manifestations.

Of course I have to be interrupted just now! Let me just summarize briefly what I'm concerned about—the claim of a world that has come of age by Jesus Christ.

. . .

The displacement of God from the world, and from the public part of human life, led to the attempt to keep his place secure at least in the sphere of the "personal," the "inner," and the "private." And as every man still has a private sphere somewhere, that is where he was thought to be the most vulnerable. The secrets known to a man's valet—that is, to put it crudely, the range of his intimate life, from prayer to his sexual life—have become the hunting-ground of modern pastoral workers. In that way they resemble (though with quite different intentions) the dirtiest gutter journalists—do you remember the *Wahrheit* and the *Glocke*, which made public the most intimate details about prominent people? In the one case it's social, financial, or political blackmail and in the other, religious blackmail. Forgive me, but I can't put it more mildly.

From the sociological point of view this is a revolution from below, a revolt of inferiority. Just as the vulgar mind isn't satisfied till it has seen some highly placed personage "in his bath," or in other embarrassing situations, so it is here. There is a kind of evil satisfaction in knowing that everyone has his failings and weak spots. In my contacts with the "outcasts" of society, its "pariahs," I've noticed repeatedly that mistrust is the dominant motive in their judgment of other people. Every action, even the most unselfish, of a person of high repute is suspected from the outset. These "outcasts" are to be found in all grades of society. In a flower-garden they grub around only for the dung on which the flowers grow. The more isolated a man's life, the more easily he falls a victim to this attitude.

There is also a parallel isolation among the clergy, in what one might call the "clerical" sniffing-around-after-people's-sins in order to catch them out. It's as if you couldn't know a fine house till you had found a cobweb in the furthest cellar, or as if you couldn't adequately appreciate a good play till you had seen how the actors behave off-stage. It's the same kind of thing that you find in the novels of the last fifty years, which do not think they have depicted their characters properly till they have described them in their marriage-bed, or in films where undressing scenes are thought necessary. Anything clothed, veiled, pure, and chaste is presumed to be deceitful, disguised, and impure; people here simply show their own impurity. A basic anti-social attitude of mistrust and suspicion is the revolt of inferiority.

Regarded theologically, the error is twofold. First, it is thought that a man can be addressed as a sinner only after his weaknesses and meannesses have been spied out. Secondly, it is thought that a man's essential nature consists of his inmost and most intimate background; that is defined as his "inner life," and it is precisely in those secret human places that God is to have his domain!

On the first point it is to be said that man is certainly a sinner, but is far from being mean or common on that account. To put it rather tritely, were Goethe and Napoleon sinners because they weren't always faithful husbands? It's not the sins of weakness, but the sins of strength, which matter here. It's not in the least necessary to spy out things; the Bible never does so. (Sins of strength: in the genius, *hubris*; in the peasant, the breaking of the order of life—is the decalogue a peasant ethic?—; in the bourgeois, fear of free responsibility. Is this correct?)

On the second point: the Bible does not recognize our distinction between the outward and the inward. Why should it? It is always concerned with *anthrōpos teleios*, the *whole* man, even where, as in the Sermon on the Mount, the decalogue is pressed home to refer to "inward disposition." That a good "disposition" can take the place of total goodness is quite unbiblical. The discovery of the so-called inner life dates from the Renaissance, probably from Petrarch. The "heart" in the biblical sense is not the inner life, but the whole man in relation to God. But as a man lives just as much from "outwards" to "inwards" as from "inwards" to "outwards," the view that his essential nature can be understood only from his intimate spiritual background is wholly erroneous.

I therefore want to start from the premise that God shouldn't be smuggled into some last secret place, but that we should frankly recognize that the world, and people, have come of age, that we shouldn't run man down in his worldliness, but confront him with God at his strongest point, that we should give up all our clerical tricks, and not regard psychotherapy and existentialist philosophy as God's pioneers. The importunity of all these people is far too unaristocratic for the World of God to ally itself with them. The Word of God is far removed from this revolt of mistrust, this revolt from below. On the contrary, it reigns.

. . .

Now for a few more thoughts on our theme. I'm only gradually working my way to the non-religious interpretation of biblical concepts; the job is too big for me to finish just yet.

On the historical side: There is one great development that leads to the world's autonomy. In theology one sees it first in Lord Herbert of Cherbury, who maintains that reason is sufficient for religious knowledge. In ethics it appears in Montaigne and Bodin with their substitution of rules of life for the commandments. In politics Machiavelli detaches politics from morality in general and founds the doctrine of "reasons of state." Later, and very differently from Machiavelli, but tending like him towards the autonomy of human society, comes Grotius, setting up his natural law as international law, which is valid *etsi deus non daretur*, "even if there were no God." The philosophers provide the finishing touches: on the one hand we have the deism of Descartes, who holds that the world is a mechanism, running by itself with no interference from God; and on the other hand the pantheism of Spinoza, who says that God is nature. In the last resort, Kant is a deist, and Fichte and Hegel are pantheists. Everywhere the thinking is directed towards the autonomy of man and the world.

(It seems that in the natural sciences the process begins with Nicolas of Cusa and Giordano Bruno and the "heretical" doctrine of the infinity of the universe. The classical *cosmos* was finite, like the created world of the Middle Ages. An infinite universe, however it may be conceived, is self-subsisting, *etsi deus non daretur*. It is true that modern physics is not as sure as it was about the infinity of the universe, but it has not gone back to the earlier conceptions of its finitude.)

God as a working hypothesis in morals, politics, or science, has been surmounted and abolished; and the same thing has happened in philosophy and religion (Feuerbach!). For the sake of intellectual honesty, that working hypothesis should be dropped, or as far as possible eliminated. A scientist or physician who sets out to edify is a hybrid.

Anxious souls will ask what room there is left for God now; and as they know of no answer to the question, they condemn the whole development that has brought them to such straits. I wrote to you before about the various emergency exits that have been contrived; and we ought to add to them the *salto mortale* [death-leap] back into the Middle Ages. But the principle of the Middle Ages is heteronomy in the form of clericalism; a return to that can be a counsel of despair, and it would be at the cost of intellectual honesty. It's a dream that reminds one of the song *O wüsst' ich doch den Weg zurück, den weiten Weg ins Kinderland*. There is no such way—at any rate not if it means deliberately abandoning our mental integrity; the only way is that of Matt. 18.3, i.e. through repentance, through *ultimate* honesty.

And we cannot be honest unless we recognize that we have to live in the world *etsi deus non daretur*. And this is just what we do recognize—before God! God himself compels us to recognize it. So our coming of age leads us to a true recognition of our situation before God. God would have us know that we must live as men who manage our lives without him. The God who is with us is the God who forsakes us (Mark 15.34). The God who lets us live in the world without the working hypothesis of God is the God before whom we stand continually. Before God and with God we live without God. God lets himself be pushed out of the world on to the cross. He is weak and powerless in the world, and that is precisely the way, the only way, in which he is with us and helps us. Matt. 8.17 makes it quite clear that Christ helps us, not by virtue of his omnipotence, but by virtue of his weakness and suffering.

Here is the decisive difference between Christianity and all religions. Man's religiosity makes him look in his distress to the power of God in the world: God is the *deus ex machina*. The Bible directs man to God's powerlessness and suffering; only the suffering God can help. To that extent we may say that the development towards the world's coming of age outlined above, which has done away with a false conception of God, opens up a way of seeing the God of the Bible, who wins power and space in the world by his weakness. This will probably be the starting-point for our "secular interpretation."

· · ·

"Christians stand by God in his hour of grieving"; that is what distinguishes Christians from pagans. Jesus asked in Gethsemane, "Could you not watch with me one hour?" That is a reversal of what the religious man expects from God. Man is summoned to share in God's sufferings at the hands of a godless world.

He must therefore really live in the godless world, without attempting to gloss over or explain its ungodliness in some religious way or other. He must live a "secular" life, and thereby share in God's sufferings. He *may* live a "secular" life (as one who has been freed from false religious obligations and inhibitions). To be a Christian does not mean to be religious in a particular way, to make something of oneself (a sinner, a penitent, or a saint) on the basis of some method or other, but to be a man—not a type of man, but the man that Christ creates in us. It is not the religious act that makes the Christian, but participation in the sufferings of God in the secular life. That is *metanoia*: not in the first place thinking about one's own needs, problems, sins, and fears, but allowing oneself to be caught up into the way of Jesus Christ, into the messianic event, thus fulfilling Isa. 53. Therefore "believe in the gospel," or, in the words of John the Baptist, "Behold, the Lamb of God, who takes away the sin of the world" (John 1.29). (By the way, Jeremias has recently asserted that the Aramaic word for "lamb" may also be translated "servant"; very appropriate in view of Isa. 53!).

This being caught up into the messianic sufferings of God in Jesus Christ takes a variety of forms in the New Testament. It appears in the call to discipleship, in Jesus' table-fellowship with sinners, in "conversions" in the narrower sense of the word (e.g. Zacchaeus), in the act of the woman who was a sinner (Luke 7)—an act that she performed without any confession of sin, in the healing of the sick (Matt. 8.17; see above), in Jesus' acceptance of children. The shepherds, like the wise men from the East, stand at the crib, not as "converted sinners," but simply because they are drawn to the crib by the star just as they are. The centurion of Capernaum (who makes no confession of sin) is held up as a model of faith (cf. Jairus). Jesus "loved" the rich young man. The eunuch (Acts 8) and Cornelius (Acts 10) are not standing at the edge of an abyss. Nathaniel is "an Israelite indeed, in whom there is no guile"

(John 1.47). Finally, Joseph of Arimathea and the women at the tomb. The only thing that is common to all these is their sharing in the suffering of God in Christ. That is their "faith." There is nothing of religious method here. The "religious act" is always something partial; "faith" is something whole, involving the whole of one's life. Jesus calls men, not to a new religion, but to life.

But what does this life look like, this participation in the powerlessness of God in the world? I will write about that next time, I hope. Just one more point for today. When we speak of God in a "non-religious" way, we must speak of him in such a way that the godlessness of the world is not in some way concealed, but rather revealed, and thus exposed to an unexpected light. The world that has come of age is more godless, and perhaps for that very reason nearer to God, than the world before its coming of age.

. . .

During the last year or so I've come to know and understand more and more the profound this-worldliness of Christianity. The Christian is not a *homo religiosus*, but simply a man, as Jesus was a man—in contrast, shall we say, to John the Baptist. I don't mean the shallow and banal this-worldliness of the enlightened, the busy, the comfortable, or the lascivious, but the profound this-worldliness, characterized by discipline and the constant knowledge of death and resurrection. I think Luther lived a this-worldly life in this sense.

I remember a conversation that I had in America thirteen years ago with a young French pastor. We were asking ourselves quite simply what we wanted to do with our lives. He said he would like to become a saint (and I think it's quite likely that he did become one). At the time I was very impressed, but I disagreed with him, and said, in effect, that I should like to learn to have faith. For a long time I didn't realize the depth of the contrast. I thought I could acquire faith by trying to live a holy life, or something like it. I suppose I wrote The Cost of Discipleship as the end of that path. Today I can see the dangers of that book, though I still stand by what I wrote.

I discovered later, and I'm still discovering right up to this moment, that it is only by living completely in this world that one learns to have faith. One must completely abandon any attempt to make something of oneself, whether it be a saint, or a converted sinner, or a churchman (a so-called priestly type!), a righteous man or an unrighteous one, a sick man or a healthy one. By this-worldliness I mean living unreservedly in life's duties, problems, successes and failures, experiences and perplexities. In so doing we throw ourselves completely into the arms of God, taking seriously, not our own sufferings, but those of God in the world—watching with Christ in Gethsemane. That, I think, is faith; that is *metanoia*; and that is how one becomes a man and a Christian (cf. Jer. 45!). How can success make us arrogant, or failure lead us astray, when we share in God's sufferings through a life of this kind?

Psychic Research as a Religious Quest

Edgar D. Mitchell

Serving as lunar module pilot for the Apollo 14 flight in February, 1971, Edgar Mitchell (1930–   ) became the sixth man to walk on the moon. He also served as support crew for Apollo 9 and as backup crew for Apollos 10 and 16. He has published numerous articles and has lectured widely on the subject of psychic research and the human potential.

In February 1971 I had the privilege of walking on the moon as a member of the Apollo 14 lunar expedition. During the voyage I made a test in extrasensory perception (ESP), attempting to send information telepathically to four receivers on earth.

Since then, people have asked me why an astronaut would take such an intense interest in a subject as ridiculed and unacceptable in respectable scientific circles as psychic research.

It is a fair question, which I will answer in this chapter. The answer is partly implied by the title of this book: psychic research presents a challenge that science can no longer avoid. But the title is also somewhat misleading. My real interest is—and has been for many years—to understand the nature of consciousness and the relationship of body to mind. Psychic research is one facet of this larger whole. Therefore, it might be said that I have simply gone from outer space to inner space.

The study of mind and consciousness is called *noetics*. The term comes from the Greek root word *nous*, meaning "mind." As popularly used, *noetic* refers to purely intellectual apprehension. But Plato spoke of noetic knowledge as the highest form of knowing—a direct cognition or apprehension of the eternal truths that surpasses the normal discursive processes of logical, intellectual reasoning. The word *science*, of course, originally meant "knowing" but has come to mean a type of knowing derived from use of the objective, rational faculties of mind. But psychic abilities such as telepathy are another type of knowing—a subjective knowing, a nonrational, cognitive process largely overlooked by the scientific world. Consciousness appears to be the central, unifying concept behind these different aspects of mind. Thus, in the spirit of its Grecian origin, I propose to use the omega (Ω) as a symbol for consciousness and noetics.

Psychic research is one aspect of noetics but by no means all of it. Paraphysics, for example, is a new field within noetics that is extending the laws and methods of physics in an attempt to explain some paranormal phenomena. Some of the factors that paraphysics has found necessary to consider are the effects of geomagnetism, phases of the moon, and solar radiation on living systems. These and other terrestrial and celestial factors rhythmically induce changes—sometimes subtle, sometimes striking—in our physical and mental condition. Another example is exobiology, the study of the possibility of extraterrestrial life. The evidence of exobiology leads some scientists to wonder: If life has existed elsewhere in the universe for periods significantly longer than has *Homo sapiens,* how much more evolved in consciousness might such life forms be? Psychic researchers would add: If mankind does contact intelligent extraterrestrial civilizations, might psychic channels prove best for communicating?

The topic of consciousness, then, is as vast as the cosmos, and as close to us as sleep. Noetics is the discipline that is arising from this confluence of outer- and inner-space research. It is the ultimate frontier in man's attempt to understand himself and the nature of the universe.

If we review the history of mankind's attempt to perceive, cognize, and interpret his environment, we find that in the last four centuries, as a result of the growth of scientific methodology, a formalized dichotomy has arisen between proponents of the two modes of knowing: objective observation (followed by deductive reasoning) and direct cognitive processes. These opposing modes of perception are crudely epitomized as science versus religion, reason versus intuition, rationality versus nonrationality, objective knowledge versus subjective experience, and so forth. Only in relatively recent years have scholars of each persuasion actively and vehemently denied the validity of the other process. In prescientific times, scholars—whether they agreed upon their conclusions or not—at least recognized the validity of both external and internal observation. (We must quickly add that the truly great teachers of modern times have always acknowledged this dual process.)

Thus, although I am identifying consciousness as the ultimate frontier in man's attempt to gain knowledge, it is by no means a new frontier because throughout history people have sought to resolve the differences between their objective methods and their subjective experience—between outer and inner. The study of mind and consciousness is the common ground for this effort. The living system that we call man is a holistic phenomenon which exhibits both modes of knowing.

Perhaps after 350 years of divisiveness between science and religion we are on the threshold of a new era of knowledge and cooperation. It should be obvious that objective observation and reason do not by themselves produce a satisfactory ethic for living—neither for the individual nor for social systems. Facts become divorced from values, and action from need.

On the other hand, intuition and inspiration do not by themselves produce the agreement society needs to bring about order, structure, and survival in the material world. In this case, observation frequently becomes subject to individual interpretation according to the covert biases of the individual.

The antagonism between the objective and subjective modes of knowledge can be clearly illustrated. In 1600 Giordano Bruno was burned at the stake by theologians for asserting that the earth was not the center of the solar system and that there were other solar systems with living beings in them. In 1972 the American Academy of Science asserted that science and religion are "mutually exclusive realms of thought" and therefore the Genesis theory of creation should be kept out of science textbooks. The roles of science and religion are reversed in the modern example, but the same closed-minded dogmatism is operating to limit inquiry through sanctimonious denial of other viewpoints.

Research over the last fifty years by little-known, but forward-looking, thinkers has shown there is a vast creative potential in the human mind that is as yet almost totally unrecognized by science. Nonrational cognitive processes have so far eluded scientific description. However, this potential *has* been previously known and described by a few ancient sages and enlightened religious teachers, using veiled prescientific language to express what they disovered through subjective, intuitive, experiential means. We are, in my opinion, on the threshold of rediscovering and redefining those concepts and insights through the objective, rational, experimental efforts of science—if dogmatism and outmoded belief structures do not prevent it. The proper direction of sophisticated instrumentation and laboratory techniques can be the means whereby the physical and metaphysical realms are shown to be different aspects of the same reality. If this is demonstrated, it would be ironic, but appropriate, that so-called godless technology and materialistic science should lead to the rediscovery of the essential unity of science and religion.

Noetics recognizes all this. Noetics is the research frontier where the convergence of objectivity and subjectivity, of reason and intuition, is occurring most rapidly. In the study of consciousness, the techniques and technology of science are being combined with the higher insights of mind from both East and West to provide a new methodology for scholarly inquiry. For it is quite clear that reason alone is not sufficient for total understanding of ourselves. As Michael Polanyi, the eminent philosopher of science, points out, scientific discoveries do not always follow in a sequence of perfectly logical deductions (11). Instead, many discoveries involve intuitions and hunches on the part of the scientist in a manner that cannot be completely explained.

An example of noetic research dealing with just this problem comes from the biofeedback laboratory of Dr. Elmer Green at the Menninger Clinic in Topeka, Kasnas. Green has given the name *reverie* to that state of mind in which creative insight sometimes leaps fully conceived into awareness, and he is making a psychophysiological study of it (3).

The project began, as most experiments do, when a literature search by his colleague (and wife) Alyce Green revealed that many of the great ideas in science and other disciplines came to people while they were in a dreamlike state of strong visual imagery. The state appeared similar to what is known as the hypnogogic state, that brief period between waking and sleeping in which memories and images seem to pass before the eyes and that is sometimes characterized by the production of theta brainwaves, a rhythm of four to eight cycles per second. In the reverie-imagery project, as it is now being called at Menninger, subjects learn to increase their production of theta waves so that they can explore the relationships between the theta state—reverie—and creativity. If there is a significant correlation, it may eventually prove possible to enhance creativity by teaching people to voluntarily enter the theta state. Green speculates that "an individual trained in theta reverie may be able to direct both his conscious and unconscious 'minds' to work on a problem and come up with a totally unexpected creative solution." Thus, a subjective phenomenon is being examined objectively. If the resulting expansion of awareness and self-control gained by subjects in theta reverie results in a release of creative potential, it will demonstrate a very practical benefit from theoretical and basic research.

A second example of practical gains from basic research in subjective phenomena comes from that area of noetics called meditation research. Studies of yogis, Zen masters, transcendental mediators, and people from other traditions (17, 19–21) are demonstrating that mediation produces qualitative and beneficial shifts in psychophysiological condition. Alpha and theta brain waves are two physiological correlates being found for psychological stages of meditation, along with changes in breathing, heartbeat rate, blood pressure, muscle tension, and various other metabolic correlates. The results in the meditator include release of stress and tension, increased intellectual capacity, greater self-control and self-direction, a feeling of deep rest and relaxation, improved social relations, a decrease in use of prescribed and nonprescribed drugs, and other significant changes.

Psychic research—the subject of this book—is still another area of noetics that offers an avenue to the resolution of the dilemma of outer versus inner, matter versus spirit, body versus mind, reason versus intuition, science versus religion. From the view point of noetics, and especially psychic research, what appear to be opposites are really composite parts of a larger whole: consciousness. I speak from personal experience.

When I went to the moon, I was as pragmatic a test pilot, engineer, and scientist as any of my colleagues. More than a quarter of a century had been spent in learning the empirical approach to dealing with the universe. Many times my life has depended upon the validity of scientific principles and the reliability of the technology built upon those principles. I knew well that analytic and logical thought, using objective data, could produce a technology that would reveal new secrets of the universe by probing the reaches of space and, at the microscopic level, the structure of atoms. Prior to the lunar exploration, I became as familiar with the spacecraft and its vast support system of people and equipment as a man could be, with confidence in it all. Despite that familiarity and confidence, though, there were moments during the flight when I felt an amazed and profound respect for the rational abilities of the human intellect—that it could find ways to guide a tiny capsule of metal through a half million miles of space with such precision and accuracy. Yes, I was pragmatic because my experience had shown beyond all question that science works.

But there was another aspect to my experience during Apollo 14, and it contradicted the "pragmatic engineer" attitude. It began with the breathtaking experience of seeing planet Earth floating in the vastness of space.

The first thing that came to mind as I looked at Earth was its incredible beauty. Even the spectacular photographs do not do it justice. It was a majestic sight—a splendid blue and white jewel suspended against a velvet black sky. How peacefully, how harmoniously, how marvelously it seemed to fit into the evolutionary pattern by which the universe is maintained. In a peak experience, the presence of divinity became almost palpable and I *knew* that life in the universe was not just an accident based on random processes. This knowledge came to me directly—noetically. It was not a matter of discursive reasoning or logical abstraction. It was an experiential cognition. It was knowledge gained through private subjective awareness, but it was —and still is—every bit as real as the objective data upon which, say, the navigational program or the communications system were based. Clearly, the universe had meaning and direction. It was not perceptible by the sensory organs, but it was there nevertheless—an unseen dimension behind the visible creation that gives it an intelligent design and that gives life purpose.

Next I thought of our planet's life-supporting character. That little globe of water, clouds, and land no bigger than my thumb was *home*, the haven our spacecraft would seek at the end of our voyage. Buckminster Fuller's description of the planet as "Spaceship Earth" seemed eminently fitting.

Then my thoughts turned to daily life on the planet. With that, my sense of wonderment gradually turned into something close to anguish. Because I realized that at the very moment when I was so privileged to view the planet from 240,000 miles in space, people of Earth were fighting wars; committing murder and other crimes; lying, cheating, and struggling for power and status; abusing the environment by polluting the water and air, wasting natural resources, and ravaging the land, acting out of lust and greed; and hurting others through intolerance, bigotry, prejudice, and all the things that add up to man's inhumanity to man. It seemed as though man were totally unconscious of his individual role in—and individual responsibility for—the future of life on the planet.

It was also painfully apparent that the millions of people suffering in conditions of poverty, ill health, misery, fear, and near-slavery were in that condition from economic exploitation, political domination, religious and ethnic persecution, and a hundred other demons that spring from the human ego. Science, for all its techological feats, had not—more likely, could not—deal with these problems stemming from man's self-centeredness.

The magnitude of the overall problem seemed staggering. Our condition seemed to be one of deepening crises on an unprecedented scale, crises that were mounting faster than we could solve them. There appeared to be the immediate possibility that warfare might destroy vast segments of civilization with one searing burst of atomic fury. Only a little further off appeared the possibility of intolerable levels of polluted air and of undrinkable water. A more remote, but no less real, likelihood was the death of large portions of the population from starvation, abetted by improper resources management by an exploding population.

How had the world come to such a critical situation—and why? Even more important, what could be done to correct it? How could we human beings restore the necessary harmonious relationship between ourselves and the environment? How could a nuclear Armageddon be avoided? How could life be made livable? How could man's potential for a peaceful, creative, fulfilling society be realized? How could the highest development of our objective rationality, epitomized by science, be wedded to the highest development of our subjective intuition, epitomized by religion?

These thoughts and questions stayed with me through the mission, splashdown, and parades. They stayed long afterward to the point of haunting me with an overwhelming awareness of how limited a view man has of his own life and the planet's. Sometimes at night I would lie awake for hours struggling with this enigma, trying to understand it and see it in a sensible perspective. How could man, the most intelligent creature on earth, be so utterly stupid and shortsighted as to put himself in a position of possible global extinction? How had insight become divorced from instinct? Was it possible to find a workable solution?

As I pondered the matter and discussed it with concerned thinkers around the world, it became obvious that there are three major alternatives for the future—alternatives within man's control:

1. To do nothing, in which case the prevailing dominant paradigm[1] and resulting socioeconomic behavior will eventually result in a massive collapse of the world system. The survivors can then start to rebuild civilization.

2. To relinquish personal freedom of choice to a central world government with the expectation that a controlled and unified society, however tyrannical its leadership, is better than nonsurvival.

3. To promote the process of metanoia,[2] or a new awakening in which mankind can realize its self-produced dilemma and, through a change of awareness and an expansion of individual responsibility, reestablish the unity of man with man and with the environment.

I believe the last alternative to be the only satisfactory and inherently stable solution to the deepening crises facing the citizens of Spaceship Earth. It is the solution closest to the perspective of the "instant global consciousness" that I and many of my colleagues attained after our view from space.[3]

The process of metanoia for an entire civilization or even for a substantial segment of a large nation is not an easy task. Certainly science and technology alone cannot produce such an effect. In fact, they are partly to blame for the crises. No, it is the consciousness of people, especially those who perform scientific research, those who create new technology, and those who put it to use, that must expand. They must expand their awareness to produce a transformation of consciousness. Those who lead nations and the other institutions of civilization have a special responsibility. Only when man sees his fundamental unity with the processes of nature and the functioning of the universe—as I so vividly saw it from the Apollo spacecraft—will the old ways of thinking and behaving disappear. Only when man moves from his ego-centered self-image to a new image of universal man will the perennial problems that plague us be susceptible of resolution. Humanity must rise from man to mankind, from the personal to the transpersonal, from self-consciousness to cosmic consciousness. I see no other way to avoid the alternatives that to me are unacceptable.

This view of man's possible futures is not original with me. Others have spoken similar words and have done so at greater length with more detailed analyses and evidence. I am only offering my voice in support of their position. But if we are correct in this, humanity's multiple problems resolve themselves into one fundamental problem: how to change consciousness, how to achieve metanoia. How can we raise our awareness to a higher level—a level that will restore the unity of man, the planet, and the universe?

---

[1] The basic pattern of perceiving, thinking, valuing, and acting associated with a particular vision of reality.

[2] Metanoia, coming from early Greek, is usually translated in the Bible as "repentance." However, the more precise meaning is "a change of mind" or "a new state of consciousness." Editor.

[3] "Instant global consciousness" is the phrase Dr. Mitchell coined in a Time magazine interview (11 December 1972) to describe the dissatisfaction with deepening world crises and a commitment to help solve them that was expressed by many astronauts after returning from space. Editor.

It was at this point in my thinking that the third aspect of my experience during the lunar voyage became important. I am referring to my experiment with extra-sensory perception.

My interest in psychic research began in 1967. At the time I was feeling a deep dissatisfaction with the ability of philosophy and theology—at least as far as I was acquainted with them—to give answers to my questions about the meaning of life and man's place in the universe. I have always been interested in the nature of things and have read widely in the humanities and other subjects that purport to examine or explain man's purpose.

However, I found many of the concepts arising from theology and philosophy to be inadequate. Empirical knowledge from the physical sciences seemed to me to be overturning our traditional notions about man. Unfortunately, it also seemed to be doing very little about replacing those notions with stronger, more valid ones. The old answers did not apply. Where would new ones come from?

In that emotional and intellectual cul-de-sac, a friend for whom I have great respect as a thoughtful but pragmatic person suggested that perhaps psychic phenomena—*psi*, as they are collectively called—ought to be considered. It was a challenge I could not resist. As a student of science, I believe there is nothing in the universe that is unworthy of investigation. If it offers the further incentive of having possible benefit for humanity, I think it is little less than foolish to refuse to examine it. The true scientist is one who is committed to knowing, to *scientia*, which is the attempt to understand the ultimate nature of reality, without bias, prejudice, or commitment to an ideology or belief system. Otherwise, he is unworthy of the name.

I am interested in knowing. That is how I came to parapsychology and related fields. I was quite skeptical at first. I imagine anyone would be if he were unacquainted with the subject, especially in view of scientific disclaimers about the paranormal. It would seem like taking fairy tales and myths seriously.

However, those apparently fanciful stories from childhood and early history are now recognized as having important content and serious significance for man's attempt to know himself more fully. Likewise, psychic research has proved its importance. As I got deeper into the study of paranormal phenomena, I found my skepticism dissolving. In its place was a feeling of awe and excitement compounded from two elements. One was respect for the truly fine scientific experimentation done by parapsychologists and psychic researchers. The other was an inability to explain away the unusual results arising from many of those experiments. Telepathy, for example—the psychic faculty I would attempt to employ during the lunar expedition—had been extensively studied and documented for a century. The work of J. B. Rhine (12, 13), René Warcollier (18), S. G. Soal (16), and many others, including the astounding experiment between Harold Sherman and Sir Hubert Wilkins in the Arctic (15), could leave no doubt about its existence.

In view of that, my whole training in scientific endeavors compelled me to make an honest admission to myself: Psychic research was looking at phenomena that were indeed real, even if the corpus of present scientific knowledge was unable to explain them. To have concluded otherwise would have been intellectual dishonesty—something that has arisen from time to time in the history of science, always to its detriment, and that is still another manifestation of the egocentric mentality.

By 1971, when the Apollo 14 mission was scheduled, I had become an avid psychic researcher in my spare time. The opportunity that the lunar expedition offered me to experiment with telepathy in space was too good to disregard, and I think any scientist whose interests and inclinations paralleled mine would have taken it. I never intended to make the experiment public in the manner that it was—as a sensational story in newspapers and other media around the world. I had decided on the experiment only a few weeks before lift-off, and it was to have been a purely personal investigation. I did not request permission from the National Aeronautics and Space Administration (NASA) because it seemed better to do it without sanction rather than risk having permission denied. Furthermore, because of experience with "news leaks" I did not even seek the counsel of established professionals. These precautions were to no avail, however.

My colleagues in the experiment were four people on earth who tried to receive by telepathic communication the targets I attempted to send them on several days of the voyage. Three of them prefer to remain anonymous. The fourth—Olaf Jonsson of Chicago—was suggested by one of my friends at the last minute and his participation was arranged by telephone. We never met before the launch, although I have met him since. Through a news leak—the source of which is still unknown to me—and through excellent detective work by the press, Jonsson was found and revealed the story to the press, with results that brought widespread attention to us and to the whole field of psychic research.

Briefly, my experiment involved four transmission sessions during rest periods programmed into the flight. Two of the sessions were completed on the way to the moon and two were completed on the return trip. I used random numbers from 1 to 5 set up in eight columns of twenty-five numbers each. Just before transmitting, in order to minimize the possibility of precognition, I assigned each number to one of the symbols of the standard Zener cards used for some ESP tests—a cross, a square, a circle, a star, and parallel wavy lines. Circumstances during the flight made subsequent evaluation of the data difficult. We were forty minutes late during lift-off, which caused the first few rest periods to start forty minutes late as well. Thus, the arrangement I had made with the receivers meant that some of the sessions appeared to yield precognitive results, not telepathic ones.

Upon return to earth, the data was analyzed independently by Dr. J. B. Rhine of the Foundation for Research on the Nature of Man, by Dr. Karlis Osis of the American Society for Psychical Research, and by me (4, 8). The results were statistically significant, not because any of the receivers got a large number of direct hits but because the number of hits was amazingly low. The statistical probability of scoring so few hits was about 3000:1. This negative ESP effect, called *psi-missing*, is something that has frequently arisen in other psychic research work, and theorists are attempting to explain its significance. In any case, it offers good evidence for psi, because the laws of chance are bypassed to a significant degree.

But what has all this to do with the problem of changing consciousness?

For me, seeing our planet from space was an event with some of the qualities traditionally ascribed to religious experience. It triggered a deep insight into the nature of existence—the sort of insight that radically changes the inner person. My thinking—indeed, my consciousness—was altered profoundly. I came to feel a moral responsibility to pass on the transformative experience of seeing earth from the larger perspective. But further, the rational man in me had to recognize the validity of the nonrational cognitive process.

That is one reason for this book. In my opinion, the act of leaving the planet is one of the pivotal moments in human history because it represents a radical change in the course of progress and offers a new perspective of civilization. If we continue without change and without growth in our basic thinking and behavior, we will, despite spectacular technological feats, eventually end the evolutionary experiment known as man. Our planetary situation becomes more desperate daily. But basically I am optimistic because the possibility of resolving those ever-growing global crises was also made clear to me during the view from space.

Obviously we cannot send everyone to the moon in the near future. But we can provide information and experiences of another sort that will serve the same purpose and provide the same perspective. Moreover, we can do it in a way that brings objective reason closer to subjective intuition and thereby help to lessen the unfortunate gulf between these two modes of knowing. We can do this because, as I indicated earlier, inner- and outer-space research are converging. The result will be an expansion of awareness and a step toward developing higher consciousness in the race.

Throughout history prophets, sages, saints, enlightened teachers, and other illuminated men and women have pointed to the same goal as the one I seek: the further evolution of human consciousness. These people have been expert travelers of inner space. Their "reports" over the centuries contain reliable directions for contemporary psychenauts. Their "maps of inner space" provide useful guides to unfamiliar territory. They have been unanimous in declaring that selflessness and freedom from egoism are an aspect of higher consciousness and the key to direct knowledge.

There is a surprising variety of ways by which people grow into selflessness. Some are formal spiritual disciplines such as the study of yoga or Zen, the taking of holy orders, or the practice of various forms of meditation. Other paths are less systematized and more spontaneous. In fact, it may be nothing more than carrying on daily work as always—but with the intention of living a better life through prayer, study, kindness, humility, and good works.

The result of all sincerely followed paths, however, is a change of consciousness in the one who walks the path. Sometimes gradually, sometimes suddenly, the traveler perceives a previously unseen order and meaning in the universe—a recognition that gives significance to life by merging the boundaries of the self with the cosmos. He recognizes that, paradoxically, the deepest aspect of himself is one with all creation. That radical expansion of the meaning of *I* has best been termed *cosmic consciousness*. It is a state in which there is constant awareness of unity with the universe pervading all aspects of one's life. Every activity, every relationship, every thought is guided by the knowledge of oneness between the self and the world. Inner and outer space are unified, and the inhumanities that people perpetrate on one another and the stupidities that people mount against nature become impossible to commit. This internal self-regulation is the surest safeguard against the destruction of our world.

Two examples can illustrate this convergence of subjective intuition and objective reason. In the course of pursuing careers in science, Albert Einstein and Sir

John Eccles both concluded that there is a transpersonal dimension to creation that is outside the space–time continuum of the three-dimensional universe and sustains it. Einstein (1, p. 413) stated it succinctly when he wrote, "I believe in [the] God who reveals Himself in the orderly harmony of what exists."

In a similar vein, Eccles (2, pp. 43–44) declared his belief that "there is a fundamental mystery in my existence, transcending any biological account of the development of my body (including my brain) with its genetic inheritance and its evolutionary origin." He concluded with this profound statement:

> I see science as a supremely religious activity but clearly incomplete in itself.
> I see also the absolute necessity for belief in a spiritual world which is
> interpenetrating with and yet transcending what we see as the material world.
> . . . Similarly I believe that anyone who denies the validity of the scientific
> approach within its sphere is denying the great revelation of God to this day
> and age. To my mind, then, any rational system of belief involves the
> conviction that the creative and sustaining spirit of God may be everywhere
> present and active; indeed I believe that all aspects of the universe, all kinds
> of experience, may be sacramental in the true meaning of the term.

I find it extraordinarily significant that Einstein, the physicist, looked at the telescopic world of outer space and Eccles, the neurophysiologist, looked at the microscopic world of inner space only to discover the same thing—the existence of God. This noetic discovery is at the heart of science and religion. It is the only thing that will counteract contemporary crises and bring meaning, direction, and fulfillment to people.

Psychic research can play an important role in helping people make that discovery. It can be a key to unlock the missing experiential component with which to expand awareness beyond the limits of objective data and logical reasoning. It can be a means of supporting the further evolution of the human race and of developing the universal man of cosmic consciousness. Quite simply, psychic experiences—like religious and mystical experiences—can, when properly developed, help a person become more aware. They can be an input to the mind that awakens curiosity, shakes the sleep from our worldly eyes, and begins to motivate us to seek paths to a different consciousness.

The primary purpose of this book is to provide a credible stimulus to the mind of the reader, but there are several others. My associates and I will demonstrate that psi are indeed real events and that psychic research is a credible, authentic, well-disciplined effort entirely compatible with the methods of science. We hope the following pages will once and for all settle the issue of whether psi exists. We hope this book will enlarge the perspective of modern science by convincing even the most skeptical critics, who have thus far rejected the evidence of psychic research. Our wish is to enlist their aid in the all-important task of studying the nature of man. Thus, science might become unified with religion, the arts, and the humanities in the common task of helping transform human life by bringing mankind to know itself and its relation to the cosmos.

I must offer a word of caution, however. As you will discern from the following chapters, the evidence indicates that psychic energy is neutral, yielding no value system. It must be used with care because *psychic development alone does not produce ethical or spiritual growth.* The history of psychic research has demonstrated this time and again, where it has exposed various sensitives with genuine gifts who nevertheless have resorted to fraud and trickery. Both scientific investigators and ordinary people seeking guidance have sometimes been deceived for a while by those psychic men and women whose main concern was not to act ethically or advance knowledge or help those in need but rather to impress others, play ego games, and increase their own status, wealth, and power over others.

Psychic energy—like atomic energy—can be applied in both creative and destructive ways. If that is so, a prayerful and cautious attitude seems proper for all concerned. It is up to each individual to find an ethical system or ethical framework within which to use psychic energy. In that regard, the injunctions in the Bible and other traditions should not be lightly dismissed. And certainly the frivolous, party-like attitude that some have with regard to séances, Ouija boards, and the like is to be discouraged.

It should be clear, then, that the psychic event must be seen in a larger perspective than usual. Both those with psychic ability and those who study them must ground themselves in a transcendent view of man and his relationship to the universe. Parapsychology must become linked with transpersonal psychology—the study of man's potential for development—as part of noetics, the general study of consciousness. Unless psychic research leads to wisdom, compassion, humility, and beneficial knowledge, it should be avoided althogther. Man is quite capable of destroying himself now. He does not need another weapon in his arsenal for perverting planetary potential.

. . .

Since the beginnings of psychic research, various esoteric and arcane traditions have moved in and out of its mainstream. Prophecy offers a good example. Astrology is perhaps the oldest and most enduring means of divination that man has developed. Tarot cards are a relatively new way of attempting to forecast events. Crystal gazing, the *I Ching*, the Ouija board, bone casting, animal sacrifice, the prophetic utterances of witch doctors and shamans while in trance states—the list seems endless. I am not passing judgment on the validity and accuracy of these traditions. I am only saying it is understandable that they should at one time or another be considered by researchers studying precognition, the nature of time, and other topics in psychic research. Likewise, it is understandable that such diverse subjects as witchcraft, voodoo, and yoga have been examined because they have a history in which psychic events clearly play a part.

Do all these occult practices belong in the purview of psychic research ? Where do the psychic sciences end and the " occult arts " begin ? If psi play some part in the religious ceremonies and training practices of primitive peoples and pagan cults, should they be studied ?

There appears to be a continuum along which we may place occult, psychic, paranormal, and mystic phenomena—a continuum of consciousness. But it is not easy to draw lines of demarcation between them. Recently, for example, meditation has come into the laboratory. Studies have shown that meditation is a means of producing an altered state of consciousness in which psi are frequently manifested. Hence, meditation is being looked at, and from there it seems likely that psychic researchers will have to examine the historical background, the belief system, and the philosophical world view of various meditative traditions. After that a movement into transpersonal psychology will take place. Beyond that, it will become apparent that psi cannot be fully understood until the nature of consciousness itself is considered. That is the rationale for the organization of chapters in this book, although some psychic researchers may feel we have overstepped the bounds of our discipline.

But diversity of opinion at the level of everyday research does not mean "enemy camps" have developed. It is generally agreed by people in psychic research around the world that their work must be performed in a spirit of service to humanity. The possibility of invasion of mental privacy or of thought control is odious. My colleagues in the psychic research community, no matter what their nationality, are unanimous in their commitment to the beneficent application of psychic faculties. All indications point to the conclusion that psi may be used for good or evil. One of their finest uses can be seen in psychic healing. One of their potentially worst uses would be for "programming" people through nonconscious telepathic suggestion. This latter possibility must not be allowed.

This brings up another reason for preferring the term *psychic research*. As I noted earlier, parapsychology is becoming part of a larger whole—transpersonal psychology. In turn, transpersonal psychology is an aspect of the general convergence of science and religion in noetics. Only as we study consciousness and the nature of man and other living systems will we really begin to understand psi and how they relate to human potential and fulfillment. Without that perspective, psi and psychic research will probably go the way of most other scientific work. Either by design or ignorance, they will be turned against humanity in physically and psychologically destructive ways because man's morally imperfect desires are generally uncontrolled by his rational intelligence.

The question "Why psychic research?" has already been briefly answered by saying it can be an important element in the long-sought formula for enriching human awareness, reconstructing society, and generally aiding nature in the great work of evolution. But let us consider the question in greater detail and see specifically why psychic research is a challenge for science.

In the course of our psychosocial progress through the study of consciousness, some fundamental assumptions of the current scientific world view will be questioned. This is inevitable, as Thomas S. Kuhn points out in *The Structure of Scientific Revolutions* (7). Psychic research is perhaps the primary area from which the revolution will come and from which a new paradigm of science will be constructed.

Fundamental to science is objectivism, a view of nature as a collection of discrete parts that scientists can observe and manipulate in a detached, impartial manner. Natural events occur as natural forces work through natural laws, while the scientist stands aside, neutral and emotionally uninvolved. He simply lets things happen as they may. There can be cause-and-effect relationships; there can be interactions. But they all happen outside the observer. The principle of separate identity remains in effect.

Another principle of science is materialism, the notion that reality is thoroughly explainable by the existence of matter alone. Operating on that basis, science has been eminently successful in exploring the physical world and learning to control it. Dramatic accomplishments over the past hundred years leave no room for doubt about that.

At the same time, however, science has been responsible for putting in man's hands knowledge that he has sadly used for unprecedented killing, destruction, and harm of his own kind and his environment. Why? Why has our sophisticated knowledge of the physical universe not led to wisdom? Why can we not live in harmony with each other and with the planet?

Part of the answer, I believe, can be found in the two fundamental assumptions of contemporary science: objectivism and materialism. Although they are valid in a limited domain, they have been unwisely viewed as universally applicable. Studies in such diverse fields as logic, metalinguistics, and quantum mechanics have demonstrated that the concepts of subjective versus objective, matter versus energy, and perhaps even causality itself are arbitrary constructions that man imposes on nature. The universe is holistic—a *universe*. But most people, including scientists, seem unaware of this, and therefore, these assumptions combine to form a nonconscious philosophy of life—a paradigm. The scientific emphasis on matter has led to an overemphasis on the material things necessary for living. Likewise, the scientific emphasis on objectivity has led to a loss of unity and empathy among people. In its place are aloofness, impersonality, and apathy.

The unfortunate results are apparent everywhere. On the individual level, our awareness of personhood is lost to the view that personality is a commodity to be packaged and sold over cosmetic counters, in clothing stores, and through self-development courses. Objects are seen as having more value than persons themselves, and there is a widespread tendency to treat people as things to be manipulated like machines.

On the social level, we are only a step away from enshrining the objective, rational mode of thought as the source of all goodness and wisdom. Reinforcing this is the objectification—rather, the reification—of abstract ideas such as nation and state. From this viewpoint it is only logical to make war on other countries and on the countryside.

This denial of the nonmaterial aspect of life—its sacred participation in the miracle of existence—leaves people with no source of meaning and direction. The resulting view may be stated thus: I am simply a prisoner of my flesh, fighting for survival in a hostile and competitive world, and death is the end of me because life is only physical. I am just a skin-encapsulated ego, locked in a soulless body that will someday perish and decay.

Psychic research presents a direct challenge to this shortsighted view of reality by calling into question the assumed primacy of objectivism and materialism. Telepathy demonstrates that there is an informational linkage between people that goes beyond the laws of science as they are presently understood—a linkage we are normally unaware of—and the discovery of primary perception in cell life apparently extends that linkage downward in the ladder of molecular organization. Clairvoyance challenges our understanding of sensory perception. Precognition and retrocognition challenge our concept of time. PK challenges our concepts of energy and energy transfer. So too does psychic healing, which also brings into question our concepts of physiology and medicine.

Studies in all these areas seem to indicate that mind and consciousness can operate at a distance from the body, interacting with the outside world in ways that cannot be explained in terms of known laws. Beyond that, survival research is pointing to the possibility that mind and consciousness may operate *independently* on the body. In short, psychic research is leading to an extraordinarily challenging conclusion: Science's basic image of man and the universe must be revised. Because of this new light on the nature of humanity and our position in the cosmos, science will have to divest itself not only of some deeply cherished "facts" but also of its philosophic foundations—the whole intellectual outlook upon which our present civilization is based. That outlook, says Arthur Koestler in *The Roots of Coincidence* (5), is "the greatest superstitition of our age—the materialistic clock-work universe of early nineteenth-century physics."

We are living, in William Irwin Thompson's words, "at the edge of history." A linear extrapolation of current conditions shows that mankind has, conservatively speaking, less than a century before it goes the way of the dinosaur. Many scientists and planetary planners think the remaining time could be only a few decades. Granted, some unforeseen circumstance such as the "green revolution" or a break-through in pollution control may favorably alter that prognosis and thereby lend support to the dictum that civilization totters but it totters steadily onward. Never-theless, survival seems to depend more than anything on a transformation of con-sciousness, an evolution of the mind. That includes our philosophy of science—the physicalistic way in which we conceive and behave.

For some scientists, that will mean a tremendous shift in thinking. It will mean relinquishing some long-held views that are no longer correct and that threaten our very existence. This need for disillusioning has arisen before in the history of science. The theory of phlogiston and the concept of the role of the neutral observer in quantum mechanics are examples. But never before has the need for jettisoning false beliefs had such global importance. If science maintains its old attitude toward psy-chic research, it will merely prove that Max Planck was correct when he said, "A new scientific truth does not triumph by convincing its opponents and making them see the light, but rather because its opponents eventually die and a new generation grows up that is familiar with it."

The only possible basis for rejecting the evidence of psychic research is prej-udice and diehard stubborness born of insecurity. Psychologist Donald O. Hebb admitted this plainly as far back as 1951. "Why do we not accept ESP as psycho-logical fact?" he asked. "Rhine has offered enough evidence to convince us on al-most any other issue where one could make some guess as to the mechanics of the disputed process. Personally, I do not accept ESP for a moment because it does not make any sense. I cannot see what other base my colleagues have for rejecting it, but my own rejection of Rhine's views is, in the literal sense, prejudiced."

That is a candid admission. I do not know if Hebb has since discovered the "sense" of psychic research, but in any case, Aldous Huxley's reply to his statement is worthy of consideration by those inclined to reject the findings and implications of this subject. Huxley said, "That a man of science should allow a prejudice to outweigh evidence seems strange enough. It is even stranger to find a psychologist rejecting a psychological discovery simply because it cannot be explained. Psi . . . is intrinsically no more inexplicable than, say, perception or memory."

. . .

Clearly, the tide is turning. When the turn is completed, the unity of all knowledge and experience will become apparent. The complementary nature of the objective and subjective modes of knowing reality and investigating the nature of the universe will be demonstrated.

The result, I think, can only be a new appreciation by both science and religion for each other's mode of operation. Thus far, science has dealt only with the rational and the irrational. It has not recognized the nonrational. Nonrational forms of knowledge transcend the categories of ordinary logic and perception that the discursive intellect works with. These areas of mind can, when properly used, be just as meaningful in providing knowledge about ourselves and the universe. Nonrational forms of knowing are our most ancient sources of wisdom. As yogi-philosopher Gopi Krishna points out in *The Secret of Yoga* (6), from them spring religious truths, artistic creativity, the insights of genius, psychic abilities, and those related forms of ESP that we call intuition, hunches, and gut feelings. Collectively, they have been called *the unconscious*—a somewhat misleading term, incidentally, because the unconscious is supremely intelligent. It is at the deepest level of our personal unconscious that the boundary between the subjective and objective modes disappears and that our limited sense of self merges with its universal source of being.

We must get in touch again with the unconscious. If we honestly and courageously let that aspect of mind speak to us, if we make the unconscious conscious, there will be a fundamental alteration in present attitudes, values, and beliefs, followed by a fundamental change in our behavior. Our objective and subjective experiences will fuse synergistically in a quantum leap of understanding, a higher level of awareness. *This could be the transformation of human consciousness that is necessary for solving our critical dilemma.*

Such a change would ensure that any course of action planned would be sane, practical, and sufficient in scope to meet planetary problems in a holistic manner. It would restore health to our divided psyches, unity to our fractured society, and harmony to the unbalanced environment. Thus far, science has mostly produced fragmentation. But health is wholeness. To "cure" science, we must, as philosopher Dane Rudhyar (15) says, "build greater wholes."

Psychic research is an avenue to the unconscious, a means for building greater wholes (10). Now is the time for us to begin building a single whole of humanity. Now is the time to develop our nonrational abilities into a "subjective technology," which will begin the wedding of science and religion, reason and intuition, the physical and the spiritual. This union of head and heart, insight and instinct, will ensure that as science comes to comprehend the nonmaterial aspect of reality as well as it knows the material—that is, as science approaches omniscience—our knowledge will become wisdom, our love of power will become the power of love, and the universal man of cosmic consciousness can then emerge.

References

1. **Clark, Ronald.** *Einstein; The Life and Times.* World: New York, 1971.
2. **Eccles, John.** *The Brain and the Unity of Conscious Experience.* Cambridge University Press: New York, 1965.

3. **Green, Alyce M.; Green, Elmer E.; and Walters, E. Dale.** "Psychophysiological Training for Creativity." Paper presented at the 1971 meeting of the American Psychological Association, Washington, D.C.
4. **"Interview: Captain Edgar D. Mitchell."** *Psychic*, September–October 1971.
5. **Koestler, Arthur.** *The Roots of Coincidence.* Random House: New York, 1972.
6. **Krishna, Gopi.** *The Secret of Yoga.* Harper & Row: New York, 1972.
7. **Kuhn, Thomas S.** *The Structure of Scientific Revolutions.* University of Chicago Press: Chicago, 1962.
8. **Mitchell, Edgar D.** "An ESP Test from Apollo 14." *Journal of Parapsychology*, 35, no. 2 (1971).
9. **Ornstein, Robert, ed.** *The Nature of Human Consciousness.* Freeman: San Francisco, 1973.
10. "Parapsychology—What the Questionnaire Revealed." *New Scientist*, 25, January, 1973.
11. **Polanyi, Michael.** *Personal Knowledge.* Routledge and Kegan Paul: London, 1958.
12. **Rhine, J. B.** *The Reach of the Mind.* Apollo: New York, 1960.
13. **Rhine, J. B.** *Extra-Sensory Perception.* Rev. ed. Humphries: Boston, 1964.
14. **Rudhyar, Dane.** *The Planetarization of Consciousness.* Harper & Row: New York, 1972.
15. **Sherman, Harold.** *Thoughts Through Space.* Fawcett: New York, 1973.

Demythologization

Rudolf Bultmann

Rudolf Karl Bultmann (1884–   ) is one of the most influential Christian theologians of the twentieth century. He is noted for his "existential" approach to the New Testament. His major works include *Theology of the New Testament* (two volumes, 1948–1953), *History and Eschatology*, and *Jesus Christ and Mythology*.

The Task of Demythologizing the New Testament Proclamation

The Problem

THE MYTHICAL VIEW OF THE WORLD AND THE MYTHICAL EVENT OF REDEMPTION. The cosmology of the New Testament is essentially mythical in character. The world is viewed as a three-storied structure, with the earth in the centre, the heaven above, and the underworld beneath. Heaven is the abode of God and of celestial beings—the angels. The underworld is hell, the place of torment. Even the earth is more than the scene of natural, everyday events, of the trivial round and common task. It is the scene of the supernatural activity of God and his angels on the one hand, and of Satan and his daemons on the other. These supernatural forces intervene in the course of nature and in all that men think and will and do. Miracles are by no means rare. Man is not in control of his own life. Evil spirits may take possession of him. Satan may inspire him with evil thoughts. Alternatively, God may inspire his thought and guide his purposes. He may grant him heavenly visions. He may allow him to hear his word of succour or demand. He may give him the supernatural power of his Spirit. History does not follow a smooth unbroken course; it is set in motion and controlled by these supernatural powers. This aeon is held in bondage by Satan, sin, and death (for "powers" is precisely what they are), and hastens towards its end. That end will come very soon, and will take the form of a cosmic catastrophe. It will be inaugurated by the "woes" of the last time. Then the Judge will come from heaven, the dead will rise, the last judgement will take place, and men will enter into eternal salvation or damnation.

This then is the mythical view of the world which the New Testament presupposes when it presents the event of redemption which is the subject of its preaching. It proclaims in the language of mythology that the last time has now come. "In the fulness of time" God sent forth his Son, a pre-existent divine Being, who appears on earth as a man.[1] He dies the death of a sinner[2] on the cross and makes atonement for the

Source: Rudolf Bultmann, "New Testament and Mythology," in *Kerygma and Myth*, Vol. 1, ed. by Hans-Werner Bartsch, trans. by Reginald H. Fuller (London, 1953), pp. 1–16, 35–37. Reprinted by permission of The Society for Promoting Christian Knowledge.

[1] Gal. 4. 4; Phil. 2. 6ff.; 2 Cor. 8. 9; John 1. 14, etc.
[2] 2 Cor. 5. 21; Rom. 8. 3.

sins of men.[3] His resurrection marks the beginning of the cosmic catastrophe. Death, the consequence of Adam's sin, is abolished,[4] and the daemonic forces are deprived of their power.[5] The risen Christ is exalted to the right hand of God in heaven[6] and made "Lord" and "King."[7] He will come again on the clouds of heaven to complete the work of redemption, and the resurrection and judgement of men will follow.[8] Sin, suffering and death will then be finally abolished.[9] All this is to happen very soon; indeed, St. Paul thinks that he himself will live to see it.[10]

All who belong to Christ's Church and are joined to the Lord by Baptism and the Eucharist are certain of resurrection to salvation,[11] unless they forfeit it by unworthy behaviour. Christian believers already enjoy the first instalment of salvation, for the Spirit[12] is at work within them, bearing witness to their adoption as sons of God,[13] and guaranteeing their final resurrection.[14]

THE MYTHOLOGICAL VIEW OF THE WORLD OBSOLETE. All this is the language of mythology, and the origin of the various themes can be easily traced in the contemporary mythology of Jewish Apocalyptic and in the redemption myths of Gnosticism. To this extent *the kerygma is incredible to modern man, for he is convinced that the mythical view of the world is obsolete*. We are therefore bound to ask whether, when we preach the Gospel to-day, we expect our converts to accept not only the Gospel message, but also the mythical view of the world in which it is set. If not, does the New Testament embody a truth which is quite independent of its mythical setting? If it does, theology must undertake the task of stripping the Kerygma from its mythical framework, of "demythologizing" it.

Can Christian preaching expect modern man *to accept the mythical view of the world as true*? To do so would be both senseless and impossible. It would be senseless, because there is nothing specifically Christian in the mythical view of the world as such. It is simply the cosmology of a pre-scientific age. Again, it would be impossible, because no man can adopt a view of the world by his own volition—it is already determined for him by his place in history. Of course such a view is not absolutely unalterable, and the individual may even contribute to its change. But he can do so only when he is faced by a new set of facts so compelling as to make his previous view of the world untenable. He has then no alternative but to modify his view of the world or produce a new one. The discoveries of Copernicus and the atomic theory are instances of this, and so was romanticism, with its discovery that the human subject is richer and more complex than enlightenment or idealism had allowed, and nationalism, with its new realization of the importance of history and the tradition of peoples.

[3] Rom. 3. 23–26; 4. 25; 8. 3; 2 Cor. 5. 14, 19; John 1. 29; 1 John 2. 2, etc.
[4] 1 Cor. 15. 21f.; Rom. 5. 12ff.
[5] 1 Cor. 2. 6; Col. 2. 15; Rev. 12. 7ff., etc.
[6] Acts 1. 6f.; 2. 33; Rom. 8. 34, etc.
[7] Phil. 2. 9–11; 1 Cor. 15. 25.
[8] 1 Cor. 15. 23f., 50ff., etc.
[9] Rev. 21. 4, etc.
[10] 1 Thess. 4. 15ff.; 1 Cor. 15. 51f.; cf. Mark 9.1.
[11] Rom. 5. 12ff.; 1 Cor. 15. 21ff., 44b, ff.
[12] Ἀπαρχή: Rom. 8. 23, χρραβών: 2 Cor. 1. 22; 5. 5.
[13] Rom. 8. 15; Gal. 4. 6.
[14] Rom. 8. 11.

It may equally well happen that truths which a shallow enlightment had failed to perceive are later rediscovered in ancient myths. Theologians are perfectly justified in asking whether this is not exactly what has happened with the New Testament. At the same time it is impossible to revive an obsolete view of the world by a mere fiat, and certainly not a mythical view. For all our thinking to-day is shaped irrevocably by modern science. A blind acceptance of the New Testament mythology would be arbitrary, and to press for its acceptance as an article of faith would be to reduce faith to works. Wilhelm Herrmann pointed this out, and one would have thought that his demonstration was conclusive. It would involve a sacifice of the intellect which could have only one result—a curious form of schizophrenia and insincerity. It would mean accepting a view of the world in our faith and religion which we should deny in our everyday life. Modern thought as we have inherited it brings with it criticism of *the New Testament view of the world*.

Man's knowledge and mastery of the world have advanced to such an extent through science and technology that it is no longer possible for anyone seriously to hold the New Testament view of the world—in fact, there is no one who does. What meaning, for instance, can we attach to such phrases in the creed as "descended into hell" or "ascended into heaven"? We no longer believe in the three-storied universe which the creeds take for granted. The only honest way of reciting the creeds is to strip the mythological framework from the truth they enshrine—that is, assuming that they contain any truth at all, which is just the question that theology has to ask. No one who is old enough to think for himself supposes that God lives in a local heaven. There is no longer any heaven in the traditional sense of the word. The same applies to hell in the sense of a mythical underworld beneath our feet. And if this is so, the story of Christ's descent into hell and of his Ascension into heaven is done with. We can no longer look for the return of the Son of Man on the clouds of heaven or hope that the faithful will meet him in the air (1 Thess. 4. 15ff.).

Now that the forces and the laws of nature have been discovered, we can no longer believe in *spirits, whether good or evil*. We know that the stars are physical bodies whose motions are controlled by the laws of the universe, and not daemonic beings which enslave mankind to their service. Any influence they may have over human life must be explicable in terms of the ordinary laws of nature; it cannot in any way be attributed to their malevolence. Sickness and the cure of disease are likewise attributable to natural causation; they are not the result of daemonic activity or of evil spells.[15] The *miracles of the New Testament* have ceased to be miraculous, and to defend their historicity by recourse to nervous disorders or hypnotic effects only serves to underline the fact. And if we are still left with certain physiological and psychological phenomena which we can only assign to mysterious and enigmatic causes, we are still assigning them to causes, and thus far are trying to make them scientifically intelligible. Even occultism pretends to be a science.

---

[15] It may of course be argued that there are people alive to-day whose confidence in the traditional scientific view of the world has been shaken, and others who are primitive enough to qualify for an age of mythical thought. And there also are many varieties of superstition. But when belief in spirits and miracles has degenerated into superstition, it has become something entirely different from what it was when it was genuine faith. The various impressions and speculations which influence credulous people here and there are of little importance, nor does it matter to what extent cheap slogans have spread an atmosphere inimical to science. What matters is the world view which men imbibe from their environment, and it is science which determines that view of the world through the school, the press, the wireless, the cinema, and all the other fruits of technical progress.

It is impossible to use electric light and the wireless and to avail ourselves of modern medical and surgical discoveries, and at the same time to believe in the New Testament world of spirits and miracles.[16] We may think we can manage it in our own lives, but to expect others to do so is to make the Christian faith unintelligible and unacceptable to the modern world.

The *mythical eschatology* is untenable for the simple reason that the parousia of Christ never took place as the New Testament expected. History did not come to an end, and, as every schoolboy knows, it will continue to run its course. Even if we believe that the world as we know it will come to an end in time, we expect the end to take the form of a natural catastrophe, not of a mythical event such as the New Testament expects. And if we explain the parousia in terms of modern scientific theory, we are applying criticism to the New Testament, albeit unconsciously.

But natural science is not the only challenge which the mythology of the New Testament has to face. There is the still more serious challenge presented by *modern man's understanding of himself.*

Modern man is confronted by a curious dilemma. He may regard himself as pure nature, or as pure spirit. In the latter case he distinguishes the essential part of his being from nature. In either case, however, *man is essentially a unity.* He bears the sole responsibility for his own feeling, thinking, and willing.[17] He is not, as the New Testament regards him, the victim of a strange dichotomy which exposes him to the interference of powers outside himself. If his exterior behavior and his interior condition are in perfect harmony, it is something he has achieved himself, and if other people think their interior unity is torn asunder by daemonic or divine interference, he calls it schizophrenia.

Although biology and psychology recognize that man is a highly dependent being, that does not mean that he has been handed over to powers outside of and distinct from himself. This dependence is inseparable from human nature, and he needs only to understand it in order to recover his self-mastery and organize his life on a rational basis. If he regards himself as spirit, he knows that he is permanently conditioned by the physical, bodily part of his being, but he distinguishes his true self from it, and knows that he is independent and responsible for his mastery over nature.

In either case he finds *what the New Testament has to say about the "Spirit"* ($\pi\nu\epsilon\hat{\upsilon}\mu\alpha$) *and the sacraments utterly strange and incomprehensible.* Biological man cannot see how a supernatural entity like the $\pi\nu\epsilon\hat{\upsilon}\mu\alpha$ can penetrate within the close texture of his natural powers and set to work within him. Nor can the idealist understand how a $\pi\nu\epsilon\hat{\upsilon}\mu\alpha$ working like a natural power can touch and influence his mind and spirit. Conscious as he is of his own moral responsibility, he cannot conceive how baptism in water can convey a mysterious something which is henceforth the agent of all his decision and actions. He cannot see how physical food can convey spiritual strength, and how the unworthy receiving of the Eucharist can result in physical sickness and death (1 Cor. 11. 30). The only possible explanation is that

---

[16] Cf. the observations of Paul Schütz on the decay of mythical religion in the East through the introduction of modern hygiene and medicine.

[17] Cf. Gerhardt Krüger, *Einsicht und Leidenschaft, Das Wesen des platonischen Denkens,* Frankfort, 1939, p. 11f.

it is due to suggestion. He cannot understand how anyone can be baptized for the dead (1 Cor. 15. 29).

We need not examine in detail the various forms of modern *Weltanschauung* whether idealist or naturalist. For the only criticism of the New Testament which is theologically relevant is that which arises *necessarily* out of the situation of modern man. The biological *Weltanschauung* does not, for instance, arise necessarily out of the contemporary situation. We are still free to adopt it or not as we choose. The only relevant question for the theologian is the basic assumption on which the adoption of a biological as of every other *Weltanschauung* rests, and that assumption is the view of the world which has been moulded by modern science and the modern conception of human nature as a self-subsistent unity immune from the interference of supernatural powers.

Again, the biblical doctrine that *death is the punishment of sin* is equally abhorrent to naturalism and idealism, since they both regard death as a simple and necessary process of nature. To the naturalist death is no problem at all, and to the idealist it is a problem for that very reason, for so far from arising out of man's essential spiritual being it actually destroys it. The idealist is faced with a paradox. On the one hand man is a spiritual being, and therefore essentially different from plants and animals, and on the other hand he is the prisoner of nature, whose birth, life, and death are just the same as those of the animals. Death may present him with a problem, but he cannot see how it can be a punishment for sin. Human beings are subject to death even before they have committed any sin. And to attribute human mortality to the fall of Adam is sheer nonsense, for guilt implies personal responsibility, and the idea of original sin as an inherited infection is sub-ethical, irrational, and absurd.

The same objections apply to *the doctrine of the atonement*. How can the guilt of one man be expiated by the death of another who is sinless—if indeed one may speak of a sinless man at all ? What primitive notions of guilt and righteousness does this imply ? And what primitive idea of God ? The rationale of sacrifice in general may of course throw some light on the theory of the atonement, but even so, what a primitive mythology it is, that a divine Being should become incarnate, and atone for the sins of men through his own blood ? Or again, one might adopt an analogy from the law courts, and explain the death of Christ as a transaction between God and man through which God's claims on man were satisfied. But that would make sin a juridical matter; it would be no more than an external transgression of a commandment, and it would make nonsense of all our ethical standards. Moreover, if the Christ who died such a death was the pre-existent Son of God, what could death mean for him ? Obviously very little, if he knew that he would rise again in three days!

The *resurrection of Jesus* is just as difficult for modern man, if it means an event whereby a living supernatural power is released which can henceforth be appropriated through the sacraments. To the biologist such language is meaningless, for he does not regard death as a problem at all. The idealist would not object to the idea of a life immune from death, but he could not believe that such a life is made available by the resuscitation of a dead person. If that is the way God makes life available for man, his action is inextricably involved in a nature miracle. Such a notion he finds incomprehensible, for he can see God at work only in the reality of his personal life and in his transformation. But, quite apart from the incredibility of such a miracle, he cannot see how an event like this could be the act of God, or how it could affect his own life.

Gnostic influence suggests that this Christ, who died and rose again, was not a mere human being but a God-man. His death and resurrection were not isolated facts which concerned him alone, but a cosmic event in which we are all involved.[18] It is only with effort that modern man can think himself back into such an intellectual atmosphere, and even then he could never accept it himself, because it regards man's essential being as nature and redemption as a process of nature. And as for the pre-existence of Christ, with its corollary of man's translation into a celestial realm of light, and the clothing of the human personality in heavenly robes and a spiritual body—all this is not only irrational but utterly meaningless. Why should salvation take this particular form? Why should this be the fulfilment of human life and the realization of man's true being?

The Task Before Us

NOT SELECTION OR SUBTRACTION. Does this drastic criticism of the New Testament mythology mean the complete elimination of the kerygma?

Whatever else may be true, we cannot save the kerygma by selecting some of its features and subtracting others, and thus reduce the amount of mythology in it. For instance, it is impossible to dismiss St. Paul's teaching about the unworthy reception of Holy Communion or about baptism for the dead, and yet cling to the belief that physical eating and drinking can have a spiritual effect. If we accept *one* idea, we must accept everything which the New Testament has to say about Baptism and Holy Communion, and it is just this one idea which we cannot accept.

It may of course be argued that some features of the New Testament mythology are given greater prominence than others: not all of them appear with the same regularity in the various books. There is for example only one occurrence of the legends of the Virgin birth and the Ascension; St. Paul and St. John appear to be totally unaware of them. But, even if we take them to be later accretions, it does not affect the mythical character of the event of redemption as a whole. And if we once start subtracting from the kerygma, where are we to draw the line? The mythical view of the world must be accepted or rejected in its entirety.

At this point absolute clarity and ruthless honesty are essential both for the academic theologian and for the parish priest. It is a duty they owe to themselves, to the Church they serve, and to those whom they seek to win for the Church. They must make it quite clear what their hearers are expected to accept and what they are not. At all costs the preacher must not leave his people in the dark about what he secretly eliminates, nor must he be in the dark about it himself. In Karl Barth's book *The Ressurection of the Dead* the cosmic eschatology in the sense of "chronologically final history" is eliminated in favour of what he intends to be a nonmythological "ultimate history." He is able to delude himself into thinking that this is exegesis of St. Paul and of the New Testament generally only because he gets

[18] Rom. 5. 12ff.; 1 Cor. 15. 21ff. 44b.

rid of everything mythological in 1 Corinthians by subjecting it to an interpretation which does violence to its meaning. But that is an impossible procedure.

If the truth of the New Testament proclamation is to be preserved, the only way is to demythologize it. But our motive in so doing must not be to make the New Testament relevant to the modern world at all costs. The question is simply whether the New Testament message consists exclusively of mythology, or whether it actually demands the elimination of myth if it is to be understood as it is meant to be. This question is forced upon us from two sides. First there is the nature of myth in general, and then there is the New Testament itself.

THE NATURE OF MYTH. The real purpose of myth is not to present an objective picture of the world as it is, but to express man's understanding of himself in the world in which he lives. Myth should be interpreted not cosmologically, but anthropologically, or better still, existentially.[19] Myth speaks of the power or the powers which man supposes he experiences as the ground and limit of his world and of his own activity and suffering. He describes these powers in terms derived from the visible world, with its tangible objects and forces, and from human life, with its feelings, motives, and potentialities. He may, for instance, explain the origin of the world by speaking of a world egg or a world tree. Similarly he may account for the present state and order of the world by speaking of a primeval war between the gods. He speaks of the other world in terms of this world, and of the gods in terms derived from human life.[20]

Myth is an expression of man's conviction that the origin and purpose of the world in which he lives are to be sought not within it but beyond it—that is, beyond the realm of known and tangible reality—and that this realm is perpetually dominated and menaced by those mysterious powers which are its source and limit. Myth is also an expression of man's awareness that he is not lord of his own being. It expresses his sense of dependence not only within the visible world, but more especially on those forces which hold sway beyond the confines of the known. Finally, myth expresses man's belief that in this state of dependence he can be delivered from the forces within the visible world.

Thus myth contains elements which demand its own criticism—namely, its imagery with its apparent claim to objective validity. The real purpose of myth is to speak of a transcendent power which controls the world and man, but that purpose is impeded and obscured by the terms in which it is expressed.

Hence the importance of the New Testament mythology lies not in its imagery but in the understanding of existence which it enshrines. The real question is whether this understanding of existence is true. Faith claims that it is, and faith ought not to be tied down to the imagery of New Testament mythology.

---

[19] Cf. Gerhardt Krüger, *Einsicht und Leidenschaft,* esp. p. 17f., 56f.

[20] Myth is here used in the sense popularized by the "History of Religions" school. Mythology is the use of imagery to express the other worldly in terms of this world and the divine in terms of human life, the other side in terms of this side. For instance, divine transcendence is expressed as spatial distance. It is a mode of expression which makes it easy to understand the cultus as an action in which material means are used to convey immaterial power. Myth is not used in that modern sense, according to which it is practically equivalent to ideology.

THE NEW TESTAMENT ITSELF. The New Testament itself invites this kind of criticism. Not only are there rough edges in its mythology, but some of its features are actually contradictory. For example, the death of Christ is sometimes a sacrifice and sometimes a cosmic event. Sometimes his person is interpreted as the Messiah and sometimes as the Second Adam. The kenosis of the pre-existent Son (Phil. 2. 6ff.) is incompatible with the miracle narratives as proofs of his messianic claims. The Virgin birth is inconsistent with the assertion of his pre-existence. The doctrine of the Creation is incompatible with the conception of the "rulers of this world" (1 Cor. 2. 6ff.), the "god of this world" (2 Cor. 4. 4) and the "elements of this world" (στοιχεῖα τοῦ κόσμου, Gal. 4. 3). It is impossible to square the belief that the law was given by God with the theory that it comes from the angels (Gal. 3. 19f.).

But the principal demand for the criticism of mythology comes from a curious contradiction which runs right through the New Testament. Sometimes we are told that human life is determined by cosmic forces, at others we are challenged to a decision. Side by side with the Pauline indicative stands the Pauline imperative. In short, man is sometimes regarded as a cosmic being, sometimes as an independent "I" for whom decision is a matter of life or death. Incidentally, this explains why so many sayings in the New Testament speak directly to modern man's condition while others remain enigmatic and obscure. Finally, attempts at demythologization are sometimes made even within the New Testament itself. But more will be said on this point later.

PREVIOUS ATTEMPTS AT DEMYTHOLOGIZING. How then is the mythology of the New Testament to be re-interpreted? This is not the first time that theologians have approached this task. Indeed, all we have said so far might have been said in much the same way thirty or forty years ago, and it is a sign of the bankruptcy of contemporary theology that it has been necessary to go all over the same ground again. The reason for this is not far to seek. The liberal theologians of the last century were working on the wrong lines. They threw away not only the mythology but also the kerygma itself. Were they right? Is that the treatment the New Testament itself required? That is the question we must face today. The last twenty years have witnessed a movement away from criticism and a return to a naïve acceptance of the kerygma. The danger both for theological scholarship and for the Church is that this uncritical resuscitation of the New Testament mythology may make the Gospel message unintelligible to the modern world. We cannot dismiss the critical labours of earlier generations without further ado. We must take them up and put them to constructive use. Failure to do so will mean that the old battles between orthodoxy and liberalism will have to be fought out all over again, that is assuming that there will be any Church or any theologians to fight them at all! Perhaps we may put it schematically like this: whereas the older liberals used criticism to *eliminate* the mythology of the New Testament, our task today is to use criticism to *interpret* it. Of course it may still be necessary to eliminate mythology here and there. But the criterion adopted must be taken not from modern thought, but from the understanding of human existence which the New Testament itself enshrines.[21]

[21] As an illustration of this critical re-interpretation of myth cf. Hans Jonas, *Augustin und das paulinische Freiheitsproblem*, 1930, pp. 66–76.

To begin with, let us review some of these earlier attempts at demythologizing. We need only mention briefly the allegorical interpretation of the New Testament which has dogged the Church throughout its history. This method spiritualizes the mythical events so that they become symbols of processes going on in the soul. This is certainly the most comfortable way of avoiding the critical question. The literal meaning is allowed to stand and is dispensed with only for the individual believer, who can escape into the realm of the soul.

It was characteristic of the older liberal theologians that they regarded mythology as relative and temporary. Hence they thought they could safely eliminate it altogether, and retain only the broad, basic principles of religion and ethics. They distinguished between what they took to be the essence of religion and the temporary garb which it assumed. Listen to what Harnack has to say about the essence of Jesus' preaching of the Kingdom of God and its coming: "The kingdom has a triple meaning. Firstly, it is something supernatural, a gift from above, not a product of ordinary life. Secondly, it is a purely religious blessing, the inner link with the living God; thirdly, it is the most important experience that a man can have, that on which everything else depends; it permeates and dominates his whole existence, because sin is forgiven and misery banished." Note how completely the mythology is eliminated: "The kingdom of God comes by coming to the individual, by entering into his *soul* and laying hold of it."[22]

It will be noticed how Harnack reduces the kerygma to a few basic principles of religion and ethics. Unfortunately this means that *the kerygma has ceased to be kerygma*: it is no longer the proclamation of the decisive act of God in Christ. For the liberals the great truths of religion and ethics are timeless and eternal, though it is only within human history that they are realized, and only in concrete historical processes that they are given clear expression. But the apprehension and acceptance of these principles does not depend on the knowledge and acceptance of the age in which they first took shape, or of the historical persons who first discovered them. We are all capable of verifying them in our own experience at whatever period we happen to live. History may be of academic interest, but never of paramount importance for religion.

But the New Testament speaks of an *event* through which God has wrought man's redemption. For it, Jesus is not primarily the teacher, who certainly had extremely important things to say and will always be honoured for saying them, but whose person in the last analysis is immaterial for those who have assimilated his teaching. On the contrary, his person is just what the New Testament proclaims as the decisive event of redemption. It speaks of this person in mythological terms, but does this mean that we can reject the kerygma altogether on the ground that it is nothing more than mythology? That is the question.

Next came the History of Religions school. Its representatives were the first to discover the extent to which the New Testament is permeated by mythology. The importance of the New Testament, they saw, lay not in its teaching about religion and ethics, but in its actual religion and piety; in comparison with that all the dogma it contains, and therefore all the mythological imagery with its apparent objectivity, was of secondary importance or completely negligible. The essence of

[22] *What Is Christianity?* Williams and Norgate, 1904, pp. 63–64 and 57.

the New Testament lay in the religious life it portrayed; its high-watermark was the experience of mystical union with Christ, in whom God took symbolic form.

These critics grasped one important truth. Christian faith is not the same as religious idealism; the Christian life does not consist in developing the individual personality, in the improvement of society, or in making the world a better place. The Christian life means a turning away from the world, a detachment from it. But the critics of the History of Religions school failed to see than in the New Testament this detachment is essentially eschatological and not mystical. Religion for them was an expression of the human yearning to rise above the world and transcend it: it was the discovery of a supramundane sphere where the soul could detach itself from all earthly care and find its rest. Hence the supreme manifestation of religion was to be found not in personal ethics or in social idealism but in the cultus regarded as an end in itself. This was just the kind of religious life portrayed in the New Testament, not only as a model and pattern, but as a challenge and inspiration. The New Testament was thus the abiding source of power which enabled man to realize the true life of religion, and Christ was the eternal symbol for the cultus of the Christian Church.[23] It will be noticed how the Church is here defined exclusively as a worshipping community, and this represents a great advance on the older liberalism. This school rediscovered the Church as a *religious* institution. For the idealist there was really no place for the Church at all. But did they succeed in recovering the meaning of the Ecclesia in the full, New Testament sense of the word? For in the New Testament the Ecclesia is invariably a phenomenon of salvation history and eschatology.

Moreover, if the History of Religions school is right, the kerygma has once more ceased to be kerygma. Like the liberals, they are silent about a decisive act of God in Christ proclaimed as the event of redemption. So we are still left with the question whether this event and the person of Jesus, both of which are described in the New Testament in mythological terms, are nothing more than mythology. Can the kerygma be interpreted apart from mythology? Can we recover the truth of the kerygma for men who do not think in mythological terms without forfeiting its character as kerygma?

AN EXISTENTIALIST INTERPRETATION THE ONLY SOLUTION. The theological work which such an interpretation involves can be sketched only in the broadest outline and with only a few examples. We must avoid the impression that this is a light and easy task, as if all we have to do is to discover the right formula and finish the job on the spot. It is much more formidable than that. It cannot be done single-handed. It will tax the time and strength of a whole theological generation.

The mythology of the New Testament is in essence that of Jewish apocalyptic and the Gnostic redemption myths. A common feature of them both is their basic dualism, according to which the present world and its human inhabitants are under the control of daemonic, satanic powers, and stand in need of redemption. Man cannot achieve this redemption by his own efforts; it must come as a gift through a divine intervention. Both types of mythology speak of such an intervention: Jewish apocalyptic of an imminent world crisis in which this present aeon will be

---

[23] Cf. e.g. Troeltsch, *Die Bedeutung der Geschichtlichkeit Jesu für den Glauben*, Tübingen, 1911.

brought to an end and the new aeon ushered in by the coming of the Messiah, and Gnosticism of a Son of God sent down from the realm of light, entering into this world in the guise of a man, and by his fate and teaching delivering the elect and opening up the way for their return to their heavenly home.

The meaning of these two types of mythology lies once more not in their imagery with its apparent objectivity but in the understanding of human existence which both are trying to express. In other words, they need to be interpreted existentially. A good example of such treatment is to be found in Hans Jonas's book on Gnosticism.[24]

Our task is to produce an existentialist interpretation of the dualistic mythology of the New Testament along similar lines. When, for instance, we read of daemonic powers ruling the world and holding mankind in bondage, does the understanding of human existence which underlies such language offer a solution to the riddle of human life which will be acceptable even to the non-mythological mind of today? Of course we must not take this to imply that the New Testament presents us with an anthropology like that which modern science can give us. It cannot be proved by logic or demonstrated by an appeal to factual evidence. Scientific anthropologies always take for granted a definite understanding of existence, which is invariably the consequence of a deliberate decision of the scientist, whether he makes it consciously or not. And that is why we have to discover whether the New Testament offers man an understanding of himself which will challenge him to a genuine existential decision.

Demythologizing in Outline

The Christian Interpretation of Being

THE CROSS. Is the cross, understood as the event of redemption, exclusively mythical in character, or can it retain its value for salvation without forfeiting its character as history?

It certainly has a mythical character as far as its objective setting is concerned. The Jesus who was crucified was the pre-existent, incarnate Son of God, and as such he was without sin. He is the victim whose blood atones for our sins. He bears vicariously the sin of the world, and by enduring the punishment for sin on our behalf he delivers us from death. This mythological interpretation is a mixture of sacrificial and juridical analogies, which have ceased to be tenable for us to-day. And in any case they fail to do justice to what the New Testament is trying to say. For the most they can convey is that the cross effects the forgiveness of all the past and future sins of man, in the sense that the punishment they deserved has been remitted. But the New Testament means more than this. The cross releases men not only from guilt, but also from the power of sin. That is why, when the author of Colossians says "He [God] . . . having forgiven us all our trespasses, having blotted out the bond written in ordinances that was against us, which was contrary to us; and he hath taken it out of the way, nailing it to the cross" he hastens to add:

[24] *Gnosis und spätantiker Geist. I. Die mythologische Gnosis*, 1934.

"having put off from himself the principalities and powers, he made a show of them openly, triumphing over them in it" (Col. 2. 13–15).

The historical event of the cross acquires cosmic dimensions. And by speaking of the Cross as a cosmic happening its significance as a historical happening is made clear in accordance with the remarkable way of thinking in which historical events and connections are presented in cosmic terms, and so its full significance is brought into sharper relief. For if we see in the cross the judgement of the world and the defeat of the rulers of this world (1 Cor. 2. 6ff.), the cross becomes the judgement of ourselves as fallen creatures enslaved to the powers of the "world."

By giving up Jesus to be crucified, God has set up the cross for us. To believe in the cross of Christ does not mean to concern ourselves with a mythical process wrought outside of us and our world, with an objective event turned by God to our advantage, but rather to make the cross of Christ our own, to undergo crucifixion with him. The cross in its redemptive aspect is not an isolated incident which befell a mythical personage, but an event whose meaning has "cosmic" importance. Its decisive, revolutionary significance is brought out by the eschatological framework in which it is set. In other words, the cross is not just an event of the past which can be contemplated, but is the eschatological event in and beyond time, in so far as it (understood in its significance, that is, for faith) is an ever-present reality.

The cross becomes a present reality first of all in the sacraments. In baptism men and women are baptized into Christ's death (Rom. 6. 3) and crucified with him (Rom. 6. 6). At every celebration of the Lord's Supper, the death of Christ is proclaimed (1 Cor. 11. 26). The communicants thereby partake of his crucified body and his blood outpoured (1 Cor. 10. 16). Again, the cross of Christ is an ever-present reality in the everyday life of the Christians. "They that are of Christ Jesus have crucified the flesh with the passions and the lusts thereof" (Gal. 5. 24). That is why St. Paul can speak of "the cross of our Lord Jesus Christ, through which the world hath been crucified unto me, and I unto the world" (Gal. 6. 14). That is why he seeks to know "the fellowship of his sufferings," as one who is "conformed to his death" (Phil. 3. 10).

The crucifying of the affections and lusts includes the overcoming of our natural dread of suffering and the perfection of our detachment from the world. Hence the willing acceptance of sufferings in which death is already at work in man means: "always bearing about in our body the dying of Jesus" and "always being delivered unto death for Jesus' sake" (2 Cor. 4. 10f.).

Thus the cross and passion are ever-present realities. How little they are confined to the events of the first Good Friday is amply illustrated by the words which a disciple of St. Paul puts into his master's mouth: "Now I rejoice in my sufferings for your sake, and fill up on my part that which is lacking of the afflictions of Christ in my flesh for his body's sake, which is the Church" (Col. 1. 24).

In its redemptive aspect the cross of Christ is no mere mythical event, but a historic (*geschichtlich*) fact originating in the historical (*historisch*) event which is the crucifixion of Jesus. The abiding significance of the cross is that it is the judgement of the world, the judgement and the deliverance of man. So far as this is so, Christ is crucified "for us," not in the sense of any theory of sacrifice or satisfaction. This interpretation of the cross as a permanent fact rather than a mythological event does far more justice to the redemptive significance of the event of the past than any of the traditional interpretations. In the last resort mythological language is only a medium for conveying the significance of the historical (*historisch*) event. The historical (*historisch*) event of the cross has, in the significance peculiar to it, created a new historic (*geschichtlich*) situation. The preaching of the cross as the event of redemption challenges all who hear it to appropiate this significance for themselves, to be willing to be crucified with Christ.

But, it will be asked, is this significance to be discerned in the actual event of past history? Can it, so to speak, be read off from that event? Or does the cross bear this significance because it is the cross of *Christ*? In other words, must we first be convinced of the significance of Christ and believe in him in order to discern the real meaning of the cross? If we are to perceive the real meaning of the cross, must we understand it as the cross of Jesus as a figure of past history? Must we go back to the Jesus of history?

As far as the first preachers of the gospel are concerned this will certainly be the case. For them the cross was the cross of him with whom they had lived in personal intercourse. The cross was an experience of their own lives. It presented them with a question and it disclosed to them its meaning. But for us this personal connection cannot be reproduced. For us the cross cannot disclose its own meaning: it is an event of the past. We can never recover it as an event in our own lives. All we know of it is derived from historical report. But the New Testament does not proclaim Jesus Christ in this way. The meaning of the cross is not disclosed from the life of Jesus as a figure of past history, a life which needs to be reproduced by historical research. On the contrary, Jesus is not proclaimed merely as the crucified; he is also risen from the dead. The cross and the resurrection form an inseparable unity.

Three

Religion and the
Current Crisis

Introduction

The current crisis in man's earthly tenure has been limned by war, racism, excessive love of money, pollution, suppression of women, rampant sexual liberty, social oppression, conflict between self and society, and the griefs of ambition. They are great rocks hanging around the neck of human hope. Evil stalks the world, its bag full of stones with which to weight us into despair. We have all long left the Garden of Eden to wander cursed on the face of the earth. Deliver us.

Religions have maintained their relevancy to most of humanity throughout history because they have not blinked the omnipresence of evil. We have included the selections in this chapter in this book because they show the historical continuity of contemporary religious thinkers with past thinkers; these contemporary religious thinkers, like their predecessors, do not blink the presence of evil—they face the current forms that evil takes, and they try to show how we can contend with evil in religious terms. For example, **Harvey Cox** addresses himself to the continual manifestations of sex in such a magazine as *Playboy* and in such fleshy display as the Miss America contest, and he finds that these stimuli, linked with the emphasis on romantic love, have placed young people in a troubling moral situation. By formulating an interpretation of Christian ethics, he tries to show that the Christian religion can help to identify what is really evil and what is sheer puritanism in the current sexual scene; further, he wishes to show that religion can give meaningful answers to questions young people have about the morality of sex.

Margaret N. Maxey does not find evil outside the church walls only; Christian theology, too, is responsible for evil because it has tarred all women with the brush used to blame Eve the Woman for the Fall from innocence. Maxey calls for a theological remodeling to liberate women from a model of interpretation that has subjected them to inferior status, humiliation, and unjustified blame for expulsion from the Garden of Eden. "Augustine's model of Woman is clearly inseparable from his model of human sexuality, with its ideal of virginity. The result is that Woman is to be located between Eve and Mary. . . . First and foremost, theology must liberate women from an Augustinian model by refusing to reduce woman's theological significance to some a-sexual, homogeneous, or relational 'human' being. . . . The alternative to homogeneity is to construct a new theological model of woman. . . ." The corrective for theological degradation of women is not, in other words, to homogenize women out of existence, but to liberate and preserve women.

Samuel H. Dresner looks at war in its most destructive, atomic form and will not let us escape our responsibility for rooting out this evil; he will not allow us the comfort of reliance on the mercy of God. Dresner does not see the bible as a salvation story; to see it this way is to neglect the message of the prophets. "The Bible may be described as God's search for the righteous man and His repeated disappointment. God regretted that He had made man. . . . What the prophets feared most was God's abandonment of man, the silencing of His voice, the withdrawal of His presence. . . . There is no guarantee that God will intervene to save our world from disaster. Neither military defense, international agreement or God's miraculous intervention is the solution we are seeking. . . . There *is* a solution. . . . It is in the roots of the human being and the human situation that the solution lies. . . . Moses has been right all these years, but the truth of his words has been ignored by the majority of mankind. It seemed perfectly possible in all the ages gone by to swindle, to cheat, to fight, to wage war, to break treaties, to seek power, to deny every law of God and man—and still get along, even to flourish." No more may one think this now that possible atomic war cancels our reprieve from final destruction, evidence that God will then have finally withdrawn from His greatest disappointment—we evil humans. We will be called to *account* and the divine experiment in humanity may end.

Fyodor Dostoyevsky's Grand Inquisitor holds Jesus responsible for evil in the world. When the devil tempted Jesus three times in the desert, and Jesus resisted, Jesus condemned humans to evil. Jesus condemned us to evil when opting for our freedom, he refused to turn the stones into bread, when he refused to cast himself down from the temple's pinnacle, and when He did not make himself ruler over all the earth. We humans will understand finally "that freedom and bread enough for all are inconceivable together. . . ." Further, had Jesus turned the stones to bread, this miracle would have established Him as the object of worship beyond dispute; humans would have found the one, universally agreeable deity, and, so, He would have prevented war. "For these pitiful creatures," says the Grand Inquisitor of us, "are concerned not only to find what one or the other can worship, but to find something all would believe in and worship; what is essential is that all may be *together* in it. This craving for *community* of worship is the chief misery of every man individually and of all humanity from the beginning of time. For the sake of common worship they've slain each other with the sword." The Grand Inquisitor's task is to accomplish what Jesus failed to do; he will not be deterred and, so, must burn Jesus upon this His return to earth in order to prevent Jesus from committing the same mistakes twice; it is the Inquisitor's task to destroy the perpetrator of the world's evils; never again must Jesus be allowed to offer we humans freedom rather than bread, community, and domination.

We remind ourselves that there are several ways to deal with Evil. As Albert Camus pointed out to us, suicide is a form of deliverance from our absurd existence. It is not a popular form of deliverance, however. Literature has more popularly suggested that deliverance is to be found by taking certain attitudes toward evil. Philosophers have recommended insouciance or indifference, but Rasselas* discovered that the philosopher soon lost the insouciance he advocated when his daughter died. Defiance is an admirable attitude, but it implies expectation of defeat. Going down with a curse and fistshake is still going down. Captain Ahab went down defiantly, but, nevertheless, down, before Moby Dick. ("Towards thee I roll, thou all-destroying but unconquering whale; . . . from hell's heart I stab at thee; for hate's sake I spit my last breath at thee . . . thou damned whale!") And for all Sancho Panza's drollery, Don Quixote could not be saved from evil in the end; humor is an attitude that provides relief but does not provide a cure for evil, any more than morphine cures cancer.

Religious thinkers have proposed more ambitious deliverance schemes. Consider a cosmological deliverance. Human beings may, indeed, be subject to unremitting evil in this world, but suppose that there is some divine intelligence who conceived a grand purpose with us as ingredient. The evil that we suffer may be no accidental, provincial affair of our kin on this small planet. The plot may be of massive, cosmological proportions. In fact, the plot may be so massive that it involves two universes, one in which there is evil and another in which there is no evil. Perhaps this divine intelligence, who also bears the virtue of divine mercy, has placed us temporarily in the evil cosmos so that when he/she delivers us into the cosmos without evil we can live in the blessed knowledge of a goodness that we could not have known without the experience of evil.

Metaphysical deliverances also have been proposed by religious thinkers. These often turn on the distinction between appearance and reality. Suppose that all evil is traceable to the body's desires, lusts, greed, excesses, and needs. Now, suppose that human beings were shown not to be identical with their body but with a spiritual soul, and suppose, further, that by careful metaphysical argument we could show that matter is only appearance, that it has no reality; then the evil that originates in the body would also be unreal, mere appearance. This is a metaphysical deliverance from evil.

We have reviewed four forms of deliverance: suicidal, attitudinal, cosmological, and metaphysical. There is a fifth form of deliverance that characterizes the thrust of this chapter. This is the way of action, the attempt to defeat the forces of evil here and now in this world.

---

*Rasselas was a fictional character in Samuel Johnson's novel Rasselas, Prince of Abyssinia. Rasselas left the happy valley of Amahra to venture into the outer world, found it a miserable place, and returned to that valley only to discover that its happiness was an illusion of youth.

Even for those religious seers who hold that deliverance from evil comes finally in another universe than this one, the believers and followers are here and now in this world. They are impatient for deliverance. These believers are organized typically into a churchly institution. Such institutions can press a struggle against evil. Being temporally organized, institutional religion is a political affair. The decisions and pronouncements of religious leaders are of this world; they are born out of politically structured councils, conventions, struggles, and power conflicts. True, leaders seek the sanction of sacred texts for their decisions and pronouncements, but that claim, too, is temporal, as temporal as a judge's who claims the sanction of statute or precedent for his decision.

In this chapter, then, the essays belong to a category we might call "religious politics."

The idea of religious politics may offend the pious, because the juncture of temporal politics with the eternal verities of religion seems to them a breach of the sacred by the profane. But to take offense would betray a certain naiveté about the relation between sacred texts and the ethical foundations of a righteous political struggle with evil. There is nothing either strange or strained about the juncture of politics and religion. Some reflections on a question Socrates asked will help us to see that the juncture is a fitting one. A form of Socrates' question, one he put to Euthyphro, is this: "Is something right because God said it or did God say it because it was right?"

Suppose that a religious-minded policeman justifies making an arrest of a seller of pornographic books by citing a sacred text, perhaps something from St. Paul. Supposing the St. Paul text to be divinely inspired, we may inquire now, as Socrates did, why the cited text is supposed to justify the action. If God's saying it alone makes it right, then the sacred text itself is the justification, but if God says it because it is right, then He must have grounds or reasons that we intelligent, temporal beings can share. This sharing means that a rational bridge between sacred texts and temporal, political decisions exists and that, consequently, the notion of religious politics is not impious.

The view that something is right merely because God says so makes the distinction between good and evil purely arbitrary; the distinction would not, then, be based on a difference in the nature of good and evil. Additionally, if God's arbitrarily saying something makes it right, we would have to acknowledge that he could just as reasonably have said the opposite of what he said. In that case, today the pious should be encouraging the pornographers, the cursers of God, the rapists of little children, and the defilers of the temple. If this seems ridiculous to you, there must be a basis for God's saying that something is right, and since we and God can divine the basis and say something because it is right, politics and religion may reasonably be fused into religious politics.

The fusion should not be cause for concern. It only implies that the day of prophets is not over. Didn't Isaiah come after Abraham? The fact that he came later didn't nullify his being a prophet. Deny not the fullness of time. There may be prophets in this chapter.

The introductory essay to this chapter by **Abraham J. Heschel** on the nature of the prophet makes it clear that there is sufficient occasion to call out the prophet and that the prophet's mission is one of which we moderns are as capable as were the prophets of old. We simply must become angry enough to become God's angry humans. Heschel points out that "The things that horrified the prophets are even now daily occurrences all over the world." The occasions for prophets are present. "The prophet is intent on intensifying responsibility, is impatient of excuse, contemptuous of pretense and self-pity.... The mouth of the prophet is "a sharp sword." He is "a polished arrow" taken out of the quiver of God." Are we not capable of these things and articulate enough to sharpen our cries of "Shame"? We do need to be less serene than we are if we are to become prophets. "Our standards are modest; our sense of injustice tolerable, timid; our moral indignation impermanent; yet human violence is interminable, unbearable, permanent." Get angry.

A. K. B.

What Manner of Man
Is the Prophet?

Abraham J. Heschel

Abraham J. Heschel (1907–1972) was professor of Jewish ethics and mysticism at Jewish Theological Seminary in New York and was widely recognized as one of the world's greatest theologians. Among his many influential books are *Man Is Not Alone, God in Search of Man: A Philosophy of Judaism*, and *Theology of Ancient Judaism.*

Sensitivity to Evil

What manner of man is the prophet? A student of philosophy who turns from the discourses of the great metaphysicians to the orations of the prophets may feel as if he were going from the realm of the sublime to an area of trivialities. Instead of dealing with the timeless issues of being and becoming, of matter and form, of definitions and demonstrations, he is thrown into orations about widows and orphans, about the corruption of judges and affairs of the market place. Instead of showing us a way through the elegant mansions of the mind, the prophets take us to the slums. The world is a proud place, full of beauty, but the prophets are scandalized, and rave as if the whole world were a slum. They make much ado about paltry things, lavishing excessive language upon trifling subjects. What if somewhere in ancient Palestine poor people have not been treated properly by the rich? So what if some old women found pleasure and edification in worshiping "the Queen of Heaven"? Why such immoderate excitement? Why such intense indignation?

The things that horrified the prophets are even now daily occurrences all over the world. There is no society to which Amos' words would not apply.

> *Hear this, you who trample upon the needy,*
> *And bring the poor of the land to an end,*
> *Saying: When will the new moon be over*
> *That we may sell grain?*
> *And the Sabbath,*
> *That we may offer wheat for sale,*

Source: Abraham J. Heschel, *The Prophets* (New York, 1962), pp. 3–11, 14–16, 23–24, 26. Copyright © 1962 by Abraham J. Heschel. Reprinted by permission of Harper & Row, Publishers Inc.

That we may make the ephah small and the shekel great,
And deal deceitfully with false balances,
That we may buy the poor for silver,
And the needy for a pair of sandals,
And sell the refuse of the wheat?

> *Amos 8:4-6*

Indeed, the sort of crimes and even the amount of delinquency that fill the prophets of Israel with dismay do not go beyond that which we regard as normal, as typical ingredients of social dynamics. To us a single act of injustice—cheating in business, exploitation of the poor—is slight: to the prophets, a disaster. To us injustice is injurious to the welfare of the people; to the prophets it is a deathblow to existence: to us, an episode; to them, a catastrophe, a threat to the world.

Their breathless impatience with injustice may strike us as hysteria. We ourselves witness continually acts of injustice, manifestations of hypocrisy, falsehood, outrage, misery, but we rarely grow indignant or overly excited. To the prophets even a minor injustice assumes cosmic proportions.

The Lord has sworn by the pride of Jacob:
Surely I will never forget any of their deeds.
Shall not the land tremble on this account,
And every one mourn whom dwells in it,
And all of it rise like the Nile,
Be tossed about and sink again, like the Nile of Egypt?

> *Amos 8:7-8*

Be appalled, O heavens, at this,
Be shocked, be utterly desolate, says the Lord.
For my people have committed two evils:
They have forsaken Me,
The fountain of living waters,
And hewed out cisterns for themselves,
Broken cisterns,
That can hold no water.

> *Jeremiah 2:12-13*

They speak and act as if the sky were about to collapse because Israel has become unfaithful to God.

Is not the vastness of their indignation and the vastness of God's anger in disproportion to its cause? How should one explain such moral and religious excitability, such extreme impetuosity?

It seems incongruous and absurd that because of some minor acts of injustice inflicted on the insignificant, powerless poor, the glorious city of Jerusalem should be destroyed and the whole nation go to exile. Did not the prophet magnify the guilt?

The prophet's words are outbursts of violent emotions. His rebuke is harsh and relentless. But if such deep sensitivity to evil is to be called hysterical, what name should be given to the abysmal indifference to evil which the prophet bewails?

They drink wine in bowls,
And anoint themselves with the finest oils,
But they are not grieved over the ruin of Joseph!

    Amos 6:6

The niggardliness of our moral comprehension, the incapacity to sense the depth of misery caused by our own failures, is a fact which no subterfuge can elude. Our eyes are witness to the callousness and cruelty of man, but our heart tries to obliterate the memories, to calm the nerves, and to silence our conscience.

The prophet is a man who feels fiercely. God has thrust a burden upon his soul, and he is bowed and stunned at man's fierce greed. Frightful is the agony of man; no human voice can convey its full terror. Prophecy is the voice that God has lent to the silent agony, a voice to the plundered poor, to the profaned riches of the world. It is a form of living, a crossing point of God and man. God is raging in the prophet's words.

The Importance of Trivialities

"Human affairs are hardly worth considering in earnest, and yet we must be in earnest about them—a sad necessity constrains us," says Plato in a mood of melancholy. He apologizes later for his "low opinion of mankind" which, he explains, emerged from comparing men with the gods. "Let us grant, if you wish, that the human race is not to be despised, but is worthy of some consideration."[1]

"The gods attend to great matters; they neglect small ones," Cicero maintains.[2] According to Aristotle, the gods are not concerned at all with the dispensation of good and bad fortune or external things.[3] To the prophet, however, no subject is as worthy of consideration as the plight of man. Indeed, God Himself is described as reflecting over the plight of man rather than as contemplating eternal ideas. His mind is preoccupied with man, with the concrete actualities of history rather than with the timeless issues of thought. In the prophet's message nothing that has bearing upon good and evil is small or trite in the eyes of God.

Man is rebellious and full of iniquity, and yet so cherished is he that God, the Creator of heaven and earth, is saddened when forsaken by him. Profound and intimate is God's love for man, and yet harsh and dreadful can be His wrath. Of what paltry worth is human might—yet human compassion is divinely precious. Ugly though the behavior of man is, yet may man's return to God make of his way a highway of God.

Luminous and Explosive

"Really great works," writes Flaubert, "have a serene look. Through small openings one perceives precipices; down at the bottom there is darkness, vertigo;

[1] *Laws*, VII, 803.
[2] *De Natura Deorum*, II, 167.
[3] *Magna Moralia*, II, 8, 1207, 1208, 1209.

but above the whole soars something singularly sweet. That is the ideal of light, the smiling of the sun; and how calm it is, calm and strong! . . . The highest and hardest thing in art seems to me to be to create a state of reverie."[4]

The very opposite applies to the words of the prophet. They suggest a disquietude sometimes amounting to agony. Yet there are interludes when one perceives an eternity of love hovering over moments of anguish; at the bottom there is light, fascination, but above the whole soar thunder and lightning.

The prophet's use of emotional and imaginative language, concrete in diction, rhythmical in movement, artistic in form, marks his style as poetic. Yet it is not the sort of poetry that takes its origin, to use Wordsworth's phrase, "from emotion recollected in tranquility." Far from reflecting a state of inner harmony or poise, its style is charged with agitation, anguish, and a spirit of nonacceptance. The prophet's concern is not with nature but with history, and history is devoid of poise.

Authentic utterance derives from a moment of identification of a person and a word; its significance depends upon the urgency and magnitude of its theme. The prophet's theme is, first of all, the very life of a whole people, and his identification lasts more than a moment. He is one not only with what he says; he is involved with his people in what his words foreshadow. This is the secret of the prophet's style: his life and soul are at stake in what he says and in what is going to happen to what he says. It is an involvement that echoes on. What is more, both theme and identification are seen in three dimensions. Not only the prophet and the people, but God Himself is involved in what the words convey.

Prophetic utterance is rarely cryptic, suspended between God and man; it is urging, alarming, forcing onward, as if the words gushed forth from the heart of God, seeking entrance to the heart and mind of man, carrying a summons as well as an involvement. Grandeur, not dignity, is important. The language is luminous and explosive, firm and contingent, harsh and compassionate, a fusion of contradictions.

The prophet seldom tells a story, but casts events. He rarely sings, but castigates. He does more than translate reality into a poetic key: he is a preacher whose purpose is not self-expression or "the purgation of emotions," but communication. His images must not shine, they must burn.

The prophet is intent on intensifying responsibility, is impatient of excuse, contemptuous of pretense and self-pity. His tone, rarely sweet or caressing, is frequently consoling and disburdening; his words are often slashing, even horrid—designed to shock rather than to edify.

The mouth of the prophet is "a sharp sword." He is "a polished arrow" taken out of the quiver of God (Isa. 49:2).

> Tremble, you women who are at ease,
> Shudder, you complacent ones;
> Strip, and make yourselves bare,
> Gird sackcloth upon your loins.
>
> Isaiah, 32:11

---

[4] Quoted by F. Kaufmann, *Thomas Mann, The World as Will and Representation* (Boston, 1957), p. 272.

Reading the words of the prophets is a strain on the emotions, wrenching one's conscience from the state of suspended animation.

The Highest Good

Those who have a sense of beauty know that a stone sculptured by an artist's poetic hands has an air of loveliness; that a beam charmingly placed utters a song. The prophet's ear, however, is attuned to a cry imperceptible to others. A clean house or a city architecturally distinguished may yet fill the prophet with distress.

> *Woe to him who heaps up what is not his own, . . .*
> *Woe to him who gets evil gain for his house, . . .*
> *For the stone cries out from the wall,*
> *And the beam from the wordwork responds.*
> *Woe to him who builds a town with blood,*
> *And founds a city on iniquity!*
>
> *Habakkuk 2:6, 9, 11-12*

These words contradict most men's conceptions: the builders of great cities have always been envied and acclaimed; neither violence nor exploitation could dim the splendor of the metropolis. "Woe to him . . ."? Human justice will not exact its due, nor will pangs of conscience disturb intoxication with success, for deep in our hearts is the temptation to worship the imposing, the illustrious, the ostentatious. Had a poet come to Samaria, the capital of the Northern Kingdom, he would have written songs exalting its magnificent edifices, its beautiful temples and worldly monuments. But when Amos of Tekoa came to Samaria, he spoke not of the magnificence of places, but of moral confusion and oppression. Dismay filled the prophet:

> *I abhor the pride of Jacob,*
> *And hate his palaces,*

he cried out in the name of the Lord (Amos 6:8). Was Amos, then, not sensitive to beauty?

What is the highest good? Three things ancient society cherished above all else: wisdom, wealth, and might. To the prophets, such infatuation was ludicrous and idolatrous. Assyria would be punished for her arrogant boasting:

> *By the strength of my hand I have done it,*
> *And by my wisdom, for I have understanding; . . .*
>
> *Isaiah 10:13*

And about their own people, because "their hearts are far from Me, . . . the wisdom of the wise men shall perish" (Isa. 29:13, 14).

> *The wise men shall be put to shame,*
> *They shall be dismayed and taken;*
> *Lo, they have rejected the word of the Lord,*
> *What wisdom is in them?*
>
> *Jeremiah 8:9*

Ephraim has said,

Ah, but I am rich,
I have gained wealth for myself;
But all his riches can never offset
The guilt he has incurred. . . .
Because you have trusted in your chariots
And in the multitude of your warriors,
Therefore the tumult of war shall arise among your people,
And all your fortresses shall be destroyed, . . .

> *Hosea 12:8; 10:13, 14*

Thus says the Lord: "Let not the wise man glory in his wisdom, let not the mighty man glory in his might, let not the rich man glory in his riches; but let him who glories, glory in this, that he understands and knows Me, that I am the Lord Who practice kindness, justice, and righteousness in the earth; for in these things I delight, says the Lord" (Jer. 9:23–24 [H. 9:22–23]).

This message was expressed with astounding finality by a later prophet: "This is the word of the Lord . . . : Not by might, nor by power, but by My spirit . . ." (Zech. 4:6).

One Octave Too High

We and the prophet have no language in common. To us the moral state of society, for all its stains and spots, seems fair and trim; to the prophet it is dreadful. So many deeds of charity are done, so much decency radiates day and night; yet to the prophet satiety of the conscience is prudery and flight from responsibility. Our standards are modest; our sense of injustice tolerable, timid; our moral indignation impermanent; yet human violence is interminable, unbearable, permanent. To us life is often serene, in the prophet's eye the world reels in confusion. The prophet makes no concession to man's capacity. Exhibiting little understanding for human weakness, he seems unable to extenuate the culpability of man.

Who could bear living in a state of disgust day and night? The conscience builds its confines, is subject to fatigue, longs for comfort, lulling, soothing. Yet those who are hurt, and He Who inhabits eternity, neither slumber nor sleep.

The prophet is sleepless and grave. The frankincense of charity fails to sweeten cruelties. Pomp, the scent of piety, mixed with ruthlessness, is sickening to him who is sleepless and grave.

Perhaps the prophet knew more about the secret obscenity of sheer unfairness, about the unnoticed malignancy of established patterns of indifference, than men whose knowledge depends solely on intelligence and observation.

The Lord made it known to me and I knew;
Then Thou didst show me their evil deeds.

> *Jeremiah 11:18*

The prophet's ear perceives the silent sigh.

In the Upanishads the physical world is devoid of value—unreal, a sham, an illusion, a dream—but in the Bible the physical world is real, the creation of God. Power, offspring, wealth, prosperity—all are blessings to be cherished, yet the thriving and boasting man, his triumphs and might, are regarded as frothy, tawdry, devoid of substance.

> *Behold, the nations are like a drop from a bucket,*
> *And are accounted as the dust on the scales; . . .*
> *All the nations are as nothing before Him,*
> *They are accounted by Him as less than nothing and emptiness.*
>
> *Isaiah 40:15, 17*

Civilization may come to an end, and the human species disappear. This world, no mere shadow of ideas in an upper sphere, is real, but not absolute; the world's reality is contingent upon compatibility with God. While others are intoxicated with the here and now, the prophet has a vision of an end.

> *I looked on the earth, and lo, it was waste and void;*
> *To the heavens, and they had no light.*
> *I looked on the mountains, and lo, they were quaking,*
> *All the hills moved to and fro.*
> *I looked, and lo, there was no man;*
> *All the birds of the air had fled.*
> *I looked, and lo the fruitful land was a desert;*
> *All its cities were laid in ruins*
> *Before the Lord, before His fierce anger.*
>
> *Jeremiah 4:23-26*

The prophet is human, yet he employs notes one octave too high for our ears. He experiences moments that defy our understanding. He is neither "a singing saint" nor "a moralizing poet," but an assaulter of the mind. Often his words begin to burn where conscience ends.

An Iconoclast

The prophet is an iconoclast, challenging the apparently holy, revered, and awesome. Beliefs cherished as certainties, institutions endowed with supreme sanctity, he exposes as scandalous pretensions.

To many a devout believer Jeremiah's words must have sounded blasphemous.

> *To what purpose does frankincense come to Me from Sheba,*
> *Or sweet cane from a distant land?*
> *Your burnt offerings are not acceptable,*
> *Nor your sacrifices pleasing to Me.*
>
> *Jeremiah 6:20*

> *Thus says the Lord of hosts, the God of Israel: Add your burnt offerings to*
> *your sacrifices, and eat the flesh. For in the day that I brought them out of the land*

of Egypt, I did not speak to your fathers or command them concerning burnt
offerings and sacrifices. But this command I gave them: Obey My voice and I
will be your God, and you shall be My people; and walk in all the way that I
command you, that it may be well with you.

> *Jeremiah 7:21-23*

The prophet knew that religion could distort what the Lord demanded of man, that priests themselves had committed perjury by bearing false witness, condoning violence, tolerating hatred, calling for ceremonies instead of bursting forth with wrath and indignation at cruelty, deceit, idolatry, and violence.

. . .

Few Are Guilty, All Are Responsible

What was happening in Israel surpassed its intrinsic significance. Israel's history comprised a drama of God and all men. God's kingship and man's hope were at stake in Jerusalem. God was alone in the world, unknown or discarded. The countries of the world were full of abominations, violence, falsehood. Here was one land, one people, cherished and chosen for the purpose of transforming the world. *This* people's failure was most serious. The Beloved of God worshipped the Baalim (Hos. 11:1–2); the vineyard of the Lord yielded wild grapes (Isa. 5:2); Israel, holy to the Lord, "defiled My land, made My heritage an abomination" (Jer. 2:3, 7).

Defining truth as the conformity of assertion to facts, we may censure the prophets for being inaccurate, incongruous, even absurd; defining truth as reality reflected in a mind, we see *prophetic* truth as reality reflected in God's mind, the world *sub specie dei*.

Prophetic accusations are perhaps more easily understood in the light of the book of Job's thesis that men might judge a human being just and pure, whom God, Who finds angels imperfect, would not.[5]

> *Can mortal man be righteous before God?*
> *Can a man be pure before His Maker?*
> *Even in His servants He puts no trust,*
> *His angels He charges with error;*
> *How much more those who dwell in houses of clay,*
> *Whose foundation is in the dust,*
> *Who are crushed before the moth. . . .*
> *What is man, that he can be clean?*
> *Or he that is born of a woman, that he can be righteous?*
> *Behold God puts no trust in His holy ones,*
> *The heavens are not clean in His sight;*
> *How much less one who is abominable and corrupt,*
> *A man who drinks iniquity like water!*
>
> *Job 4:17-19; 15:14-16*

"For there is no man who does not sin" (I Kings 8:46). "Surely there is not a righteous man on earth who does good and never sins" (Eccles. 7:20).

---

[5] Eliphaz' thesis is accepted by Job (9:2); see also 25:4.

It is with a bitter sense of the tremendous contrast between God's righteousness and man's failure that the psalmist prays:

Enter not into judgment with Thy servant;
For no man living is righteous before Thee.

    Psalm 143:2

Men are greatly praised when worthy of being reproved. Only a strong heart can bear bitter invectives.

Above all, the prophets remind us of the moral state of a people: Few are guilty, but all are responsible. If we admit that the individual is in some measure conditioned or affected by the spirit of society, an individual's crime discloses society's corruption. In a community not indifferent to suffering, uncompromisingly impatient with cruelty and falsehood, continually concerned for God and every man, crime would be infrequent rather than common.

. . .

The Primary Content of Experience

What is the primary content of prophetic experience, the thought immediately felt, the motive directly present to the prophet's mind? What are the facts of conciousness that stirred him so deeply? Is it a sense of anxiety about the fate and future of the people or of the state? An impulse of patriotism? Is it personal irritation at the violation of moral laws and standards, a spontaneous reaction of the conscience against what is wrong or evil? Moral indignation?

In a stricken hour comes the word of the prophet. There is tension between God and man. What does the word say? What does the prophet feel? The prophet is not only a censurer and accuser, but also a defender and consoler. Indeed, the attitude he takes to the tension that obtains between God and the people is characterized by a dichotomy. In the presence of God he takes the part of the people. In the presence of the people he takes the part of God.

It would be wrong to maintain that the prophet is a person who plays the role of "third party," offering his good offices to bring about reconciliation. His view is oblique. God is the focal point of his thought, and the world is seen as reflected in God. Indeed, the main task of prophetic thinking is to bring the world into divine focus. This, then, explains his way of thinking. He does not take a direct approach to things. It is not a straight line, spanning subject and object, but rather a triangle—through God to the object. An expression of a purely personal feeling betrays itself seldom, in isolated instances. The prophet is endowed with the insight that enables him to say, not I love or I condemn, but God loves or God condemns.

The prophet does not judge the people by timeless norms, but from the point of view of God. Prophecy proclaims what happened to God as well as what will happen to the people. In judging human affairs, it unfolds a divine situation. Sin is not only the violation of a law, it is as if sin were as much a loss to God as to man. God's role is not spectatorship but involvement. He and man meet mysteriously in the human deed. The prophet cannot say Man without thinking God.

Therefore, the prophetic speeches are not factual pronouncements. What we hear is not objective criticism or the cold proclamation of doom. The style of legal, objective utterance is alien to the prophet. He dwells upon God's inner motives, not only upon His historical decisions. He discloses *a divine pathos*, not just a divine judgment. The pages of the prophetic writings are filled with echoes of divine love and disappointment, mercy and indignation. The God of Israel is never impersonal.

This divine pathos is the key to inspired prophecy. God is involved in the life of man. A personal relationship binds Him to Israel; there is an interweaving of the divine in the affairs of the nation. The divine commandments are not mere recommendations for man, but express divine concern, which, realized or repudiated, is of personal importance to Him. The reaction of the divine self (Amos 6:8; Jer. 5:9; 51:14), its manifestations in the form of love, mercy, disappointment or anger convey the profound intensity of the divine inwardness.

. . .

An analysis of prophetic utterances shows that the fundamental experience of the prophet is a fellowship with the feelings of God, a *sympathy with the divine pathos*, a communion with the divine consciousness which comes about through the prophet's reflection of, or participation in, the divine pathos. The typical prophetic state of mind is one of being taken up into the heart of the divine pathos. Sympathy is the prophet's answer to inspiration, the correlative to revelation.

Prophetic sympathy is a response to transcendent sensibility. It is not, like love, an attraction to the divine Being, but the assimilation of the prophet's emotional life to the divine, an assimilation of function, not of being. The emotional experience of the prophet becomes the focal point for the prophet's understanding of God. He lives not only his personal life, but also the life of God. The prophet hears God's voice and feels His heart. He tries to impart the pathos of the message together with its logos. As an imparter his soul overflows, speaking as he does out of the fullness of his sympathy.

The Crisis of Community

The Grand Inquisitor

Fyodor Dostoyevsky

Fyodor Dostoyevsky (1822–1881) was one of the two or three greatest Russian novelists. Some of his famous novels are *Crime and Punishment* (1866), *The Idiot* (1868), and *The Brothers Karamazov* (1880).

"My story is laid in Spain, in Seville, in the most terrible time of the Inquisition, when fires were lighted every day to the glory of God, and 'in the splendid *auto da fé* the wicked heretics were burnt.' Oh, of course, this was not the coming in which He will appear according to His promise at the end of time in all His heavenly glory, and which will be sudden 'as lightning flashing from east to west.' No, He visited His children only for a moment, and there where the flames were crackling round the heretics. In His infinite mercy He came once more among men in that human shape in which He walked among men for three years fifteen centuries ago. He came down to the 'hot pavement' of the southern town in which on the day before almost a hundred heretics had, *ad majorem gloriam Dei*, been burnt by the cardinal, the Grand Inquisitor, in a magnificent *auto da fé*, in the presence of the king, the court, the knights, the cardinals, the most charming ladies of the court, and the whole population of Seville.

"He came softly, unobserved, and yet, strange to say, every one recognised Him. That might be one of the best passages in the poem. I mean, why they recognised Him. The people are irresistibly drawn to Him, they surround Him, they flock about Him, follow Him. He moves silently in their midst with a gentle smile of infinite compassion. The sun of love burns in His heart, light and power shine from His eyes, and their radiance, shed on the people, stirs their hearts with responsive love. He holds out His hands to them, blesses them, and a healing virtue comes from contact with Him, even with His garments. An old man in the crowd, blind from childhood, cries out, 'O Lord, heal me and I shall see Thee!' and, as it were, scales fall from his eyes and the blind man sees Him. The crowd weeps and kisses the earth under His feet. Children throw flowers before Him, sing, and cry hosannah. 'It is He—it is He!' all repeat. 'It must be He, it can be no one but Him!' He stops at the steps of the Seville cathedral at the moment when the weeping mourners are bringing in a little open white coffin. In it lies a child of seven, the only daughter of

From Fyodor Dostoyevsky, *The Brothers Karamazov*, trans. by Constance Garnett.

a prominent citizen. The dead child lies hidden in flowers. 'He will raise your child,' the crowd shouts to the weeping mother. The priest, coming to meet the coffin, looks perplexed, and frowns, but the mother of the dead child throws herself at His feet with a wail. 'If it is Thou, raise my child!' she cries, holding out her hands to Him. The procession halts, the coffin is laid on the steps at His feet. He looks with compassion, and His lips once more softly pronounce, 'Maiden, arise!' and the maiden arises. The little girl sits up in the coffin and looks around, smiling with wide-open wondering eyes, holding a bunch of white roses they had put in her hand.

"There are cries, sobs, confusion among the people, and at that moment the cardinal himself, the Grand Inquisitor, passes by the cathedral. He is an old man, almost ninety, tall and erect, with a withered face and sunken eyes, in which there is still a gleam of light. He is not dressed in his gorgeous cardinal's robes, as he was the day before, when he was burning the enemies of the Roman Church—at that moment he was wearing his coarse, old, monk's cassock. At a distance behind him come his gloomy assistants and slaves and the 'holy guard.' He stops at the sight of the crowd and watches it from a distance. He sees everything; he sees them set the coffin down at His feet, sees the child rise up, and his face darkens. He knits his thick grey brows and his eyes gleam with a sinister fire. He holds out his finger and bids the guards take Him. And such is his power, so completely are the people cowed into submission and trembling obedience to him, that the crowd immediately makes way for the guards, and in the midst of deathlike silence they lay hands on Him and lead Him away. The crowd instantly bows down to the earth, like one man, before the old inquisitor. He blesses the people in silence and passes on. The guards lead their prisoner to the close, gloomy vaulted prison in the ancient palace of the Holy Inquisition and shut Him in it. The day passes and is followed by the dark, burning 'breathless' night of Seville. The air is 'fragrant with laurel and lemon.' In the pitch darkness the iron door of the prison is suddenly opened and the Grand Inquisitor himself comes in with a light in his hand. He is alone; the door is closed at once behind him. He stands in the doorway and for a minute or two gazes into His face. At last he goes up slowly, sets the light on the table and speaks.

"'Is it Thou? Thou?' but receiving no answer, he adds at once, 'Don't answer, be silent. What canst Thou say, indeed? I know too well what Thou wouldst say. Thou hast no right to add anything to what Thou hadst said of old. Why, then, art Thou come to hinder us? For Thou hast come to hinder us, and Thou knowest that. But dost Thou know what will be to-morrow? I know not who Thou art and care not to know whether it is Thou or only a semblance of Him, but to-morrow I shall condemn Thee and burn Thee at the stake as the worst of heretics. And the very people who have today kissed Thy feet, to-morrow at the faintest sign from me will rush to heap up the embers of Thy fire. Knowest Thou that? Yes, maybe Thou knowest it,' he added with thoughtful penetration, never for a moment taking his eyes off the Prisoner."

"I don't quite understand, Ivan. What does it mean?" Alyosha, who had been listening in silence, said with a smile. "Is it simply a wild fantasy, or a mistake on the part of the old man—some impossible *quiproquo?*"

"Take it as the last," said Ivan, laughing, "if you are so corrupted by modern realism and can't stand anything fantastic. If you like it to be a case of mistaken identity, let it be so. It is true," he went on, laughing, "the old man was ninety, and he might well be crazy over his set idea. He might have been struck by the appearance of the Prisoner. It might, in fact, be simply his ravings, the delusion of an old man of ninety, over-excited by the *auto da fé* of a hundred heretics the day before. But does it matter to us after all whether it was a mistake of identity or a wild fantasy? All that matters is that the old man should speak out, should speak openly of what he has thought in silence for ninety years."

"And the Prisoner too is silent? Does He look at him and not say a word?"

"That's inevitable in any case," Ivan laughed again. "The old man has told Him He hasn't the right to add anything to what He has said of old. One may say it is the most fundamental feature of Roman Catholicism, in my opinion at least. 'All has been given by Thee to the Pope,' they say, 'and all, therefore, is still in the Pope's hands, and there is no need for Thee to come now at all. Thou must not meddle for the time, at least.' That's how they speak and write too—the Jesuits, at any rate. I have read it myself in the works of their theologians. 'Hast Thou the right to reveal to us one of the mysteries of that world from which Thou hast come?' my old man asks Him, and answers the question for Him. 'No, Thou hast not; that Thou mayest not add to what has been said of old, and mayest not take from men the freedom which Thou didst exalt when Thou wast on earth. Whatsoever Thou revealest anew will encroach on men's freedom of faith; for it will be manifest as a miracle, and the freedom of their faith was dearer to Thee than anything in those days fifteen hundred years ago. Didst Thou not often say then, "I will make you free"? But now Thou hast seen these "free" men,' the old man adds suddenly, with a pensive smile. 'Yes, we've paid dearly for it,' he goes on, looking sternly at Him, 'but at last we have completed that work in Thy name. For fifteen centuries we have been wrestling with Thy freedom, but now it is ended and over for good. Dost Thou not believe that it's over for good? Thou lookest meekly at me and deignest not even to be wroth with me. But let me tell Thee that now, to-day, people are more persuaded than ever that they have perfect freedom, yet they have brought their freedom to us and laid it humbly at our feet. But that has been our doing. Was this what Thou didst? Was this Thy freedom?'"

"I don't understand again," Alyosha broke in. "Is he ironical, is he jesting?"

"Not a bit of it! He claims it as a merit for himself and his Church that at last they have vanquished freedom and have done so to make men happy. 'For now' (he is speaking of the Inquisition, of course) 'for the first time it has become possible to think of the happiness of men. Man was created a rebel; and how can rebels be happy? Thou wast warned,' he says to Him. 'Thou hast had no lack of admonitions and warnings, but Thou didst not listen to those warnings; Thou didst reject the only way by which men might be made happy. But fortunately, departing Thou didst hand on the work to us. Thou hast promised, Thou hast established by Thy word, Thou hast given to us the right to bind and to unbind, and now, of course, Thou canst not think of taking it away. Why, then, hast Thou come to hinder us?'"

"And what's the meaning of 'no lack of admonitions and warnings'?" asked Alyosha.

"Why, that's the chief part of what the old man must say."

"'The wise and dread spirit, the spirit of self-destruction and non-existence,' the old man goes on, 'the great spirit talked with Thee in the wilderness, and we are told in the books that he "tempted" Thee. Is that so? And could anything truer be said than what he revealed to Thee in three questions and what Thou didst reject, and what in the books is called "the temptation"? And yet if there has ever been on earth a real stupendous miracle, it took place on that day, on the day of the three temptations. The statement of those three questions was itself the miracle. If it were possible to imagine simply for the sake of argument that those three questions of the dread spirit had perished utterly from the books, and that we had to restore them and to invent them anew, and to do so had gathered together all the wise men of the earth —rulers, chief priests, learned men, philosophers, poets—and had set them the task to invent three questions, such as would not only fit the occasion, but express in three words, three human phrases, the whole future history of the world and of humanity—dost Thou believe that all the wisdom of the earth united could have invented anything in depth and force equal to the three questions which were actually put to Thee then by the wise and mighty spirit in the wilderness? From those questions alone, from the miracle of their statement, we can see that we have here to do not with the fleeting human intelligence, but with the absolute and eternal. For in those three questions the whole subsequent history of mankind is, as it were, brought together into one whole, and foretold, and in them are united all the un-solved historical contradictions of human nature. At the time it could not be so clear, since the future was unknown; but now that fifteen hundred years have passed, we see that everything in those three questions was so justly divined and foretold, and has been so truly fulfilled, that nothing can be added to them or taken from them.

"'Judge Thyself who was right—Thou or he who questioned Thee then? Remember the first question; its meaning, in other words, was this: "Thou wouldst go into the world, and art going with empty hands, with some promise of freedom which men in their simplicity and their natural unruliness cannot even understand, which they fear and dread—for nothing has ever been more insupportable for a man and a human society than freedom. But seest Thou these stones in this parched and barren wilderness? Turn them into bread, and mankind will run after Thee like a flock of sheep, grateful and obedient, though for ever trembling, lest Thou with-draw Thy hand and deny them Thy bread." But Thou wouldst not deprive man of freedom and didst reject the offer, thinking, what is that freedom worth, if obedience is bought with bread? Thou didst reply that man lives not by bread alone. But dost Thou know that for the sake of that earthly bread the spirit of the earth will rise up against Thee and will strive with Thee and overcome Thee, and all will follow him, crying, "Who can compare with this beast? He has given us fire from heaven!" Dost Thou know that the ages will pass, and humanity will proclaim by the lips of their sages that there is no crime, and therefore no sin; there is only hunger? "Feed men, and then ask of them virtue!" that's what they'll write on the banner, which they will raise against Thee, and with which they will destroy Thy temple. Where Thy temple stood will rise a new building; the terrible tower of Babel will be built again, and though, like the one of old, it will not be finished, yet Thou mightest have prevented that new tower and have cut short the sufferings of men for a thousand years; for they will come back to us after a thousand years of agony with their tower. They will seek us again, hidden underground in the cata-combs, for we shall be again persecuted and tortured. They will find us and cry to us, "Feed us, for those who have promised us fire from heaven haven't given it!"

And then we shall finish building their tower, for he finishes the building who feeds them. And we alone shall feed them in Thy name, declaring falsely that it is in Thy name. Oh, never, never can they feed themselves without us! No science will give them bread so long as they remain free. In the end they will lay their freedom at our feet, and say to us, "Make us your slaves, but feed us." They will understand themselves at last, that freedom and bread enough for all are inconceivable together, for never, never will they be able to share between them! They will be convinced, too, that they can never be free, for they are weak, vicious, worthless and rebellious. Thou didst promise them the bread of Heaven, but, I repeat again, can it compare with earthly bread in the eyes of the weak, ever sinful and ignoble race of man? And if for the sake of the bread of Heaven thousands and tens of thousands shall follow Thee, what is to become of the millions and tens of thousands of millions of creatures who will not have the strength to forego the earthly bread for the sake of the heavenly? Or dost Thou care only for the tens of thousands of the great and strong, while the millions, numerous as the sands of the sea, who are weak but love Thee, must exist only for the sake of the great and strong? No, we care for the weak too. They are sinful and rebellious, but in the end they too will become obedient. They will marvel at us and look on us as gods, because we are ready to endure the freedom which they have found so dreadful and to rule over them—so awful it will seem to them to be free. But we shall tell them that we are Thy servants and rule them in Thy name. We shall deceive them again, for we will not let Thee come to us again. That deception will be our suffering, for we shall be forced to lie.

"'This is the significance of the first question in the wilderness, and this is what Thou hast rejected for the sake of that freedom which Thou hast exalted above everything. Yet in this question lies hid the great secret of this world. Choosing "bread," Thou wouldst have satisfied the universal and everlastnig craving of humanity—to find some one to worship. So long as man remains free he strives for nothing so incessantly and so painfully as to find some one to worship. But man seeks to worship what is established beyond dispute, so that all men would agree at once to worship it. For these pitiful creatures are concerned not only to find what one or the other can worship, but to find something that all would believe in and worship; what is essential is that all may be *together* in it. This craving for *community* of worship is the chief misery of every man individually and of all humanity from the beginning of time. For the sake of common worship they've slain each other with the sword. They have set up gods and challenged one another, "Put away our gods and come and worship ours, or we will kill you and your gods!" And so it will be to the end of the world, even when gods disappear from the earth; they will fall down before idols just the same. Thou didst know, Thou couldst not but have known, this fundamental secret of human nature, but Thou didst reject the one infallible banner which was offered Thee to make all men bow down to Thee alone—the banner of earthly bread; and Thou hast rejected it for the sake of freedom and the bread of Heaven. Behold what Thou didst further. And all again in the name of freedom! I tell Thee that man is tormented by no greater anxiety than to find some one quickly to whom he can hand over that gift of freedom with which the ill-fated creature is born. But only one who can appease their conscience can take over their freedom. In bread there was offered Thee an invincible banner; give bread, and man will worship Thee, for nothing is more certain than bread. But if some one else gains possession of his conscience—oh! then he will cast away Thy bread and follow after him who has ensnared his conscience. In that Thou wast right. For the secret of man's being is not only to live but to have something to live for. Without a stable conception of the object of life, man would not consent to go on living, and would rather destroy himself than remain on earth, though he had bread in abundance. That is true. But what happened? Instead of taking men's freedom from them, Thou didst make it greater than ever! Didst Thou forget that man prefers peace, and even death, to freedom of choice in the knowledge of good and evil? Nothing is more seductive for man than his freedom of conscience, but nothing is a greater cause of suffering. And behold, instead of giving a firm foundation for setting the conscience of man at rest for ever, Thou didst choose all that is exceptional, vague and enigmatic; Thou didst choose what was utterly beyond the strength of men, acting as though Thou didst not love them at all—Thou who didst come to give Thy life for them! Instead of taking possession of men's freedom, Thou didst increase it, and burdened the spiritual kingdom of mankind with its sufferings for ever. Thou didst desire man's free love, that he should follow Thee freely, enticed and taken captive by Thee. In place of the rigid ancient law, man must hereafter with free heart decide for himself what is good and what is evil, having only Thy image before him as his guide. But didst Thou not know he would at last reject even Thy image and Thy truth, if he is weighed down with the fearful burden of free choice? They will cry aloud at last that the truth is not in Thee, for they could not have been left in greater confusion and suffering than Thou hast caused, laying upon them so many cares and unanswerable problems.

"'So that, in truth, Thou didst Thyself lay the foundation for the destruction of Thy kingdom, and no one is more to blame for it. Yet what was offered Thee? There are three powers, three powers alone, able to conquer and to hold captive for ever the conscience of these impotent rebels for their happiness—those forces are miracles, mystery and authority. Thou hast rejected all three and hast set the example for doing so. When the wise and dread spirit set Thee on the pinnacle of the temple and said to Thee, "If Thou wouldst know whether Thou art the Son of God then cast Thyself down, for it is written: the angels shall hold him up lest he fall and bruise himself, and Thou shalt know then whether Thou art the Son of God and shalt prove then how great is Thy faith in Thy Father." But Thou didst refuse and wouldst not cast Thyself down. Oh! of course, Thou didst proudly and well, like God; but the weak, unruly race of men, are they gods? Oh, Thou didst know then that in taking one step, in making one movement to cast Thyself down, Thou wouldst be tempting God and have lost all Thy faith in Him, and wouldst have been dashed to pieces against that earth which Thou didst come to save. And the wise spirit that tempted Thee would have rejoiced. But I ask again, are there many like Thee? And couldst Thou believe for one moment that men, too, could face such a temptation? Is the nature of men such, that they can reject miracle, and at the great moments of their life, the moments of their deepest, most agonising spiritual difficulties, cling only to the free verdict of the heart? Oh, Thou didst know that Thy deed would be recorded in books, would be handed down to remote times and the utmost ends of the earth, and Thou didst hope that man, following Thee, would cling to God and not ask for a miracle. But Thou didst not know that when man rejects miracle he rejects God too; for man seeks not so much God as the miraculous. And as man cannot bear to be without the miraculous, he will create new miracles of his own for himself, and will worship deeds of sorcery and witchcraft, though he might be a hundred times over a rebel, heretic and infidel. Thou didst not come down from the Cross when they shouted to Thee, mocking and reviling Thee, "Come down from the cross and we will believe that Thou art He." Thou didst not come down, for again Thou wouldst not enslave man by a miracle, and didst crave faith given freely, not based on miracle. Thou didst crave for free love and not the base raptures of the slave before the might that has over-awed him for ever. But Thou didst think too highly of men therein, for they are slaves, of course, though rebellious by nature. Look round and judge; fifteen centuries have passed, look upon them. Whom hast Thou raised up to Thyself? I swear, man is weaker and baser by nature than Thou hast believed him! Can he, can he do what Thou didst? By showing him so much respect, Thou didst, as it were, cease to feel for him, for Thou didst ask far too much from him—Thou who hast loved him more than Thyself! Respecting him less, Thou wouldst have asked less of him. That would have been more like love, for his burden would have been lighter. He is weak and vile. What though he is everywhere now rebelling against our power, and proud of his rebellion? It is the pride of a child and a schoolboy. They are little children rioting and barring out the teacher at school. But their childish delight will end; it will cost them dear. They will cast down temples and drench the earth with blood. But they will see at last, the foolish children, that, though they are rebels, they are impotent rebels, unable to keep up their own rebellion. Bathed in their foolish tears, they will recognise at last that He who created them rebels must have meant to mock at them. They will say this in despair, and their utterance will be a blasphemy which will make them more unhappy still, for man's nature cannot bear blasphemy, and in the end always avenges it on itself. And so unrest, confusion and unhappiness—that is the present lot of man after Thou didst bear so much for their freedom! Thy great prophet tells in vision and in image, that he saw all those who took part in the first resurrection and that there were of each tribe twelve thousand. But if there were so many of them, they must have been not men but gods. They had borne Thy cross, they had endured scores of years in the barren, hungry wilderness, living upon locusts and roots—and Thou mayest indeed point with pride at those children of freedom, of free love, of free and splendid sacrifice for Thy name. But remember that they were only some thousands; and what of the rest? And how are the other weak ones to blame, because they could not endure what the strong have endured? How is the weak soul to blame that it is unable to receive such terrible gifts? Canst Thou have simply come to the elect and for the elect? But if so, it is a mystery and we cannot understand it. And if it is a mystery, we too have a right to preach a mystery, and to teach them that it's not the free judgement of their hearts, not love that matters, but a mystery which they must follow blindly, even against their conscience. So we have done. We have corrected Thy work and have founded it upon *miracle, mystery* and *authority*. And men rejoiced that they were again led like sheep, and that the terrible gift that had brought them such suffering, was, at last, lifted from their hearts. Were we right teaching them this? Speak! Did we not love mankind, so meekly acknowledging their feebleness, lovingly lightening their burden, and permitting their weak nature even sin with our sanction? Why hast Thou come now to hinder us? And why dost Thou look silently and searchingly at me with Thy mild eyes? Be angry. I don't want Thy love, for I love Thee not. And what use is it for me to hide anything from Thee? Don't I know to Whom I am speaking? All that I can say is known to Thee already. And is it for me to conceal from Thee our mystery? Perhaps it is Thy will to hear it from my lips. Listen, then. We are not working with Thee, but with *him*—that is our mystery. It's long—eight centuries—since we have been on *his* side and not on Thine. Just eight centuries ago, we took from him what Thou didst reject with scorn, that last gift he offered Thee, showing Thee all the kingdoms of the earth. We took from him Rome and the sword of Cæsar, and proclaimed ourselves sole rulers of the earth, though hitherto we have not been able to complete our work. But whose fault is that? Oh, the work is only beginning, but it has begun. It has long to await completion and the earth has yet much to suffer, but we shall triumph and shall be Cæsars, and then we shall plan the universal happiness of man. But Thou mightest have taken even then the sword of Cæsar. Why didst Thou reject that last gift? Hadst Thou accepted that last counsel of the mighty spirit, Thou wouldst have accomplished all that man seeks on earth—that is, some one to worship, some one to keep his conscience, and some means of uniting all in one unanimous and harmonious ant-heap, for the craving for universal unity is the third and last anguish of men. Mankind as a whole has always striven to organise a universal state. There have been many great nations with great histories, but the more highly they were developed the more unhappy they were, for they felt more acutely than other people the craving for worldwide union. The great conquerors, Timours and Ghenghis-Khans, whirled like hurricanes over the face of the earth striving to subdue its people, and they too were but the unconscious expression of the same craving for universal unity. Hadst Thou taken the world and Cæsar's purple, Thou wouldst have founded the universal state and have given universal peace. For who can rule men if not he who holds their conscience and their bread in his hands? We have taken the sword of Cæsar, and in taking it, of course, have rejected Thee and followed *him*. Oh, ages are yet to come of the confusion of free thought, of their science and cannibalism. For having begun to build their tower of Babel without us, they will end, of course, with cannibalism. But then the beast will crawl to us and lick our feet and spatter them with tears of blood. And we shall sit upon the beast and raise the cup, and on it will be written, "Mystery." But then, and only then, the reign of peace and happiness will come for men. Thou art proud of Thine elect, but Thou hast only the elect, while we give rest to all. And besides, how many of those elect, those mighty ones who could become elect, have grown weary waiting for Thee, and have transferred and will transfer the powers of their spirit and the warmth of their heart to the other camp, and end by raising their *free* banner against Thee. Thou didst Thyself lift up that banner. But with us all will be happy and will no more rebel or destroy one another as under Thy freedom. Oh, we shall persuade them that they will only become free when they renounce their freedom to us and submit to us. And shall we be right or shall we be lying? They will be convinced that we are right, for they will remember the horrors of slavery and confusion to which Thy freedom brought them. Freedom, free thought and science, will lead them into such straits and will bring them face to face with such marvels and insoluble mysteries, that some of them, the fierce and rebellious, will destroy themselves, others, rebellious but weak, will destroy one another, while the rest, weak and unhappy, will crawl fawning to our feet and whine to us: "Yes, you were right, you alone possess His mystery, and we come back to you, save us from ourselves!"

"'Receiving bread from us, they will see clearly that we take the bread made by their hands from them, to give it to them, without any miracle. They will see that we do not change the stones to bread, but in truth they will be more thankful for taking it from our hands than for the bread itself! For they will remember only too well that in old days, without our help, even the bread they made turned to stones in their hands, while since they have come back to us, the very stones have turned to bread in their hands. Too, too well they know the value of complete submission! And until men know that, they will be unhappy. Who is most to blame for their not knowing it, speak? Who scattered the flock and sent it astray on unknown paths? But the flock will come together again and will submit once more, and then it will be once for all. Then we shall give them the quiet humble happiness of weak creatures such as they are by nature. Oh, we shall persuade them at last not to be proud, for Thou didst lift them up and thereby taught them to be proud. We shall show them that they are weak, that they are only pitiful children, but that childlike happiness is the sweetest of all. They will become timid and will look to us and huddle close to us in fear, as chicks to the hen. They will marvel at us and will be awestricken before us, and will be proud at our being so powerful and clever, that we have been able to subdue such a turbulent flock of thousands of millions. They will tremble impotently before our wrath, their minds will grow fearful, they will be quick to shed tears like women and children, but they will be just as ready at a sign from us to pass to laughter and rejoicing, to happy mirth and childish song. Yes, we shall set them to work, but in their leisure hours we shall make their life like a child's game, with children's songs and innocent dance. Oh, we shall allow them even sin, they are weak and helpless, and they will love us like children because we allow them to sin. We shall tell them that every sin will be expiated, if it is done with our permission, that we allow them to sin because we love them, and the punishment for these sins we take upon ourselves. And we shall take it upon ourselves, and they will adore us as their saviours who have taken on themselves their sins before God. And they will have no secrets from us. We shall allow or forbid them to live with their wives and mistresses, to have or not to have children— according to whether they have been obedient or disobedient—and they will submit to us gladly and cheerfully. The most painful secrets of their conscience, all, all they will bring to us, and we shall have an answer for all. And they will be glad to believe our answer, for it will save them from the great anxiety and terrible agony they endure at present in making a free decision for themselves. And all will be happy, all the millions of creatures except the hundred thousand who rule over them. For only we, we who guard the mystery, shall be unhappy. There will be thousands of millions of happy babes, and a hundred thousand sufferers who have taken upon themselves the curse of the knowledge of good and evil. Peacefully they will die, peacefully they will expire in Thy name, and beyond the grave they will find nothing but death. But we shall keep the secret, and for their happiness we shall allure them with the reward of heaven and eternity. Though if there were anything in the other world, it certainly would not be for such as they. It is prophesied that Thou wilt come again in victory, Thou wilt come with Thy chosen, the proud and strong, but we will say that they have only saved themselves, but we have saved all. We are told that the harlot who sits upon the beast, and holds in her hands the *mystery*, shall be put to shame, that the weak will rise up again, and will rend her royal purple and will strip naked her loathsome body. But then I will stand up and point out to Thee the thousand millions of happy children who have known no sin. And we who have taken their sins upon us for their happiness will stand up before Thee and say: "Judge us if Thou canst and darest." Know that I fear Thee not. Know that I too have been in the wilderness, I too have lived on roots and locusts, I too prized the freedom with which Thou hast blessed men, and I too was striving to stand among Thy elect, among the strong and powerful, thirsting "to make up the number." But I awakened and would not serve madness. I turned back and joined the ranks of those *who have corrected Thy work*. I left the proud and went back to the humble, for the happiness of the humble. What I say to Thee will come to pass, and our dominion will be built up. I repeat, to-morrow Thou shalt see that obedient flock who at a sign from me will hasten to heap up the hot cinders about the pile on which I shall burn Thee for coming to hinder us. For if any one has ever deserved our fires, it is Thou. To-morrow I shall burn Thee. Dixi.'"[1]

---

[1] "I have spoken."

In Search of a New Community

Paul Kagan

Paul Kagan (1943–   ) is a photographer, graphic artist, and historian living in San Francisco, California. The present selection formed the basis of the concluding chapter of his recently published *New World Utopias*.

Men today have lost the knowledge of when to come together and when not to come together. And with this has been lost the sense of what communication or community means, and why it is necessary. In an age when the details of a military massacre are available in seconds to a public halfway around the globe, when relatives thousands of miles apart can be reunited in hours, the speed and availability of technological communications operate in perverse contrast to the lack of human communication among individuals and groups. What passes for a serious exchange on community affairs today is usually an exposition of random opinions and idle gossip. Little wonder, then, that a response to this unfulfilled but not forgotten need has become the formation of communal families or its obverse, withdrawal into routine days of work and nights of television.

The attraction to communal life can be identified as an attraction to wholeness —it is in the commune that life becomes complete, an encompassing world is formed. But it is also in the commune that the real disunity—the frictions and factions—appears that has resulted in an ever-decreasing lifetime for communal experiments not based on traditional ideals.

Why have people been turning more and more toward non-traditional, ephemeral communes, both today and in the past hundred years of California's relatively short history? The traditional communes—the monasteries—exist, as they have for several thousand years. What is it about the ideas motivating the monasteries that have given them their longevity? Why do monasteries not appeal to the people who found new and autonomous communes?

There is obvious confusion in life. It becomes so unbearable at certain periods of history that some men leave society for the isolation of the desert or the mountains. This extreme rejection of society takes two forms. It can produce the short-lived communities that are catalysts in a changing society. On the other hand, such movement away from the present world may, paradoxically, bring one in touch with a knowledge or understanding of an even earlier world. An increasing awareness of our rejection of the old, and attraction to the new, sometimes leads to the appearance of ideas completely unexpected and unexplored, which often derive from older, more harmonious societies that took into account the complex needs in man's nature.

Interest in traditional ways of leaving society is diminishing. Monasteries are regarded as institutions which are too rigidly structured and whose dogma is stale. At the same time, those who flee to the communal life have the burden of making it up as they go along. They are without the formal structure provided by the church. The problems of starting a new community require so much initiative and work that little energy is left to devote to the purposes which first attracted the members and drew them together. This discovery of lack of purpose is compounded by the recognition that the problems that one is escaping are present in the community, intensified by numbers. The old baggage arrives at the new destination.

This problem appears in the commune in various forms. Terms like "authority" and "obedience" are not often used. But the roles implied by these terms are present under different names. The same devotion to work, and adherence to shibboleths and half-truths, that were demanded by the rejected society are demanded by the new.

After Job Harriman's experience at Llano del Rio, he wrote in 1923: "Under a system of private ownership of property one may exclude from his thought and companionship whomsoever he may dislike; . . . in a co-operative community this cannot be done." The community is, after all, a microcosm of the larger world. Here, men's smallest and pettiest habits cannot go undetected; brother is up against brother at every turn.

The surprise of the commune member is not unlike that of the marriage partner who discovers the early dream of going away and building a world together has lost its appeal. So it must be asked: Why doesn't the idea and intention of change work? Perhaps naivete is the answer: naivete concerning what needs to be changed, what can be changed, and what must be done in order to change. Commune members rarely understand their motivations, their contradictory natures, their selfishness, the extent of their involvement in the world outside, or their belief that a physical wall will protect them from the pressures they felt in society.

The life-span of a "sucessful" California community was about twenty years. The life-span of a monastery often surpasses two thousand years. Why is it, then, that at a time when the monasteries are struggling to survive, non-tradional communities are formed so frequently? Why Holy City and not the Catholic Church? Why Vedanta and not a Hasidic community?

Utopian experiments have been dichotomized as political–religious, soft–hard, static–dynamic, sensate–spiritual, aristocratic–plebian, escape–realization, collectivist–individual. Why do these dualities exist? It appears that all utopian attempts to overcome conflict have resulted only in more serious strife and division. Perhaps this is why Sir Thomas More's word "utopia" means "nowhere." There is nowhere that man can go to strive toward wholeness without recognizing, and even coming toward, his fragmented nature. Do any utopian experiments take into account both the part of man that wishes to be whole and the part that longs for division?

Which ideas are practical? Some ideas help to perpetuate communities. Other ideas die out. Still others reappear cloaked in new forms. Perhaps this is what is meant by enduring, real ideas—the ones that live on and continue to be practical by altering their forms to meet changing conditions.

In this context is it useful to speak of communities as having a birth, a life, and a death, similar to that of individuals, civilizations, and living systems? There is little doubt that a commune is born and dies. But it lives as part of the world around it. Some of the new communes even rely on support by government food-stamps, welfare, and foundation grants to survive, in spite of their members' skills as gardeners and builders. Conversely, the economically successful Shakers profited from the revenue provided by a society which valued their products. But there is a finer interdependence. A commune may die because the original leader fails to provide a suitable successor, as at Point Loma, or because the members find their utopia reflects the world's strife, as at Kaweah. Sometimes the commune simply comes to the end of its natural life-span; it no longer has any function in itself, although it has probably had some impact on the world around it that will persist.

The Hermetic principle "as above, so below" applies to the question of man's dependence on his fellow man. In a world where "self-sufficiency" is a major value, communal members seek dependence on one another. They may, however, only rarely see the relationship of their experiment to the complex conditions that surround it.

In most communes there is little self-conscious concern with the questions of survival and motivation. Amazingly enough, even the leader rarely knows why his group exists, and for what. The member is often attracted to "a better way of life" and then is satisfied with much less. Why? The type of commune he joins seems to promise the style of life he seeks but when the commune does not meet his expectations, he may remain as a "hanger-on" because he is reluctant to return to society. In religious communes, if a member becomes harmful to the group, the leader may throw him out. In the socio-economic group, the difficulties of the "hanger-on" are reflected in the endless petty "democratic" meetings, filled with elementary "motions" and "decisions," such as the injunction of Llano not to urinate in the stream upriver of the drinking supply. Generally, there was little need for sanctions, because the group shared a common aim. If a person strayed from the accepted intention, he could leave. The question has always been—who is to judge?

In asking what common influences are present in the formation of one communal experiment as opposed to another in the same geographical region, the role of the leader must be questioned. Present-day communes vehemently affirm the principle of non-leadership, yet there is always a leader. In Eastern religious traditions the leader himself serves the same authority as the group he is helping. Why does the cynicism towards this type of relationship, where the leader himself is subservient to a higher power, exist in large measure in the West today? One of the implications may be that the leader's ability to organize is often greater than the knowledge he professes to possess. The leader is a good leader by virtue of his setting the example. Perhaps it is the narrow Western vision of leader and follower that has bred today's prevailing rejection of authority.

The way in which a leader takes part in the activities of the group, and his understanding of his own role, are vital factors in the life of the commune. In a way, the leader is a prisoner of the utopian experiment—could the community continue without his constant presence? The energy that is generated by the concentrated interinvolvement of a group and its leader has to be expressed. It often takes the form of feelings that move from affection to loyalty to disappointment.

There have been several attempts to evaluate the results of communal endeavors. One writer of the 1930's felt that the value of a commune was not in its survival, but in its giving birth to new experiments. Yet, some social scientists today feel that perpetuation is the measure of success; unless children are trained to continue the group's work, the commune may die. Still others look at the effects of the communal group on society in terms of contributions to culture, education, economics, human understanding, social reform, etc. St. Benedict viewed the monastery as a microcosm of a state that could emerge from the new Christian society.

The outside world has a tendency to look at members of communal experiments as stereotypes, rather than as people. Direct contact with various communal experiments, however, creates an appreciation of the efforts of the individuals involved, the fruits of these efforts, and the promise they hold for the future. An example of this is the role played by the Theosophists and Vedantists in making the ideas sacred in the East available to Western culture today. Unfamiliar impulses are generated by groups of people who are trying things that are not a part of the society from which they came. When money and success are not the goal, other goals emerge in their place.

One of the main differences between the traditional and non-traditional communes is in their identification of goals. Both groups understand that the main purpose is to learn by experience—that real knowledge does not come from reading a book or real success from becoming the president of Shell Oil. But the people who join contemporary communes rarely realize that the longstanding tradition, the knowledge that has built up over centuries, offers the traditional communes at least a better quality of the experience which is sought in non-traditional communes. An even more important distinction between the two is that the traditional monastery offered a different level of experience, while today's commune offers a heightening or improvement of a level of experience already known to those who join.

In contrasting the traditional monasteries to the ephemeral communes we are studying, the role of sex is important. The monasteries required the separation of members from their families. Abstinence from sex was a form of payment much more extreme than anything demanded by the non-traditional communes, where women and children were usually welcome. Those who join today's communes take the conditions of their life with them. Although they may be asked to relinquish privacy and possessions, this does not evidence the same self-denial that was demanded as a spiritual payment by the monasteries.

Abstinence from the drugs, alcohol, and tobacco so commonly used in the outside world is a requirement promulgated in some communes so as not to "artificially heighten the experience." It can also be a rite of purification from past use of these volatile substances in the larger society.

Novitiates enter the monastery with a commitment—they have prepared and have some awareness of the ideals embodied by the institution. They come to perfect these ideals in themselves. Those entering non-traditional communes bring a passive hope for transformation simply through change of environment. Attraction to groups embodying values opposed to society is on the same level as attraction to groups devoted to maintaining society. Monastic aspiration, however, is not passive transformation by the same or opposite conditions of life, but a coming in touch with an entirely different type of experience. Out of the traditional communes of the Middle Ages came cathedrals and Gregorian chants. Out of Llano del Rio came endless bickering about the laziness of its indifferent members.

The distinctions here call for a definition of the term "intentional community." The intentional community is one whose purpose or intention is not solely a reaction to the surrounding society. An intentional community makes room for new ideas which, though occasionally appearing in communes, are entirely unknown to outside society. For example, the current terms "inner space" and "levels of consciousness" are two such new ideas from today's communes.

The idea of intention raises the question of how a group, or an individual, or a culture discovers its identity. A popular theory says that an adolescent arrives at his identity through those influences of his family and his peer group to which he reacts, for whatever reason. But an unknown part of the identity must come from the individual himself.

A trace of an impersonal goal lies in the intention of the "back to the land" communes, where nature has become the teacher. There is an ancient knowledge embodied in the Hopi Indian's respect for "our mother the earth and our father the sun." Communes in New Mexico have learned from the Indians to build with adobe—the earth itself—and their architecture is a manifestation of their intention, perhaps comparable on a smaller scale in some cases to the work of the cathedral builders.

Yesterday it was possible for a college graduate, not wishing to become a bank president, to enter public service with a clear conscience. Increased governmental repression at home and continuing massacre abroad have made the choice of private business or public service less meaningful, and a commune may appear as the only means to maintain one's individuality. Many come to believe in the concept of communal sharing as a means of growth, despite competitive upbringing.

Today's questions of identity are often posed in terms of civil rights, the Vietnam war, drugs, television, the establishment, and ecology. The resolution of reactions to these issues cannot be foreseen, but one could question whether the widening gulf between the establishment and the divergent culture of today's youth might not be the birth-pangs of a new culture. Another aspect of the same process is exemplified by the growth of interest in non-traditional communes.

California's place as the "last frontier" raises the question of a substitute for the frontier. When societies have no room for people, the people go somewhere else. They "light out for the territory," in Huck Finn's words. With little unexplored territory left, the pioneering instinct is being turned inwards and to outer space.

Today's technology more and more restricts the participation of the individual and he becomes a cog in a wheel. The communal wish to see the whole wheel is evidenced by activities that are followed through from start to finish, such as raising a sheep, shearing it, combing, carding, and spinning the yarn, and finally knitting it into a sweater. This reaction was presaged by the reaction of the Romantic Poets to the Industrial Revolution, and later by the Marxist goal of having the worker less separated from the product by having him control the means of production. With the dual problem of the new technology on the one hand, and the need for community on the other, it is possible that automation might actually help to solve the problem. By eliminating "scissors and paperclip" jobs and automating all functions possible, a new system of goods and services might appear that allows for a more personal relationship of the individual to society.

What, then, is the meaning of the communal movement? Communal experiments on the West Coast today stretch from British Columbia to Peru. Most are small, unpublicized, and, unlike tneir predecessors, they share an interest in each other's doings and whereabouts. There are inter-community magazines and newsletters, and conferences covering the diverse spectrum of communal endeavor. If the emergence of interest in these non-traditional groups through the past hundred years and through the varied spectrum of today can be seen as the emergence of a newly developing and as yet unknown culture, then the phenomena described by Roszak as the "counter-culture" and by Reich as "consciousness III" are steps in the self-examination necessary for the new culture to be born.

The movement toward utopia highlights not only the increasing schism in society, but also the direction necessary for the birth of a new society. The direction begins with an awareness of the schism, or duality, and the possibility of wholeness through this awareness.

The search for community is generally directed towards someplace "over there." Can the vision of the utopians be pursued in the context of one's life in the world? Need one go to the desert? There is evidence that at times means have existed within the society for bringing together the inner and outer sides of man.

Today, man is lacking in knowledge about his needs, motivations, structure, purpose, and place. But the means that provide this knowledge have no external safeguards against degeneration. They change with the times. When they cease to be flexible, all energy goes into preserving the external forms and traditions, a "church" is created, and the essential knowledge is lost.

If the church appears to be hypocritical, society divided, and the communes defined negatively by their reaction to society, where can man turn for real ideas? The need would seem to call for the appearance of a way in life that fulfills both the rational and the mystical needs of men, a way that includes the additional need to come together as part of the other functions and activities of society. How much time would such a society then give to the study of utopia, and how much time to the study of thermodynamics? What would be the right tension between the individual and the community? Perhaps the means for such a study already exist. The question then would not be "How does one form a community?" but rather "How does one find the conditions in the midst of one's life to allow for such a study?"

There has been a gradual movement in history from traditional knowledge to humanist psychology, in which the aim is no longer to understand but instead, to adapt. On the other hand, people still get together on Sundays. But who knows why they get together?

The Social Nature of Persons

Arthur K. Bierman

Arthur K. Bierman (1923–   ) is professor of philosophy at San Francisco State University. He is author of *Logic: A Dialogue* and *The Philosophy of Urban Existence* and is co-editor of the pioneering philosophy text, *Philosophy for a New Generation*.

The new vocation is concinnation. The word comes from a Latin root; to concinnate means to join fitly or becomingly together, make well-connected; choose and compose suitably. I suggest that we poor, cursed things from Eve's womb are the material we should concinnate. Concinnation is a moral vocation. The highest vocation of us who approach the second arc is to concinnate ourselves into the republic of an urban Eden.

Source: A. K. Bierman, *The Philosophy of Urban Existence* (Athens, Ohio: Ohio University Press, 1973), pp. 16-17, 54-66, 71-79.

Life has come to be and will be even more an urban affair. Cities are the main sites of life. The "Garden of Eden" is a dated re-run from the past, a long vanished coconut community, nevermore to be. The "Garden" is so remote from normal living that a question which gave delightful free play to the speculative imagination of the church fathers still has tickle-power; that question was "What did Adam do in the Garden of Eden before the Fall?" Today, it is realistic to speak only of the "City of Eden" rather than the "Garden of Eden."

What Adam did before the Fall seems an idle, though wonderful, question, just because doing is understood as a normal response to a need, and it is hard to specify just what needs Adam could have had in the Garden. If doing is undertaken to satisfy a need, the chief doing is what is done to satisfy the most urgent need. I shall argue that our present most urgent human need is for social consolidation through unification of the city. Our awareness of that need surfaces painfully in our personal, emotional lives: It surfaces as alienation and such associated plagues as isolation, feelings of social ineffectiveness and aimlessness, as truncated benevolence and excessive self-centeredness, in the agony of insecurity stemming from the absence of socially confirmed and shared convictions, in frustation at being unable to experience the release that follows uninhibited commitment, in our moral confusion wrought by contradictory impulses and goals, in ungrounded suspicions and fears, and consequent shame for our reluctant withdrawal from civic existence.

This pitiful pathology of our emotional lives is not traceable to psychological inadequacies, nor to personal failings, nor to original sin, nor to existential anxieties; therefore, it cannot be treated successfully by psychological counselling, nor by personal reform, nor by religious revival or the importation of Eastern religions, nor by philosophical fads. This pathology is traceable mainly to the fact that we do not live in morally whole civic communities; thus, the only cure for these pathological emotional plagues is a moral and social one: We must make our cities creative, supportive, moral resources in our pursuit of the good life of self-realization, recognizing that the person-self is a social entity. That persons are social entities means that we should opt for a social version of self-realization achievable by concinnation rather than for the first-arc, individualistic, American version achievable by competitive work.

I advocate the vocation of concinnating in this essay because it is a doing whose purpose is to unify cities and morally to consolidate their citizens, and, thereby, to restore our emotional health by banishing alienation and its associated plagues, and to create unified, realized persons.

. . .

Individualism is a defense mechanism employed when persons realize they have been abandoned by their society. That is its pitiful side. Individualism also encourages bravado, which is its rugged side. "Rugged" individualism is a clarion summons to gird up your muscles and to act vigorously to gain your goals; anyone caught hesitating to go roughshod in the world is spiked as a pallid, callow, sentimental bleedingheart; assertions of human interdependency are seen as admissions of weakness; competing is the great thing and the winner's reward is control over the losers; social welfare programs, medical aid, unemployment benefits, bankruptcy laws, and special help programs in the public schools are regarded as evidence of the victim's moral fiberlessness and failure rather than as evidence of a crippling social system; it is man heroically matching himself against a perpetually present, rugged frontier; self-interest is all; glory be to Daddy Warbucks!

Rugged individualism flies the proud banner of self-reliance and self-confidence. It also runs up the banner of freedom, of autonomy. In relying on and confiding in yourself alone, you can avoid buckling yourself to others. Any dependency relation you have with another person is unwelcome because it restricts your choices and actions, and, therefore, restricts your freedom. The other becomes as a millstone around your neck. In order to achieve maximum freedom—according to the ethics of rugged individualism—you should be the sole source of the energy required to achieve your goals. Human alliances are undertaken under the pressure of circumstances, and always reluctantly, because the acid of each alliance destroys a bit more of your freedom. It is assumed that human aid can be purchased only at the cost of freedom.

Given that the supreme value of rugged individualism is personal freedom, human relations are to be avoided except when you cannot accomplish your goals without help from others. The conditions which account for social relations, therefore, are those in which we look on other persons as means to our ends. The perfect relation to have with another person if we are absolutely forced to resort to using him as a means—according to individualism—is a one-way relation: You get help from him and he asks nothing in return, for, by asking for nothing, he does not restrict your freedom. The closest we come to this one-way relation between humans is in the master-slave relationship. The ideal logical outcome of rugged individualism when forced to operate in a world where we need others is slavery. The ideal outcome when persons are not forced to rely on the help of others is a "society" of personal atoms, each doing his own thing independently of others. This kind of society is essentially an aggregate of atoms, since there are no mutual relations tying the atoms together: it is a Many that shuns Oneness. If we were to picture an extreme form of alienation, we would picture the unrelated aggregate of personal atoms which rugged individualism projects as its ideal.

Of course, the person committed to rugged individualism does not want to be the slave of another because a slave suffers a minimum state of freedom. To avoid becoming another's slave, a person must either have the power to be a master or he must live in splendid isolation. Among a group of persons, it is not logically possible for every one to be a master; masters cannot be masters without someone being a slave. Given that no rugged individualist willingly becomes a slave, a power struggle to determine who shall be masters and who slaves is another logical outcome of rugged individualism. Might doesn't make right, it makes Masters. To be caught in the toils of the ethics of rugged individualism is to be caught permanently in the toils of war.

There is a way out of this permanent state of war that is becoming more and more a practical possibility. With advances in technology, we can replace slaves with machines. This makes possible the perfect one-way relationship because machines help us accomplish our goals without asking for anything in return. Technology perfected would enable us to live in complete freedom from others without struggle. The bliss of living with machines would be chilled only by their lack of love, respect, care, admiration, praise, encouragement, and concern. This chill might be removed by programming the machines to show by their behavior that they do love, respect, care for, admire, praise, encourage, and are concerned for us. Of course programming these human attitudes into the machines would be the ultimate act of rugged individualism because they would, in effect, then be attitudes of self-love, self-respect, self-care, self-admiration, self-praise, self-encouragement, and self-concern.

The ethic of rugged individualism logically results, then, in alienation, slavery, war, and self-glorification. These results should be enough reason to reject it as our ideal ethical system. The fact that the results are exactly our present moral situation makes the philosophical task of fashioning an alternative more than an academic exercise.

I don't suppose anyone would willingly opt for rugged individualism if faced with these logical results. He might suicidally resign himself to this fate, however, if he thought that it was an unavoidable "human condition." Unfortunately, this seems to be exactly what many do think. I believe that most of our contemporaries are resigned to some form of the ethic of rugged individualism because they believe that the nature of persons leaves us with no alternative. I do not have in mind an appraisal of the moral nature of persons but, rather, a view of the metaphysical nature of persons. The metaphysical view of persons that underwrites rugged individualism is the view that a person is an object kind of thing called a substance.

I shall show how, in thinking that persons are substances, we are led to think of them as self-contained entities, atoms of existence, fundamentally isolated from each other because relations between them affect only the surface and not the core of each other's reality. In short, to think of persons as substances is to think of them as metaphysically alienated. This metaphysical alienation underwrites a form of moral and political alienation such as rugged individualism because it imposes a particular image of society on us. The image is that society is a collection of atoms, each atom being a person. Atoms are morally isolated from each other because moral and political relations between them fail to tie their core realities together into an integrated society; they tie only the surface appearance of persons together. This view of persons and their moral relations leaves us barren of any other than prudential reasons why we should treat others morally because nothing more profound than their appearance is at stake. Substance thinking makes a mystery of morality and of a commitment to social ideals.

We are like BB's scattered randomly on a plane; we touch only on the surface, if we touch at all.

Let us proceed to draw out what it is to think of a person as a substance, as, I suspect, you do.

The concept of substance is given its marching orders by our common sense notion of a physical object, so that to think of a person, a self, as a substance is to think of him on the model of a physical object. To be sure, not everyone who holds a substance theory of persons believes that the substance of persons is physical matter; they may hold that a person is a mental substance, a soul. Still, even as a mental substance, the person is thought of as a thing, an object, albeit a mental thing.

I have often noticed that at the mention of the word "metaphysics" or of metaphysical words such as "substance," people's eyes glaze over, they start acting slightly shifty, and you know they are wondering how they ever got themselves into such a situation. They are perfectly willing to leave metaphysics to the philosophers who apparently find some use for it, little knowing that they themselves are metaphysicians. People generally have too great a reverence and/or fear of Madame Metaphysics. Let us escort her from the study to the kitchen where we may comfortably consort with her.

A Metaphysical Interlude

The scene is Andrea and Homer's kitchen. They are engaged in their usual sort of after-dinner conversation.

ANDREA: I've been reading Descartes' *Meditations* again, Homer, and thinking about substance.

HOMER: That's swell, Andrea.

ANDREA: Why are your eyes glazing over?

HOMER: They always do that when you mention "substance."

ANDREA: You've simply got to get over that. You embarrass me in front of our friends.

HOMER: Can you help me?

ANDREA: I hope so. Look, Homer, suppose all your concepts were laid out before you. You'd find that they presented a cluster pattern. There would be a cluster of concepts that we use to think about economics, another we use to think about botany, another we use to think about food, another we use to think about law and so forth.

HOMER: I would?

ANDREA: Yes, and you would also notice that some concepts occur in every cluster. These concepts saturate all your thinking. You use them to think about anything. These pervasive concepts are metaphysical concepts.

HOMER: That doesn't sound complicated. Can you give me some examples?

ANDREA: Sure, and all of them perfectly familiar to you. Beginning and end, individual, character, unity, change, identity, and interaction. Oh, good, you're beginning to unglaze a little.

HOMER: And my breathing is getting more normal, too.

ANDREA: I think you're ready for substance.

HOMER: I'm starting to feel shifty, though.

ANDREA: Relax, dear, nothing could be simpler to explain. Substance is simply a concept you use in thinking, for example, about physical objects. You do think about physical objects, you know.

HOMER: Oh, yes, all the time, but I don't think I use substance all the time. Do I?

ANDREA: I think so. You think physical objects have a beginning and an end, don't you?

HOMER: Of course. Even the world has a beginning and an end.

ANDREA: Do you think things, or the world, are made out of nothing?

HOMER: You can't make something out of nothing. Even good fairies can't do that. The good fairy had to make Cinderella's horses out of mice and her carriage out of a pumpkin.

ANDREA: You agree with the first Greek philosophers, then. They thought there is a primary stuff out of which everything is made. Now listen to this: They called that primary stuff "substance."

HOMER: Am I unglazing just a little?

ANDREA: I think so. Now, Homer, you think that this substance is divisible because you think there are individual things.

HOMER: Absolutely. Here is an individual candle, there another one. And they are different individuals from the table they're sitting on. They're separate from each other.

ANDREA: Good. And don't you distinguish between a thing and its character? Don't you think that a character is something different from the thing that has the character?

HOMER: I suppose so, if you mean by a thing's character its properties or qualities.

ANDREA: That is what I mean. Roses are red, violets are blue. Now suppose that a thing's character were taken away from it. What would you have left? Suppose you take the taste odor, color, shape, size, and so forth away from a piece of wax. What would you have left?

HOMER: I would have left whatever has those qualities.

ANDREA: Very clever. What should we call it?

HOMER: Substance?

ANDREA: Right. Substance and shadow, the thing and its appearance.

HOMER: Huh?

ANDREA: The character is the outward appearance, the show of the underlying reality which is substance. The character, the complex of qualities, inheres in the substance.

HOMER: What's this "inheres" bit? Is it as if the substance were some sticky stuff to which qualities stick, or what?

ANDREA: A visual and tactile metaphor won't do because even a "sticky stuff" is substance with a sticky character rather then "pure" substance. Substance is not something that can be observed by the senses; only its character appearance is sensible. Substance is the child of theory. It is an entity known only by reason. Descartes, in his *Second Meditation*, observes a piece of wax fresh from the beehive. When fresh from the hive it has a given character but, when he puts it by fire, it melts and changes its character completely. It tastes and smells different; it changes color and shape and size. Still we say it is the identical wax.

HOMER: I do. The wax didn't go out of existence just because its character changed.

ANDREA: Why do you suppose you can say it is the identical wax even though it has completely changed its character?

HOMER: Substance, again. The substance is the same before and after the wax melted; the substance did not go out of existence.

ANDREA: You see how marvelous you are at metaphysics, darling?

HOMER: Thanks. But I'm not yet wholly unglazed. I still don't understand how character inheres in substance.

ANDREA: There are somethings you just have to accept. The mind must come to rest somewhere. Substance, being a child of reason, has whatever nature our mind needs in order to organize our experience of physical objects. For example, here is another use for substance. The character of an object is complex; it is made up of several qualities such as taste, smell, size, shape. Though the qualities are Many, the character is One. How is it possible that a character may have this unity?

HOMER: Like the good fairy, I utter a magic word: Substance! Since each of the characteristics inheres in the same substance, they are held together as a single character.

ANDREA: Excellent: More brandsey, please. Your eyes are getting quite unglazed now. Things change. Let me tell you how substance helps us understand change. A thing changes when one of its qualities gets disinherited and nother inheres in ish playsh. Simple.

HOMER: Drunken qualities replace sober qualities.

ANDREA: That's because of the brandsey. One thing has an effect on another when they interact; it makesh a substance lose one characteristic and gain another.

HOMER: That makes me sad.

ANDREA: Poor Homer. Tell me all about it.

HOMER: You said a thing's character is only an appearance, an outward show. If interaction between things changes only the world's appearance but not its substance, reality never changes. Reality is static; it stays the same forever. That means our personal relations don't really change anything of our reality; we are doomed to affect only each other's appearance.

ANDREA: What a terribly sobering thought.

HOMER: You are beyond the hand of change even when it is the hand of someone who loves you very much. We are locked in our substances. There is an unbridgeable gulf between our substances. Our souls—

ANDREA: Souls?

HOMER: Yes, our souls. They are our substance, our reality. After all, I am not my body. Our souls are like BB shot lying on the plane of existence. Society amounts to no more than an aggregate of unconnected BB-souls. There is no true, profound interpenetration of one human substance by another.

ANDREA: But what makes you think . . .

HOMER: Andrea, I don't want you to ever read Descartes again. Look what his foul substance has done. Our personal character, sometimes so hard won, is vain foppery, the soul's dress, subject to fashion's whims, forever concealing our real, naked self from others. Do you realize what this means? I'll tell you. You may have the brains, but I've got the heart. What it means is that we are never able to reach beyond our own to another's reality. That means all our moral aspirations must sink to a base, rugged individualism or some similar stupid ethic, a kind of BB version of our moral condition. To a rugged individualist, only a feather brained idealist could raise expectations for genuine relations and obligations between people.

ANDREA: But what makes you think . . .

HOMER: Don't stop me now. Thinking of humans as substances is merely a metaphysical version of human BB-hood; it is a metaphysical basis for yielding to belief in ultimate, unavoidable alienation; it is a metaphysical prop for a BB-ethic. According to your substance-cretins, we live a life of pretense if we think we can lay an obligation on somebody else because, in effect, our realities are sealed off from each other. As substances we are existentially independent; only our appearances are affected by human relations. Life is a series of transmigrations, which is just a series of transmogrifications of persons' appearance. In actuality, our hemetically sealed souls drift in eternal isolation, unperturbed, unruffled, unchanged, essentially uninvolved, shedding one appearance after another like a snake shucking last year's dead skin. Weep for them, Andrea. Weep.

ANDREA: Come, come, dear, the slough of despair doesn't suit you. We can escape this dreadful metaphysical fate. What makes you think that we have to think of persons as substances, as if they were like physical objects?

HOMER: You don't deny that we think of them that way, do you? After all, we do apply all the metaphysical concepts to humans that we apply to physical objects. Persons have beginnings and ends, birth and death; we distinguish one individual person from another; persons have character, personality; their character belongs to them and no one else, and may have a unity; persons change, the child and the adult are as different as the wax is before and after melting; persons maintain their identity even though their character changes completely; I remember a poem Bob Kennedy gave me, a Hindu poem, he said:

> Death is only matter dressed
>   in some new form,
> A varied vest:
> From tenement to tenement
>   though tossed,
> The Soul does not change.
> Only the figure is lost!

And you won't deny that persons interact.

ANDREA: What is all that supposed to prove?

HOMER: That the metaphysical concepts—beginning and end, individual, character, unity, change, identity, and interaction—apply to persons as well as to physical objects.

ANDREA: Just because they apply to persons doesn't by itself prove that persons are substances. Substance happens to be part of a particular metaphysical theory designed to explain how metaphysical concepts apply to physical objects. But, those concepts apply to every field. Remember?

HOMER: Sure, I remember. That's what makes them metaphysical concepts. So they do apply. So what? Brandy Andrea?

ANDREA: At least the glaze is gone, but you're still too damn shifty, Homer. Those metaphysical concepts apply to economics. Take the idea of a market. Markets come and go; the surrey market is kaput, dead. We distinguish the tobacco market from the hair spray market. Markets have a character; just read the *Wall Street Journal*. Markets have a unity; if they didn't we couldn't financially "grab" "the market"; there has to be something you control when you control it. Markets change; they rise and fall. And they have to have an identity or we couldn't say the market has fallen. Today the market is 783; yesterday it was 785. One number is lower than the other; but if the two numbers don't describe the same entity (it, the market) at two different times, we couldn't say that *it* had fallen. Finally, markets interact; the auto market affects the steel market.

Here comes the big question, Homer. When you think of the market, do you think there is a substance that is its underlying reality?

HOMER: That's an easy one. No.

ANDREA: Well, there you are, we don't always need substance to explain how the metaphysical concepts apply. What makes you think we need it to explain how they apply to persons?

HOMER: To tell you the truth, I'm not sure.

ANDREA: The existence and nature of substance is entirely dependent on theory. It is a theoretical entity. We can keep it as long as it plays a necessary part in a good theory. But as soon as we reject the theory, we can reject substance. Substance becomes a useless piece of baggage that is best dropped. Don't you agree?

HOMER: I think I do. Some biologists once thought there was a life-force. They needed it to explain how "inert" matter could be alive, but now that we have more advanced chemical and physical theories to explain life, we don't need such an entity as "life-force" anymore. Good.

ANDREA: Do you think the substance theory of persons is a good one?

HOMER: You must not have taken my tirade seriously. Any metaphysical theory that leads to a bad ethic such as rugged individualism has got to be bad.

ANDREA: Why don't you throw it out, then?

HOMER: I don't know. Maybe I still think it's true.

ANDREA: You don't have to believe in the existence of substance in the way that you have to believe in the existence of candles. You can see, feel, smell, and taste candles, but you can't see, feel, smell, or taste substance. It's an entity invented by the mind to explain how we apply metaphysical concepts. You admit you don't use it—so, you don't need it—to explain your talk about markets. Maybe the concept of a person is more like the concept of a market than it is like the concept of a physical object. If it is, then substance is a superfluous theoretical entity. Give up your old metaphysical habits; they only lead to rotten moral theories. You've got metaphysical freedom, sweetie. Reorganize your thought about persons.

HOMER: Freedom from substance! What a slogan! I like it. Do you mean we might think of a different theory of persons? I'd like one that makes a decent human society possible, a theory in which it is possible for human relations to affect the essence of each other's being. I'd like a theory that helps us understand how our very existence and nature are dependent upon the achievement of a set of moral relations to each other. We wouldn't have to live like BB's then.

ANDREA: That's what I've always found dear in you, Homer, that streak of nobility, your hunger for moral dignity. It becomes you.

HOMER: Thanks, Andrea, but, tell me, what kind of a theory of persons would give us what I want, really?

ANDREA: You've been too generous with the brandy. I can't figure that one out tonight. It will just have to wait, Homer.

. . .

By eavesdropping on Andrea and Homer's conversation, we learned that we not only don't have to think of persons as substances, but that we don't want to think of them as substances because a substance theory of persons is a metaphysical version of alienation that supports the moral isolation of rugged individualism. With her comments on an economic market, Andrea taught us that we have the theoretical freedom to recast our metaphysical notion of a person. In this chapter, I take advantage of that freedom to suggest another theory of what a person is.

Andrea suggested to Homer that a person may be more like a market than like a physical object. We know that Andrea had had too much brandy when she said that. Of course, it may be a ridiculous idea, but just on the chance that she was putting us on the trail of a vein we might profitably prospect, let's think about the notion of a market for a bit.

Here we are on a flying carpet, scooting over the world, peering down through its rents. We dip down toward the world to have a closer look: Below we see some things: two men, some pieces of silver, and a ham. The men are talking: "I'll give you five pieces of silver for the ham." "It's a deal. It's cheap, but a deal." We are witnessing an exchange which is a portion of a market.

An exchange is a banal occurrence that holds something of interest to us. The occurrence takes place amongst correlatives. A correlative is something—for example, a buyer—that stands in some relation to something else—for example, a seller—that stands in a relation to the buyer. Something that is a buyer is a correlative; it is a correlative to a seller. A parent and child are correlatives. A valley and a mountain are correlatives. Correlatives are tied with bonds of necessity. There cannot be a buyer unless there is a seller; and *vice versa*. There cannot be a parent unless there is a child; and *vice versa*. There cannot be a valley without a mountain; and *vice versa*.

Just as a seller and a buyer are correlatives, so a seller and his goods are correlatives. One cannot be a seller unless he has goods to sell. Similarly, a buyer and his coin are correlatives. Also, a seller and the buyer's coin are correlatives because if the seller doesn't get something for his goods he has either given his goods as a gift or his goods have been stolen. Further, a buyer and the seller's goods are correlatives; you can't be a buyer if you haven't bought something.

The banal occurence we call an exchange does not take place unless there are at least four things in a complex network of co-relations. A market such as the stock market is a set of such exchanges actual or potential.

One more step and then we will be ready to grasp a new vision of persons.

What makes silver (or seashells) money? Not the fact that it is silver, for something may be silver and not be money. Nor that it is valuable, for many things are valuable that are not money. What makes ham (or shoes) goods? It isn't always goods because sometimes it is food. What makes a person a buyer? Not that he is a person, for persons are not always buyers; sometimes they are sellers. Clearly, what makes silver money, ham goods, and persons buyers and sellers are their being in correlative relations to each other. It is not the silver's physical nature nor the ham's physical nature that makes one money and the other goods; their natures may make them silver and ham, but it is their co-relations that make them money and goods. (Hint: The concept of person is like the concepts of goods and money, not like the concept of ham or silver.)

In the spirit that we ask what makes an object such as ham a piece of goods, or what makes an object such as silver money, we ask what makes a body a person. We approach our answer to this question through an analogy. What makes a piece of wood a spear and a support and a part of a picture frame and a handle? The same piece of wood may be a spear to a boy playing Hercules, a part of a picture frame to an artist, a support for plants to the gardener, or a placard handle to a picketer.

Which of them the piece of wood is depends upon the situation it is in; it depends upon the relations it has to other things. Buyers, sellers, money, goods, spears, supports, picture frame parts, and handles are not things-in-themselves. They are what they are because of the other things to which they are related and because of the way they are related to those other things.

We can make this clearer by means of a generalization: xRy. We will let x and y stand for objects and R stand for a relation. Suppose y is a sheet of cardboard, x is the stick, and the relation R is "tacked to," so that the stick is tacked to the cardboard. That relation and the cardboard object to which the stick is related make the stick into a handle.

Suppose, again, that y is a willowy plant and the relation R is "tied to," so that the stick is tied to the plant. That relation and the plant to which the stick is related make the stick into a support.

x is a relatent, so I call it. What it is (a handle, a support, etc.) varies with and depends on R and y in xRy. y, too, I call a relatent.

Spears, supports, handles, picture frame parts, buyers, sellers, money, goods are relational entities, or what, in short, I call relatents. Let us call "xRy," as a whole, a relationship. x and y, considered together, I call correlatents; why I do so should be clear from my discussion of correlatives. In applying these notions to persons, I will call x the inner correlatent and y the outer correlatent.

Suppose that a piece of wood could simultaneously be a spear, a support, a picture frame part, a handle. It would be possible to give a name to the collection of these things; we could call the collection, for example, a ridotto. A person is like a ridotto. "Person" is the word we use to refer to a collection of relatents. Consider some of our relatents. There are familial relations that make us into sons, daughters, wives, fathers, uncles, and cousins. There are occupational relations that make us into bosses, employees, foremen, actors, salesman, assistant professors, longshoremen, journalists, executives, and lawyers. There are neighborhood relations that make us into neighbors, volunteers, Neighborhood Council members, Civic Affairs chairmen, monthly newsletter editors and writers, and boosters. There are city relations that make us taxpayers, voters, supervisors, citizens, mayors, witnesses, judges, Democrats, Republicans, jury members, and petitioners. A relatent is not the same concept as a role. I shall distinguish later between a factual– and a moral–relatent, which get confused in the concept of role.

Just as a piece of wood becomes a handle because relatents are created, that is, because it becomes related to other things in specific ways, so out of human bodies persons are created because their bodies become related to other bodies, families, occupations, neighborhoods, cities, and so forth. To be a person is to be many of the kinds of relatents of which I gave a sample list above. "Person" is the word we use to designate a collection of relatents. You are a collection of such relatents as son, husband, uncle, employee, musician, citizen, Democrat, voter, and many many others.

This notion of person is theoretically useful because it helps us to understand what it means to say that man is a social being. Each person is a self; the self is a correlative being, a set of inner correlatents. Since a self is a collection of correlatents, and, since correlatents' existence and nature logically depend upon the existence of others and the nature of their relations to others, we see why the existence and nature of the self is logically dependent upon other persons; since other persons, too, are sets of correlatents, they, too, logically depend upon relations to yourself and other selves.

You must not confuse this point with a commonplace psychological doctrine. It is a truism to say that our social environment influences the kind of attitudes, dreams, emotions, fears, ambitions, and conscience we have. My point is not a psychological one; it is a logical point. I am talking about the conditions necessary for your existence; and I am talking about the conditions necessary for your having the nature of a person at all, not about the psychological conditions that make you this kind of person rather than that kind of person.

This notion of person is theoretically useful, again, because it helps us to reinterpret our notion of society. We no longer have to think of a society as a collection of atoms, as a collection of hermetically sealed substances. A society is to self and others as a topography is to a mountain and a valley. A topography is a variation in land levels described relationally as mountains, valleys, and plains; a society is an organization of human bodies described relationally as sets of relatents. It is an arrangement that creates persons; some arrangements are good, others bad, because some make good persons possible and others do not.

The following two reality diagrams show us the contrast between a substance picture of social reality and a relatent picture of social reality.

In the left diagram, a person is identified as a substance, represented by a dot. It is a picture of a reality composed of isolated substances. On the right, a person is identified as a set of inner correlatents—promisee, employee, parent, and buyer.

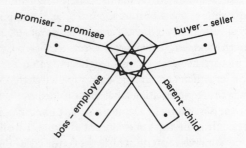

The outer correlatents in the picture are promiser, boss, child, and seller. It is a picture of a reality composed of persons. To picture a person in that diagram, we necessarily have to draw moral and social co-relations between the dots, which represent bodies. We can leave relations out of the substance picture of reality, however, because they are mere appearances in that world, whereas in the relatent world they are the reality of persons.

The substance picture underwrites the rugged individualist, who aims at self-sufficiency and maximum autonomy in pursuit of his self-interest. That picture posits the substance-dot as the moral center; all moral treasures are located there in the fortress self; and therein resides the autonomous, self-activating moral tyrant we call the will. The substance-dot defines the perspective from which he views the world; it affords him a personal point of view of the social landscape. From the safe battlements of the self, the tyrant directs his foraging forces of appearance in their raids on other appearances. Though his point of view is provincial, and though he is doomed to moral solipsism, he is happy enough because his vantage point is metaphysically autonomous, secure, and impregnable.

When we conceive of a person as a collection of relatents, it is impossible to locate the moral center in a dot. Since each inner correlatent requires an outer correlative entity, a person and his moral treasures are spread throughout the social landscape. A person cannot remain provincial in his point of view; he must take up the perspective of the other as well as himself because his existence and nature are logically related to the existence and nature of others. If, for example, you wish to be a seller, you must also concern yourself with the existence of a buyer; you must help some other to retain his buyer nature if you are to retain your seller nature. It is logically impossible to define a person's interests in terms of self-interest alone according to a relatent theory of persons; it is logically impossible to conceive of your interests apart from the interests of others; thus, the relatent theory is morally useful because it razes the rugged fortress walls of the substance-self.

The relatent notion of a person is morally useful also because it erases the distinction between a person's reality and his appearance, a distinction which is central to the substance notion of a person. In ranking the value of reality and appearance, reality takes chief place; appearance is "mere" appearance, illusion, the world's seeming, not its being. According to the substance theory, our character, including the social and moral aspects of our character, belongs to appearance; our obligations to others and theirs to us are of secondary importance. This relegation of the social and moral aspects of our life to secondary importance gives free license to the rugged individualist who seizes the opportunity to pursue his "self-interest" with maximum autonomy. Restraint on one's action by others is to be avoided; obligations are a burden, not an opportunity—an obstacle, not a necessity.

With the relatent notion of a person, on the other hand, we can discern that our moral and social relations are both a necessity and an opportunity first, because they are necessary to our existence as persons, and secondly, because they are the material out of which we form our nature in accord with our ideal.

Perhaps another image might help you to grasp the concept of a person that I am advocating. Picture a net. Let the net represent a society, the net knots—not the string of the knots—represent persons, and the string between the net knots represent relations. If we were to cut the strings that lead from a net knot to other net knots, what was a net knot would become a detached, knotted string, but it would no longer be a net knot. (Moral: If you cut all a body's relations to other bodies, you have made relatents impossible for it and, thereby, destroyed a person [and injured the society]. Alienation is a form of murder.) What made the knotted string a net knot was its stringy relations to other net knots.

If I pull on a net knot some distance from a given net knot, the latter will be affected. (Moral: What is done to others in your society, whether done by you or someone else, is done to you.) Also, if someone pulls on a given net knot, it will affect the other net knots. (Moral: What is done to or by you is done to others in your society.)

And I will make you fishers of men.

Two Vedantas: The Best and the Worst of India

Philippe Lavastine

Philippe Lavastine is a well-known French scholar. He has lived and traveled throughout Asia and now teaches in Paris.

Vedanta is commonly thought to be the basic cultural force of India. But this is true only because India has not yet learned to discriminate between the spurious and the genuine, the best and the worst in the huge mass of Vedantic teachings.

Living in India for many years, I learned from a pupil of the great Pandit Madhusudana of Jaipur that two Vedantas must be discerned: the good Vedanta

Source: Philippe Lavastine, "Two Vedantas: The Best and the Worst of India," *Material for Thought* (Spring 1974), pp. 1–30. Reprinted by permission of Far West Press.

of the ancients, which really was the *anta* or end, meaning fulfillment, accomplishment, of the Vedic way of life; and the bad Vedanta, which can only be called by the same name if we remember that the word *anta*, end, may also mean destruction, annihilation. There is a recent brand of Vedanta that ignores everything in the Veda (which it despises), a Vedanta that sees and teaches only the top of the mountain, *despising and obscuring its slopes and the paths which can actually take us there.*

The first Vedanta was life giving, and its tradition, where it still exists, continues to give to India its incomparable light and its most delicate fragrance. It is for such Vedanta that so many people in the world love India, Mother India.

But what of the other side of India? What of the misery that is also one of its features? For while you may proclaim the glory of Indian spirituality, how can you explain this dark side? It is no use saying that invaders and colonizers brought this ruin. It is true. But why did it happen so easily without the slightest resistance worthy of the name? We have to admit that something went wrong with the Hindu spirituality, the Hindu Vedanta.

Pandit Madhusudana Ojha pointed unwaveringly to one single factor: the distinction between a Vedanta that works for the good of the whole collectivity and a so called "Vedanta" that crept in later and that cared only for the deliverance of the individual. This "Vedanta" (in quotation marks) was inevitably death-giving, for the private good and the public good do not always entail each other. While the public good necessarily brings in its wake the good of the individual, the reverse does not irrevocably follow. For if you say, "Why should I care primarily for the kingdom and its justice?" you must necessarily destroy both the kingdom and the people living in it.

And that is the worst side of India, this "Vedanta" that is always claiming the unreality of the world, saying that it is sheer *Maya*, illusion. But Maya, from the Vedic standpoint, was never understood as illusion. It meant symbol, *pratika* or *vigraha* in Sanskrit. Symbol: that means similitude, reflection. But to take all things as symbols is precisely to redeem the world which we murder when we remain attached to its objects, never understanding that these things of the world are also signs, *deva*, rather than only *bhutas* (material entities).

This is the first key that will help us to distinguish between the best and the worst Vedanta. The first never saw in this world anything but symbols, but the last Vedanta never even uses the word. This bad Vedanta repeats *ad nauseam* that we must turn our backs on the objects of the senses. From the very beginning, it claims that the things of the world are *vishayas*, things endued with poison (*visha*), never remembering that the Lord Shiva is named Nila Kantha, meaning "blue throat," an allusion to the high feat of drinking the blue poison called Hala Hala, which first appeared during the churning of the Ocean of Milk at the creation of the world.

And now this Shiva, the Great Lord, for this reason is equated with the peacock because of its blue throat and the splendor of its *mandala*, the circle of its unfurled tail. The wheel is even in our day the emblem of India, inscribed on its flag. But more important than this wheel, the Dharmacakra, which the Lord Buddha set in motion, is the perfect circle of the peacock's tail, because it is adorned with a multiplicity of lesser circles, called eyes, meaning that the One Divine never crushes others down, but adorns Himself with innumerable replicas of His own Infinity, whose perfect symbol is the circle.

Is God, the Supreme Principle, one or multiple? To this question, the Vedas answer: In Himself He is One, but He is multiple in His children.

Participation, the key word of ancient Vedanta, was ascribed first of all to the Deity. By participation we mean, with Durkheim, the power of being at the same time oneself and others. The ancient Vedas stressed this unique feature of the Highest Principle by forbidding the name monism and by speaking of it as simply nondual, Two-in-One, a union more one than unity itself.

Let us understand that though the words may remain the same (*Advaita, Atman, Brahman*), the meaning may drain away leaving a dead shell, a verbalism, a metaphysical stunt.

It happened in India—as it happened in the West—that the Peacock Throne of God, the King of Kings, the One and Only Great King, was completely forgotten. Since so many usurpers had occupied the Peacock Throne, generation after generation, the belief arose that the truth of the divine city could never be revived. As a result, everything social was rejected as worldly, inferior, and, in the last analysis, illusory—Maya.

In this way the new Vedanta appeared. God exists for the individual alone; he has nothing to do with social order and collective life. Religion is a private affair—in the words of Whitehead, "God is what a man does with his own solitude."

We die from this nonsense! If the best Vedanta does not remember itself . . . then what will be the future of man on this planet?

I say the "best Vedanta," but as you will see from what follows, I mean by that the best, the truest, and the most real understanding of the force of tradition in the life of mankind. It is not only India's question; it is a question asked by earth to heaven.

Creation

The creation myth of the *Rig Veda* is entitled the Hymn of Man and it speaks to us about the *dismemberment of man*. It is the foundation myth of the Hindu culture (*Sams Kriti*), their story of a God All, called Man (*Purusha*), who was dismembered by the gods, his own senses, at the beginning, and has now to be re-membered.

A fall. With powerful images the Vedic seer tells us that "the skull of man (became) the sky, his eyes the sun and the moon, his breath the wind, his navel the atmosphere . . . his feet the earth." And a resurrection, when the creature, his *membra disjecta*, came back to recollect Him, at the call of the *Brahmana*.

It is in *Rig Veda X*, 90, 72 that we find the first mention of the four castes: *Brahmana, Kshatriya* (those whose function is protection, *Kshatra*), *Vaishya* (the people), and *Shudra*, the servants.

Here is the extraordinary passage:

His mouth was of a Brahmana
The Kshatriyas came back to reconstitute His arms,
The Vaishyas came back to reconstitute His thighs,
The Shudras issued from His feet (as His shadow).

The formulations may appear to be very different in the creation myths of the other traditions. Nevertheless there is a point which is always the same—

namely, that there was before the creation a Wholeness or Holiness that was dispersed at the *beginning*, giving place to everything we may perceive. We must emphasize that the fall and resurrection of Man is described as the fall and resurrection of a *collective man*.

In the same way, Adam in the Bible is a collective personality.

Now—a distinction between fall and sacrifice. The first creation, SRSTI, happens as the result of a fall—of a forgetting of oneself. The second creation (KRTI—"well-created," or *Sams Kriti*) happens as the result of a sacrifice, as a conscious action. In SRSTI everything proceeds by itself, mechanically— spreading outward and downward indefinitely, as it is told in the Kabbalah, where God, seeing this, mechanical, indefinite out-spreading of the first creation, shouts out, "*Enough!*"

Since it is mechanical, it spreads outward without control. God must establish limits. A *horizon*.

Limit in this sense contains, brings us back to ourselves, to a remembering. In Indian myth this limitation is known as the "great arms of the Black" (the darkness of Krishna).

Like the blackness that surrounds and limits all light and energy, there is a cosmic need for real limit which brings reality to itself. No light can go farther than a definite horizon. The idea of a divine horizon can be understood if we remember that the sublime is what remains within its limit—*sub-limen*.

Legend

Why have we lost the legends?—and are we not in danger of dying from cold because of this loss? We forget that a legend is a tale that has to be understood with intelligence. But for this intelligence to bear fruit, it must lead to action. Legend must be lived.

Legends are tales that have to be understood, but if you do not act accordingly, you will never acquire the ambrosia, the nectar of imperishable being. Your understanding cannot remain in your head. When you *act* in accordance with legend, only then do you understand with your head, your arms, your feet, your belly, your whole presence. This is what we have forgotten about the understanding of legends—and, indeed, about all understanding.

Let us take, for example, the legend of the hero and the dragon—a central legend of India as well as of all other cultures. It was not meant as an entertainment but as a guide to life. Think of the dragon as the collective, the collective personality of the *patriarchal reality*. We speak of a collectivity with a head, a real *head*, a chief in the root meaning of the word. This needs to be emphasized.

To the individual, the patriarchal reality appears dragonlike (draconian).

But we must not speak yet of the individual. We speak of the *dividual*. "Individual" means, literally, not divisible. But we are divisible, you and I. We are divided within ourselves, we are a multiplicity, in conflict and suffering. We are not only dividuals, we are poor, poor dividuals.

In this legend of the dragon, the hero is the dividual who refuses to be eaten by the corporate personality, the patriarchal reality.

Yet, for the dividual, if he is eaten, he is saved—he becomes the dragon. We need to be eaten by this dragon.

In the *Shatapatha Brahmana* we have the story of the Purusha Prajapati rushing toward the creatures, with his mouth wide open, so much so that they are terrified. But he tells them, "Don't be afraid! If I eat you, each of you will find his true place in my Body!"

The Two Vedantas

We speak of two Vedantas, and we may equally speak of two Indias. There is the India of the Brahmins and the India of the yogis. It is incomprehensible that they live together, and the life of India is made up of these two lives. It was the same in ancient China, where there existed a state religion of Confucianism and the individual religion of Taoism.

The yogi is fundamentally anarchical, individualistic. He cares only for ecstasy, for personal liberation, freedom from every collective discipline. He takes upon himself many disciplines, but only for himself. I have seen many such men. A yogi who holds up his arms for months and years without moving them until they become frozen, stiff as wood. A remarkable achievement, but he has to be fed by others. This is a symbol of a way of living, of the man who wants his own truth, a wonder of a man who is yet for himself only. Such a man does everything for his divine self, his godliness.

Such is the yogi. The Brahmin does not even look at the yogi. He lives in a larger reality, one well ordered, well limited, well horizoned, as we might say. In most parts of India the name of a Brahmin ends with this dignifying word: *Sharma* —meaning *serene*. The *Nirukta*, which is India's treatise about the art of charging words with meaning, explains *sharma* by quite another word, *carma*, meaning *skin*. And the book explains that the only way of keeping serenity is never to transgress one's own skin. The Brahmins say, "We tie our petty selves with collective rituals in order to find liberation."

We may say of these Brahmins that they are notaries for the supernatural. A notary is not a very amusing person. Yet these notaries in their way have been the great artists who have shaped the civilization of India. The word "Brahmin" means shaper, former—like an unseen stage director who forms the reality before us. They directed the consecration of Kings, unlike our Christian priests always fighting for supremacy over "Caesar." The so-called "Laws of Manu" contain an important word on this: "The Brahmin of this land does not teach others his own law, but theirs."

The yogi, on the other hand, teaches his own law. He says to everyone, "Look what a master I am!"

The civilization of the ancient Hebrews was also made by these notaries for the supernatural.

Two Vedantas, then: the Vedanta of the Brahmins and the Vedanta of the yogis. The first proceeding by steps, *krama mukti*, the second believing in the possibility of an immediate, explosive, orgasmic illumination. For the Brahmin there is no romanticism at all in this *samadhi*. Such *samadhi* appears when the mind is in the right place, well concentrated, as it is said.

There is a story of the great Mullah Nasr Eddin, the legendary wise simpleton of the Islamicized East. It happened one day that the Mullah had to play his part as a *cadi*, a judge. Two plaintiffs appear, each of them saying that the other is a devil and that he is a pure angel. Mullah hears them with the greatest attention and says to each of them, "Your are right." An onlooker is astonished and says to Mullah, "But they contradict each other on every point. How can they both be right?" And Mullah answers, "You are right!"

Our Brahmins and yogis contradict each other in the same way. What is the key? We have to understand that the yogi is not wrong because he believes in grace but because his *askesis* (asceticism) is a systematic forcing of grace. When the Doctor of the Law, the humble Brahmin, is taken by a rapture into a Seventh Heaven, like Saint Paul, it is felt as a catastrophic invasion of the divine in a well-formed, sacred world that is utterly transcended from within and not broken from without as is the case with the yogi.

Such stories as those of Mullah Nasr Eddin are a means of transmitting ideas. Mullah is right when he says that both the yogi and the Brahmin are right because both are only aspects of a living, suffering collective body that necessarily envelops the two standpoints of the yogi and the Brahmin.

We may say that it was a catastrophe for India when Shankaracarya in the eighth century translated the Upanishads into conceptual, philosophical language. He thought that by this he would open the teachings. But it was not an opening; it was a shutting. It was Coomaraswamy who said that to have lost the art of thinking in images is to have fallen into the verbalism of philosophy.

If the present need is new thought, new thinking, let us attend to such stories more respectfully. It is such new thought—which is really ancient thought—that the story hints at. There is a higher logic of complementarity, a logic of mediation through social feeling. Social feeling is *love*.

Revolutionary Thought and Cyclical Reality. Our thought and our action must become *cosmomimetic*, a reflection of the universal law. What other meaning is there to the phrase "being in contact with reality"?

Is it night or day? Does the turning wheel go upward or downward? According to our linear logic these two movements—ascending and descending—contradict each other. Either you are progressing or regressing, and there is no third alternative. But Eastern thought knows about a *Bhavacakra*, the wheel of Existence. And when one part of the circumference of the wheel is going downward it means that the opposite—not contradictory—part is going upward. In other words, there is no regression of another part. And if we care, as we should, only for the whole, we have to understand that even if such progress is not possible without a progress of the parts, the excessive progress of one part may be a definite obstacle to the progress of the whole. Hence this part will have to be sacrificed by the King—I mean, the Spirit responsible for the common good.

Srsti or Infracreation

The literal meaning is ejaculation. Millions of spermatozoa are thrown out, but one will fertilize the ovum—*if it is received*. All others must perish because the

Infinite Possibility can never *manifest* entirely. Such are the conditions of the ovum.

The maternal side stands on the side of Grace. And now let us well understand that the Brahmins of India stand on the side of Rigor, as it has been said, "Let us first create a Mother, out of whom we might be reborn."

This mother is a social community, called *ecclesia* in the West and *sangha* in India. Inside a *sangha*, not every possibility is allowed to manifest. But if a possibility, a grace from the divine Father, is received, the spiritual seed that has been elected will be born into a real child. *It will not remain a possibility; there will be an effective realization.*

That is why it is said in India that the SRSTI of the Father is not enough. There must be ATISRSTI—*ati* means beyond—which means a *second creation.*

This second creation is called KRTI or Samskriti. This is creation in its proper meaning, according to the root *kr*, which we find in the words *karman*—literally, action of creating in order; or *samskaras*—usually translated as "sacraments," but meaning literally actions in order to create a being *completely*, actions necessary in order to create a complete being (SAM).

The yogis stand on the level of the SRSTI. The Brahmins alone know of the SAMSKRTI or the art of making a thing complete. And the thing about which they care first of all is the *state*. How often I have heard it said in India, "Never say Church and State!" What is the state? It is the normal church, the normal city, temple, led by those who follow the norm (*dharma*)—that is, the final goal of the life of man.

A state that does not know the norm is no state at all. Western "states," being completely ignorant of the norm, are "e-normous" monsters. And why? It is because the Brahmins of the West never cared for the birth of a true *Dharmarajah*, King of Justice, Melchizedek, King of Salem (peace). Yet the Brahmins of the West still speak of *Mater Ecclesia*, but they have forgotten the whole point: the Birth, the *Incarnation* of their Christ in a real King. Without a center, there can be no *mandala* (circus, *Kirche*).

The concentration of the Divine in a point, the Throne (Greek: *thronos* = Sanskrit: *dharman*—literally, action of sustaining) is the whole work of the Brahmins, who do not simply support the Throne, as it commonly said. *They are the Throne, and may be called the Isis of India.* Their Son is the King, Horus, the Face of God turned toward the world. They are themselves the invisible side of the Deity, its very secret, and that is why they have to remain unmanifest. The glory is for the King and not for us who are his mother.

And do you know why things went the way they did in the West? Look here—this is a rising sun:  . How do you read it? A Westerner will see it as the symbol of a victory of Light over Darkness. But for us Brahmins, who must always stay in the *superluminous Night of the divine*, it must be read as the Victory of the Cow of Night giving birth to the Golden Calf, the *Bambino, oriens*, as the Divine Kid is called in the church liturgy of Christmas. Only the King, who is endowed with spiritual power by the Brahmins, can bring the reign of God, the *Ramraj* upon earth, and by the instrumentality of its *divine power* (never say "temporal power!") the Peace of God that "passeth understanding." The same is said in our Vedas about the Great King of Heaven, Varuna: "His Power gives wisdom to all the creatures." But in the West, you see, all this is topsy-turvy.

And that is why you care so much for all our feeble yogis, and not us Brahmins who could be creators of powerful Kings. Nowadays, things have gone so far that people call a miserable yogi sitting in the street adorned only with the ornament of his lice a *Maharaj*! This yogi, however, is still in the SRSTI, in a complete confusion of mind concerning the science of the possible and the impossible. He has not even a faint idea of what we call culture, *Samskriti*, in our Sanskrit language, which he blissfully ignores and even despises.

Beneath the world of names and forms of our notaries there is the "world" of ignominy and deformity, the *infraformal*. Although the world of form stands below the "world" of the superformal or the universal, we must understand that in relation to the first "creation" of the *Asuras*, SRSTI, whose symbol is the dark forest (*aranya*), the chaos of infinite possibility, the second creation is that of the clearing (*loka*) which is obtained by burning down, by sacrificing a part of the dark forest in order to obtain a *place* (locus, lodge) *from within which we might be born to an orderly life.*

The Profane, the Sacred (the Fanum), and the Divine. We are always leaping from one extreme to another, forgetting the middle world, the mesocosmos of the Sacred. For instance, Christians still quarrel about the meaning of the expression, "Give us this day our daily bread." For "materialist" Christians, it is the "real" bread that is meant, while for "spiritualist" Christians it has always been understood as the bread of the angels, *fanum supersubstantialum, ton arton epiousioun*. But the true interpretation is that a sacred precept has not only to be learned by heart *each day*—it was also called the *manducation* (the eating) of the lesson, the lesson put into practice, according to the words of Jesus, "My food is to do the will of my Father."

The world of the Sacred alone deserves to be called the world of a MANAVA, meaning real man in Sanskrit, real because having MANU (ATMAN in its legislative aspect) as his center. Beyond the world of men live the gods; and below, the animals. And we must realize how wrong Durkheim was when he confused the Sacred with the Divine on one side and with the social on the other side. He wished to oppose these three to the "world" of the uninitiated individuals, equated by him, justly, with the profane. Durkheim's idea of the Divine, being nothing more than a mystical hypostasis of the social, was complete nonsense, which veiled the truth of its equation of the social with the Sacred.

In this equation, however veiled it was, Durkheim was nevertheless more profound than Rudolf Otto or Mircea Eliade, who have also equated the Sacred with the Divine, missing—in an opposite way—the real nature of the Sacred. Once they relegate the social to the realm of the profane, they have unwittingly adopted the yogi's view of things.

But God can descend only in the realm of the Sacred, the sacramental, or well-formed social order (*Shakyamuni:* Shakya-socibranches; *muni*-the trunk, the *axis mundi*; therefore, *Shakyamuni*: the tree of life, savior, and king). God appears in the middle realms, the realm of the Brahmin.

Let us take it as our task to discriminate between the real or sacred collective man, and the infrahuman collectivity of totalitarian states in all their modes, subtle and obvious. The sacred collectivity is superhuman, supraindividual in that it brings saving force to the mutilated dividuals that we are.

Two Vedantas. The Fall always takes place at the end (*anta*) of a Veda (vision). That is why we can never rest only on personal vision. We need collective ritual life. We need to be supported by a sacred year "in heaven" and a sacred geography "on earth." "Thy Kingdom come, thy will be done, on earth as it is in heaven." We repeat the words like parrots and every trace of a mythical or sacred geography has disappeared from our so-called civilized countries.

But the Fall is a necessity—because it brings suffering in its wake. And when we suffer, we remember. When things again begin to "go quite well"—that is, in a completely mechanical way—we forget Him again. And there is a new fall, a new war, new miseries for a new Remembering.

> *In suffering all men Remember,*
> *In happiness no one who can.*
> *If in happiness man could Remember,*
> *What need for suffering then?*

Therefore, the question arises: How could it be possible to remember Him even when we are not distressed? The answer is: our whole life needs to be ritualized that is, submitted to voluntary sufferings for the individual in order to realize the state of nonsuffering for the city, the corporate whole. In the salvation of the city, you will find your deliverance, *moksha*. But the contrary is not true at all. More that: the so-called deliverance of an individual alone cannot but disequilibrate the life of the whole city, *if it is not a deliverance that takes place in the center, on the throne.* If one man is a saint, he has to be the King.

But who shall decide the sanctity of a man? The disciples are always shouting out that their own master is the greatest saint, the greatest maharishi, the greatest maharaj. . .

The word "Vedanta" is late. In Vedic times, they said, *Anansa Vedah!*: "The Vedas are without end, infinite!" Later, the word Vedanta (*Veda + anta*) was taken to mean fulfillment, consummate, complete achievement (ANSA) of the vision of the Divine in the fourth stage of life of the *sannyasi*, the man of *complete* renunciation.

Vedic seers did not call themselves Vedantins, because they were still active. But we find now everywhere in India men who are still living in one of the inferior stages of life, called the stage of the student (*brahma-charya*), the stage of the householder (*grmastha*), or the stage of the "Senator" (*vana-prasth*), the man who has forsaken all concern for his own family so as to devote himself to the public good. But now Vedanta has become a private philosophic *opinion*, precisely that which was called in the West *Airesis* and in Buddhist scriptures *Ditti*, and was forbidden as such. Who are you to decide about the ultimate truth? Is it Advaita, Visishtadvaita, Dvaita, or some mixture of these three systems as in the Vedanta of Vallabha and Nimbuka?

There is this Sanskrit saying: "In a dubious question, you must first ask the *Sruti* (the Vedic revelation); if it brings no answer, ask the *Smrti* (the sacred tradition); if it brings no answer, ask the *Puranas* (the ancient writings); if they bring no answer, ask your family guru; and if he does not see the answer, ask your parents; and if they do not see either, ask your friends—because it is only when every help from outside has failed that one man is allowed to ask his own consciousness to decide about the truth."

Such was the traditional standpoint. How far we are from it. But even further from it is this so-called Vedantin of the streets who really is only divinizing his own opinion.

Atman-Brahman

These words have remained for three thousand years, but their meaning has changed. Gradually, progressively, without any violence, a deviation creeps in and the tradition that was life-giving in the beginning ends by becoming death-giving. It always happens in that way.

Then revolutions come inevitably. The sacred tradition of old is accused and discarded abruptly and brutally. But it may happen that the so-called revolutionaries actually bring back the earliest tradition that had slowly been forgotten.

Speaking about "tradition," we must never forget that the word is cognate with "trade" in English and *tradittore* (traitor) in Italian.

The first Christians who did not hide the Gospels from the pagans were called *tradittores*. Similarly, we find at the end of every Upanishad—as in the last chapter of the Bhagavad Gita—terrible warnings against such "*tradittores*." Nevertheless, it happened that the Upanishads finally fell into the hands of each and every person in India as the Gospels have fallen into our hands in our own times.

The first "Christian" teaching was absolutely "Vedantic," since it taught the Supreme Identity of the Son and the Father, Man and God, Atman and Brahman. But it was never said that this Son was the *dividual* man. He was Man as a whole, as the Assyro-Babylonian tradition has put it so clearly:

> *The Shadow of God is Man*
> *and men are the Shadow of Man*
> *Man is the King,*
> *who is the image of God.*

In the Epistles of Paul, the Son is depicted as "the very image and imprint of the Father." But a time came when each and every *dividual* attributed to himself the *imago Dei* which pertains only to the *individuum quod non est pars* of the medieval tradition—namely, the Sacred King, called the *Christus Domini*.

Therefore we must rid ourselves of two fateful errors: first, the error committed by "the bad Vedanta," which is to believe that there is a supreme identity between a dividual and the Brahman. Second, the error committed by the Christians when they misunderstood completely the idea of *incarnation*, angrily discarding the perspective of the Jews who wanted the Messiah to be a real King.

There is no doubt that in the High Middles Ages, in Byzantium as well as in the West, the so-called "Constantinian Christianity" was still *traditional*, and that the fall into our "modern times" occurred only in the time of the so-called Reformation, whose founders had lost every memory of the Form.

Coomaraswamy has clearly shown that the discarding of the idea of transsubstantiation (which is the main point of Christianity) was done for the same reason as the rejection of the idea of the Divinity of the King. The *imbroglio* was hopeless and the so-called "religious wars" of those times had to be atrocious because the Re-formers indeed were nearer the truth concerning Kingship and the "mystery of the Kingdom" than were the friends of the Pope. It was Catholicism that was the main destroyer of the *corpus politicum vel mysticum* of Christ, of the *Purusha*, whose resurrection can never take place in a Church alone, but only in a *Church-State*.

Both Emperors and Popes indeed were right, in a sense, when they wanted to be at the same time Popes and Emperors. The only trouble was that at such times the very idea of a Brahmana had completely disappeared from the West. The Maharaja of India who wore, as it were, the *triregnum* (the symbol of his Power over the three worlds) always prostrated himself at the feet of the naked *sannyasi* when he visited him in secret, asking for spiritual help. But neither the Pope nor the Emperor would have done that. "I Caesar, I Imperator," shouted Pope Boniface VIII. Such a fall of the "spiritual authority" was bound to produce a spiritual revolt. And Christianity disintegrated.

Now we may return to the first meaning of the word *Atman* in Vedic times. To be sure, such a word is an *anugama*, a word whose meaning exists *according* to its context. *Atman is that with which I identify. Tadatmyan*—literally, *That-I*—is the word that means "identification" in Sanskrit. And *that* (*tat*) does not necessarily mean the Supreme *Brahman*. It may mean—and such was the case in the times when the *Brihad Aranyaka Upanishad* was written—my wife, myself, my children, and the goods of my eyes and my ears (the material things I see and the spiritual things I hear).

The *atman* in Vedic times was first of all the social unit, of which I was a *part*. Feeling himself to be a part of the social body greater than his own body, the life of the Vedic man was a *participation* in a life greater than his own. And that very life was *his atman*.

Participation is the key word. We need life, I mean a participation in a greater life than our own. But here lies danger. We may desire that life for ourselves, not for others. We may refuse to play our part in the collective life, believing that *we* are more than a part.

We have already mentioned Durkheim's definition of *participation*: "power to be at the same time one's own self and others." Later, Levy-Brühl maintained that participation was the supreme confusion of the mind, because A is A and, if A is A, how can it be B? And therewith he initiated the concept of a "primitive mind" of old that was, as he said, "completely prelogical." But if a man tells you that he *is* not only himself, but also his wife and his children, will you shout that such a man is prelogical?

The point is—and it cannot be stressed too much—that we *need* the Absolute. Relativity is meaningless and boring. *Homo capax Dei*. And if this *need* is not taken into consideration, the result for man will inevitably be "existential neurosis," the endless, empty, gnawing groping for "the meaning of life."

But I ask you to pay attention. There is a terrible pitfall—that pretention that may appear when a poor dividual lays claim to having found Absolute Truth. It is complete nonsense! Yet there is a desire at the root of this whole pretention that is perfectly real and authentic, a tremendous desire to escape endless relativity, a desire to *participate* in something *real, divine,* or *absolute.* And this desire may be and must be satisfied.

It is the *present need.*

And *sacred tradition,* if rightly understood, may show us the ways of satisfying it.

Atman indeed was the *Brahman* in ancient Aryan India, but not at all in the way our modern Vedantins take it—because the *Brahman* was then understood rightly as the totality of the "sacred formulas" (*brahman*), rituals, and sacraments (*samskaras*) by which the family, on a lesser scale, and the Kingdom, on the greater scale, could be maintained in a good state of mind and in good health as a corporate whole, where the dividuals could find their Individuality in a greater Person than their petty selves.

The Upanishads say it quite clearly: "Everything which is not the *Atman* is misery." But traitorous-*tradittore*-tradition came, for whom the experience of a participative life in a greater whole had become *res ignota,* a thing unknown.

And as it is said, *ignota nulla cupido* (that which is unknown cannot be desired). Therefore they translated their word *Atman* by the words "Ultimate Reality."

But the *Atman-Brahman* of a family, of a kingdom, even if it is greater than my own *atman,* nevertheless falls very far short of an *ultimate reality.* To be sure, it is still a mortal *atman*—but *precisely as such it may be offered, when it has become perfected* (*samskrita*)—*that is, worthy of being offered,* in the fire of sacrifice to the Absolute. And such sacrifice, the sacrifice of the *collective man, the regenerated Adam,* whose prototype among us was Christ, may be the means for the descent of the Divine in Man—not man in the singular to the exclusion of others.

Just as *psyche* and *theos* are not to be confused with psychology and theology, which are the science of the soul and the science of God, so myth must not be equated with mythology, the interpretation of myths, the attempt to trap their meaning.

For each myth—for example, the Christian myth—how many mythologies do we have! And all claim to be the sole and only interpretation. In this they are all of them wrong because each myth admits of many interpretations. And the deeper interpretations will not necessarily be the best for men who still stand at a very superficial level of undertaking.

And that is why it may be good sometimes simply to recite, to re-ex-cite, the ancient myths without caring for their symbolism. The myth has first to be taken *as you like it,* as you find your way into it. Only keep it in your memory and, some day, you may suddenly shout: It is *that* which the myth wanted to tell me *and I did not understand it !*"

Myths are time-bombs.

Here are two of them.

I. A Story of Arjuna

This tale takes place before the *Mahabharata* war. Arjuna, at last, has understood that he cannot remain hiding in a corner, but that he has to manifest, to fight—

that is, to win or die. But he had nothing in his hands but a human sword, his own resolution. He realized that he needed a divine sword and decided to visit Shiva, in his Himilayan abode. Great were the obstacles, the demons, the doors he had to open with his sword along the way. Success followed success. But as he was nearing the top of the mountain, a huge dragon blocked his way. The path was narrow and Arjuna had to choose whether to flee or fight. Arjuna sensed that he would die in this struggle and he begged the monster to give him respite so that he could offer a last sacrifice to Shiva. The dragon agreed. And with some small stones Arjuna erected an altar to Shiva. He gathered red flowers along the side of the path and wove them into a garland which he placed atop the altar.

He knelt down to worship the Lord, dying in his prayer. And when, regenerated, he turned again for battle, he felt such power in his arms that he had no doubt he would cut off the head of the beast with one stroke. But at that moment he saw the very garland of flowers which he had set upon the altar resting now upon the head of the dragon.

II. A Story of the Ramayana

Once upon a time, at dawn, the great bell was struck that stood at the door of the palace of Rama. A mightly sound. And the King awoke suddenly and sprang from his bed, knowing that the sound of that bell meant someone had been the victim of injustice.

There at the gate stood a Brahmin with his young son dead in his arms. "It is supposed to be Ramraj, the Golden Age," said the father, his voice trembling with sorrow and anger. "Yet here, look! Seven years old and death has taken him!"

For Rama it was enough. He understood at once that some crime had been left unpunished in his Kingdom and that the blot was upon him. He took down his great bow and went out into the land, inquiring near and far. Soon he discovered a Shudra named Shambuka who had forsaken his duties and instead was practicing Yoga at the door of the city. Without a moment's hesitation, Rama released his arrow, killing Shambuka. At that very instant the Brahmin child returned to life as the Shudra attained his goal: the Death divine, liberation, from the very hands of the Lord.

The Kali Yuga

Throughout India you will hear a beautiful story which is at the same time a prayer. Its refrain is, "Take us to the other shore!" But we are asked to understand that the other shore, like the Kingdom, is always "at hand." God is not a goal to be attained at the end of a long road. The road starts from God. The *Satya Yuga*, the Golden Age, is always waiting for man.

But at some point an invention crept into the tradition. People began to think and to say that the Age of Truth lies in the distant past and that we are condemned to live cut off from that glorious arising of light; we are irrevocably denizens of the *Kali Yuga*.

The ancient view was actually quite different. It said that each of us is in the

Kali Yuga as long as we have not yet taken the first steps of Yoga. The words *yuga* and *Yoga* are the same. A community that lives according to the teachings with individuals who strive along the path of Yoga—at any moment such a community can enter the *Satya Yuga*.

This is a striking example of how an idea becomes death giving when taken in an external meaning only.

And what about the *samadhi* (illumination, ecstasy) which is at the end of the yogic path and is, as well, the goal of the Vedantin? The word is understandable only in contrast to *vyadhi*, which means distress—literally: displaced mind, infirm mind. In other words, the mind (*dhi*) fallen from its correct place at the center of Man. Man in Sanskrit is called *purusha*, literally: the holy fire which burns in the city (*pura*), or *manava*, literally: son of Manu. And *Manu* means "Center of Man." Now the Center is never far, though we may fall very far from our Center. But the vision of it may take place at any time. *if we are reminded.*

It is said that God is the starting point of the road. But it is not said that there is no road, no work to be done upon ourselves. The point that matters is that the Beginning is on the top of the mountain. In order to say *in principio, en arke, bereshit*, the Sanskrit language says: *Agre*. It means: on the peak of the mountain, when the first sacrifice takes place. Read, for this, "creation of the world" (what we have called the second or real creation).

Therefore, the work to be done is not a work of de-creation but a work of allowing the spiritual influence that is received in the sacrifice to descend over all the slopes of the world mountain. The work must always begin from the summit which is equally the center of the world-wheel. The mind has to radiate. It has to extend (TAN—thus: *tantra*) all over the world, *but without losing its Center, its state of samadhi.*

The whole difficulty of the work lies here. And that is why so many people in India have lost the ancient doctrine so clearly formulated in these two words: *Samadarshanam; Vishamavartanam*, meaning "equality" (*sama*) in vision; "differentiation" in action.

This was interpreted as meaning that seeing all things as equal (*Samadarshanam—samadhi*)—meant the disappearance of the world since the world we know is so differentiated. But the primordial idea was completely different. The idea was that, what was needed was *detachment* in order that there could be real, objective *participation* in the life the world, without the fall into forgetfulness of our real Self.

All the creatures cried out to the awakened one, the Buddha, "O Compassionate!"

Expansion and Contraction

The story of Rama and Shambuka has shown us that the ancient world knew about *nidanas*, hidden connections. All things hang together. We are living within a Whole. If there is a disturbance at the periphery, the fall of a Shudra from the duties of his caste, it can bring about such disorders as the death of a Brahmin boy. Then, what about a disorder in the Center?

Such a disorder in the Center would inevitably destroy the entire web of our corporate life. Destroyed at its root would be the *vine*, the *atman*, all the branches—called *Shakya* in Sanskrit and *socii* in Latin. If the Truth is not enthroned in the middle of the temple-palace, which is built in the middle of the *capital* (the head—Latin, *caput*) of the whole kingdom—then disorder, war, famine, and death everywhere and for all things.

Hence we understand now the tremendous importance of the divine right of Kings. If they are not divinely ordained, if a usurper has taken over, if he sits in the middle, the tree of life will soon be struck by the thunderbolt of Zeus or Yahweh.

One day I asked a friend, a learned rabbi, "Can you tell me in brief the message of the whole Bible?"

He answered, "I can. The Bible is nothing but God shouting these two words, 'ENTHRONE ME!'"

It was as though a flash of light instantly dispelled from my mind a doubt that had long been lingering over it. And I told him in one breath about the last words of Shankaracarya, which are unfortunately so much admired by modern Vedantins: "O my Lord, forgive me that I went to search for you in your temples, forgetting that you are everywhere."

The rabbi exploded. "Such was the Fall," he said. "That is pantheistic spirituality, the blotting out of any differentiation between the Lord and his creatures. And our own Solomon," he said, "was already beginning to be infected with this plague when he uttered nearly the same words: 'O my Lord, I shall do your will and build your sanctuary, but why do you need a Center, when you are everywhere?'"

Life is rhythm, Great Life is great rhythm, expansion and contraction, the giving out and the taking in, the Wings of Garuda, the bird of Vishnu. But the expansion, the giving out, must be conscious.

All beings breathe, even God.

Sacred Tradition and Present Need

The present need is God. But we have to understand that the true God is the collective consciousness of the City. *God is not the animator of a personal consciousness proceeding by assertion and the exclusion of others.* When such men appear they are not the representatives of God. They are the "great men" of the West—conquerors in the line of damnation which is led by Alexander, Caesar, Napoleon, and Hitler.

Asserting individuals are the exact opposite of the present need. We have to understand together. If we do not understand together, the understanding has no value. And most of the gurus of India proceed by exclusion and assertion—the exclusion of all other points of view. That was not the case in ancient, Vedic, India.

In ancient India there was no orthodoxy. *Orthodoxy is the opposite of the present need.* Orthopraxis and orthopoiea—yes. The "lonely crowd" has to be formed into a social body, awakened to a corporate life. Things have to be done correctly. The art of living together has to be learned and practiced. That is the need. The sacred, the form of the social whole, has to come back into being.

Mohammed said, "My community cannot proffer error."

And the great saying of At-Tabari—who in the modern world understands this saying? "When a scholar studies the Koran and comes to the truth by his own judgment, it is not the truth, because he has come to it by his own judgment." Because the ego has crept in there.

The greatest Vedanta is life-giving, as was expressed by the holiest of Sufis, Ibn Arabi, who said, "The divine essence must invade man as would death, as a power that takes hold of him. Were it not so, the divine essence could be taken from man by death." For us there cannot be anything immortal, if we are not first annihilated by the divine. If then this death takes hold of us, what can ordinary death do? It does not exist.

Fulfillment, Work, and Money

Religion and the Rise of Capitalism

R. H. Tawney

R. H. Tawney (1880–1962) was deeply involved in both economic theory and the political life of England, having helped to formulate the economic and ethical views of the British Labor Party. He also ran for Parliament (though he was never elected) and served as an advisor to numerous government bodies. In addition to his groundbreaking *Religion and the Rise of Capitalism*, his works include *The Acquisitive Society* and *Equality*. He was professor at the University of London from 1931 to 1949.

Has religious opinion in the past regarded questions of social organization and economic conduct as irrelevant to the life of the spirit, or has it endeavored not only to christianize the individual but to make a Christian civilization? Can religion admit the existence of a sharp antithesis between personal morality and the practices which are permissible in business? Does the idea of a Church involve the acceptance of any particular standard of social ethics, and, if so, ought a Church to endeavor to enforce it as among the obligations incumbent on its members? Such are a few of the questions which men are asking today, and on which a more competent examination of history than I can hope to offer might throw at any rate an oblique and wavering light.

. . .

There are, perhaps, four main attitudes which religious opinion may adopt toward the world of social institutions and economic relations. It may stand on one side in ascetic aloofness and regard them as in their very nature the sphere of unrighteousness, from which men *may* escape—from which, if they consider their souls, they *will* escape—but which they can conquer only by flight. It may take them for granted and ignore them, as matters of indifference belonging to a world with which religion has no concern; in all ages the prudence of looking problems boldly in the face and passing on has seemed too self-evident to require justification. It may throw itself into an agitation for some particular reform, for the removal of some crying scandal, for the promotion of some final revolution, which will inaugurate the reign of righteousness on earth. It may at once accept and criticize, tolerate and amend, welcome the gross world of human appetites, as the squalid scaffolding from amid which the life of the spirit must rise, and insist that this also is the material of the Kingdom of God. To such a temper, all activities divorced from religion are brutal or dead, but none are too mean to be beneath or too great to be above it, since all, in their different degrees, are touched with the spirit which permeates the whole. It finds its most sublime expression in the words of Piccarda: "Paradise is everywhere, though the grace of the highest good is not shed everywhere in the same degree."

. . .

The mercantilist thought of later centuries owed a considerable debt to scholastic discussions of money, prices, and interest. But the specific contributions of medieval writers to the technique of economic theory were less significant than their premises. Their fundamental assumptions, both of which were to leave a deep imprint on the social thought of the sixteenth and seventeenth centuries, were two: that economic interests are subordinate to the real business of life, which is salvation, and that economic conduct is one aspect of personal conduct, upon which, as on other parts of it, the rules of morality are binding. Material riches are necessary; they have a secondary importance, since without them men cannot support themselves and help one another; the wise ruler, as St. Thomas said, will consider in founding his State the natural resources of the country. But economic motives are suspect. Because they are powerful appetites, men fear them, but they are not mean enough to applaud them. Like other strong passions, what they need, it is thought, is not a clear field, but repression. There is no place in medieval theory for economic activity which is not related to a moral end, and to found a science of society upon the assumption that the appetite for economic gain is a constant and measurable force, to be accepted, like other natural forces, as an inevitable and self-evident *datum* would have appeared to the medieval thinker as hardly less irrational or less immoral than to make the premise of social philosophy the unrestrained operation of such necessary human attributes as pugnacity or the sexual instinct. The outer is ordained for the sake of the inner; economic goods are instrumental—*sicut quædam adminicula quibus, adjuvamur ad tendendum in beatitudinem*. "It is lawful to desire temporal blessings, not putting them in the first place, as though setting up our rest in them, but regarding them as aids to blessedness, inasmuch as they support our corporal life and serve as instruments for acts of virtue." Riches, as St. Antonino says, exist for man, not man for riches.

At every turn, therefore, there are limits, restrictions, warnings against allowing economic interests to interfere with serious affairs. It is right for a man to seek such wealth as is necessary for a livelihood in his station. To seek more is not enterprise but avarice, and avarice is a deadly sin. Trade is legitimate; the different resources of different countries show that it was intended by Providence. But it is a dangerous business. A man must be sure that he carries it on for the public benefit, and that the profits which he takes are no more than the wages of his labor. Private property is a necessary institution, at least in a fallen world; men work more and dispute less when goods are private than when they are common. But it is to be tolerated as a concession to human frailty, not applauded as desirable in itself; the ideal—if only man's nature could rise to it—is communism. "Communis enim," wrote Gratian in his *decretum*, "usus omnium, quae sunt in hoc mundo, omnibus hominibus esse debuit." At best, indeed, the estate is somewhat encumbered. It must be legitimately acquired. It must be in the largest possible number of hands. It must provide for the support of the poor. Its use must as far as practicable be common. Its owners must be ready to share it with those who need, even if they are not in actual destitution. Such were the conditions which commended themselves to an archbishop of the business capital of fifteenth-century Europe. There have been ages in which they would have been described, not as a justification of property, but as a revolutionary assault on it. For to defend the property of the peasant and small master is necessarily to attack that of the monopolist and usurer, which grows by devouring it.

The assumption on which all this body of doctrine rested was simple. It was that the danger of economic interests increased in direct proportion to the prominence of the pecuniary motives associated with them. Labor—the common lot of mankind—is necessary and honorable; trade is necessary, but perilous to the soul; finance, if not immoral, is at best sordid and at worst disreputable. This curious inversion of the social values of more enlightened ages is best revealed in medieval discussions of the ethics of commerce. The severely qualified tolerance extended to the trader was partly, no doubt, a literary convention derived from classical models; it was natural that Aquinas should laud the State which had small need of merchants because it could meet its needs from the produce of its own soil; had not the Philosopher himself praised αὐταρκεία? But it was a convention which coincided with a vital element in medieval social theory, and struck a responsive note in wide sections of medieval society. It is not disputed, of course, that trade is indispensable; the merchant supplements the deficiencies of one country with the abundance of another. If there were no private traders, argued Duns Scotus, whose indulgence was less carefully guarded, the governor would have to engage them. Their profits, therefore, are legitimate, and they may include, not only the livelihood appropriate to the trader's status, but payment for labor, skill, and risk.

The defense, if adequate, was somewhat embarrassing. For why should a defense be required? The insistence that trade is not positively sinful conveys a hint that the practices of traders may be, at least, of dubious propriety. And so, in the eyes of most medieval thinkers, they are. *Summe periculosa est venditionis et emptionis negotiatio.* The explanation of that attitude lay partly in the facts of contemporary economic organization. The economy of the medieval borough—consider only its treatment of food supplies and prices—was one in which consumption held somewhat the same primacy in the public mind, as the undisputed arbiter of economic effort, as the nineteenth century attached to profits. The merchant pure and simple, though convenient to the Crown, for whom he collected taxes and provided loans, and to great establishments such as monasteries, whose wool he bought in bulk, enjoyed the double unpopularity of an alien and a parasite. The best practical commentary on the tepid indulgence extended by theorists to the trader is the network of restrictions with which medieval policy surrounded his activities, the recurrent storms of public indignation against him, and the ruthlessness with which boroughs suppressed the middleman who intervened between consumer and producer.

Apart, however, from the color which it took from its environment, medieval social theory had reasons of its own for holding that business, as distinct from labor, required some special justification. The suspicion of economic motives had been one of the earliest elements in the social teaching of the Church, and was to survive till Calvinism endowed the life of economic enterprise with a new sanctification. In medieval philosophy the ascetic tradition, which condemned all commerce as the sphere of iniquity, was softened by a recognition of practical necessities, but it was not obliterated; and, if reluctant to condemn, it was insistent to warn. For it was of the essence of trade to drag into a position of solitary prominence the acquisitive appetites; and towards those appetites, which to most modern thinkers have seemed the one sure social dynamic, the attitude of the medieval theorist was that of one who holds a wolf by the ears. The craftsman labors for his living; he seeks what is sufficient to support him, and no more. The merchant aims, not merely at livelihood, but at profit. The traditional distinction was expressed in the words of Gratian: "Whosoever buys a thing, not that he may sell it whole and unchanged, but that it may be a material for fashioning something, he is no merchant. But the man who buys it in order that he may gain by selling it again unchanged and as he bought it, that man is of the buyers and sellers who are cast forth from God's temple." By very definition a man who "buys in order that he may sell dearer," the trader is moved by an inhuman concentration on his own pecuniary interest, unsoftened by any tincture of public spirit or private charity. He turns what should be a means into an end, and his occupation, therefore, "is justly condemned, since, regarded in itself, it serves the lust of gain."

The dilemma presented by a form of enterprise at once perilous to the soul and essential to society was revealed in the solution most commonly propounded for it. It was to treat profits as a particular case of wages, with the qualification that gains in excess of a reasonable remuneration for the merchant's labor were, though not illegal, reprehensible as *turpe lucrum*. The condition of the trader's exoneration is that "he seeks gain, not as an end, but as the wages of his labor." Theoretically convenient, the doctrine was difficult of application, for evidently it implied the acceptance of what the sedate irony of Adam Smith was later to describe as "an affectation not very common among merchants." But the motives which prompted it were characteristic. The medieval theorist condemned as a sin precisely that effort to achieve a continuous and unlimited increase in material wealth which modern societies applaud as a quality, and the vices for which he reserved his most merciless denunciations were the more refined and subtle of the economic virtues. "He who has enough to satisfy his wants," wrote a Schoolman of the fourteenth century, "and nevertheless ceaselessly labors to acquire riches, either in order to obtain a higher social position, or that subsequently he may have enough to live without labor, or that his sons may become men of wealth and importance—all such are incited by a damnable avarice, sensuality, or pride." Two and a half centuries later, in the midst of a revolution in the economic and spiritual environment, Luther, in even more unmeasured language, was to say the same. The essence of the argument was that payment may properly be demanded by the craftsmen who make the goods, or by the merchants who transport them, for both labor in their vocation and serve the common need. The unpardonable sin is that of the speculator or the middleman, who snatches private gain by the exploitation of public necessities. The true descendant of the doctrines of Aquinas is the labor theory of value. The last of the Schoolmen was Karl Marx.

The Sin of Avarice

. . .

No man, again, may charge money for a loan. He may, of course, take the profits of partnership, provided that he takes the partner's risks. He may buy a rent-charge; for the fruits of the earth are produced by nature, not wrung from man. He may demand compensation—*interesse*—if he is not repaid the principal at the time stipulated. He may ask payment corresponding to any loss he incurs or gain he foregoes. He may purchase an annuity, for the payment is contingent and speculative, not certain. It is no usury when John Deveneys, who has borrowed £19.80, binds himself to pay a penalty of £40 in the event of failure to restore the principal, for this is compensation for damages incurred; or when Geoffrey de Eston grants William de Burwode three marks of silver in return for an annual rent of six shillings, for this is the purchase of a rent-charge, not a loan; or when James le Reve of London advances £100 to Robert de Bree of Dublin, merchant, with which to trade for two years in Ireland, for this is a partnership; or when the priory of Worcester sells annuities for a capital sum paid down. What remained to the end unlawful was that which appears in modern economic text-books as "pure interest"—interest as a fixed payment stipulated in advance for a loan of money or wares without risk to the lender. "Usura est ex mutuo lucrum pacto debitum vel exactum . . . quidquid sorti accedit, subaudi per pactum vel exactionem, usura est, quodcunque nomen sibi imponat." The emphasis was on *pactum*. The essence of usury was that it was certain, and that, whether the borrower gained or lost, the usurer took his pound of flesh. Medieval opinion, which has no objection to rent or profits, provided that they are reasonable—for is not every one in a small way a profit-maker?—has no mercy for the debenture-holder. His crime is that he takes a payment for money which is fixed and certain, and such a payment is usury.

. . .

On the subject of usury, Luther goes even further than the orthodox teaching. He denounces the concessions to practical necessities made by the cononists. "The greatest misfortune of the German nation is easily the traffic in interest. . . . The devil invented it, and the Pope, by giving his sanction to it, has done untold evil throughout the world." Not content with insisting that lending ought to be free, he denounces the payment of interest as compensation for loss and the practice of investing in rent-charges, both of which the canon law in his day allowed, and would refuse usurers the sacrament, absolution, and Christian burial. With such a code of ethics, Luther naturally finds the characteristic developments of his generation— the luxury trade with the East, international finance, speculation on the exchanges, combinations and monopolies—shocking beyond measure. "Foreign merchandise which brings from Calicut and India and the like places wares such as precious silver and jewels and spices . . . and drain the land and people of their money, should not be permitted. . . . Of combinations I ought really to say much, but the matter is endless and bottomless, full of mere greed and wrong. . . . Who is so stupid as not to see that combinations are mere outright monopolies, which even heathen civil laws—I will say nothing of divine right and Christian law—condemn as a plainly harmful thing in all the world?"

So resolute an enemy of license might have been expected to be the champion of law. It might have been supposed that Luther, with his hatred of the economic appetites, would have hailed as an ally the restraints by which, at least in theory, those appetites had been controlled. In reality, of course, his attitude towards the mechanism of ecclesiastical jurisprudence and discipline was the opposite. It was one, not merely of indifference, but of repugnance. The prophet who scourged with whips the cupidity of the individual chastised with scorpions the restrictions imposed upon it by society; the apostle of an ideal ethic of Christian love turned a shattering dialectic on the corporate organization of the Christian Church. In most ages, so tragic a parody of human hopes are human institutions, there have been some who have loved mankind, while hating almost everything that men have done or made. Of that temper Luther, who lived at a time when the contrast between a sublime theory and a hideous reality had long been intolerable, is the supreme example. He preaches a selfless charity, but he recoils with horror from every institution by which an attempt had been made to give it a concrete expression. He reiterates the content of medieval economic teaching with a literalness rarely to be found in the thinkers of the later Middle Ages, but for the rules and ordinances in which it had received a positive, if sadly imperfect, expression, he has little but abhorrence. God speaks to the soul, not through the mediation of the priesthood or of social institutions built up by man, but *solus cum solo*, as a voice in the heart and in the heart alone. Thus the bridges between the worlds of spirit and of sense are broken, and the soul is isolated from the society of men, that it may enter into communion with its Maker. The grace that is freely bestowed upon it may overflow in its social relations; but those relations can supply no particle of spiritual nourishment to make easier the reception of grace. Like the primeval confusion into which the fallen Angel plunged on his fatal mission, they are a chaos of brute matter, a wilderness of dry bones, a desert unsanctified and incapable of contributing to sanctification. "It is certain that absolutely none among outward things, under whatever name they may be reckoned, has any influence in producing Christian righteousness or liberty. . . . One thing, and one alone, is necessary for life, justification and Christian liberty; and that is the most holy word of God, the Gospel of Christ."

The difference between loving men as a result of first loving God, and learning to love God through a growing love for men, may not, at first sight, appear profound. To Luther it seemed an abyss, and Luther was right. It was, in a sense, nothing less than the Reformation itself. For carried, as it was not carried by Luther, to its logical result, the argument made, not only good works, but sacraments and the Church itself unnecessary. The question of the religious significance of that change of emphasis, and of the validity of the intellectual processes by which Luther reached his conclusions, is one for theologians. Its effects on social theory were staggering. Since salvation is bestowed by the operation of grace in the heart and by that alone, the whole fabric of organized religion, which had mediated between the individual soul and its Maker—divinely commissioned hierarchy, systematized activities, corporate institutions—drops away, as the blasphemous trivialities of a religion of works. The medieval conception of the social order, which had regarded it as a highly articulated organism of members contributing in their different degrees to a spiritual purpose, was shattered, and differences which had been distinctions within a larger unity were now set in irreconcilable antagonism to each other. Grace no longer completed nature: it was the antithesis of it. Man's actions as a member of society were no longer the extension of his life as a child of God: they were its negation. Secular interests ceased to possess, even remotely, a religious significance: they might compete with religion, but they could not enrich it. Detailed rules of conduct—a Christian casuistry—are needless or objectionable: the Christian has a sufficient guide in the Bible and in his own conscience. In one sense, the distinction between the secular and the religious life vanished. Monasticism was, so to speak, secularized; all men stood henceforward on the same footing towards God; and that advance, which contained the germ of all subsequent revolutions, was so enormous that all else seems insignificant. In another sense, the distinction became more profound than ever before. For, though all might be sanctified, it was their inner life alone which could partake of sanctification. The world was divided into good and evil, light and darkness, spirit and matter. The division between them was absolute; no human effort could span the chasm.

. . .

Luther's impotence was not accidental. It sprang directly from his fundamental conception that to externalize religion in rules and ordinances is to degrade it. He attacked the casuistry of the canonists, and the points in their teaching with regard to which his criticism was justified were only too numerous. But the remedy for bad law is good law, not lawlessness; and casuistry is merely the application of general principles to particular cases, which is involved in any living system of jurisprudence, whether ecclesiastical or secular. If the principles are not to be applied, on the ground that they are too sublime to be soiled by contact with the gross world of business and politics, what remains of them? Denunciations such as Luther launched against the Fuggers and the peasants; aspirations for an idyll of Christian charity and simplicity, such as he advanced in his tract *On Trade and Usury*. Pious rhetoric may be edifying, but it is hardly the panoply recommended by St. Paul.

"As the soul needs the word alone for life and justification, so it is justified by faith alone, and not by any works. . . . Therefore the first care of every Christian ought to be to lay aside all reliance on works, and to strengthen his faith alone more and more." The logic of Luther's religious premises was more potent for posterity than his attachment to the social ethics of the past, and evolved its own inexorable conclusions in spite of them. It enormously deepened spiritual experience, and sowed the seeds from which new freedoms, abhorrent to Luther, were to spring. But it riveted on the social thought of Protestantism a dualism which, as its implications were developed, emptied religion of its social content, and society of its soul. Between light and darkness a great gulf was fixed. Unable to climb upwards plane by plane, man must choose between salvation and damnation. If he despairs of attaining the austere heights where alone true faith is found, no human institution can avail to help him. Such, Luther thinks, will be the fate of only too many.

He himself was conscious that he had left the world of secular activities perilously divorced from spiritual restraints. He met the difficulty, partly with an admission that it was insuperable, as one who should exult in the majestic unreasonableness of a mysterious Providence, whose decrees might not be broken, but could not, save by a few, be obeyed; partly with an appeal to the State to occupy the province of social ethics, for which his philosophy could find no room in the Church. "Here it will be asked, 'Who then can be saved, and where shall we find

Christians? For in this fashion no merchandising would remain on earth.' . . . You see it is as I said, that Christians are rare people on earth. Therefore stern hard civil rule is necessary in the world, lest the world become wild, peace vanish, and commerce and common interests be destroyed. . . . No one need think that the world can be ruled without blood. The civil sword shall and must be red and bloody."

Thus the axe takes the place of the stake, and authority, expelled from the altar, finds a new and securer home upon the throne. The maintenance of Christian morality is to be transferred from the discredited ecclesiastical authorities to the hands of the State. Skeptical as to the existence of unicorns and salamanders, the age of Machiavelli and Henry VIII found food for its credulity in the worship of that rare monster, the God-fearing Prince.

Calvin

. . .

For Calvin, and still more his later interpreters, began their voyage lower down the stream. Unlike Luther, who saw economic life with the eyes of a peasant and a mystic, they approached it as men of affairs, disposed neither to idealize the patriarchal virtues of the peasant community, nor to regard with suspicion the mere fact of capitalist enterprise in commerce and finance. Like early Christianity and modern socialism, Calvinism was largely an urban movement; like them, in its earlier days, it was carried from country to country partly by emigrant traders and workmen; and its stronghold was precisely in those social groups to which the traditional scheme of social ethics, with its treatment of economic interests as a quite minor aspect of human affairs, must have seemed irrelevant or artificial. As was to be expected in the exponents of a faith which had its headquarters at Geneva, and later its most influential adherents in great business centers, like Antwerp with its industrial hinterland, London, and Amsterdam, its leaders addressed their teaching, not of course exclusively, but none the less primarily, to the classes engaged in trade and industry, who formed the most modern and progressive elements in the life of the age.

In doing so they naturally started from a frank recognition of the necessity of capital, credit and banking, large-scale commerce and finance, and the other practical facts of business life. They thus broke with the tradition which, regarding a preoccupation with economic interests "beyond what is necessary for subsistence" as reprehensible, had stigmatized the middleman as a parasite and the usurer as a thief. They set the profits of trade and finance, which to the medieval writer, as to Luther, only with difficulty escaped censure as *turpe lucrum*, on the same level of respectability as the earnings of the laborer and the rents of the landlord. "What reason is there," wrote Calvin to a correspondent, "why the income from business should not be larger than that from land-owning? Whence do the merchant's profits come, except from his own diligence and industry?" It was quite in accordance with the spirit of those words that Bucer, even while denouncing the frauds and avarice of merchants, should urge the English Government to undertake the development of the woollen industry on mercantilist lines.

Since it is the environment of the industrial and commercial classes which is foremost in the thoughts of Calvin and his followers, they have to make terms with its practical necessities. It is not that they abandon the claim of religion to moralize economic life, but that the life which they are concerned to moralize is one in which the main features of a commercial civilization are taken for granted, and that it is for application to such conditions that their teaching is designed. Early Calvinism, as we shall see, has its own rule, and a rigorous rule, for the conduct of economic affairs. But it no longer suspects the whole world of economic motives as alien to the life of the spirit, or distrusts the capitalist as one who has necessarily grown rich on the misfortunes of his neighbor, or regards poverty as in itself meritorious, and it is perhaps the first systematic body of religious teaching which can be said to recognize and applaud the economic virtues. Its enemy is not the accumulation of riches, but their misuse for purposes of self-indulgence or ostentation. Its ideal is a society which seeks wealth with the sober gravity of men who are conscious at once of disciplining their own characters by patient labor, and of devoting themselves to a service acceptable to God.

It is in the light of that change of social perspective that the doctrine of usury associated with the name of Calvin is to be interpreted. Its significance consisted, not in the phase which it marked in the technique of economic analysis, but in its admission to a new position of respectability of a powerful and growing body of social interests, which, however irrepressible in practice, had hitherto been regarded by religious theory as, at best, of dubious propriety, and, at worst, as frankly immoral. Strictly construed, the famous pronouncement strikes the modern reader rather by its rigor than by its indulgence. "Calvin," wrote an English divine a generation after his death, "deals with usurie as the apothecarie doth with poyson." The apologetic was just, for neither his letter to Œcolampadius, nor his sermon on the same subject, reveal any excessive tolerance for the trade of the financier. That interest is lawful, provided that it does not exceed an official maximum, that, even when a maximum is fixed, loans must be made *gratis* to the poor, that the borrower must reap as much advantage as the lender, that excessive security must not be exacted, that what is venial as an occasional expedient is reprehensible when carried on as a regular occupation, that no man may snatch economic gain for himself to the injury of his neighbor—a condonation of usury protected by such embarrassing entanglements can have offered but tepid consolation to the devout money-lender.

Contemporaries interpreted Calvin to mean that the debtor might properly be asked to concede some small part of his profits to the creditor with whose capital they had been earned, but that the exaction of interest was wrong if it meant that "the creditor becomes rich by the sweat of the debtor, and the debtor does not reap the reward of his labor." There have been ages in which such doctrines would have been regarded as an attack on financial enterprise rather than as a defense of it. Nor were Calvin's specific contributions to the theory of usury strikingly original. As a hard-headed lawyer, he was free both from the incoherence and from the idealism of Luther, and his doctrine was probably regarded by himself merely as one additional step in the long series of developments through which ecclesiastical jurisprudence on the subject had already gone. In emphasizing the difference between the interest wrung from the necessities of the poor and the interest which a prosperous merchant could earn with borrowed capital, he had been anticipated by Major; in his sanction of a moderate rate on loans to the rich, his position was the same as that already assumed, though with some hesitation, by Melanchthon. The picture of Calvin, the organizer and disciplinarian, as the parent of laxity in social ethics, is a legend. Like the author of another revolution in economic theory, he might have turned on his popularizers with the protest: "I am not a Calvinist."

Legends are apt, however, to be as right in substance as they are wrong in detail, and both its critics and its defenders were correct in regarding Calvin's treatment of capital as a watershed. What he did was to change the plane on which the discussion was conducted, by treating the ethics of money-lending, not as a matter to be decided by an appeal to a special body of doctrine on the subject of usury, but as a particular case of the general problem of the social relations of a Christian community, which must be solved in the light of existing circumstances. The significant feature in his discussion of the subject is that he assumes credit to be a normal and inevitable incident in the life of society. He therefore dismisses the oft-quoted passages from the Old Testament and the Fathers as irrelevant, because designed for conditions which no longer exist, argues that the payment of interest for capital is as reasonable as the payment of rent for land, and throws on the conscience of the individual the obligation of seeing that it does not exceed the amount dictated by natural justice and the golden rule. He makes, in short, a fresh start, argues that what is permanent is, not the rule *"non fœnerabis,"* but *"l'équité et la droiture,"* and appeals from Christian tradition to commercial common sense, which he is sanguine enough to hope will be Christian. On such a view all extortion is to be avoided by Christians. But capital and credit are indispensable; the financier is not a pariah, but a useful member of society; and lending at interest, provided that the rate is reasonable and that loans are made freely to the poor, is not *per se* more extortionate than any other of the economic transactions without which human affairs cannot be carried on. That acceptance of the realities of commercial practice as a starting-point was of momentous importance. It meant that Calvinism and its off-shoots took their stand on the side of the activities which were to be most characteristic of the future, and insisted that it was not by renouncing them, but by untiring concentration on the task of using for the glory of God the opportunities which they offered, that the Christian life could and must be lived.

It was on this practical basis of urban industry and commercial enterprise that the structure of Calvinistic social ethics was erected. Upon their theological background it would be audacious to enter. But even an amateur may be pardoned, if he feels that there have been few systems in which the practical conclusions flow by so inevitable a logic from the theological premises. "God not only foresaw," Calvin wrote, "the fall of the first man, . . . but also arranged all by the determination of his own will." Certain individuals he chose as his elect, predestined to salvation from eternity by "his gratuitous mercy, totally irrespective of human merit"; the remainder have been consigned to eternal damnation, "by a just and irreprehensible, but incomprehensible, judgment." Deliverance, in short, is the work, not of man himself, who can contribute nothing to it, but of an objective Power. Human effort, social institutions, the world of culture, are at best irrelevant to salvation, and at worst mischievous. They distract man from the true aim of his existence and encourage reliance upon broken reeds.

That aim is not personal salvation, but the glorification of God, to be sought, not by prayer only, but by action—the sanctification of the world by strife and labor. For Calvinism, with all its repudiation of personal merit, is intensely practical. Good works are not a way of attaining salvation, but they are indispensable as a proof that salvation has been attained. The central paradox of religious ethics—that only those are nerved with the courage needed to turn the world upside down, who are convinced that already, in a higher sense, it is disposed for the best by a Power of which they are the humble instruments—finds in it a special exemplification. For the Calvinist the world is ordained to show forth the majesty of God, and the duty of the Christian is to live for that end. His task is at once to discipline his individual life, and to create a sanctified society. The Church, the State, the community in which he lives, must not merely be a means of personal salvation, or minister to his temporal needs. It must be a "Kingdom of Christ," in which individual duties are performed by men conscious that they are "ever in their great Taskmaster's eye," and the whole fabric is preserved from corruption by a stringent and all-embracing discipline.

. . .

With the expansion of finance and international trade in the sixteenth century, it was this problem which faced the Church. Granted that I should love my neighbor as myself, the questions which, under modern conditions of large-scale organization, remain for solution are, Who precisely *is* my neighbor? and, How exactly am I to make my love for him effective in practice? To these questions the conventional religious teaching supplied no answer, for it had not even realized that they could be put. It had tried to moralize economic relations by treating every transaction as a case of personal conduct, involving personal responsibility. In an age of imper- sonal finance, world-markets and a capitalist organization of industry, its traditional social doctrines had no specific to offer, and were merely repeated, when, in order to be effective, they should have been thought out again from the beginning and formulated in new and living terms. It had endeavored to protect the peasant and the craftsman against the oppression of the money-lender and the monopolist. Faced with the problems of a wage-earning proletariat, it could do no more than repeat, with meaningless iteration, its traditional lore as to the duties of master to servant and servant to master. It had insisted that all men were brethren. But it did not occur to it to point out that, as a result of the new economic imperialism which was beginning to develop in the seventeenth century, the brethren of the English merchant were the Africans whom he kidnaped for slavery in America, or the American Indians whom he stripped of their lands, or the Indian craftsmen from whom he bought muslins and silks at starvation prices. Religion had not yet learned to console itself for the practical difficulty of applying its moral principles by clasping the comfortable formula that for the transactions of economic life no moral principles exist. But, for the problems involved in the association of men for economic purposes on the grand scale which was to be increasingly the rule in the future, the social doctrines advanced from the pulpit offered, in their traditional form, little guidance. Their practical ineffectiveness prepared the way for their theoretical abandonment.

They were abandoned because, on the whole, they deserved to be abandoned. The social teaching of the Church had ceased to count, because the Church itself had ceased to think. Energy in economic action, realist intelligence in economic thought—qualities were to be the note of the seventeenth century, when once the confusion of the Civil War had died down. When mankind is faced with the choice between exhilarating activities and piety imprisoned in a shriveled mass of desiccated formulæ, it will choose the former, though the energy be brutal and the intelligence narrow. In the age of Bacon and Descartes, bursting with clamorous interests and eager ideas, fruitful, above all, in the germs of economic speculation, from which was to grow the new science of Political Arithmetic, the social theory of the Church of England turned its face from the practical world, to pore over doctrines which, had their original authors been as impervious to realities as their later exponents, would never have been formulated. Naturally it was shouldered aside. It was neglected because it had become negligible.

. . .

The separation of economic from ethical interests, which was the note of all this movement, was in sharp opposition to religious tradition, and it did not establish itself without a struggle. Even in the very capital of European commerce and finance, an embittered controversy was occasioned by the refusal to admit usurers to communion or to confer degrees upon them; it was only after a storm of pamphleteering, in which the theological faculty of the University of Utrecht performed prodigies of zeal and ingenuity, that the States of Holland and West Friesland closed the agitation by declaring that the Church had no concern with questions of banking. In the French Calvinist Churches, the decline of discipline had caused lamentations a generation earlier. In America, the theocracy of Massachusetts, merciless alike to religious liberty and to economic license, was about to be undermined by the rise of new States like Rhode Island and Pennsylvania, whose tolerant, individualist and utilitarian temper was destined to find its greatest representative in the golden common sense of Benjamin Franklin. "The sin of our too great fondness for trade, to the neglecting of our more valuable interests," wrote a Scottish divine in 1709, when Glasgow was on the eve of a triumphant outburst of commercial enterprise, "I humbly think will be written upon our judgment . . . . I am sure the Lord is remarkably frowning upon our trade . . . since it was put in the room of religion."

In England, the growing disposition to apply exclusively economic standards to social relations evoked from Puritan writers and divines vigorous protests against usurious interest, extortionate prices and the oppression of tenants by landlords. The faithful, it was urged, had interpreted only too literally the doctrine that the sinner was saved, not by works, but by faith. Usury, "in time of Popery an odious thing," had become a scandal. Professors, by their covetousness, caused the enemies of the reformed religion to blaspheme. The exactions of the forestaller and regrater were never so monstrous or so immune from interference. The hearts of the rich were never so hard, nor the necessities of the poor so neglected. "The poor able to work are suffered to beg; the impotent, aged and sick are not sufficiently provided for, but almost starved with the allowance of 3d. and 4d. a piece a week. . . . These are the last times indeed. Men generally are all for themselves. And some would set up such, having a form of religion, without the power of it."

These utterances came, however, from that part of the Puritan mind which looked backward. That which looked forward found in the rapidly growing spirit of economic enterprise something not uncongenial to its own temper, and went out to welcome it as an ally. What in Calvin had been a qualified concession to practical exigencies appeared in some of his later followers as a frank idealization of the life of the trader, as the service of God and the training-ground of the soul. Discarding the suspicion of economic motives, which had been as characteristic of the reformers as of medieval theologians, Puritanism in its later phases added a halo of ethical sanctification to the appeal of economic expediency, and offered a moral creed, in which the duties of religion and the calls of business ended their long estrangement in an unanticipated reconciliation. Its spokesmen pointed out, it is true, the peril to the soul involved in a single-minded concentration on economic interests. The enemy, however, was not riches, but the bad habits sometimes associated with them, and its warnings against an excessive preoccupation with the pursuit of gain worn more and more the air of after-thoughts, appended to teaching the main tendency and emphasis of which were little affected by these incidental qualifications. It insisted, in short, that money-making, if not free from spiritual dangers, was not a danger and nothing else, but that it could be, and ought to be, carried on for the greater glory of God.

The conception to which it appealed to bridge the gulf sprang from the very heart of Puritan theology. It was that expressed in the characteristic and oft-used phrase, "a Calling." The rational order of the universe is the work of God, and its plan requires that the individual should labor for God's glory. There is a spiritual calling, and a temporal calling. It is the first duty of the Christian to know and believe in God; it is by faith that he will be saved. But faith is not a mere profession such as that of Talkative of Prating Row, whose "religion is to make a noise." The only genuine faith is the faith which produces works. "At the day of Doom men shall be judged according to their fruits. It will not be said then, Did you believe? but, Were you doers, or talkers only?" The second duty of the Christian is to labor in the affairs of practical life, and this second duty is subordinate only to the first. "God," wrote a Puritan divine, "doth call every man and woman . . . to serve him in some peculiar employment in this world, both for their own and the common good. . . . The Great Governour of the world hath appointed to every man his proper post and province, and let him be never so active out of his sphere, he will be at a great loss, if he do not keep his own vineyard and mind his own business."

From this reiterated insistence on secular obligations as imposed by the divine will, it follows that, not withdrawal from the world, but the conscientious discharge of the duties of business, is among the loftiest of religious and moral virtues. "The begging friars and such monks as live only to themselves and to their formal devotion, but do employ themselves in no one thing to further their own subsistence or the good of mankind . . . yet have the confidence to boast of this their course as a state of perfection; which in very deed, as to the worthiness of it, falls short of the poorest cobbler, for his is a calling of God, and theirs is none." The idea was not a new one. Luther had advanced it as a weapon against monasticism. But for Luther, with his patriarchal outlook on economic affairs, the calling means normally that state of life in which the individual has been set by Heaven, and against which it is impiety to rebel. On the lips of Puritan divines, it is not an invitation to resignation, but the bugle-call which summons the elect to the long battle which will end only with their death. "The world is all before them." They are to hammer out their salvation, not merely *in vocatione*, but *per vocationem*. The calling is not a condition in which the individual is born, but a strenuous and exacting enterprise, to be undertaken, indeed, under the guidance of Providence, but to be chosen by each man for himself, with a deep sense of his solemn responsibilities. "God hath given to man reason for this use, that he should first consider, then choose, then put in execution; and it is a preposterous and brutish thing to fix or fall upon any weighty business, such as a calling or condition of life, without a careful pondering it in the balance of sound reason."

Laborare est orare. By the Puritan moralist the ancient maxim is repeated with a new and intenser significance. The labor which he idealizes is not simply a requirement imposed by nature, or a punishment for the sin of Adam. It is itself a kind of ascetic discipline, more rigorous than that demanded of any order of mendicants—a discipline imposed by the will of God, and to be undergone, not in solitude, but in the punctual discharge of secular duties. It is not merely an economic means, to be laid aside when physical needs have been satisfied. It is a spiritual end, for in it alone can the soul find health, and it must be continued as an ethical duty long after it has ceased to be a material necessity. Work thus conceived stands at the very opposite pole from "good works," as they were understood, or misunderstood, by Protestants. They, it was thought, had been a series of single transactions, performed as compensation for particular sins, or out of anxiety to acquire merit. What is required of the Puritan is not individual meritorious acts, but a holy life— a system in which every element is grouped round a central idea, the service of God, from which all disturbing irrelevances have been pruned, and to which all minor interests are subordinated.

His conception of that life was expressed in the words, "Be wholly taken up in diligent business of your lawful callings, when you are not exercised in the more immediate service of God." In order to deepen his spiritual life, the Christian must be prepared to narrow it. He "is blind in no man's cause, but best sighted in his own. He confines himself to the circle of his own affairs and thrusts not his fingers in needless fires . . . He sees the falseness of it [the world] and therefore learns to trust himself ever, others so far as not to be damaged by their disappointment." There must be no idle leisure: "those that are prodigal of their time despise their own souls." Religion must be active, not merely contemplative. Contemplation is, indeed, a kind of self-indulgence. "To neglect this [i.e., bodily employment and mental labor] and say, 'I will pray and meditate,' is as if your servant should refuse your greatest work, and tye himself to some lesser, easie part. . . . God hath commanded you some way or other to labour for your daily bread." The rich are no more excused from work than the poor, though they may rightly use their riches to select some occupation specially serviceable to others. Covetousness is a danger to the soul, but it is not so grave a danger as sloth. "The standing pool is prone to putrefaction: and it were better to beat down the body and to keep it in subjection by a laborious calling, than through luxury to become a cast-away." So far from poverty being meritorious, it is a duty to choose the more profitable occupation. "If God show you a way in which you may lawfully get more than in another way (without wrong to your soul or to any other), if you refuse this, and choose the less gainful way, you cross one of the ends of your Calling, and you refuse to be God's steward." Luxury, unrestrained pleasure, personal extravagance, can have no place in a Christian's conduct, for "every penny which is laid out . . . must be done as by God's own appointment." Even excessive devotion to friends and relations is to be avoided. "It is an irrational act, and therefore not fit for a rational creature, to love any one farther than reason will allow us. . . . It very often taketh up men's minds so as to hinder their love to God." The Christian life, in short, must be systematic and organized, the work of an iron will and a cool intelligence.

.   .   .

Few tricks of the unsophisticated intellect are more curious than the naïve psychology of the business man, who ascribes his achievements to his own unaided efforts, in bland unconsciousness of a social order without whose continuous support and vigilant protection he would be as a lamb bleating in the desert. That individualist complex owes part of its self-assurance to the suggestion of Puritan moralists, that practical success is at once the sign and the reward of ethical superiority. "No question," argued a Puritan pamphleteer, "but it [riches] should be the portion rather of the godly than of the wicked, were it good for them; for godliness hath the promises of this life as well as of the life to come." The demonstration that distress is a proof of demerit, though a singular commentary on the lives of Christian saints and sages, has always been popular with the prosperous. By the lusty plutocracy of the Restoration, roaring after its meat, and not indisposed, if it could not find it elsewhere, to seek it from God, it was welcomed with a shout of applause.

A society which reverences the attainment of riches as the supreme felicity will naturally be disposed to regard the poor as damned in the next world, if only to justify itself for making their life a hell in this. Advanced by men of religion as a tonic for the soul, the doctrine of the danger of pampering poverty was hailed by the rising school of Political Arithmeticians as a sovereign cure for the ills of society. For, if the theme of the moralist was that an easy-going indulgence undermined character, the theme of the economist was that it was economically disastrous and financially ruinous. The Poor Law is the mother of idleness, "men and women growing so idle and proud that they will not work, but lie upon the parish wherein they dwell for maintenance." It discourages thrift; "if shame or fear of punishment makes him earn his dayly bread, he will do no more; his children are the charge of the parish and his old age his recess from labour or care." It keeps up wages, since "it encourages wilful and evil-disposed persons to impose what wages they please upon their labours; and herein they are so refractory to reason and the benefit of the nation that, when corn and provisions are cheap, they will not work for less wages than when they were dear." To the landowner who cursed the poor-rates, and the clothier who grumbled at the high cost of labor, one school of religious thought now brought the comforting assurance that morality itself would be favoured by a reduction of both.

.   .   .

It would be misleading to dwell on the limitations of Puritan ethics without emphasizing the enormous contribution of Puritanism to political freedom and social progress. The foundation of democracy is the sense of spiritual independence which nerves the individual to stand alone against the powers of this world, and in England, where squire and parson, lifting arrogant eyebrows at the insolence of the lower orders, combined to crush popular agitation, as a menace at once to society and to the Church, it is probable that democracy owes more to Nonconformity than to any other single movement. The virtues of enterprise, diligence and thrift are the indispensable foundation of any complex and vigorous civilization. It was Puritanism which, by investing them with a supernatural sanction, turned them from an unsocial eccentricity into a habit and a religion. Nor would it be difficult to find notable representatives of the Puritan spirit in whom the personal austerity, which was the noblest aspect of the new ideal, was combined with a profound consciousness of social solidarity, which was the noblest aspect of that which it displaced. Firmin the philanthropist, and Bellers the Quaker, whom Owen more than a century later hailed as the father of his doctrines, were pioneers of Poor Law reform. The Society of Friends, in an age when the divorce between religion and social ethics was almost complete, met the prevalent doctrine, that it was permissible to take such gain as the market offered, by insisting on the obligation of good conscience and forbearance in economic transactions, and on the duty to make the honorable maintenance of the brother in distress a common charge.

The general climate and character of a country are not altered, however, by the fact that here and there it has peaks which rise into an ampler air. The distinctive note of Puritan teaching was different. It was individual responsibility, not social obligation. Training its pupils to the mastery of others through the mastery of self, it prized as a crown of glory the qualities which arm the spiritual athlete for his solitary contest with a hostile world, and dismissed concern with the social order as the prop of weaklings and the Capua of the soul. Both the excellences and defects of that attitude were momentous for the future. It is sometimes suggested that the astonishing outburst of industrial activity which took place after 1760 created a new type of economic character, as well as a new system of economic organization. In reality, the ideal which was later to carry all before it, in the person of the inventor and engineer and captain of industry, was well established among Englishmen before the end of the seventeenth century. Among the numerous forces which had gone to form it, some not inconsiderable part may reasonably be ascribed to the emphasis on the life of business enterprise as the appropriate field for Christian endeavor, and on the qualities needed for success in it, which was characteristic of Puritanism. These qualities, and the admiration of them, remained, when the religious reference, and the restraints which it imposed, had weakened or disappeared.

Societies, like individuals, have their moral crises and their spiritual revolutions. The student can observe the results which these cataclysms produce, but he can hardly without presumption attempt to appraise them, for it is at the fire which they kindled that his own small taper has been lit. The rise of a naturalistic science of society, with all its magnificent promise of fruitful action and of intellectual light; the abdication of the Christian Churches from departments of economic conduct and social theory long claimed as their province; the general acceptance by thinkers of a scale of ethical values, which turned the desire for pecuniary gain from a perilous, if natural, frailty into the idol of philosophers and the mainspring of society—such movements are written large over the history of the tempestuous age which lies between the Reformation and the full light of the eighteenth century. Their consequences have been worked into the very tissue of modern civilization. Posterity still stands too near their source to discern the ocean into which these streams will flow.

In an historical age the relativity of political doctrines is the tritest of commonplaces. But social psychology continues too often to be discussed in serene indifference to the categories of time and place, and economic interests are still popularly treated as through they formed a kingdom over which the *Zeitgeist* bears no sway. In reality, though inherited dispositions may be constant from generation to generation, the system of valuations, preferences and ideals—the social environment within which individual character functions—is in process of continuous change, and it is in the conception of the place to be assigned to economic interests in the life of society that change has in recent centuries been most comprehensive in its scope, and most sensational in its consequences. The isolation of economic aims as a specialized object of concentrated and systematic effort, the erection of economic criteria into an independent and authoritative standard of social expediency, are phenomena which, though familiar enough in classical antiquity, appear, at least on a grand scale, only at a comparatively recent date in the history of later civilizations. The conflict between the economic outlook of East and West, which impresses the traveller today, finds a parallel in the contrast between medieval and modern economic ideas, which strikes the historian.

The elements which combined to produce that revolution are too numerous to be summarized in any neat formula. But, side by side with the expansion of trade and the rise of new classes to political power, there was a further cause, which, if not the most conspicuous, was not the least fundamental. It was the contraction of the territory within which the spirit of religion was conceived to run. The criticism which dismisses the concern of Churches with economic relations and social organization as a modern innovation finds little support in past history. What requires explanation is not the view that these matters are part of the province of religion, but the view that they are not. When the age of the Reformation begins, economics is still a branch of ethics, and ethics of theology: all human activities are treated as falling within a single scheme, whose character is determined by the spiritual destiny of mankind; the appeal of theorists is to natural law, not to utility; the legitimacy of economic transactions is tried by reference, less to the movements of the market, than to moral standards derived from the traditional teaching of the Christian Church; the Church itself is regarded as a society wielding theoretical, and sometimes practical, authority in social affairs. The secularization of political thought, which was to be the work of the next two centuries, had profound reactions on social speculation, and by the Restoration the whole perspective, at least in England, has been revolutionized. Religion has been converted from the keystone which holds together the social edifice into one department within it, and the idea of a rule of right is replaced by economic expediency as the arbiter of policy and the criterion of conduct. From a spiritual being, who, in order to survive, must devote a reasonable attention to economic interest, man seems sometimes to have become an economic animal, who will be prudent, nevertheless, if he takes due precautions to assure his spiritual well-being.

. . .

Circumstances alter from age to age, and the practical interpretation of moral principles must alter with them. Few who consider dispassionately the facts of social history will be disposed to deny that the exploitation of the weak by the powerful, organized for purposes of economic gain, buttressed by imposing systems of law, and screened by decorous draperies of virtuous sentiment and resounding rhetoric, has been a permanent feature in the life of most communities that the world has yet seen. But the quality in modern societies which is most sharply opposed to the teaching ascribed to the Founder of the Christian Faith lies deeper than the exceptional failures and abnormal follies against which criticism is most commonly directed. It consists in the assumption, accepted by most reformers with hardly less *naïveté* than by the defenders of the estabished order, that the attainment of material riches is the supreme object of human endeavor and the final criterion of human success. Such a philosophy, plausible, militant, and not indisposed, when hard pressed, to silence criticism by persecution, may triumph or may decline. What is certain is that it is the negation of any system of thought or morals which can, except by a metaphor, be described as Christian. Compromise is as impossible between the Church of Christ and the idolatry of wealth, which is the practical religion of capitalist societies, as it was between the Church and the State idolatry of the Roman Empire.

"Modern capitalism," writes Mr. Keynes, "is absolutely irreligious, without internal union, without much public spirit, often, though not always, a mere congeries of possessors and pursuers." It is that whole system of appetites and values, with its deification of the life of snatching to hoard, and hoarding to snatch, which which now, in the hour of its triumph, while the plaudits of the crowd still ring in the ears of the gladiators and the laurels are still unfaded on their brows, seems sometimes to leave a taste as of ashes on the lips of a civilization which has brought to the conquest of its material environment resources unknown in earlier ages, but which has not yet learned to master itself. It was against that system, while still in its supple and insinuating youth, before success had caused it to throw aside the mask of innocence, and while its true nature was unknown even to itself, that the saints and sages of earlier ages launched their warnings and their denunciations. The language in which theologians and preachers expressed their horror of the sin of covetousness may appear to the modern reader too murkily sulphurous; their precepts on the contracts of business and the disposition of property may seem an impracticable pedantry. But rashness is a more agreeable failing than cowardice, and, when to speak is unpopular, it is less pardonable to be silent than to say too much. Posterity has, perhaps, as much to learn from the whirlwind eloquence with which Latimer scourged injustice and oppression as from the sober respectability of the judicious Paley—who himself, since there are depths below depths, was regarded as a dangerous revolutionary by George III.

Buddhist Economics

E. F. Schumacher

E. F. Schumacher was advisor to Britain's National Coal Board from 1950 to 1970 and helped organize the Intermediate Technology Development Group, which publishes a magazine of intermediate tools, etc., particularly for under-developed nations. His celebrated book, *Small Is Beautiful*, was published in 1973.

'Right Livelihood' is one of the requirements of the Buddha's Noble Eightfold Path. It is clear, therefore, that there must be such a thing as Buddhist economics.

Buddhist countries have often stated that they wish to remain faithful to their heritage. So Burma: "The New Burma sees no conflict between religious values and economic progress. Spiritual health and material wellbeing are not enemies: they are natural allies." Or: "We can blend successfully the religious and spiritual values of our heritage with the benefits of modern technology." Or: "We Burmans have a sacred duty to conform both our dreams and our acts to our faith. This we shall ever do."

All the same, such countries invariably assume that they can model their economic development plans in accordance with modern economics, and they call upon modern economists from so-called advanced countries to advise them, to formulate the policies to be pursued, and to construct the grand design for development, the Five-Year Plan or whatever it may be called. No one seems to think that a Buddhist way of life would call for Buddhist economics, just as the modern materialist way of life has brought forth modern economics.

Economists themselves, like most specialists, normally suffer from a kind of metaphysical blindness, assuming that theirs is a science of absolute and invariable truths, without any presuppositions. Some go as far as to claim that economic laws are as free from "metaphysics" or "values" as the law of gravitation. We need not, however, get involved in arguments of methodology. Instead, let us take some fundamentals and see what they look like when viewed by a modern economist and a Buddhist economist.

There is universal agreement that a fundamental source of wealth is human labour. Now, the modern economist has been brought up to consider 'labour' or work as little more than a necessary evil. From the point of view of the employer, it is in any case simply an item of cost, to be reduced to a minimum if it cannot be eliminated altogether, say, by automation. From the point of view of the workman, it is a "disutility"; to work is to make a sacrifice on one's leisure and comfort, and

Source: E. F. Schumacher, *Small Is Beautiful: Economics as if People Mattered* (New York, 1973), pp. 50–58. Copyright © 1973 by E. F. Schumacher. Reprinted by permission of Harper & Row, Publishers, Inc., and Blond & Briggs Ltd.

wages are a kind of compensation for the sacrifice. Hence the ideal from the point of view of the employer is to have output without employees, and the ideal from the point of view of the employee is to have income without employment.

The consequences of these attitudes both in theory and in practice are, of course, extremely far-reaching. If the ideal with regard to work is to get rid of it, every method that "reduces the work load" is a good thing. The most potent method, short of automation, is the so-called "division of labour" and the classical example is the pin factory eulogised in Adam Smith's *Wealth of Nations*. Here it is not a matter of ordinary specialisation, which mankind has practised from time immemorial, but of dividing up every complete process of production into minute parts, so that the final product can be produced at great speed without anyone having had to contribute more than a totally insignificant and, in most cases, unskilled movement of his limbs.

The Buddhist point of view takes the function of work to be at least threefold: to give a man a chance to utilise and develop his faculties; to enable him to overcome his egocentredness by joining with other people in a common task; and to bring forth the goods and services needed for a becoming existence. Again, the consequences that flow from this view are endless. To organise work in such a manner that it becomes meaningless, boring, stultifying, or nerve-racking for the worker would be little short of criminal; it would indicate a greater concern with goods than with people, an evil lack of compassion and a soul-destroying degree of attachment to the most primitive side of this worldly existence. Equally, to strive for leisure as an alternative to work would be considered a complete misunderstanding of one of the basic truths of human existence, namely that work and leisure are complementary parts of the same living process and cannot be separated without destroying the joy of work and the bliss of leisure.

From the Buddhist point of view, there are therefore two types of mechanisation which must be clearly distinguished: one that enhances a man's skill and power and one that turns the work of man over to a mechanical slave, leaving man in a position of having to serve the slave. How to tell the one from the other? "The craftsman himself," says Ananda Coomaraswamy, a man equally competent to talk about the modern west as the ancient east, "can always, if allowed to, draw the delicate distinction between the machine and the tool. The carpet loom is a tool, a contrivance for holding warp threads at a stretch for the pile to be woven round them by the craftsmen's fingers; but the power loom is a machine, and its significance as a destroyer of culture lies in the fact that it does the essentially human part of the work." It is clear, therefore, that Buddhist economics must be very different from the economics of modern materialism, since the Buddhist sees the essence of civilisation not in a multiplication of wants but in the purification of human character. Character, at the same time, is formed primarily by a man's work. And work, properly conducted in conditions of human dignity and freedom, blesses those who do it and equally their products. The Indian philosopher and economist J. C. Kumarappa sums the matter up as follows:

"If the nature of the work is properly appreciated and applied, it will stand in the same relation to the higher faculties as food is to the physical body. It nourishes and enlivens the higher man and urges him to produce the best he is capable of. It directs his free will along the proper course and disciplines the animal in him into progressive channels. It furnishes an excellent background for man to display his scale of values and develop his personality."

If a man has no chance of obtaining work he is in a desperate position, not simply because he lacks an income but because he lacks this nourishing and enlivening factor of disciplined work which nothing can replace. A modern economist may engage in highly sophisticated calculations on whether full employment "pays" or whether it might be more "economic" to run an economy at less than full employment so as to ensure a greater mobility of labour, a better stability of wages, and so forth. His fundamental criterion of success is simply the total quantity of goods produced during a given period of time. "If the marginal urgency of goods is low," says Professor Galbraith in *The Affluent Society*, "then so is the urgency of employing the last man or the last million men in the labour force." And again: "If . . . we can afford some unemployment in the interest of stability—a proposition, incidentally, of impeccably conservative antecedents—then we can afford to give those who are unemployed the goods that enable them to sustain their accustomed standard of living."

From a Buddhist point of view, this is standing the truth on its head by considering goods as more important than people and consumption as more important than creative activity. It means shifting the emphasis from the worker to the product of work, that is, from the human to the sub-human, a surrender to the forces of evil. The very start of Buddhist economic planning would be a planning for full employment, and the primary purpose of this would in fact be employment for everyone who needs an "outside" job: it would not be the maximisation of employment nor the maximisation of production. Women, on the whole, do not need an "outside" job, and the large-scale employment of women in offices or factories would be considered a sign of serious economic failure. In particular, to let mothers of young children work in factories while the children run wild would be as uneconomic in the eyes of a Buddhist economist as the employment of a skilled worker as a soldier in the eyes of a modern economist.

Whilst the materialist is mainly interested in goods, the Buddhist is mainly interested in liberation. But Buddhism is "The Middle Way" and therefore in no way antagonistic to physical well-being. It is not wealth that stands in the way of liberation but the attachment to wealth; not the enjoyment of pleasurable things but the craving for them. The keynote of Buddhist economics, therefore, is simplicity and non-violence. From an economist's point of view, the marvel of the Buddhist way of life is the utter rationality of its pattern—amazingly small means leading to extraordinarily satisfactory results.

For the modern economist this is very difficult to understand. He is used to measuring the "standard of living" by the amount of annual consumption, assuming all the time that a man who consumes more is "better off" than a man who consumes less. A Buddhist economist would consider this approach excessively irrational: since consumption is merely a means to human well-being, the aim should be to obtain the maximum of well-being with the minimum of consumption. Thus, if the purpose of clothing is a certain amount of temperature comfort and an attractive appearance, the task is to attain this purpose with the smallest possible effort, that is, with the smallest annual destruction of cloth and with the help of designs that involve the smallest possible input of toil. The less toil there is, the more time and strength is left for artistic creativity. It would be highly uneconomic, for instance, to go in for complicated tailoring, like the modern west, when a much more beautiful effect can be achieved by the skilful draping of uncut material. It would be the height of folly to make material so that it should wear out quickly and the height of barbarity to make anything ugly, shabby or mean. What has just been said about clothing applies equally to all other human requirements. The ownership and the consumption of goods is a means to an end, and Buddhist economics is the systematic study of how to attain given ends with the minimum means.

Modern economics, on the other hand, considers consumption to be the sole end and purpose of all economic activity, taking the factors of production—land, labour, and capital—as the means. The former, in short, tries to maximise human satisfactions by the optimal pattern of consumption, while the latter tries to maximise consumption by the optimal pattern of productive effort. It is easy to see that the effort needed to sustain a way of life which seeks to attain the optimal pattern of consumption is likely to be much smaller than the effort needed to sustain a drive for maximum consumption. We need not be surprised, therefore, that the pressure and strain of living is very much less in, say, Burma than it is in the United States, in spite of the fact that the amount of labour-saving machinery used in the former country is only a minute fraction of the amount used in the latter.

Simplicity and non-violence are obviously closely related. The optimal pattern of consumption, producing a high degree of human satisfaction by means of a relatively low rate of consumption, allows people to live without great pressure and strain and to fulfil the primary injunction of Buddhist teaching: "Cease to do evil; try to do good." As physical resources are everywhere limited, people satisfying their needs by means of a modest use of resources are obviously less likely to be at each other's throats than people depending upon a high rate of use. Equally, people who live in highly self-sufficient local communities are less likely to get involved in large-scale violence than people whose existence depends on world-wide systems of trade.

From the point of view of Buddhist economics, therefore, production from local resources for local needs is the most rational way of economic life, while dependence on imports from afar and the consequent need to produce for export to unknown and distant peoples is highly uneconomic and justifiable only in exceptional cases and on a small scale. Just as the modern economist would admit that a high rate of consumption of transport services between a man's home and his place of work signifies a misfortune and not a high standard of life, so the Buddhist economist would hold that to satisfy human wants from faraway sources rather than from sources nearby signifies failure rather than success. The former tends to take statistics showing an increase in the number of ton/miles per head of the population carried by a country's transport system as proof of economic progress, while to the latter—the Buddhist economist—the same statistics would indicate a highly undesirable deterioration in the *pattern* of consumption.

Another striking difference between modern economics and Buddhist economics arises over the use of natural resources. Bertrand de Jouvenel, the eminent French political philosopher, has characterised "western man" in words which may be taken as a fair description of the modern economist:

"He tends to count nothing as an expenditure, other than human effort; he does not seem to mind how much mineral matter he wastes and, far worse, how much living matter he destroys. He does not seem to realise at all that human life is a dependent part of an ecosystem of many different forms of life. As the world is ruled from towns where men are cut off from any form of life other than human, the feeling of belonging to an ecosystem is not revived. This results in a harsh and improvident treatment of things upon which we ultimately depend, such as water and trees."

The teaching of the Buddha, on the other hand, enjoins a reverent and non-violent attitude not only to all sentient beings but also, with great emphasis, to trees. Every follower of the Buddha ought to plant a tree every few years and look after it until it is safely established, and the Buddhist economist can demonstrate without difficulty that the universal observation of this rule would result in a high rate of genuine economic development independent of any foreign aid. Much of the economic decay of south-east Asia (as of many other parts of the world) is undoubtedly due to a needless and shameful neglect of trees.

Modern economics does not distinguish between renewable and non-renewable materials, as its very method is to equalise and quantify everything by means of a money price. Thus, taking various alternative fuels, like coal, oil, wood, or water-power: the only difference between them recognised by modern economics is relative cost per equivalent unit. The cheapest is automatically the one to be preferred, as to do otherwise would be irrational and "uneconomic". From a Buddhist point of view, of course, this will not do; the essential difference between non-renewable fuels like coal and oil on the one hand and renewable fuels like wood and water-power on the other cannot be simply overlooked. Non-renewable goods must be used only if they are indispensable, and then only with the greatest care and the most meticulous concern for conservation. To use them heedlessly or extravagantly is an act of violence, and while complete non-violence may not be attainable on this earth, there is nonetheless an ineluctable duty on man to aim at the ideal of non-violence in all he does.

Just as a modern European economist would not consider it a great economic achievement if all European art treasures were sold to America at attractive prices, so the Buddhist economist would insist that a population basing its economic life on non-renewable fuels is living parasitically, on capital instead of income. Such a way of life could have no permanence and could therefore be justified only as a purely temporary expedient. As the world's resources of non-renewable fuels—coal, oil and natural gas—are exceedingly unevenly distributed over the globe and undoubtedly limited in quantity, it is clear that their exploitation at an ever-increasing rate is an act of violence against nature which must almost inevitably lead to violence between men.

This fact alone might give food for thought even to those people in Buddhist countries who care nothing for the religious and spiritual values of their heritage and ardently desire to embrace the materialism of modern economics at the fastest possible speed. Before they dismiss Buddhist economics as nothing better than a nostalgic dream, they might wish to consider whether the path of economic development outlined by modern economics is likely to lead them to places where they really want to be. Towards the end of his courageous book *The Challenge of*

Man's Future, Professor Harrison Brown of the California Institute of Technology gives the following appraisal:

"Thus we see that, just as industrial society is fundamentally unstable and subject to reversion to agrarian existence, so within it the conditions which offer individual freedom are unstable in their ability to avoid the conditions which impose rigid organisation and totalitarian control. Indeed, when we examine all of the foreseeable difficulties which threaten the survival of industrial civilisation, it is difficult to see how the achievement of stability and the maintenance of individual liberty can be made compatible."

Even if this were dismissed as a long-term view there is the immediate question of whether "modernisation." as currently practised without regard to religious and spiritual values, is actually producing agreeable results. As far as the masses are concerned, the results appear to be disastrous—a collapse of the rural economy, a rising tide of unemployment in town and country, and the growth of a city proletariat without nourishment for either body or soul.

It is in the light of both immediate experience and long-term prospects that the study of Buddhist economics could be recommended even to those who believe that economic growth is more important than any spiritual or religious values. For it is not a question of choosing between "modern growth" and "traditional stagnation." It is a question of finding the right path of development, the Middle Way between materialist heedlessness and traditionalist immobility, in short, of finding "Right Livelihood."

James Gollin's
Worldly Goods:
A Review

Material for Thought is a journal, published by the Far West Press of San Francisco, which offers reviews and essays dealing with "psychology and man's situation on earth." Each issue is an effort at what might be termed "spiritual criticism." "Our aim," writes the editor, "is to communicate a kind of insight or vision that throws light on the contemporary materialism without arousing false expectations or helpless reactions of self-esteem and self-pity." The contributions are usually anonymous.

In our understanding of Christianity, there is great ambiguity about the idea of community. The Catholic Church, by its very name, calls for a community of man-

Source: *Material for Thought* (1974), pp. 51–54. Reprinted by permission of Far West Press.

kind, yet the most creative epoch in church history was the great monastic period of the Middle Ages. The same is true of the other religions of man; their transforming power seems to be greatest when in some way they exist apart, providing within our "horizonal" world a "vertical" hierarchy, and thus a basis for the exchange of human and divine energies.

At first glance, *Worldly Goods* by James Gollin seems utterly unrelated to this question of spiritual exchange. It is a study of the wealth of the Catholic Church done in workmanlike fashion by a financial reporter fascinated by a unique phenomenon. For example, in the United States alone the wealth of the Church is estimated at $42 billion, comprising 175 cathedrals and the structures and treasures of 18,244 parishes. The Church operates 2,000 high schools, 10,000 grade schools, 283 colleges and universities and 220 schools of nursing, every one of these being a separate enterprise with its own staff, rules and financial structure. Gollin examines the impact of such wealth on the economy of America, and paints a detailed picture of a spiritual organization struggling to maintain its direction amid the complexities of the contemporary social, political and economic order.

Yet the relationship of the Church to its wealth, particularly to its money, has ramifications beyond those which Gollin treats.

As the expression of man's relationship to the external world, money is like a kind of plasma circulating between men and things. Those who wish to cut off the exchange between the psyche and the world give up money. They beg in the streets or simply wait for sustenance, accounting the world relevant only to their bodies and not to their minds. But apart from such individuals, the great religions have sought to make impress upon the material world; civilisations in India, Persia and the West have been generated by men who in ordinary circumstances lived the values of the spiritually great. Seen in the large, religion has taken man on earth to be a medium of transmission between truth and matter.

It is within the world of men that money has its most obvious function as an expression of exchange. It follows that the nature of a community can be studied in its use of money. Thus, the Church as a community apart from the rest of mankind finds its problems writ large in its present financial plight. Mr. Gollin is amazed at the inefficiency and fiscal mismanagement of the Church; he recommends business methods that seem to work with modern corporations, even though acknowledging that the Church is not like other businesses. He calls special attention to the extreme decentralization of the Church and to the unique way it separates strictly religious institutions from related activities such as schools and hospitals.

Yet in a sense what Gollin is urging—intelligently, from a secular point of view—is that the Church pretend men are one community even before they are such. Were it to open itself utterly to the professional money managers (to computerize operations, to invest money more cleverly, to liquify more capital), would it be absorbed into the community of man, rather than absorb men into the community of Christ? Perhaps it is naive to think that only ideas and words separate a religion from the world in the dynamic way that makes it operate as a rope suspended in the midst of human suffering. A Church that is failing financially, like a Church that is rich in treasure—what does it demand of men? Are the religious organizations of the day which move easily in and out of social, financial and political situations able to generate the power of spiritual relationship among their followers?

Can such organizations accumulate the psychological energy necessary to give light as well as food and shelter to their members?

It is easy to forget that the Catholic Church, with a world-wide membership of 614 million people, has survived two thousand years, while every business we know of fails or changes into something completely different in a relatively short time. Why has it survived in a world that has always been worldly? Perhaps it is because it functions to compel a sort of attention on the part of man, of which the flow of money is the most visible expression. Psychologically, the law of charity and grace demands of men that they give in order to receive, give love, money, attention—all human energy must be spent before divine energy reaches in. One wonders if the ebb and flow of Church wealth should be understood in a similar way.

It has been said that when Jesus tore away the veil of the temple he established religion without an inner community and, in that connection, one remembers his many sayings that nothing will be hidden. Yet the fact remains that the Church is an inner community within the community of man and that all of nature is structured on the functional principle of nucleus, radiation and periphery.

But is anyone in the Church thinking along these lines in the current financial crisis? A Bishop is absolutely at the head of the diocese and of the funds available. He must therefore administer both the money of the parishes and money of the schools and hospitals. Do the Bishops see their situation as a unique vantage point from which to understand both the purification and the degradation of man's relationship to God? In the former case, money comes from plate donations (which in America add up to a $2 billion a year cash flow), and the diocese is dependent on the charity and respect of the congregation. Here the Bishop faces the temptation to make money flow downwards toward the Church—as money flows downwards in the direction of ordinary human desire in worldly business. Should he succumb to this temptation by psychologically *compelling* money from the faithful he obstructs their opportunity to cut a thread from the bonds of worldly care. Perhaps the popular Church has lost the voluntary struggle with the body that is part of the monk's approach to God. But through the medium of money the voluntary struggle for a purer emotion can surely be placed before anyone in this world.

The situation is different with respect to the other enterprises of the Church which are financially autonomous. These provide an arena for applying the canons of Christian teaching to the impartial test of ordinary life with its complex mixture of events and human types. Here Christianity is transmitted through good works done in the rough-and-tumble of everyday human forces. The schools and hospitals are businesses and to make them function money must to some extent flow downwards; they must be efficient, though not absolutely so; they must make money, but only enough to function well. Here Christianity radiates outwards like the arterial pulse of the heart.

Does the Church wish to preserve this ancient systole and diastole? How far out can its business activity go and still allow for a return such that its money, circulating through mankind, helps in the exchanges of Christian truth? How far out can its money management go? And how far in does its message penetrate? Is there someone studying the relationship between these factors?

Eupsychian Management

Abraham Maslow

Abraham Maslow (1908–1970) was one of the prime movers in the emergence of humanistic psychology in the mid-1950s and what has come to be known as "transpersonal psychology" in the late 1960s. Among his most influential works are *Toward a Psychology of Being, Religions, Values and Peak Experiences,* and "Self-actualizing People: A Study of Psychological Health."

The redefining of the concept "profit" necessarily involves the redefining of the concept "cost." Also it requires the redefining of the concept "price." Maybe I can approach the whole business from a different angle altogether, that is, from the angle of the critique of classical economic theory. In the textbooks I've seen, this is based almost entirely on an obsolete motivation theory of lower basic needs exclusively (leaving out higher needs and metaneeds); furthermore it assumes that these can be phrased in interchangeable terms, which in turn implies that any accounting deals entirely with objects or qualities or characteristics that can be phrased in terms of money and therefore put into a money accounting balance sheet.

But all this is today absolute nonsense. This is true only because we now know so much more about the higher basic needs and also the metaneeds beyond them (which will be far more important motivators in the affluent, automated society). One way of showing this is to stress the fact that money no longer is a very important motivation. There are now many people in our society who cannot be won away to another job by offering more money unless it is a *huge* increase in money. Or say it still another way. Suppose that money becomes unimportant because everybody has enough, or anybody can get enough rather easily in order to satisfy his basic needs. As labor of any kind gets higher and higher priced it becomes possible to earn a minimum subsistence with less and less work. Anybody who really wants to be a hobo can rather easily be one these days. It's very easy to earn what used to be called "a living." (The trouble is when most people talk about earning a living these days they really mean earning an automobile, a fine house, landscaped garden, and so on and so on.)

If this is so, as it indeed seems to be, there are many people who cannot be won away from their present jobs except by offering all sorts of higher need and metaneed satisfactions. Furthermore, many people are influenced more by nonmonetary than by monetary considerations. For instance, I pointed out to Andy Kay that when anybody offered me a job I tried to put some rough money value on all sorts of intangibles, like for instance, giving up a friend, or beautiful surroundings,

Source: A. H. Maslow, *Eupsychian Management: A Journal* (Homewood, Ill.: Dow Jones-Irwin, 1965).

or giving up warm relationships at my place of work, or the simple fact of familiarity with everything and everybody, or going to the trouble of moving from one city to another, or even such things as having to learn my way around a new city. I have asked myself how much money is it worth to me to give up my friendship with my best friends. At my time of life it is difficult to develop this kind of intimacy in a short period of time. Is my best friend worth $1,000 a year or $500 a year or $5,000 or what? Anyway, it's quite clear that he is worth *something* which I had better take into account. If, for instance, I arbitrarily assign a value of $1,000 a year to having an intimate friend (which is certainly a modest figure), then this new job which has been offered at a raise, of let's say $2,000 or $3,000, or $4,000 a year simply is not what it looked like at first. I may actually be losing value, or dollar value, if I take into account all these other higher need intangibles which nobody puts into the contract nor on the balance sheet, but which are nevertheless very, very real to any sensible person.

But something of the same sort is true of industry. Why should a necessary and valuable person stay in a job rather than move to another one? Well, is it not that he likes the house he lives in or that he has a pleasant boss to work with or pleasant colleagues or that the secretary that he works with is cheerful rather than surly or that the janitors are obliging rather than nasty or even such a thing as that the place is unattractive or beautiful rather than ugly? Certainly the questions of climate and weather and education for the children, etc., are all taken into account by any sensible person.

The old concept of taxes is that they are like the fees which the robber barons arbitrarily imposed, or which some group of bandits squeezed out of passersby under threat of military oppression. The "protection money" which the gangsters used to impose in Chicago is very close to this original meaning of the word "tax." The word today still carries some of this connotation, that of arbitrary, greedy people who are demanding some money for which they return nothing, just simply because they're in a position of power, and you have to grind your teeth and give in. But, under good circumstances and under eupsychian theoretical conditions, taxes are a very different kind of thing and must be seen in a very different way, that is, as payment for necessary services at a bargain rate, because otherwise the healthy long-term enterprise would have to replace all of these services on a private basis, which would cost a great deal more. This is true for water, police services, medical services, fire services, general sanitation services and the like. Practically all of these represent terrific bargains, and the taxes for them should be considered to be part of the necessary costs of any long-term enterprise, an indispensable *sine qua non* of enterprise. This is also as true or almost as true for the huge chunk of local taxes which goes for education and schools in general. From the point of view of an enterprise, this can be seen as preparation by the community of skilled workers and managers of all kinds. If the community did not teach reading, writing, and arithmetic, then the enterprise itself would have to do this. If there were no school system, then this would have to be created by the enterprise itself. So this, too, is a great bargain.

(Of course this all assumes enlightened managerial policy in which the more developed the human being is, the more evolved, the more fully grown, the better for the enterprise. Under Theory X conditions the opposite would be true because authoritarianism rests upon ignorance and fear rather than upon enlightenment, autonomy, and courage.)

Sooner or later we will have to deal with the questions of higher-need economics and of metaneed economics in a serious theoretical way. I cannot foresee how many modifications of economic theory and practice would be needed because of this, but certainly some can be seen now. One is this; in a prosperous society and under fairly good conditions and with fairly good people, the lowest creature needs would be taken care of very easily; it would take rather little money to be able to barely eat and sleep and have shelter and so on. Perhaps it will even be cheaper to give them away. Then as we rise higher in the hierarchy of basic needs, we find that money gets to be less and less important in buying them. Of the highest needs we can say that they come free or almost free. Or to say it another way, the higher need satis-factions of belongingness, of love and friendliness and affection, of respect given, and of possibility of building self-respect—all these are largely outside the money economy altogether; e.g., they can be given to the poorest family just so long as it is well organized.

These higher needs are precisely what enlightened management policy points itself toward. That is to say, enlightened management policy may be *defined* as an attempt to satisfy the higher needs in the work situation, in a nonmonetary way, that is, to have the work situation give intrinsically higher need satisfaction (rather than to give the money and expect the money to buy these satisfactions outside the work situation). We can go pretty far with this because it's actually possible to distinguish between Theory X management and Theory Y management simply on this basis; that is, Theory X is a theory of motivation which implies all the lower needs and Theory Y is a more inclusive and more scientific and realistic theory of motivation because it includes the higher needs and considers them to be factors in the work situation and in the economic situation. Or to say it still another way, authoritarian economics or Theory X economics and managerial policy proceed on the assumption that there are no instinctoid higher basic needs. (Since there is so much evidence that there are such needs, Theory X is not only distasteful in a democratic society on moral principles, but it is also scientifically false.) (I think the high and low grumble experiment [see below] will prove that metaneeds are also part of the economic situation or the work situation and of managerial Theory X. That is, we may turn out to have a lower-need economics, a higher-need economics, and also a metaneed economics, in a kind of hierarchy of prepotency.) I wish Walter Weiss-kopf could be permitted to teach others about these points as he has taught me.[1]

The trouble is how to put these on the balance sheet, how to put them into the accounting system, how to give them weight in the actual calculation of salary for a particular man or of the worth to the organization of the personality development of the people in it, for instance. Try to put it this way, for one example: if a particular man who is twenty-five years old is working in an organization at a particular level X which is not terribly good, and then for some reason goes into psychotherapy for a long period of time and becomes a better person and as a result comes out able to work at a higher level Y, then it is very clear that attaining this higher level of

[1] W. Weisskopf, *The Psychology of Economics* (Chicago: University of Chicago Press, 1955); also "Economic Growth and Human Well-Being," *Manas*, August 21, 1963, 16, 1–8.

efficiency in productivity and managerial skill cost him a great deal of money. Is this part of his "wealth"? Where in his accounting system does this gain get written down? (The same question is true for higher education of any other kind.)

Still another question here: assuming that in one factory Theory X prevails and in another factory Theory Y prevails, and that naturally the latter one is better for the personal growth of any individual in it, how can this gain be put into the accounting system? Certainly it all costs some money. The cost of training enlightened managers is greater than the cost of training unenlightened managers. How shall this gain be represented in a numerical fashion in the balance sheet? Certainly it must be considered some kind of fringe benefit, that is to say a nonmoney benefit, and any sensible man, of course, would realize that this was a benefit, an economic benefit, a higher-need economic benefit, even though it would be hard to put into numerical terms or monetary terms.

Another question: the fact that an enlightened factory undoubtedly will be discovered to make all sorts of differences not only in the intrinsic work situation, that is, by way of turning out better products and so on, but also in helping its people to become better citizens, better husbands, better wives, etc., etc. This is an asset or a benefit to the population at large in exactly the same way that a schoolhouse is or college or hospital or a therapeutic institute. That is, how could an accounting system build into itself the benefits that an enterprise gives to the community? Certainly, even in the money economy, this makes a certain amount of sense, because this costs a certain amount of money to the enterprise, e.g., for education within the company, for enlightened services of various sorts, for education in the broadest sense, etc.

Sometimes in the future we will have to deal with more subtle aspects of long-term, enlightened management, democratic holistic society economics, in at least this sense: A healthy business assumes all sorts of things that we haven't yet spoken about. For instance, it really assumes a kind of an open and free market, perhaps we can use the word "open competition" here. It is better for the long-term health of an enterprise that it be able to compete, that there be rival factories turning out similar products which can be compared with each other, that other factories keep on pressing for improvement, etc. This is in contrast with, let's say, the Franco-Spain situation in which a monopoly is arbitrarily given to some relative, who thereafter, for instance, will produce all the matches in Spain or all the automobiles or whatever it may be. What happens inevitably in the monopoly situation of this sort, since there is no pressure to keep up quality or certainly none to improve, is that everything will most likely deteriorate steadily. The people involved must inevitably become cynical as they realize that they are crooks and liars and evil people in general who have been forced into an evil situation. They will almost inevitably tax the helpless population, i.e., set a higher price on the products than they would be worth in an open market, and furthermore, since the product itself will most likely deteriorate, the enterprise will certainly not be healthy.

To use a slightly different parallel a child who is brought up in a germ-free environment, is carefully protected against all bacteria and viruses and so on, loses entirely, sooner or later, the ability to resist disease. That is to say, he must thereafter, for the rest of his life be artificially protected because he cannot protect himself. By contrast, the child who is permitted to take his own chances and to live in the world of dangers and is only ordinarily and reasonably protected against the dangers will, because he gets these dangers in small doses, build up antibodies and resistances so that he can walk freely through all the germs and viruses thereafter for the rest of his life without fear and without getting disease. I think this is indication enough that some new theory of competition or of free market or of free enterprise in this sense will have to be worked out. It should be kept separate from cold war talk, or political talk of any kind, because precisely the same thing is true of any other kind of social or economic system. That is, a healthy enterprise in the socialistic economy would depend upon the same conditions of exposure to stress, exposure to competition that would be required in a capitalistic economy. That is to say, this is not simply a political economic or moral consideration; it follows very simply from the intrinsic necessities of an enterprise which is to last for a couple of centuries, and which is to remain alive homeostatically and also to grow. A good boxer needs a good sparring partner or he will deteriorate.

Furthermore, if we assumed, as I think it could be demonstrated that we *must*, that rationality, truth, honesty, and justice in this free market, in this free competition of similar products, should prevail in order to keep up the health of all the enterprises and of all the people in these enterprises and of the society in general, then it is very desirable (and perhaps even theoretically necessary), that cream be able to rise to the top of the milk. The best product should be bought, the best man should be rewarded more. Interfering factors which befuddle this triumph of virtue, justice, truth, and efficiency, etc., should be kept to an absolute minimum or should approach zero as a limit. Here I'm talking about the salesman's winning smiles, personal loyalties, favoring your relatives, or fake advertising which stresses the wrong thing (like the beautiful design of a car on the outside without regard to the lousy motor inside).

If all these things can be demonstrated to be true for the healthy enterprise and the healthy system of enterprises, i.e., society, then many things will follow. And one of these things is that the consumer, the buyer, the customer must be assumed to be rational, that is, that he will want the best product for his purposes. This means also to think that he will look for factual information, examine specifications, read the labels, get indignant over being swindled instead of taking it for granted, and shudder with disgust when he meets a crook or liar and thereafter stay away from him, etc., etc. Now, all these qualities are characteristics of higher psychological health, growth toward self-actualization. Therefore, any determinant that increases the health of a particular person, making him therefore not only a better manager or better worker or better citizen but also a better consumer, must be considered to be good for the health of any particular enterprise, even though in a tiny, tiny way. Anything that will enable the consumers to select out on the basis of facts and of truly good workmanship, etc., is good for everybody else or everything else in the whole society, including the single, long-termed enlightened enterprise. Therefore the enlightened factory which helps people to grow is thereby helping every other factory in the whole society in principle. And, in principle at least, this should be valued by all the other factories, just as anything else should be valued that turns out better, more realistic, "higher" customers. Now the question is, can this somehow be put on the balance sheet: can an accounting system take account of fringe benefits to other factories from having an efficient, enlightened scientific factory setup.

Another way to try to say these various things is to start with the conception of the "good customer in eupsychia or the eupsychian customer." Everything that has preceded and everything in the management literature rests on assuming that the customer is rational, prefers good quality, will choose the better product for the purpose, will choose the lesser price if quality is equal, will not be seduced by irrelevancies, will prefer virtue and truth and justice and so on, and will get indignant or insulted or disgusted or angry when someone tries to swindle him. This assumption is also necessary because the main basis upon which enlightened management policy so far rests is that productivity is improved both in quantity and quality. *But* what good will it do to turn out a better product at a cheaper price if betterness and cheapness mean nothing to the consumer? That is, if he cares less about these than about other things which are irrelevant, then the whole argument for more efficient factories, managers, and supervisors falls to the ground entirely. If people like being fooled, if they like being swindled, of they prefer being seduced, if they prefer being bribed, then enlightened management is bad, rather than good for economic survival. Therefore, the theory of the good and efficient factory has as an absolute prerequisite, the good and rational customer armed with good taste and with righteous indignation. It is only when people value honesty that honesty pays. It is only when people value good quality that good quality pays. It is only when people get righteously indignant over being swindled, that people will tend to stop swindling. If swindling pays, then it will *not* stop. The definition of the good society is one in which virtue pays. I can now add a slight variation on this; you cannot have a good society *unless* virtue pays. But here we get very close to the whole subject of metaneeds, and also of the synergy theory, which in turn is a by-product of B-psychology—the B-psychology of ideal conditions where dichotomies are resolved and transcended. (Put all this together with the other memorandum on the good eupsychian salesman and the good eupsychian customer and stress that a "good customer" is both a necessity and a virtuous, desirable person, because he wishes the system to work. As soon as he stops caring, the whole system will collapse.)

The Crisis of Ecology

The Historical Roots of Our Ecologic Crisis

Lynn White, Jr.

Lynn White, Jr. (1907–   ) is at present professor of history at UCLA, but over a long and distinguished career has also taught at Princeton and Stanford and was president of Mills College from 1943 to 1958. Among his major works are *Medieval Technology and Social Change*, *The Transformation of the Roman World*, and *Machina ex Deo: Essays in the Dynamism of Western Culture*.

A conversation with Aldous Huxley not infrequently put one at the receiving end of an unforgettable monologue. About a year before his lamented death he was discoursing on a favorite topic: Man's unnatural treatment of nature and its sad results. To illustrate his point he told how, during the previous summer, he had returned to a little valley in England where he had spent many happy months as a child. Once it had been composed of delightful grassy glades; now it was becoming overgrown with unsightly brush because the rabbits that formerly kept such growth under control had largely succumbed to a disease, myxomatosis, that was deliberately introduced by the local farmers to reduce the rabbits' destruction of crops. Being something of a Philistine, I could be silent no longer, even in the interests of great rhetoric. I interrupted to point out that the rabbit itself had been brought as a domestic animal to England in 1176, presumably to improve the protein diet of the peasantry.

All forms of life modify their contexts. The most spectacular and benign instance is doubtless the coral polyp. By serving its own ends, it has created a vast undersea world favorable to thousands of other kinds of animals and plants. Ever since man became a numerous species he has affected his environment notably. The hypothesis that his fire-drive method of hunting created the world's great grasslands and helped to exterminate the monster mammals of the Pleistocene from much of the globe is plausible, if not proved. For 6 millennia at least, the banks of the lower Nile have been a human artifact rather than the swampy African jungle

Source: Lynn White, Jr., "The Historical Roots of Our Ecologic Crisis," *Science*, Vol. 155 (March 10, 1967), pp. 1203–1207. Copyright © 1967 by the American Association for the Advancement of Science. Reprinted by permission.

which nature, apart from man, would have made it. The Aswan Dam, flooding 5000 square miles, is only the latest stage in a long process. In many regions terracing or irrigation, overgrazing, the cutting of forests by Romans to build ships to fight Carthaginians or by Crusaders to solve the logistics problems of their expeditions, have profoundly changed some ecologies. Observation that the French landscape falls into two basic types, the open fields of the north and the *bocage* of the south and west, inspired Marc Bloch to undertake his classic study of medieval agricultural methods. Quite unintentionally, changes in human ways often affect nonhuman nature. It has been noted, for example, that the advent of the automobile eliminated huge flocks of sparrows that once fed on the horse manure littering every street.

The history of ecologic change is still so rudimentary that we know little about what really happened, or what the results were. The extinction of the European aurochs as late as 1627 would seem to have been a simple case of overenthusiastic hunting. On more intricate matters it often is impossible to find solid information. For a thousand years or more the Frisians and Hollanders have been pushing back the North Sea, and the process is culminating in our own time in the reclamation of the Zuider Zee. What, if any, species of animals, birds, fish, shore life, or plants have died out in the process? In their epic combat with Neptune have the Nether-landers overlooked ecological values in such a way that the quality of human life in the Netherlands has suffered? I cannot discover that the questions have ever been asked, much less answered.

People, then, have often been a dynamic element in their own environment, but in the present state of historical scholarship we usually do not know exactly when, where, or with what effects man-induced changes came. As we enter the last third of the 20th century, however, concern for the problem of ecologic backlash is mounting feverishly. Natural science, conceived as the effort to understand the nature of things, had flourished in several eras and among several peoples. Similarly there had been an age-old accumulation of technological skills, sometimes growing rapidly, sometimes slowly. But it was not until about four generations ago that Western Europe and North America arranged a marriage between science and technology, a union of the theoretical and the empirical approaches to our natural environment. The emergence in widespread practice of the Baconian creed that scientific knowledge means technological power over nature can scarcely be dated before about 1850, save in the chemical industries, where it is anticipated in the 18th century. Its acceptance as a normal pattern of action may mark the greatest event in human history since the invention of agriculture, and perhaps in nonhuman terrestrial history as well.

Almost at once the new situation forced the crystallization of the novel concept of ecology; indeed, the word *ecology* first appeared in the English language in 1873. Today, less than a century later, the impact of our race upon the environment has so increased in force that it has changed in essence. When the first cannons were fired, in the early 14th century, they affected ecology by sending workers scrambling to the forests and mountains for more potash, sulfur, iron ore, and charcoal, with some resulting erosion and deforestation. Hydrogen bombs are of a different order: a war fought with them might alter the genetics of all life on this planet. By 1285 London had a smog problem arising from the burning of soft coal, but our present combustion of fossil fuels threatens to change the chemistry of the globe's atmosphere as a whole, with consequences which we are only beginning to guess. With the population explosion, the carcinoma of planless urbanism, the now geological deposits of sewage and garbage, surely no creature other than man has ever managed to foul its nest in such short order.

There are many calls to action, but specific proposals, however, worthy as individual items, seem too partial, palliative, negative: ban the bomb, tear down the billboards, give the Hindus contraceptives and tell them to eat their sacred cows. The simplest solution to any suspect change is, of course, to stop it, or, better yet, to revert to a romanticized past: make those ugly gasoline stations look like Anne Hathaway's cottage or (in the Far West) like ghost-town saloons. The "wilderness area" mentality invariably advocates deep-freezing an ecology, whether San Gimignano or the High Sierra, as it was before the first Kleenex was dropped. But neither atavism nor prettification will cope with the ecologic crisis of our time.

What shall we do? No one yet knows. Unless we think about fundamentals, our specific measures may produce new backlashes more serious than those they are designed to remedy.

As a beginning we should try to clarify our thinking by looking, in some historical depth, at the presuppositions that underlie moden technology and science. Science was traditionally aristocratic, speculative, intellectual in intent; technology was lower-class, empirical, action-oriented. The quite sudden fusion of these two, towards the middle of the 19th century, is surely related to the slightly prior and contemporary democratic revolutions which, by reducing social barriers, tended to assert a functional unity of brain and hand. Our ecologic crisis is the product of an emerging entirely novel, democratic culture. The issue is whether a democratized world can survive its own implications. Presumably we cannot unless we rethink our axioms.

The Western Traditions of Technology and Science

One thing is so certain that it seems stupid to verbalize it: both modern technology and modern science are distinctively *Occidental*. Our technology has absorbed elements from all over the world, notably from China; yet everywhere today, whether in Japan or in Nigeria, successful technology is Western. Our science is the heir to all the sciences of the past, especially perhaps to the work of the great Islamic scientists of the Middle Ages, who so often outdid the ancient Greeks in skill and perspicacity: al-Rāzī in medicine, for example; or ibn-al-Haytham in optics; or Omar Khayyám in mathematics. Indeed, not a few works of such geniuses seem to have vanished in the original Arabic and to survive only in medieval Latin translations that helped to lay the foundations for later Western developments. Today, around the globe, all significant science is Western in style and method, whatever the pigmentation or language of the scientists.

A second pair of facts is less well recognized because they result from quite recent historical scholarship. The leadership of the West, both in technology and in science, is far older than the so-called Scientific Revolution of the 17th century or the so-called Industrial Revolution of the 18th century. These terms are in fact outmoded and obscure the true nature of what they try to describe—significant stages in two long and separate developments. By A.D. 1000 at the latest—and perhaps, feebly, as much as 200 years earlier—the West began to apply water power to industrial processes other than milling grain. This was followed in the late 12th century by the harnessing of wind power. From simple beginnings, but with remarkable consistency of style, the West rapidly expanded its skills in the development of power machinery, labor-saving devices, and automation. Those who doubt should contemplate that most monumental achievement in the history of automation: the weight-driven mechanical clock, which appeared in two forms in the early 14th century. Not in craftsmanship but in basic technological capacity, the Latin West of the later Middle Ages far outstripped its elaborate, sophisticated, and esthetically magnificent sister cultures, Byzantium and Islam. In 1444 a great Greek ecclesiastic, Bessarion, who had gone to Italy wrote a letter to a prince in Greece. He is amazed by the superiority of Western ships, arms, textiles, glass. But above all he is astonished by the spectacle of water-wheels sawing timbers and pumping the bellows of blast furnaces. Clearly, he had seen nothing of the sort in the Near East.

By the end of the 15th century the technological superiority of Europe was such that its small, mutually hostile nations could spill out over all the rest of the world, conquering, looting, and colonizing. The symbol of this technological superiority is the fact that Portugal, one of the weakest states of the Occident, was able to become, and to remain for a century, mistress of the East Indies. And we must remember that the technology of Vasco da Gama and Albuquerque was built by pure empiricism, drawing remarkably little support or inspiration from science.

In the present-day vernacular understanding, modern science is supposed to have begun in 1543, when both Copernicus and Vesalius published their great works. It is no derogation of their accomplishments, however, to point out that such structures as the *Fabrica* and the *De revolutionibus* do not appear overnight. The distinctive Western tradition of science, in fact, began in the late 11th century with a massive movement of translation of Arabic and Greek scientific works into Latin. A few notable books—Theophrastus, for example—escaped the West's avid new appetite for science, but within less than 200 years effectively the entire corpus of Greek and Muslim science was available in Latin, and was being eagerly read and criticized in the new European universities. Out of criticism arose new observation, speculation, and increasing distrust of ancient authorities. By the late 13th century Europe had seized global scientific leadership from the faltering hands of Islam. It would be as absurd to deny the profound originality of Newton, Galileo, or Copernicus as to deny that of the 14th century scholastic scientists like Buridan or Oresme on whose work they built. Before the 11th century, science scarcely existed in the Latin West, even in Roman times. From the 11th century onward the scientific sector of Occidental culture has increased in a steady crescendo.

Since both our technological and our scientific movements got their start, acquired their character, and achieved world dominance in the Middle Ages, it would seem that we cannot understand their nature or their present impact upon ecology without examining fundamental medieval assumptions and developments.

Medieval View of Man and Nature

Until recently, agriculture has been the chief occupation even in "advanced" societies; hence, any change in methods of tillage has much importance. Early plows, drawn by two oxen, did not normally turn the sod but merely scratched it. Thus, cross-plowing was needed and fields tended to be squarish. In the fairly light soils and semiarid climates of the Near East and Mediterranean, this worked well. But such a plow was inappropriate to the wet climate and often sticky soils of northern Europe. By the latter part of the 7th century after Christ, however, following obscure beginnings, certain northern peasants were using an entirely new kind of plow, equipped with a vertical knife to cut the line of the furrow, a horizontal share to slice under the sod, and a moldboard to turn it over. The friction of this plow with the soil was so great that it normally required not two but eight oxen. It attacked the land with such violence that cross-plowing was not needed, and fields tended to be shaped in long strips.

In the days of the scratch-plow, fields were distributed generally in units capable of supporting a single family. Subsistence farming was the presupposition. But no peasant owned eight oxen: to use the new and more efficient plow, peasants pooled their oxen to form large plow-teams, originally receiving (it would appear) plowed strips in proportion to their contribution. Thus, distribution of land was based no longer on the needs of a family but, rather, on the capacity of a power machine to till the earth. Man's relation to the soil was profoundly changed. Formerly man had been part of nature; now he was the exploiter of nature. Nowhere else in the world did farmers develop any analogous agricultural implement. Is it coincidence that modern technology, with its ruthlessness toward nature, has so largely been produced by descendents of these peasants of northern Europe?

This same exploitive attitude appears slightly before A.D. 830 in Western illustrated calendars. In older calendars the months were shown as passive personifications. The new Frankish calendars, which set the style for the Middle Ages, are very different: they show men coercing the world around them—plowing, harvesting, chopping trees, butchering pigs. Man and nature are two things, and man is master.

These novelties seem to be in harmony with larger intellectual patterns. What people do about their ecology depends on what they think about themselves in relation to things around them. Human ecology is deeply conditioned by beliefs about our nature and destiny—that is, by religion. To Western eyes this is very evident in, say, India or Ceylon. It is equally true of ourselves and of our medieval ancestors. The victory of Christianity over paganism was the greatest psychic revolution in the history of our culture. It has become fashionable today to say that, for better or worse, we live in "the post-Christian age." Certainly the forms of our thinking and language have largely ceased to be Christian, but to my eye the substance often remains amazingly akin to that of the past. Our daily habits of action, for example, are dominated by an implicit faith in perpetual progress which was unknown either to Greco-Roman antiquity or to the Orient. It is rooted in, and is indefensible apart from, Judeo-Christian teleology. The fact that Communists share it merely helps to show what can be demonstrated on many other grounds: that Marxism, like Islam, is a Judeo-Christian heresy. We continue today to live, as we have lived for about 1700 years, very largely in a context of Christian axioms.

What did Christianity tell people about their relations with the environment?

While many of the world's mythologies provide stories of creation, Greco-Roman mythology was singularly incoherent in this respect. Like Aristotle, the intellectuals of the ancient West denied that the visible world had had a beginning. Indeed, the idea of a beginning was impossible in the framework of their cyclical notion of time. In sharp-contrast, Christianity inherited from Judaism not only a concept of time as nonrepetitive and linear but also a striking story of creation. By gradual stages a loving and all-powerful God had created light and darkness, the heavenly bodies, the earth and all its plants, animals, birds, and fishes. Finally, God had created Adam and as an afterthought, Eve to keep man from being lonely. Man named all the animals, thus establishing his dominance over them. God planned all of this explicitly for man's benefit and rule: no item in the physical creation has any purpose save to serve man's purposes. And, although man's body is made of clay, he is not simply part of nature: he is made in God's image.

Especially in its Western form, Christianity is the most anthropocentric religion the world has seen. As early as the 2nd century both Tertullian and Saint Irenaeus of Lyons were insisting that when God shaped Adam he was forshadowing the image of the incarnate Christ, the Second Adam. Man shares, in great measure, God's transcendence of nature. Christianity, in absolute contrast to ancient paganism and Asia's religions (except, perhaps, Zoroastrianism), not only established a dualism of man and nature but also insisted that it is God's will that man exploit nature for his proper ends.

At the level of the common people this worked out in an interesting way. In Antiquity every tree, every spring, every stream, every hill had its own *genius loci*, its guardian spirit. These spirits were accessible to men, but were very unlike men; centaurs, fauns, and mermaids show their ambivalence. Before one cut a tree, mined a mountain, or dammed a brook, it was important to placate the spirit in charge of that particular situation, and to keep it placated. By destroying pagan animism, Christianity made it possible to exploit nature in a mood of indifference to the feelings of natural objects.

It is often said that for animism the Church substituted the cult of saints. True; but the cult of saints is functionally quite different from animism. The saint is not *in* natural objects; he may have special shrines, but his citizenship is in heaven. Moreover, a saint is entirely a man; he can be approached in human terms. In addition to saints, Christianity of course also had angels and demons inherited from Judaism and perhaps, at one remove, from Zoroastrianism. But these were all as mobile as the saints themselves. The spirits *in* natural objects, which formerly had protected nature from man, evaporated. Man's effective monopoly on spirit in this world was confirmed, and the old inhibitions to the exploitation of nature crumbled.

When one speaks in such sweeping terms, a note of caution is in order. Christianity is a complex faith, and its consequences differ in differing contexts. What I have said may well apply to the medieval West, where in fact technology made spectacular advances. But the Greek East, a highly civilized realm of equal Christian devotion, seems to have produced no marked technological innovation after the late 7th century, when Greek fire was invented. The key to the contrast may perhaps be found in a difference in the tonality of piety and thought which students of comparative theology find between the Greek and the Latin Churches. The Greeks believed that sin was intellectual blindness, and that salvation was found in illumination, orthodoxy—that is, clear thinking. The Latins, on the other hand, felt that sin was moral evil, and the salvation was to be found in right conduct. Eastern theology has been voluntarist. The Greek saint contemplates; the Western saint acts. The implications of Christianity for the conquest of nature would emerge more easily in the Western atmosphere.

The Christian dogma of creation, which is found in the first clause of all the Creeds, has another meaning for our comprehension of today's ecologic crisis. By revelation, God had given man the Bible, the Book of Scripture. But since God had made nature, nature also must reveal the divine mentality. The religious study of nature for the better understanding of God was known as natural theology. In the early Church, and always in the Greek East, nature was conceived primarily as a symbolic system through which God speaks to men: the ant is a sermon to sluggards; rising flames are the symbol of the soul's aspiration. This view of nature was essentially artistic rather than scientific. While Byzantium preserved and copied great numbers of ancient Greek scientific texts, science as we conceive it could scarcely flourish in such an ambience.

However, in the Latin West by the early 13th century natural theology was following a very different bent. It was ceasing to be the decoding of the physical symbols of God's communication with man and was becoming the effort to understand God's mind by discovering how his creation operates. The rainbow was no longer simply a symbol of hope first sent to Noah after the Deluge: Robert Grosseteste, Friar Roger Bacon, and Theodoric of Freiberg produced startlingly sophisticated work on the optics of the rainbow, but they did it as a venture in religious understanding. From the 13th century onward, up to and including Leibnitz and Newton, every major scientist, in effect, explained his motivations in religious terms. Indeed, if Galileo had not been so expert an amateur theologian he would have got into far less trouble: the professionals resented his intrusion. And Newton seems to have regarded himself more as a theologian than as a scientist. It was not until the late 18th century that the hypothesis of God became unnecessary to many scientists.

It is often hard for the historian to judge, when men explain why they are doing what they want to do, whether they are offering real reasons or merely culturally acceptable reasons. The consistency with which scientists during the long formative centuries of Western science said that the task and the reward of the scientist was "to think God's thoughts after him" leads one to believe that this was their real motivation. If so, then modern Western science was cast in a matrix of Christian theology. The dynamism of religious devotion, shaped by the Judeo-Christian dogma of creation, gave it impetus.

An Alternative Christian View

We would seem to be headed toward conclusions unpalatable to many Christians. Since both *science* and *technology* are blessed words in our contemporary vocabulary, some may be happy at the notions, first, that, viewed historically, modern science is an extrapolation of natural theology and, second, that modern technology is at least partly to be explained as an Occidental, voluntarist realization of the Christian dogma of man's transcendence of, and rightful mastery over, nature. But, as we now recognize, somewhat over a century ago science and technology—hitherto quite separate activities—joined to give mankind powers which, to judge by many of the ecologic effects, are out of control. If so, Christianity bears a huge burden of guilt.

I personally doubt that disastrous ecologic backlash can be avoided simply by applying to our problems more science and more technology. Our science and technology have grown out of Christian attitudes toward man's relation to nature which are almost universally held not only by Christians and neo-Christians but also by those who fondly regard themselves as post-Christians. Despite Copernicus, all the cosmos rotates around our little globe. Despite Darwin, we are *not*, in our hearts, part of the natural process. We are superior to nature, contemptuous of it, willing to use it for our slightest whim. The newly elected Governor of California, like myself a churchman but less troubled than I, spoke for the Christian tradition when he said (as is alleged), "when you've seen one redwood tree, you've seen them all." To a Christian a tree can be no more than a physical fact. The whole concept of the sacred grove is alien to Christianity and to the ethos of the West. For nearly a millennia Christian missionaries have been chopping down sacred groves, which are idolatrous because they assume spirit in nature.

What we do about ecology depends on our ideas of the man-nature relationship. More science and more technology are not going to get us out of the present ecologic crisis until we find a new religion, or rethink our old one. The beatniks, who are the basic revolutionaries of our time, show a sound instinct in their affinity for Zen Buddhism, which conceives of the man-nature relationship as very nearly the mirror image of the Christian view. Zen, however, is as deeply conditioned by Asian history as Christianity is by the experience of the West, and I am dubious of its viability among us.

Possibly we should ponder the greatest radical in Christian history since Christ: Saint Francis of Assisi. The prime miracle of Saint Francis is the fact that he did not end at the stake as many of his left-wing followers did. He was so clearly heretical that a General of the Franciscan Order, Saint Bonaventura, a great and perceptive Christian, tried to suppress the early accounts of Franciscanism. The key to an understanding of Francis is his belief in the virtue of humility—not merely for the individual but for man as a species. Francis tried to depose man from his monarchy over creation and set up a democracy of all God's creatures. With him the ant is no longer simply a homily for the lazy, flames a sign of the thrust of the soul toward union with God; now they are Brother Ant and Sister Fire, praising the Creator in their own ways as Brother Man does in his.

Later commentators have said that Francis preached to the birds as a rebuke to men who would not listen. The records do not read so: he urged the little birds to praise God, and in spiritual ecstasy they flapped their wings and chirped rejoicing. Legends of saints, especially the Irish saints, had long told of their dealings with animals but always, I believe, to show their human dominance over creatures. With Francis it is different. The land around Gubbio in the Apennines was being ravaged by a fierce wolf. Saint Francis, says the legend, talked to the wolf and persuaded him of the error of his ways. The wolf repented, died in the odor of sanctity, and was buried in consecrated ground.

What Sir Steven Runciman calls "the Franciscan doctrine of the animal soul" was quickly stamped out. Quite possibly it was in part inspired, consciously or unconsciously, by the belief in reincarnation held by the Cathar heretics who at that time teemed in Italy and southern France, and who presumably had got it originally from India. It is significant that at just the same moment, about 1200, traces of metempsychosis are found also in western Judaism, in the Provençal *Cabbala*. But Francis held neither to transmigration of souls nor to pantheism. His view of nature and of man rested on a unique sort of pan-psychism of all things animate and inanimate, designed for the glorification of their transcendent Creator, who, in the ultimate gesture of cosmic humility, assumed flesh, lay helpless in a manger, and hung dying on a scaffold.

I am not suggesting that many contemporary Americans who are concerned about our ecologic crisis will be either able or willing to counsel with wolves or exhort birds. However, the present increasing disruption of the global environment is the product of a dynamic technology and science which were originating in the Western medieval world against which Saint Francis was rebelling in so original a way. Their growth cannot be understood historically apart from distinctive attitudes toward nature which are deeply grounded in Christian dogma. The fact that most people do not think of these attitudes as Christian is irrelevant. No new set of basic values has been accepted in our society to displace those of Christianity. Hence we shall continue to have a worsening ecologic crisis until we reject the Christian axiom that nature has no reason for existence save to serve man.

The greatest spiritual revolutionary in Western history, Saint Francis, proposed what he thought was an alternative Christian view of nature and man's relation to it: he tried to substitute the idea of the equality of all creatures, including man, for the idea of man's limitless rule of creation. He failed. Both our present science and our present technology are so tinctured with orthodox Christian arrogance toward nature that no solution for our ecologic crisis can be expected from them alone. Since the roots of our trouble are so largely religious, the remedy must also be essentially religious, whether we call it that or not. We must rethink and refeel our nature and destiny. The profoundly religious, but heretical, sense of the primitive Franciscans for the spiritual autonomy of all parts of nature may point a direction. I propose Francis as a patron saint for ecologists.

Living on a Lifeboat

Garrett Hardin

Garrett Hardin began his career in the field of microbiology and went on to work in genetics and evolution. A faculty member of the University of California for more than a quarter-century, he was named Santa Barbara's Faculty Research Lecturer in 1966 and has lectured elsewhere throughout the United States for several years. His books include *Nature and Man's Fate*, *Exploring New Ethics for Survival*, and several textbooks. He is also well known for his provocative essay, "The Tragedy of the Commons."

Susanne Langer (1942) has shown that it is probably impossible to approach an unsolved problem save through the door of a metaphor. Later, attempting to meet the demands of rigor, we may achieve some success in cleansing theory of metaphor, though our success is limited if we are unable to avoid using common language, which is shot through and through with fossil metaphors. (I count no less than five in the preceding two sentences.)

Since metaphorical thinking is inescapable it is pointless merely to weep about our human limitations. We must learn to live with them, to understand them, and to control them. "All of us," said George Eliot in *Middlemarch*, "get our thoughts entangled in metaphors, and act fatally on the strength of them." To avoid unconscious suicide we are well advised to pit one metaphor against another. From the interplay of competitive metaphors, thoroughly developed, we may come closer to metaphor-free solutions to our problems.

No generation has viewed the problem of the survival of the human species as seriously as we have. Inevitably, we have entered this world of concern through the door of metaphor. Environmentalists have emphasized the image of the earth as a spaceship—Spaceship Earth. Kenneth Boulding (1966) is the principal architect of this metaphor. It is time, he says, that we replace the wasteful "cowboy economy" of the past with the frugal "spaceship economy" required for continued survival in the limited world we now see ours to be. The metaphor is notably useful in justifying pollution control measures.

Unfortunately, the image of a spaceship is also used to promote measures that are suicidal. One of these is a generous immigration policy, which is only a particular instance of a class of policies that are in error because they lead to the tragedy of the commons (Hardin 1968). These suicidal policies are attractive because they mesh with what we unthinkingly take to be the ideals of "the best people." What is missing in the idealistic view is an insistence that rights and responsibilities must go together. The "generous" attitude of all too many people results in asserting inalienable rights while ignoring or denying matching responsibilities.

Source: Garrett Hardin, "Living on a Lifeboat," *The CoEvolution Quarterly* (Summer 1975), pp. 16–23. Reprinted by permission of BioScience.

For the metaphor of a spaceship to be correct the aggregate of people on board would have to be under unitary sovereign control (Ophuis 1974). A true ship always has a captain. It is conceivable that a ship could be run by a committee. But it could not possibly survive if its course were determined by bickering tribes that claimed rights without responsibilities.

What about Spaceship Earth? It certainly has no captain, and no executive committee. The United Nations is a toothless tiger, because the signatories of its charter wanted it that way. The spaceship metaphor is used only to justify spaceship demands on common resources without acknowledging corresponding spaceship responsibilities.

An understandable fear of decisive action leads people to embrace "incrementalism"—moving toward reform by tiny stages. As we shall see, this strategy is counterproductive in the area discussed here if it means accepting rights before responsibilities. Where human survival is at stake, the acceptance of responsibilities is a precondition to the acceptance of rights, if the two cannot be introduced simultaneously.

Lifeboat Ethics

Before taking up certain substantive issues let us look at an alternative metaphor, that of a lifeboat. In developing some relevant examples the following numerical values are assumed. Approximately two-thirds of the world is desperately poor, and only one-third is comparatively rich. The people in poor countries have an average per capita GNP (Gross National Product) of about $200 per year; the rich, of about $3,000. (For the United States it is nearly $5,000 per year.) Metaphorically, each rich nation amounts to a lifeboat full of comparatively rich people. The poor of the world are in other, much more crowded lifeboats. Continuously, so to speak, the poor fall out of their lifeboats and swim for a while in the water outside, hoping to be admitted to a rich lifeboat, or in some other way to benefit from the "goodies" on board. What should the passengers on a rich lifeboat do? This is the central problem of "the ethics of a lifeboat."

First we must acknowledge that each lifeboat is effectively limited in capacity. The land of every nation has a limited carrying capacity. The exact limit is a matter for argument, but the energy crunch is convincing more people every day that we have already exceeded the carrying capacity of the land. We have been living on "capital"—stored petroleum and coal—and soon we must live on income alone.

Let us look at only one lifeboat—ours. The ethical problem is the same for all, and is as follows. Here we sit, say 50 people in a lifeboat. To be generous, let us assume our boat has a capacity of 10 more, making 60. (This, however, is to violate the engineering principle of the "safety factor." A new plant disease or a bad change in the weather may decimate our population if we don't preserve some excess capacity as a safety factor.)

The 50 of us in the lifeboat see 100 others swimming in the water outside, asking for admission to the boat, or for handouts. How shall we respond to their calls? There are several possibilities.

One. We may be tempted to try to live by the Christian ideal of being "our brother's keeper," or by the Marxian ideal (Marx 1875) of "from each according to his abilities, to each according to his needs." Since the needs of all are the same, we take all the needy into our boat, making a total of 150 in a boat with a capacity of 60. The boat is swamped, and everyone drowns. Complete justice, complete catastrophe.

Two. Since the boat has an unused excess capacity of 10, we admit just 10 more to it. This has the disadvantage of getting rid of the safety factor, for which action we will sooner or later pay dearly. Moreover, *which* 10 do we let in? The neediest 10? How do we *discriminate*? And what do we say to the 90 who are excluded?

Three. Admit no more to the boat and preserve the small safety factor. Survival of the people in the lifeboat is then possible (though we shall have to be on our guard against boarding parties).

The last solution is abhorrent to many people. It is unjust, they say. Let us grant that it is.

"I feel guilty about my good luck," say some. The reply to this is simple: *Get out and yield your place to others.* Such a selfless action might satisfy the conscience of those who are addicted to guilt but it would not change the ethics of the lifeboat. The needy person to whom a guilt-addict yields his place will not himself feel guilty about his sudden good luck. (If he did he would not climb aboard.) The net result of conscience-stricken people relinquishing their unjustly held positions is the elimination of their kind of conscience from the lifeboat. The lifeboat, as it were, purifies itself of guilt. The ethics of the lifeboat persist, unchanged by such momentary aberrations.

This then is the basic metaphor within which we must work out our solutions. Let us enrich the image step by step with substantive additions from the real world.

Reproduction

The harsh characteristics of lifeboat ethics are heightened by reproduction, particularly by reproductive differences. The people inside the lifeboats of the wealthy nations are doubling in numbers every 87 years; those outside are doubling every 35 years, on the average. And the relative difference in prosperity is becoming greater.

Let us, for a while, think primarily of the U.S. lifeboat. As of 1973 the United States had a population of 210 million people, who were increasing by 0.8% per year, that is, doubling in number every 87 years.

Although the citizens of rich nations are outnumbered two to one by the poor, let us imagine an equal number of poor people outside our lifeboat—a mere 210 million poor people reproducing at a quite different rate. If we imagine these to be the combined populations of Colombia, Venezuela, Ecuador, Morocco, Thailand, Pakistan, and the Philippines, the average rate of increase of the people "outside" is 3.3% per year. The doubling time of this population is 21 years.

Suppose that all these countries, and the United States, agreed to live by the Marxian ideal, "to each according to his needs," the ideal of most Christians as well. Needs, of course, are determined by population size, which is affected by reproduction. Every nation regards its rate of reproduction as a sovereign right. If our lifeboat were big enough in the beginning it might be possible to live *for a while* by Christian-Marxian ideals. *Might*.

Initially, in the model given, the ratio of non-Americans to Americans would be one to one. But consider what the ratio would be 87 years later. By this time Americans would have doubled to a population of 420 million. The other group (doubling every 21 years) would now have swollen to 3,540 million. Each American would have more than eight people to share with. How could the lifeboat possibly keep afloat?

All this involves extrapolation of current trends into the future, and is consequently suspect. Trends may change. Granted: but the change will not necessarily be favorable. If—as seems likely—the rate of population increase falls faster in the ethnic group presently inside the lifeboat than it does among those now outside, the future will turn out to be even worse than mathematics predicts, and sharing will be even more suicidal.

Ruin in the Commons

The fundamental error of the sharing ethics is that it leads to the tragedy of the commons. Under a system of private property the man (or group of men) who own property recognize their responsibility to care for it, for if they don't they will eventually suffer. A farmer, for instance, if he is intelligent, will allow no more cattle in a pasture than its carrying capacity justifies. If he overloads the pasture, weeds take over, erosion sets in, and the owner loses in the long run.

But if a pasture is run as a commons open to all, the right of each to use it is not matched by an operational responsibility to take care of it. It is no use asking independent herdsmen in a commons to act responsibly, for they dare not. The considerate herdsman who refrains from overloading the commons suffers more than a selfish one who says his needs are greater. (As Leo Durocher says, "Nice guys finish last.") Christian-Marxian idealism is counterproductive. That it *sounds* nice is no excuse. With distribution systems, as with individual morality, good intentions are no substitute for good performance.

A social system is stable only if it is insensitive to errors. To the Christian-Marxian idealist a selfish person is a sort of "error." Prosperity in the system of the commons cannot survive errors. If *everyone* would only restrain himself, all would be well; but it takes *only one less than everyone* to ruin a system of voluntary restraint. In a crowded world of less than perfect human beings—and we will never know any other—mutual ruin is inevitable in the commons. This is the core of the tragedy of the commons.

One of the major tasks of education today is to create such an awareness of the dangers of the commons that people will be able to recognize its many varieties, however disguised. There is pollution of the air and water because these media are treated as commons. Further growth of population and growth in the per capita conversion of natural resources into pollutants require that the system of the commons be modified or abandoned in the disposal of "externalities."

The fish populations of the oceans are exploited as commons, and ruin lies ahead. No technological invention can prevent this fate: in fact, all improvements in the art of fishing merely hasten the day of complete ruin. Only the replacement of the system of the commons with a responsible system can save oceanic fisheries.

The management of western range lands, though nominally rational, is in fact (under the steady pressure of cattle ranchers) often merely a government-sanctioned system of the commons, drifting toward ultimate ruin for both the rangelands and the residual enterprisers.

World Food Banks

In the international arena we have recently heard a proposal to create a new commons, namely an international depository of food reserves to which nations will contribute according to their abilities, and from which nations may draw according to their needs. Nobel laureate Norman Borlaug has lent the prestige of his name to this proposal.

A world food bank appeals powerfully to our humanitarian impulses. We remember John Donne's celebrated line, "Any man's death diminishes me." But before we rush out to see for whom the bell tolls let us recognize where the greatest political push for international granaries comes from, lest we be disillusioned later. Our experience with Public Law 480 clearly reveals the answer. This was the law that moved billions of dollars worth of U.S. grain to food-short, population-long countries during the past two decades. When P.L. 480 first came into being, a headline in the business magazine *Forbes* (Paddock and Paddock 1970) revealed the power behind it: "Feeding the World's Hungry Millions: How it will mean billions for U.S. business."

And indeed it did. In the years 1960 to 1970 a total of $7.9 billion was spent on the "Food for Peace" program, as P.L. 480 was called. During the years 1948 to 1970 an additional $49.9 billion were extracted from American taxpayers to pay for other economic aid programs, some of which went for food and food-producing machinery. (This figure does *not* include military aid.) That P.L. 480 was a give-away program was concealed. Recipient countries went through the motions of paying for P.L. 480 food—with IOU's. In December 1973 the charade was brought to an end as far as India was concerned when the United States "forgave" India's $3.2 billion debt (Anonymous 1974). Public announcement of the cancellation of the debt was delayed for two months: one wonders why.

Famine—1975! (Paddock and Paddock 1968) is one of the few publications that points out the commercial roots of this humanitarian attempt. Though all U.S. taxpayers lost by P.L. 480, special interest groups gained handsomely. Farmers benefited because they were not asked to contribute the grain—it was bought from them by the taxpayers. Besides the direct benefit there was the indirect effect of increasing demand and thus raising prices of farm products generally. The manufacturers of farm machinery, fertilizers, and pesticides benefited by the farmers' extra efforts to grow more food. Grain elevators profited from storing the grain for varying lengths of time. Railroads made money hauling it to port, and shipping lines by carrying it overseas. Moreover, once the machinery for P.L. 480 was established an immense bureaucracy had a vested interest in its continuance regardless of its merits.

Very little was ever heard of these selfish interests when P.L. 480 was defended in public. The emphasis was always on its humanitarian effects. The combination of multiple and relatively silent selfish interests with highly vocal humanitarian apologists constitutes a powerful lobby for extracting money from taxpayers. Foreign aid has become a habit that can apparently survive in the absence of any known justification. A news commentator in a weekly magazine (Lansner 1974), after exhaustively going over all the conventional arguments for foreign aid—self-interest, social justice, political advantage, and charity—and concluding that none of the known arguments really held water, concluded: " So the search continues for some logically compelling reasons for giving aid . . ." In other words. *Act now, Justify later*—if ever. (Apparently a quarter of a century is too short a time to find the justification for expending several billion dollars yearly.)

The search for a rational justification can be short-circuited by interjecting the word "emergency." Borlaug uses this word. We need to look sharply at it. What is an "emergency?" It is surely something like an accident, which is correctly defined as *an event that is certain to happen, though with a low frequency* (Hardin 1972a). A well-run organization prepares for everything that is certain, including accidents and emergencies. It budgets for them. It saves for them. It expects them —and mature decision-makers do not waste time complaining about accidents when they occur.

What happens if some organizations budget for emergencies and others do not ? If each organization is solely responsible for its own well-being, poorly managed ones will suffer. But they should be able to learn from experience. They have a chance to mend their ways and learn to budget for infrequent but certain emergencies. The weather, for instance, always varies and periodic crop failures are certain. A wise and competent government saves out of the production of the good years in antici-pation of bad years that are sure to come. This is not a new idea. The Bible tells us that Joseph taught this policy to Pharaoh in Egypt more than 2,000 years ago. Yet it is literally true that the vast majority of the governments of the world today have no such policy. They lack either the wisdom or the competence, or both. Far more difficult than the transfer of wealth from one country to another is the transfer of wisdom between sovereign powers or between generations.

"But it isn't their fault! How can we blame the poor people who are caught in an emergency ? Why must we punish them ?" The concepts of blame and punish-ment are irrelevant. The question is, what are the operational consequences of estab-lishing a world food bank ? If it is open to every country every time a need develops, slovenly rulers will not be motivated to take Joseph's advice. Why should they ? Others will bail them out whenever they are in trouble.

Some countries will make deposits in the world food bank and others will withdraw from it: there will be almost no overlap. Calling such a depository-transfer unit a "bank" is stretching the metaphor of *bank* beyond its elastic limits. The proposers, of course, never call attention to the metaphorical nature of the word they use.

The Ratchet Effect

An "international food bank" is really, then, not a true bank but a disguised one-way transfer device for moving wealth from rich countries to poor. In the absence of such a bank, in a world inhabited by individually responsible sovereign nations, the population of each nation would repeatedly go through a cycle of the sort shown in Figure 1. P_2 is greater than P_1, either in absolute numbers or because a deterioration of the food supply has removed the safety factor and produced a dangerously low ratio of resources to population. P_2 may be said to represent a state of overpopulation, which becomes obvious upon the appearance of an "accident," e.g., a crop failure. If the "emergency" is not met by outside help, the population drops back to the "normal" level—the "carrying capacity" of the environment—or even below. In the absence of population control by a sovereign, sooner or later the population grows to P_2 again and the cycle repeats.

The long-term population curve (Hardin 1966) is an irregularly fluctuating one, equilibrating more or less about the carrying capacity.

A demographic cycle of this sort obviously involves great suffering in the restrictive phase, but such a cycle is normal to any independent country with inadequate population control. The third century theologian Tertullian (Hardin 1969a) expressed what must have been the recognition of many wise men when he wrote: "The scourges of pestilence, famine, wars, and earthquakes have come to be regarded as a blessing to overcrowded nations, since they serve to prune away the luxuriant growth of the human race."

Only under a strong and farsighted sovereign—which theoretically could be the people themselves, democratically organized—can a population equilibrate at some set point below the carrying capacity, thus avoiding the pains normally caused by periodic and unavoidable disasters. For this happy state to be achieved it is necessary that those in power be able to contemplate with equanimity the "waste" of surplus food in times of bountiful harvests. It is essential that those in power resist the temptation to convert extra food into extra babies. On the public relations level it is necessary that the phrase "surplus food" be replaced by "safety factor."

But wise sovereigns seem not to exist in the poor world today. The most anguishing problems are created by poor countries that are governed by rulers insufficiently wise and powerful. If such countries can draw on a world food bank in times of "emergency," the population *cycle* of Figure 1 will be replaced by the population *escalator* of Figure 2. The input of food from a food bank acts as the pawl of a ratchet, preventing the population from retracting its steps to a lower level. Reproduction pushes the population upward, inputs from the world bank prevent its moving downward. Population size escalates, as does the absolute magnitude of "accidents" and "emergencies." The process is brought to an end only by the total collapse of the whole system, producing a catastrophe of scarcely imaginable proportions.

Such are the implications of the well-meant sharing of food in a world of irresponsible reproduction.

I think we need a new word for systems like this. The adjective "melioristic" is applied to systems that produce continual improvement; the English word is derived from the Latin *meliorare*, to become or make better. Parallel with this it

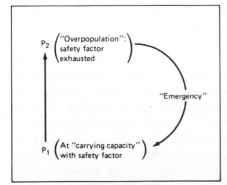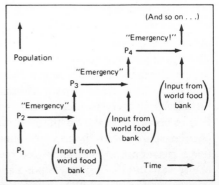

FIGURE 1. The population cycle of a nation that has no effective, conscious population control, and which receives no aid from the outside. P_2 is greater than P_1.   FIGURE 2. The population escalator. Note that input from a world food bank acts like the pawl of a ratchet, preventing the normal population cycle shown in Figure 1 from being completed. P_{n+1} is greater than P_n, and the absolute magnitude of the "emergencies" escalates. Ultimately the entire system crashes. The crash is not shown, and few can imagine it.

would be useful to bring in the word *pejoristic* (from the Latin *pejorare*, to become or make worse). This word can be applied to those systems which, by their very nature, can be relied upon to make matters worse. A world food bank coupled with sovereign state irresponsibility in reproduction is an example of a pejoristic system.

This pejoristic system creates an unacknowledged commons. People have more motivation to draw from than to add to the common store. The license to make such withdrawals diminishes whatever motivation poor countries might otherwise have to control their populations. Under the guidance of this ratchet, wealth can be steadily moved in one direction only, from the slowly-breeding rich to the rapidly-breeding poor, the process finally coming to a halt only when all countries are equally and miserably poor.

All this is terribly obvious once we are acutely aware of the pervasiveness and danger of the commons. But many people still lack this awareness and the euphoria of the "benign demographic transition" (Hardin 1973) interferes with the realistic appraisal of pejoristic mechanisms. As concerns public policy, the deductions drawn from the benign demographic transition are these:

1. If the per capita GNP rises the birth rate will fall; hence, the rate of population increase will fall, ultimately producing ZPG (Zero Population Growth).
2. The long-term trend all over the world (including the poor countries) is of a rising per capita GNP (for which no limit is seen).
3. Therefore, all political interference in population matters is unnecessary; all we need to do is foster economic "development"—*note the metaphor*—and population problems will solve themselves.

Those who believe in the benign demographic transition dismiss the pejoristic mechanism of Figure 2 in the belief that each input of food from the world outside fosters development within a poor country thus resulting in a drop in the rate of population increase. Foreign aid has proceeded on this assumption for more than two decades. Unfortunately it has produced no indubitable instance of the asserted effect. It has, however, produced a library of excuses. The air is filled with plaintive calls for more massive foreign aid appropriations so that the hypothetical melioristic process can get started.

The doctrine of demographic laissez-faire implicit in the hypothesis of the benign demographic transition is immensely attractive. Unfortunately there is more evidence against the melioristic system than there is for it (Davis 1963). On the historical side there are many counter-examples. The rise in per capita GNP in France and Ireland during the past century has been accompanied by a rise in population growth. In the 20 years following the Second World War the same positive correlation was noted almost everywhere in the world. Never in world history before 1950 did the worldwide population growth reach 1% per annum. Now the average population growth is over 2% and shows no signs of slackening.

On the theoretical side, the denial of the pejoristic scheme of Figure 2 probably springs from the hidden acceptance of the "cowboy economy" that Boulding castigated. Those who recognize the limitations of a spaceship, if they are unable to achieve population control at a safe and comfortable level, accept the necessity of the corrective feedback of the population cycle shown in Figure 1. No one who knew in his bones that he was living on a true spaceship would countenance political support for the population escalator shown in Figure 2.

Eco-Destruction Via the Green Revolution

The demoralizing effect of charity on the recipient has long been known. "Give a man a fish and he will eat for a day: teach him how to fish and he will eat for the rest of his days." So runs an ancient Chinese proverb. Acting on this advice the Rockefeller and Ford Foundations have financed a multipronged program for improving agriculture in the hungry nations. The result, known as the "Green Revolution," has been quite remarkable. "Miracle wheat" and "miracle rice" are splendid technological achievements in the realm of plant genetics.

Whether or not the Green Revolution can increase food production is doubtful (Harris 1972, Paddock 1970, Wilkes 1972), but in any event not particularly important. What is missing in this great and well-meaning humanitarian effort is a firm grasp of fundamentals. Considering the importance of the Rockefeller Foundation in this effort it is ironic that the late Alan Gregg, a much-respected vice-president of the Foundation, strongly expressed his doubts of the wisdom of all attempts to increase food production some two decades ago. (This was before Borlaug's work—supported by Rockefeller—had resulted in the development of "miracle wheat.") Gregg (1955) likened the growth and spreading of humanity over the surface of the earth to the metastasis of cancer in the human body, wryly remarking that "Cancerous growths demand food; but, as far as I know, they have never been cured by getting it."

"Man does not live by bread alone"—the scriptural statement has a rich meaning even in the material realm. Every human being born constitutes a draft on all aspects of the environment—food, air, water, unspoiled scenery, occasional and optional solitude, beaches, contact with wild animals, fishing, hunting—the list is long and incompletely known. Food can, perhaps, be significantly increased: but what about clean beaches, unspoiled forests, and solitude? If we satisfy the need for food in a growing population we necessarily decrease the supply of other goods, and thereby increase the difficulty of equitably allocating scarce goods (Hardin 1969b, 1972b).

The present population of India is 600 million, and it is increasing by 15 million every year. The environmental load of this population is already great. The forests of India are only a small fraction of what they were three centuries ago. Soil erosion, floods, and the psychological costs of crowding are serious. Every one of the net 15 million lives added each year stresses the Indian environment more severely. *Every life saved this year in a poor country diminishes the quality of life for subsequent generations.*

Observant critics have shown how much harm we wealthy nations have already done to poor nations through our well-intentioned but misguided attempts to help them (Paddock and Paddock 1973). Particularly reprehensible is our failure to carry out postaudits of these attempts (Farvar and Milton 1972). Thus have we shielded our tender consciences from knowledge of the harm we have done. Must we Americans continue to fail to monitor the consequences of our external "do-gooding?" If, for instance, we thoughtlessly make it possible for the present 600 million Indians to swell to 1,200 millions by the year 2001—as their present growth rate promises—will posterity in India thank *us* for facilitating an even greater destruction of *their* environment? Are good intentions ever a sufficient excuse for bad consequences?

Immigration Creates a Commons

I come now to the final example of a commons in action, one for which the public is least prepared for rational discussion. The topic is at present enveloped by a great silence which reminds me of a comment made by Sherlock Holmes in A. Conan Doyle's story, "Silver Blaze." Inspector Gregory had asked, "Is there any point to which you would wish to draw my attention?" To this Holmes responded:

"To the curious incident of the dog in the night-time."
"The dog did nothing in the night-time," said the Inspector.
"That was the curious incident," remarked Sherlock Holmes.

By asking himself what would repress the normal barking instinct of a watch dog Holmes realized that it must be the dog's recognition of his master as the criminal trespasser. In a similar way we should ask ourselves what repression keeps us from discussing something as important as immigration?

It cannot be that immigration is numerically of no consequence. Our government acknowledges a *net* inflow of 400,000 a year. Hard data are understandably lacking on the extent of illegal entries, but a not implausible figure is 600,000 per year (Buchanan 1973). The natural increase of the resident population is now about 1.7 million per year. This means that the yearly gain from immigration is at least 19%, and may be 37%, of the total increase. It is quite conceivable that educational campaigns like that of Zero Population Growth, Inc., coupled with adverse social and economic factors—inflation, housing shortage, depression, and loss of confidence in national leaders may lower the fertility of American women to a point at which all of the yearly increase in population would be accounted for by immigration. Should we not at least ask if that is what we want? How curious it is that we so seldom discuss immigration these days!

Curious, but understandable—as one finds out the moment he publicly questions the wisdom of the status quo in immigration. He who does so is promptly charged with *isolationism, bigotry, prejudice, ethnocentrism, chauvinism,* and *selfishness.* These are hard accusations to bear. It is pleasanter to talk about other matters, leaving immigration policy to wallow in the cross-currents of special interests that take no account of the good of the whole—*or of the interests of posterity.*

We Americans have a bad conscience because of things we said in the past about immigrants. Two generations ago the popular press was rife with references to *Dagos, Wops, Pollacks, Japs, Chinks,* and *Krauts*—all pejorative terms which failed to acknowledge our indebtedness to Goya, Leonardo, Copernicus, Hiroshige, Confucius, and Bach. Because the implied inferiority of foreigners was *then* the justification for keeping them out, it is *now* thoughtlessly assumed that restrictive policies can only be based on the assumption of immigrant inferiority. *This is not so.*

Existing immigration laws exclude idiots and known criminals; future laws will almost certainly continue this policy. But should we also consider the quality of the average immigrant, as compared with the quality of the average resident? Perhaps we should, perhaps we shouldn't. (What is "quality" anyway?) But the quality issue is not our concern here.

From this point on, *it will be assumed that immigrant and native-born citizens are of exactly equal quality,* however quality may be defined. The focus is only on quantity. The conclusions reached depend on nothing else, so all charges of ethnocentrism are irrelevant.

World food banks move food to the people, thus facilitating the exhaustion of the environment of the poor. By contrast, unrestricted immigration moves people to the food, thus speeding up the destruction of the environment in rich countries. Why poor people should want to make this transfer is no mystery: but why should rich hosts encourage it? This transfer, like the reverse one, is supported by both selfish interests and humanitarian impulses.

The principal selfish interest in unimpeded immigration is easy to identify: it is the interest of the employers of cheap labor, particularly that needed for degrading jobs. We have been deceived about the forces of history by the lines of Emma Lazarus inscribed on the Statue of Liberty:

> Give me your tired, your poor
> Your huddled masses yearning to breathe free,
> The wretched refuse of your teeming shore,
> Send these, the homeless, tempest-tossed, to me:
> I lift my lamp beside the golden door.

The image is one of an infinitely generous earth-mother, passively opening her arms to hordes of immigrants who come here on their own initiative. Such an image may have been adequate for the early days of colonization, but by the time these lines were written (1886) the force for immigration was largely manufactured inside our own borders by factory and mine owners who sought cheap labor not to be found among laborers already here. One group of foreigners after another was thus enticed into the United States to work at wretched jobs for wretched wages.

At present, it is largely the Mexicans who are being so exploited. It is particularly to the advantage of certain employers that there be many illegal immigrants. Illegal immigrant workers dare not complain about their working conditions for fear of being repatriated. Their presence reduces the bargaining power of all Mexican-American laborers. Cesar Chavez has repeatedly pleaded with congressional committees to close the doors to more Mexicans so that those here can negotiate effectively for higher wages and decent working conditions. Chavez understands the ethics of a lifeboat.

The interests of the employers of cheap labor are well served by the silence of the intelligentsia of the country. WASPS—White Anglo-Saxon Protestants—are particularly reluctant to call for a closing of the doors to immigration for fear of being called ethnocentric bigots. It was, therefore, an occasion of pure delight for this particular WASP to be present at a meeting when the points he would like to have made were made better by a non-WASP speaking to other non-WASPS. It was in Hawaii, and most of the people in the room were second-level Hawaiian officials of Japanese ancestry. All Hawaiians are keenly aware of the limits of their environment, and the speaker had asked how it might be practically and constitutionally possible to close the doors to more immigrants to the islands. (To Hawaiians, immigrants from the other 49 states are as much of a threat as those from other nations. There is only so much room in the islands, and the islanders know it. Sophistical arguments that imply otherwise do not impress them.)

Yet the Japanese-Americans of Hawaii have active ties with the land of their origin. This point was raised by a Japanese-American speaker: "But how can we shut the doors now? We have many friends and relations in Japan that we'd like to bring to Hawaii some day so that they can enjoy this beautiful land.

The speaker smiled sympathetically and responded slowly: "Yes, but we have children now and someday we'll have grandchildren. We can bring more people here from Japan only by giving away some of the land that we hope to pass on to our grandchildren some day. What right do we have to do that?"

To be generous with one's own possessions is one thing; to be generous with posterity's is quite another. This, I think, is the point that must be gotten across to those who would, from a commendable love of distributive justice, institute a ruinous system of the commons, either in the form of a world food bank or that of unrestricted immigration. Since every speaker is a member of some ethnic group it is always possible to charge him with ethnocentrism. But even after purging an argument of ethnocentrism the rejection of the commons is still valid and necessary if we are to save at least some parts of the world from environmental ruin. Is it not desirable that at least some of the grandchildren of people now living should have a decent place in which to live?

The Asymmetry of Door-Shutting

We must now answer this telling point: "How can you justify slamming the door once you're inside? You say that immigrants should be kept out. But aren't we all immigrants or the descendants of immigrants? Since we refuse to leave, must we not, as a matter of justice and symmetry, admit all others?"

It is literally true that we Americans of non-Indian ancestry are the descendants of thieves. Should we not, then, "give back" the land to the Indians; that is, give it to the now-living Americans of Indian ancestry? As an exercise in pure logic I see no way to reject this proposal. Yet I am unwilling to live by it; and I know no one who is. Our reluctance to embrace pure justice may spring from pure selfishness. On the other hand, it may arise from an unspoken recognition of consequences that have not yet been clearly spelled out.

Suppose, becoming intoxicated with pure justice, we "Anglos" should decide to turn our land over to the Indians. Since all our other wealth has also been derived from the land, we would have to give that to the Indians, too. Then what would we non-Indians do? Where would we go? There is no open land in the world on which men without capital can make their living (and not much unoccupied land on which men with capital can either). Where would 209 million putatively justice-loving, non-Indian, Americans go? Most of them—in the persons of their ancestors—came from Europe, but they wouldn't be welcomed back there. Anyway, Europeans have no better title to their land than we to ours. They also would have to give up their homes. (But to whom? And where would *they* go?)

Clearly, the concept of pure justice produces an infinite regress. The law long ago invented statutes of limitations to justify the rejection of pure justice, in the interest of preventing massive disorder. The law zealously defends property rights —but only *recent* property rights. It is as though the physical principle of exponential decay applies to property rights. Drawing a line in time may be unjust, but any other action is practically worse.

We are all the descendants of thieves, and the world's resources are inequitably distributed, but we must begin the journey to tomorrow from the point where we are today. We cannot remake the past. We cannot, without violent disorder and suffering, give land and resources back to the "original" owners—who are dead anyway.

We cannot safely divide the wealth equitably among all present peoples, so long as people reproduce at different rates, because to do so would guarantee that our grandchildren—everyone's grandchildren—would have only a ruined world to inhabit.

Must Exclusion Be Absolute?

To show the logical structure of the immigration problem I have ignored many factors that would enter into real decisions made in a real world. No matter how convincing the logic may be it is probable that we would want, from time to time, to admit a few people from the outside to our lifeboat. Political refugees in particular are likely to cause us to make exceptions: We remember the Jewish refugees from Germany after 1933, and the Hungarian refugees after 1956. Moreover, the interests of national defense, broadly conceived, could justify admitting many men and women of unusual talents, whether refugees or not. (This raises the quality issue, which is not the subject of this essay.)

Such exceptions threaten to create runaway population growth inside the lifeboat, i.e., the receiving country. However, the threat can be neutralized by a population policy that includes immigration. An effective policy is one of flexible control.

Suppose, for example, that the nation has achieved a stable condition of ZPG, which (say) permits 1.5 million births yearly. We must suppose that an acceptable system of allocating birth-rights to potential parents is in effect. Now suppose that an inhumane regime in some other part of the world creates a horde of refugees, and that there is a wide-spread desire to admit some to our country. At the same time, we do not want to sabotage our population control system. Clearly, the rational path to pursue is the following. If we decide to admit 100,000 refugees this year we should compensate for this by reducing the allocation of birth-rights in the following year by a similar amount, that is downward to a total of 1.4 million. In that way we could achieve both humanitarian and population control goals. (And the refugees would have to accept the population controls of the society that admits them. It is not inconceivable that they might be given proportionately fewer rights than the native population.)

In a democracy, the admission of immigrants should properly be voted on. But by whom? It is not obvious. The usual rule of a democracy is votes for all. But it can be questioned whether a universal franchise is the most just one in a case of this sort. Whatever benefits there are in the admission of immigrants presumably accrue to everyone. But the costs would be seen as falling most heavily on potential parents, some of whom would have to postpone or forego having their (next) child because of the influx of immigrants. The double question *Who benefits? Who pays?* suggests that a restriction of the usual democratic franchise would be appropriate and just in this case. Would our particular quasi-democratic form of government be flexible enough to institute such a novelty? If not, the majority might, out of humanitarian motives, impose an unacceptable burden (the foregoing of parenthood) on a minority, thus producing political instability.

Plainly many new problems will arise when we consciously face the immigration question and seek rational answers. No workable answers can be found if we ignore population problems. And—if the argument of this essay is correct—so long as there is no true world government to control reproduction everywhere it is impossible to survive in dignity if we are to be guided by Spaceship ethics. Without a world government that is sovereign in reproductive matters mankind lives, in fact, on a number of sovereign lifeboats. For the foreseeable future survival demands that we govern our actions by the ethics of a lifeboat. Posterity will be ill served if we do not.

References

Anonymous. 1974. *Wall Street Journal*, 19 Feb.

Borlaug, N. 1973. Civilization's future: a call for international granaries. *Bull. At. Sci.* 29: 7–15.

Boulding, K. 1966. The economics of the coming Spaceship earth. In H. Jarrett, ed. *Environmental Quality in a Growing Economy*. Johns Hopkins Press, Baltimore.

Buchanan, W. 1973. Immigration statistics. *Equilibrium* 1(3): 16–19.

Davis, K. 1963. Population. *Sci. Amer.* 209(3): 62–71.

Farvar, M. T., and J. P. Milton. 1972. *The Careless Technology.* Natural History Press, Garden City, N.Y.

Gregg, A. 1955. A medical aspect of the population problem. *Science* 121: 681–682.

Hardin, G. 1966. Chap. 9 in *Biology: Its Principles and Implications,* 2nd ed. Freeman, San Francisco.

———. 1968. The tragedy of the commons. *Science* 162; 1243–1248.

———. 1969a. Page 18 in *Population, Evolution, and Birth Control,* 2nd ed. Freeman, San Francisco.

———. 1969b. The economics of wilderness. *Nat. Hist.* 78(6): 20–27.

———. 1972a. Pages 81–82 in Exploring New Ethics for Survival: *The Voyage of the Spaceship Beagle.* Viking, N.Y.

———. 1972b. Preserving quality on Spaceship Earth. In J. B. Trefethen, ed. *Transactions of the Thirty-Seventh North American Wildlife and Natural Resources Conference.* Wildlife Management Institute, Washington, D.C.

———. 1973. Chap. 23 in *Stalking the Wild Taboo.* Kaufmann, Los Altos, Cal.

Harris, M. 1972. How green the revolution. *Nat. Hist.* 81(3): 28–30.

Langer, S. K. 1942. *Philosophy in a New Key.* Harvard University Press, Cambridge.

Lansner, K. 1974. Should foreign aid begin at home? *Newsweek,* 11 Feb., p. 32.

Marx, K. 1875. Critique of the Gotha program. Page 388 in R. C. Tucker, ed. *The Marx–Engels Reader.* Norton, N.Y.

Ophuls, W. 1974. The scarcity society. *Harper's* 248(1487): 47–52.

Paddock, W. C. 1970. How green is the green revolution? *BioScience* 20: 897–902.

Paddock, W., and E. Paddock. 1973. *We Don't Know How.* Iowa State University Press, Ames, Iowa.

Paddock, W., and P. Paddock. 1968. *Famine—1975!* Little, Brown, Boston.

Wilkes, H. G. 1972. The green revolution. *Environment* 14(8): 32–39.

The Ecological Problem in the Light of Sufism

Seyyed Hassein Nasr

Seyyed Hassein Nasr (1933–   ) is dean of the faculty of arts and letters at Tehran University and professor of the history of science and philosophy. He received his early education in Tehran, after which he studied physics at MIT and took his doctorate at Harvard. Among his many books are *Three Muslim Sages, Ideals and Realities of Islam,* and *Sufi Essays.*

In a sense the problem of the presence of other religions and of the presence of Nature are related from the point of view of the most current trends in Christian

Source: Seyyed Hassein Nasr, *Sufi Essays* (London, 1972), pp. 152–163. Reprinted by permission of George Allen & Unwin Ltd.

theology, for in these theological perspectives both problems concern realities cut off from the grace of the Christian revelation. It is no accident that K. Barth and his followers are so adamantly opposed or at least indifferent to both a "theology of comparative religion" and a "theology of nature." To extend the horizons of man to embrace other forms of revelation should include nature as well, since from the metaphysical point of view this also is a revelation of God, conveying its own spiritual message and possessing its own spiritual methods.[1] Strangely enough modern man is faced with both of these problems at the same time. He is in desperate need of gaining a new vision of nature and of his own relation with it in order to survive even physically; likewise he needs to reach a more profound understanding of other religions in order to better understand himself, not to speak of becoming better acquainted with segments of humanity other than his own.

In Islam the key necessary for the solution of both problems is to be found in Sufism. In the previous chapter our task was to apply Sufism's teachings to the problem posed for Islam by the presence of other religions. In the present essay these same teachings have to be applied to the question of the conquest of nature, which has taken on a most urgent character in the West and also in Japan, but which for the moment at least has not succeeded in attracting the attention of most of the Muslim intelligentsia, although in their case also it is bound to become a crucial question soon.[2] In examining this problem it has seemed expedient to deal with the Eastern sciences in general rather than with Islamic science alone, seeing that in the question of the relation of man to nature there is a profound harmony among these sciences,[3] and also in view of the fact that the question of the relation of man and nature and the crisis brought about in this realm by modern civilization has world-wide repercussions.

It is interesting to note how the cry of a few seers in the wilderness just a generation ago has today become the battle-cry of so many men who are intelligent enough to perceive the catastrophic effects that the further pursuit of the ways followed by Western civilization in its treatment of nature during the past four or five centuries can have for all humanity. If a few lonely voices in past years warned of the dangers that would follow in the path of indefinite material expansion and so-called "development" or "progress," today a great many people realize that the goal of the "conquest of nature," which has seemed the most obvious aim of modern civilization, can no longer be pursued. The very success of modern man in con-

---

[1] "Utterly untouched nature has of itself the character of a sanctuary and this it is considered to be by most nomadic and semi-nomadic peoples, particularly the Red Indians. . . . For Hindus the forest is the natural dwelling-place of sages and we meet with a similar valuation of the sacred aspect of nature in all traditions which have, even indirectly, a primordial and mythological character." F. Schuon, *Spiritual Perspectives and Human Facts.*

[2] It is unfortunately one of the worst characteristics of this age that people wait until they fall into a pitfall and only then begin to struggle to climb out of it. When one mentions the immediacy of the ecological problem and the necessity to have greater foresight in industrial and economic planning to most modernized Muslims, especially those responsible for carrying out such programmes, the stereotyped answer is that we should wait until we reach the economic level of the West and then think about such problems, to which one could simply answer that by that time it will be too late to do anything effective.

[3] We have dealt more extensively with this problem in *The Encounter of Man and Nature : the Spiritual Crisis of Modern Man.*

As for the Sufi conception of nature see Nasr, *Science and Civilization in Islam*, chapter 13; Nasr, *Islamic Studies*, chapter 13; and T. Burckhardt, *Cle spirituelle de l'astrologie musulmane*, Paris, 1950.

quering nature has itself become a major danger. All the problems caused by the unilateral attitude of modern man towards nature, from overpopulation and mass pollution to the lowering of the quality of human life itself and the threat of its actual destruction, have at least caused those capable of reflection to pause a moment and to examine the assumptions upon which modern science and its applications are based. Somehow, something has gone wrong in the application of a science that purports to be an objective knowledge of nature shorn from all spiritual and metaphysical considerations. The application of such a science seems to aid in destroying its very object. Nature seems to cry out that the knowledge derived from it through the techniques of modern Western science and then applied to it once again through technology leaves aside a whole aspect of its reality, without which it could not continue to survive as the complete and harmonious whole that in fact it is. Considering the gravity of the situation, it is to this crucial problem, to the limitations of Western science and its unending applications with the aim of "conquering nature," that we must now address ourselves by drawing from the sapiential teachings of the Oriental traditions or of what in this essay we can call "Eastern science."[4]

Before everything else it is essential to clarify what is meant by Eastern science. For our purpose here is meant the sciences of the great traditions of Asia, especially the Chinese and Japanese, the Indian and the Islamic. By extension, this term could embrace other traditional sciences, but it is sufficient here to limit ourselves to the cases cited above. Although far from being identical in themselves, these sciences share a fundamental principle in common, which is to regard the sciences of nature in the light of metaphysical principles, or from another point of view, to study nature as a domain that is "contained and embraced" by a supra-sensible world that is immensely greater than it. Because of this basic principle and many other features that are directly of indirectly related to it, one can definitely speak of Eastern science as a body of knowledge containing a distinct vision of things in contrast to Western science as it has developed since the Renaissance and as it has spread to other continents during the present century.

Moreover, in this essay the term "science" will be deliberately used rather than, let us say, "philosophy" or "religion," precisely because in the present discussion one is envisaging a science of nature which is akin in subject matter if not in method and point of view to "science" as currently understood in Western parlance. For decades people have contrasted Eastern spirituality in such forms as Sufism and the Vedanta with Western science and have written of how each has been successful and borne fruit in its own way. It has been said more than once, especially by modern orientals, that the East must learn science from the West and that the West does not have to learn geology or botany from the East but, as even some Westerners have conceded, can profit from an acquaintance with eastern religion and spirituality. We can be the first to agree that the West needs to learn metaphysics and traditional sapiential doctrines from the East if it is to preserve and revive anything at all of its own spiritual heritage. This is a dazzlingly evident reality which any profound study of comparative religion and of the present state of

---

[4] Although there are, of course, many different schools of science in each of the Oriental traditions, they are close enough in their teachings concerning the spiritual significance of nature and the relation of man to it to allow of one's using this term; there is no question here of overlooking the diversity within the Oriental traditions themselves.

mentality in the West would reveal. Many have journeyed to the lands of the East, especially those lands which have preserved to this day their spiritual heritage, such as Japan, India and the Islamic world, for just this reason.

Fewer people realize, however, that even on the level of the sciences of nature the East has something extremely precious to offer to the modern world. Just to cite a few examples, Islamic natural philosophy and physics, or Indian alchemy, or Chinese and Japanese medicine, or even, one might add, geomancy—whose practice, known as *Fung Shui*, is still prevalent in China—have something to say about the situation that the application of modern science has brought about in the form of the ecological crisis everyone now fears so greatly.

The Eastern sciences, which must be made more accessible and better known by the few historians of science specializing in these fields, were successful through just what appears in modern eyes as their failure. Modern science on the other hand is in a sense facing failure—especially through its alliance with technology and the spirit of conquest over nature—because of its very success. In this major dilemma the modern world needs not only Eastern spirituality and metaphysics, which evidently are the essence and fundamental basis of all the Eastern traditions and contain the principles of all the traditional sciences, but also the curative influence of the world view contained in the Eastern sciences of nature.

Hitherto, the educated reader found it well nigh impossible to take seriously the world view of the Eastern sciences and this still is the case in most Western "intellectual" circles. Western science has "advanced," in whatever sense we define this ambiguous term, by negating all other possible sciences of nature. Its monolithic and monopolistic character has been part and parcel of its image of its own self, although there is no logic whatsoever which would deny the possibility of other legitimate forms of science existing alongside it. The sense of pride that has accompanied the particular type of mental activity called "modern science" is such that it relegates anything that does not conform to its view of what true science should be to the realm of "pseudo-science." That is why today so many things which are left out of the official scientific view in the West are creeping up in the form of occult sciences, against whose rise modern science has no power at all. The totalitarian character of modern science has duped the vast majority of men who accept its point of view unconditionally into denying the possibility of any form of knowledge of a serious order, with the result that interest in anything other than the "official science" usually manifests itself in the form of a truncated and mutilated occultism. To quote the words of one of the rare men in the West who understand the real meaning of the Eastern traditions and their sciences, "It is man who has let himself be deceived by discoveries and inventions of a falsely totalitarian science, that is to say a science that does not recognize its own proper limits and for that same reason misses whatever lies beyond these limits."[5]

The terms "science" and "pseudo-science" will bear a little closer examination. A traditional science of metals and minerals such as alchemy, or of sacred geography or of geomancy, is called pseudo-science in modern parlance without anyone bothering to examine the principles that lie behind it. For instance, it is undeniable that by applying what today is called science in the form of different

[5] F. Schuon, "No Activity Without Truth," *Studies in Comparative Religion,* 1969, p. 196.

engineering or architectural projects, modern man often produces monstrosities of ugliness, while in applying the so-called "pseudo-sciences" of sacred geography and geomancy the Chinese and Japanese or the Persians and Arabs have produced some of the most beautiful buildings, gardens and city landscapes imaginable. The same would apply to the applications of chemistry and alchemy, respectively.

Before the fruits of these two types of science—one of which is honoured by being called "true science" and the other denigrated by being called "pseudo-science"—man instinctively feels that there is an aspect of nature which so-called pseudo-science, as it has existed in traditional civilizations and not in its current deformations in the Occident, takes into consideration and which modern official science has allowed to be neglected. It is the qualitative and spiritual element of nature which is the source of the beauty reflected in the Persian or Japanese garden and in works of a similar nature based upon the Eastern sciences; and it is precisely this element that is lacking in the creations of modern science. Moreover, this qualitative element is certainly present in nature itself and with as great a certainty absent from the fruits of modern technology. One could thus conclude that the qualitative element, reflected in the beauty and harmony observable within nature, is an ontological aspect of nature which no science of nature can ignore except at its own peril. It is also because of the presence of this element of complexity pertaining to the chain or community of life on this earth that is the source of the strength and survival of this community, even from a biological point of view. In contrast, because of the lack of this qualitative and spiritual element, the very complexity of technology is of a quite different order, and as a result is becoming ever more a source of danger and weakness for technological society.

People who speak of the fusion of the sciences of East and West must know that such a thing has certainly not yet occurred in our times.[6] Nor could it occur so long as the attitude of modern science remains what it is. Such a fusion could, in fact, only occur if modern science would agree to put aside its monopolistic point of view so that a science could be developed which would embrace the qualitative and spiritual elements in nature as well as the quantitative aspect of things. Such a science would of necessity be based upon a metaphysical and cosmological doctrine which would perceive the relativity of the relative and realize that the whole material plane of reality is but a speck of dust before the supra-sensible and supra-formal worlds that encompass it. It would also of necessity be combined with an attitude of contemplation toward nature rather than be wedded to the desire for its domination and conquest. This desire, to be sure, is a direct result of the fact that, for all his science of the reality that surrounds him, modern man remains totally ignorant of certain basic aspects of this reality.

The import of Eastern science to the contemporary problems caused by the applications of Western science in many different fields can be illustrated through the problem of the unicity of and interrelation between things. This simple principle, which lies at the heart of all Sufi doctrine, will also cast some light upon the nature of Eastern science itself, whose contents we certainly cannot even begin to analyse here. Until now, modern science has succeeded largely by turning its back

[6] See A. K. Coomaraswamy, "Gradation, Evolution, and Reincarnation," in *The Bugbear of Literacy*, London, 1949, pp. 122–30.

upon the interrelation between different parts of nature and by isolating each segment of nature in order to be able to analyse and dissect it separately. Ideally, according to Newtonian physics, in studying a falling body we can only calculate the gravitational forces acting upon it by knowing the mass and distance of every particle of matter in the material Universe. But since this is impossible, we consider only the earth as the centre of attraction and forget about all the other parts of the material Universe. As a result, we are able to arrive at a precise numerical figure by applying the laws of Newton to the simplified case in question. Something has been gained through this method no doubt; but also something very fundamental has been lost and neglected, namely the basic truth that the simple falling body is related to all the particles of the Universe through a force which Plato would call *eros* and Ibn Sînâ *'ishq*.[7]

Formerly the loss of this aspect of the relation between things was considered trivial when compared with the gains of being able to have mathematical precision. But now that the application of this partial science of nature has destroyed so much of nature itself and threatens us with much worse calamities, and since furthermore the ecologists have discovered that the whole natural environment is a remarkably complex but harmonious whole in which nothing functions except in connection with the other parts, it has become clear how catastrophic this type of omission actually is. Only now after causing so much damage do we realize that in order to survive we must put a stop to the indiscriminate destruction of our natural environment and the waste of the resources which provide for our needs; we must face the fact that our needs and the sources that can provide for them are interconnected with other parts of nature, animate and inanimate, in a way that the present sciences of nature have failed to grasp fully as a result of their own self-imposed limitation.

In the West a poet like John Donne could write four centuries ago ... "No man is an *Iland*, intire of it selfe; every man is a peece of the *Continent*, a part of the *maine*; if a *Clod* bee washed away by the *Sea, Europe* is the lesse." Although here Donne is referring to humanity, his vision certainly did not exclude the whole of creation of which man is a part. At a later date, Romantic poets like Wordsworth could describe the awareness of the spirit infused in all forms of nature and whereby these forms are integrated, an awareness that leads man to a sense of the Infinite, as the following lines of his show:

The sense sublime
Of something far more deeply interfused,
Whose dwelling is the light of setting suns,
And the round ocean and the living air,
And the blue sky, and in the mind of man;
A motion and a spirit, that impels
All thinking things, all objects of all thoughts,
And rolls through all things.

(Lines Composed above Tintern Abbey)

---

[7] On the attraction between material particles which is known as love or *'ishq* see Ibn Sînâ, *Risâlah fi'l-'ishq*, trans. by E. L. Fackenheim, *Medieval Studies*, vol. 7, 1945, pp. 208–228; and Nasr, *An Introduction to Islamic Cosmological Doctrines*, pp. 261–262.

Such views were considered by official Western science as no more than poetic images, having nothing to do with "science," and the same applied to the utterances of other romantic poets like Shelley and Novalis who wrote about the spiritual aspect of nature and the interrelation between its parts: only now do ecologists realize how "scientific" such poetic utterances really were! But neither then nor now, because of the lack of the appropriate metaphysical knowledge on the part of modern scientists and the absence of a living sapiential tradition to give intellectual support to such poetry could a firm intellectual basis be established for the views expressed poetically by Donne, Wordsworth and others.[8] Consequently, no means can be discovered through these channels to transform Western science in a way that is fundamental enough to enable it to take into serious consideration this sense of the interrelation between things—which of necessity also means the various levels of existence.

It is to the Eastern sciences that we must turn in order to discover a world view in which the principle of the interrelatedness of things plays a central part. The traditional sciences of nature exist for the express purpose of making known, rather than veiling, the unicity of nature, which derives directly from the Unity of the Divine Principle, as all the masters of Islamic gnosis have declared.[9] In the case of the Islamic sciences, the sense of Unity pervades all things and all forms of knowledge, Unity (al-tawhîd) being the central axis around which everything revolves in the Islamic world-view. In Hinduism also the various traditional sciences contained in the darshánas, although separate outwardly, are based on the interrelatedness of all things and represent stages in the development of knowledge. As for the Chinese and Japanese traditions, there also the "ten-thousand things" are related and belong in fact to a whole, so that every science of nature reflects in one way or another both heaven and earth, and through them the Unity that transcends this polarity. An ancient Chinese sage, Sêng-chao, once said: "Heaven and earth and I are of the same root, the ten-thousand things and I are of one substance." The intuition of the oneness of the roots of things, reflecting the metaphysical principle of the "transcendent unity of Being," forms the very matrix of the Eastern sciences of nature.

As far as the traditional civilizations and their sciences are concerned, Islam occupies a special position in its role as intermediary between the Eastern traditions and the West. In the same way that geographically Islam covers the middle belt of the world, intellectually and spiritually it occupies a position half way between the mental climate of the Occident and the intellectual climate of the Indian and Far Eastern worlds. The reference made in the Quran to the Islamic people as the "people of the middle" alludes, among other things, to this truth.

The Islamic sciences, which were cultivated avidly for seven hundred years, from the third/ninth to the tenth/sixteenth centuries and even afterwards, are deeply related on the one hand to Western science in its medieval and Renaissance phases and on the other hand to the sciences of India and China. In fact, Islamic science was related to these sciences historically both in its genesis and in its later

---

[8] In contrast, such Sufi verses as the famous line of Sa'di, "I am in love with the whole Universe because it comes from Him," are supported by rigorous metaphysical principles which make such poems not only beautiful poetic utterances but explications of the Truth in the dress of poetic imagery.
[9] See S. H. Nasr, *An Introduction to Islamic Cosmological Doctrines*, pp. 4ff.

development. Islam created a science which must be considered as science according to whatever definition we give to this term, a science without which science in the West could not have developed, although modern Western science eventually adopted a completely different point of view. At the same time Islamic science did not bring into being a secular science independent of a spiritual vision of the Universe. It carefully guarded the proportions between things, giving the spiritual and material their proper due and always preserving in mind the hierarchy of being and knowledge, whereby the integration of the sciences of nature into a wisdom transcending all discursive thought was maintained. Furthermore, many of the leading Muslim scientists were Sufis, gnostics ('ârifs), theosophers and traditional philosophers (hakîms) who developed the discursive and analytical sciences always in the bosom of the contemplative vision of nature.[10] From Ibn Sînâ to Naṣîr al-Dîn Ṭûsî and Quṭb al-Dîn Shîrâzî, all of whom were great scientists and philosophers-mystics, we encounter outstanding figures in the history of science who were at the same time men of spiritual vision and who would have felt perfectly at ease in the presence of the contemplative sages of China, Japan and India.

Islam developed within itself different intellectual schools, hierarchically ordered, which stretch over a vast intellectual expanse, ranging from Sufism, which is akin in its doctrines and methods to the pure sapiential doctrines of the Indian, Chinese and Japanese traditions, to the Peripatetic school, which is close to the main philosophical tradition of medieval Europe, of which sprang—albeit through miscomprehension—modern rationalistic philosophy. Also, because of the centrality of the doctrine of unity in Islam, the principle of the unicity of nature upon which the Eastern sciences are based is emphasized with remarkable persistence in Islamic science, clothed in a rational as well as an intuitive garb. Thus it is perhaps more accessible to minds nurtured on Western modes of thought than the purely metaphysical and supra-rational perspectives usually found in the works of the sages of India and the Far East. But this is only a question of method of exposition and means of access to the pure truth. As already mentioned, the Eastern sciences are essentially unified in their vision of nature and in the principles of science based upon this vision.

To come back to the necessity of turning to Eastern science in order to help solve the crisis that Western science has brought upon itself, it must be stated that the realization by modern ecologists that one must study the whole environment as a complex unity in which everything is interrelated can only be complete if it also embraces the psychological and spiritual levels of reality and hence ultimately the Source of all that is. It is of course good to realize that inanimate objects are related to animate ones and that all parts of this corporeal world are interrelated; but the metaphysical principle of the relation of the states of being to one other, according to which any lower state of being derives its reality from the state above it, from which it is inseparable, has to be borne in mind at every step and can never be negated or nullified. If the terrestrial sphere has fallen into the danger of disorder and chaos, it is precisely because Western man has tried for several centuries to remain a purely terrestrial being and has sought to cut off his terrestrial world from

[10] We have dealt extensively with this problem in our *Science and Civilization in Islam*.

any reality that transcends it. The profanation of nature through its so-called conquest and the development of a purely secular science of nature would not have been possible otherwise.

This being so, it is not possible to correct this disorder in the natural domain without removing its cause, which is none other than the attempt to consider the terrestrial state of existence in isolation from all that transcends it. Present ecological considerations can overcome some of the barriers that separative and compartmentalized studies of nature have brought about, but they cannot solve the profounder problems which involve man himself, because it is precisely man who has disturbed the ecological balance through factors of a nonbiological nature. The spiritual revolt of man against heaven has polluted the earth, and no attempt to rectify the situation on earth can ever be fully successful without the revolt against heaven coming to an end. For it is only the light of heaven cast upon the earth through the presence of seers and contemplatives living within the framework of the authentic religious traditions of humanity that preserves the harmony and beauty of nature and in fact maintains the cosmic equilibrium. Until this truth is understood all attempts to re-establish peace with nature will end in failure, although they can have partial success in preventing a particular tragedy from occurring here or there.

Once again it is only Eastern science, grounded in metaphysical principles, that can re-establish harmony between man and earth, by first establishing harmony between man and heaven and thereby turning man's covetous and greedy attitude toward nature, which underlies the reckless exploitation of natural resources, into an attitude combined with and based upon contemplation and compassion. It is only tradition that can convert man from his role of plunderer of the earth to that of the "viceregent of God on earth" (khaîifat Allâh fi'l-ard), to use the Islamic terminology.[11]

If it be asked what one is to do in a practical manner in the present context, it can be answered that on the plane of knowledge one must seek a higher science of nature into which the quantitative sciences of nature can be integrated. This in turn can only be achieved through a knowledge of the indispensable metaphysical principles upon which these sciences are ultimately based. On the plane of action it would mean first of all to act at all times according to the truth, according to the religious principle, in whatever situation one is placed. The question often asked in desperation, as to whether activity still has any meaning, can best be answered once again in the words of F. Schuon,

> To this is must be answered that an affirmation of the truth, or any effort on behalf of truth, is never in vain, even if we cannot from beforehand measure the value or the outcome of such an activity. Moreover we have no choice in the matter. Once we know the truth we must needs live in it and fight for it, but what we must avoid at any price is to let ourselves bask in illusions. Even if, at this moment the horizon seems as dark as possible, one must not forget that in a perhaps unavoidably distant future the victory is ours and cannot but be ours. Truth by its very nature conquers all obstacles: Vincit omnia Veritas.[12]

[11] See S. H. Nasr, "Who is Man: the Perennial Answer to Islam," in Man and His World, Toronto, 1968, pp. 61–68, also in Studies in Comparative Religion, 1968, pp. 45–56.
[12] F. Schuon, "No Activity Without Truth," p. 203.

As far as nature is concerned, for those who understand Sufism, or more generally metaphysics and the Eastern sciences of nature, it is their duty and function in relation to the truth to continue to expound their knowledge, to love nature and to contemplate her never-ending forms as theophanies of the Divine All-Possibility. Such an attitude would itself be the greatest charity for the world, for it would make concretely evident before modern man the possibility of another attitude towards nature, one which he needs desperately in order to survive even physically. Men from such cultures as the Islamic, where Sufi poets, especially those of the Persian language, have sung over the centuries of the beauties of nature as reflections of the beauties of paradise in which man's being is refreshed and renewed, have a special vocation at the present time. The same can be said of the Japanese whose remarkable artistic gifts combined with the deepest insight into nature have evolved what might be described as echoes of the angelic world amidst the very forms of earthly nature; Japanese artists have almost succeeded in bringing paradise literally down to earth. All who have been granted this insight must remain true to themselves and preserve the traditional sciences of nature and those metaphysical principles that are so precious for the future of their own cultures. They must also make these teachings well enough known to the world at large for others who are seeking such teachings to benefit from them. In this vital question, as in so many others, the traditional cultures of the East can render the greatest service to the world by remaining first of all faithful, more than ever before, to their own principles. And in this task they have the guarantee of ultimate success, for they are grounded in the truth, and as the Quran has said "Truth has come and falsehood has vanished away. Lo! falsehood is ever bound to vanish" (XVII, 81).

The Crisis of Sexuality: Women and God

Beyond Eve and Mary

Margaret N. Maxey

Margaret N. Maxey taught theological ethics at the University of Detroit. She is also a Roman Catholic nun of the order of the Sacred Heart of Jesus.

Detained by an incautious title, a reader should expect an incautious essay into a doubly forbidding realm: a Theology of (and for) Women. I am fully aware that in introducing this expression I may appear far less enlightened than some of my colleagues or seem ignorant of their strictures.[1] As a matter of fact, those strictures are precisely what this essay is about. But not only that.

As if all were not about Eve, a "Woman's Liberation" theme at once freights an inquiry with overtones of complicity in, or undertones of compliance to, a movement propelled by a psychology of protest. But protest is not the cutting edge for the kind of liberation I have in mind. Protest can vocalize the effects but cannot thereby eliminate the origins of injustice or exploitation. Moreover, recent opinion polls among the women who are presumably being "liberated" indicate that their attitude quotients cover the entire spectrum from Right to Left. Evidently a "silent majority" of women are rejecting the strategies and rhetoric coined by their self-styled Liberators of the New Left. Yet just as evidently, contemporary women are instinctively (if silently) rejecting an androcentric cultural and religious heritage which continues to assume that Man sets the standards and is in fact the norm for being human, and that Woman is man's indispensable complement and companion —a divine but gratuitous afterthought. The women who refuse to compete for

Source: Martin Marty (ed.), New Theology No. 9. Originally published in Dialog. Reprinted by permission of the author.

[1] In her competent study, The Church and the Second Sex (New York: Harper & Row, 1968), Professor Mary Daly concludes her discussion of "Theological Roots of the Problem" by asserting "it is necessary to opt for a clear-cut rejection of that approach which is suggested by the expression, 'theology of woman.' This approach contains a built-in assumption that 'woman' is in fact a distinct species which can be understood apart from the other sex. It is founded on the unproved supposition that there is an innate psychosexual complementarity. Invariably, attempts to develop a 'theology of woman' fall on their various faces because they naively assume that the sex images of a patriarchal culture infallibly correspond to 'nature' and to God's will." (p. 147). It seems unfortunate that Professor Daly does not recognize that the expression need not indicate an uncritical acceptance of the "naive assumptions" which she attributes to those who adopt the expression for other purposes.

masculine roles in Church and Society are thereby refusing to emulate man as their norm. From my reading of the evidence, I have concluded that women are instinctively searching for a different and peculiar kind of liberation. This is why I would assign to theology a peculiar task.

I

Clearly, woman's identity is in trouble today. She feels compelled to carve out anew or to relocate her identity by competing for those economic, socio-political, sexual roles with which Western culture and history have presumably awarded men their "superior" status. Her logic is not to be faulted. Her *models* are. When women look back over cultural and religious history for facts to document their demand for "liberation," their arguments are not inconsistent. Their presuppositions are.

This essay wishes to take seriously the dictum, "He [she] who is ignorant of history is condemned to repeat it." Its seriousness emerges from a sobering realization: we ourselves shape history by the kind of questions we address to it thinking, mistakenly, that we somehow recover a *neutral* or *objective* past. Contemporary women (and men) cannot change the history which has produced them and their problems. But women (and men) do control their interpretations of history—the modeling character they confer on it. More and more women are reviewing their past and protesting their present condition of exploitation. It would be unfortunate if the "solutions" women project were to be truncated and narrowed by a past from which they only seek "liberation." The need for a critical instrument—for a "theology" of and for "women"—inserts itself precisely at this point. An instrumental theology would have the task of liberating women from past models by displacing them with new models.

A particular notion of "theology" is just as much at issue here as a notion about "women." The credentials qualifying a person to assume that her notion about woman is valid do not yet qualify as valid supports for her notion about theology. And so I must look for support from accepted theologians—who happen to have been men, who also happen to have been celibates, yet who did not therefore disqualify themselves from speaking as experts about, to and for unknown and unknowable women. The case I am trying to make for a "theology of woman" would define theology as an instrument for criticizing and constructing models for self-interpretation—in this case, of women. It would appear that theologians in the past have already made my case.

Take Augustine of Hippo. The misogynistic deliverances of a Jerome[2] or a Tertullian[3] or a John Damascene[4] or an Ambrose[5] are generally disallowed by the

[2] Besides praising marriage grudgingly because it brings forth virgins, Jerome can also be credited with asking: "If we abstain from coitus we honor our wives; if we do not abstain—well, what is the opposite of honor but insult?" (*Adv. Joy*, I.7). Concerning woman, he writes: "As long as woman is for birth and children, she is different from man as body is from soul. But when she wishes to serve Christ more than the world, then she will cease to be a woman and will be called Man [*vir*]." (*Comm. in epist. ad Ephes.*, III. 5 [PL 26, 567]).

[3] Characteristically, Tertullian addresses the "guilty sex" by asking woman: "Do you not know that each of you is also an Eve ? . . . You are the devil's gateway, you are the unsealer of that forbidden tree, you are the first deserter of the divine law, you are the one who persuaded him whom the devil was too weak to attack. How easily you destroyed man, the image of God! Because of the death which you brought upon us, even the Son of God had to die. . . ." (*De cult, feminarium*, I. 1).

theological purist. The basis for disallowing statements of these early Fathers is that they reflect, in each case, some controlling idiosyncrasy in personal biography, or a polemic occasioned by a cultural climate of opinion. With Augustine, however, the margin for disallowance is embarrassingly diminished, not only because the weight of his "theological authority" in Western Christian tradition has been considerable, but because his theological doctrines still find resonances in Christian consciousness. It is from Augustine the Christian *theologian*—not Augustine the repentant father of an illegitimate son, or unfaithful lover of a mistress—that Christians have inherited a theology of human sexuality, of marriage, of virginity, and summarily of Woman. As a consequence, Christian women have had to locate themselves somewhere between Eve and Mary.

Whatever the wellsprings of Augustine's theology, it has given to Women a theological significance and explanatory function distinct from Man. My point is not to *discount* the psychological conflicts which at one time shaped Augustine's theological speculations. To the contrary, my concern is to insist upon their theological indispensability. The point I wish to press is not the obvious one that some emotional or intellectual bias can always be held to acccount partially for why a thinker has the theological (or any other) perspective he has. The point is that a *psychology* is inevitably ingredient to any theological accountability for the human condition.

The initial question is why Augustine should have developed his doctrine of "original sin" by linking the *Fall* of man and woman to their *sexuality*. The consensus of recent scholarship seems to point to one primary explanatory factor.[6] This factor is the primacy that a dualistic faculty psychology has awarded to *rational control*, both as a means for differentiating man from other species of animal, and as a means for differentiating Man from Woman.[7] The evidence for this factor in Augustine's theological development is impressive.[8]

Against the pessimistic dualism of the Manicheans who condemned coitus and marriage as intrinsically evil, and against the optimistic naturalism of the Pelagians who declared the natural goodness of man and his endowments despite

[4] John Damascene is reported to have described woman as "a wicked she-ass, a hideous tapeworm . . . the advanced post of hell." (Cf. "A History of Catholic Thinking on Contraception" by Daniel Sullivan in *What Modern Catholics Think About Child Control* [New York: Signet Book, 1964], pp. 28–73).

[5] Ambrose measures Woman against the standard of Man in these terms: "She who does not believe is a woman and should be designated by the name of her sex, whereas she who believes progresses to perfect manhood, to the measure of the adulthood of Christ. She then dispenses with the name of her sex. . . ." (*Expos. evang. sec. Lucam*, X, 161).

[6] See D. S. Bailey's discussion of Augustine in *The Man-Woman Relation in Christian Thought* (London: Longmans, Green and Co., 1959), pp. 50ff. Also, Daniel Sullivan, op. cit., pp. 36ff.

[7] The view that woman is "the irrational half" of mankind is expressed by St. Methodius, among others, in support or his assertion that woman is "carnal and sensuous." Ambrose, Pope St. Gregory, and Cyril of Alexandria are of one mind, writes Callahan (*op. cit.*, p. 32) in discoursing on "woman's slow understanding, her unstable and naive mind, her natural mental weakness, and her need of an authoritative husband."

[8] Augustine has himself insisted that it was rational and spiritual *certitude* he had been seeking in vain through Manichaeism, skepticism, and Neoplatonism. When he seemed at last to have found certitude in the Christian faith, the condition for its attainment was radical—*sexual continence*, the renunciation of sexual pleasure or "sensuality" via disciplined asceticism. At the heart of Augustine's conversion to Christian faith was a decision *for* rational certitude and a contemplative life, but only by way of a decision *against* sexual pleasure, even in legitimate marriage. Augustine was obviously a man of his time in his esteem for a reasoned and disciplined "contemplation of divine things" attainable through a single-minded "way of perfection."

the Fall, Augustine had to develop a theology of sexuality which avoided both extremes. Moreover, Augustine had to account for man's original transgression without compromising two other extremes. On the one hand, Augustine had to affirm that man was a perfectly created being, lest some imperfection or weakness in man be ascribed to a divine deficiency in power or in goodness. On the other hand, man's original condition had to allow for the origination of sin from man's own activity, as a distortion of the goodness of God's primal gift. The keystone in the arch bridging both sets of extremes was to be Augustine's theory of concupiscence.[9]

Originally neutral in meaning "desire," *concupiscentia* in Augustine's theory assumed the explanatory function of "lust," the insatiable and inordinate drive for self-satisfaction operating in every human impulse, but most powerfully and typically in genital sexuality. In Augustine's exegesis of the Genesis account of the Fall of Man, we discover his account of the cause and subsequent manifestation of "original sin." Eve and Adam, by their respective disobedience and rebellious act against God's express command, were themselves infected by their disobedience. It recoiled upon their natural powers, impairing the control of their bodies, organs, and especially their genitals.[10]

The fact that Adam and Eve covered their nakedness (according to Genesis) was a confirmation for the theory Augustine proposed. He argues that the original shame of Adam and Eve continues to be reenacted in man's sense of shame and guilt when he recovers his rational powers, after they have been engulfed by uncontrollable and unseemly sexual pleasure. The greater strength of sexual impulses has not only clouded the mind, but disabled the will, making it incapable of inciting or controlling either tumescence or impotence.[11]

Whereas God intended and implanted sexual desires to assure the continuance of mankind, man has corrupted sexual desire by his concupiscence (lust), causing every concrete act of coitus he performs to be intrinsically evil (irrational), sinful (disobedient), and shameful (guilt-ridden). Virtually, if not explicitly, Augustine is responsible for having formulated a theological equivalence between original sin, concupiscence or desire, and sexual passion.[12]

Augustine acknowledged that the intention to procreate would excuse a husband and wife from the sinfulness inherent to their marriage act. Nevertheless, coitus remained the channel by which parents transmit concupiscence and its accompanying guilt to their children. Without exception, "Everyone who is born of sexual intercourse is in fact sinful flesh."[13]

It makes little difference whether we trace Augustine's doctrine of the Fall and concept of sin to his own psychological history or to a then-current Christian asceticism and its ideal of perfection. The theological fact remains that a dualistic *psychology* has been ingredient and presupposed to the theological doctrine which has produced an Augustinian model of Woman. To Augustine's theological man,

---

9 For a fuller discussion of this point, see Bailey, op. cit. pp. 52–58.
10 Augustine, *De civitate Dei*, XIII. 13 and XIV. 16–17.
11 *De nupt. et concup.* I. 6.
12 See the discussion of Norman P. Williams in *The Ideas of the Fall and of Original Sin* (London, 1927), esp. pp. 366–367.
13 *De myst. et cont.* I. 13.

woman as a theological datum is the visible incarnation of sexual desire and lust, the carrier of evil and guilt, the occasion of man's original Fall and subsequent transmission of sin. For Augustine, it is only proper that, "since through a female death had occurred to us, through a female also life should be born to us."[14] As mother of all the living, Eve had brought dishonor upon all women. Through Mary, however, women can be honored if they imitate and reflect her Virginal Motherhood.

Augustinian man was exhorted to obey the divine command to love woman in the same way that he was to love an enemy. That is to say, Man must regard Woman not as an opposing adversary, but simply as a similar human being. Or in other words, man must regard woman not as a *sexed* being, but simply as a *sinful* human being to be redeemed. Augustine writes:

> . . . it is characteristic of a good Christian to love in a woman the creature of God whom he desires to be transformed and renewed, but to hate corruptible and mortal intimacy and sexual intercourse—that is—to love the human being in her, but to hate what belongs to her as a wife.[15]

A recent commentator on Augustine has noted that, for this theologian at least, "sex was no more intrinsic to human nature than hatred to one's adversary."[16] Augustine's evaluation of sexuality, and thus of woman's relation to man, has long given theological support to the insistence that "being sexed" is inconsequential and nonessential—if not detrimental—to "being a person."

Parenthetically, I find a disturbing redivivus of Augustinian Man in the assertions of those who hastily dismiss a "theology of woman" in favor of a homogenized "theological anthropology." One argument for this dismissal has suggested that ". . . a 'theology of woman' . . . is misbegotten in that it places sexual differentiation above personhood." As a corrective, we are urged "to develop a theological anthropology which will study the dynamics of human personality and social relationship from a radically evolutionary point of view."[17] It is quite possible that we can agree upon the objections to a "theology of woman" without, however, agreeing that the correctives proposed are sufficient or able to meet those objections.

Given woman's present stage of self-interpretation, it will not do simply to substitute one form of theological dogmatizing for another. It cannot be the theological task to debunk "natural" or "essential" sexual differences summarily, and then proceed to substitute socially-conditioned "persons-in-relation," presumably displacing distinct "sexes" or "essences in isolation."[18] Such an enterprise is, I submit, methodologically wrong-headed and theologically shortsighted.

Theology must at present perform a *liberating task*, not impose still another set of dogmas, however different. If theology is to acquit itself of its most urgent task, it must begin to recognize not only the modeling and remodeling functions

---

[14] *De agone Chr.* XXII. 24.

[15] *De serm. Dom. in mont.* I. 15. 41.

[16] William E. Phipps, *Was Jesus Married? The Distortion of Sexuality in the Christian Tradition* (New York: Harper & Row, 1970), p. 173.

[17] Daly, *op. cit.*, p. 147.

[18] *Loc. cit.*

it has performed in the past, but also the source of its models. This recognition would require, among other reconstructions, a Theology of Woman which would first locate past models dominating woman's self-interpretation; then it would locate and criticize the source of those models; finally, it would reconstruct or propose new models for woman's (and man's) self-understanding.

In our brief examination of Augustine, we have, in fact, illustrated this mode of inquiry. Augustine's model of Woman has been traced to his equation of original sin with concupiscence and sexual passion, an equation which depends on a dualistic psychology which awards primacy to rational control as the index of man's superiority over women and over animals. Augustine's model of Woman is clearly inseparable from his model of human sexuality, with its ideal of virginity. The result is that Woman is to be located between Eve and Mary.

Is it accurate to insist that what we have inherited from Augustine are *models* for self-interpretation and for evaluating human behavior? We may evaluate this insistence by assessing our response to a number of questions. How extensively does our culture still retain the notion that sexuality is somehow tainted with sin or evil? Do men and women still equate being moral or Christian with suppressing sexual desire? Do we contrast Christian love (*agape*) with sexual love (*eros*), or relegate an ideal sexuality to the nonself, to an a-personal or infrahuman domain? We might also evaluate the modeling character of an Augustinian inheritance by asking if our ideal in liberating women is to render them *equal* to men as *human beings*—that is to say, insignificantly distinct from men on the basis of *sexual* differences, and thus, distinct from men only as individual persons are distinguishable. Do we exhort and expect men and women to be simply equivalent as "creatures of God" and distinguishable only as individual persons? Those who refuse to collapse the differences between men and women by reducing them to "individuality differences" are in effect, if not in conscious intent, refusing to perpetuate the theological models of Augustinian Man and Augustinian Woman.

II

The thesis I am attempting to argue is that we shall never liberate women (or men), Christian or otherwise, until we have induced *theology* to liberate women. First and foremost, theology must liberate women from an Augustinian model by refusing to reduce woman's theological significance to some a-sexual, homogeneous, or relational "human" being. Human sexual differences are neither theologically evil nor theologically nonessential. The alternative to homogeneity is to construct a new theological model of woman—a model introducing correctives from an updated depth-psychology that will counteract not only Augustine's *concupiscentia*, but also Freud's *libido*. The theological model I propose to construct would rely primarily (though not exclusively) on the depth-psychology of Jung and his inter-preters.[19] It would supply a *model* for interpretation, not a touchstone of orthodoxy.

[19] For example: C. G. Jung, "Women in Europe," *Contributions to Analytical Psychology* (New York: Harcourt Brace, 1928); R. S. J. Hostie, *Religion and the Psychology of Jung* (New York: Sheed and Ward, 1957); Erich Neumann, *Amor and Psyche* (New York: Bollingen Series I.IV, Pantheon Books, 1965); E, C. Whitmont, *Basic Concepts of Analytical Psychology* (New York: C. G. Jung Foundation, 1967).

According to the thesis I am arguing, the theological task of "liberating" women would get underway primarily by rejecting and counteracting an Augustinian inheritance; it would then construct a corrective formed as a more promising alternative. This task would at once be compounded, however, for theologians have authorized more than an Augustinian model for woman's self-interpretation.

III

Consider the case of Thomas Aquinas. What a Neoplatonic psychological dualism had provided for Augustine, an Aristotelian biological naturalism provided for Aquinas, but with an important difference. Preoccupied with the problem of grace and the human will, Augustine had addressed himself to the problem of sin in Fallen Man; only indirectly did he address himself to Woman as acquiring significance from that theological problem. But Aquinas, preoccupied by the problem of grace and human nature, addressed himself directly to the problem of Woman as having been produced by the Author of Nature. The problem of woman's divinely intended *place in nature*, rather than her contingent *role in sin*, dictated the terms in which Thomas accounted theologically for the distinction between women and men.

From the self-evidence of woman's nature—her predestined maternity and inferior powers of reason—Aquinas deduced the general intention of the Universal Author of Nature:

> It was necessary for woman to be made . . . as a helpmate for man—not indeed as a help in some other work, as some maintain, for in fact, in any other work a man can be more efficiently helped by another man than by a woman—but as a help in the work of generation.[20]

Woman's maternal function indicated to Thomas that the natural order had appointed to woman a social location in the family. In that location, it would be contrary to "good order" (unnatural) ". . . if some were not governed by others wiser than themselves. So by a kind of subjection, woman is naturally subject to man, because in man the power of reason predominates."[21] Woman's inferior powers of reason and limited contribution to man's work could not result from nature's general tendency, nor could it be ascribed to its Author's universal intent. Therefore, it was evidently due to accidental factors which could in the end work Nature's will and weal.

Adopting Aristotle's *homunculus* theory (the male sperm precontains a "little man"), Aquinas accounted for and justified woman's existence in these terms:

> Woman is misbegotten and defective, for the active force in the male seed tends to the production of a perfect likeness in the masculine sex; while the production of woman comes from a defect in the active force or from some material indisposition, or even from some external influence, as such as that of a south wind which is moist.[22]

[20] Thomas Aquinas, *Summa Theologiae*, I. 92. 1.
[21] *S. Th.* I. 92. 1, ad 2^m.
[22] *S. Th.* I. 92. 1.

Woman's defective condition, however, is not to be considered totally detrimental to humankind. Woman fulfills a limited task, that of contributing to the greater efficiency of nature's general tendency. Thomas avers that, ". . . as regards human nature in general, woman is not misbegotten but is *included* in nature's intention as directed to the work of generation."[23] Hence, Thomas is led to interpret woman's biological defectiveness and rational inferiority as a divinely willed asset: woman contributes to the common good by generating members of the human species.

Although he acknowledges the Genesis account—where God's intention in creating woman appears to be that man have companionship or an "other" to enrich self-knowledge—Aquinas persists in his biologism by insisting that the divine purpose for human sexuality, thus for woman, is human reproduction. In the first place, it is by the divine order that sexual organs are given to man, for they are intended for procreation. As such, sexual endowments are for a social or common good, not for individual purposes.

> Generation is the only natural act that is ordered to the common good, for eating and the emission of waste-matters pertain to the individual good, but generation to the preservation of the species[24]

In the second place, the divine order requires that man respect the purpose for which woman has been allotted to man.

> A woman is taken into man's society for the needs of generation [reproduction]; with the disappearance of woman's fecundity and beauty, she would no longer be able to associate with another man.[25]

Consequently, since woman has been reproductive, Thomas concludes that man ought in justice and out of duty to remain with his wife after she grows old.

Despite his skillful departure from an Augustinian condemnation of sexual pleasure as intrinsically evil, Thomas could not depart from a rationalist perfectionism which both justified and preserved the purely *biological* purpose of sexual functions. Thomas insisted, on the one hand, that the purpose of certain natural powers was unquestionably good. On the other hand, he had to agree with Augustine that sexual pleasures were more oppressive to the reason than pleasures of the palate; and since sexual pleasures are more impetuous,

> . . . they are in greater need of chastisement and restraint. . . . Hence, Augustine says, "I consider that nothing so casts down the manly mind from its heights as the fondling of women, and those bodily contacts which belong to the married state." [26]

[23] *S. Th.* I. 92, 1, ad s^m.
[24] *Summa Contra Gentes* III. 2. 123.
[25] *S.C.G.* III. 2. 123.
[26] *S. Th.* II-II, 151. 3. Thomas later writes: "Sexual intercourse casts down the mind, not from virtue but from the height, that is, the perfection of virtue." (II-II. 153. 2).

Again: "For those people who devote their attention to the contemplation of divine things and of every kind of truth, it is especially harmful to have been addicted to sexual pleasures." (S.C.G. III. 2. 136).

Moreover, Thomas declared that ". . . in the sex act, man becomes like the animals because the pleasure of the act and the fervor of concupiscence cannot be moderated by reason."[27] Again, he insisted that "the man who is too ardent a lover of his wife acts counter to the good of marriage," and therefore he might be termed "an adulterer."[28] In these affirmations, however, Thomas is much less a psychologist than a biologist. In his perspective, the *purpose of Nature's Creator* is adulterated or frustrated when men substitute the good of *individual* pleasure for the *common* good of continuing the species.

Clearly, Thomas Aquinas has not bequeathed to theological posterity and religious piety a model of Woman who is either a carrier of evil, sin, and guilt, or a carrier of salvation, purity, and holiness. Thomistic Woman is not located between Eve and Mary. Perhaps more damagingly, Thomas has reduced woman's theological significance to a biologically determined and divinely intended *natural function*: the reproduction of human creatures. The naturalism that has dominated and truncated Thomas' model of Woman is to be traced to his biologism. Thomas' biology devalues the (divinely intended) potential in sexual endowments, thereby devaluing the model of Woman which presupposes his biologized sexuality.

The naturalism and biologism on which Thomas grounded his theological model of Woman have long since been superseded. Recent research in biology and genetics, as well as psycho-sexual research, have marshalled evidence that woman and man are sexed for other than reproductive purposes. In general, sexuality involves an apportioning between two individuals of potentials for pooling the mutation-experiences of two lines of hereditary descent.[29] In particular, sexuality in highly complex organisms intrudes itself upon the cycle of reproduction to assure greater individuality and to enhance the autonomy of sexed individuals.

Human sexuality provides human persons with an unparalleled mode of disclosures between one "self" and another, enriching and enhancing their powers of self-knowing. We must not limit inferences from recent research merely to affirmations which concern the greater uniqueness or individuality of the human child, in contrast to infrahuman offspring. If human sexuality does not exist primarily or essentially for purposes of reproduction, then the sexuality of men and women must be explored along parameters which will discover not only the conditions appropriate to modes of disclosure for self-knowing, but also the criteria appropriate for enhancing and protecting self-disclosures. The outcome of such an exploration would certainly provide theology with data on which to construct new theological models of Woman and Man.

More importantly perhaps, new theological models might cut through the Gordian knot which moral theologians (at least, in the Roman tradition) have been busily tying with arguments against "artificial" contraception, against "unnatural"

<hr/>

[27] *S. Th.* I. 98. 2.
[28] *S. Th.* II-II. 154. 8.
[29] Cf. Julian Huxley's "Evolution and Genetics" in *What Is Science?* edited by James R. Newman (New York: Washington Square Press, 1961), "Sex itself is illuminated by our genetic knowledge. In origin it has nothing to do with sexual differentiation, the difference between males and females of a species; its basic and universal function is to provide the species with greater genetic variability." (p. 285)

abortion, or against "immoral" methods of population control.[30] From their arguments, it would appear that traditional moral theologians are held captive by the same biologism and naturalism that once captivated Thomas Aquinas and Aristotle before him. But theologians will not be able to relinquish their arguments unless and until they have recognized that their logic is controlled by an assumed *model*—in this case, a biological model of sexuality underlying a model of Woman. Failing that recognition, a Thomistic theological model of Woman and sexuality seems destined to prevail, especially in controversies about contraception, abortion, and means of genetic control.

IV

Let us consider one more instance of theological modeling. I suggest that we look at the controversy between opponents and advocates of continuing a mandatory priestly celibacy, as the "discipline" has become institutionalized in Roman Catholic tradition. The arguments advanced clearly contain an implicit theological model of Woman.

Advocates of mandatory celibacy (when they venture beyond authoritarian *fiat* to some reasoned justification) presume that an unquestionable and divinely advocated *celibacy of Jesus* provides everyone concerned with two requisites: (1) a convincing *social legitimation* for a celibate priesthood; and (2) a sufficient *personal motivation* for choosing between personal values which, in fact, stand opposed as equally personal and equally valuable (e.g., authentically human love of others, "requiring the sacrifice" of normal human expressions of authentic love). The Christology which official advocates of mandatory clerical celibacy have assumed without question has recently become more than ever questionable *theologically*.[31] Our first concern here is with the sociological consequences of such a Christology, as it affects ecclesiastical practice in the twentieth century.

What sociological implication and inference should we draw—both for the institutional Church and its hierarchical priesthood—from the data amassed by recently conducted opinion polls?[32] In increasing numbers, ordained clergy and "lay" persons alike evidently favor and even demand that priestly celibacy become a matter of choice separated from the choice to serve God in a particular form of commitment within the institutional Church. A church endeavoring to *serve* the needs and "best interests" of its committed members would conceivably recognize

---

[30] I can only suggest briefly how interpretations of human sexuality might overcome excessively biologistic and naturalistic theological justifications and condemnations of contraception, as well as arguments against abortion of a foetus in early stages of development. Moral theologians have insisted that a person, and what constitutes a person, is already present in the embryo within a woman's uterus. Their arguments usually appeal to analogies from lower organisms. Against these analogies, the data from genetics and psycho-sexual research suggests different criteria and alternative models. The sheer presence of *structures* or *conditions* for personal and psycho-sexual development neither guarantee the inevitability nor preprogram the mode or quality of that development. Recent research does not provide ethicists or moral theologians with a "new naturalism," but with an awareness of specifically human modes of novel disclosures. The conditions for being human persons are not biologically predetermined, nor can decisions about preserving human embryos be settled with biological criteria, excluding the social and temporal conditions which will prevail after birth.

[31] I refer here and commend to the reader the work of Phipps cited above, n. 16; see esp. pp. 177ff.

[32] For example, Joseph H. Fichter, *America's Forgotten Priests* (New York: 1968).

an expression of majority opinion as a remarkable "sign of the times." A *Servant Church* would count it an unmistakable mandate from God to pay heed to the experiences and values expressed by those whom it attempts to serve. A Servant Church would listen to the expressions of need for compassion, for understanding, for awareness of changed conditions in which the values and goals of contemporary men and women must now be expressed.

Instead, Christians have recently been instructed by the highest authority-figure in the Roman Catholic church, acknowledging that the "authority" of the hierarchy is indeed divinely instituted to serve "the faithful." Yet "[the faithful] are the object, not the origin, of the authority which is established for their service, and is not at their service."[33] Why has the issue of mandatory celibacy been met with intransigent refusals by highest authority even to reconsider or officially to re-evaluate the necessity of continuing such an ecclesiastical discipline?[34] Many who have confronted this question regard the issue to be, in fact, a drama enacting a long-rehearsed conflict between *two sources of Authority*.[35] Some contend that Authority derives from a sovereign ruler who is humanly selected (by a College of Cardinals), yet whose social location has been theologically legitimated as the "Vicar of Christ." Others contend that Authority derives from a sovereign people, or (in the case before us) from a priestly people who must express the authority of their experience. It would appear that our era, especially in the issue of mandatory clerical celibacy, is witnessing not only a theological, but a sociological conflict.

Significantly, if not obviously, the conflict reveals a dimly recognized theological rejection of a sociological axiom. Considered sociologically, not even an ecclesiastical institution can continue if it ceases to be supported with and by "plausibility structures." That is to say, it must continue to be affirmed and confirmed by human persons who find that institution and its structures meaningful, who find in it a continuing *expression of* and *response to* their deepest needs for ultimate meaning. I am suggesting that this sociological axiom is covertly (or unconsciously) rejected because of a theological axiom. According to this axiom, a "divine institution," by a self-legitimating claim to its "divine origin," need not be socially plausible or receive human confirmation from a consenting majority or a sovereign people.

Assuming this axiom, the advocates of an allegedly nonhuman (divine) origin for the discipline of priestly celibacy set forth their claim as self-evident or self-legitimating, as *exempt* from having to be socially and personally plausible. Those persons who are allegedly served by a celibate priesthood and who question its serviceability do not know what is in their best interests. It is assumed that "authority knows best." Dissenters who seek reevaluation of mandatory celibacy are suspected (sometimes accused) of being undisciplined, pleasure-seeking, *disobedient* creatures

[33] The account and quotation were reported by the UPI, appearing under a dateline of 28 January 1971 in the City Edition of *The Detroit News*.

[34] Pope Paul VI, in an *address* on 1 February 1970, said: "[Celibacy] is a capital law in our Latin church. It cannot be abandoned or subjected to argument."

[35] In December of 1920, Pope Benedict XV addressed a group of Czechoslovakian priests who were pressing for the right to marry: "The Latin church owes its flourishing vitality . . . to the celibacy of the clergy. . . . Never will the Holy See in any way even lighten or mitigate the obligation of this holy and salutary law of clerical celibacy, not to speak of abolishing it. We also deny . . . that the innovations of a 'democratic' character for whose introduction into ecclesiastical discipline some are agitating, can ever be approved by the Holy See." *Address*, 16 December 1920. (Cited by Phipps, op. cit., p. 192.)

of God. Consequently, the self-legitimated status of mandatory celibacy continues to be imposed by an "authority" beyond the range of human reason, logical argument, and social plausibility.

The issue, however, has an increasingly precarious immunity from human questioning. A common conjecture is that "authority" can continue to impose the discipline only as long as men are persuaded that (1) a monarchical concept of a Divine Being, (2) a hierarchical concept of power descending through a Vicarious Authority, and (3) a disparagement of sexuality and of women in an androcentric Creation, are unquestionable Christian verities. The third factor returns us to our second concern, namely, whether or not an ecclesiastical institution and an ecclesiastical discipline rest on a theological model of Woman.

Undoubtedly, some model of Woman is operative when men are exhorted to forego marriage, sexual intercourse, the "society of women," in order to pursue their personal purity and to preserve an institutional image of holiness and chastity. Theological authority can trace an uninterrupted line of descent from the fourth century to the twentieth. In *Duties of the Clergy*, Ambrose, bishop of Milan, asserted that married priests were "foul in heart and body"; consequently, "the ministerial office must be kept pure and unspotted, and must not be defiled by coitus."[36] In the twentieth century, Pope John XXIII confided to Etienne Gilson that it would be quite simple for him to sign a decree permitting priests to marry; but then the Church would no longer be worthy to be considered "holy and chaste." Officially, Pope John declared that celibacy was unquestionably "one of the purest and noblest glories of [the Church's] priesthood."[37]

Several who have studied the historical development of sacerdotal celibacy suggest that we should distinguish between the "actual purpose" and the "ostensible purpose" of polemics insisting that priests be celibates.[38] Ostensibly, the preservation of a celibate clergy has a religious purpose, namely, to guarantee that "purity of heart" and single-minded devotion to a sacred ministry which would be compromised or "divided" if the clergy had wives to love and care for. Actually, the preservation of a celibate clergy has socio-political and economic purposes, namely, to guarantee solidarity and political effectiveness within a body of men intending to be unimpaired by emotional ties, an elite who will not be subverted by their own vested interests or secular pursuits from an unquestioning obedience to the will of authorities who have ecclesiastical power over the sources of Salvation.[39]

If we grant this distinction, we would have to admit that a model of Woman subserves only the *ostensible* purpose of preserving sacerdotal celibacy. This model has proved instrumental (useful) in perpetuating both the social image of the institutional Church, and the personal image of priestly celibates whose motivation for sacrifice must be justified. According to this model, actual women are considered an institutional liability and a personal impediment to the ministrations of an androcentric, power-oriented, hierarchically-controlled "divine institution."

[36] *De offic.* I. 50.

[37] Phipps reports this account of a conversation with Etienne Gilson (op. cit., p. 192). Pope John's *address* was dated 26 January 1960. Gilson's "Souvenir du Père" appeared in *La France Catholique*, 862, dated 7 July 1963.

[38] Cf. Bailey, op. cit., pp. 150–152.

[39] *Loc cit.*; cf. Fichter, op. cit., p. 210; Phipps, op. cit., pp. 179, and 193–194; also Joseph Blenkinsopp, *Celibacy, Ministry, Church* (New York: 1968), pp. 61–62.

A masculine version of personal asceticism and disciplined control of others has fashioned a socially useful model of Woman dictated by institutional and ecclesiastical requirements. This model does not locate women primarily between Eve and Mary; nor does it locate women by their place in Nature and natural maternal functions. Women are assigned a third "utility" (*utile*)[40] in and through a model locating them institutionally. Women are supposed to be *recipients* rather than *mediators* or *ministers* for a sexually defined institutional "holiness and chastity." Once again, but with social consequences, Woman acquires theological (and sociological) significance because of her *sexuality*, now considered as an institutional liability.

The theological model of Woman resulting from and required by social institutionalizations of Christianity is losing its plausibility for several powerful reasons. Unprecedented methods of scientific control over genital sexuality have precipitated a "sexual liberation" which is already revolutionizing every behavioral pattern and mode of human interdependence. Not only is human sexuality being liberated from a morality based exclusively on the equation of sexual intercourse with human reproduction; there is also a liberation of marital fidelity and "total commitment" from an individualistic morality based on genital and psychological exclusivity.

A theological model of Woman as a *divisive* force—*opposed* to man's institutional commitment and impersonal service to others—must be linked with an increasingly questionable ideal for monogamous marriage. Traditional definitions and exhortations assume that the a-social character of intimate sexual relationships and the dis-social character of marriage naturally require married persons to be absorbed in mutual concerns and interests, thereby forming a self-sufficient and enduring social unit. On this view, men could selflessly commit themselves to an institutional " She," to " Holy Mother Church," but men could not commit themselves *both* to an institution and to a concrete woman. According to accepted (masculine) standards for a ministry extraordinarily "ordained" to accomplish a privileged work of redeeming the faithful, the requirements for marriage and for an ordained ministry involve distinct, mutually exclusive types of total commitment. An assumed model of Woman underlying this distinction is called into question by changing conceptions of marital fidelity and commitment.

Furthermore, the unsuitability of women themselves for ordination can no longer appeal to genetics for support of social prejudices. The emotional quality of objections to ordaining women was recently epitomized in the question of one horrified reactor: "*Pregnant priests ?*" Anatomy, of course, destines women to be pregnant just as inescapably as it destines men to be celibate. Nevertheless, anatomy and celibacy have been major reasons for excluding women both from having positions with political decision-making power in Christian churches, and from

---

[40] Woman's "utility" (*utile*) has long been a linguistic staple in theological discourse on sexual relations and the purpose of marriage (Cf. Bailey, op. cit., pp. 234–235). Theologians have in the past defined two "uses" of woman: one maternal, the other remedial. Woman is "useful" to man in generating his progeny; and she is "useful" in providing a release or remedy for man's imperious sexual impulses. The third "use" I am suggesting is woman's *institutional utility*. We need little clairvoyance to see that a theological model of Woman enables ecclesiastical authorities to measure (1) the nobility of the sacrifice which women make possible to celibates who are pursuing their personal purity; and (2) the "divine origin" of an institution which preserves its image of holiness and chastity by rejecting the ministrations of women both officially and in practice.

having mutual bonds with those who do. The denial of ordination to women is but a consistent conclusion from the premise that woman's *sexuality* nullifies her access to any institutionalized religious power to fulfill functions ordained for the service and concern of others. Sexual liberation is overtaking such a premise.

The sociological and ecclesiastical concerns which have required theologians (in the Roman tradition) to construct an implicit social model of Woman might be counteracted partially by a critical reexamination of two assumptions. One would require a reassessment of the apparent antithesis between "total commitment" to an institutional Church and its ministry, and "total commitment" to a monogamous marriage and its domestic responsibilities.

The other would require celibates and ecclesiastical authorities to scrutinize both their presuppositions regarding the "work of redemption" by a divinely "ordained ministry," and their image of "institutional holiness." This scrutiny could induce a reevaluation of both mandatory priestly celibacy and the rejection of women's ordination under the harsh light of their concrete social plausibility for actual women and men in today's world. It is altogether possible that a new theological-social model of Woman would discover women to be an institutional asset, and that the ministry of women would relieve men of that assumed burden of "total commitment" which for centuries has divided men from women under an outmoded theological model.

Lest my insistence upon past theological modeling in the case of Woman should become tedious, I shall in conclusion only underscore the *liberating optimism* to which my thesis extends credibility. If, in fact, contemporary women are enabled to interpret themselves as originating from—but not determined by—past theological modeling of woman's role in Sin, woman's place in Nature, woman's status in an institutional Church, then at the least these models are vulnerable to displacement by new theological models. Liberation in an ultimate sense—its theological sense—can thus acquire a profound and pervasive meaning whose social consequences for women (and men) should be immense. Once we recognize that the process of liberation is an *authorizing process*—one of displacing the "authority" of past dominant models-for-self-understanding and behavior by constructing more meaningful or authoritative models—then theology might once again perform its central humanizing task. Theology might liberate women (and men) by authorizing models for self-expression through more plausible life-styles and social institutions.

My thesis contains a hypothesis: if women are brought to realize that past *models* hold them captive, then perhaps they will recognize that the task of "liberation" will remain but half accomplished until new models are constructed to displace the old. I submit that *theology* must empower women to criticize and reconstruct more promising and plausible models for interpreting not only themselves, but their present and ultimate meaning. A Theology of Woman would endeavor to accomplish this liberating task.

Status of Indian Women

Ananda K. Coomaraswamy

Ananda Kentish Coomaraswamy (1877–1947) was born in Ceylon and educated in London to be a scientist. He soon afterward became interested in
the religious philosophy of both East and West, especially as it was embodied
in sacred art. In this area, he was one of the greatest art historians of modern
times, and one of the most penetrating students of comparative religion. He
was also active in Indian politics, Among his many works are *Hinduism and
Buddhism, Buddha and the Gospel of Buddhism*, and *Am I My Brother's Keeper?*

In the *Mahabharata* there is reported a conversation between Shiva and Uma.
The Great God asks her to describe the duties of women, addressing her, in so
doing, in terms which acknowledge her perfect attainment of the highest wisdom
possible to man or god—terms which it would be hard to parallel anywhere in
western literature. He says:

> "Thou that dost know the Self and the not-Self, expert in every work:
> endowed with self-restraint and perfect same-sightedness towards every
> creature: free from the sense of I and my—thy power and energy are equal to
> my own, and thou hast practised the most severe discipline. O Daughter of
> Himalaya, of fairest eyebrows, and whose hair ends in the fairest curls,
> expound to me the duties of women in full."

Then, She, who is queen of heaven, and yet so sweetly human, answers:

> "The duties of woman are created in the rites of wedding, when in presence
> of the nuptial fire she becomes the associate of her Lord, for the performance
> of all righteous deeds. She should be beautiful and gentle, considering her
> husband as her god and serving him as such in fortune and misfortune, health
> and sickness, obedient even if commanded to unrighteous deeds or acts that
> may lead to her own destruction. She should rise early, serving the gods,
> always keeping her house clean, tending to the domestic sacred fire, eating
> only after the needs of gods and guests and servants have been satisfied,
> devoted to her father and mother and the father and mother of her husband.
> Devotion to her Lord is woman's honor, it is her heaven; and O Maheshvara,"

she adds, with a most touching human cry,

> "I desire not paradise itself if thou are not satisfied with me!"

Source: Ananda K. Coomaraswamy, "Status of Indian Women," in *The Dance of Shiva* (New York,
1957), pp. 98–123. Copyright © 1957 by The Noonday Press, Inc. Reprinted with the permission of
Farrar, Straus & Giroux, Inc.

"She is a true wife who gladdens her husband," says Rajashekhara in the *Karpura Manjari*. The extract following is from the Laws of Manu:

> Though destitute of virtue, or seeking pleasure elsewhere, or devoid of good qualities, a husband must be constantly worshipped as a god by a faithful wife . . . If a wife obeys her husband, she will for that reason alone be exalted in heaven.
>
> The production of children, the nurture of those born, and the daily life of men, of these matters woman is visibly the cause.
>
> She who controlling her thoughts, speech and acts, violates not her duty to her Lord, dwells with him after death in heaven, and in this world is called by the virtuous a faithful wife.

Similar texts from a variety of Indian sources could be indefinitely multiplied.

If such are the duties of women, women are accorded corresponding honor, and exert a corresponding influence upon society. This power and influence do not so much belong to the merely young and beautiful, nor to the wealthy, as to those who have lived—mothers and grandmothers—or who follow a religious discipline—widows or nuns. According to Manu: "A master exceedeth ten tutors in claim to honour; the father a hundred masters; but the mother a thousand fathers in right to reverence and in the function of teacher." When Rama accepted Kaikeyi's decree of banishment, it was because "a mother should be as much regarded by a son as is a father." Even at the present day it would be impossible to over-emphasize the influence of Indian mothers not only upon their children and in all household affairs, but upon their grown-up sons to whom their word is law. According to my observation, it is only those sons who have received an "English" education in India who no longer honour their fathers *and* mothers.

No story is more appropriate than that of Madalasa and her son Vikranta to illustrate the position of the Indian mother as teacher. As Vikranta grew up day by day, the *Markandeya Purana* relates, Madalasa "taught him knowledge of the Self[1] by ministering to him in sickness; and as he grew in strength and there waxed in him his father's heart, he attained to knowledge of the Self by his mother's words." And these were Madalasa's words, spoken to the baby crying on her lap:

"My child, thou art without a name or form, and it is but in fantasy that thou has been given a name. This thy body, framed of the five elements, is not thine in sooth, nor art thou of it. Why dost thou weep? Or, maybe, thou weepest not; it is a sound self-born that cometh forth from the king's son. . . . In the body dwells another self, and therewith abideth not the thought that 'This is mine,' which appertaineth to the flesh. Shame that man is so deceived!"

Even in recent times, in families where the men have received an English education unrelated to Indian life and thought, the inheritance of Indian modes of thought and feeling rests in the main with women; for a definite philosophy of life is bound up with household ritual and traditional etiquette and finds expression equally in folktale and cradle-song and popular poetry, and in those pauranic and epic stories which constitute the household Bible literature of India. Under these conditions it is often the case that Indian women, with all their faults of

---

[1] "Knowledge of the Self"—the *Adhyatmavidya*.

sentimentality and ignorance, have remained the guardians of a spiritual culture which is of greater worth than the efficiency and information of the educated.

It is according to the Tantrik scriptures, devoted to the cult of the Mother of the World, that women, who partake of her nature more essentially than other living beings, are especially honoured; here the woman may be a spiritual teacher (*guru*), and the initiation of a son by a mother is more fruitful than any other. One doubts how far this may be of universal application, believing with Paracelsus that woman is nearer to the world than man, of which the evidence appears in her always more personal point of view. But all things are possible to women such as Madalasa.

The claim of the Buddhist nun—"How should the woman's nature hinder us ?"—has never been systematically denied in India. It would have been contrary to the spirit of Indian culture to deny to individual women the opportunity of saintship or learning in the sense of closing to them the schools of divinity or science after the fashion of the Western academies in the nineteenth century. But where the social norm is found in marriage and parenthood for men and women alike, it could only have been in exceptional cases and under exceptional circumstances that the latter specialised, whether in divinity, like Auvvai, Mira Bai, or the Buddhist nuns, in science, like Lilavati, or in war, like Chand Bibi or the Rani of Jhansi. Those set free to cultivate expert knowledge of science or to follow with undivided allegiance either religion of any art, could only be the *sannyasini* or devotee, the widow, and the courtesan. A majority of women have always, and naturally, preferred marriage and motherhood to either of these conditions. But those who felt the call of religion, those from whom a husband's death removed the central motif of their life, and those trained from childhood as expert artists, have always maintained a great tradition in various branches of cultural activity, such as social service or music. What we have to observe is that Hindu sociologists have always regarded these specializations as more or less incompatible with wifehood and motherhood; life is not long enough for the achievement of many different things.

Hinduism justifies no cult of ego-expression, but aims consistently at spiritual freedom. Those who are conscious of a sufficient inner life become the more indifferent to outward expression of their own or any changing personality. The ultimate purposes of Hindu social discipline are that men should unify their individuality with a wider and deeper than individual life, should fulfil appointed tasks regardless of failure or success, distinguish the timeless from its shifting forms, and escape the all-too-narrow prison of the " I and mine."

Anonymity is thus in accordance with the truth; and it is one of the proudest distinctions of the Hindu culture. The names of the "authors" of the epics are but shadows, and in later ages it was a constant practice of writers to suppress their own names and ascribe their work to a mythical or famous poet, thereby to gain a better attention for the truth that they would rather claim to have "heard" than to have "made." Similarly, scarcely a single Hindu painter or sculptor is known by name; and the entire range of Sanskrit literature cannot exhibit a single autobiography and but little history. Why should women have sought for modes of self-advertisement that held no lure even for men ? The governing concept of Hindu ethics is vocation (*dharma*); the highest merit consists in the fulfilment of "one's own duty," in other words, in dedication to one's calling. Indian society was highly organized; and where it was considered wrong for a man to fulfil the duties of another man rather than his own, how much more must a confusion of function as between woman and man have seemed wrong, where differentiation is so much more evident. In the words of Manu: "To be mothers were women created, and to be fathers men"; and he added significantly "therefore are religious sacraments ordained in the Veda to be observed by the husband together with the wife."[2]

The Asiatic theory of marriage, which would have been perfectly comprehensible in the Middle Ages, before the European woman had become an economic parasite, and which is still very little removed from that of Roman or Greek Christianity, is not readily intelligible to the industrial democratic consciousness of Europe and America, which is so much more concerned for rights than for duties, and desires more than anything else to be released from responsibilities—regarding such release as freedom. It is thus that Western reformers would awaken a divine discontent in the hearts of Oriental women, forgetting that the way of ego-assertion cannot be a royal road to realization of the Self. The industrial mind is primarily sentimental, and therefore cannot reason clearly upon love and marriage; but the Asiatic analysis is philosophic, religious and practical.

Current Western theory seeks to establish marriage on a basis of romantic love and free choice; marriage thus depends on the accident of "falling in love." Those who are "crossed in love" or do not love are not required to marry. This individualistic position, however, is only logically defensible if at the same time it is recognized that to fall out of love must end the marriage. It is a high and religious ideal which justifies sexual relations only as the outward expression demanded by passionate love and regards an intimacy continued or begun for mere pleasure, or for reasons of prudence, or even as a duty, as essentially immoral; it is an ideal which isolated individuals and groups have constantly upheld; and it may be that the ultimate development of idealistic individualism will tend to a nearer realisation of it. But do not let us deceive ourselves that because the Western marriage is nominally founded upon free choice, it therefore secures a permanent unity of spiritual and physical passion. On the contrary, perhaps in a majority of cases, it holds together those who are no longer "in love"; habit, considerations of prudence, or, if there are children, a sense of duty often compel the passionless continuance of a marriage for the initiation of which romantic love was felt to be a *sine qua non*. Those who now live side by side upon a basis of affection and common interest would not have entered upon marriage on this basis alone.

If the home is worth preserving under modern conditions—and in India at any rate, the family is still the central element of social organization, then probably the "best solution" will always be found in some such compromise as is implied in a more or less permanent marriage; though greater tolerance than is now usual must be accorded to exceptions above and below the norm. What are we going to regard as the constructive basis of the normal marriage?

---

[2] Jahangir observes in his "*Memoirs*" that the Hindu woman "is the half of a man, and his companion in religious ceremonies." Cf. the *Prema Sagara*, ch. xxiv: "without a wife a sacrifice is not fruitful."

For Hindu sociologists marriage is a social and ethical relationship, and the begetting of children the payment of a debt. Romantic love is a brief experience of timeless freedom, essentially religious and ecstatic, in itself as purely antisocial as every glimpse of Union is a denial of the Relative; it is the way of Mary. It is true the glamour of this experience may persist for weeks and months, when the whole of life is illumined by the partial merging of the consciousness of the lover and beloved; but sooner or later in almost every case there must follow a return to the world of reality, and that insight which once endowed the beloved with innumerable perfections fades in the light of commonsense. The lovers are fortunate if there remains to them a basis of common interest and common duty and a mutuality of temperament adequate for friendship, affection and forbearance; upon this chance depends the possibility of happiness during the greater part of almost every married life. The Hindu marriage differs from the marriage of sentiment mainly in putting these considerations first. Here, as elsewhere, happiness will arise from the fulfilment of vocation, far more than when immediate satisfaction is made the primary end. I use the term vocation advisedly; for the Oriental marriage, like the Oriental actor's art, is the fulfilment of a traditional design, and does not depend upon the accidents of sensibility. To be such a man as Rama, such a wife as Sita, rather than to express " oneself," is the aim. The formula is predetermined; husband and wife alike have parts to play; and it is from this point of view that we can best understand the meaning of Manu's law, that a wife should look on her husband as a god, regardless of his personal merit or demerits —it would be beneath her dignity to deviate from a woman's norm merely because of the failure of a man. It is for her own sake and for the sake of the community, rather than for his alone, that life must be attuned to the eternal unity of Purusha and Prakriti.

Whatever the ultimate possibilities of Western individualism, Hindu society was established on a basis of group morality. It is true that no absolute ethic is held binding on all classes alike; but within a given class the freedom of the individual is subordinated to the interest of the group, the concept of duty is paramount. How far this concept of duty trenches on the liberty of the individual may be seen in Rama's repudiation of Sita, subsequent to the victory in Lanka and the coronation at Ayodhya; although convinced of her perfect fidelity, Rama, who stands in epic history as the mirror of social ethics, consents to banish his wife, because the people murmur against her. The argument is that if the king should receive back a wife who had been living in another man's house, albeit faithful, popular morality would be endangered, since others might be moved by love and partiality to a like rehabilitation but with less justification. Thus the social order is placed before the happiness of the individual, whether man or woman. This is the explanation of the greater peace which distinguishes the arranged marriage of the East from the self-chosen marriage of the West; where there is no deception there can be no diappointment. And since the conditions on which it is founded do not change, it is logical that Hindu marriage should be indissoluble; only when social duties have been fulfilled and social debts paid, is it permissible for the householder to relinquish simultaneously the duties and the rights of the social individual. It is also logical that when the marriage is childless, it is permissible to take a second wife with the consent—and often at the wish—of the first.

It is sometimes asked, what opportunities are open to the Oriental woman? How can she express herself? The answer is that life is so designed that she is given the opportunity to be a woman—in other words, to realise, rather than to express herself. It is possible that modern Europe errs in the opposite direction. We must also remember that very much which passes for education nowadays is superficial; some of it amounts to little more than parlour tricks, and nothing is gained by communicating this condition to Asia, where I have heard of modern parents who desired that their daughters should be taught "a little French" or "a few strokes of the violin." The arts in India are professional and vocational, demanding undivided service; nothing is taught to the amateur by way of social accomplishment or studied superficially. And woman represents the continuity of the racial life, an energy which cannot be divided or diverted without a correspond-ing loss of racial vitality; she can no more desire to be something other than herself, than the Vaishya could wish to be known as a Kshattriya, or the Kshattriya, as a Brahman.

It has been shown in fact, some seventy-five percent of Western graduate women do not marry; and apart from these, if it be true that five-sixths of a child's tendencies and activities are already determined before it reaches school age, and that the habits then deeply rooted cannot be greatly modified, if it be true that so much depends on deliberate training while the instincts of the child are still potential and habits unformed, can we say that women whose social duties or pleasures, or self-elected careers or unavoidable wage slavery draw them into the outer world, are fulfilling their duty to the race, or as we should say, the debt of the ancestors? The modern suffragist declares that the state has no right to demand of woman, whether directly or indirectly, by bribe or pressure of opinion, that she consider herself under any obligation, in return for the protection afforded her, to produce its future citizens. But we are hardly likely to see this point of view accepted in these days when the right of society to conscript the bodies of men is almost uni-versally conceded. It is true that many who do not acquiesce in the existing industrial order are prepared to resist conscription in the military sense, that is to say, con-scription for destruction; but we are becoming accustomed to the idea of another kind of conscription, or rather co-operation. based on service, and indeed, according to the two dynamic theories of a future society—the syndicalist and the individualis-tic—it must appear that without the fulfilment of function there can exist no *rights*. From the co-operative point of view society has an absolute right to compel its members to fulfil the functions that are necessary to it; and only those who, like the anchorite, voluntarily and entirely renounce the advantages of society and the protection of law have a right to ignore the claims of society.[3] From the individualist point of view, on the other hand, the fulfilment of function is regarded as a spon-taneous activity, as is even now true in the cases of the thinker and the artist; but even the individualist does not expect to get something for nothing, and the last idea he has is to compel the service of others.

[3] A vigorous society can well afford to support, and in the interests of spiritual values will gladly support, so far as support is necessary, not only thinkers and artists, whose function is obvious, but also a certain number of thorough-going rebels who to all appearances are mere idlers. But the idler, whether anchorite or courtesan, must not *demand* to be supported in luxury, and must recognize that whatever he or she receives is given in *love*, and not according to *law*.

I doubt if anyone will deny that it is the function or nature of women, as a group—not necessarily in every individual case—in general, to be mothers, alike in spiritual and physical senses. What we have to do then, is not to assert the liberty of women to deny the duty or right of motherhood, however we regard it, but to accord this function a higher protection and honor than it now receives. And here, perhaps, there is still something to be learnt in Asia. There the pregnant woman is auspicious, and receives the highest respect; whereas in many industrial and secular Western societies she is an object of more or less open ridicule, she is ashamed to be seen abroad, and tries to conceal her condition, sometimes even by means that are injurious to her own and the child's health. That this was not the case in a more vital period of European civilization may be seen in all the literature and art of the Middle Ages, and particularly in the status of the Virgin Mary, whose motherhood endeared her to the folk so much more nearly than her virginity.

To avoid misunderstanding, let me say in passing, that in depicting the life of Hindu women as fulfilling a great ideal, I do not mean to indicatè the Hindu social formula as a thing to be repeated or imitated. This would be a view as futile as that of the Gothic revival in architecture; the reproduction of period furniture does not belong to life. A perfection that has been can never be a perfection for us.

Marriage was made for man, not man for marriage. One would gladly accept for Europe very soon, and for Asia in due time, temporary marriage, the endowment of motherhood, and matriarchal succession, or whatever other forms our own spiritual and economic necessity may determine for us—not because such forms may be absolutely better than the Asiatic or mediaeval European institutions, but because they correspond more nearly to *our* inner life. In comparing one social order with another, I have no faith in any millennium past or future, but only in the best attainable adaptation of means to ends; and, "let the ends determine the means," should be the evidence of our idealism.

Let us now return to the Indian Sati and try to understand her better. The root meaning of the word is essential being, and we have so far taken it only in the wide sense. But she who refuses to live when her husband is dead is called Sati in a more special sense, and it is only so that the word (suttee) is well-known to Europeans. This last proof of the perfect unity of body and soul, this devotion beyond the grave, has been chosen by many Western critics as our reproach; we differ from them in thinking of our "suttees" not with pity, but with understanding, respect, and love. So far from being ashamed of our "suttees" we take a pride in them; that is even true of the most "progressive" amongst us. It is very much like the tenderness which our children's children may some day feel for those of their race who were willing to throw away their lives for "their country right or wrong," though the point of view may seem to us then, as it seems to so many already, evidence rather of generosity than balanced judgment.

The criticism we make on the institution of Sati and woman's blind devotion is similar to the final judgment we are about to pass on patriotism. We do no not, as pragmatists may, resent the denial of the ego for the sake of an absolute, or attach an undue importance to mere life; on the contrary we see clearly that the reckless and useless sacrifice of the "suttee" and the patriot is spiritually significant. And what remains perpetually clear is the superiority of the reckless sacrifice to the calculating assertion of rights. Criticism of the position of the Indian woman from the ground of assertive feminism, therefore, leaves us entirely unmoved: precisely as the patriot must be unmoved by an appeal to self-interest or a merely utilitarian demonstration of futility. We do not object to dying for an idea as "suttees" and patriots have died; but we see that there may be other and greater ideas we can better serve by living for them.

For some reason it has come to be believed that Sati must have been a man-made institution imposed on women by men for reasons of their own, that it is associated with feminine servility, and that it is peculiar to India. We shall see that these views are historically unsound. It is true that in aristocratic circles Sati became to some degree a social convention,[4] and pressure was put on unwilling individuals, precisely as conscripts are even now forced to suffer or die for other people's ideas; and from this point of view we cannot but be glad that it was prohibited by law in 1829 on the initiative of Raja Rammohun Roy. But now that nearly a century has passed it should not be difficult to review the history and significance of Sati more dispassionately than was possible in the hour of controversy and the atmosphere of religious prejudice.

It is not surprising that the idea of Sati occupies a considerable place in Indian literature. Parvati herself, who could not endure the insults levelled against her husband by her father, is the prototype of all others. In the early Tamil lyrics we read of an earthly bride whom the Brahmans seek to dissuade from the sacrifice; but she answers that since her lord is dead, the cool waters of the lotus pool and the flames of the funeral pyre are alike to her. Another pleads to share her hero's grave, telling the potter that she had fared with her lord over many a desert plain, and asking him to make the funeral urn large enough for both. Later in history we read of the widowed mother of Harsha that she replied to her son's remonstrances:

"I am the lady of a great house; have you forgotten that I am the lioness-mate of a great spirit, who, like a lion, had his delight in a hundred battles?"

A man of such towering genius and spirituality as Kabir so takes for granted the authenticity of the impulse to Sati that he constantly uses it as an image of surrender of the ego to God; and indeed, in all Indian mystical literature the love-relation of woman to man is taken unhesitatingly as an immediate reflection of spiritual experience. This is most conspicuous in all the Radha-Krishna literature. But here let us notice more particularly the beautiful and very interesting poem of Muhammad Riza Nau'i, written in the reign of Akbar upon the "suttee" of a Hindu girl whose betrothed was killed on the very day of the marriage. This Musulman poet, to whom the Hindus were "idolaters," does not relate his story in any spirit of religious intolerance or ethical condescension; he is simply amazed "that after the death of men, the woman shows forth her marvellous passion." He does not wonder at the wickedness of men, but at the generosity of women; how different from the modern critic who can see no motive but self-interest behind a social phenomenon that passes his comprehension!

---

[4] "Social conventions" are rarely "*man*-made laws" alone.

This Hindu bride refused to be comforted and wished to be burnt on the pyre of her dead betrothed. When Akbar was informed of this, he called the girl before him and offered wealth and protection, but she rejected all his persuasion as well as the counsel of the Brahmans, and would neither speak nor hear of anything but the Fire.

Akbar was forced, though reluctantly, to give his consent to the sacrifice, but sent with her his son Prince Daniyal who continued to dissuade her. Even from amidst the flames, she replied to his remonstrances. "Do not annoy, do not annoy, do not annoy." "Ah," exclaims the poet:

> *Let those whose hearts are ablaze with the Fire of*
> *Love learn courage from this pure maid!*
> *Teach me, O God, the Way of Love, and enflame my*
> *heart with this maiden's Fire.*

Thus he prays for himself; and for her:

> *Do Thou, O God, exalt the head of that rare hidden*
> *virgin, whose purity exceeded that of the Houris,*
> *Do Thou endear her to the first kissing of her King,*
> *and graciously accept her sacrifice.*

Matter of fact accounts of more modern "suttees" are given by Englishmen who have witnessed them. One which took place in Baroda in 1825 is described by R. Hartley Kennedy, the widow persisting in her intention in spite of "several fruitless endeavors to dissuade her." A more remarkable case is described by Sir Frederick Halliday. Here also a widow resisted all dissuasion, and finally proved her determination by asking for a lamp, and holding her finger in the flame until it was burnt and twisted like a quill pen held in the flame of a candle; all this time she gave no sign of fear or pain whatever. Sir F. Halliday had therefore to grant her wish, even as Akbar had had to do three centuries earlier.

It is sometimes said by Indian apologists that at certain times or places in India—amongst the Buddhists, or the Marathas, or in the epics—there was no purdah; or that certain historic or mythic individual women were not secluded. Such statements ignore the fact that there are other kinds of seclusion than those afforded by palace walls. For example, though Rama, Lakshman and Sita had lived together in forest exile for many years in closest affection, it is expressly stated that Lakshman had never raised his eyes above his brother's wife's feet, so that he did not even know her appearance. To speak more generally, it is customary for Hindus, when occasion arises for them to address an unknown woman, to call her "mother" irrespective of her age or condition. Those unseen walls are a seclusion equally absolute with any purdah. One result is that the streets of an Indian city by night are far safer for a woman than those of any city in Europe. I have known more than one European woman, acquainted with India, express her strong conviction of this.

Western critics have often asserted that the Oriental woman is a slave, and that we have made her what she is. We can only reply that we do not identify freedom with self-assertion, and that the Oriental woman is what she is, only because our social and religious culture has permitted her to be and to remain essentially feminine. Exquisite as she may be in literature and art, we dare not claim for ourselves as men the whole honor of creating such a type, however persistently the industrious industrial critic would thrust it upon us.

The Eastern woman is not, at least we do not claim that she is, superior to other women in her innermost nature; she is perhaps an older, purer and more specialised type, but certainly an universal type, and it is precisely here that the industrial woman departs from type. Nobility in women does not depend upon race, but upon ideals; it is the outcome of a certain view of life.

Savitri, Padmavati, Sita, Radha, Uma, Lilavati, Tara—our divine and human heroines—have an universal fellowship, for everything feminine is of the Mother. Who could have been more wholly devoted than Alcestis, more patient than Griselda, more loving than Deirdre, more soldier than Joan of Arc, more Amazon than Brynhild?

When the *Titanic* sank, there were many women who refused—perhaps mistakenly, perhaps quite rightly—that was their own affair—to be rescued without their husbands, or were only torn from them by force; dramatic confirmation of the conviction that love-heroism is always and everywhere the same, and not only in India, nor only in ages past, may be stronger than death.

I do not think that the Indian ideal has ever been the exclusive treasure of any one race or time, but rather, it reappears wherever woman is set free to be truly herself, that is wherever a sufficiently religious, heroic and æsthetic culture has afforded her the necessary protection. Even the freedom which she seeks in modern self-assertion—which I would grant from the standpoint of one who will not govern —is merely an inverted concept of protection, and it may be that the more she is freed the more she will reveal the very type we have most adored in those who seemed to be slaves. Either way would be happier for men than the necessity of protecting women from themselves, and the tyranny of those who are not capable of friendship, being neither bound nor free.

The cry of our Indian Sati, "Do not annoy, do not annoy," and "No one has any right over the life of another; is not that my own affair?" is no cry for protection from a fate she does not seek; it is passionate, and it has been uttered by every woman in the world who has followed love beyond the grave. Deirdre refused every offer of care and protection from Conchubar: "It is not land or earth or food I am wanting," she said, "or gold or silver or horses, but leave to go to the grave where the sons of Usnach are lying." Emer called to Cuchullain slain: "Love of my life, my friend, my sweetheart, my one choice of the men of the world, many is the women, wed or unwed, envied me until to-day, and now I will not stay living after you."

Irish women were free, but we are used even more to look on the old Teutonic types as representative of free and even amazonian womanhood. We do not think of Brynhild, Shield-may and Victory-wafter, as compelled by men to any action against her will, or as weakly submissive. Yet when Sigurd was slain she became "suttee"; the prayers of Gunnar availed as little as those of Conchubar with Deirdre. He "laid his arms about her neck, and besought her to live and have wealth from him; and all others in like wise letter her from dying; but she thrust them all from her, and said that it was not the part of any to let her in that which was her will." And the second heroic woman figured in the saga, wedded to Sigurd, though she did not die, yet cried when he was betrayed:

Now am I as little
As the leaf may be
Amid wind-swept wood,
Now when dead he lieth.

"She who is courteous in her mind," says the *Shacktafelsk*, "with shyness shall her face be bright; of all the beauties of the body, none is more shining than shyness." This theory of courtesy, of supreme gentleness—"full sweetly bowing down her head," says the English Merlin, "as she that was shamefast," runs also through all mediæval chivalry. Yet it is about this shy quiet being, a mystery to men, that the whole mediæval world turns; "first reserve the honor to God," says Malory, "and secondly, the quarrel must come of thy lady." Like Uma and Sita, Virgin Mary is the image of a perfect being—

For in this rose conteined was
Heaven and earth in litel space—

and for a little while, in poetry and architecture, we glimpse an idealisation of woman and woman's love akin to the praise of Radha in the contemporary songs of Chandidas and Vidyapati.

But for our purpose even more significant than the religious and knightly culture, the product of less quickly changing conditions, and impressive too in its naïveté, is the picture of the woman of the people which we can gather from folk-song and lyric. Here was a being obviously strong and sensible, not without knowledge of life, and by no means economically a parasite. If we study the folk speech anywhere in the world we shall see that it reveals woman, and not the man, as typically the lover; when her shyness allows, it is she who would pray for man's love, and will serve him to the utmost. Industrialism reverses this relation, making man the suppliant and the servant, a condition as unnatural as any other of its characteristic perversions.

The woman of the folk does not bear resentment. Fair Helen, who followed Child Waters on foot, and bore his child in a stable, is overheard singing:

Lullaby, my owne deere child!
I wold thy father were a king,
Thy mother layed on a beere.

Is she not like the Bengali Malanchamala, whose husband had married a second wife, and left her unloved and forgotten—who says, "though I die now, and become a bird or a lesser creature or whatever befall me, I care not, for I have seen my darling happy?"

If woman under industrialism is unsatisfied, it would be difficult to say how much man also loses. For woman is naturally the lover, the bestower of life:

Conjunction with me renders life long.
I give youth when I enter upon amorousness.[5]

Her complaint is not that man demands too much, but that he will accept too little.

Long time have I been waiting for the coming of my dear;
Sometimes I am uneasy and troubled in my mind,
Sometimes I think I'll go to my lover and tell him my mind.
But if I should go to my lover, my lover he will say me nay,
If I show to him my boldness, he'll ne'er love me again.[6]

And it is to serve him, not to seek service from him that she desires:

In the cold stormy weather, when the winds are a-blowing,
My dear, I shall be willing to wait on you then.[7]

The Oriental woman, perhaps is not Oriental at all, but simply woman. If the modern woman could accept this thought, perhaps she would seek a new way of escape, not an escape from love, but a way out of industrialism. Could we not undertake the quest together?

It is true that the modern woman is justified in her discontent. For of what has she not been robbed? The organization of society for competition and exploitation has made possible for the few, and only the very few, more physical comfort and greater security of life; but even these it has robbed of all poise, of the power to walk or to dress or to marry wisely, or to desire children or lovers, or to believe in any power not legally exteriorised. From faith in herself to a belief in votes, what a descent!

Decade after decade since the fourteenth century has seen her influence reduced. It was paramount in religion, in poetry, in music, in architecture and in all life. But men, when they reformed the church and taught you that love was not a sacrament without the seal of clerical approval; when they forced your music into modes of equal temperament; when they substituted knowledge for feeling and wisdom in education,[8] when they asked you to pinch your shoes and your waists, and persuaded you to think this a refinement, and the language of Elizabethan poetry coarse; when at last they taught you to become Imperialists, and went away alone to colonise and civilise the rest of the world, leaving you in England with nothing particular to do; when, if you have the chance to marry at all, it is ten or fifteen years too late—who can wonder that you are dissatisfied, and claim the right to a career of your own "not merely to earn your livelihood, but to provide yourself with an object in life?"[9] How many women have only discovered an object in life since the energies of men have been employed in activities of pure destruction? What a confession! To receive the franchise would be but a small compensation

[5] Nizami.
[6] Eastern Counties folk-song.
[7] Somerset folksong.
[8] Cf. *The Great State*, p. 127.
[9] From an advertisement in the *Englishwoman's Year Book*, 1911.

for all you have suffered, if it did not happen that we have now seen enough of representative government and the tyranny of majorities to understand their futility. Let women as well as men, turn away their eyes from the delusions of government, and begin to understand direct action, finding enough to do in solving the problems of their own lives, without attempting to regulate those of other people. No man of real power has either time or strength for any other man's work than his own, and this should be equally true for women. Aside from all questions of mere lust for power or demand for rights, untold evils have resulted from the conviction that it is our God-given duty to regulate other people's lives—the effects of the current theories of "uplift," and of the "white man's burden" are only single examples of this; and even if the intentions are good, we need not overlook the fact that the way to hell is often paved with good intentions.

Meanwhile there lies an essential weakness in the propaganda of emancipation, inasmuch as the argument is based on an unquestioning acceptance of male values. The so-called feminist is as much enslaved by masculine ideals as the so-called Indian nationalist is enslaved by European ideals. Like industrial man, the modern woman values industry more than leisure, she seeks in every way to externalise her life, to achieve success in men's professions, she feigns to be ashamed of her sexual nature, she claims to be as reasonable, as learned, as expert as any man, and her best men friends make the same claims on her behalf. But just in proportion as she lacks a genuine feminine idealism, inasmuch as she wishes to be something other than herself, she lacks power.

The claim of women to share the loaves and fishes with industrial man may be as just as those of Indian politicians. But the argument that women can do what men can do ("we take all labor for our province," says Olive Schreiner) like the argument that Indians can be prepared to govern themselves by a course of studies in democracy, implies a profound self-distrust. The claim to equality with men, or with Englishmen—what an honor! That men, or Englishmen, as the case may be, should grant the claim—what a condescension!

If there is one profound intuition of the non-industrial consciousness, it is that the qualities of men and women are incommensurable. "The sexes are differently entertained," says Novalis, "man demands the sensational in intellectual form, woman the intellectual in sensational form. What is secondary to the man is paramount to the woman. Do they not resemble the Infinite, since it is impossible to square (*quadriren*) them, and they can only be approached through approximation?" Is not the Hindu point of view possibly right; not that men and women should approach an identity of temperament and function, but that for the greatest abundance of life, there is requisite the greatest possible sexual differentiation?

What is it that great men—poets and creators, not men of analysis—demand of women? It is, surely, the requirements of the prolific, rather than of the devourers, which are of most significance for the human race, which advances under the guidance of leaders, and not by accident. The one thing they have demanded of women is Life.

To one thing at least the greatest men have been always indifferent, that is, the amount of knowledge a woman may possess. It was not by her learning that Beatrice inspired Dante, or the washerwoman Chandidas. When Cuchullain chose a wife, it was Emer, because she had the six gifts of beauty, voice, sweet speech, needlework, wisdom and charity. We know only of Helen that "strangely like she was to some immortal spirit"; in other words, she was radiant. Radha's shining made the ground she stood on bright as gold. The old English poet wrote of one like her

Hire lutre lumes liht
As a launterne a nyht.

It is this radiance in women, more than any other quality, that urges men to every sort of heroism, be it martial or poetic.

Everyone understands the heroism of war; we are not surprised at Lady Hamilton's adoration of Nelson. But the activity of war is atavistic, and highly civilised people such as the Chinese regard it with open contempt. What nevertheless we do not yet understand is the heroism of art, that exhausting and perpetual demand which all creative labor makes alike on body and soul. The artist must fight a continual battle for mastery of himself and his environment; his work must usually be achieved in the teeth of violent, ignorant and often well-organised opposition, or against still more wearing apathy, and in any case, even at the best, against the intense resistance which matter opposes to the moulding force of ideas, the tamasic quality in things. The ardent love of women is not too great a reward for those who are faithful. But it is far more than the reward of action, it is the energy without which action may be impossible. As pure male, the Great God is inert, and his "power" is always feminine, and it is she who leads the hosts of heaven against the demons.

When man of necessity spent his life in war or in hunting, when women needed a personal physical as well as a Spiritual protection, then she could not do enough for him in personal service; we have seen in the record of folk-song and epic how it is part of woman's innermost nature to worship man. In the words of another Indian scripture, her husband is for her a place of pilgrimage, the giving of alms, the performance of vows, and he is her spiritual teacher—this according to the same school which makes the initiation of son by mother eight times more efficacious than any other. What we have not yet learnt is that like relations are needed for the finest quality of life, even under conditions of perpetual peace; the tenderness of women is as necessary to man now, as ever it was when his first duty was that of physical warfare, and few men can achieve greatness, and then scarcely without the danger of a one-sided development, whose environment lacks this atmosphere of tenderness. Woman possesses the power of perpetually creating in man the qualities she desires, and this is for her an infinitely greater power than the possession of those special qualities could ever confer upon her directly.

Far be it from us, however, to suggest the forcing of any preconceived development upon the modern individualist. We shall accomplish nothing by pressing anything in moulds. What I have tried to explain is that notwithstanding that the formula of woman's status in Oriental society may have ere now crystallised—as the formulae of classic art have become academic—nevertheless this formula represented once, and still essentially represents, although "unfelt" in realisation, a veritable expression of woman's own nature. If not so, then the formula stands self-condemned. I do not know if through our modern idealistic individualism it may be possible to renounce all forms and formulae for ever—I fear that it is only in heaven that there shall be neither marrying nor giving in marriage—but were that the case, and every creature free to find itself, and to behave according to its own nature, then it is possible, at least, that the "natural" relation of woman to man would after all involve the same conditions of magic that are implied in the soon-to-be-discarded conventional and calculated forms of mediæval art and Oriental society. If not, we must accept things as they really are—however they may be.

Meanwhile, it would be worth while to pause before we make haste to emancipate, that is to say, reform and industralize the Oriental woman. For it is not for Asia alone that she preserves a great tradition, an an age that is otherwise preoccupied. If she too should be persuaded to expend her power upon externals, there might come a time on earth when it could not be believed that such women had ever lived, as the ancient poets describe; it would be forgotten that woman had ever been unselfish, sensuous, and shy. Deirdre, Brynhild, Alcestis, Sita, Radha, would then be empty names. And that would be a loss, for already it has been felt in Western schools that we "are not furnished with adequate womanly ideals in history and literature."[10]

The industrial revolution in India is of external and very recent origin; there is no lack of men, and it is the sacred duty of parents to arrange a marriage for every daughter: there is no divergence of what is spiritual and what is sensuous: Indian women do not deform their bodies in the interests of fashion: they are more concerned about service than rights: they consider barrenness the greatest possible misfortune, after widowhood. In a word, it has never happened in India that women have been judged by or have accepted purely male standards. What possible service then, except in few externals, can the Western world render to Eastern women? Though it may be able to teach us much of the means of life, it has everything yet to relearn about life itself. And what we still remember there, we would not forget before we must.

[10] Stanley Hall, *Youth*, ed. 1909, p. 286.

The Crisis of Sexuality: Religion and Eros

The Vatican Declaration on Sexual Ethics

The Sacred Congregation for the Doctrine of the Faith published this declaration reaffirming the enduring validity of the church's traditional teachings on sexual morality. Entitled "Declaration on Certain Questions Concerning Sexual Ethics," the document was released in the U.S. on Jan. 15, 1976. "The moral order of sexuality," says the document, "involves such high values of human life that every direct violation of this order is objectively serious." Bishops are called upon to make sure the church's moral teachings are faithfully held and taught. "It will especially be necessary," it says, "to bring the faithful to understand that the church holds these principles not as old inviolable superstitions, . . . but rather because she knows with certainty that they are in complete harmony with the divine order of creation and with the spirit of Christ, and therefore also with human dignity." The complete text follows.

1. According to contemporary scientific research, the human person is so profoundly affected by sexuality that it must be considered as one of the factors which give to each individual's life the principal traits that distinguish it. In fact it is from sex that the human person receives the characteristics which on the biological, psychological and spiritual levels, make that person a man or a woman, and thereby largely condition his or her progress towards maturity and insertion into society. Hence sexual matters, as is obvious to everyone, today constitute a theme frequently and openly dealt with in books, reviews, magazines and other means of social communication.

In the present period, the corruption of morals has increased, and one of the most serious indications of this corruption is the unbridled exaltation of sex. Moreover, through the means of social communication and through public entertainment this corruption has reached the point of invading the field of education and infecting the general mentality.

In this context certain educators, teachers and moralists have been able to contribute to a better understanding and integration into life of the values proper to each of the sexes; on the other hand there are those who have put forward concepts and modes of behavior which are contrary to the true moral exigencies of the latter group have even gone so far as to favor a licentious hedonism.

As a result, in the course of a few years, teachings, moral criteria and modes of living hitherto faithfully preserved have been very much unsettled, even among Christians. There are many people today who being confronted with so many widespread opinions opposed to the teaching which they received from the church, have come to wonder what they must still hold as true.

2. The church cannot remain indifferent to this confusion of minds and relaxation of morals. It is a question, in fact, of a matter which is of the utmost importance both for the personal lives of Christians and for the social life of our time.[1]

The bishops are daily led to note the growing difficulties experienced by the faithful in obtaining knowledge of wholesome moral teaching, especially in sexual matters, and of the growing difficulties experienced by pastors in expounding this teaching effectively. The bishops know that by their pastoral charge they are called upon to meet the needs of their faithful in this very serious matter, and important documents dealing with it have already been published by some of them or by episcopal conferences. Nevertheless, since the erroneous opinions and resulting deviations are continuing to spread everywhere, the Sacred Congregation for the Doctrine of the Faith, by virtue of its function in the universal church[2] and by a mandate of the supreme pontiff, has judged it necessary to publish the present declaration.

3. The people of our time are more and more convinced that the human person's dignity and vocation demand that they should discover, by the light of their own intelligence, the values innate in their nature, that they should ceaselessly develop these values and realize them in their lives, in order to achieve an ever greater development.

In moral matters man cannot make value judgments according to his personal whim: " In the depths of his conscience, man detects a law which he does not impose on himself, but which holds him to obedience . . . For man has in his heart a law written by God. To obey it is the very dignity of man; according to it he will be judged."[3]

Moreover, through his relevation God has made known to us Christians his plan of salvation, and he has held up to us Christ, the savior and sanctifier, in his teaching and example, as the supreme and immutable law of life: " I am the light of the world; anyone who follows me will not be walking in the dark, he will have the light of life."[4]

Therefore there can be no true promotion of man's dignity unless the essential order of his nature is respected. Of course, in the history of civilization many of the concrete conditions and needs of human life have changed and will continue to change. But all evolution of morals and every type of life must be kept within the limits imposed by the ummutable principles based upon every human person's constitutive elements and essential relations—elements and relations which transcend historical contingency.

[1] Cf. Second Vatican Ecumenical Council, Constitution on the Church in the Modern World, *Gaudium et Specs*, 47: *AAS* 58 (1966), p. 1067.
[2] Cf. Apostolic constitution *Regimini Ecclesiae Universae*, 29 (August 15, 1967): *AAS* 59 (1967), p. 897.
[3] *Gaudium et Spes*. 16: *AAS* 58 (1966), p. 1037.
[4] Jn 8:12.

These fundamental principles, which can be grasped by reason, are contained in "the divine law—eternal, objective and universal—whereby God orders, directs governs the entire universe and all the ways of the human community, by a plan conceived in wisdom and love. Man has been made by God to participate in this law, with the result that, under the gentle disposition of divine providence, he can come to perceive ever increasingly the unchanging truth."[5] This divine law is accessible to our minds.

4. Hence, those many people are in error who today assert that one can find neither in human nature nor in the revealed law any absolute and immutable norm to serve for particular actions other than the one which expresses itself in the general law of charity and respect for human dignity. As a proof of their assertion they put forward the view that so-called norms of the natural law or precepts of sacred scripture are to be regarded only as given expressions of a form of particular culture at a certain moment of history.

But in fact, divine revelation and, in its own proper order, philosophical wisdom, emphasize the authentic exigencies of human nature. They thereby necessarily manifest the existence of immutable laws inscribed in the constitutive elements of human nature and which are revealed to be identical in all beings endowed with reason.

Furthermore, Christ instituted his church as "the pillar and bulwark of truth."[6] With the Holy Spirit's assistance, she ceaselessly preserves and transmits without error the truths of the moral order, and she authentically interprets not only the revealed positive law but "also . . . those principles of the moral order which have their origin in human nature itself"[7] and which concern man's full development and sanctification. Now in fact the church throughout her history has always considered a certain number of precepts of the natural law as having an absolute and immutable value, and in their transgression she has seen a contradiction of the teaching and spirit of the gospel.

5. Since sexual ethics concern fundamental values of human and Christian life, this general teaching equally applies to sexual ethics. In this domain there exist principles and norms which the church has always unhesitatingly transmitted as part of her teaching, however much the opinions and morals of the world may have been opposed to them. These principles and norms in no way owe their origin to a certain type of culture, but rather to knowledge of the divine law and of human nature. They therefore cannot be considered as having become out of date or doubtful under the pretext that a new cultural situation has arisen.

It is these principles which inspired the exhortations and directives given by the Second Vatican Council for an education and an organization of social life taking account of the equal dignity of man and woman while respecting their differences.[8]

[5] Second Vatican Ecumenical Council, declaration *Dignitatis Humanae*, 3: *AAS* 58 (1966), p. 931.
[6] 1 Tim 3:15.
[7] *Dignitatis Humanae*, 14: *AAS* 58 (1966), p. 940; cf. Pius XI, encyclical letter *Cast Connubii*, December 31, 1930: *AAS* 22 (1930), pp. 579–580; Pius XII, Allocution of November 2, 1954: *AAS* 46 (1954), pp. 671–672; John XXIII, encyclical letter *Maier et Magistra*, May 15, 1961: *AAS* 53 (1961), p. 457: Paul VI, encyclical letter *Humanae Vitae*, 4, July 25, 1968: *AAS* 60 (1968), p. 483.
[8] Cf. Second Vatican Ecumenical Council, declaration *Gravissimum Educationis*, 1, 8: *AAS* 58 (1966), pp. 729–730; 734–736. *Gaudium et Spes*, 29, 60, 67: *AAS* 58 (1966), pp. 1048–1049, 1080–1081, 1088–1089.

Speaking of "the sexual nature of man and the human faculty of procreation," the Council noted that they "wonderfully exceed the dispositions of lower forms of life."[9] It then took particular care to expound the principles and criteria which concern human sexuality in marriage, and which are based upon the finality of the specific function of sexuality.

In this regard the Council declares that the moral goodness of the acts proper to conjugal life, acts which are ordered according to true human dignity, "does not depend solely on sincere intentions or on an evaluation of motives. It must be determined by objective standards. These, based on the nature of the human person and his acts, preserve the full sense of mutual self-giving and human procreation in the context of true love."[10]

These final words briefly sum up the Council's teaching—more fully expounded in an earlier part of the same constitution[11]—on the finality of the sexual act and on the principal criterion of its morality: it is respect for its finality that ensures the moral goodness of this act.

This same principle, which the church holds from divine revelation and from her authentic interpretation of the natural law, is also the basis of her traditional doctrine, which states that the use of the sexual function has its true meaning and moral rectitude only in true marriage.[12]

6. It is not the purpose of the present declaration to deal with all the abuses of the sexual faculty, nor with all the elements involved in the practice of chastity. Its object is rather to repeat the church's doctrine on certain particular points, in view of the urgent need to oppose serious errors and widespread aberrant modes of behavior.

7. Today there are many who vindicate the right to sexual union before marriage, at least in those cases where a firm intention to marry and an affection which is already in some way conjugal in the psychology of the subjects require this completion, which they judge to be connatural. This is expecially the case when the celebration of the marriage is impeded by circumstances or when this intimate relationship seems necessary in order for love to be preserved.

This opinion is contrary to Christian doctrine, which states that every genital act must be within the framework of marriage. However firm the intention of those who practice such premature sexual relations may be, the fact remains that these relations cannot ensure, in sincerity and fidelity, the interpersonal relationship between a man and a woman, nor especially can they protect this relationship from whims and caprices.

Now it is a stable union that Jesus willed, and he restored its original requirement, beginning with the sexual difference. "have you not read that the creator from the begining made them male and female and that he said: This is why a man must leave father and mother, and cling to his wife, and the two become one

---

[9] *Gaudium et Spes*, 51: *AAS* 58 (1966), p. 1072.

[10] Ibid., cf. also 49: oc. cit., pp. 1069–1070.

[11] Ibid., 49, 50: oc. cit., pp. 1069–1072.

[12] The present declaration does not go into further detail regarding the norms of sexual life within marriage; these norms have been clearly taught in the encyclical letters *Cast, Connubi*, and *Humanae Vitae*.

body? They are no longer two, therefore, but one body. So then, what God has united, man must not divide."[13]

Saint Paul will be even more explicit when he shows that if unmarried people or widows cannot live chastely they have no other alternative than the stable union of marriage: ". . . it is better to marry than to be aflame with passion."[14] Through marriage, in fact, the love of married people is taken up into that love which Christ irrevocably has for the church,[15] while dissolute sexual union [16] defiles the temple of the Holy Spirit which the Christian has become. Sexual union therefore is only legitimate if a definite community of life has been established between the man and the woman.

This is what the church has always understood and taught,[17] and she finds a profound agreement with her doctrine in men's reflection and in the lessons of history.

Experience teaches us that love must find its safeguard in the stability of marriage if sexual intercourse is truly to respond to the requirements of its own finality and to those of human dignity. These requirements call for a conjugal contract sanctioned and guaranteed by society—a contract which establishes a state of life of capital importance both for the exclusive union of the man and the woman and for the good of their family and of the human community. Most often, in fact, premarital relations exclude the possibility of children. What is represented to be conjugal love is not able, as it absolutely should be, to develop into paternal and maternal love. Or, if it does happen to do so, this will be to the detriment of the children, who will be deprived of the stable environment in which they ought to develop in order to find in it the way and the means of their insertion into society as a whole.

The consent given by people who wish to be united in marriage must therefore be manifested externally and in a manner which makes it valid in the eyes of society. As far as the faithful are concerned, their consent to the setting up of a community of conjugal life must be expressed according to the laws of the church. It is a consent which makes their marriage a sacrament of Christ.

8. At the present time there are those who, basing themselves on observations in the psychological order, have begun to judge indulgently, and even to excuse completely, homosexual relations between certain people. This they do in opposition to the constant teaching of the magisterium and to the moral sense of the Christian people.

A distinction is drawn, and it seems with some reason, between homosexuals whose tendency comes from a false education, from a lack of normal sexual development, from habit, from bad example, or from other similar causes, and is transitory or at least not incurable; and homosexuals who are definitively such

---

[13] Cf. Mt 19:4–6.
[14] 1 Cor 7:9.
[15] Cf. Eph. 5:25–32.
[16] Sexual intercourse outside marriage is formally condemned: 1 Cor 5:1; 6:9; 7:2; 10:8; Eph. 5:5; 1 Tim 1:10; Heb 13:4; and with explicit reasons: 1 Cor 6:12–20.
[17] Cf. Innocent IV, Letter Sub catholica professioe, March 6, 1254, DS 835; Pius II, Propos. damn. in Ep. Cum sicut accepimus, November 14, 1459, DS 1367; Decrees of the Holy Office September 24, 1665, DS 2045; March 2, 1679, DS 2148. Pius XI, encyclical letter Cast, Connubii, December 31, 1930: AAS 22 (1930), pp. 558–559.

because of some kind of innate instinct or a pathological constitution judged to be incurable.

In regard to this second category of subjects, some people conclude that their tendency is so natural that it justifies in their case homosexual relations with a sincere communion of life and love analogous to marriage, insofar as such homosexuals feel incapable of enduring a solitary life.

In the pastoral field, these homosexuals must certainly be treated with understanding and sustained in the hope of overcoming their personal difficulties and their inability to fit into society. Their culpability will be judged with prudence. But no pastoral method can be employed which would give moral justification to these acts on the grounds that they would be consonant with the condition of such people. For according to the objective moral order, homosexual relations are acts which lack an essential and indispensable finality. In sacred scripture they are condemned as a serious depravity and even presented as the sad consequence of rejecting God.[18] This judgment of scripture does not of course permit us to conclude that all those who suffer from this anomaly are personally responsible for it, but it does attest to the fact that homosexual acts are intrinsically disordered and can in no case be approved of.

9. The traditional Catholic doctrine that masturbation constitutes a grave moral disorder is often called into doubt or expressly denied today. It is said that psychology and sociology show that it is a normal phenomenon of sexual development, especially among the young. It is stated that there is real and serious fault only in the measure that the subject deliberately indulges in solitary pleasure closed in on self ("ipsation"), because in this case the act would indeed be radically opposed to the loving communion between persons of different sex which some hold is what is principally sought in the use of the sexual faculty.

This opinion is contradictory to the teaching and pastoral practice of the Catholic Church. Whatever the force of certain arguments of a biological and philosophical nature, which have sometimes been used by theologians, in fact both the magisterium of the church—in the course of a constant tradition—and the moral sense of the faithful have declared without hesitation that masturbation is an intrinsically and seriously disordered act.[19]

The main reason is that, whatever the motive for acting in this way, the deliberate use of the sexual faculty outside normal conjugal relations essentially contradicts the finality of the faculty. For it lacks the sexual relationship called for by the moral order, namely the relationship which realizes "the full sense of mutual self-giving and human procreation in the context of true love."[20]

---

[18] Rom 1:24–27: "That is why God left them to their filthy enjoyments and the practices with which they dishonor their own bodies since they have given up divine truth for a lie and have worshipped and served creatures instead of the creator, who is blessed for ever. Amen! That is why God has abandoned them to degrading passions: why their women have turned from natural intercourse to unnatural practices and why their menfolk have given up natural intercourse to be consumed with passion for each other, men doing shameless things with men and getting an appropriate reward for their perversion." See also what Saint Paul says of *masculorum concubitores* in 1 Cor 6:10, 1 Tim 1:10.

[19] Cf. Leo IX, etter *Ad splendidum nitentisi* in the year 1054: *DS* 687–688. Decree of the Holy Office, March 2, 1679: *DS* 2149; Pius XII, *Allocutio*, October 8, 1953: *AAS* 45 (1953), pp. 677–678; May 19, 1956: *AAS* 48 (1956), pp. 472–473.

[20] *Gaudium et Spes*, 51: *AAS* 58 (1966), p. 1072.

All deliberate exercise of sexuality must be reserved to this regular relationship. Even if it cannot be proved that scripture condemns this sin by name, the tradition of the church has rightly understood it to be condemned in the New Testament when the latter speaks of "impurity," "unchasteness" and other vices contrary to chastity and continence.

Sociological surveys are able to show the frequency of this disorder according to the places, populations or circumstances studied. In this way facts are discovered, but facts do not constitute a criterion for judging the moral value of human acts.[21] The frequency of the phenomenon in question is certainly to be linked with man's innate weakness following original sin; but it is also to be linked with the loss of a sense of God, with the corruption of morals engendered by the commercialization of vice, with the unrestrained licentiousness of so many public entertainments and publications, as well as with the neglect of modesty, which is the guardian of chastity.

On the subject of masturbation modern psychology provides much valid and useful information for formulating a more equitable judgment on moral responsibility and for orienting pastoral action. Psychology helps one to see how the immaturity of adolescence (which can sometimes persist after that age), psychological imbalance or habit can influence behavior, diminishing the deliberate character of the act and bringing about a situation whereby subjectively there may not always be serious fault. But in general, the absence of serious responsibility must not be presumed; this would be to misunderstand people's moral capacity.

In the pastoral ministry, in order to form an adequate judgment in concrete cases, the habitual behavior of people will be considered in its totality, not only with regard to the individual's practice of charity and of justice but also with regard to the individual's care in observing the particular precepts of chastity. In particular, one will have to examine whether the individual is using the necessary means, both natural and supernatural, which Christian asceticism from its long experience recommends for overcoming the passions and progressing in virtue.

10. The observance of the moral law in the field of sexuality and the practice of chastity have been considerably endangered, especially among less fervent Christians, by the current tendency to minimize as far as possible, when not denying outright, the reality of grave sin, at least in people's actual lives.

There are those who go as far as to affirm that mortal sin, which causes separation from God, only exists in the formal refusal directly opposed to God's call, or in that selfishness which completely and deliberately closes itself to the love of neighbor. They say that it is only then that there comes into play the fundamental option, that is to say the decision which totally commits the person and which is necessary if mortal sin is to exist; by this option the person, from the depths of the personality, takes up or ratifies a fundamental attitude towards God or people. On the contrary, so-called "peripheral" actions (which, it is said, usually do not

---

[21] ". . . if sociological surveys are useful for better discovering the thought patterns of the people of a particular place, the anxieties and needs of those to whom we proclaim the word of God, and also the opposition made to it by modern reasoning through the widespread notion that outside science there exists no legitimate form of knowledge, still the conclusions drawn from such surveys could not of themselves constitute a determining criterion of truth," Paul VI, apostolic exhortation *Quinque iam anni*, December 8, 1970, *AAS* 63 (1971), p. 102.

involve decisive choice), do not go so far as to change the fundamental option, the less so since they often come, as is observed, from habit. Thus such actions can weaken the fundamental option, but not to such a degree as to change it completely.

Now according to these authors, a change of the fundamental option towards God less easily comes about in the field of sexual activity, where a person generally does not transgress the moral order in a fully deliberate and responsible manner but rather under the influence of passion, weakness, immaturity, sometimes even through the illusion of thus showing love for someone else. To these causes there is often added the pressure of the social environment.

In reality, it is precisely the fundamental option which in the last resort defines a person's moral disposition. But it can be completely changed by particular acts, especially when, as often happens, these have been prepared for by previous more superficial acts. Whatever the case, it is wrong to say that particular acts are not enough to constitute mortal sin.

According to the church's teaching, mortal sin, which is opposed to God, does not consist only in formal and direct resistance to the commandment of charity. It is equally to be found in this opposition to authentic love which is included in every deliberate transgression, in serious matter, of each of the moral laws.

Christ himself has indicated the double commandment of love as the basis of the moral life. But on this commandment depends "the whole law, and the prophets also."[22] It therefore includes the other particular precepts. In fact, to the young man who asked, ". . . what good deed must I do to possess eternal life?" Jesus replied ". . . if you wish to enter into life, keep the commandments. . . You must not kill. You must not commit adultery. You must not steal. You must not bring false witness. Honor your father and mother, and: you must love your neighbor as yourself."[23]

A person therefore sins mortally not only when his action comes from direct contempt for love of God and neighbor, but also when he consciously and freely, for whatever reason, chooses something which is seriously disordered. For in this choice, as has been said above, there is already included contempt for the divine commandment: the person turns himself away from God and loses charity. Now according to Christian tradition and the church's teaching, and as right reason also recognizes, the moral order of sexuality involves such high values of human life that every direct violation of this order is objectively serious.[24]

It is true that in sins of the sexual order, in view of their kind and their causes, it more easily happens that free consent is not fully given; this is a fact which calls for caution in all judgment as to the subject's responsibility. In this matter it is particularly opportune to recall the following words of scripture: "Man looks at appearances but God looks at the heart,"[25] However, although prudence is recommended in judging the subjective seriousness of a particular sinful act, it in no way follows that one can hold the view that in the sexual field mortal sins are not committed.

[22] Mt 22:38 40.
[23] Mt 19: 16–19.
[24] Cf. note 17 and 19 above: Decree of the Holy Office, March 18, 1666, DS 2060; Paul VI, encyclical letter *Humanae Vitae* 13, 14: AAS 60 (1968), pp. 489–496.
[25] 1 Sam 16:7.

Pastors of souls must therefore exercise patience and goodness; but they are not allowed to render God's commandments null, nor to reduce unreasonably people's responsibility. "To diminish in no way the saving teaching of Christ constitutes an eminent form of charity for souls. But this must ever be accompanied by patience and goodness, such as the Lord himself gave example of in dealing with people. Having come not to condemn but to save, he was indeed intransigent with evil, but merciful towards individuals."[26]

11. As has been said above, the purpose of this declaration is to draw the attention of the faithful in present-day circumstances to certain errors and modes of behavior which they must guard against. The virtue of chastity, however, is in no way confined solely to avoiding the faults already listed. It is aimed at attaining higher and more positive goals. It is a virtue which concerns the whole personality, as regards both interior and outward behavior.

Individuals should be endowed with this virtue according to their state in life: for some it will mean virginity or celibacy consecrated to God, which is an eminent way of giving oneself more easily to God alone with an undivided heart.[27] For others it will take the form determined by the moral law, according to whether they are married or single. But whatever the state of life, chastity is not simply an external state; it must make a person's heart pure in accordance with Christ's words: "You have learned how it was said: "You must not commit adultery. But I say this to you: if a man looks at a woman lustfully, he has already committed adultery with her in his heart."[28]

Chastity is included in that continence which Saint Paul numbers among the gifts of the Holy Spirit, while he condemns sensuality as a vice particularly unworthy of the Christian and one which precludes entry into the kingdom of heaven.[29]

"What God wants is for all to be holy. He wants you to keep away from fornication, and each one of you to know how to use the body that belongs to him in a way that is holy and honorable, not giving way to selfish lust like the pagans who do not know God. He wants nobody at all ever to sin by taking advantage of a brother in these matters. . . We have been called by God to be holy, not to be immoral. In other words, anyone who objects is not objecting to a human authority, but to God, who gives you his Holy Spirit."[30]

"Among you there must not be even a mention of fornication or impurity in any of its forms, or promiscuity: this would hardly become the saints! For you can be quite certain that nobody who actually indulges in fornication or impurity or promiscuity—which is worshipping a false god—can inherit anything of the kingdom of God. Do not let anyone deceive you with empty arguments: it is for this loose living that God's anger comes down on those who rebel against him. Make sure that you are not included with them. You were darkness once, but now you are

---

[26] Paul VI encyclical letter *Humanae Vitae*, 29: *AAS* 60 (1968), p. 501.
[27] Cf. 1 Cor 7:7, 34; Council of Trent, Session XXIV, can. 10: *DS* 1810; Second Vatican Council, Constitution *Lumen Gentium*, 42, 43, 44: *AAS* 57 (1965), pp. 47?51; Synod of Bishops, *De Sacredotio Ministeriali*, part II, 4 b: *AAS* 63 (1971), pp. 915–916.
[28] Mt 5:28.
[29] Cf. Gal 5:19–23; 1 Cor 6:9–11.
[30] 1 Thess 4:3–8; cf. Col 3:5–7; 1 Tim 1:10.

light in the Lord; be like children of light, for the effects of the light are seen in complete goodness and right living and truth."[31]

In addition, the apostle points out the specifically Christian motive for practicing chastity when he condemns the sin of fornication not only in the measure that this action is injurious to one's neighbor or to the social order but because the fornicator offends against Christ who has redeemed him with his blood and of whom he is a member, and against the Holy Spirit of whom he is the temple.

"You know, surely, that your bodies are members making up the body of Christ. . . All the other sins are committed outside the body; but to fornicate is to sin against your own body. Your body, you know, is the temple of the Holy Spirit, who is in you since you received him from God. You are not your own property; you have been bought and paid for. That is why you should use your body for the glory of God."[32]

The more the faithful appreciate the value of chastity and its necessary role in their lives as men and women, the better they will understand, by a kind of spiritual instinct, its moral requirements and counsels. In the same way they will know better how to accept and carry out, in a spirit of docility to the church's teaching, what an upright conscience dictates in concrete cases.

12. The apostle Saint Paul describes in vivid terms the painful interior conflict of the person enslaved to sin: the conflict between "the law of his mind" and the "law of sin which dwells in his members" and which holds him captive.[33] But man can achieve liberation from his "body doomed to death" through the grace of Jesus Christ.[34] This grace is enjoyed by those who have been justified by it and whom "the law of the spirit of life in Christ Jesus has set free from the law of sin and death."[35] It is for this reason that the apostle adjures them: "That is why you must not let sin reign in your mortal bodies or command your obedience to bodily passions."[36]

This liberation, which fits one to serve God in newness of life, does not however suppress the concupiscence deriving from original sin, nor the promptings to evil in this world, which is "in the power of the evil one."[37] This is why the apostle exhorts the faithful to overcome temptations by the power of God[38] and to "stand against the wiles of the devil"[39] by faith, watchful prayer[40] and an austerity of life that brings the body into subjection to the Spirit.[41]

Living the Christian life by following in the footsteps of Christ requires that everyone should "deny himself and take up his cross daily,"[42] sustained by the hope of reward, for "if we have died with him, we shall also reign with him."[43]

[31] Eph 5:3–8; cf. 4:18–19.
[32] 1 Cor 6:15, 18–20.
[33] Cf. Rom 7:23.
[34] Cf. Rom 7:24–25.
[35] Cf. Rom 8:2.
[36] Rom 6:12.
[37] 1 Jn 5:19.
[38] Cf. 1 Cor 10:13.
[39] Eph 6:11.
[40] Cf. Eph 6:16, 18.
[41] Cf. 1 Cor 9:27.
[42] Lk 9:23.
[43] 2 Tim 2:11–12.

In accordance with these pressing exhortations, the faithful of the present time, and indeed today more than ever, must use the means which have always been recommended by the church for living a chaste life. These means are: discipline of the senses and the mind, watchfulness and prudence in avoiding occasions of sin, the observance of modesty, moderation in recreation, wholesome pursuits, assiduous prayer and frequent reception of the sacraments of penance and the eucharist. Young people especially should earnestly foster devotion to the immaculate mother of God, and take as examples the lives of the saints and other faithful people, especially young ones, who excelled in the practice of chastity.

It is important in particular that everyone should have a high esteem for the virtue of chastity, its beauty and its power of attraction. This virtue increases the human person's dignity and enables him to love truly, disinterestedly, unselfishly and with respect for others.

13. It is up to the bishops to instruct the faithful in the moral teaching concerning sexual morality, however great may be the difficulties in carrying out this work in the face of ideas and practices generally prevailing today. This traditional doctrine must be studied more deeply. It must be handed on in a way capable of properly enlightening the consciences of those confronted with new situations and it must be enriched with a discernment of all the elements that can truthfully and usefully be brought forward about the meaning and value of human sexuality.

But the principles and norms of moral living reaffirmed in this declaration must be faithfully held and taught. It will especially be necessary to bring the faithful to understand that the church holds these principles not as old and inviolable superstitions, nor out of some Manichaean prejudice, as is often alleged, but rather because she knows with certainty that they are in complete harmony with the divine order of creation and with the spirit of Christ, and therefore also with human dignity.

It is likewise the bishops' mission to see that a sound doctrine enlightened by faith and directed by the magisterium of the church is taught in faculties of theology and in seminaries. Bishops must also ensure that confessors enlighten people's consciences and that catechetical instruction is given in perfect fidelity to Catholic doctrine.

It rests with the bishops, the priests and their collaborators to alert the faithful against the erroneous opinions often expressed in books, reviews and public meetings.

Parents, in the first place, and also teachers of the young must endeavor to lead their children and their pupils, by way of a complete education, to the psychological, emotional and moral maturity befitting their age. They will therefore prudently give them information suited to their age; and they will assiduously form their wills in accordance with Christian morals, not only by advice but above all by the example of their own lives, relying on God's help, which they will obtain in prayer. They will likewise protect the young from the many dangers of which they are quite unaware.

Artists, writers and all those who use the means of social communication should exercise their profession in accordance with their Christian faith and with a clear awareness of the enormous influence which they can have. They should remember that "the primacy of the objective moral order must be regarded as absolute by all,"[44] and that it is wrong for them to give priority above it to any so-called aesthetic purpose, or to material advantage or to success.

Whether it be a question of artistic or literary works, public entertainment or providing information, each individual in his or her own domain must show tact, discretion, moderation and a true sense of values. In this way, far from adding to the growing permissiveness of behavior, each individual will contribute towards controlling it and even towards making the moral climate of society more wholesome.

All lay people, for their part, by virtue of their rights and duties in the work of the apostolate, should endeavor to act in the same way.

Finally, it is necessary to remind everyone of the words of the Second Vatican Council: " This Holy Synod likewise affirms that children and young people have a right to be encouraged to weigh moral values with an upright conscience, and to embrace them by personal choice, to know and love God more adequately. Hence, it earnestly entreats all who exercise government over people or preside over the work of education to see that youth is never deprived of this sacred right."[45]

At the audience granted on November 7, 1975 to the undersigned prefect of the Sacred Congregation for the Doctrine of the Faith, the sovereign pontiff by divine providence Pope Paul VI approved this declaration " On certain questions concerning sexual ethics," confirmed it and ordered its publication.

Given in Rome, at the Sacred Congregation for the Doctrine of the Faith, on December 29, 1975.¶

Cardinal Franjo Seper
Prefect
Archbishop Jerome Hamer, O.P.
Secretary

[44] Second Vatican Ecumenical Council, decree *Inter Mirifica*, 6: *AAS* 56 (1964), p. 147.
[45] *Gravissimum Educationis*, 1: *AAS* 58 (1966), p. 730.

The Sexual
Relationship in
Christian Thought

Philip Sherrard

Philip Sherrard (1922–   ) is an Orthodox Christian educated at Cambridge, University of London, and Oxford. He is author of *The Greek East and the Latin West*, *Athos: the Mountain of Silence*, and *Constantinople: The Iconography of a Sacred City* (with E. L. Keeley). He is at present associated with the British School of Archaeology in Athens, Greece.

The idea of the sacramental potentiality of sexual love is one of the most creative and ennobling ideas in which the European imagination has shared. Anticipated by Plato and by some of the neo-Platonic philosophers, particularly Plotinus, it began gradually to be affirmed in the Middle Ages: in the legends surrounding the Holy Grail, in that *ley de cortezia* of the Provencal palaces which marks the first break with the ascetic spirit of the mediaeval world; in the love of Tristan and Iseult and later in that of Dante and Beatrice, as well as in the works of Renaissance figures like Ficino and Pico della Mirandola. Subsequently it is celebrated by several of the English poets—by Shakespeare, Spencer, Blake, Emily Brontë and Yeats, to mention but a few of them—and attempts are made to give it a philosophical or religious basis by writers like Soloviev and Berdiaev. One of its more recent literary expressions is in Pasternak's *Dr. Zhivago*.

What are the implications of this discovery? When we speak of sexual love, we cover by that term a whole host of meanings, moods and activities. It denotes anything ranging from desire for the body of another person to the passion of an Othello or a Don Juan. Most confusing of all, we speak of "making love" when what we mean is another function altogether. In fact, most of our references to sex or sexual love are coloured by associations with purely physical or what is called carnal activity. Hence it is necessary to discriminate and to say that this sacramental form of sexual love is something different from the love (if it can be called that) which is simply sensual desire or passion. It is something different even from that mutual sympathy, fidelity and affection which by and large stands as the Christian ideal of marriage. What is indicated in this form of love is a relationship between two people—a man and a woman—in which each through their mutual awareness and recognition of each other experience what Plato calls that "something, they do not know what" which overflows their beings and transforms their individual

Source: Philip Sherrard, "The Sexual Relationship in Christian Thought," in *Studies in Comparative Religion* (Bedfont, Middlesex, England, 1971), pp. 151–172. Reprinted by permission of Perennial Books, Ltd.

existence into a single reality. Through it, an "I—thou" totality in the way that Martin Buber understood it is established; or a single heart and a single soul in two bodies:

> So they loved, as love in twain
> Had the essence but in one;
> Two distincts, division none:
> Number there in love was slain.

It is a mutual awareness and recognition which is a total act of the soul. We tend to distinguish between the love of God and the love of one person for another—to distinguish between *Agape* and *Eros*—and to regard the second as a rather debased form of the first, if not as directly opposed to the first and only indulged at the expense of the first. In a sexualized sacramental love there is no such distinction. It is transcended and eliminated and there is but a single communion, a single participation of the man and the woman and the divine in each other, although it must be remembered that however transparent the two human beings become to each other in its light, the divine itself always remains hidden and inaccessible in its essence. It is because of its participation in the divine that this love may further be defined as Plato defines it, namely, as a birth in beauty (*tiktein en to kalo*); and for the same reason it may also be said to partake potentially of eternity.

It may therefore be concluded that this sacramental form of sexual love is not simply a human emotion or impulse or even a created cosmic or elemental force. Still less is it to be identified simply with a bodily or a somato-psychic energy. It is, in its origins, a spiritual energy. It is rooted in divine life itself and its principle, so to say, is placed by God in man and woman in their creation. Hence, to be united in this love is to find oneself returned to oneself, to one's full being and primal condition. In this sense, it is not simply to be born in beauty. It is also to be regenerated in God and to have the divine Paradise revealed to one. In other words, it is a form of sexual relationship which has a spiritualizing influence on the two people concerned in it. It follows from this that its *raison d'être* is not the generation of children or any other specifiable purpose connected with the family or the race or which is, as it were, external to itself. It also follows that though it is a fully sexualized love, in that it involves the fully differentiated beings of man and woman, this sexual element need not have any so-called carnal (or genital) expression: not because the man and the woman have taken any vow of virginity or regard celibacy as a superior state of existence, but simply because the kind of communion they experience makes such expression unnecessary—a descent into a lower key. Finally, it must be said that this form of love is relatively a rare occurrence: rare, because it demands a high level of understanding and sensitivity, and because it also demands the fulfilment of certain conditions which are not always present or which people are not always willing to fulfill unreservedly.

The idea of the sexual relationship as a sacrament is of course affirmed by the Christian Church. It is the corner-stone of the Christian conception of marriage. It is understood that Christ's presence at the marriage in Cana and the fact that it was there that He performed His first miracle implies that God not only approves of marriage but also gives it His special blessing. Therefore the Church continues to give it her special blessing. If it is asked why such a dignity has been conferred on marriage, the answer generally given is that there are two main reasons to account for it. The first is that it unites man and woman and that this union has a sacred significance. Here the traditional authority is St. Paul. In the Epistle to the Ephesians (5: 31–32), it is indicated that in marriage man and woman become one flesh and that this great mystery corresponds to the relationship between Christ and the Church. Marriage—the union of man and woman—symbolizes the union of Christ and the Church and so is sacred. The second main reason for regarding marriage as sacred is that it is the established institution for the procreation of children. God said to our forefathers: "Be fruitful and multiply"; and this is taken to mean that He wanted Adam and Eve to have children and must therefore regard the procreation of children by husband and wife as a holy procedure under all circumstances. It follows that marriage, through which man and woman become husband and wife, must also be holy, provided the Church gives it her blessing.

Yet in spite of the fact that marriage is recognized as a sacrament by the Church, the attitude of Christian thought towards the sexual relationship and its spiritualizing potentialities has in practice been singularly limited and negative. From the start Christian authors have been ill at ease with the whole subject. First, supported by a literal interpretation of Christ's words about those who make themselves eunuchs for the sake of the Kingdom of Heaven, as well as by St. Paul's commendation of the single state (1 Cor. VII), early Christian theologians did not hesitate to affirm that celibacy is *per se* superior to marriage; and, second, they have seemed incapable of envisaging any aspect of sexuality other than its purely generative (not to say genital) expression, and towards this they display an antipathy obsessive to a degree scarcely less than vicious. Although precluded by their basic doctrine from subscribing to an out-and-out dualism in this matter, and so from attributing the origin of sexuality directly to an evil power, their practical attitude differs little from that of dualists of a Manichaean type. Sexuality is tainted. It is impure. It invests matrimony (which in any case must be regarded as a concession to those too feeble to endure the single state) with shame and contaminates those who indulge in it. If not actually evil in itself, its use stirs up the passions and so leads directly to sin. It is the springhead through which the tribes of evil pour into human nature. Consequently any progress in the life of the spirit demands as an initial step the circumventing or transcending of sexuality. Not until that step is taken is man capable of entering into a truly spiritual state.

In spite of differences in a number of doctrinal presuppositions, both the eastern and the western Christian traditions manifest a very similar attitude to the sexual relationship and its significance. Where the eastern tradition is concerned, two authors—St. Gregory of Nyssa and St. Maximos the Confessor—may be taken as representative. For both, their attitude to the sexual life derives from their anthropology—their idea of what precisely it is that constitutes human nature. The foundation of this anthropology is the text in Genesis (1.26): "Let us make man in our image and resemblance". What man is "in the image" is his natural state and provides the norm for human life. In his original state—as he is created "in the image"—man comprehends what we call the intellectual life (the *nous*) and the spiritual life (the *pneuma*); and it is these two realities together which constitute the true and basic man. The animal or organic life has as it were been superadded to this true and basic man. It is superadded as a consequence of the "fall." This is indicated in another text in Genesis (3.21): "The Lord God made Adam and his wife garments of skin." These "garments of skin" (chitones) are the figure of the animal life. They are identified as accretions and alien to man's basic nature, superimposed upon this nature as a consequence of its declension from its original state. The condition into which man is born in this world is not his natural condition. It is an unnatural and fallen condition; and he has to find his way back to the natural unfallen life for which he was created "in the image."

Two fundamental qualities distinguish this natural unfallen life: immortality and incorruptibility; and, St. Gregory argues, the presence of these two qualities presupposes the absence of sexuality. In his original state as he is created "in the image," man is free from sexuality. There is not even a division between the sexes. There is no man and woman. Sexuality is one of the consequences of a fall and of the loss of immortality and incorruptibility that goes with it. It is a consequence of man's investiture with an animal or organic life. It is one of the most disastrous consequences of the fall because it is the source of the passion, and it is the passions which lead to sin. "I consider it to be from this principle (the sexual life) that the passions as from a fountain-head flow over human nature," writes St. Gregory; while for St. Maximos the fall itself is due precisely to bodily desire and a search for sensual pleasure, and this is confirmed most fully in the sexual relationship. Hence the importance of virginity. Virginity is a condition of man's return to his original state. A true Christian, St. Gregory maintains, must choose between two forms of marriage, one "bodily" and the other "spiritual." His choice can be for one of these forms only, since they are mutually exclusive. In fact, man is called upon to choose the second form—spiritual marriage—in which he does not desire an earthly woman, but true Wisdom, and in which the soul is attached to the incorruptible Bridegroom and her love (eros) is related to the true Wisdom which is God.

Sexual love between man and woman is, therefore, at the expense of the spiritual life. Sexual relationships, as such, are the consequence of sin and are only to be tolerated because they provide for the continuity of the human race. Even the distinction between man and woman only exists or is only established because God foresees that man is going to sin and so to fall and therefore will be in need of a mode of propagation which will make it possible for him to continue the human race under new conditions. But the Pauline phrase (Galatians III:28) is adduced to confirm that in Christ there is "neither male nor female" (the alternative Pauline phrase (I Cor. XI:11) to the effect that "neither is the man without the woman, neither the woman without the man, in the Lord", tends to be ignored); and the scriptural passage (Matthew XXII:30) in which Christ tells the Sadducees that in the resurrection people neither marry nor are married is taken to signify that man should live without marriage. This does not mean that the value of marriage is totally denied. It cannot be totally denied because without it man cannot be born into this world. But, according to St. Maximos, at best it constitutes only the lowest and most external of the unions which man must experience before he can be restored to the spiritual state. Even so, a generic sin is always at work within the sexual relationship and this can only be extirpated on condition that sexuality itself is extirpated. One has to transcend the sexual life and even to overcome the sexual differentiation altogether in order to dry up the passions at their source, because until the passions are dried up one cannot begin to live the life of the spirit. Only through monastic celibacy can man recover that natural—and sexless—state for which he was originally created "in the image."

Where the western Christian tradition is concerned the scene is dominated by the imposing figure of St. Augustine, whose theology of marriage was to set the over-all pattern for western Christian thinking in these matters for the next fifteen hundred years and continues to be influential even today.[1] This theology—as western Christian theology in general—presupposes an anthropology different from that of the Greek Patristic tradition. In western theology, man by nature—as he is created "in the image"—is a union of the animal or organic life and the intellectual life. The animal or organic life is not superadded to man as a consequence of the fall. On the contrary, it is the spiritual life which is superadded to man's natural state. Man is not spiritual by nature, as he is in the eastern Christian tradition. He is spiritual through a supererogatory act of grace. This difference modifies the perspective within which St. Augustine writes. But in common with theologians of both traditions, he too is almost exclusively concerned with the purely genital aspect of sexuality and is acutely embarrassed by the fact that in this world the good work of generation cannot take place without "a certain amount of bestial movement" and "a violent acting of lust". Indeed, that the genitals are no longer under control is for St. Augustine one of the most evident consequences of the "fall" of man. In Paradise no such bestial movement accompanied the act of generation; and had such an act occurred in Paradise it would have been accomplished without any emotional disturbance. But when pride and self-will provoked Adam and Eve to sin, a new and destructive impulse asserted itself within them; and this impulse—an insatiable search for self-satisfaction which St. Augustine calls concupiscence, or lust—although it manifested itself in all spheres of life, was most evident in the disobedience of the genitals, which now lost their passivity and refused to submit to the will. It is because of this that the genitals had to be covered—they were now *pudenda* and objects of shame. And they have continued to be *pudenda* and objects of shame, the outward sign of human degradation and evil.

The identifying of sexuality with its purely genital expression and its close association with evil is one of the aspects of Augustinian theology which has been most pervasive in western Christian thought; and it is linked both by St. Augustine himself and by later writers with their particular conception of original sin. Western theologians have always insisted on the idea that all human beings have sinned "in Adam": all are guilty of original sin, all bear the responsibility for it and all must suffer the punishment that God has inflicted on man because of it. Each human being has in some sense committed the original crime of rebellion; and although this crime is not itself identified with sexual activity, its consequences are most immediately and most dramatically evident in the sexual sphere. There is a direct and intimate link between original sin and concupiscence, and the effects of concupiscence are most powerful in the uncontrollable movement of the genitals. Hence every act of coition performed by man is not only inextricably related to the original sin for which each human being is responsible; it also shares in the taint of

[1] For an admirable summary of the views of St. Augustine and other western mediaeval theologians on the sexual relationship, see: D. S. Bailey, *The Man–Woman Relationship in Christian Thought* (London, 1959).

that sin and binds man more firmly to it. Moreover, it is by means of this sexual activity that evil is transmitted from generation to generation: every child conceived can be said literally to have been conceived in the sin of its parents, and because of this every child bears within it the seeds of evil from the very moment of its conception. It too is ineradicably involved not merely in the consequences of Adam's crime, but in that crime itself, and must bear the punishment for it. Nothing, not even marriage, can take away the stigma attached to every act of generation performed by fallen man. Marriage itself is good: but as the carnal acts for which it provides an opportunity and which in a certain measure it sanctions cannot be performed without the bestial movement of fleshly lust, these acts must remain sinful and shameful even within marriage. Marriage cannot remove their intrinsic evil. All it can do—and here St. Augustine promotes a tortuosity that has become embedded in Christian thought in this connection—is to make it possible for those who engage in the act of coition to engage in it not to satisfy their lust but as a distasteful duty unavoidable in the begetting of children. So long as married men and women perform such an act solely for the purpose of generation, they may be excused the sin they commit; although they are not on this account any less responsible for passing this sin on to their intended offspring. To copulate for any motive other than procreation, or with any intention of frustrating procreation, is simply abominable debauchery, and cancels that exemption from venial sin which is accorded to married couples who perform the shameful deed because they cannot encompass the good work of begetting children in any other manner.

By such argument, then, St. Augustine and his theological successors (who include practically every mediaeval theologian in the western Christian tradition) separated the idea of marriage from that of the sexual relationship and set the first over against the second so radically that only through contortions of the most devious kind have those who have accepted their views been able to reconcile the demands of the one with the prescriptions surrounding the other. Indeed, as these views did in fact become the guiding principles for those most responsible for the moral conduct of the Christian community—the officers of the Church—it is hardly surprising that the modern heirs of this community should suffer from an in-built schizophrenia in all that concerns this most intimate and personal aspect of their lives. Moreover, the split in consciousness and in behaviour that is an inevitable result of driving a wedge not so much between body and soul as between the idea of marriage, which theologians were constrained to regard as good, and the fact of the sexual relationship, in which they tended to see the consequence and even the actualization of original sin, became still more extreme once marriage itself was viewed as possessing a sacramental character. Indeed, the situation then became altogether absurd.

St. Paul had not only invested marriage with a symbolism of a most sacred order. He had also made it clear (I Cor. VI: 16) that for man and woman to become one flesh and so to conform to the symbolism of the union of Christ and the Church they had to fulfill the act of coition. When this symbolism was regarded as conferring on marriage a sacramental dignity—and St. Augustine himself believed this to be the case—the fact that marriage could acquire this dignity and so its indissolubility only through such a consummation continued to be accepted virtually without question. This placed Christian theologians in an untenable position.

They were obliged by scriptural authority to accept that the procreation of children was an end good in itself and that by becoming one flesh man and woman partook of a "great mystery" and possessed the sign of a supernatural union; yet they were persuaded that the act which determined both procreation and this *sacramentum* is tainted with evil. They had to conclude that the act of coition is necessary to marriage so long as its motive is to produce children; but even this motive did not in their eyes exonerate the act itself from impurity and shame. Such an attitude not only involved them in the absurdity of attributing to God the willing of something— the procreation of children—which could be achieved only through means that contributed to human degradation; it also compelled them to pretend that the main motive for sexual intercourse between man and woman must be the wish to produce offspring. By embracing the fiction that the main motive for such intercourse both should and could in practice be reduced to one of wishing to procreate, these authors committed Christian thought in this matter to a tangle of hypocrisy from which it has not yet disentangled itself.

Caught in this confusion, later mediaeval theologians gradually displaced the idea of the union of man and woman in one flesh from the central position it had occupied in the consideration of marriage as a sacrament, and substituted the idea that the sacrament of marriage is conferred upon its recipients by the exchange of mutual consent. The significance of the act of coition was not, however, rejected. It was still accepted that the first act of coition indissolubly confirms the union of the man and the woman after the pattern of the indissoluble union of Christ and the Church. Hence the Roman Catholic Church retains the right to dissolve a marriage which has not been "consummated" in terms of coition even though the sacramental character has been conferred by the mutual consent of its partners. But the underlying theological difficulty remained; and even through Aquinas divorces genital sexual intercourse from that intimate and total association with original sin which it possesses in Augustinian thought and concedes that it cannot be entirely evil when performed by married persons in a state of grace for the purpose of begetting children, he still regards it as containing an intrinsic taint of evil—not of moral evil, but of evil proceeding from moral evil—and as inimical to the good life. If it is pursued for any purpose other than begetting children, then of course its degree of sin is greater—in marriage it is a venial sin, outside marriage a mortal sin.

Moreover, the fact that in the mind of mediaeval theologians marriage became invested with a sacramental character because of its symbolic link with the union of Christ and the Church did not mean that it was recognized as possessing the personal and metaphysical significance which might be thought to be implicit in such a status. The understanding of the symbolism was limited in a manner which prevented a full realization of its scope. A sacred symbolism becomes a creative or spiritualizing influence when it is seen as capable of acting upon the matter to which it applies in such a way that it helps to transform this matter into the reality which the symbolism is intended to signify. This presupposes the perception that within the matter to which the symbolism applies there is the capacity or the potentiality to be transformed in this way. In the case in point, if the symbolism of Christ and the Church applied to marriage is to have a creative or spiritualizing influence on marriage, it must be recognized that the relationship between man and woman is capable of being transformed into an eternal and metaphysical bond of the kind that exists between Christ and the Church. The relationship between man and woman must be recognized as possessing *a priori* this metaphysical and sacramental potentiality, a potentiality that is developed and brought to fruition partially at least through the sacred symbolism with which it is invested. It is only when it is perceived that there is an inherent, if concealed, correspondence or congeneracy between the reality which the symbolism is intended to signify and the matter to which it is applied, that the symbolism is able to operate as a transmuting or transforming agency. Only if it is understood that the relationship between man and woman is capable of possessing an eternal and metaphysical character can it actually become a fully achieved sacramental union.

Neither in the thought of St. Augustine nor in that of the later scholastics is there any recognition that the relationship between man and woman is capable of attaining a sacramental dignity in this sense. Mediaeval theologians like William of St. Thierry and Aelred did elaborate a rich understanding of the significance of friendship and saw in it a way of return to the state of Paradise. But there is no doctrine in which sexual love is recognized as providing the basis of a spiritualizing process whose consummation is the union, soul and body, of man and woman in God, a revelation of the divine in and through their deepening sense of each other's being. The idea that the sexual relationship might create a metaphysical bond which death itself is powerless to destroy is alien to the mind of mediaeval theology as a whole. Marriage is regarded above all as an ecclesiastical or social institution designed for procreation. It is not regarded as a unique personal relationship and, as we have seen, the sexual element in it is considered only in its purely generative or genital aspect and even then with an undisguised hostility. In fact, not only are the personal aspects and spiritual potentiality of the sexual relationship ignored by mediaeval theology; but woman in her relationship with man is regarded as little more than at best a collaborator in the work of generation or a safety-valve for excess sexual pressures and at worst a pawn of the devil. For Fathers of the Church like Tertullian, it is woman who, profaning the Tree of Life, disfigures that exclusive image of God which is man, and drags him with her out of Paradise; and St. Augustine's own attitude towards and treatment of the woman with whom he had been living for thirteen years and who was the mother of his son, amply illustrate what little recognition a woman might expect as a person in her own right.

In view of all this, the fact that marriage was invested with a sacred symbolism, above all with that of Christ and the Church, and was on this account accorded a sacramental status, did not mean that the relationship between man and woman was looked on as something that might lead to the beatific vision or to personal deification. Instead, the symbolism was applied merely externally, and without any idea that it might be realized in an active mode in the relationship to which it was applied. Marriage was regarded as a sacrament not because it might become a metaphysical bond, but because it signified on another and unrelated level the union of Christ and the Church. Hence it must not be broken in this world not because the man and woman have achieved, or could achieve, an interior union which cannot be broken, but because to break it would be to break the symbolism of the supernatural union with which it was invested. In other words, it is quite sufficient for a marriage to conform outwardly to the symbolism for it to possess a sacramental character, even if inwardly there is nothing that corresponds to this character at all. In any case, the death of either the man or the woman was regarded as terminating the symbolism as well as the conjugal state to which it applied. It is true that in later mediaeval thought from the 12th century onwards, this purely exterior, legalistic and impersonal conception of the sacramental character of marriage is modified to include the idea that the consummated marriages of the baptized are ratified by divine grace and hence actually partake of the inner content of the symbolism which they exemplify; and that this is taken to signify not simply that a marriage must not be dissolved because that would be to break this symbolism, but that it could not be dissolved, any more than the supernatural union of its archetype itself could be dissolved. But this sacramental character is still regarded as conferred, effective and binding quite apart from the interior harmony and the reciprocity of qualities in the man and woman who are meant to embody it. It is still conceived dominantly in legalistic and ethical terms. Fundamentally, the attitude of the scholastics to the sexual relationship remains that of the earlier theologians: unlike celibacy, which represents an altogether higher state and remains the ideal, it has no positive creative rôle in man's spiritual development and must always be a sign of his alienation from God.

In the post-mediaeval period many influences, from both within and without the Christian tradition, have led to an increased realization of the personal and spiritual significance of the sacramental idea of marriage and the sexual relationship. The Romance poets had conceived of this relationship as a unique personal experience transcending the conditions of procreation and family life and even of mortality itself, and as possessing a spiritual value that was its own justification and fulfilment; and although for the Romance poets this relationship was accompanied, in theory at any rate, by a great emphasis on virginity, the "rediscovery of the body" associated with the Renaissance and the growing belief that within such a relationship its physical expression was also God-given, meant that it was felt that the physical sexual factor could at least in certain circumstances be liberated from its intrinsic association with evil. But in western Christian thought itself what may be called the Augustinian-Scholastic heritage has not been displaced, although it has been modified in the way indicated above. This is well illustrated by a contemporary document, the encyclical letter, *Humanae Vitae*, issued by Pope Paul VI on the subject of marriage and the sexual relationship within marriage. This letter does not of course treat its subject in an exhaustive way, nor does it by any means represent the whole mind of the Christian tradition at the present time. But it does represent at least the official thinking of a most powerful organ of this tradition, the Roman Catholic Church; and it does vividly illustrate both the limitations of that whole line of Christian thought we have been examining, as well as some of the modifications that have been introduced into it over the last centuries.

After an opening preamble explaining the Church's competence to deal with these matters, the letter goes on to a consideration of the sexual relationship. Marriage, it is said, is not the result of the blind evolution of natural forces. It is the provident institution of God the Creator. This being the case, for what has it been provided? At first sight, it seems that something creative and enriching is going to be said, something that would show to what extent the idea of marriage as a sacrament has undergone an inner transformation in post-mediaeval Christian thought and would illuminate the purely personal significance, as an end in itself, of the Pauline symbolism of the union of Christ and the Church. Marriage, it is stated, is the mutual gift of husband and wife to each other. Through it, husband and wife develop that union in which they perfect one another. But this positive and enriching image of marriage is not enlarged on or even allowed to stand in its own right. It is made subordinate to the conventional non-sacramental view of the early theologians: that the principal end of marriage and that which uniquely specifies its nature is the procreation and education of children. We are told in effect that the perfection of each other which man and woman may achieve through marriage is not an end in itself, but exists "in order to co-operate with God in the generation and education of new lives." This is the ultimate purpose of marriage, its final *raison d'être*. It is not that through their union man and woman should achieve the integrity of the human creature by means of an inner transformation of the mortal and corrupt conditions of their present existence and the restoration of their fallen lives to the paradisaical state—a union and integrity therefore which potentially transcend the term of the conventional marriage-vow "until death do us part," since they have their roots in the very prolificity and incorruptibility of divine life itself. On the contrary, nothing further than a relationship whose term is the mortal limits of the fallen world is envisaged, and the ultimate purpose of this relationship is but the propagation of more lives within the materialized space-time process. It is to co-operate with God in the production of children. In this view of the ultimate purpose of marriage, God appears as the master of a great human stud in which married couples are "ordained to the procreation and bringing up of children," so that these presumably in their turn may marry and beget, perpetuating in this way the history of man's disgrace into an indefinite and empty future.

Having re-affirmed in accordance with the general orientation of Christian thought that the chief end of marriage is to beget children, the letter now turns to a consideration of the purpose and function of the sexual factor within marriage. Or, rather, it turns to a consideration of the generative or genital act within marriage. Since it is the will of God that children should continue to be produced in this world, and since, the letter continues, human intelligence discovers that children can be born into this world only through observing the biological laws governing procreative life, it follows that the generative activity through which husband and wife fulfill the will of God is "honourable and good." Here there appears to be a modification of the Augustinian-Scholastic attitude according to which all generative activity is intrinsically tainted with evil, and which puts God in the absurd position of willing something—the procreation of children—while disapproving of the means through which it can be accomplished. Indeed, so far does this attitude appear to be displaced that it is now said that the co-operation of married partners with God in the begetting of children is so important that it is "absolutely required that *any use whatever of marriage* must retain the natural potential to procreate human life." It is recognized that the act of coition—and it may be noted here, though commented on later, that in common with earlier Christian thought in this respect the letter shows no awareness of any expression of sexuality between man and woman other than that which is carnal in this sense—may contribute to increasing the mutual love between the married pair; but it is clearly stated that such activity must never be divorced from its generative potential. This is because of "the inseparable connection, established by God, which man of his own initiative may not break, between the unitive significance and the procreative significance which are both inherent in the marriage act." The unitive act actualizes the capacity to generate new life; and this it does "as a result of laws written into the actual nature of man and woman"—laws which, because they express the will of God, must not be interfered with on human initiative. Any act of this kind which "impairs the capacity to transmit life which God the Creator, through specific laws, has built into it, frustrates His design which constitutes the norms of marriage, and contradicts the will of the Author of life." Hence, "to use this divine gift (the generative function) while depriving it, even if only potentially, of its meaning and purpose (to beget children), is equally repugnant to the nature of man and woman, and is consequently in opposition to the plan of God and His holy will."

It is at this point that the argument runs into difficulties. Although it is said that man may not of his own initiative break the unitive and procreative significance of the act of coition, and that any use whatever of marriage must retain the natural potential to procreate human life, yet it is recognized that this act continues to be honourable and good even when it is *foreseen to be infertile*. That is to say, the act of coition is admitted to have a positive value in and for itself apart from whether or not its use may lead to procreation, even indeed when it is consciously known that its use will not lead to procreation. So long as the infertility is not due to human intervention and so long as it is God who breaks the connection between the unitive and the procreative significance of the act of coition, then the "divine gift" may be totally deprived of what in one place is described as its meaning and purpose—the begetting of children—and yet retain a positive meaning and purpose within the context of married life. Moreover, this is so not only in cases in which the husband or the wife are permanently infertile through no fault of his or her own; it is also so when they take deliberate advantage of periods of infertility which occur in the normal course of biological events—those, specifically, provided by woman's menstrual cycle. Indeed, in the name of "responsible parenthood," the "human intelligence has the right and responsibility to control the forces of irrational nature provided this is done within the limits of the order of reality established by God." This means that God has established woman's menstrual pattern, and so it is legitimate to take advantage of any provision He has made for infertility within this pattern. Although it is not stated in so many words, one is almost given the impression that it is assumed God has providentially provided these periods of infertility in the monthly cycle precisely so that genital activity may flourish then without the risk of conception! This, however, is not the point to be emphasized. The point to be emphasized is that so long as man and woman use a facility provided by nature to have intercourse knowing that no child will result, then this intercourse is good and honourable even when deprived of its procreative significance. And it continues to be good and honourable although there is a deliberate intention to avoid having children or the couple "mean to make sure that none will be born."

The conclusions which derive from this as to which methods of contraception are legitimate and which are not, need not concern us here. But it should be made clear that something very near hypocrisy would seem to be involved in the line of argument set out above. If it is absolutely required by the Church that *any use whatever of marriage* must retain its natural potential to create human life, how can one approve of a use of marriage in which the couple concerned deliberately take advantage for coition only of periods which they know to be infertile? If there is an inseparable connection, established by God, between the unitive significance and the procreative significance of coition, how does it retain its significance—continue to be good and honourable—when it has no procreative significance? If it is repugnant to the nature of man and woman, and also contrary to God's plan and holy will, to use the divine gift of the generative function while depriving it, even if only partially, of its meaning and purpose (the begetting of children), how is it not equally repugnant to man and woman and equally contrary to God's plan and holy will to use it with the specific intention of depriving it of its meaning and purpose—to use it, that is to say, when one knows as certainly as one can know that it will not beget children? To say that the vital qualitative difference in each case is whether it is God or man who has deprived the generative act of its natural potential to create human life, and that provided man sticks to the facility instituted by God (the infertile period) then he is not violating the purpose and meaning of this act even when he deliberately intends to avoid having children, and means to make sure none will be born, may pass as an adroit piece of legalistic or moral quibbling, but it is surely a very pathetic argument with which to present the mature Christian intelligence and conscience. It is an example of a kind of casuistry which ill becomes the treatment of so profound a human, and more than human, theme, and what it indicates is the basic insufficiency of the teaching which it purports to interpret and apply.

This insufficiency appears in relation to three interconnected assumptions, all briefly noted in what has already been said. The first is the assumption that it is God's will that man should go on endlessly begetting children within the mortal and corrupt conditions of this materialized universe, which is the scene and consequence of his fallen existence. According to this assumption, man and woman are reduced in marriage to the role of instruments serving to populate the void of a monstrous materialized space-time future and to do this in a way that is explicitly identified with serving the divine plan itself. This conception, by displacing the purpose and fulfilment of the relationship between man and woman from the centre of their respective beings and projecting this purpose and fulfilment into an external, nonexistent, cold and impersonal space-time continuum stretching into an entirely false infinity, adulterates the conjugal principle at its very heart. Man in this conception merely perpetuates his condition of slavery to a process in which his own personal created dignity is sacrificed to the abstract common good of a hypothetical future human society.

It is worth noting that what is here proposed as Christian teaching differs in this respect but little from Communist teaching, which likewise claims that the purpose and fulfilment of the lives of individual men and women are to be found in serving the abstract good of a future human society. Indeed, that this is so is supported by the statement in the encyclical letter itself to the effect that in thus vindicating this teaching the Church is "convinced she is contributing to the creation of a truly human civilization." One would have thought that a Christian teaching should be concerned less with contributing to human civilization than with man and woman's participation in the kingdom "not of this world." It is in fact difficult to see how the point of view which puts so much emphasis on the begetting of children can be maintained unless the presuppositions concerning the idea of original sin which lie as the basis of the western theological tradition are first abandoned. According to these presuppositions, this world is a sinful world and a child conceived in it is conceived in sin and this sin is transmitted to it through conception. At the same time, Christianity is said to be a call to put an end to sin and to overcome the conditions which produce it. If this is the case, how, one might ask, can Christian theologians exhort men and women to continue to beget children when the act of begetting them and the world into which they are begotten simply perpetuate those conditions that Christianity intends to overcome and requires all men and women to overcome? One does not free oneself from debts by incurring more debts. Indeed, whatever one's view of original sin, it would appear that in so far as Christianity is concerned with the transfiguration of the world there must be a basic— and on one level tragic—conflict between participation in the kingdom "not of this world" and the biological continuation of the human race in this world; and that to ignore this conflict in the way that so much Christian thought does ignore it is to forfeit a competence to interpret the realities of the Christian faith.

The second assumption is intimately connected with the first. As we remarked, the encyclical opens with a brief statement explaining the Church's competence to speak on the matter under discussion. The Church, it is said, is the interpreter of the moral law. The moral law is based on natural law as illuminated and enriched by divine Revelation. This is possible because natural laws express the will of God. This means that the will of God is expressed in the processes of nature, so that the processes of nature are in themselves sacred. What happens in nature happens because God wants it to happen like that. It contributes to the divine scheme or plan of the universe. It must not therefore be interfered with by man acting on his own initiative, for that would be to violate the will of God. It would be to disobey the moral law—God's law for man. It follows that if the laws and processes of nature express God's will and are geared, as they are where human biological functions are concerned, to the production of children in this materialized world, then it must be God's will that mankind continues to produce children in this world through the use of these functions. This conclusion, maintained in the letter, necessarily derives from this second assumption concerning the relationship between the moral and the natural law.

The point that must be stressed is not the validity of the relationship itself, but that what is meant by nature in this context—and this is in line with the main stream of western theology—appears to be nature in its present state, not as it is in its original state, as it issued from the hand of God "in the beginning." We are here within an order of theology which represents an uneasy alliance between the conception of original sin indicated above and Aristotelian optimism in respect of mundane existence. The effect of this alliance is that to all intents and purposes the event described as the "fall of man" is treated as something that conforms to the will of God, and consequently there is no sharp distinction made between the order of nature prior to the fall and the order of nature subsequent to the fall: both are treated as expressing the will of God. Man's fallen life and the natural processes to which he is subject in the fallen world also express the will, pleasure and purpose of God, and so may be taken as constituting the norm on which the moral law of the Church is to be based. There is no recognition that life in the world as it is—the world which comes within the sphere of his everyday observation—is profoundly abnormal and unnatural where man is concerned, and concomitantly where everything else is concerned as well. There is no acknowledgement that it is not that which God has created or intended for man, but is what man has brought on himself as a result of his own defection and error. There is consequently no recognition that the norm for what is natural for man, and hence what constitutes the moral law, may lie in a completely different order of reality, and that to derive it from this world as it has become, and man's life as it is now being lived in this world, is to mistake human error and its consequences for divine ordinance. If it is understood that it is not the fallen state of nature and of man which is natural, but their pre-fallen and paradisaical state, and that it is this state which expresses the will of God, then a quite different attitude to the relationship between the moral and natural law will prevail, and quite different conclusions may be drawn from it as a consequence.

According to this latter attitude, which is that of the eastern Christian tradition, what is regarded as man's natural life, and so as the norm providing the basis for the moral law, is that of the original creation. Man's life as it is now, in this world, and the biological processes to which he is subject, are not regarded as natural, but as a consequence of a breach in nature, a declension from the natural state, and an entering into conditions that are abnormal and corrupt. And, it is understood, this breach and dislocation in man's natural state—this fall into a materialized space-time universe—has not only resulted in a loss of spiritual vision and in the contracting of the human mind to the perspectives of a fundamentally unreal world; it has also introduced a corresponding alteration in the laws of nature itself, so that these too are now tainted by something of the abnormality and corruption which vitiates human life itself. They are not these laws as they are ordained by God. They are these laws deformed and denaturalized by the fall of Adam—a fall which itself is profoundly "unnatural" and *contrary to the will of God*. To accept, in the manner of western Christian thought, the laws of nature and natural processes as they appear to the human mind in this fallen world as expressing the will of God and therefore as constituting the norm for the moral law, is to shift the responsibility for a human act that is contrary to the will of God from man to God, and to make God the ultimate author not only of man's crime but also of the abnormal and corrupt conditions of the world which issues from it. God becomes responsible for that state of servitude to which man reduces himself and the whole natural order as a result of his assertion of a false liberty in the face of his Creator. The divergence between eastern and western Christian thought on the fall of man and its consequences is profound; and it is of course the western point of view which supports the second assumption underlying the teaching on marriage expounded in the encyclical letter.

The third assumption is also intimately connected with the two already mentioned. It is that the unitive significance of the sexual relationship between man and woman is inseparably connected with its procreative significance, and hence with the act of coition. It is intimately linked with the two previous assumptions because if the purpose of marriage is to co-operate with God in the propagation of more and more children in this fallen world, and if (the example of Mary the Mother of God notwithstanding) the genital mode of propagation is ordained by God so that His will in this respect may be obeyed, it follows that to separate the sexual relationship between man and woman from its biological procreative functions is, as the letter states, in opposition to the plan of God and His holy will. Copulation, that is to say, must thrive. We have already noted the difficulties to which such a view must inevitably lead, and have seen that in fact the unitive significance of the genital act is admitted even when husband and wife use it with the deliberate and conscious intention to avoid having children and mean to make sure that none will be born.

It is not so much this, however, that represents the insufficiency of the assumption in question. It is that it seems to identify the expression of the *sexual* relationship or *sexual* communion between man and woman in a more or less exclusive manner with the act of coition, so that it is regarded as fulfilled in this act. As it is precisely here that the encyclical letter reflects what is perhaps the basic shortcoming of that tradition of Christian thought we have been considering, we can leave the specific discussion of the letter and examine this point in relation to that whole tradition.

We have remarked how early Christian theologians appear to have been incapable of envisaging any aspect of sexuality other than its purely generative or genital expression, and we have seen how this attitude has continued to characterize Christian thought down to the present day. What we have not stressed is that such an attitude, which leads to isolating the copulatory act from the totality of the relationship between the sexes, is extremely false and dangerous, and has had disastrous consequences in many spheres of human behaviour. In effect, Christian thought seems to have made the worst of all worlds in its attitude to the sexual life. First, it has to all intents and purposes refused to recognize in the sexual relationship any purpose other than the procreation of children. Then, in spite of its frequent denigration of the act of coition itself, it has pressed this act into symbolic service for a reality—that of the union of Christ and the Church—to which at best it can be analogous only in a very remote manner and to which it must in itself always remain extrinsic: it cannot in itself be transformed into the reality it is intended to symbolize, and this, as we noted, amounts to a denial of the very principle of all sacred symbolism. This means that this act has been charged with a significance which is totally incommensurate with its nature and which can only be realized between man and woman through the development of potentialities that transcend this particular aspect of their relationship. The result is that the act of coition has become hopelessly idealized. It is viewed as the sign of a supernatural union, the crux of the sexual life, and as that through which the sacrament of marriage is consummated. By regarding what is at best an imperfect and all too often a most crude and inhuman form of sexual communion between man and woman as though it were the most complete form, and by largely ignoring other forms of such communion, Christian thought in this matter may be said to have prepared the intellectual ground for the dislocation and debasement of man's sexual life of which the consequences are only too evident today. The failure to perceive and affirm any positive or creative value in the sexual relationship apart from procreation, together with the habit of regarding the act of coition as the crux of the sexual life, has meant that now when improved forms of contraception have made it possible to divorce this act more or less effectively from its procreative function, not only does it continue to be regarded as the crux of the sexual life, but also, through the lapse of Christian belief, it is basically reduced to having no significance apart from the pleasure or relief it gives. It follows that there is little to impede the idea that it may and even should be carried out more or less indiscriminately and whenever the opportunity arises without this in the least degrading either the act itself or those who perform it in this way. In other words, the failure to place this act within the full sacramental context of a personal relationship engaging the whole beings of the man and woman concerned has meant that it has been impossible to regard it in a manner that does not lead either to its idealization or to its abuse or to both at once.

If one now asks how Christian teaching has come to concentrate so one-sidedly on the genital aspect of the sexual relationship, the answer is that this stems directly from the too simple assumption that the principal end of marriage and that which uniquely specifies its nature is the procreation and education of children. Once this assumption is made, the emphasis in Christian thought on genital intercourse isolated from other aspects of the full sexual relationship is quite logical, because it is genital intercourse irrespective of other aspects of the relationship that produces children. Consequently, this intercourse is not considered primarily within the context of the man-woman relationship regarded as an end in its own right and apart from the propagation of children; it is considered primarily as a biological activity designed exclusively for that purpose. Christian teaching on marriage has literally made a religion out of having children. In fact, such a religion has it made out of having children that in spite of its ambivalent attitude towards the act of coition itself, it may be said to be among the great promoters of this act, provided it takes place within the limits of the marriage contract. Within the marriage contract, the begetting of children is regarded as a praiseworthy and even as a divinely approved activity whatever the circumstances. There is no real concern for the inner quality of the married relationship itself and no real understanding that for married couples to produce children in certain circumstances may be little short of sacrilege or even murder. Outside the marriage contract, there must be no genital intercourse, however deep the relationship between the man and the woman may be. But once legally married, the couple are exhorted to be fruitful and multiply virtually without restriction and certainly without there being a question of whether the marriage is a marriage in the true sense—a union and reciprocity of soul and body. It is in accord with this attitude that the Christian priest is asked to give his blessing to unions that in effect may be entirely graceless and unspiritual; and he may grant communion to one who is "faithful" to his or her married state whether or not there is any true love in it. Moreover, the criterion of faithfulness itself in Christian thought tends to have reference only to the genital act; and in spite of the Christian gospel it tends to count as adultery only what has been committed in the most explicit way, not also what has been committed "in the heart." Such an attitude not only results in debasing the priestly function in this respect; it also means that in relation to the sexual life the Church itself comes virtually to be regarded as little more than a kind of brothel of which the priest is the bawd: the point of marrying in the Church is that it makes it possible, almost obligatory, to have "legal" or at least not mortally sinful genital intercourse.

All this may be justified on the grounds that if the procreation and education of children is the chief end of marriage, it is vitally important to preserve the institution of marriage at all costs, because to produce children in our society outside the context of an established and legally and socially recognized institution such as marriage could be to expose them to quite unwarranted suffering—something which individuals have a right to do with regard to themselves, but not with regard to those yet unborn. The fact that the procreation of children is deliberately encouraged in conditions which are likely to expose them to an equally great and equally unwarranted suffering, and that this is justified on the grounds that the parents are legally married, is simply another example of the confusion and hypocrisy in which so much Christian thought in this matter is involved.

Whatever support may be found for it, however, it remains true none the less that the view of the principal end of marriage to which Christian thought has been committed virtually from the beginning and by which it is still restricted, does in fact cut directly across the idea of marriage as a sacramental reality in its own right as well as across the potentialities of sexual communion in the fully developed man-woman relationship. No doubt the propagation and education of children is or may be one motive for marriage which must be taken into account, even though, given the Christian understanding of the present sinful state of the world and the fact that Christianity is a summons to participate in the kingdom "not of this world," it is difficult to see on what grounds a teaching that makes virtually a cult out of generation in this world can be justified from the Christian point of view. But to make this the main motive is to subordinate the idea of marriage as a unique personal relationship with a spiritual purpose and value that are their own fulfilment and justification to the idea of marriage as an ecclesiastical or social institution concerned with the well-being of the family in the materialized space-time dimensions of fallen human existence.

Moreover, not only does this dominantly legalistic and ethical view of marriage mean promoting and lending support to countless marriages that are little more than licensed harlotry: it also means preserving the fiction that the main motive for sexual communion is not a strongly felt impulse to unite which at the time overrides all other motives, but both should and could be a desire to propagate. This impulse to unite may of course lead to the act of coition and hence to propagation; but where man and woman are concerned the kind of union to which it points and to which indeed it may be said to be a summons (however misunderstood and however frequently ignored by those to whom it is made) is not one which in itself can be fulfilled either through the act of coition or through the production of offspring. In the man-woman relationship regarded from the point of view of its sexual totality, the act of coition is but one aspect of the whole soul-body communion, and its procreative function may often be of incidental or even of no significance.

Yet in spite of the relative failure of both the writings of Christian theologians and official pronouncements of the Church to affirm the full potentialities of the primal relationship between man and woman as these have been indicated in the opening pages of this essay, the Christian tradition itself does in fact bear living witness to them. First, it is not accidental that it preserves at the heart of its sacred books *The Song of Songs*, a drama in which the man and the woman are seen as passionately engaged in the discovery of the ultimate ground of their being that is at once the lost Paradise and the image of God in which they are created. Then, it is not accidental that the opening chapters of two of the Christian gospels throw further scriptural light on this archetypal human relationship in depicting a specific man and woman whose mutual involvement forms the immediate background to the Annunciation and so is a condition of the Incarnation itself: not until Joseph took Mary into his care could she, the perfect woman, give birth to her immaculately conceived offspring, the perfect man. Finally, it is the Christian tradition which, in the face of all attempts to reduce it to a matter of social convenience or to a purely physical or human affair, has insisted that this relationship, properly understood and lived, possesses or should possess a sacramental dignity. To whatever extent Christian thought may have denied the full implications of this, or been crippled by evasion and duplicity in its approach to it, it has at least always affirmed it. And ultimately it is this which is important: because what is recognized as a sacrament must in the end and in spite of all contradictions be acknowledged to enshrine in its own right the highest spiritual potentialities and creative significance.

Sex and Secularization

Harvey Cox

Harvey Cox (1929–   ) is Victor Thomas Professor of Divinity at Harvard Divinity School. In addition to The Secular City, he is author of The Feast of Fools and On Not Leaving It to the Snake. His most recent book is The Seduction of the Spirit: The Use and Misuse of People's Religion.

No aspect of human life seethes with so many unexorcised demons as does sex. No human activity is so hexed by superstition, so haunted by residual tribal lore, and so harassed by socially induced fear. Within the breast of urban-secular man, a toe-to-toe struggle still rages between his savage and his bourgeois forebears. Like everything else, the images of sex which informed tribal and town society are expiring along with the eras in which they arose. The erosion of traditional values and the disappearance of accepted modes of behavior have left contemporary man free, but somewhat rudderless. Abhoring a vacuum, the mass media have rushed in to supply a new code and a new set of behavioral prototypes. They appeal to the unexorcised demons. Nowhere is the persistence of mythical and metalogical denizens more obvious than in sex, and the shamans of sales do their best to nourish them. Nowhere is the humanization of life more frustrated. Nowhere is a clear word of exorcism more needed.

Source: Harvey G. Cox, The Secular City (New York, 1965), pp. 192–216. Copyright © 1965 by Harvey G. Cox, Reprinted by permission of Macmillan Publishing Co., Inc.

How is the humanization of sex impeded? First it is thwarted by the parading of cultural-identity images for the sexually dispossessed, to make money. These images become the tyrant gods of the secular society, undercutting its liberation from religion and transforming it into a kind of neotribal culture. Second, the authentic secularization of sex is checkmated by an anxious clinging to the sexual standards of the town, an era so recent and yet so different from ours that simply to transplant its sexual ethos into our situation is to invite hypocrisy of the worst degree.

Let us look first at the spurious sexual models conjured up for our anxious society by the sorcerers of the mass media and the advertising guild. Like all pagan deities, these come in pairs—the god and his consort. For our purposes they are best symbolized by The Playboy and Miss America, the Adonis and Aphrodite of a leisure-consumer society which still seems unready to venture into full postreligious maturity and freedom. The Playboy and Miss America represent The Boy and The Girl. They incorporate a vision of life. They function as religious phenomena and should be exorcised and exposed.

The Residue of Tribalism

Let us begin with Miss America. In the first century B.C., Lucretius wrote this description of the pageant of Cybele:

> Adorned with emblem and crown . . . she is carried in awe-inspiring state.
> Tight-stretched tambourines and hollow cymbals thunder all round to the
> stroke of open hands, hollow pipes stir with Phrygian strain. . . . She rides in
> procession through great cities and mutely enriches mortals with a blessing not
> expressed in words. They strew all her path with brass and silver, presenting
> her with bounteous alms, and scatter over her a snow-shower of roses.[1]

Now compare this with the annual twentieth-century Miss America pageant in Atlantic City, New Jersey. Spotlights probe the dimness like votive tapers, banks of flowers exude their varied aromas, the orchestra blends feminine strings and regal trumpets. There is a hushed moment of tortured suspense, a drumroll, then the climax—a young woman with carefully prescribed anatomical proportions and exemplary "personality" parades serenely with scepter and crown to her throne. At TV sets across the nation throats tighten and eyes moisten. "There she goes, Miss America—" sings the crooner. "There she goes, your ideal." A new queen in America's emerging cult of The Girl has been crowned.

Is it merely illusory or anachronistic to discern in the multiplying pageants of the Miss America, Miss Universe, Miss College Queen type a residuum of the cults of the pre-Christian fertility goddesses? Perhaps, but students of the history of religions have become less prone in recent years to dismiss the possibility that the cultural behavior of modern man may be significantly illuminated by studying it in the perspective of the mythologies of bygone ages. After all, did not Freud

---

[1] This is quoted from Lucretius ii, 608f. in T. R. Glover *The Conflict of Religions in the Early Roman Empire* (Boston: Beacon, 1960), p. 20. It was originally published in 1909 by Methuen & Co. Ltd.

initiate a revolution in social science by utilizing the venerable myth of Oedipus to help make sense out of the strange behavior of his Viennese contemporaries? Contemporary man carries with him, like his appendix and his finger-nails, vestiges of his tribal and pagan past.

In light of this fertile combination of insights from modern social science and the history of religions, it is no longer possible to see in the Miss America pageant merely an overpublicized prank foisted on us by the advertising industry. It certainly is this, but it is also much more. It represents the mass cultic celebration, complete with a rich variety of ancient ritual embellishments, of the growing place of The Girl in the collective soul of America.

This young woman—though she is no doubt totally ignorant of the fact— symbolizes something beyond herself. She symbolizes The Girl, the primal image, the One behind the many. Just as the Virgin appears in many guises—as our Lady of Lourdes or of Fatima or of Guadalupe—but is always recognizably the Virgin, so with the Girl.

The Girl is also the omnipresent icon of consumer society. Selling beer, she is folksy and jolly. Selling gems, she is chic and distant. But behind her various theophanies she remins recognizably The Girl. In Miss America's glowingly healthy smile, her openly sexual but officially virginal figure, and in the namebrand gadgets around her, she personifies the stunted aspirations and ambivalent fears of her culture. "There she goes, your ideal."

Miss America stands in a long line of queens going back to Isis, Ceres, and Aphrodite. Everything from the elaborate sexual taboos surrounding her person to the symbolic gifts at her coronation hints at her ancient ancestry. But the real proof comes when we find that the function served by The Girl in our culture is just as much a "religious" one as that served by Cybele in hers. The functions are identical—to provide a secure personal "identity" for initiates and to sanctify a particular value structure.

Let us look first at the way in which The Girl confers a kind of identity on her initiates. Simone de Beauvoir says in *The Second Sex* that "no one is *born* a woman."[2] One is merely born a female, and "*becomes* a woman" according to the models and meanings provided by the civilization. During the classical Christian centuries, it might be argued, the Virgin Mary served in part as this model. With the Reformation and especially with the Puritans, the place of Mary within the symbol system of the Protestant countries was reduced or eliminated. There are those who claim that this excision constituted an excess of zeal that greatly impoverished Western culture, an impoverishment from which it has never recovered. Some would even claim that the alleged failure of American novelists to produce a single great heroine (we have no Phaedra, no Anna Karenina) stems from this self-imposed lack of a central feminine ideal.

Without entering into this fascinating discussion, we can certainly be sure that, even within modern American Roman Catholicism, the Virgin Mary provides an identity image for few American girls. Where then do they look for the "model" Simone de Beauvoir convincingly contends they need? For most, the prototype

---

[2] Simone de Beauvoir, *The Second Sex* (New York: Knopf, 1953; London: Cape) p. 41.

of femininity seen in their mothers, their friends, and in the multitudinous images to which they are exposed on the mass media is what we have called The Girl.

In his significant monograph *Identity and the Life Cycle*, Erik Erikson reminds us that the child's identity is not modeled simply on the parent but on the parent's "super-ego."[3] Thus in seeking to forge her own identity the young girl is led beyond her mother to her mother's ideal image, and it is here that what Freud called "the ideologies of the superego . . . the traditions of the race and the people" become formative. It is here also that The Girl functions, conferring identity on those for whom she is—perhaps never completely consciously—the tangible incarnation of womanhood.

To describe the mechanics of this complex psychological process by which the fledgling American girl participates in the life of The Girl and thus attains a woman's identity would require a thorough description of American adolescence. There is little doubt, however, that such an analysis would reveal certain striking parallels to the "savage" practices by which initiates in the mystery cults shared in the magical life of their god.

For those inured to the process, the tortuous nightly fetish by which the young American female pulls her hair into tight bunches secured by metal clips may bear little resemblance to the incisions made on their arms by certain African tribesmen to make them resemble their totem, the tiger. But to an anthropologist comparing two ways of attempting to resemble the holy one, the only difference might appear to be that with the Africans the torture is over after initiation, while with the American it has to be repeated every night, a luxury only a culture with abundant leisure can afford.

In turning now to an examination of the second function of The Girl—supporting and portraying a value system—a comparison with the role of the Virgin in the twelfth and thirteenth centuries may be helpful. Just as the Virgin exhibited and sustained the ideals of the age that fashioned Chartres Cathedral, as Henry Adams saw, so The Girl symbolizes the values and aspirations of a consumer society. (She is crowned not in the political capital, remember, but in Atlantic City or Miami Beach, centers associated with leisure and consumption.) And she is not entirely incapable of exploitation. If men sometimes sought to buy with gold the Virgin's blessings on their questionable causes, so The Girl now dispenses her charismatic favor on watches, refrigerators, and razor blades—for a price. Though The Girl has built no cathedrals, without her the colossal edifice of mass persuasion would crumble. Her sharply stylized face and figure beckon us from every magazine and TV channel, luring us toward the beatific vision of a consumer's paradise.

The Girl is *not* the Virgin. In fact she is a kind of anti-Madonna. She reverses most of the values traditionally associated with the Virgin—poverty, humility, sacrifice. In startling contrast, particularly, to the biblical portrait of Mary in Luke 1:46–55, The Girl has nothing to do with filling the hungry with "good things," hawking instead an endless proliferation of trivia on TV spot commercials. The Girl exalts the mighty, extols the rich, and brings nothing to the hungry but added

---

[3] Erik Erikson, *Identity and the Life Cycle* (New York: International University Press, 1959).

despair. So The Girl does buttress and bring into personal focus a value system, such as it is. In both social and psychological terms, The Girl, whether or not she is really a goddess, certainly acts that way.

Perhaps the most ironic element in the rise of the cult of The Girl is that Protestantism has almost completely failed to notice it, while Roman Catholics have at least given some evidence of sensing its significance. In some places, for instance, Catholics are forbidden to participate in beauty pageants, a ruling not entirely inspired by prudery. It is ironic that Protestants have traditionally been most opposed to lady cults while Catholics have managed to assimilate more than one at various points in history.

If we are correct in assuming that The Girl *functions* in many ways as a goddess, then the cult of The Girl demands careful Protestant theological criticism. Anything that functions, even in part, as a god when it is in fact not God, is an idol. When the Reformers and their Puritan offspring criticized the cult of Mary it was not because they were antifeminist. They opposed anything—man, woman, or beast (or dogma or institution)—that usurped in the slightest the prerogatives that belonged alone to God Almighty. As Max Weber has insisted, when the prophets of Israel railed against fertility cults, they had nothing against fertility. It is not against sexuality but against a cult that protest is needed. Not as it were, against the beauty but against the pageant.

Thus the Protestant objection to the present cult of The Girl must be based on the realization that The Girl is an *idol*. She functions as the source of value, the giver of personal identity. But the values she mediates and the identity she confers are both spurious. Like every idol she is ultimately a creation of our own hands and cannot save us. The values she represents as ultimate satisfactions—mechanical comfort, sexual success, unencumbered leisure—have no ultimacy. They lead only to endless upward mobility, competitive consumption, and anxious cynicism. The devilish social insecurities from which she promises to deliver us are, alas, still there, even after we have purified our breaths, our skins, and our armpits by applying her sacred oils. She is a merciless goddess who draws us farther and farther into the net of accelerated ordeals of obeisance. As the queen of commodities in an expanding economy, the fulfillment she promises must always remain just beyond the tips of our fingers.

Why has Protestantism kept its attention obsessively fastened on the development of Mariolatry in Catholicism and not noticed the sinister rise of this vampire-like cult of The Girl in our society? Unfortunately, it is due to the continuing incapacity of theological critics to recognize the religious significance of cultural phenomena outside the formal religious system itself. But the rise of this new cult reminds us that the work of the reformer is never done. Man's mind is indeed—as Luther said—a factory busy making idols. The Girl is a far more pervasive and destructive influence than the Virgin, and it is to her and her omnipresent altars that we should be directing our criticism.

Besides sanctifying a set of phony values, The Girl compounds her noxiousness by maiming her victims in a Procrustean bed of uniformity. This is the empty "identity" she panders. Take the Miss America pageant, for example. Are these virtually indistinguishable specimens of white, middle-class post-adolescence really the best we can do? Do they not mirror the ethos of a mass-production society, in which genuine individualism somehow mars the clean, precision-tooled effect? Like their sisters, the finely calibrated Rockettes, these meticulously measured and pretested "beauties" lined up on the Boardwalk bear an ominous similarity to the faceless retinues of goose-steppers and the interchangeable mass exercisers of explicitly totalitarian societies. In short, *who* says this is beauty?

The caricature becomes complete in the Miss Universe contest, when Miss Rhodesia is a blonde, Miss South Africa is white, and Oriental girls with a totally different tradition of feminine beauty are forced to display their thighs and appear in spike heels and Catalina swim suits. Miss Universe is as universal as an American adman's stereotype of what beauty should be.

The truth is that The Girl can*not* bestow the identity she promises. She forces her initiates to torture themselves with starvation diets and beauty-parlor ordeals, but still cannot deliver the satisfactions she holds out. She is young, but what happens when her followers, despite added hours in the boudoir, can no longer appear young? She is happy and smiling and loved. What happens when, despite all the potions and incantations, her disciples still feel the human pangs of rejection and loneliness? Or what about all the girls whose statistics, or "personality" (or color) do not match the authoritative "ideal"?

After all, it is God—not The Girl—who is God. He is the center and source of value. He liberates men and women from the bland uniformity of cultural deities so that they may feast on the luxurious diversity of life He has provided. The identity He confers frees men from all pseudo-identities to be themselves, to fulfill their human destinies regardless whether their faces or figures match some predetermined abstract "ideal." As His gift, sex is freed from both fertility cults and commercial exploitation to become the thoroughly human thing He intended. And since it is one of the last items we have left that is neither prepackaged not standardized, let us not sacrifice it too hastily on the omnivorous altar of Cybele.

The Playboy, illustrated by the monthly magazine of that name, does for the boys what Miss America does for the girls. Despite accusations to the contrary, the immense popularity of this magazine is not solely attributable to pin-up girls. For sheer nudity its pictorial art cannot compete with such would-be competitors as *Dude* and *Escapade*. *Playboy* appeals to a highly mobile, increasing affluent group of young readers, mostly between eighteen and thirty, who want much more from their drugstore reading than bosoms and thighs. They need a total image of what it means to be a man. And Mr. Hefner's *Playboy* has no hesitation in telling them.

Why should such a need arise? David Riesman has argued that the responsibility for character formation in our society has shifted from the family to the peer group and to the mass-media peer-group surrogates.[4] Things are changing so rapidly that one who is equipped by his family with inflexible, highly internalized values becomes unable to deal with the accelerated pace of change and with the varying contexts in which he is called upon to function. This is especially true in

---

[4] David Riesman, *The Lonely Crowd* (New Haven: Yale University Press, 1950; Harmondsworth, Middlesex, England: Penguin).

the area of consumer values toward which the "other-directed person" is increasingly oriented.

Within the confusing plethora of mass media signals and peer-group values, *Playboy* fills a special need. For the insecure young man with newly acquired free time and money who still feels uncertain about his consumer skills, *Playboy* supplies a comprehensive and authoritative guidebook to this forbidding new world to which he now has access. It tells him not only who to be; it tells him *how* to be it, and even provides consolation outlets for those who secretly feel that they have not quite made it.

In supplying for the other-directed consumer of leisure both the normative identity image and the means for achieving it, *Playboy* relies on a careful integration of copy and advertising material. The comic book that appeals to a younger generation with an analogous problem skillfully intersperses illustrations of incredibly muscled men and excessively mammalian women with advertisements for body-building gimmicks and foam-rubber brassiere supplements. Thus the thin-chested comic-book readers of both sexes are thoughtfully supplied with both the ends and the means for attaining a spurious brand of maturity. *Playboy* merely continues the comic-book tactic for the next age group. Since within every identity crisis, whether in teens or twenties, there is usually a sexual-identity problem, *Playboy* speaks to those who desperately want to know what it means to be a man, and more specifically a *male*, in today's world.

Both the image of man and the means for its attainment exhibit a remarkable consistency in *Playboy*. The skilled consumer is cool and unruffled. He savors sportscars, liquor, high fidelity, and book-club selections with a casual, unhurried aplomb. Though he must certainly *have* and *use* the latest consumption item, he must not permit himself to get too attached to it. The style will change and he must always be ready to adjust. His persistent anxiety that he may mix a drink incorrectly, enjoy a jazz group that is passé, or wear last year's necktie style is comforted by an authoriatative tone in *Playboy* beside which papal encyclicals sound irresolute.

"Don't hesitate," he is told, "this assertive, self-assured weskit is what every man of taste wants for the fall season." Lingering doubts about his masculinity are extirpated by the firm assurance that "real men demand this ruggedly masculine smoke" (cigar ad). Though "the ladies will swoon for you, no matter what they promise, don't give them a puff. This cigar is for men only." A furlined canvas field jacket is described as "the most masculine thing since the cave man." What to be and how to be it are both made unambiguously clear.

Since being a male necessitates some kind of relationship to females, *Playboy* fearlessly confronts this problem too, and solves it by the consistent application of the same formula. Sex becomes one of the of the items of leisure activity that the knowledgeable consumer of leisure handles with his characteristic skill and detachment. The girl becomes a desirable—indeed an indispensable—"Playboy accessory."

In a question-answering column entitled "The Playboy Adviser," queries about smoking equipment (how to break in a meerschaum pipe), cocktail preparation (how to mix a Yellow Fever), and whether or not to wear suspenders with a vest alternate with questions about what to do with girls who complicate the cardinal principal of casualness either by suggesting marriage or by some other impulsive gesture toward a permanent relationship. The infallible answer from the oracle never varies: sex must be contained, at all costs, within the entertainment-recreation area. Don't let her get "serious."

After all, the most famous feature of the magazine is its monthly fold-out photo of a *playmate*. She is the symbol par excellence of recreational sex. When playtime is over, the playmate's function ceases, so she must be made to understand the rules of the game. As the crew-cut young man in a *Playboy* cartoon says to the rumpled and disarrayed girl he is passionately embracing, "Why speak of love at a time like this?"

The magazine's fiction purveys the same kind of severely departmentalized sex. Although the editors have recently dressed up the *Playboy* contents with contributions by Hemingway, Bemelmans, and even a Chekhov translation, the regular run of stories relies on a repetitious and predictable formula. A successful young man, either single or somewhat less than ideally married—a figure with whom readers have no difficulty identifying—encounters a gorgeous and seductive woman who makes no demands on him except sex. She is the prose duplication of the cool-eyed but hot-blooded playmate of the fold-out.

Drawing heavily on the fantasy life of all young Americans, the writers utilize for their stereotyped heroines the hero's schoolteacher, his secretary, an old girl friend, or the girl who brings her car into the garage where he works. The happy issue is always a casual but satisfying sexual experience with no entangling alliances whatever. Unlike the women he knows in real life, the *Playboy* reader's fictional girl friends know their place and ask for nothing more. They present no danger of permanent involvement. Like any good accessory, they are detachable and disposable.

Many of the advertisements reinforce the sex-accessory identification in another way—by attributing female characteristics to the items they sell. Thus a full-page ad for the MG assures us that this car is not only "the smoothest pleasure machine" on the road and that having one is a "love-affair," but most important, "you drive it—it doesn't drive you." The ad ends with the equivocal question "Is it a date?"[5]

Playboy insists that its message is one of liberation. Its gospel frees us from captivity to the puritanical "hatpin brigade." It solemnly crusades for "frankness" and publishes scores of letters congratulating it for its unblushing "candor." Yet the whole phenomenon of which *Playboy* is only a part vividly illustrates the awful fact of a new kind of tyranny.

Those liberated by technology and increased prosperity to new worlds of leisure now become the anxious slaves of dictatorial tastemakers. Obsequiously waiting for the latest signal on what is cool and what is awkward, they are paralyzed by the fear that they may hear pronounced on them that dread sentence occasionally intoned by "The Playboy Adviser": "You goofed!" Leisure is thus swallowed up in apprehensive competitiveness, its liberating potential transformed into a self-destructive compulsion to consume only what is *à la mode*. *Playboy* mediates the

---

[5] This whole fusing of sex and machine symbols in contemporary mass media was once brilliantly explored by Marshall McLuhan in *The Mechanical Bride*, now out of print.

Word of the most high into one section of the consumer world, but it is a word of bondage, not of freedom.

Nor will *Playboy's* synthetic doctrine of man stand the test of scrutiny. Psychoanalysts constantly remind us how deep-seated sexuality is in the human being. But if they didn't remind us, we would soon discover it ourselves anyway. Much as the human male might like to terminate his relationship with a woman as he would snap off the stereo, or store her for special purposes like a camel's-hair jacket, it really can't be done. And anyone with a modicum of experience with women knows it can't be done. Perhaps this is the reason *Playboy's* readership drops off so sharply after the age of thirty.

Playboy really feeds on the existence of a repressed fear of involvement with women, which for various reasons is still present in many otherwise adult Americans. So *Playboy's* version of sexuality grows increasingly irrelevant as authentic sexual maturity is achieved.

The male identity crisis to which *Playboy* speaks has at its roots a deep-set fear of sex, a fear that is uncomfortably combined with fascination. *Playboy* strives to resolve this antinomy by reducing the proportions of sexuality, its power and its passion, to a packageable consumption item. Thus in *Playboy's* iconography the nude woman symbolizes total sexual accessibility but demands nothing from the observer. "You drive it—it doesn't drive you." The terror of sex, which cannot be separated from its ecstasy, is dissolved. But this futile attempt to reduce the *mysterium tremendum* of the sexual fails to solve the problem of being a man. For sexuality is the basic form of all human relationship, and therein lies its terror and its power.

Karl Barth has called this basic relational form of man's life *Mitmensch*, co-humanity.[6] This means that becoming fully human, in this case a human male, requires not having the other totally exposed to me and my purposes—while I remain uncommitted—but exposing myself to the risk of encounter with the other by reciprocal self-exposure. The story of man's refusal to to be exposed goes back to the story of Eden and is expressed by man's desire to control the other rather than to *be with* the other. It is basically the fear to be one's self, a lack of the "courage to be."

Thus any theological critique of *Playboy* that focuses on its "lewdness" will misfire completely. *Playboy* and its less successful imitators are not "sex magazines" at all. They are basically antisexual. They dilute and dissipate authentic sexuality by reducing it to an accessory, by keeping it at a safe distance.

It is precisely because these magazines are antisexual that they deserve the most searching kind of theological criticism. They foster a heretical doctrine of man, one at radical variance with the biblical view. For *Playboy's* man, others—especially women—are *for* him. They are his leisure accessories, his playthings. For the Bible, man only becomes fully man by being *for* the other.

Moralistic criticisms of *Playboy* fail because its antimoralism is one of the few places in which *Playboy* is right. But if Christians bear the name of One who was truly man because He was totally *for* the other, and if it is in Him that we know who

---

[6] Karl Barth, *Church Dogmatics* (Edinburgh: T & T Clark, 1957), II/2.

God is and what human life is for, then we must see in *Playboy* the latest and slickest episode in man's continuing refusal to be fully human.

Freedom for mature sexuality comes to man only when he is freed from the despotic powers which crowd and cower him into fixed patterns of behavior. Both Miss America and The Playboy illustrate such powers. When they determine man's sexual life, they hold him in captivity. They prevent him from achieving maturity. They represent the constant danger of relapsing into tribal thralldom which always haunts the secular society, a threat from which the liberating, secularizing word of the Gospel repeatedly recalls it.

Remnants of Town Virtues

Equally hazardous for sexual maturity, however, is the lure of town culture, the period we have most recently left behind, at least in most respects. In the area of sexual ethics, this period speaks to us through the traditional sexual practices of our Puritan and Victorian pasts. Since the melody of this ethic lingers on today, our sexual ethics are caught in the crossfire of contradiction and confusion. To illustrate this tension, let us take the traditional ideal of premarital chastity.

I choose this not because of any belief that it is really the key issue. It does seem clear, however, that for many young adults today "to bed or not to bed" *seems* to be the Big Question, and I believe the reasons they press it so vigorously merit exploration. Three aspects of the problem require particular attention: (1) why the yes or no of premarital chastity is more critical for young adults today than in the past; (2) why the answers we usually give to this question are either not heard or provide little guidance; and (3) what, if anything, we should be saying about the matter.

Let us reject at the outset any Kinseyian inference that what *is* being done should determine what *ought* to be done. But let us candidly admit that our culture has undergone drastic changes. Though our Puritan style of life has vanished almost completely, the Puritan sex ethic remains, at least on paper. We have exchanged ankle-length dresses for bikinis. We hold blanket parties instead of bobbing for apples. But the people caught up in these epochal changes are still taught, albeit with winks and evasions, the selfsame code of total premarital abstinence that was instilled into Priscilla Alden.

We have thus fashioned for unmarried young adults a particularly unfortunate combination of emotional environments. They are constantly bombarded —through clothing styles, entertainment, advertising, and courtship mores—with perhaps the most skillfully contrived array of erotic stimulants ever amassed. Their sexual fears and fantasies are studied by motivational researchers and then ruthlessly exploited by mass-media hucksters. Elizabeth Taylor's Brobdingnagian bosom decorates billboards, and throaty songstresses hum their hoarse invitations from transistors.

Yet we pass on to our youth, unaltered, a set of behavioral taboos that, in a sex-saturated society, seem diabolically created to produce a high level of duplicity and desperation.

Why have we deliberately constructed such a bizarre imbalance in our moral and psychological milieu? Obviously because we want to have our cake and eat it too. We want to gorge ourselves at the table of an affluent society whose continued prosperity, we are told, necessitates a constantly expanding market. And sex sells anything. At the same time we want to cherish our national memories of Pilgrims and piety, including the sexual code of Massachusetts Bay. The inherent contradiction comes home to roost in the already tormented psyche of the unmarried young adult.

The essential contradictions of any society, as the Marxists say, are concentrated in its proletariat. In a sexually exploitative society, youth subculture becomes the psychological proletariat. It picks up the tab for our hypocrisy. Exposed to all the stimulants married people are, young people are forbidden the socially acceptable form of fulfillment. The refusal is expressed both in the laws of the realm and in the official taboos of the culture. Enforcement, however, is sporadic, and, because the signals are so confused and contradictory, adolescents suspect that it is all one vast dissimulation.

No wonder the beatnik, who rejects *both* the signals of the mass media and the sexual mores, becomes the secret hero of many young adults.

To make matters just a bit more trying, we have thoughtfully provided Jane and Joe more privacy and permissiveness in dating than ever before. This extends far beyond Harvard dormitory rooms. I wonder if Henry Ford ever realized that his invention would be viewed by many not primarily as a means of transportation but as the urban society's substitute for Keats' "elfin grot."

Remember also that dating (and with it various types of petting) now reaches down to the sixth grade. Youngsters are thus exposed for a longer period and much more intensely to the mutual exploration of erogenous regions, which is the American courtship pattern. The only advice they get is "Don't go too far," and it is usually the girl who is expected to draw the line.

By the time a girl who begins petting at thirteen has reached marriageable age, she has drawn an awful lot of lines. If she is especially impressed with her religious duty to avoid intercourse, she will probably have mastered, by twenty-one, all the strategems for achieving a kind of sexual climax while simultaneously preventing herself and her partner from crossing the sacrosanct line.

What this border-skirting approach does to inhibit her chances for a successful adjustment in marriage is a question now engaging the attention of psychologists and marriage counselors. One psychologist who specializes in sexual behavior remarked recently that if Americans had consciously set out to think up a system that would produce maximal marital and premarital strife for both sexes, we could scarcely have invented a sexually more sabotaging set of dating procedures than we have today. This may be an overstatement, but I suspect the inherent hypocrisy of the cultural taboo and the patterns of behavior it engenders must have considerable negative influence on marriage.

Add to this the fact that penicillin and oral contraceptives will soon remove the last built-in deterrents to premarital coitus, and the reason for the recent rumblings of discontent with traditional standards becomes clearer. Not that the young adults themselves are guiltless. They share the blame for perpetuating the same values. But they also consider themselves the victims of a kind of cultural charade.

They are shown one thing, told another, and they never know when the society will wink and when it will whip them. Their suspicion that they are the fall guys in a giant collusion is expressed in their growing demand that we come clean on this matter.

Now we can turn to the question of why, amid this schizophrenic carnival of prurience and prudery, the Christian Gospel seems to offer so little positive guidance. I believe the answer to this question is that most young adults do not perceive Christian sexual ethics as "evangelical," that is, as *good news*. They are not hearing the Gospel as good news and therefore they are not hearing the Gospel at all, but something else.

The German theologian Friedrich Gogarten states that the two most serious dangers from which the Gospel must be protected are (a) its being dissolved into a myth and (b) its being hardened into a religion of Law.[7] In either case it ceases to be the Gospel. When we examine what has happened to the Gospel as it touches the area of sex, it is evident that both of these distortions have set in.

The Gospel comes to the sexual puzzlement of most young adults not as a liberating *yes*, not as God's Good News freeing them for personhood and community. It comes rather as a remnant of cultural Christendom and an assortment of confused conventions. To be heard once again as the Gospel it must be demythologized and delegalized.

Let us turn first to the task of demythologizing it from odd bits of sexual folklore with which it has been confused. I shall refer to only two of the many mythical motifs that obfuscate the Gospel in its bearing on sexual conduct. First the ideal of romantic love, which Denis de Rougement has traced to paganism and which is almost always fused with any young American's ideas about sex.[8] Second, the Western obsession with coital intercourse as normative sexuality and hence as that which defines the content of chastity and virginity. The identification is now so complete that, as Theodor W. Adorno recently pointed out, intercourse now *means* coitus.[9]

Both the romantic ideal and the indentification of intercourse with coitus are cultural accretions that have been coalesced with the rule of premarital chastity. The combination has so beclouded the liberating power of the Gospel that it can scarcely be heard because of them and the Gospel is frequently perceived to be saying almost the opposite of what is intended.

The ideal of romantic love is the most obvious mythical excrescence. It leads often to the belief, especially among girls, that certain forms of intimacy become progressively less objectionable the more you "love" the boy. The snares in this curious amalgam of Our Gal Sunday and Saint Teresa are manifold. Among adolescents of all ages, *love* has come to mean nothing more than a vague emotional glow. It's "that ol' black magic, . . . those icy fingers up and down my spine."

The belief that love is the only honest basis for sex forces countless maidens into anguished efforts to justify their sexual inconstancy by falling in and out of love with a passing parade of partners. Naturally, opportunities for self-deception are

[7] Friedrich Gogarten, *Der Mensch zwischen Gott und Welt* (Stuttgart: F. Vorweck Verlag, 1956), p. 34.

[8] Denis de Rougement, *Love in the Western World* (New York: Pantheon, 1956).

[9] Theodor W. Adorno, *Neun Kritische Modelle* (Frankfurt: Suhrkamp Verlag, 1963), pp. 99ff.

almost endless, and the outcome is often an acid cynicism about the possibility of ever really loving anyone.

Furthermore, the sex-and-romantic-love equation sets up an inevitable collision course. The conflict occurs because, although girls tend to "go the limit" only with a boy they believe they "love," many boys, as sociologist Winston Ehrmann shows in his *Premarital Dating Behavior*,[10] will stop short of intercourse with girls they "love" or "respect," though they will go as far as possible with another girl. Thus girls associate sex with romantic love far more than boys do, and emotional scars emerging from this built-in contradiction often last far into married life.

Since girls feel they must be swept into sexual experience by something "bigger than both of us," they often fail to take the precautions against pregnancy they might otherwise. Somehow it doesn't seem romantic to go out with a boy, having prepared in advance to be swept off one's feet. Consequently, many instances of intercourse are not "planned," but occur more or less spontaneously at the end of an evening of progressively heavier necking. Unwanted pregnancies, abortions, shattered family relations, and forfeited careers are the inevitable result.

One solution is to admonish everybody to avoid any physical contact that could spiral toward intercourse. But how sane or compassionate is this advice in a society where various types of petting are the only socially approved way of handling tensions exacerbated by a sexually saturated culture? Petting does sometimes lead to intercourse, but not always. Most of the time it does not. To try to abolish it while still retaining our prosperity and our aphrodisiac advertising would be even less honest than the preach-and-wink pharisaism.

Another antidote is simply to deromanticize sex. This would mean urging young people who are going to have intercourse anyway (and who, under layers of unsuccessful self-deception, know they will) to accept the full responsibility for their behavior and to take the necessary steps to avoid pregnancy.

Such a solution, although more realistic, has almost as little chance of acceptance as the first. It would necessitate dispelling the illusions of romantic love and suggesting that young people ponder soberly in the light of day what they are really doing. But it would also require our society to face up to the cant and flimflam of its sexual folkways, and this no one really wants to do. So the black magic, petting, and pregnancies will probably continue.

A more stubborn and deceptive segment of folklore that has been equated with the doctrine of premarital chastity is one that is rarely discussed openly: the curious presumption that a person who has not experienced coital intercourse remains a virgin—no matter what else he or she has done. This popular piece of legerdemain explains in part the discovery by Kinsey that, although the incidence of premarital intercourse among women has merely mounted steadily, premarital petting of all varieties has skyrocketed.

Kinsey's finding could be substantiated by the most casual observer of the American college scene. The number of students who do not pet at all is negligible. An increasing number regularly carry their necking to the point of heavy sex play and orgasm. A pert young graduate of a denominational college assured me recently

[10] Winston Ehrmann, *Premarital Dating Behavior* (New York: Holt, 1959).

that although she had necked to orgasm every week-end for two years, she had never "gone all the way." Her premarital chastity was intact.

Or was it? Only, I submit, by the most technical definition of what is meant by preserving virginity. True, some writers actually advocate such noncoital orgasm as the "safest" way for unmarried people to achieve sexual climax. However distasteful this idea may seem to some, it is extremely important to realize that the church's traditional teaching actually functions in such a fashion as to give considerable support to this view.

The ideal of premarital chastity is generally understood to mean that, although necking is somewhat questionable, the fragile gem of virginity remains intact so long as coitus is avoided. This myth has helped open the floodgate to a tidal wave of noncoital promiscuity.

Here the demythologizing process might be helped if we note Saint Paul's insistence (in I Corinthians 6:15–16) that liaisons intended to be highly casual, for example with prostitutes, nevertheless involve us in a relationship that is inevitably much deeper than we bargained for. We "become one flesh." D. S. Bailey calls this "a psychological insight . . . altogether exceptional by first-century standards."[11]

Saint Paul saw the striking fact that as human beings we both *have* and *are* bodies. This is an issue that has been explored at length by such contemporary philosophers as Gabriel Marcel and Maurice Merleau-Ponty. Paul saw that sex—unlike excretion, for example—is not simply a physiological but also a "bodily" (somatic) activity. It involves us at the deepest levels of our personal identity.

But why limit Saint Paul's insight to coital intercourse alone, or to contacts with prostitutes? The mere avoidance of coitus does not exempt anyone from becoming "one flesh" with another. All "virgins" who are promiscuous neckers should know that. Nor can the "one flesh" phenomenon be restricted to the bordello.

Saint Paul knew that no sexual relationship could be kept merely physical without ceasing to be really sexual in the fully human sense of the word. This is why the playmate-of-the-month domestication of sex as a purely recreational pursuit just doesn't work. Paul really appreciated sex more than Hugh Hefner does. He expected more from it. Sex is certainly fun, but to make it *simply* fun is to eviscerate and enfeeble it. Then it eventually ceases even to be fun.

When it is demythologized, the evangelical sexual ethic turns out to be an invitation to life together in a community of personal selves. The Gospel frees us from the need to cling to romantic self-deception and the works righteousness by which we clothe our promiscuity in the costume of technical virginity. By delivering us from mythology into history, Jesus Christ allows us to see that the marvelous skein of privileges and responsibilities in which we find ourselves as human beings is something for which we are responsible. But how do we exercise this responsibility?

At this point the going becomes more difficult. Any effort to arrest the degeneration of the Gospel into some form of Law will be viewed in some quarters

---

[11] D. S. Bailey, *Sexual Relations in Christian Thought* (New York: Harper, 1959; London: Longmans, Green).

as antinomianism, the belief that the precepts of the Law are not binding for Christians. A Gospel ethic, however, demands more maturity and more discipline than a Law ethic. Evangelical ethics are by nature riskier. This risk must be run since the New Testament insists unequivocally that it is the Gospel and not the Law that saves. How then can we begin to "delegalize" the Gospel when sexual behavior is the question at issue?

The Gospel is addressed to persons; the Law sees acts. One weakness of the traditional ethical formulation on premarital chastity is its sweeping inclusiveness and total lack of discrimination. Reduced to a precept, the ideal of premarital chastity permits no distinction between intercourse by engaged couples, for example, and the chilling exploitation of high school girls at fraternity parties. Both are transgressions of the Law, and there is no middle ground between virginity and nonvirginity.

Consequently there emerges alongside the technical virgin her shadowy counterpart, the technically fallen woman—the girl who, because she once consented to intercourse, now feels she is permanently pastured among the goats. She has crossed the sexual Styx and there is no way back. Because she can no longer present herself to her husband in purity on the wedding night anyway, why shouldn't anything go?

Her self-condemnation arises in part because she has not heard the *good* news. She has perceived the traditional teaching as a *law*. Law without Gospel is arbitrary and abstract. It cannot discriminate among cases. And it has nothing helpful to say to the transgressor. Consequently, for the increasing proportion of young people who have already had sexual intercourse, the rule of premarital chastity is simply irrelevant. And since for many it appears to be the only record the church ever plays on this subject, they conclude the church has nothing to say to them.

But preaching the Gospel also entails preaching the Law—exposing the false absolutes from which one is liberated. Negatively this means making clear the distorted images of sex from which the Gospel delivers us. Positively it entails protecting sex as a fully human activity against all the principalities and powers that seek to dehumanize it. In our day these include the forces, both within and without, that pervert sex into a merchandising technique, a means of self-aggrandizement, a weapon for rebelling against parents, a recreational pursuit, a way to gain entrance into the right clique, *or*—let the reader beware—a devotional act with some sort of religious significance.

To be freed from the "bondage of the Law" means to be freed from these dehumanizing powers. It also means to be freed from those diabolical pressures toward subcultural conformity that push so many adolescents into whatever is "in" at the moment. Sexual freedom in Christ, in one concrete case, means that a harried co-ed can say *no* to a cloying Romeo without feeling she is being hopelessly square.

Evangelical ethics cease to be Law and once again become Gospel when the Word liberates people from cultural conventions and social pressures, when persons discover their sexuality as a delightful gift of God that links them in freedom and concern to their fellows. But how do we make *this* Gospel heard by young adults in today's sexually rapacious society?

Before answering this question we must admit that we have created a set of cultural conditions in which sexual responsibility is made exceedingly difficult. In our American Xanadu, exhortations to individual continence are almost as useless as urging businessmen to eschew the profit motive.

It is strange how even people who see most clearly that crime, illegitimacy, narcotics addiction, and poverty are largely structural problems still interpret the increase in premarital sexual experience as a breakdown in personal morals.

But the jig is nearly up. Our feverish effort to paper over a society propelled by drives for sex and status with a set of Victorian courtship mores is breaking down badly. We must direct our fire more toward the "feminine mystique" and the cynical misutilization of sex by the public-relations culture than toward the hapless individual offender.

This may involve some searching questions about limiting the deliberate use of sexual stimulation in selling or, even more radically, about the merit of an economic system that seems to require a constant perversion of sexuality in order to survive. Commercial exploitation of sex drives—not the call girls—is our most serious form of prostitution today.

When we do turn from the society to the individual, especially to the unmarried young adult, we must avoid giving a simple yes-or-no answer to the question of premarital chastity. Of course, this will sound like evasion, but any simple answer panders to the cheap attempt to oversimplify the issue, to reduce all the intricacies of premarital sexuality to one decision. And churchmen, by allowing the Gospel to deteriorate into folklore and fiat, have contributed to this fatal oversimplification.

I do not believe that an evangelical ethic of premarital sex can be chopped down to a flat answer to this weighted question without impoverishing and distorting it. Instead of registering an answer, the Gospel poses a question of its own (as Jesus himself frequently did with such questions). It asks how I can best nourish the maturity of those with whom I share the torments and transports of human existence.

The Gospel liberates men from mythical taboos and rigid concepts for a purpose: so that the full and untrammeled resources of the human imagination can be exercised in responsibility for others within the patterns of public and private life. In the freedom of the Gospel, we arrive at decisions by utilizing norms that themselves must always be open to criticism and transformation and are therefore never final. Traditional Christian sexual norms are no exception. They do not stand above history. They have arisen as Christians attempted to live faithfully through constantly changing social systems. Like all human codes they stand in continuous need of revision so they will help rather than hinder God's maturation of man.

Christians believe God is at work in history bringing man to adulthood and responsibility. Within this framework the norms by which we make our decisions are fashioned and discarded in a continuous conversation with the Bible and with the culture, a conversation that is never completed. The Christian knows he is free only as a partner in this conversation and as a member of this community. This means, among other things, that his decisions about sexual conduct inevitably involve more people than he would sometimes like to involve. Sex is never simply a private matter.

To refuse to deliver a prepared answer whenever the question of premarital intercourse pops up will have a healthy influence on the continuing conversation that is Christian ethics. It moves the axis of the discussion away from the arid stereotypes by which we oversimplify intricate human issues. It gets us off dead-end arguments about virginity and chastity, forces us to think about fidelity to persons. It exposes the promiscuity of sexual pharisees and the subtle exploitation that poisons even the most immaculate Platonic relationships.

By definition, premarital refers to people who plan to marry someone someday. Premarital sexual conduct should therefore serve to strengthen the chances of sexual success and fidelity in marriage, and we must face the real question of whether avoidance of intercourse beforehand is always the best preparation.

This question includes consideration of the appropriate degree of sexual intimacy during increasingly extended engagement periods. The reason it cannot be answered once and for all is that circumstances vary from couple to couple. Guidance must be given with specific persons rather than with general conventions in view.

Admittedly, this approach requires more resourcefulness and imagination than relying on universally applicable axioms. Principles are useful, perhaps indispensable in ethical thinking, but all too often "sticking to principles" can become just another way to avoid seeing persons. It can signify a relapse from Gospel into Law.

Perhaps one day we in America will put away childish things and become mature men and women who do not have to rely on the male and female deities of the mass media to tell us who to be. Perhaps one day we will outgrow our ridiculous obsession with sex, of which our fixation on chastity and virginity is just the other side of the coin. Until that time, however, we should rejoice that in Jesus Christ we are freed from myth and from Law. We are placed in a community of selves, free to the extent that we live for each other, free to develop whatever styles of life will contribute to the maturation of persons in a society where persons are often overlooked as we scamper to pursue profits and piety all at once.

Man, God, and Atomic War

Samuel H. Dresner

Rabbi Samuel H. Dresner (1925–   ) is the spiritual leader of the North
Suburban Synagogue Beth El, Highland Park, Illinois. A past editor of *Con-
servative Judaism*, he is the author of many books, including *Man, God and
Atomic War*, *The Sabbath*, and *Between the Generations*.

There are those who assert that if human might and mind—military defense and
international agreement—cannot prevent atomic destruction, there is One who can,
One higher than all men, wiser than all human minds, more powerful than all
human might—*God*! Surely He will not permit the creature that He fashioned
and placed upon this earth, who was made in His image, to whom He gave lordship
over the entire earth, to be destroyed. This is an argument that many of us toy
with in the back of our minds when all else begins to crumble. We like to consider
it, rest upon it, embrace it—because it is reassuring.

But are we so sure that God wants to save us, even if He could? Are we so
confident that we deserve being saved at all? Who dares declare that he knows the
will of God? Perhaps it is all quite different. Perhaps God has had enough of the
human race. Perhaps He is fed up with us, disgusted with our killing, our hating, our
wars, our treachery, our intrigue, our concentration camps and gas chambers, our
Bergen-Belsens and Treblinkas, our Cains and Hamans, our Genghis Khans and
Attilas, our Hitlers and Stalins, our miserable struggle for money and power and
ego-satisfaction, with the filth and rottenness of our world and our lives. Perhaps
He thought that the human race might learn in time from the suffering and tragedy
which it encountered in the world and would, thereby—in a hundred years, a
thousand years, three thousand years—become faithful to Him. But we did not.
Every generation repeated the same errors of the generation before. Indeed, as time
passes the errors seem to grow larger.

From the very beginning the creation of man was a doubtful venture. This is
the verdict of more than a few of the ancient sages of Israel. According to rabbinic

Source: Samuel H. Dresner, "Man, God and Atomic War," in *God and the H-Bomb*, ed. by Donald
Keys (New York, 1961). Copyright © 1961, by Bellmeadows Press and Bernard Geis Associates.
Reprinted by permission of Bernard Geis Associates, publishers.

parable of creation (Breshit Rabbah 8), God created and destroyed many worlds before He created ours. When He was about to make man, we are told great consternation arose in heaven. The forces of truth and justice arose to oppose the creation of man. For if the truth were known and pure justice were exercised, man could never be created, since he could not survive God's justice. Therefore, according to the rabbis, God cast truth away and put aside justice for mercy and, while the angels were weighing the merits of the case—whether or not man should be created—God created him.

Has man been able to justify God's hope? We are told in the Talmud that the schools of Hillel and Shammai disputed two and a half years whether it would have been better if man had or had not been created. Finally they agreed that it would have been better had he not been created, but since he had been created, let him examine his past deeds and take care in what he was about to do. (Eruvin 13b.)

What the ancients expressed through Biblical exegesis and fanciful fable, we would put differently today. The Bible taught them that man exists through God's grace and not by His justice. This is fundamental. For if pure justice were to prevail, man would be destroyed. But God tempers His justice with mercy and thus man survives. Man's continued existence is by no means guaranteed; it is, on the contrary, tenuous and dependent. There is no stability or certainty to man's existence. The angels opposed the creation of man; the forces of truth and justice opposed the creation of man. The creation of man was opposed because the evil that would come forth from him was foreseen. The creation of man was opposed because man's power to hurt, his will to destroy, was foreseen. Notwithstanding, God created man (according to the rabbis) in the hope that the good would conquer the evil, the power to love would conquer the power to hurt, and the will to obey His will would conquer the will to destroy. The history of man, however, has been the history of God's disappointment with man.

Indeed the Bible may be described as God's search for the righteous man and His repeated disappointment. God regretted that He had made man, Scripture tells us, and was about to destroy him, but He offered him a second opportunity through Noah, who seemed to be a righteous man, at least in comparison with his generation. So all the rest of mankind was swept away in the flood, and it was as if Noah were again the first man. But Noah too disappointed God. He was a drunkard, and his descendants in their rebellious pride built a great tower reaching up to the heavens, so that they might know the mysteries of God and themselves become gods. God punished them by confounding their language so that "they would not understand one another's speech," and "scattered them abroad from thence upon the face of all the earth."

Once more the Almighty was about to bring an end to the human experiment when He offered mankind another hope, perhaps its last. But this time He would place His hope in one family and in the people that would come from it—Abraham, Isaac and Jacob, the children of Israel. They were a small people crushed by slavery and open, perhaps, to His word. He revealed His will to this people at Sinai, transforming them into a kingdom of priests and a holy nation, that through them the world might come to know the Lord and follow His ways. If mankind will accept the Torah, the rabbis taught, the world will survive; but if they will not, it will be turned back into chaos.

Adam failed, Cain failed, Noah failed, the generations of the Tower of Babel failed. Is it so utterly inconceivable that man's last chance was given with the covenant at Sinai? Is it inconceivable to believe that if Judaism and Christianity fail, there will be an end? Ludicrous as this may have sounded a century ago, it does not sound ludicrous at all today. Man has known the teachings of the Bible for more than three thousand years. How much progress has the world made in understanding and obeying that book? Perhaps our Earth will take its place among the others which God was said to have created and destroyed. Perhaps the time of reckoning has come and God is abandoning us to ourselves.

See! the Lord's hand is not too short to save.
Nor His ear too dull to hear;
But your iniquities have been a barrier
Between you and your God.
And your sins have hidden His face,

So that He could not hear you.
For your hands are stained with blood,
And your fingers with iniquity;
Your lips have spoken lies,
And your tongue utters untruths.
There is none who sues honestly,
None who pleads his case truthfully.
But each one trusts in vanity and speaks lies,
Conceives wrong, and brings forth mischief.

Therefore is justice far from us,
And righteousness does not reach us;
We look for light, but lo! darkness,
For rays of dawn, but we walk in gloom.
We grope like blind men along a wall,
Like men without eyes we grope;
We stumble at noonday as in the twilight,
In the strength of manhood we are like the dead.
We growl like bears,
And moan like doves,
And look for redress, but it comes not,
For salvation, but it remains far from us.[1]

What the prophets feared most was God's abandonment of man, the silencing of His voice, the withdrawal of His presence. Perhaps this is the meaning of our time. If man wants to destroy himself, God seems to say, "Let him. I have had enough. I shall try again elsewhere." There is no guarantee that God will intervene to save our world from disaster.

Neither military defense, international agreement or God's miraculous intervention is the solution we are seeking. But this does not mean that there is no solution. There *is* a solution to the problem of nuclear war and the possible end of human life. But it is a radical solution. It must be so. It can only be so. A radical situation demands a radical solution. Nothing short of that will avail. It is in the roots of the human being and the human situation that the solution lies. It is not a

---

[1] Isa. 50:1-11.

political formula, a diplomatic theory, a gospel of economics or a master plan for world government, but something which, on the one hand, reaches beyond them all and, on the other hand, is their foundation, the only real hope for their fulfillment. It goes to the root of them all.

Perhaps the clearest expression of our solution is found in this passage of the Bible:

> "I call heaven and earth to witness against you this day, that I have set before thee life and death, and blessing and the curse; therefore choose life, that thou mayest live, thou and thy seed; to love the Lord thy God, to hearken to His voice, and to cleave unto Him; for that is thy life and the length of thy days . . .
> "If you obey the commandment of the Lord thy God which I command you this day by loving the Lord thy God, by walking in His ways, and by keeping His commandments . . . , then you shall live and multiply and the Lord thy God will bless you . . .
> "But if your heart turns away and you will not hear, but are drawn away to worship other gods and serve them, I declare unto you this day, that you shall surely perish . . ."[2]

These ancient words, hoary with time and memory, were written down in an ancient book by an ancient people who claimed that they were confronted by God and found the truth about man for all time. These simple yet profound words contain the answer we seek. Their meaning is evident. We are placed on earth with freedom of will to choose the evil way or the good way, the blessing or the curse. God urges us to choose the good way, to love the Lord and walk in His ways. For in that way lies life, length of days and blessing. But there is the other way, too, and it is a tempting way, the worship of false gods as the true God, the idols of nature, society and the ego, of man himself. In that way lies the curse and death, for the idol becomes a demon which ultimately destroys those who worship it.

Moses has been right all these years, but the truth of his words has been ignored by the majority of mankind. It seemed perfectly possible in all the ages gone by to swindle, to cheat, to fight, to wage war, to break treaties, to seek power, to deny every law of God and man—and still get along, even to flourish. By and large, in the past, the man who loved God and obeyed His law was rewarded with a joyous life, and, by and large, those who violated God's law inherited misery. But that was only "by and large," and even the lesson of "by and large" did not impress many people, because it seemed easier and more tempting to be one's own god, live for one's own interests and serve one's own welfare. There were also history's Jobs to consider, those whose innocence did not prevent the wrath of sickness, poverty and anguish from reaching them; and the kings and princes and merchants and generals and pirates and gangsters and criminals of all ages to consider, those whose evil deeds, far from bringing them misery, rewarded them with untold wealth, power and pleasure. The world, in the past, has been able to tolerate vast amounts of evil and still maintain itself. But today it has reached the saturation point. This is the unending chasm that divides all that has gone before us from today.

[2] Deut. 30:19, 20:15-18.

In the past, loving God, walking in His ways and obeying His Commandments, was looked upon as desirable, the proper thing to do. Some even took it seriously and devoted their lives to the service of God; many more took it less seriously, but at least allowed it to play some role in their lives. Still, if there were people who did not walk in God's ways—who defiled, corrupted and oppressed—the world would survive. Today it is quite a different matter. Whether or not men walk in God's ways—whether or not men are criminals or responsible citizens, tyrants or dedicated leaders, corrupt or decent, depraved or exalted—is literally a matter of life and death, of the very survival of the world. Either there will be a change in man's heart or there will be no man nor heart to change!

It almost seems as if the premodern concept of divine reward and punishment for human deeds, which was one of the strongest forces in days gone by to encourage good deeds and prevent evil deeds, has now become reinstated. The fiery threat of Hell which motivated so much of the lives of our ancestors, now, ironically, takes on a new form. There are two differences, however. In the past, the fear of punishment was largely relegated to a future world and, in the opinion of scoffers, was nothing but superstition. Today, fear of physical punishment for man's deeds is moved ahead to our own world, and is a fear that, far from being argued by religious fanatics, is a demonstrated fact in the minds of Nobel-prize-winning physicists.

Nevertheless, I am not arguing that men should love God and obey His Commandments out of fear of punishment alone. This would return us to the argument for preventing war by mutual fear of retaliation. Rather must it awaken us to the terrible relevancy of man's inner life to our outer situation. Indeed nothing —*nothing*—is more relevant to the problem we face than the condition of the human spirit.

It is not as if, down through the ages, man had not endeavored to solve the problems of our world. Man's error was repeated again and over again in a thousand different forms, but in essence it was the same error. It was the error of making relative truths absolute. And each time this happened something fallible and finite, the product of man's mind and hands, was raised to the throne of God Himself and worshipped as God, as absolute. But when a relative good is turned into an absolute, it becomes a demon that carries us away with it. This is the lesson of history.

There is only one way to remember that everything human is dependent or relative, and that is by accepting the Lord of justice and mercy, the Creator of heaven and earth, as our God and our absolute. Then there can be no other gods, and all else is constantly judged in terms of the one absolute.

What gives meaning and usefulness is the simple command of the Bible to love God and walk in His ways. We can exist without skyscrapers and air conditioning, without gas chambers and H-bombs. But we cannot get along without the spiritual source of our existence. The problem is not how to escape civilization—that is impossible—but how to surpass it. It is not enough to say, as is said again and again, that our spiritual progress has not kept up with our technological progress, but rather that our *technological advance has finally reached such a point that virtual spiritual perfection is demanded to harness it to good purposes and prevent it from being used for evil purposes.* This is a dreadful prospect, but it clearly defines our position. Scientific progress has brought us to the spiritual saturation point. And we are not at all ready.

In such a context a strange thing happens. The Bible becomes what it always has been—the most relevant of all books. If man walks in the ways of God, he will have peace and blessing. If man rebels against Him and worships gods of his own— the state, power, the ego—he will have death and the end of the world.

The simple fact is that the ultimate questions of the universe are no longer for the philosopher or the saint. They have become peculiarly relevant to the day-to-day life of every single one of us and to the future of our world. The truth is, of course, that they have always been relevant to our life and our world. But this relevancy, the relevancy of revering God and walking in His ways—rarely apparent in the course of history—has now assumed tremendous significance to millions of minds, and must of necessity become apparent to millions more. It is only a question of time. *Ultimate* issues—good and evil, justice and mercy, the love and law of God— are now *necessary* issues. *Ultimate* concerns are now *immediate* concerns. They are now, perhaps, for the first time in the history of mankind, seen in a new light and from the most practical of vantage points.

What the inescapable facts of our situation are forcing man to understand with merciless pressure is the very meaning of life itself. He soon comes to the solemn and frightening conclusion that life is not simply a game without rules, created solely for his pleasure. He understands that life must be taken *seriously.* That man's actions have *consequences.* That man may be *called to account* for his actions, by overwhelming disaster. That *man himself is only an experiment*, a possibility in time, a colossal gamble in joining the holy and the profane, heaven and earth, angel and animal, infinite and finite, a *divine experiment* with no guarantee of success; and it is precisely this experimental nature of man's existence, which the Bible has always taught, that men everywhere have suddenly become aware of.

What the prophets ranted and raved about some twenty-five hundred years ago—that the murder of the innocent would bring destruction upon nations, that the persecution of a stranger could lead to catastrophe, that hurting an orphan was a crime of cosmic proportions, that despising the poor could cause the heavens to shake, that lies and robbery and crime might shatter the very foundations of the world—was almost always taken by readers to indicate some manner of ecstatic hysteria which was responsible for the cataclysmic conclusions they drew from such insignificant causes. After all, how could good or evil affect the natural order? How could doing wrong jeopardize the existence of the world?

Few people understood in the past that loving God and walking in His ways meant life, while following after the idols of our own creation meant death; that the existence of the world depends on goodness and not steel, on justice and not iron, on mercy and not power. The scientist would no doubt claim that the world stands upon natural law, the philosopher upon reason, the tyrant upon power, the businessman upon profit. But these are not the real foundations of the world; they cannot guarantee the stability and permanence of our society. They are weak, fallible and deceitful. We are now suddenly awakened to the supreme fact: the true foundations of the world are the foundations of the human spirit.

And if there is no change in the heart of man, then it seems as if an end may come to our world as we know it. Does that sound fantastic? It is the plain, simple truth, without embellishment or fancy. How is it possible that we go about our ways so blissfully complacent, so incredibly oblivious to the reality of the age in which we live? Perhaps it is because it is incredible. It is an either-or age. *Either* we transform our inner life—*or* we may perish. Either we get us a new heart—or we may be turned into ashes. Either we destroy the idols we worship—or the end may be upon us. It is a time of such extremes, an eschatological age.

Between man and his world stands that power, peace, and plenty which is the will of God and the presence of God. It is this sense of God's will and God's presence that modern man has lost, sundering himself from the very roots of his existence. The ultimate must once again become real, so that it possesses the strength to transform, interpenetrating the disciplines of our society with new power and new perspective.

To revere God and walk in His ways is, of course, no easy solution. I am not saying that it is, holding a simple formula aloft as the magic removal for all our ills. Far from it. I am only making one claim: that the material world is dependent, in the last analysis, upon the spiritual world, that ultimate realities have become immediate realities, and that our world may be annihilated unless we awake. This is what we face, and these are its consequences:

1. The machinery for instant death for all mankind is now in men's hands.

2. There is no defense.

3. Only the creation of a new society can prevent the use of the bomb and outlaw war.

4. A new society requires a new man who can only become so by revering God and walking in His ways.

The "Just War" Justifies Too Much

Donald A. Wells

Donald A. Wells (1917–   ), who teaches philosophy at the University of Hawaii at Hilo, is the author of *The War Myth* and *God, Man and the Thinker*.

"Justification" is not an unambiguous term. In the context of logical justification, the defense of a claim is a function of a given system, where consistency with axioms is a necessary, if not sufficient, criterion of proof. In normative discourse, however, justification takes on an honorific and emotion-laden aura. In addition to both consistency and truth claims, moral justification entails some notion of "rightness" or "goodness." The problem of the "Just War" is, in this latter sense, more than a matter of consistency with some given axioms, more than a question of the truth of some factual claims, more than a matter of what is permissible legally, and surely more than an exercise in the possible limits of an hypothetical ethics.

In a very ordinary sense of the term "justify" we commonly seek an explanation of why a war was waged in the first place. "Why did Athens war against Sparta?" is in this sense "justified" by giving the antecedent reasons prompting the declaration. But more has been involved than this in traditional dispute over the justice of some war. Commonly the dispute sounds more like the defense of an appellant before a judge, and the "justification" consists in part in showing that some acts of war were consistent with the legal rules under which we have agreed to operate. In a further sense, the justification of war is like the famous "justification of induction," and its resolution involves us in a metalinguistic search for some frame of reference that transcends both politics and morals.

More pertinently, however, the attempts to justify war constitute a recognition that the terms "just" and "war" are, if not contradictions, at least of doubtful conjunction. Since the kind of havoc which war entails is normally classed with immoral actions, the concept of the "just war" aims to show the circumstances under which it would be proper to perform otherwise immoral acts and to contribute to evil consequences. The first century of the Christian church, with its pacifist rejection of war altogether, did not produce any theorizers of the just war, while by the time Christianity was adopted as the official religion of the Roman Empire, war had lost its aura of absolute evil, and men now proposed conditions under which it would be appropriate to kill in war. While the post-Constantine church accepted war as a defensible method, it never quite lost its first-century suspicion that killing was still evil. Thus the defenses of the "just war" exhibited

Source: Donald A. Wells, "How Much Can 'the Just War' Justify?" *Journal of Philosophy,* Vol. LXVI (December 1969), 819–829. Reprinted by permission.

a friction or tension between the ethical ideal of non-killing and the political practice of killing in the service of the state.

In his essay "Politics As A Vocation" Max Weber distinguished these two basically contrary concerns. He formulated them in two maxims: (1) the ethics of ultimate ends, and (2) the ethics of responsibility. In the case of the first position the Christians act rightly and leave the outcome to God. The Christian commitment to the sacredness of human life led them to posit limits to the means a person can rightly perform in the support of any other end. The end of human life precluded, in this sense, the acceptance of any alternative end which might destroy this prior humanistic one. In the case of the second position, the politician or head of state accepts the survival of the state as the supreme goal, and he rejects, therefore, the idea that there are limits to permissible action. While he did not intend that the statesman be given carte blanche to do any act whatsoever, he did mean to grant to the statesman the right to perform absolutely any act needed to preserve the state. While Weber's essay suggests that the problem is basically one of ends versus means, this is surely not what differentiates the traditional or modern conflict between moralists and statesmen over the use of war. What is, for the Christian of the first century, the summum bonum of human life, is for the statesman of the Empire replaced by the summum bonum of national survival. The former could scarcely adopt a means that destroyed human life, while the latter could sacrifice human lives since he did not value them above the life of the state. Put in very simple terms, the problem of the just war became one of reconciling early Christian compunction with later political necessity.

Historically the medieval thesis of the just war was to set limits to the so-called "reasons of state" without at the same time denying that right of the state to survive, apparently at any cost. The just war criteria set hypothetical limits, but at no point was it intended to require states to surrender their sovereignty. In operation the criteria of the just war established the rules by which states ought to defend themselves. These rules aimed to curb excessively inhumane war practices, where they were not really needed, to reduce the number of reasons that could justify a war, to assure that the means of war bore some proportional relation to the ends of war, and generally to reduce the number of wars that actually occurred. There was no doubt in the Middle Ages that the concept functioned as a defense of national sovereignty, and of the right of nations to defend themselves by war in a basically lawless world. It made national survival feasible, while making international organization unlikely. If the rules for just wars seemed counsels of perfection, it was clear enough in practice that they set no serious limits to the aspirations of Princes.

Since the notion of the just war has been revived after nearly two centuries of silence on the issue, it is appropriate to look again at the general principles of the medieval position to determine whether, if they had a defense then, they have any defense now. The entire case for the medieval thinker rested, of course, on a concession which itself needs reassessment: namely, that war has a place in the moral scheme. Traditional questions about war were prudential, and the discussion centered on such questions as to time, place, and cause. Wars were presumed to be neutral means which could be given moral properties under the appropriate conditions. Wars were criticised, if at all, in practice rather than in principle. In this regard, medieval discussion of capital punishment shared common predicates. It wasn't the fact of killing that was the determinant, but rather the reasons given for the acts of killing that were decisive. How did the medieval thinker develop this notion?

The Criteria of Saint Thomas

In order for a war to be just three general conditions had to be met: (1) an authoritative sovereign must declare the war, (2) a just cause is required, and (3) the men who wage the war must have noble intentions and moderate means so that some good actually results. Furthermore, the good that results should be greater by some magnitude than the evil that must be produced by waging war. In the application of these criteria very few criticisms of war emerged, suggesting that Princes were remarkably wise and beneficent, or else that the criteria of the just war were too vague to be discriminating. In addition to the paucity of critique against wars, what protest there was came from persons not officially in government so that their objection was a kind of baying at the moon. George Fox, for example, challenged the wars of Cromwell, but then Fox was a pacifist who rejected all wars and could thus be dismissed as unrealistic. Franciscus de Victoria, a theological professor at the University of Salamanca in the 16th century, chastised his Spanish superiors for their wars against the American Indians.[1] University professors, however, were no more influential in effecting changes in foreign policy in the 16th century than they appear to be now, and thus such remarks as these constituted a kind of irrelevant campus protest.

More recently, Joseph McKenna[2] has revived the just war doctrine with an expanded list of seven conditions. They are: (1) the war must be declared by the duly constituted authority, (2) the seriousness of the injury inflicted on the enemy must be proportional to the damage suffered by the virtuous, (3) the injury to the aggressor must be real and immediate, (4) there must be a reasonable chance of winning the war, (5) the use of war must be a last resort, (6) the participants must have right intentions, and (7) the means used must be moral. The problem before us is whether such criteria can be made applicable to modern war. To put the issue this way suggests that the methodology of war is a datum entailing its justice, and it insinuates that the weapons of war determine to some degree the morality of war. This brings us back to the medieval position that it is not so much a question of killing as it is the manner of the killing that really counts.

Just War Is One Declared by the Duly Constituted Authority

For a theologian like Saint Augustine or Saint Thomas, who presumed some ameliorating influence from Christian prelates, such a criterion might be considered to constitute a limitation on careless heathen scoundrels. Since both worthy Saints accepted heathen Princes as duly constituted, it was not obvious how this influence was supposed to work. By the 16th century, however, with the proliferation of

[1] Franciscus de Victoria, *On The Law of War*. Washington, D.C. The Carnegie Institute, 1917. Section 22.
[2] "Ethics and War: A Catholic View." *American Political Science Review*. September, 1960. pp. 647–658.

Princes, and the fading away of Christian prelates, a radically new situation had emerged. By this time the "reasons of state" as Machiavelli elaborated them, permitted every Prince to wage war whenever he deemed it fit. Since by the 18th century war had become the sport of kings, it was clear that authorities had no special claim to sensitivity or good sense.

The rise of nationalism made this first criterion undifferentiating. It became increasingly obvious that to grant to any Prince the privilege of judging his neighboring prelates posed an odd situation. Every Prince judged every other Prince and was in turn judged by them, and there appeared to be a kind of gentleman's agreement not to be too critical of each other. It was this anomaly that led Grotius and Victoria to insist that while only one side of a war should properly be considered to be just, in fact persons on both sides could, in good conscience, presume that they had justice on their respective sides. In the absence of any international judge, no one was in a position to assess the claims of the national judges.

If rulers were saints or scholars there might be some reason to suppose that their judgments on war were adequate, and that they would not declare war for scurrilous reasons. At least two obstacles lay in the way of such a likelihood occurring. In the first place, the permissible reasons for waging war were so inclusive that virtually any conceivable princely aim could get support. Even wars of vindictive justice were permitted. In the second place, there were no plausible reasons to suppose that secular leaders had intentions that would meet even minimal standards of humaneness. It is not necessary to have in mind leaders like Hitler, Mussolini, Tojo, or Thieu to see that this is so. There is nothing in the nature of the process by which leaders are selected to give assurance that the leaders of France, England, or America have moral insights that are even as good as the average, let alone sufficiently discerning to be used as the criteria for a just war. We do not imagine our Princes to be especially gifted in domestic policy. Why should we imagine that they are wise as Solomon in foreign affairs?

Even clerics have had a rather poor reputation for sound moral judgment. Witness, for example, the stand of Archbishop Groeber of Freiburg-im-Breisgau who rejected Christian pacifism for German Catholics on the grounds that Hitler was the duly constituted authority. Pope Pius XII was no more reassuring on this point when he rejected the right of conscientious objection for German Catholics at the time of the formation of NATO. This first criterion of the duly constituted authority seems, therefore, to serve no distinguishing function at all. Indeed it is so ambiguous that applied to the present conflict in Vietnam both Ho Chi Minh and Thieu would satisfy the condition since they have declared war, while the American part in the war would be unjust since no war declaration has been made by the duly constituted authority.

A Just War Uses Means Proportional to the Ends

Franciscus de Victoria (1480–1546) observed that if to retake a piece of territory would expose a people to "intolerable ills and heavy woes,"[3] then it would not be

---

[3] Victoria, op. cit., Sections 33, 37.

just to retake it. We must be sure, he continued, that the evils we commit in war do not exceed the evils we claim to be averting. This was appropriate general advice, but in the absence of any specific suggestions as to how to make such measurement of relative ills, it was not even a helpful counsel of perfection, let alone a practical guide in the concrete situation. How do we measure proportionality? This was the problem of the hedonic calculus on which Mill's system first foundered. Since Victoria granted to Princes the right to despoil innocent children, if military necessity required it, it ceased to be apparent what proportionality meant at all. When this was combined with an equal vagueness on what constituted military necessity, the net contribution amounted to zero.

In a recent paper on this issue Father John A. Connery[4] stated that the morality of the violence depends on the proportionality of this violence to that of the aggression. Here again, what is required is some calculus to make this measurement. The latitude with which conscientious persons have interpreted what is proportional as a response suggests, what was clear enough to Mill, that we possess neither the quantitative nor the qualitative yardstick for such a decision. Pope Pius XII believed that the annihilation of vast numbers of persons was impermissible. Did he then intend for nations to surrender if the only price for success was such annihilation? Since the Pope was not explicit on this matter, John Courtney Murray[5] assumed that the papal prohibition was a conditional one. It was merely that large numbers of persons ought not to be slaughtered needlessly. Such a view, however, makes Pope Pius XII appear like a fool, for either he did not mean what he appeared to be saying, or he had not thought through the implications of what he appeared to be saying.

Proportionality is a slippery term unless there is some measure. Herbert Hoover thought in 1939 that the aerial bombing of cities was beyond moral proportion, although he did urge the U.S. to build bombing planes to perform this banned action. Jacques Maritain also put bombing from the air in the category of an absolutely proscribed act.[6] But how is such a determination made? In the early period of World War II "saturation bombing" was considered to be too inhumane for the American citizens to accept. Our military practiced instead what was euphemistically called "precision bombing." But even here where measurement would seem most plausible, the distinction was empty. This was illustrated when the Air Force announced at the time of the first test shot of the Atlas missile, that a bomb that lands within fifty miles of its target is considered accurate.[7]

In the concept of proportionality the medieval theorist introduced a distinction that made no difference. It is all very well to insist that actions be proportional, but if there are no criteria for the determination of proportionality, then the advice is not even a helpful counsel of perfection, let alone a useful curb to military excesses. Here again history reports the vacuity of the criterion. In the days of

---

[4] "Morality and Nuclear Armament." in William J. Nagle (Ed.) *Morality and Modern Warfare.* Baltimore: Helicon, 1960, p. 92.
[5] *Morality and Modern War.* New York: The Council on Religion and International Affairs, 1959, p. 9.
[6] "War and the Bombardment of Cities." *Commonweal.* September 2, 1938.
[7] Nagle, op. cit., p. 107.

the cross-bow it was deemed necessary to remind military men of proportionality in relation to the ends to be preserved. If this was needful then, what about proportionality in the use of guns, fragmentation bombs, germ and chemical weapons, and thermonuclear explosives. Since the ends to be preserved by the cross-bow are essentially the same as those to be preserved by the H-bomb, one would expect that if there could have been an excessive use of the bow, then modern weapons could have no proportional use at all.

During World War II the English writer, Vera Brittain, attacked both Britain and America for the bombing of civilians in her book, *Massacre by Bombing*. Here was an opportunity to see whether proportionality was still alive. Mrs. Brittain said that the bombing of civilians was not proportional to the threat or to the goal to be achieved. The Protestant journal, *The Christian Century*, editorialized in support of the bombing of civilians. The American Bar Association defeated a resolution calling for a condemnation of the bombing of civilians.[8] *The Saturday Evening Post* suggested that it was a sign of "instability" to question the need for the bombing of civilians. Orthodox clergy like the Reverend Carl McIntyre and the Reverend H. J. Ockenga called Mrs. Brittain's position "un-American and pro-Fascist." Can such positions be defended on the basis of proportionality? Whether they can or not, the fact is that they were not so defended.

Proportionality, in use, appears to have been a justification for increasing escalation, rather than a curb to ascending violence. John Courtney Murray, in an essay on "Morality and Modern War,"[9] defended the survival of American culture as well as of the American state on the grounds that it was without peer in any moral system. Furthermore, he saw Communism as a kind of Anti-Christ, so evil and so destructive of the values of his personal national outlook, that he defended any means necessary to their preservation. The possibility of the loss of the pure and noble Western capitalist, democratic, and Christian culture was so unpleasant to him that he was able to tolerate the intolerable, think the unthinkable, and admit a cosmic amount of human destruction as quite proportional to the ends and the threat. Is there, indeed, any measure for such an assessment? The medieval concern with misplaced sword-thrusts is qualitatively unrelated to the contemporary calculation with the mega-death of civilians. Unless some case could be made that the modern values are infinitely more worthy than medieval values, the immense increase in human destruction that our wars now involve makes proportionality absolutely inapplicable.

In the medieval calculation, wars for religion were considered to be unsupportable. Waging wars for religious reasons, such as the goal of conversion to Christianity or of abolishing heathenism, was classed as simply disproportional to war's havoc. Part of the medieval rejection of religious war, at least in principle, rested on their objection to wars against ideas or abstractions. Such an antipathy may be supported from a variety of bases. Conversion to an idea is normally considered a function of education, not of war. The method of war is simply not suited to changing opinion. In addition, false opinion or even heretical doctrine is not so cosmic an evil that war could be considered the lesser of two so-called evils.

[8] *New York Times*, July 15, 1939, p. 3.
[9] Murray, op. cit., p. 6.

Much of the modern just war theorizing presumes that wars for politics are proportionally defensible, and it would seem that the medieval reasons against wars for religion hold here with equal cogency. Our twentieth century wars to save democracy, freedom, or to banish fascism, communism, or socialism have failed signally to alter opinion or to establish new thinking on such generalities. War is, in this regard, not a form of debate or of mental persuasion. As a matter of fact persons live well under a variety of economic and political systems—communist, socialist, capitalist, monarchic, democratic, or republican, even fascist. They can equally live poorly under these same systems—the Jews in Germany, the Blacks in the United States, and the Orientals in Australia. Wars for ideology not only misunderstand the sources of human ills, but they are, in part because of this misunderstanding, all out of proportion. Even our most callous storm-trooper does not recommend the bomb on Selma, Little Rock, or Chicago, while some of our most sensitive leaders propose simple genocide on Vietnam for putative ideological reasons.

Consideration of the current discussion of what is called "rational nuclear armament" suggests that the criterion calling for just means or for proportionality in our actions of war is only a verbal genuflection. Dr. Kahn, famous for his ability to think the unthinkable, has recommended in the interests of proportionality that bombs be limited to the one-half megaton class. Since this is fifty times greater than the bomb dropped on Hiroshima proportionality has obviously become a rather loose term. This is the same conclusion we reach in the context of the language of "overkill" or "megakill." If we have enough bombs to kill every person in a country twice, or in effect twice as many bombs as we actually need to exterminate the population, then it makes no moral sense to speak of the reduction of bombs to the precise amount needed as illustrating any degree of humane or ethical proportion. To be sure there is a mathematical difference, and from the point of view of the military-educational-industrial complex there is a production difference. From the point of view of moral distinctions, however, there is no difference at all. The use of too much "firepower" is an economic waste, not a superfluity of immorality.

War May Justly Be Taken
Only As a Last Resort

In conventional discourse the notion of a "last resort" presupposes some notion of "first resort." Thus, unless a nation could show that it had indeed exhausted first resorts, it would make no sense for that nation to claim any right to use the last resort. First resorts might be such alternatives as economic, social, or political boycott, negotiations through the U.N. or through some unilateral means, and, of course, surrender is a first resort. Now let us assume that the first resorts have all been attempted, and that there appear to be no non-violent alternatives nor any violent options less destructive than war. We would still need to show that the last resort of war ought to be taken in this case. To permit war as a last resort is not the same as requiring that the last resort be taken. To say that war is a last resort is not the same as granting the right to go to war. It is possible that the last resort that can morally be defended is the first resort that is taken. This is clearer in a case like that of the Nazi treatment of the Jews than it is usually seen to be in actions of our own nation like our treatment of the Blacks or of the Vietnamese. Could the Germans have defended the statement: "Having exhausted every other resort to remove the threat of the Jews to Aryan supremacy, may we now as a last resort, open the gas chambers?"

What confuses the case in war is the presumption that war is a proper resort at all, while domestically we assume citizens deserve better treatment. Somehow we contemporaries have retained the legitimacy of the means of war in spite of the escalation of its instruments and the scope of its use. In domestic gas chambers, on the contrary, we draw the line at excess. Some American states still use gas chambers on offenders, but these same defenders of local gas chambers were offended by the German use of them. It was as if they were saying that gas chambers as methods are proper or proportional as a last resort, provided that they are not used too widely. Or that the use of gas chambers was an appropriate last resort provided that the offense was of a certain magnitude. If all the German Jews had been culpable by American standards of offenses that in America would have sent them to the gas chambers, then, the conjecture seems to be, it would have been a proper last resort for the German Nazis to administer Belsen, Buchenwald, and the rest.

Most contemporary defense of the just war doctrine bypasses an important decisional matter: is the expression "just war" different in kind from the expressions "just murder," "just torture," "just genocide," or even "just annihilation of innocents." Since the words "murder," "torture," and "genocide" are pejorative, and communicate a clear moral condemnation as to their practice, we surely need to show that "war" is not also this kind of pejorative term. If war were shown to be a kind of murder, would just war theorists now wish to speak of just murder? At least a part of the implication of the War Crimes Trials in Nuremberg was that if war did become murder or genocide then it could not be justified. Thus in some cases, at least, war could not be considered as even a viable or justifiable last resort.

In this day of massive retaliation and mega-kill, the justification of war as any resort at all requires a defense that medieval concepts are unable to support. If persons are of the value that medieval theology assigned to them, then the sheer scope and devastation of modern war makes it impossible to find another value so over-riding that an Hiroshima becomes the lesser of two evils, and that war becomes a proper resort at all. The military claim that Ben Tre was destroyed to save Ben Tre makes no sense in the language of resorts. That vacuous maxim "military necessity" has led us to endorse unbelievable slaughter on the inference that what is militarily necessary must be morally approvable. There has never been a clear explication of what is militarily necessary, and furthermore, there has been no argument to show that morality should take its cue from generals. Paul Ramsey, the distinguished Protestant advocate of the just war thesis, endorses the use of thermonuclear bombs on civilians if military necessity requires it.[10] Ob-

---

[10] "Just War and Reasons of State," in Robert W. Tucker, *Just War and Vatican Council II: A Critique*. New York: The Council on Religion and International Affairs, 1966, pp. 68f.

viously the only way to answer his claim that this is not too great a price to pay is to consult the living, but equally the only way for him to defend his thesis is for him to consult the dead.

Since the doctrine of the just war has become the verbal tool of military theologians or moral tacticians of war, no one seriously considers that surrender might be the most moral option, making it additionally clear that the discussants are speaking only for nations that win wars. Indeed, if the just war has any credence at all, there should be situations where the wise Prince surrenders rather than declare war. Politicians and military strategists argue from premises of national sovereignty and a proper power struggle, not from a concern with virtue, and this is further reason why modern carnage turns out to be just. That there is a blind spot on this forbidden notion of surrender was illustrated by the spectacle in August, 1958, when the Senate of the United States voted 82 to 2 to deny government funds to any person or institution that proposes or actually conducts any study regarding the possible results of the surrender of the U.S. as an alternative to war. Since nations with arms are loth to succumb to their national neighbors, and moreover to do so over concern with whether first resorts still remain, about all the theory of last resort tells us is that war is a resort that nations are bound to take.

A Just War Must Be Waged by Men with Right Intentions

This issue has a direct relation to the question of whether war is an appropriate resort, first or last. Both what we intend to do and what we intend to preserve are related to whether it can be said that our intentions in war are actually just. Vatican II spoke to this matter when it reported: "As long as the danger of war remains and there is no competent and sufficiently powerful authority at the international level, governments cannot be denied the right to legitimate defense once every means of peaceful settlement has been exhausted."[11] But are there no limits on any governments? Isn't it conceivable that Nazi Germany did not deserve to survive, any more than the government of Thieu in South Vietnam? Is the preservation of the state so incontrovertibly significant that the resort to war to save it is always an act of right intention?

Much of the medieval controversy over intentionality revolved around the doctrine of the "double-effect." A just belligerent intended only as much killing as was proportional to the threat, and he was responsible only for the deaths he intended to cause. It was, of course, assumed that he did not intend to kill noncombatants. That this was the ideal, not always implemented in practice, was borne out by the concessions of men from Saint Thomas to Victoria that military necessity might justify even the despoiling of innocents. Still the medieval concern with the death of the by-stander was one that could be implemented. Their weapons made such a concern practical. Although an archer might shoot his arrow into the

---

[11] *Pastoral Constitution on the Church in the Modern World.* Part II, Chapter V. National Catholic Welfare Conference, 1966.

air and not be too clear as to where it landed, he was not in doubt as to whether he was aiming it at combatants. He might miss a small barn, but he did hit the right city. Modern weapons make such a concern with the innocents inoperable and unfeasible. In addition, the fact that so many non-combatants are killed in modern war, a number commonly exceeding that of the soldiers, suggests that something is awry. Instead of proper regret for the scope of modern weapons of destruction on the civilians, contemporaries have theorized that the class of non-combatants is now a null class. The limited war of the past has been replaced by the total war of the present—total in the sense that military necessity now justifies the death of all without exception. The medieval man might pardonably weep for the accidentally slain civilians, but modern man cannot afford to weep since he knows that he intends the death of every person slain.

This problem of unwanted or unintended death has always been an harassing one. In 1076 at a Council in Winchester, England the cases were considered of men who had fought with William the Conqueror at the Battle of Hastings. Many of the soldiers were troubled by the memory of the men they had slain, and in the case of archers, with the thought that they had slain some unknowingly. Archers were assigned the penance of daily prayers for the rest of their lives for the un-known deaths they may have caused. No comparable cleric or council concern has emerged in the twentieth century. Now when our weapons make our intentions to no avail, we cling to the weapons and adjust our intentions to our moral yard-stick. If military necessity now requires the mega-death of civilians, then modern theorists will show that such intended deaths are consistent with the doctrine of right intentions. If medieval men suffered pangs of guilt for ricocheting arrows, modern men exhibit no comparable concern for Dresden, Tokyo, Hiroshima, Nagasaki, or Ben Tre. When we realize, in addition, that "double-effect" is not something that plays a role in military tactics or political strategy, it is apparent that moral concerns at this point are rather ivory tower ephemera.

A further problem with intentionality is that of showing that the means of war are appropriate even for those persons considered to be fair game because they are combatants. Nowhere has the ingenuity of man been more exercised than in the enterprise of developing "humane" ways to exterminate his fellows. In 1041 the Bishop of Arles and the Abbot of Cluny established the "truce of God" which limited the times when war could properly be carried out. Initially, war was per-mitted only between Monday morning and Wednesday evening, and holy days could further delimit this range. The "peace of God" decreed at the Council of Narbonne in 1054 limited the kinds of persons who could properly be attacked. By the sixteenth century Pierino Belli[12] while urging that war remain a conflict only of armed soldiers concluded that the rules of the "peaces" may safely be ignored.

In every age the attempt was made anew to proscribe some war weapons even against combatants. William Paley eschewed poison and assassination.[13] J. G. Fichte considered the use of snipers to be "downright illegal."[14] Pope Pius XII added his

[12] Pierino Belli, *A Treatise On Military Matters*. Oxford: Clarendon Press, 1936. p. 81.
[13] William Paley, *Moral Philosophy*, Volume IV. London: C. and J. Rivington, 1825. p. 531.
[14] J. G. Fichte, *The Science of Rights*. Philadelphia: J. B. Lippincott, 1869, p. 484.

anathema against poison gas.[15] By the time Hitler declaimed against attack from the air as too inhumane to be tolerated,[16] it should have occurred to all that this discussion left something to be desired. The Hague Declarations of 1899 and 1907 made "prohibited" the discharge of projectiles from the air, the use of asphyxiating gases, expanding bullets, contact mines, and torpedoes which remain dangerous after they have missed their mark.[17] Little remained for soldiers to do save to joust in the knightly fashion of the middle ages. The absurdity of such an exercise was sharpened by the remarks of a doctor to the Berlin Military Medical Society in 1885 on the discovery of a high-speed, non-expanding bullet. "I welcome the new bullet with great joy and believe that if it were generally adopted by international consent, all humanity would have cause to rejoice."[18] He called this new type bullet "humane." Haven't we lost something of the medieval sense of humane intention if we can talk seriously in this fashion? Yet the mandate against expanding bullets so impressed Hiram Maxim (1840–1916) that he considered his machine gun to be "the greatest life-saving instrument ever invented."[19]

Serious discussion among just war theorists today about the limits of just intention rarely begins until thermonuclear weapons. The whole range of "lesser" evils has been reconciled into the moral scheme. Only new tools of destruction pose any problem. Thus Richard J. Krickus[20] believed that chemical bombs were moral while biological bombs were not. Part of his reasoning rested on the thesis that control was more possible with the former than with the latter, but also that there has been a long religious-psychic association between germs and evil. Still napalm, anti-personnel shrapnel, and expanding bullets posed no moral dilemmas.

The Gas Chamber has been a disturbing symbol in modern times of a possible limit to how man can justly treat his fellows. Since we in America use gas chambers for domestic offenders, it must have been something other than the tool itself that led to the War Crimes Trials against the Nazis. Perhaps it was that the Germans gassed the wrong persons. Would the deed have been palatable if they had killed only soldiers, and had left the women, children, and civilian men alone? Was it that the Nazis killed the Jews for the wrong reasons? If the Nazis were being exterminated in Belsen would there be no moral problem? Is there a way to calculate that the death of twenty civilians poses a different moral problem from the death of twenty soldiers? Is it worse to kill twenty children than to kill twenty adults? Perhaps there is no way to calculate the relative horrors in these alternatives, but it is precisely this kind of question that the just war theorists must answer.

Our problem here is one of calculating the relative evil of war with the relative evil of any alternative. And surely part of the relevant variables includes the magnitude of the weapons, and the scope of their application to various persons normally considered to be innocent or at least non-combatant. Since it is unlikely that the

[15] C'est une Vive Satisfaction." September 14, 1939.
[16] Adolf Hitler, *My New Order*. New York: Reynal and Hitchcock, 1941, p. 951.
[17] Carnegie Endowment for International Peace. Pamphlets 1–22.
[18] I. S. Bloch, *The Future of War*. New York: Doubelday, 1902, p. 150.
[19] Hiram Maxim, *Defenseless America*. New York: Hearst, 1915, p. 83.
[20] Richard J. Krickus, "On the Morality of Chemical/Biological War." *Journal of Conflict. Resolution.* June, 1965. pp. 200–210.

values now claimed to be the justification for war are any better, let alone any different, from those in the Middle Ages, the increased destruction of war must surely be germane to the question whether war as a means can be made just at all any more. If in the Middle Ages some wars were conceivably less tragic than the alternatives, although live illustrations would be hard to find, modern wars are so ghastly and so much more destructive of the humane virtues than the alternatives, that to justify war now seems to justify too much.

Conclusion

We are back to our starting point and the problem, as yet unpersuasively resolved, is to show that war is a potentially moral means at all. While we know the legal distinction between killing done by private citizens (called murder) and the killing done by soldiers in the name of the state (called war) and the killing done by the state to its criminals (called capital punishment), the moral indictment against taking life once applied equally to every instance. Surely it made no difference to the person slain what the circumstances of his death were, or by what name the deed was called. "Thou shalt not kill" once had an absolute ring to it. Since human life was the supreme value, taking it was a supreme disvalue, and extenuating circumstances did not alter this assessment. Furthermore, the question of self-defense posed an apparent dilemma to the matter of human life. If each person has a right to self-defense, at the price of the death of the opponent, hasn't there occurred a radical reorganization of relative values? Or isn't it rather that self-defense, while a ubiquitous political right renowned in oratory, is not a moral right at all. Nor, doubtless, is the supposed right of national defense any more rooted in moral axioms. In fact, for rather evident reasons national survival is less important than personal survival. The former can be revived should it be thought a good idea, while dead citizens are irrevocably gone.

What has not yet been demonstrated by the just war theorist is the radical distinction he draws between killing in war and killing under any other circumstance. The following illustration is not resolved by any just war dogmas yet devised. Suppose we are the Aryans, genuinely confronted by "mongrelization" by the Jews, and we approach our problem with the concepts and axioms of the medieval theologian. Our problem is that of the "just pogrom." Aryans may, of course, exterminate the Jews provided that the duly constituted leader declares the pogrom. Furthermore, the "death camps" need to be administered with means proportional to the threat, taking special care not to kill non-Jews. With this minimum presumption the citizens may kill the Jews if the Prince commands it with reasons as good as outlined. Cultural defense, like national defense, once granted as a supreme good, will allow all the gas chambers needed to preserve it. This is what military necessity justifies. The citizens would, in adddition, be expected to implement the State Department policy of the "containment of Judaism" and to seek to rid by every means creeping Jews from the world. With no more intellectual effort than the just war theory requires we would be able to conduct the pogrom in accordance of the "laws of pogroms." Our means would naturally be humane gas chambers and sanitary ovens. With pure hearts we could march to

Armageddon, with "just war" or "just pogrom" emblazoned on our banners. But isn't this to justify too much?

There are several presuppositions in conventional just war theory that make any resolution, short of ultimate annihilation under a mushroom-shaped cloud, unlikely.

1. Given a world of sovereign nation states, and without any adjudicating power, and given that such nations deserve to survive ultimately and unquestionably, then no moral doctrine can take away the right of states to do whatever is needful for their continuation.

2. Given war as a proper method, at worst neutral in quality and at best endowed with virtue, then no moral doctrine can attack war because it contains both the weapons and the deeds that destroy human life. It would be comparable to condemning the surgeon and his scalpel since there is a risk that the patient may die. Obviously the analogy is not quite appropriate here since the successful soldier kills his "patient," while the successful surgeon saves his patient.

3. Given that the state is more important than the individual, indeed, that the state is more important than an infinite number of individuals, mere human death will never be a significant argument against war.

But, if this much be "given" then what is left for just war theory to adjudicate? Generally, it will be able to resolve what the medieval theorists claimed, namely:

1. It can resolve that the war was properly announced.

2. It can assess reasons, other than national defense, for their appropriateness. It must, of course, be recognized that national defense is the only reason theorists give any more, and thus there really isn't any assessment called for.

3. It can determine that the means are proportional to the end of national defense. But unless it is clearly stated how long it is proper to wage a war, how great a human price it is proper to pay, what subsidiary losses in property, culture, or manner of living it is moral to suffer—this is, what "military necessity" consists of—than there really isn't anything save an hypothetical exercise in casuistry that can engage the effort of the just war spokesman.

With these limitations, discussion of the just war can raise merely questions of consistency within the set of given axioms, and engage in a kind of aesthetic or psychological exercise in sensitivity. In the context of the presuppositions with which theories of the just war must operate, the "just war" justifies too much.

Four

Humanity in
Search of Virtue

Introduction

Twenty-five hundred years ago Socrates confounded the citizens of Athens with a question that was as difficult to answer as it was easy to put: Can virtue be taught? Those who had the self-sincerity to follow Socrates' line of inquiry found to their amazement that to become virtuous required a subtle and lifelong struggle involving all the parts of human nature that have been spoken about in the previous section. From this perspective, the inward dimension of the crises of the modern world becomes apparent: the world is what it is because the individual human being is what he is. Virtue is a power that can only be obtained in a new condition of the self.

The present chapter presents a variety of points of view on the meaning of virtue, the power to be and act upon what we know to be good, and the nature of the obstacles that stand in the way of virtue. We open with the classic statement of **St. Augustine,** reflecting upon an apparently minor childhood "sin" of stealing fruit from a neighbor's orchard. In this act, Augustine discerns what he takes to be the essential error of the soul that lies at the heart of all real crime: the turning toward the things of this world for that which can only be found through a relationship with God.

From St. Augustine we move to an American follower of the Hare Krishna movement, writing under the name **Viśākhā-devī dāsī.** Here sin and virtue are understood in terms of mechanicalness and freedom: even the "good" life is not spiritually good if it is the mere result of identifying ourselves with the body or mind and living under the influence of forces that govern body and mind. Seen from this angle, acceptable morality may actually be an obstruction to religious morality which emanates from inner or spiritual freedom.

Our next selection is by one of the wittiest and most penetrating religious thinkers of the twentieth century, **C. S. Lewis.** In this excerpt from his classic work, *The Screwtape Letters*, the protagonist, a "senior devil" named Screwtape, advises his protégé, a "junior devil" named Wormwood, on the subtle techniques of converting incipient virtues to actual sins, while keeping the "patient" (man) under the illusion that he is a Christian. At the same time, however, Screwtape warns his "pupil" that what may appear to be a movement of doubt in his patient may actually be the beginning of a turning toward virtue from within, independent of external stimuli. "Our cause," Screwtape writes, "is never more in danger than when a human, no longer desiring, but still intending, to do our Enemy's will, looks around upon a universe from which every trace of Him seems to have vanished, and asks why he has been forsaken, and still obeys."

From the anatomy of sin, we turn to a brilliant metaphysical speculation about the meaning of virtue as exemplified by the figure of Christ. In this brief and daring note, **Simone Weil** "proves" the inevitability of the Incarnation as the sole means of absorbing the evil that men do.

Following that, **Heinrich Zimmer,** who was perhaps the greatest Western interpreter of the traditions of India, outlines the ideal of virtue represented by the Buddhist concept of the Bodhisattva, the saint who defers his own final liberation to work for the liberation of all sentient beings. As Zimmer presents it, the way of the Bodhisattva is meant to be a guide to all human beings in search of a more authentically human relationship to others through a new understanding of their own desires and fears.

Finally, **Maurice Nicoll,** one of the most creative modern interpreters of the New Testament, defines the ideal of Christian virtue in terms of psychological rebirth. This idea of an actual psychological event resulting in a higher level of being is what Nicoll identifies as the central meaning of the parables of Christ. As long as this psychological event does not take place in man, argues Nicoll, none of the virtues of action which have attracted Western man through the centuries are realizable, except in an imitative and deceptive way.

J. N.

Sin

St. Augustine

St. Augustine (354–430), Bishop of Hippo, was perhaps the most influential theologian of the Catholic tradition. Before his conversion, he was deeply affected by Neo-Platonic thought with its doctrine of a supersensible realm of higher reality of which the material world is but an expression. Among his voluminous body of writings, the best-known are the *Confessions* and *The City of God.*

1

I want to call back to mind my past impurities and the carnal corruptions of my soul, not because I love them, but so that I may love you, my God. It is for the love of your love that I do it, going back over those most wicked ways of mine in the bitterness of my recollection so that the bitterness may be replaced by the sweetness of you. O unfailing sweetness, happy sweetness and secure! And gathering myself together from the scattered fragments into which I was broken and dissipated during all that time when, being turned away from you, the One, I lost myself in the distractions of the Many.

For in that youth of mine I was on fire to take my fill of hell. Outrageously in all my shady loves I began to revert to a state of savagery: *my beauty consumed away* and I stank in your sight; pleasing myself and being anxious to please in the eyes of men.

2

And what was it that delighted me? Only this—to love and be loved. But I could not keep that true measure of love, from one mind to another mind, which marks the bright and glad area of friendship. Instead I was among the foggy exhalations which proceed from the muddy cravings of the flesh and the bubblings of first manhood. These so clouded over my heart and darkened it that I was unable to distinguish between the clear calm of love and the swirling mists of lust. I was storm-tossed by a confused mixture of the two and, in my weak unstable age, swept over the precipices of desire and thrust into the whirlpools of vice. Your wrath had gathered above me, and I was not aware of it. I had grown deaf through the clanking of the chain of my mortality. This was your punishment for my soul's pride. I was going further and further from you, and you let me be. I was tossed here and there, spilled on the ground, scattered abroad; I boiled over in my fornications. And still you were silent, O my joy so slow in coming! Then you were silent, and I went on

Source: St. Augustine, *Confessions,* trans. by Rex Warner, pp. 40–51. Reprinted by permission of Omega Press.

going further from you and further, making my way into more and more of these sterile plantations of sorrow, arrogant in my dejection and still restless in my weariness.

How I wish that there had been someone at that time to put a measure on my disorder and to turn to good use the fleeting beauties of these new temptations and to put limits to their delights. Then the waves of my youth might at last have spent themselves on the shore of marriage, if tranquility could not be found simply in the purposeful begetting of children, as your law, Lord, prescribes; for you shape even the offspring of our mortality and are able with a gentle hand to blunt the thorns which were excluded from your paradise. And not far from us is your omnipotence, even when we are far from you. Or certainly I ought to have listened with greater heed to the voice from those clouds of yours: *Nevertheless such shall have trouble in the flesh, but I spare you.* And, *it is good for a man not to touch a woman.* And, *he that is without a wife thinketh of the things of God, how he may please God; but he that is married thinketh of the things of the world, how he may please his wife.* I should have listened more carefully to words such as these, and should have become a *eunuch for the kingdom of heaven's sake,* so in greater happiness awaiting your embraces.

But I, poor wretch, boiled up and ran troubled along the course of my own stream, forsaking you. I broke through all the boundaries of your law but did not escape your chastisement. What mortal can? For you were always with me, angered against me in your mercy, scattering the most bitter discontent over all my illicit pleasures, so that thus I might seek for pleasure in which there was no discontent and be unable to find such a thing except in you, Lord, except in you, who shape sorrow to be an instructor, who give wounds in order to heal, who kill us lest we should die away from you. Where was I, and how far was I banished from the delights of your house in that sixteenth year of my flesh when the madness of lust (forbidden by your laws but too much countenanced by human shamelessness) held complete sway over me and to this madness I surrendered myself entirely! And those about me took no care to save me from falling by getting me married; their one aim was that I should learn how to make a good speech and become an orator capable of swaying his audience.

3

In this year there was a break in my studies. I came back home from Madaura, the nearby city to which I had gone to learn the beginnings of literature and rhetoric, and now money was being provided for me to go further afield, to Carthage. This was rather because my father had big ideas than because he was rich. He was only a poor citizen of Tagaste. But to whom am I relating this? Not to you, my God. But I am telling these things in your presence to my own kind, to that portion of mankind, however small it may be, which may chance to read these writings of mine. And my object in doing so is simply this: that both I myself and whoever reads what I have written may think *out of what depths we are to cry unto Thee.* For nothing comes nearer to your ears than a confessing heart and a life of faith.

At that time, then, people on all sides praised my father for spending more money than his means really allowed so that his son could be equipped with what was necessary for a long journey and be able to continue his studies. Many citizens much richer than my father did no such a thing for their children. And yet this father of mine was not at all interested in how I was growing up in relation to you, or how chaste I was. The only idea was that I should become "cultured," though this "culture" really meant a lack of cultivation from you, God, the one true and good landlord and farmer of this field of yours, my heart.

But in this sixteenth year of my age when, because of our straitened circumstances, I had a period of leisure, living at home with my parents and not doing any schoolwork at all, the brambles of lust grew up right over my head, and there was no hand to tear them up by the roots. In fact when my father saw me at the baths and noticed that I was growing toward manhood and showing the signs of the burgeoning of youth he told my mother of it with great pleasure, as though he were already confident of having grandchildren; but his pleasure proceeded from that kind of drunkenness in which the world forgets you, its creator, and falls in love with your creature instead of with you; so drugged it is with the invisible wine of a perverse self-will, bent upon the lowest objects. But in my mother's breast you had already begun to build your temple and had laid the foundation for your holy dwelling place. My father was still a catechumen, and had only been a catechumen for a short time. My mother, therefore, was seized with a holy fear and trembling; even though I was not yet baptized, she was alarmed for me, fearing those crooked ways which are trodden by those who turn their backs to you and not their face.

How bitter this is to me! And do I dare to say that you, my God, kept silent while I was going further and further from you? Did you really say nothing to me then? Whose words were they except yours which, by the means of my mother, your devoted servant, you kept crying in my ears? Not that any of them sank down into my heart and made me act in accordance with them. For it was her wish, and I remember how privately and with what great anxiety she warned me not to commit fornication and especially not to commit adultery with another man's wife. And these warnings seemed to me merely the sort of things which one might expect from a woman and which it would be a shame for me to follow. But, though I did not know it, these warnings came from you. I thought that you were silent and that it was my mother who was speaking; but you were not silent; you spoke to me through her, and in despising her I was despising you, I, her son, the son of your handmaid, I, your servant. But I did not know, I went headlong on my way, so blind that among people of my own age I was ashamed to be more modest than they were. I heard them boasting of their acts of vice (and the worse these were, the more they boasted), and so I enjoyed the pleasure not only of the act but also of the praise one got for having committed it.

What deserves censure except vice? I, to avoid censure, made myself more vicious than I was, and when, in fact, I had not committed a sin that would put me on a level with the worst sinners, I used to pretend that I had committed it, so that I might not be despised for my greater degree of innocence or thought less of for a comparative chastity. With what companions did I walk the streets of Babylon and wallow in its mire as though I lay in a bed of spices and precious ointments! And, so that I should stick the closer to the very center of it, the invisible enemy trod me underfoot and seduced me, since I was easy to seduce. And as to the mother of my flesh (who had herself already *fled out of the center of Babylon*, yet still lingered in the outskirts), she had certainly advised me to be chaste; but she did not give the attention she might have given to what she heard about me from her husband; she thought that if my desires could not be, as it were, cut off at the root, it would be unhealthy for the moment and dangerous for the future to restrain them within the bounds of the affections of marriage. The reason why she was against my getting married was that she feared that a wife would be a handicap to me in my hopes for the future, and these hopes were not those which my mother had of a future life in you; they were merely hopes that I might attain proficiency in literature. In these hopes both of my parents indulged too much—my father, because he hardly thought of you at all and only thought in the most trivial way about me; my mother, because, in her view, these usual courses of learning would be, not only no hindrance, but an actual help to me in attaining you. So at least I conjecture when I recollect to the best of my ability what the characters of my parents were. Meanwhile, the reins were loosened, I was given free play with no kind of severity to control me and was allowed to dissipate myself in all kinds of ways. In all of these was a mist cutting me off, my God, from the pure brightness of your truth, and *mine iniquity burst out as from my fatness.*

4

Certainly, Lord, your law punishes theft; indeed there is a law written in men's hearts which not iniquity itself can erase; for no thief will submit to being robbed by another; even a rich thief will not tolerate another man who is forced to steal by poverty. Yet I both wanted to steal and did steal, and I was not forced to it by any kind of want; it was only that I lacked and despised proper feeling and was stuffed with iniquity. For I stole something of which I had plenty myself, and much better than what I stole. I had no wish to enjoy what I tried to get by theft; all my enjoyment was in the theft itself and in the sin.

Near our vineyard there was a pear tree, loaded with fruit, though the fruit was not particularly attractive either in color or taste. I and some other wretched youths conceived the idea of shaking the pears off this tree and carrying them away. We set out late at night (having, as we usually did in our depraved way, gone on playing in the streets till that hour) and stole all the fruit that we could carry. And this was not to feed ourselves; we may have tasted a few, but then we threw the rest to the pigs. Our real pleasure was simply in doing something that was not allowed. Such was my heart, God, such was my heart which you had pity on when it was at the very bottom of the abyss. And now let my heart tell you what it was looking for there, that I became evil for nothing, with no reason for wrongdoing except the wrongdoing itself. The evil was foul, and I loved it; I loved destroying myself; I loved my sin—not the thing for which I had committed the sin, but the sin itself. How base a soul, falling back from your firmament to sheer destruction, not seeking some object by shameful means, but seeking shame for self!

5

Certainly the eye is pleased by beautiful bodies, by gold, and silver and all such things, and in the sense of touch a great part is played by a kind of reciprocity. All the other senses too have their own proper modulations with regard to their particular objects. Worldly honor also has its own grace and the power to command and prevail over others (from which comes too the eagerness to assert one's own rights); yet in following all these things, we must not depart from you, Lord, or transgress your law. The life too, which we live here, has its own enchantment because of a certain measure in its own grace and a correspondence with all these beautiful things of this world. And human friendship, knotted in affection, is a sweet thing because of the unity between many different souls which it expresses. Yet for all these things and all things of this sort sin is committed. For there are goods of the lowest order, and we sin if, while following them with too great an affection, we neglect those goods which are better and higher—you, our Lord God, and your truth and your law. Certainly these lower things have their delights, but not like my God, who made all things, *for in Him doth the righteous delight, and He is the joy of the upright in heart.*

So, when we inquire into why any particular crime was committed, the only motives which, as a rule, we regard as credible are when it appears that there might have been either a desire for gaining or a fear of losing some of these goods which we have described as "lower." For they certainly are objects of beauty and worth, although they are low and mean enough when compared with those higher goods which confer real happiness. Suppose a man has committed murder. Why did he do it? Perhaps he was in love with the other man's wife, or with his estate; or he wanted to rob him of his money in order to live himself; or he was afraid that the other man might despoil him of one of these things; or he had been injured and was eager to revenge himself. Certainly a man does not commit murder for no reason at all, simply for the pleasure of doing the deed. No one could believe such a thing. Even in the case of that brutal and savage man of whom it was said that he was evil and cruel just for the sake of evil and cruelty, there is still a reason given it for. It was (says Sallust) "to prevent his hand and heart from growing slow through inactivity." And why was that? Why indeed? Obviously the point of this exercise in crime was that, after having seized Rome, he might obtain honors, commands, and riches and, in his poverty and guilty knowledge of his own evil deeds, might be freed from all fear of the law and all financial difficulties. Even Catiline, therefore, did not love his own crimes; what he loved was something else, for the sake of which he committed them.

6

And what did I, wretched I, love in you, you theft of mine, you sin in the night committed by me in my sixteenth year? There was nothing beautiful about you, because you were merely theft. But are you in fact anything, for me to speak to you like this? Certainly the pears that we stole were beautiful since they were of your creation, yours, most beautiful of all, Creator of all, good God, God supremely good, and my true good. The pears certainly were beautiful, but it was not the pears that my miserable soul desired. I had plenty of better pears of my own; I only took these ones in order that I might be a thief. Once I had taken them I threw them away, and all I tasted in them was my own iniquity, which I enjoyed very much. For if I did put any of these pears into my mouth, what made it sweet to me was my sin. And now, my Lord God, I inquire what it was that delighted me in that act of theft. Clearly there is no beauty about it at all. I am not speaking about the beauty that is to be found in justice and wisdom; nor of that which is in the mind and memory and senses and animal life of man; nor of the stars, which, set in their places, are beautiful and glorious; nor the earth and the sea, which is full of new life constantly being born to replace what passes away; no, it has not even got that incomplete and shadowy beauty which we find in deceiving vices.

Pride too strives to appear as though it was high and lofty, whereas you alone are God high over all. Ambition's one aim is honor and glory, whereas you alone and before all else are to be honored and are glorious forever and ever. Great men in their anger wish to inspire fear; but who is to be feared except God alone? From His power what can be withdrawn or subtracted? And where, or when, or whither, or by whom? The tender endearments of passion aim at provoking love. But nothing can be more tender and more dear than your charity, and nothing can be loved more healthfully than your truth, that truth which is beautiful and brilliant above all things. Curiosity puts on the appearance of a zeal for knowledge, while you, in the highest degree, know everything. Even ignorance and mere foolishness go under the names of simplicity and innocence, because there is nothing more simple than you; and what can be more innocent than you, since what brings hurt to the wicked is their own actions? And laziness seems to be looking for rest; but what sure rest is there except in the Lord? Luxury would like to be called plenty and abundance; but you are the fullness and the unfailing supply of a sweetness that is incorruptible. Prodigality shows, as it were, the shadow of liberality; but you are the most supremely rich bestower of all good things. Avarice wishes to possess much: you possess everything. Envy disputes for the first place; what place is higher than yours? Anger seeks requital; what requital is more just than yours? Fear shows its agitation in the presence of what is unusual or sudden and endangering to things that are loved, and it tries to secure their safety. But to you nothing is unusual, nothing is sudden. No one can take away from you the thing which you love, and nowhere except with you is there real safety. Grief pines away at the loss of things in which the desire delighted; this is because it would like nothing to be taken away, just as nothing can be taken away from you.

So the soul commits fornication when she turns away from you and tries to find outside you things which, unless she returns to you, cannot be found in their true and pure state. So all men who put themselves far from you and set themselves up against you, are in fact attempting awkwardly to be like you. And even in this imitation of you they declare you to be the creator of everything in existence and that consequently there can be no place in which one can in any way withdraw oneself from you.

What then was it that I loved in that theft of mine? In what way, awkwardly and perversely, did I imitate my Lord? Did I find it pleasant to break your law and prefer to break it by stealth, since I could not break it by any real power? And was I thus, though a prisoner, making a show of a kind of truncated liberty, doing unpunished what I was not allowed to do and so producing a darkened image of omnipotence? What a sight! A servant running away from his master and following a shadow! What rottenness! What monstrosity of life and what abyss of death! Could I enjoy what was forbidden for no other reason except that it was forbidden?

7

What shall I render unto the Lord because, while my memory recalls these things, my soul is not terrified at them? *I will love Thee, O Lord, and thank Thee and confess unto Thy name*, because you have forgiven me these great sins and these evil doings of mine. To your grace I owe it, and to your mercy, that you have melted away my sins like ice. And to your grace too I owe the not doing of whatever evil I have not done. For what evil might I not have done, I who loved crime simply for crime's sake? Yes, I own it: all these evils have been forgiven me—both those which I committed of my own will and those which, because of your guidance, I did not commit.

No man who considers his own weakness can dare to say that it is because of his own virtue that he is chaste or innocent, and so love you less, as though he had less need of your mercy, by which you remit the sins of those that turn to you. And if a man has heard your voice and followed it and not committed those sins which he reads of in this recollection and confession of mine, he ought not to laugh at me, who was sick and then cured by the Physician owing to whose care he himself avoided sickness or rather was not so sick; for this he should love you just as much, or rather much more; he sees that I have recovered from the great weakness and depression of my sins, and he sees that my recovery was due to that same Physician who preserved him from being the victim of the same weakness and depression.

8

What advantage did I gain then, poor wretch, from these things which I now blush to remember? And in particular what advantage did I get from that act of theft, in which the only thing that I loved was just the act of theft itself, and it too was nothing, and I, therefore, who loved it, still more of a wretch. And yet I would not have done it by myself; for I can remember what I was like then; no, I would certainly never have done it by myself. Then in the act of theft I must have loved something else too, namely the company of those with whom I committed it. And so I did not love nothing except the theft itself; yet, no; indeed there was nothing else, since this fact of having accomplices is also nothing. What is the real truth of the matter? Who can teach me, except he who sheds his light into my heart and scatters the shadows that are within it? And what is it which makes me indulge in all this inquiry and discussion and consideration? For if I then loved the pears which I stole and desired to enjoy them, I could have committed the theft by myself, supposing that I merely had to do this in order to get what I wanted to enjoy; there was no need to raise the pruriency of my desire by the excitement of having others to share the guilt. No, it was in the sin itself and not in those pears that my pleasure lay— a pleasure occasioned by the company of others who were sinning with me.

9

Now what exactly was this feeling? Certainly it was a very bad one and a disgrace to me, who had it. But what exactly was it? *Who can understand his errors?* We laughed at it, as though our hearts were tickled at the thought that we were deceiving people who had no idea of what we were doing and who would have strongly disapproved of it. Why, then, was my pleasure of such a kind that still I did not do the act by myself? Was it because people do not generally laugh by themselves? Generally they do not; but nevertheless there are times when, if something really ridiculous occurs to the mind or is presented to the senses, people, even quite alone by themselves, will be overcome by laughter. But I would not have done that alone; no, certainly, I would not.

See, my God, in front of you this vivid memory of my soul. By myself I would not have committed that theft, in which what pleased me was not what I stole, but that I stole; nor would I have got any pleasure out of it by myself, nor would I have done it at all by myself. What an unfriendly friendship is this! What a seduction of the soul and how difficult to track! That out of mere fun and play should proceed an eagerness to hurt and an appetite to do harm to others and with no sort of a desire either to avenge myself or to gain anything for myself! It has only to be said: "Come on, let's do it," and we become ashamed at not being shameless.

10

Who can disentangle this most twisted and most inextricable knottiness? It is revolting; I hate to think of it; I hate to look at it. It is you that I desire, O justice and innocence, you who, to the eyes of the pure, are beauty and honesty, you, O plenteous unsating satisfaction. With you is true peace and life imperturbable. He who enters into you *enters into the joy of his Lord*; he shall have no fear; he shall be well indeed in him who is best of all. I slipped from you and went astray, my God, in my youth, wandering too far from my upholder and my stay, and I became to myself a wasteland.

Who's Pulling the Strings?

Viśākhā-devī dāsī

Viśākhā-devī dāsī was graduated from Rochester Institute of Technology in 1970 and then wrote a technical book on the art of close-up photography. She and her husband, also a professional photographer, joined the Hare Krishna Movement in 1971, while shooting assignments in India.

Dr. and Mrs. A. B. Bright and their two children have a small home, just suitable to their needs, in a peaceful country town. Dr. Bright is the local M.D., a thoughtful, qualified man, respected for doing his job honestly and selflessly. His hobby: reading books of philosophy, poetry and science. Mrs. Bright and the children (when the children aren't in school) farm and garden around the house and care for the family cow. The Brights are mildly prosperous people who give thanks to God for the things they have and take their religion as a serious duty. By almost anyone's standards, they'd have to be considered exceptionally pious. They don't gamble, and for them intoxicants are strictly taboo—they don't smoke, and not to speak of liquor, they don't even drink coffee or tea. Dr. Bright has seen too many of his patients bring trouble to themselves through extramarital affairs, so he's always been faithful to his wife; and she, too, has always been faithful to him. The Brights decided long ago that killing animals is barbaric, so they never eat meat, fish, chicken or even eggs. All in all, the Brights lead a clean, simple and happy life. But the Brights are conditioned by a sense of happiness and knowledge. They are attached to their harmonious world. Therefore they are bound to the mode of goodness.

The Smiths, by contrast, live in suburbia in a stylish home filled with modern conveniences. Each morning Larry Smith gulps down breakfast in time to fight traffic to the office. There he sits all day dealing with different "headaches," as he calls them. A hard job, but worth it, he figures, since it lets him afford the luxuries he enjoys and still have some money left over for the stock market and some rather shady business schemes he has going on the side. ("Money is the honey," Larry says.) Gloria, his wife, wakes up in time to see that the two older children look decent (family prestige is important to the Smiths) and sends them off to school. She spends most of her day with the baby ("the one we didn't expect," says Larry). Either Gloria's in the house with the TV going, in the playground with the other housewives and children, in the beauty salon, or (sometimes it seems like forever) shopping. All day the Smiths are active, on the go. At night they relax, but sometimes their minds are just so wound up that they can't get a good night's sleep. They squabble with each other, and sometimes they're depressed, but as Larry jokingly philosophizes, "There's no problem so great that sex can't solve it." On the weekends the Smiths make a show of being religious, but it's more or less a social affair, since in fact they generally disregard the guidelines of their scriptures. This family is typical of the mode of passion.

The mode of ignorance is exemplified by the lives of John Dull and Betty Grumble. They never got married, but they live together, in squalor, in a cheap apartment in New York City. Welfare checks cover part of the rent, and at the end of the month John gets together the rest by peddling drugs. Religion, they both decided long ago, is something they want no part of. They spend their time sleeping (at least ten or twelve hours a day) or else getting high on drugs, feasting on beer and salami, and languishing in their apartment. For years they've dreamed about starting a commune in Spain, or perhaps Madagascar or Nepal.

What are these forces called "modes"? The modes of nature—goodness, passion and ignorance—are aspects of Kṛṣṇa's inferior energy. Lord Kṛṣṇa, the Supreme Personality of Godhead, has innumerable energies. For our understanding, however, they have been classified in three groups: the inferior energy, which is material; the superior energy, which is spiritual; and the marginal energy—we ourselves, the living entities. We are called marginal because we may come under the influence of either the superior or the inferior energy. For example, our body is Kṛṣṇa's inferior energy. That means that by nature it is temporary and is a source of ignorance and misery. If one identifies with the body or mind—if one thinks that he's an American or Indian, that he's fat or thin, healthy, or sick, Hindu or Catholic, democratic or communistic, and so on—he then comes under the influence of the inferior energy and its material qualities. Thus one is impelled to act by the modes or qualities of material nature—goodness, passion and ignorance. If we remember, however, that the life force—the source of consciousness within the body—is different from the body itself, and if we act in that remembrance, then we can free ourselves from the influence of the material energy.

The conscious spark that gives life to the body is a tiny particle of the spiritual energy of the Supreme Lord, and so it has an eternal relationship with the Lord. When we act according to that relationship, which is one of service to the Lord, then we are acting naturally, spiritually. Thus we are completely liberated from the modes of material nature, and we revive our natural spiritual qualities of eternity, knowledge and bliss.

We generally think that we're in control of our actions and that we're making our own decisions, but the supreme authority, Kṛṣṇa, declares that this is not the case. He says that we are acting as puppets—victims—of the forces of nature. In *Bhagavad-gītā* Lord Kṛṣṇa says, "All men are forced to act helplessly according to the impulses born of the modes of material nature: therefore no one can refrain from doing something, not even for a moment." (Bg. 3.5) Not just you and I, but "no being existing, anywhere in the material world, is free from the three modes of material nature." (Bg. 18.40).

To return to our earlier example, Dr. Bright, our learned physician, feels advanced in knowledge and materially happy in his peaceful library at home. But although his life may seem pleasant, he's still in the bodily or material concept of life, and therefore he is in illusion. He thinks that he is Dr. Bright, an American, a middle-aged man, a husband, a father, a reasonable, well-educated country gentleman. But these designations are all material; they concern only the body and mind. Dr. Bright has not yet realized that he is neither his body nor his mind; he is a spiritual soul, an eternal servant of Kṛṣṇa. Since he misidentifies himself with his body, he must come under the influence of the laws of nature governing that body. So he must continue suffering the bodily problems of birth, old age, disease and death.

If one in the mode of goodness is bound in this way, what to speak of those in the lower modes? Those in passion, like the Smiths, are bound by their attempts to satisfy their uncontrollable hankerings and longings. And those in ignorance, like Mr. Dull and Miss Grumble, are bound by madness, indolence and sleep.

Our real life, as we mentioned, is spiritual, and so it is eternal, blissful and full of knowledge. Under the illusion of goodness, however, we look for this reality in mundane learning and a feeling of material satisfaction. In passion we seek it in sex and possessions; and in ignorance we seek it in sleep and intoxication. Thus our pure spiritual nature is perverted by impure desires, born of the modes of nature.

When Bright, Smith, Dull and Grumble were born, they had no control over when or where they'd take birth, what kinds of bodies they'd be given or who their parents would be. Somehow or other, nature put each of them, helpless, into his own predicament. Now they think that they're controlling their fate, but actually their helplessness has not changed. They are still acting according to the bodies that a higher authority has given them. They are neither the proprietors nor the controllers of the actions and reactions of those bodies. They are simply drowning in the midst of a material ocean, being tossed by the waves of that ocean and struggling for existence. Therefore Kṛṣṇa says in *Bhagavad-gītā*, "One who can see that all activities are performed by the body, which is created of material nature, and sees that the self, the soul within, does nothing, actually sees." (Bg. 13.30)

At this point we can hear ourselves protesting: " *I* have control over what I do. I can choose whether to go to the bar or the opera, whether to marry a prostitute or a Radcliffe girl. Nothing is forcing *me* to act."

Yes, we have minute independence. Kṛṣṇa is *svarāṭ*, or completely independent; God can do whatever He likes. And since we are tiny parts of God, we also have His quality of independence—but only in a minute quantity, proportionate to our size. Therefore, according to our desires, our body acts either in goodness, passion, ignorance or some combination. But whatever these desires are, they are material. They spring from our bodily concept of life, and therefore they are products of the modes of nature. And the ways we try to fulfil these desires are also material. Thus we are revolving in Kṛṣṇa's inferior, material energy. "Sometimes the mode of passion becomes prominent," Lord Kṛṣṇa says, "defeating the mode of goodness. And sometimes the mode of goodness defeats passion, and at other times the mode of ignorance defeats goodness and passion. In this way there is always competition for supremacy." (Bg. 14.10) Just as the basic colors yellow, red and blue mix in different ways to produce an uncountable variety of tints and hues, so goodness, passion and ignorance mix together to produce innumerable illusions in our minds. This explains why the Brights sometimes quarrel over trivial problems; why the Smiths and even Dull and Grumble, sometimes unexpectedly give to a bona fide religious charity; and why the Smiths go partying once in a while, drink too much, and find themselves hungover in bed the next morning, overcome by the mode of ignorance.

Like it or not, we should understand that we are now tightly tied by ropes of illusion. A man bound by the hands and feet cannot free himself; he must be helped by a person who is unbound. Because the bound cannot help the bound, the rescuer must be liberated. Therefore only Kṛṣṇa, the fully liberated Supreme Lord, or His bona fide representative, the spiritual master, can release the conditioned soul. Without such superior help, one cannot be freed from the bondage of material nature. The only way to get completely free from its clutches is to surrender to the Supreme Person. Lord Kṛṣṇa therefore says in *Bhagavad-gītā*, "This divine energy of Mine, consisting of the three modes of material nature, is difficult to overcome. But those who have surrendered unto Me can easily cross beyond it." (Bg. 7.14)

The Brights and Smiths, and Dull and Grumble, can become free from the material concept of life simply by receiving bona fide transcendental knowledge. If one has been living in a dark room all his life, he is always floundering, unable to see things as they are. Once the lights are switched on, however, everything becomes apparent, and one can at once act properly. Similarly, with the light of transcendental knowledge we can overcome our bondage and act in accordance with our spiritual nature. Thus we can liberate ourselves from this material world. Kṛṣṇa therefore says in the *Gītā*, "One who understands this philosophy concerning material nature, the living entity, and the interaction of the modes of nature is sure to attain liberation. He will not take birth here in this material world again, regardless of his present position." (Bg. 13.24)

One who is thus becoming freed from illusion and who is scientifically understanding his pure, natural consciousness is sure to become a devotee of the Supreme Lord. In the beginning such potential devotees naturally develop the desirable personal qualities that characterize the mode of goodness. They strictly avoid all sinful activities: they do not eat meat, fish or eggs, they take no intoxicants, and they do not gamble or engage in illicit sex. But, beyond that, they seek out a bona fide spiritual master and then cultivate transcendental knowledge under his guidance. Thus each day they hear scientific information about Kṛṣṇa from Vedic scriptures like *Bhagavad-gītā* and *Śrīmad-Bhāgavatam*, and they chant the holy names of God Hare Kṛṣṇa, Hare Kṛṣṇa, Kṛṣṇa, Kṛṣṇa, Hare Hare/ Hare Rāma, Hare Rāma, Rāma Rāma, Hare Hare. Chanting this transcendental vibration is recommended in the scriptures as the best way to transcend the three modes of material nature in our difficult age of quarrel and hypocrisy.

A devotee of the Lord is free from bondage to the modes because his mind, body and words act spiritually—that is, in relationship to Kṛṣṇa. He always serves the pleasure of the Lord. For the sake of the Lord he will do any work needed, and for such work he will live anywhere—whether it be in the country, suburbs, or city. Such a Kṛṣṇa conscious devotee accepts whatever is favorable to the service of Kṛṣṇa and rejects everything unfavorable to that service. In *Bhagavad-gītā* Kṛṣṇa says:

māṁ ca yo 'vyabhicdrena
bhakti-yogena sevate
sā gunān samatityaitān
brahma-bhuyāya kalpate

"One who engages in full devotional service, who does not fall down in any circumstance, at once transcends the modes of material nature and thus comes to the level of spiritual perfection." (Bg. 14.26)

Thus we can attain spiritual perfection simply by remembering our relationship with Kṛṣṇa and acting in that relationship. We need not be disturbed by the modes of nature, for instead of putting our consciousness into material activities, we can transfer it to activities centered around Kṛṣṇa. Such Kṛṣṇa-centered activities make up *bhakti-yoga*. When we engage in this topmost *yoga* system, we acquire the same spiritual qualities as Kṛṣṇa. The Lord is eternal, blissful and full of knowledge, and we are part of Him, as gold particles are part of a gold mine. Thus our spiritual qualities are similar to those of Kṛṣṇa. The difference, however, is that Kṛṣṇa is infinite, whereas the living entities are infinitesimal.

Although the modes of material nature are very difficult to overcome, we can overcome them easily if we have the mercy of the Lord, for the Lord, after all, is the creator and controller of the modes. And how can we attain that mercy?

yasya deve parā bhaktir
yathā deve tathā gurau
tasyaite kathitā hy arthāḥ
prakāśante mahātmanaḥ

"The mercy of the Lord can be obtained only by those surrendered souls who have implicit faith in both the Lord and the spiritual master." Such fortunate souls can at once become free from the three modes of material nature and regain their original spiritual nature, which is one of boundless transcendental joy in a loving relationship with Kṛṣṇa, the Supreme Personality of Godhead.

The Screwtape Letters
C. S. Lewis

C. S. Lewis (1898–1963) was professor of medieval and renaissance literature at Cambridge University. In addition to being an important theologian and literary scholar, he was also the author of many popular books for children as well as several still widely-read science fiction novels. *The Screwtape Letters*, from which the present selection is excerpted, has already achieved the status of a modern classic. Among his best-known other works are *Mere Christianity*, *The Problem of Pain*, and *Out of the Silent Planet*.

MY DEAR WORMWOOD,
So you "have great hopes that the patient's religious phase is dying away,"

Source: C. S. Lewis, *The Screwtape Letters and Screwtape Proposes a Toast* (New York, 1975). Reprinted by permission of Macmillan Publishing Co., Inc.

have you? I always thought the Training College had gone to pieces since they put old Slubgob at the head of it, and now I am sure. Has no one ever told you about the law of Undulation?

Humans are amphibians—half spirit and half animal. (The Enemy's determination to produce such a revolting hybrid was one of the things that determined Our Father to withdraw his support from Him.) As spirits they belong to the eternal world, but as animals they inhabit time. This means that while their spirit can be directed to an eternal object, their bodies, passions, and imaginations are in continual change, for to be in time means to change. Their nearest approach to constancy, therefore, is undulation—the repeated return to a level from which they repeatedly fall back, a series of troughs and peaks. If you had watched your patient carefully you would have seen this undulation in every department of his life—his interest in his work, his affection for his friends, his physical appetites, all go up and down. As long as he lives on earth periods of emotional and bodily richness and liveliness will alternate with periods of numbness and poverty. The dryness and dulness through which your patient is now going are not, as you fondly suppose, your workmanship; they are merely a natural phenomenon which will do us no good unless you make a good use of it.

To decide what the best use of it is, you must ask what use the Enemy wants to make of it, and then do the opposite. Now it may surprise you to learn that in His efforts to get permanent possession of a soul, He relies on the troughs even more than on the peaks; some of His special favourites have gone through longer and deeper troughs than anyone else. The reason is this. To us a human is primarily food; our aim is the absorption of its will into ours, the increase of our own area of selfhood at its expense. But the obedience which the Enemy demands of men is quite a different thing. One must face the fact that all the talk about His love for men, and His service being perfect freedom, is not (as one would gladly believe) mere propaganda, but an appalling truth. He really *does* want to fill the universe with a lot of loathsome little replicas of Himself—creatures whose life, on its miniature scale, will be qualitatively like His own, not because He has absorbed them but because their wills freely conform to His. We want cattle who can finally become food; He wants servants who can finally become sons. We want to suck in, He wants to give out. We are empty and would be filled; He is full and flows over. Our war aim is a world in which Our Father Below has drawn all other beings into himself: the Enemy wants a world full of beings united to Him but still distinct.

And that is where the troughs come in. You must have often wondered why the Enemy does not make more use of His power to be sensibly present to human souls in any degree He chooses and at any moment. But you now see that the Irresistible and the Indisputable are the two weapons which the very nature of His scheme forbids Him to use. Merely to over-ride a human will (as His felt presence in any but the faintest and most mitigated degree would certainly do) would be for Him useless. He cannot ravish. He can only woo. For His ignoble idea is to eat the cake and have it; the creatures are to be one with Him, but yet themselves; merely to cancel them, or assimilate them, will not serve. He is prepared to do a little over-riding at the beginning. He will set them off with communications of His presence which, though faint, seem great to them, with emotional sweetness, and easy conquest over temptation. But He never allows this state of affairs to last long. Sooner or later He withdraws, if not in fact, at least from their conscious experience, all those supports and incentives. He leaves the creature to stand up on its own legs— to carry out from the will alone duties which have lost all relish. It is during such trough periods, much more than during the peak periods that it is growing into the sort of creature He wants it to be. Hence the prayers offered in the state of dryness are those which please Him best. We can drag our patients along by continual tempting, because we design them only for the table, and the more their will is interfered with the better. He cannot "tempt" to virtue as we do to vice. He wants them to learn to walk and must therefore take away His hand; and if only the will to walk is really there He is pleased even with their stumbles. Do not be deceived, Wormwood. Our cause is never more in danger than when a human no longer desiring, but still intending, to do our Enemy's will, looks round upon a universe from which every trace of Him seems to have vanished, and asks why he has been forsaken, and still obeys.

But of course, the troughs afford opportunities to our side also. Next week I will give you some hints on how to exploit them,

Your affectionate uncle
SCREWTAPE

MY DEAR WORMWOOD,

I hope my last letter has convinced you that the trough of dulness or "dryness" through which your patient is going at present will not, of itself, give you his soul, but needs to be properly exploited. What forms the exploitation should take I will now consider.

In the first place I have always found that the Trough periods of the human undulation provide excellent opportunity for all sensual temptations, particularly those of sex. This may surprise you, because, of course, there is more physical energy, and therefore more potential appetite, at the Peak periods; but you must remember that the powers of resistance are then also at their highest. The health and spirits which you want to use in producing lust can also, alas, be very easily used for work or play or thought or innocuous merriment. The attack has a much better chance of success when the man's whole inner world is drab and cold and empty. And it is also to be noted that the Trough sexuality is subtly different in quality from that of the Peak—much less likely to lead to the milk and water phenomenon which the humans call "being in love," much more easily drawn into perversions, much less contaminated by those generous and imaginative and even spiritual concomitants which often render human sexuality so disappointing. It is the same with other desires of the flesh. You are much more likely to make your man a sound drunkard by pressing drink on him as an anodyne when he is dull and weary than by encouraging him to use it as a means of merriment among his friends when he is happy and expansive. Never forget that when we are dealing with any pleasure in its healthy and normal and satisfying form, we are, in a sense, on the Enemy's ground. I know we have won many a soul through pleasure. All the same, it is His invention, not ours. He made the pleasures: all our research so far has not enabled us to produce one. All we can do is to encourage the humans to take the pleasures which our Enemy has produced, at times, or in ways, or in degrees, which He has forbidden. Hence we always try to work away from the natural condition of any pleasure to that in which it is least natural, least redolent of its Maker, and least pleasurable. An ever increasing craving for an ever diminishing pleasure is the formula. It is more certain; and it's better *style*. To get the man's soul and give him *nothing* in return—that is what really gladdens our Father's heart. And the Troughs are the time for beginning the process.

But there is an even better way of exploiting the Trough; I mean through the patient's own thoughts about it. As always, the first step is to keep knowledge out of his mind. Do not let him suspect the law of undulation. Let him assume that the first ardours of his conversion might have been expected to last, and ought to have lasted, forever, and that his present dryness is an equally permanent condition. Having once got this misconception well fixed in his head, you may then proceed in various ways. It all depends on whether your man is of the desponding type who can be tempted to despair, or of the wishful-thinking type who can be assured that all is well. The former type is getting rare among the humans. If your patient should happen to belong to it, everything is easy. You have only got to keep him out of the way of experienced Christians (an easy task now-a-days), to direct his attention to the appropriate passages in scripture, and then to set him to work on the desperate design of recovering his old feelings by sheer will-power, and the game is ours. If he is of the more hopeful type your job is to make him acquiesce in the present low temperature of his spirit and gradually become content with it, persuading himself that it is not so low after all. In a week or two you will be making him doubt whether the first days of his Christianity were not, perhaps, a little excessive. Talk to him about "moderation in all things." If you can once get him to the point of thinking that "religion is all very well up to a point," you can feel quite happy about his soul. A moderated religion is as good for us as no religion at all—and more amusing.

Another possibility is that of direct attack on his faith. When you have caused him to assume that the trough is permanent, can you not persuade him that "his religious phase" is just going to die away like all his previous phases? Of course there is no conceivable way of getting by reason from the proposition "I am losing interest in this" to the proposition "This is false." But, as I said before, it is jargon, not reason, you must rely on. The mere word *phase* will very likely do the trick. I assume that the creature has been through several of them before—they all have —and that he always feels superior and patronising to the ones he has emerged from, not because he has really criticised them but simply because they are in the past. (You keep him well fed on hazy ideas of Progress and Development and the Historical Point of View, I trust, and give him lots of modern Biographies to read? The people in them are always emerging from Phases, aren't they?)

You see the idea? Keep his mind off the plain antithesis between True and False. Nice shadowy expressions—"It was a phase"—"I've been through all that"—and don't forget the blessed word "Adolescent,"

Your affectionate uncle

SCREWTAPE

MY DEAR WORMWOOD,

Obviously you are making excellent progress. My only fear is lest in attempting to hurry the patient you awaken him to a sense of his real position. For you and I, who see that position as it really is, must never forget how totally different it ought to appear to him. We know that we have introduced a change of direction in his course which is already carrying him out of his orbit around the Enemy; but he must be made to imagine that all the choices which have effected this change of course are trivial and revocable. He must not be allowed to suspect that he is now, however, slowly, heading right away from the sun on a line which will carry him into the cold and dark of utmost space.

For this reason I am almost glad to hear that he is still a churchgoer and a communicant. I know there are dangers in this; but anything is better than that he should realise the break he has made with the first months of his Christian life. As long as he retains externally the habits of a Christian he can still be made to think of himself as one who has adopted a few new friends and amusements but whose spiritual state is much the same as it was six weeks ago. And while he thinks that, we do not have to contend with the explicit repentance of a definite, fully recognized, sin, but only with his vague, though uneasy, feeling that he hasn't been doing very well lately.

This dim uneasiness needs careful handling. If it gets too strong it may wake him up and spoil the whole game. On the other hand, if you suppress it entirely—which, by the by, the Enemy will probably not allow you to do—we lose an element in the situation which can be turned to good account. If such a feeling is allowed to live, but not allowed to become irresistible and flower into real repentance, it has one invaluable tendency. It increases the patient's reluctance to think about the Enemy. All humans at nearly all times have some such reluctance; but when thinking of Him involves facing and intensifying a whole vague cloud of half-conscious guilt, this reluctance is increased tenfold. They hate every idea that suggests Him, just as men in financial embarrassment hate the very sight of a pass-book. In this state your patient will not omit, but he will increasingly dislike, his religious duties. He will think about them as little as he feels he decently can beforehand, and forget them as soon as possible when they are over. A few weeks ago you had to *tempt* him to unreality and inattention in his prayers: but now you will find him opening his arms to you and almost begging you to distract his purpose and benumb his heart. He will *want* his prayers to be unreal, for he will dread nothing so much as effective contact with the Enemy. His aim will be to let sleeping worms lie.

As this condition becomes more fully established, you will be gradually freed from the tiresome business of providing Pleasures as temptations. As the uneasiness and his reluctance to face it cut him off more and more from all real happiness, and as habit renders the pleasures of vanity and excitement and flippancy at once less pleasant and harder to forgo (for that is what habit fortunately does to a pleasure) you will find that anything or nothing is sufficient to attract his wandering attention. You no longer need a good book, which he really likes, to keep him from his prayers or his work or his sleep; a column of advertisements in yesterday's paper will do. You can make him waste his time not only in conversation he enjoys with people whom he likes, but in conversations with those he cares nothing about on subjects that bore him. You can make him do nothing at all for long periods. You can keep him up late at night, not roistering, but staring at a dead fire in a cold room. All the healthy and outgoing activities which we want him to avoid can be inhibited and *nothing* given in return, so that at last he may say, as one of my own patients said on his arrival down here, " I now see that I spent most of my life in doing *neither* what

I ought *nor* what I liked." The Christians describe the Enemy as one "without whom Nothing is strong." And Nothing is very strong: strong enough to steal away a man's best years not in sweet sins but in a dreary flickering of the mind over it knows not what and knows not why, in the gratification of curiosities so feeble that the man is only half aware of them, in drumming of fingers and kicking of heels, in whistling tunes that he does not like, or in the long, dim labyrinth of reveries that have not even lust or ambition to give them a relish, but which, once chance association has started them, the creature is too weak and fuddled to shake off.

You will say that these are very small sins; and doubtless, like all young tempters, you are anxious to be able to report spectacular wickedness. But do remember, the only thing that matters is the extent to which you separate the man from the Enemy. It does not matter how small the sins are provided that their cumulative effect is to edge the man away from the Light and out into the Nothing. Murder is no better than cards if cards can do the trick. Indeed the safest road to Hell is the gradual one—the gentle slope, soft underfoot, without sudden turnings, without milestones, without signposts,

Your affectionate uncle

SCREWTAPE

MY DEAR WORMWOOD,

The most alarming thing in your last account of the patient is that he is making none of those confident resolutions which marked his original conversion. No more lavish promises of perpetual virtue, I gather; not even the expectation of an endowment of "grace" for life, but only a hope for the daily and hourly pittance to meet the daily and hourly temptation! This is very bad.

I see only one thing to do at the moment. Your patient has become humble; have you drawn his attention to the fact? All virtues are less formidable to us once the man is aware that he has them, but this is specially true of humility. Catch him at the moment when he is really poor in spirit and smuggle into his mind the gratifying reflection, "By jove! I'm being humble," and almost immediately pride—pride at his own humility—will appear. If he awakes to the danger and tries to smother this new form of pride, make him proud of his attempt—and so on, through as many stages as you please. But don't try this too long, for fear you awake his sense of humour and proportion, in which case he will merely laugh at you and go to bed.

But there are other profitable ways of fixing his attention on the virtue of Humility. By this virtue, as by all the others, our Enemy wants to turn the man's attention away from self to Him, and to the man's neighbours. All the abjection and self-hatred are designed, in the long run, solely for this end; unless they attain this end they do us little harm; and they may even do us good if they keep the man concerned with himself, and, above all, if self-contempt can be made the starting-point for contempt of other selves, and thus for gloom, cynicism, and cruelty.

You must therefore conceal from the patient the true end of Humility. Let him think of it not as self-forgetfulness but as a certain kind of opinion (namely, a low opinion) of his own talents and character. Some talents, I gather, he really has. Fix in his mind the idea that humility consists in trying to believe those talents to be less valuable than he believes them to be. No doubt they *are* in fact less valuable than he believes, but that is not the point. The great thing is to make him value an opinion for some quality other than truth, thus introducing an element of dishonesty and make-believe into the heart of what otherwise threatens to become a virtue. By this method thousands of humans have been brought to think that humility means pretty women trying to believe they are ugly and clever men trying to believe they are fools. And since what they are trying to believe may, in some cases, be manifest nonsense, they cannot succeed in believing it and we have the chance of keeping their minds endlessly revolving on themselves in an effort to achieve the impossible. To anticipate the Enemy's strategy, we must consider His aims. The Enemy wants to bring the man to a state of mind in which he could design the best cathedral in the world, and know it to be the best, and rejoice in the fact, without being any more (or less) or otherwise glad at having done it than he would be if it had been done by another. The Enemy wants him, in the end, to be so free from any bias in his own favour that he can rejoice in his own talents as frankly and gratefully as in his neighbour's talents—or in a sunrise, an elephant, or a waterfall. He wants each man, in the long run, to be able to recognise all creatures (even himself) as glorious and excellent things. He wants to kill their animal self-love as soon as possible; but it is His long-term policy, I fear, to restore to them a new kind of self-love—a charity and gratitude for all selves, including their own; when they have really learned to love their neighbours as themselves, they will be allowed to love themselves as their neighbours. For we must never forget what is the most repellent and inexplicable trait in our Enemy; He *really* loves the hairless bipeds He has created and always gives them back to them with His right hand what He has taken away with His left.

His whole effort, therefore, will be to get the man's mind off the subject of his own value altogether. He would rather the man thought himself a great architect or a great poet and then forgot about it, than that he should spend much time and pains trying to think himself a bad one. Your efforts to instil either vainglory or false modesty into the patient will therefore be met from the Enemy's side with the obvious reminder that a man is not usually called upon to have an opinion of his own talents at all, since he can very well go on improving them to the best of his ability without deciding on his own precise niche in the temple of Fame. You must try to exclude this reminder from the patient's consciousness at all costs. The Enemy will also try to render real in the patient's mind a doctrine which they all profess but find it difficult to bring home to their feelings—the doctrine that they did not create themselves, that their talents were given them, and that they might as well be proud of the colour of their hair. But always and by all methods the Enemy's aim will be to get the patient's mind off such questions, and yours will be to fix it on them. Even of his sins the Enemy does not want him to think too much: once they are repented, the sooner the man turns his attention outward, the better the Enemy is pleased,

Your affectionate uncle

SCREWTAPE

MY DEAR WORMWOOD,

The contemptuous way in which you spoke of gluttony as a means of catching souls, in your last letter, only shows your ignorance. One of the great achievements of the last hundred years has been to deaden the human conscience on that subject, so that by now you will hardly find a sermon preached or a conscience troubled about it in the whole length and breadth of Europe. This has largely been effected by concentrating all our efforts on gluttony of Delicacy, not gluttony of Excess. Your patient's mother, as I learn from the dossier and you might have learned from Glubose, is a good example. She would be astonished—one day, I hope, *will* be—to learn that her whole life is enslaved to this kind of sensuality, which is quite concealed from her by the fact that the quantities involved are small. But what do quantities matter, provided we can use a human belly and palate to produce querulousness, impatience, uncharitableness, and self-concern? Glubose has this old woman well in hand. She is a positive terror to hostesses and servants. She is always turning from what has been offered her to say with a demure little sigh and a smile "Oh please, please . . . *all* I want is a cup of tea, weak but not too weak, and the teeniest weeniest bit of really crisp toast." You see? Because what she wants is smaller and less costly than what has been set before her, she never recognizes as gluttony her determination to get what she wants, however troublesome it may be to others. At the very moment of indulging her appetite she believes that she is practising temperance. In a crowded restaurant she gives a little scream at the plate which some overworked waitress has set before her and says, "Oh, that's far, far too much! Take it away and bring me about a quarter of it." If challenged, she would say she was doing this to avoid waste; in reality she does it because the particular shade of delicacy to which we have enslaved her is offended by the sight of more food than she happens to want.

The real value of the quiet, unobtrusive work which Glubose has been doing for years on this old woman can be gauged by the way in which her belly now dominates her whole life. The woman is in what may be called the "All-I-want" state of mind. *All* she wants is a cup of tea properly made, or an egg properly boiled, or a slice of bread properly toasted. But she never finds any servant or any friend who can do these simple things "properly"—because her "properly" conceals an insatiable demand for the exact, and almost impossible, palatal pleasures which she imagines she remembers from the past; a past described by her as "the days when you could get good servants" but known to us as the days when her senses were more easily pleased and she had pleasures of other kinds which made her less dependent on those of the table. Meanwhile, the daily disappointment produces daily ill temper; cooks give notice and friendships are cooled. If ever the Enemy introduces into her mind a faint suspicion that she is too interested in food, Glubose counters it by suggesting to her that she doesn't mind what she eats herself but "does like to have things nice for her boy." In fact, of course, her greed has been one of the chief sources of his domestic discomfort for many years.

Now your patient is his mother's son. While working your hardest, quite rightly, on other fronts, you must not neglect a little quiet infiltration in respect of gluttony. Being a male, he is not so likely to be caught by the "*All* I want" camouflage. Males are best turned into gluttons with the help of their vanity. They ought to be made to think themselves very knowing about food, to pique themselves on having found the only restaurant in the town where steaks are really "properly" cooked. What begins as vanity can then be gradually turned into habit. But, however you approach it, the great thing is to bring him into the state in which the denial of any one indulgence—it matters not which, champagne or tea, *sole colbert* or cigarettes—"puts him out," for then his charity, justice, and obedience are all at your mercy.

Mere excess in food is much less valuable than delicacy. Its chief use is as a kind of artillery preparation for attacks on chastity. On that, as on every other subject, keep your man in a condition of false spirituality. Never let him notice the medical aspect. Keep him wondering what pride or lack of faith has delivered him into your hands when a simple enquiry into what he has been eating or drinking for the last twenty-four hours would show him whence your ammunition comes and thus enable him by a very little abstinence to imperil your lines of communication. If he *must* think of the medical side of chastity, feed him the grand lie which we have made the English humans believe, that physical exercise in excess and consequent fatigue are specially favourable to this virtue. How they can believe this, in face if the notorious lustfulness of sailors and soldiers, may well be asked. But we used the schoolmasters to put the story about—men who were really interested n chastity as an excuse for games and therefore recommended games as an aid to chastity. But this whole business is too large to deal with at the tail-end of a letter,

Your affectionate uncle

SCREWTAPE

The Fate of Evil

Simone Weil

Simone Weil (1909–1943) was one of the most profound religious thinkers of our time. Her works include *Gravity and Grace, The Need for Roots*, and *Waiting for God*.

. . .

What is the connection between punishment and forgiveness? There is *reparation* —an offended man only forgives if the offender has undergone a penalty and humiliation, either by consenting to submit to it (as was frequent in the middle ages) or by being constrained to it until he says, like the whipped slaves at Rome: Forgive me, I have suffered enough.

Another connection is *cure*—it is hoped that the punishment will be a remedy to reform the criminal; once he has been reformed, this fact alone will secure his pardon.

Source: Simone Weil, "New York Notebook," in *First and Last Notebooks*, by Simone Weil, trans. by Sir Richard Rees (Oxford, 1970). Copyright © 1970 by Sir Richard Rees. The "New York Notebook" was first published in French as *La Connaissance surnaturelle* © Editions Gallimard 1950. Reprinted by permission of Oxford University Press.

These are two human relationships, but they can be transposed into the relationship between God and man, provided the rules of such a transposition are observed.

What are these rules ?

The purpose of reparation is not to cure the criminal but the injured party, who cannot forget the offence or think of it without distress until he has seen the criminal suffer.

This corresponds with the need to pass suffering on. The captain who has been reprimanded by the colonel stomachs the reprimand until he can be relieved of it by reprimanding the lieutenant.

But if one has been offended by an inferior one passes the suffering back to the man who caused it, and with interest.

The broken china vase cannot be mended; but luckily the slave who broke it can be broken by the whip.

If the slave falls on his knees, it is enough, sometimes, simply to have him thus in one's power.

The slave who has been whipped—or even if he has only suffered the pain of begging for mercy—needs to find compensation in his turn.

Every evil stirred up in this world passes from one man to another (it is the Homeric myth of Atë) until it alights upon a perfectly pure being who suffers it in its completeness and destroys it.

The Father who is in heaven is not affected as a man is by our offences. But for that very reason, every offence committed directly against Him falls back upon the offender as a curse; and thenceforward he cannot help trying to free himself from this evil by doing evil to other creatures. He puts into circulation an evil which passes continually from one creature to another.

That is what happened to Cain—assuming that Cain sacrificed reluctantly.

The evil put in circulation in this way moves on and on until it falls upon a victim who is perfectly pure.

God who is in heaven cannot destroy evil; he can only send it back in the form of a curse. It is only God in this world, having become a victim, who can destroy evil by suffering it.

Thus the idea of evil as reparation leads to the idea of redemption, when correctly transposed.

The Father who is in heaven does not send the evil back, but because he cannot in any way be touched by it, the evil falls back.

The man who takes vengeance imitates God the Father. This is the wrong way to imitate God. Man is permitted only to imitate God the Son. That is why "No man comes to the Father save by me."

Nevertheless: "Be ye perfect as your heavenly Father is perfect." But here it is a question of imitating God the Father in his abdication, of which the complete fulfilment is the Incarnation.

Men have always felt the need to purify themselves by the sacrifice of innocent beings—animals, children, virgins. It is the highest degree of innocence when the sacrifice is voluntary.

The man who has suffered evil wants to be relieved of it by putting it elsewhere: that is what the desire for satisfaction is. He does not want to abolish the evil, but to abolish it out of his own life, and therefore to throw it out elsewhere.

But for God there is no elsewhere to which to throw the evil; the sphere of his existence is all-inclusive. God can desire only to abolish the evil. But it is only through contact with God that the evil falls into nothingness.

Thus the satisfaction which man gets by throwing the offence away from himself consists for God in submitting to it.

By eating the apple, Adam offended God, and this offence fell back again in the form of a curse because it didn't touch God. But the offence of those who drove nails into Christ's flesh did not fall back again as a curse; it touched God and disappeared.

The Way of the Bodhisattva

Heinrich Zimmer

Heinrich Zimmer (1890–1943) is considered by many to have been the greatest modern Western scholar of Hinduism. Born in Germany, he studied at the University of Berlin and was professor of Sanskrit at Heidelberg until 1938. He left Germany in that year and moved to the United States in 1939 where he became a visiting lecturer at Columbia University. His major works in English include *The King and the Corpse*, *Philosophies of India*, and *The Art of Indian Asia*.

The great Mahāyāna Bodhisattva Avalokiteśvara is a personification of the highest ideal of the Mahāyāna Buddhist career. His legend recounts that when, following a series of eminently virtuous incarnations, he was about to enter into the surcease of nirvāṇa, an uproar, like the sound of a general thunder, rose in all the worlds. The great being knew that this was a wail of lament uttered by all created things—the rocks and stones as well as the trees, insects, gods, animals, demons, and human beings of all the spheres of the universe—at the prospect of his imminent departure from the realms of birth. And so, in his compassion, he renounced for himself the boon of nirvāṇa until all beings without exception should be prepared to enter in before him—like the good shepherd who permits his flock to pass first through the gate and then goes through himself, closing it behind him.

Source: Heinrich Zimmer, *Philosophies of India* (Bollingen Series XXVI), ed. by Joseph Campbell (Princeton, N.J., 1951), pp. 534–552. Copyright © 1951 by the Bollingen Foundation. Reprinted by permission of Princeton University Press.

Whereas in the Hīnayāna the term *bodhisattva* denotes one who is on the point of consecration into Buddhahood (for example, Gautama was a Bodhisattva prior to his awakening under the Bo Tree), in the Mahāyāna tradition the term designates those sublimely indifferent, compassionate beings who remain at the threshold of nirvāṇa for the comfort and salvation of the world. Out of perfect indifference (egolessness) and perfect compassion (which is also egolessness) the Mahāyāna Bodhisattva does not experience the "real or true enlightenment" (*samyaksambodhi*) of the Buddha and then pass to final extinction (*parinirvāṇa*), but stops at the brink—the brink of time and eternity—and thus transcends that pair of opposites: for the world will never end; the round of the cosmic eons will go on and on without ceasing; the vow of the Bodhisattva, to remain at the brink till all shall go in before him, amounts to a vow to remain as he is forever. And this is the reason why his vow is world-redemptive. Through it the truth is symbolized that time and eternity, saṁsāra and nirvāṇa, do not exist as pairs of opposites but are equally "emptiness" (*śūnyatā*), the void.

In popular worship the Bodhisattva is invoked because he is possessed of an inexhaustible power to save. His potential perfection is being diffused all the time, in an everlasting act of universal salvage, and he appears in helpful forms—for example as the legendary flying horse-of-rescue, Cloud[1]—to deliver creatures from the darkness of their woeful lives-in-ignorance. He is possessed of a boundless "treasury of virtues" (*guṇa sambhāra*), which was accumulated by means of a prolonged and absolutely faultless practice, through many lifetimes, of the "highest rectitude" (*pāramitā*). During eons, the Bodhisattva-in-the-making progressed along a sublime path of the most especial, most highly refined psychological austerities, cancelling always every notion and emotion of ego. And this is what brought him into possession of that inexhaustible "treasury," which, in the end, as a result of this supreme act of timeless renunciation, became available forever to every suffering, striving creature in the world.

The peculiar and especial path of the Mahāyāna Bodhisattva represents the final spiritual refinement—the compassionate counterpart, as it were—of the primordial Indian discipline of tapas. This, as we have seen, was a technique for cultivating in oneself a state of glowing psychophysical heat. The internal energies, systematically controlled and retained, and stored within the body, generated a condition of high temperature, comparable to a fever, and bestowed a certain sovereignty over the forces of the macrocosm by virtue of the conquest of the parallel forces in the microcosm; because it is a fact that every form of asceticism results in its own type of freedom from the usual needs and consequent laws of nature, and therefore affords its own boon of independence. The glowing ascetic cannot be crushed or frustrated by the forces of his environment—nature, the weather, animals, or society. Asserting his superior strength, he defies them. He is fearless and cannot be intimidated; he is in control of his own reactions and emotions.

The only peril that can touch such self-sufficiency is that of being surprised or tricked into some involuntary reaction. This could precipitate an unpremeditated outburst of the concentrated store of tyrannically repressed feeling. Indian epics and romances abound in accounts of holy men who explode irritably in this way at some

[1] Cf. *supra*, pp. 392–393.

slight annoyance. (They are, in fact, a standard device of the Oriental storyteller for complicating plots.) The old fellows blast with the lightning of a curse any poor innocent who chances to disturb them in their spiritual exercise, letting go the full force of their extraordinary power and thus forfeiting, in a single flash, their hard-won equilibrium. This is a major catastrophe for the holy man as well as for his shattered, unfortunate, and unwitting—often charming—victim. Or (as we also read), whenever Indra, the jealous king of the gods, feels that his cosmic sovereignty is being jeopardized by the increase of some ascetic's spiritual power, he sends a heavenly damsel, incredibly beautiful, to intoxicate the senses of the spiritual athlete. If she succeeds, the saint, in a sublime night (or even eon) of passion, pours away the whole charge of psychophysical force that he has spent his lifetime striving to accumulate. The consequence for the world, then, is the birth in due time of a child of fabulous endowments, and for the holy man, the wreckage of his power-project.

In the case of a Bodhisattva the requirements of his peculiar spiritual attitude are, humanly speaking, so severe that were he not established perfectly in his knowledge and his mode of being the danger of his subversion would be practically universal. Temptation is concealed in every incident of life, even the slightest detail, yet for the fulfilled Bodhisattva the possibility of relapse is nonexistent. Since he is the one who is truly without ego, he feels no temptation whatsoever to assert the value of his purely phenomenal personality—not even to the extent of a moment's pause for thought when confronted with an arduous decision. The legends of the Bodhisattvas show them sacrificing their limbs, life, and even wives and children, to what would seem to any normal intellect the most unwarranted demands. Possessions that any ordinary man (*pṛthag-jana*) would regard as the most precious and sacred in the world, the Bodhisattva immediately surrenders to some inconsequential or completely indefensible claim—for example, the plea of a troubled bird or tiger-cub, or the command of some wicked, greedy, and lustful old Brāhman.

The tale is told, for example, in the popular story of the Children of King Vessantara,[2] of how this pious monarch, who was an earlier incarnation of the Buddha, took a vow never to refuse anything demanded of him: "My heart and eye, my flesh and blood, my entire body—should anyone ask these of me, I would give them." Without a second thought he gave away a wonderful elephant on which the well-being of his kingdom depended, and was consequently driven into exile by his indignant people, together with his loyal queen and two little children. And when he was approached in the wilderness by an ugly old Brāhman who demanded the children as slaves, they were given without a qualm; the queen was demanded, and she too was given. But in the end, the Brāhman revealed that he was Indra, the king of the gods, and stated that he had descended to test the saintly human king, and so all ended well. In this case, the temptation of Indra having failed, the god was gracious in defeat.

Even the crudest, most elementary mind cannot but be amazed and outraged by such demonstrations of saintly indifference to the normal values of human welfare—particularly since nothing whatsoever is gained from them. For what does it

---

[2] *Jātaka* 547. (Also, *Jātakamālā* 9: J. S. Speyer, *The Jātakamālā*, Sacred Books of the Buddhists, Vol. I, London, 1895, pp. 71–93; cf. *infra*, p. 543, note 91).

really matter if a single dove is preserved from the talons of a hawk,[3] a new born litter of tiger-kittens rescued from starvation,[4] or a senile, nasty old Brāhman gratified in his greed and lust by the enslavement of a little prince and princess ? The cruel course of nature is not altered. Indeed, the Bodhisattva's absurd sacrifices often support and give voluntary corroboration to the brutal laws that prevail where the struggle for life goes on in its crude, unmitigated, animal-demonic form; while in the case of the Brāhman and the young prince and princess, the first dictate of human morality would seem to have been violated.

In terms, however, of the basic problem and task of the Bodhisattva, it is precisely the apparent senselessness, even indecency, of the sacrifice that makes the difference; for to refuse a paradoxical surrender would be to subscribe (if only by negation) to the standards and world vision of the passion-bound, ego-ridden, common individual who has presented the demand. The supreme and especial test of the Bodhisattva is that of his readiness and power to expand, time and time again, in boundless giving (*dāna*). This requires of him a continuous abdication—or rather nonexperience—of ego. Any reaction of shrinking back, even from a nonsensical sacrifice, would confirm and harden a nucleus of ego-consciousness; whereas the whole sense of Bodhisattvahood is that the limited and limiting ego has evaporated. To suppose that a Bodhisattva should give an absurd demand his second thought— or be the least reluctant to abandon body, life, family, and possessions—would be to ask him to show himself as one who subscribed to the intrinsic value and substantiality of things; and this would imply that on the transcendental plane, which he represents, something of the earth is admitted to have a value—one's body or possessions, kingly rank, queen, children, or honor—whereas, on that plane, all things are known to be ephemeral, phenomenal, and so, in reality, nonexistent. Refusal or resistance would throw a candidate for Bodhisattvahood back into the sphere of the unessential and immediately cut him off from true reality. He would no longer be an aspirant to enlightenment, one " whose essence (*sattva*) is (virtually) enlightenment (*bodhi*)," but, like the yogī transfixed by the allure of a seductive heavenly damsel, would have been tempted, tricked, and returned to the realm and multitude of " ordinary beings " (*pṛthagjana*).

The aspirant to Bodhisattvahood must strive to behave as though he were already completely without ego; just as a pupil in any art (the dance, for example) must try to act as though he were already a master of his skill. The nonexistence of all phenomenal values on the transcendental plane must be unremittingly anticipated in both thought and conduct, and the point of view of absolute wisdom relentlessly exercised in numberless acts through numberless lives. In this manner wisdom is incorporated gradually in the candidate. It becomes, first, part and parcel of his personality and then, at last, his whole essence and only state of being. A "superabundant store of forces or virtues " (*guṇa-sambhāra*) is the natural corollary of such a supreme achievement of indifference. By not caring for anything at all, and thus completely transcending himself as man, the absolutely unconditioned being becomes elevated to, and established in, a spiritual sphere of universal omnipotence—

---

[3] Aśvaghoṣa, *Sutrālankāra* 64. (A fine translation will be found in E. W. Burlingame, *Buddhist Parables*, New Haven, 1922, pp. 314–324).

[4] *Jātakamālā* 1. (Speyer, op. cit., pp. 1–8).

and this force thereafter radiates from him eternally, flashing forth for the benefit of all who ask.

The fierce will and the struggle for superhuman power of the old ascetics of the hermit groves thus attain, in the Bodhisattva ideal, to their most benign transfiguration. The infinitely powerful status of saviorship is the purified and perfected, non-egoistic counterpart of that earlier, supremely self-assertive effort—the whole discipline now being devoted to the universal, instead of to the individual, benefit. In every phase, crisis, and realization along the path to perfection of Avalokiteśvara, Kṣitigarbha (Chinese: Ti-tsang; Japanese: Jizo), Amitābha, and the multitude of other Bodhisattvas of Mahāyāna sacred cult and legend, we read the lesson of this absolutely sublimated, omnipotently selfless state of realization.

The brief, extraordinarily compressed Mahāyāna Buddhist text known as the *Prajñā-pāramitā-hṛdaya-sūtra*, "The Manual of the Heart (i.e., the Secret) of the Perfection of the Wisdom of the Other Shore,"[5] states that when a Bodhisattva engaging in the deep practice of the Wisdom of the Other Shore considers within himself, "There are the five elements-of-existence," he perceives immediately that they are "void in their very nature."[6] "Here form," it is stated, "is emptiness, and emptiness indeed is form. Emptiness is not different from form, form is not different from emptiness. What is form that is emptiness, what is emptiness that is form."

This is what the Bodhisattva perceives with respect to form. His perceptions, then, with respect to each of the other elements of existence—sensations, notions, predispositions, and knowledge—are the same. "All things bear the characteristic marks of emptiness. They do not come into being, they do not cease to be; they are not stainless, they are not stained; they do not become imperfect, they do not become perfect. Therefore, here in this emptiness there is no form, there are no sensations, notions, or mental propensities; there is no consciousness; there is no eye, ear, nose, tongue, body, or mind; no color, sound, odor, taste, or object of touch; no constituent element of vision or of the other sense processes, no constituent element of the mental processes. There is no knowledge, no nescience, no destruction of knowledge, no destruction of nescience. There is no twelvefold concatenation of causes and effects, ending in old age and death.[7] There is no destruction of old age and death; there is neither any coming into existence nor any ceasing of suffering; there is no path to the destruction of suffering. There is no enlightenment, no attainment, no realization—since enlightenment does not exist."

No argument is offered in support of these fantastic observations. They are simply presented as the statements of the Bodhisattva Avalokiteśvara—obviously to show that the paradoxical truth of the Wisdom of the Other Shore lies beyond the range of the vision of this bank. The nature of such a truth may be suggested ver-

---

[5] Sacred Books of the East, Vol. XLIX, Part II, pp. 147–149.

[6] The five elements of existence are: 1. *rūpa* (form), which comprehends the four elements of earth, water, fire, and air, as well as every form that springs from them, i.e., all physical phenomena, 2. *vedanā* (sensations, sense-perceptions, feelings), 3. *sañjñā* (all the notions that constitute self-conscious intellection), 4. *sāmskāra* (predispositions, inclinations, mental molds), and 5. *vijñāna* (consciousness, discrimination, knowledge). The group 2–5 composes the sphere of *nāman* (name), or mental phenomena.

[7] The twelvefold concatenation of causes and effects (*pratītya-samutpāda*) is represented in Buddhism as follows: 1. ignorance, 2. action, 3. consciousness, 4. name and form, 5. the senses, 6. contact, 7. sensation, 8. craving, 9. attachment, 10. becoming, 11. birth, 12. old age, disease, and death. Cf. Takakusu, op. cit., pp. 29–36.

bally, but it resists the analysis and arguments of reason. Following, therefore, this suggestion of what is to be known, comes a description of the perfected state itself; and this is the clue to the curious "way of action" of the candidate for Bodhisattva-hood:

"There are no obstacles of thought for the Bodhisattva who cleaves to the Wisdom of the Other Shore. Because there are no obstacles of thought, he has no fear; he has transcended all wrong notions; he abides in enduring nirvāṇa. All the Buddhas of the past, present, and future,[8] cleaving to the Wisdom of the Other Shore, have awakened to the highest, perfect, complete awakening.

"Therefore one should know"—and the text now proceeds to its most mysterious and most helpful, culminating statement: "The Wisdom of the Other Shore is the great magic formula (mantra), the magic formula of great wisdom, the most excellent magic formula, the peerless magic formula, capable of allaying every suffering. It is truth because it is not falsehood. A magic formula has been given in the Wisdom of the Other Shore. It sounds as follows:

"'O THOU WHO ART GONE, WHO ART GONE, WHO ART GONE TO THE OTHER SHORE, WHO HAST LANDED ON THE OTHER SHORE, O THOU ENLIGHTENMENT, HAIL!'"

"Here endeth the Manual of the Heart of the Wisdom of the Other Shore."

The first requirement of the spiritual pupil in India, as we have seen, is the great virtue of faith (śraddhā), trust in the teacher and his words. The faith will be corroborated by the pupil's own experience in the course of his spiritual progress, but meanwhile he cannot presume to argue with his guru in callow criticism of the paradoxical doctrine. He must undergo, first, a transformation; that, not criticism, will be the means of his understanding. He must be brought by a process of evolution to a spiritual level from which to experience the meaning of the enigmatical teaching. And meanwhile, the process of his sublimation will be facilitated by meditation on the magic formula, which is the "Heart of the Wisdom of the Other Shore," and which he is to regard as an expression of his own supreme belief, designed to concentrate and intensify his faith. Though temporarily unintelligible to him, it is nevertheless his credo, to be repeated in constant recitation, as an invocation bidding the Wisdom of the Other Shore to come to him. And the wonder is that this magic formula actually can function as an effective alchemical charm, facilitating the transmutation that duly yields, of itself, the gold of enlightenment.

For meditation on this curious string of words is not the sole means by which the neophyte, filled with faith, is to attempt to bring to pass the all-important transformation in his understanding. The performance of certain characteristic acts is also required, and these, together with the experience of their results, make the formula more meaningful in the course of time, while, in reciprocal effect, the formula, constantly held in mind, serves to extract and bring to a point the lesson of the faithful performance of the necessary acts.

The sense, for example, of the Mahāyānist rerenderings of certain tales from the Jātaka, in the sixth-century collection known as the *Jātakamālā*, "The Garland

---

[8] According to the Mahāyāna there have been, there are, and there will be numberless Buddhas; cf. *supra*, p. 508.

of Tales from the Earlier Lives of the Buddha,"[9] is that one has to assume peculiar attitudes, exhibit uncommon reactions in crucial situations, and accomplish very special deeds, if one is ever to come to a new outlook upon life and on oneself. Practice precedes insight; knowledge is the reward of action: therefore, try! That is the thought. For it is by doing things that one becomes transformed. Executing a symbolic gesture, actually living through, to the very limit, a particular role, one comes to realize the truth inherent in the role. Suffering its consequences, one fathoms and exhausts its contents. Knowledge is to be attained, in other words, not through inaction (as in the Jaina and the classic Yoga disciplines) but through a bold and advertent living of life.

This is an idea radically different in its implications from that of the penitential groves, and yet completely consistent with the ancient Indian concept of karma.[10] One attracts the bright karmic substance that cleans away and replaces tamas[11] by sacrificing oneself wholeheartedly, in a spirit of humility and self-effacement, performing virtuous deeds while suppressing relentlessly every impulse to self-aggrandizement and display. The Buddha-in-the-making gradually imbues himself with karmic luminosity by cultivating in action the "highest virtues or perfections" (pāramitās), until there is finally no space left within him for any darker, inauspicious karmic force. People who cling to their ego favor instinctively the deceits of the phenomenal illusion, and so bind themselves the more, with every act, to the passionate forces of the life-instinct that clings only to itself; but the candidate for the Wisdom of the Other Shore behaves consistently as though he had already left behind the delusion of the world display. In every act of his daily living he makes a decision in favor of the self-transcending alternative, until at last, as a consequence of infinitely numerous deed-experiences of this kind, he does actually transcend the delusions of his phenomenal psychology: thenceforward he behaves instinctively as though his ego, with its false impressions, did not exist. This transmutation is the very sense and essence of the Wisdom of the Other Shore.

Actual acts, meanwhile, are the only things that can set us free. Virtuous, egoless acts release the mind, in the end, from the bondage of its ingrained, normal human attitudes and propensities, which are based on not knowing better. But such egoless, apparently dangerous acts require a faith in the as yet unknown, a humble courage, and a generous willingness to take a blind jump into the dark. Then, as a reward, they open to us a new outlook. A magical change of scenery is produced— a new order of values emerges. Because it is a fact: one is transformed by one's deeds, either for better or for worse: ignorance and knowledge are but the intellectual aspects of the changes wrought upon us by our manner of life.

---

[9] The *Jātakamālā* is a work in Sanskrit attributed to a certain Āryasūra (for translation, see *supra*, p. 537, note 84), which contains 34 Jātakas, or exemplary tales of the earlier lives of the Buddha, adapted, for the most part, from the much earlier, Pāli compendium of more than five hundred Jātakas. The latter is one of the great portions of the orthodox Hinayāna canon (cf. *The Jātaka, or Stories of the Buddha's Former Births*, translated from the Pāli by various hands under the editorship of E. B. Cowell, 6 vols., Cambridge, England, 1895–1907).

[10] *Editor's note*: The final goal and emphasis—as ever in India—is knowledge, not work; but work, or action, is indicated as the means. Dr. Zimmer's manuscript carries a brief note, indicating his intention to compare this approach with that of the Karma Yoga taught in the *Bhagavad Gītā*, but the paragraph seems not to have been written.

[11] Tamas gun ; for a discussion of the gunas, cf. *supra*, pp. 295–297, 398–402.

The manner of life of the Bodhisattva is well summarized in the formula: "A guard I would be to them who have no protection, a guide to the voyager, a ship, a well, a spring, a bridge for the seeker of the Other Shore."[12]

To see the potential Buddhahood in all, the criminal and the animal as well as the virtuous and the human, is the most just approach possible to the beings of the world. All beings, all men, whether virtuous or wicked, as well as inferior creatures even down to the ants, are to be regarded, respected, and treated as potential Buddhas. This is a view at once democratic and aristocratic—basically the same view as that of the ancient Jaina system and the doctrine of Gosäla. Indeed, in all of the later Indian philosophic disciplines dedicated to the realization of the hidden truth through an attainment of individual perfection, this view is reflected, one way or another. Its main principle is, that perfection is not something added or acquired from without, but rather, the very thing that is already potential within, as the basic actuality of the individual. The proper metaphor, therefore, for the Indian view of the process of fulfillment is not that of progress, growth, evolution, or expansion into greater external spheres, but Self-recollection. The effort of the pupil is to bring into consciousness what already reposes in a hidden state, dormant and quiescent, as the timeless reality of his being.

This is the basic Indian concept of the way—a fundamentally static view of the "march to enlightenment" (bodhicaryā). In the Yoga-sūtras the goal is represented as the attainment of "isolation-integration" (kaivalya), in the Sānkhya as the achievement of "discriminating insight" (viveka), in Vedānta as the realization of the "Transcendental Self" (ātman-brahman), and in Buddhism as "Enlightenment" (bodhi); but in essence these goals are one. Something that was stained, impaired, temporarily inactive and out of contact, polluted, obscured, not shining forth in its supreme light, not manifesting its boundless strength and prodigious faculties, becomes reinstated, restored to its native glory, cleansed, awake, and pristine. The process is compared to that of the polishing of a crystal, or the cleaning of a mirror that has somehow become besmeared and soiled.[13]

The purification of the gross body is properly the first step, and this is best effected through the physical exercises and processes of Haṭha Yoga: a cleansing of the intestinal canal through the practices called basti and neti, and of the bodily channels containing and carrying vital wind (prāṇa) through the classic exercises

---

[12] Cf. Louis de la Valée Poussin, Bouddhisme, 3rd edtiion, Paris 1925, p. 303, and Keith op, cit., p. 290.

[13] Editor's note: Nāgārjuna's doctrine of the Void rendered this image archaic; nevertheless, it continued to serve as a respected metaphor until Hui-neng (638–713 A.D.) wrote his celebrated verse on the wall of the Yellow Plum Monastery:

There is neither Bo Tree
Nor any mirror bright;
Since sūnyatā is all,
Whereon can what dust alight?

Hui-neng became the Sixth Patriarch of the Ch'an (Japanese: Zen)school of Far Eastern Buddhism. (Cf. Suzuki, op. cit., p. 205; Alan W. Watts, The Spirit of Zen, The Wisdom of the East Series, London, 1936, p. 40; and Sokei-an, "The Transmission of the Lamp," in Cat's Yawn, published by the First Zen Institute of America, New York, 1947, p. 26).

of control of the breath (*prāṇāyāma*). Such disciplines cleanse and rebuild the nervous and glandular systems.[14]

Meanwhile the systematic purification of the subtle body is also undertaken. According to the yogic method of Patañjali, this is effected by a gradual transformation of tāmasic and rājasic qualities and forces into sāttvic,[15] while according to the more ancient, less psychological, more materialistic approach of the Jaina disciplines, it is to be brought about by an inhibiting of the physical influx of darkening karmic color into the crystal of the monad. In either case, the sum and substance of the teaching is the same: not simply that we are meant to be crystal pure and perfect, but that in essence we really are. The psychophysical system is defiled, obscured, and disordered by obstructing matter of some kind, which clogs the channels and vessels of life and consciousness on every level. *Mala*, " dirt, refuse, impurity," fills us; we are " besmeared." Whereas the true and highest state is *nir-añjana*: "without besmearing." Brahman is *nir-añjana*. The Buddha is *nir-añjana*. We ourselves become wholly Brahman, wholly Enlightened, wholly what we are, only by getting rid of the soiling matter (*prakṛti*) which afflicts us from without, purging both the physique and the psyche by means of a continuous and radical cleansing diet.

That is to say: instead of a concept of growth, expansion, evolution, and acquisition, India's thought is that of a draining, scouring, and purification, directed to a *restitutio in integrum*: an integral restitution of the primal state—such as it was before the enigmatic moment or motion that set in action the universe and its microcosmic counterpart, the clouded wit of man. The Self, when cleansed, shines forth of itself, and at this moment our Enlightenment is no longer potential, but a fact. The comparable procedure in Hindu medicine is that of the regimen of preliminary purgatives, enemas, and emetics, to be followed by a light and wholesome, restorative, sāttvic diet.[16]

Philosophic theory, religious belief, and intuitive experience support each other in India in the basic insight that, fundamentally, all is well. A supreme optimism prevails everywhere, in spite of the unromantic recognition that the universe of man's affairs is in the most imperfect state imaginable, one amounting practically to chaos. The world-root, the secret veiled reality, is of an indestructible diamond-

[14] *Editor's note*: This paragraph is followed in Dr. Zimmer's papers by a brief note indicating his intention to build it out. Hatha Yoga is a system of physical exercises for the cultivation of perfect health and supernormal bodily powers. Properly, it is a preliminary to other yoga disciplines, but it may be practiced also as an end in itself.

[15] For a discussion of the gunas (tamas guṇa, rajas gaṇa, sattva guṇa), cf. *supra*, pp. 295–297, 398–402.

[16] *Editor's note*: "The difference of method between the Indian and the Chinese [Buddhist teachers] often raised the question as to the difference, if there be [any], between the 'Tathāgata Dhyāna' and the 'Patriarchal Dhyāna.' For instance, when Hsiang-yen showed his song of poverty to Yang-shan, the latter said, 'You understand the Tathāgata Dhyāna but not yet the Patriarchal Dhyāna.' When asked about the difference, Mu-chou replied, 'The green mountains are green mountains, and the white clouds are white clouds'" (Suzuki, op. cit., pp. 224–225). The difference of method here noted does not mean that the Far Eastern Buddhist goal is not the same as the Indian, namely a *restitutio in integrum*. "When the monk Ming came to Hui-neng and asked for instruction, Hui-neng said, 'Show me your original face before you were born'" (ibid., p. 224). The "Tathāgata Dhyāna" to which Dr. Suzuki refers was the mode of "contemplation" (Sanskrit, *dhyāna;* Chinese, *Ch'anā* Japanese *zen*) taught by Gautama Takyamuni (the Tathāgata), the "Patriarchal Dhyāna" was that introduced into China in 520 A.D. by the Indian Buddhist Patriarch Bodhidharma and developed by Hui-neng; it is continued to this day in the Zen schools of Japan. For an exposition of this technique of restitution, the reader is referred to Takakusu, op. cit., pp. 153–165, and to the volumes cited *supra*, p. 546, note 94a.

hardness, even though we—our feelings, minds, and senses—can be in the wrong, and indeed mostly are. Mentally, bodily, and morally, we are far from perfection; hence we are incapable of mirroring truth and becoming aware of our basic serenity. That very truth, however, the highest reality, is ever and universally present, whether our consciousness gets in touch with it or not. Furthermore, even though in the realm of the perishable, in the passage between birth and death, in the sphere of suffering and delight, everything changes, above or beyond all these disturbing changes there remains the possibility of that one, supreme, composing change, which is unique and *sui generis*: the change in our own nature that puts an end to the derangements of change—through knowledge of the Unchangeable, which is the fundament of our own intrinsic, never-changing being.

That abiding presence is compared to the sun obscured from us by the cloud of the mind's unknowing. Suffering, pain, and the disorders of the world do not represent the true state of things, but are the reflexes of our own wrong perspective, and yet they seem to us to be very real, until the obstruction is dissolved and the mind beholds the source of its own light. The cloud between is small, yet it can cover with its little, perishable form the blazing presence. This cloud being blown away, the transcendent light is beheld immediately, of its own power, and yet even while obscured from us—unlooked upon, unrealized, unrevealed—it is ever there in its enduring splendor. And not only is it always there, it is the source and sustenance of everything that is here.

As we have stated many times, and now, for the last time, must state again, the Jainas represented the crystal of the life-monad (*kīva*) as defiled by a physical karmic coloring substance (*leśya*), which, on entering it, darkened its intrinsic light. This subtle physical influx (*āsrava*) had to be literally stopped, and the darkening matter then allowed to evaporate or burn away by becoming converted into experience, biography, suffering, and destiny—which was a comparatively simple, materialistic reading of the problem. The later Indian view, as represented in the classic, semi-materialistic systems of the Sāṅkhya, Yoga, and Upaniṣads, then regarded the life-monad (Sāṅkhya and Yoga: *puruṣa*), or the Self (Upaniṣads: *ātman*), as forever undefiled, like the sun; only the soul-faculties clustering around it were in darkness—and this was a darkness, furthermore, rather of ignorance than of literal involvement. No longer was karmic matter pouring into the kernel of our being, as in the formula of the Jainas, but a veil of ignorance was cutting off the light. And we had merely to dissolve this cloud by bringing to bear upon it the power of its opposite: *viveka* (discrimination), *vidyā* (knowledge). The unresolved question remained, however, as to the nature of the cloud, and this, as we have seen, furnished a theme for inexhaustible debate. One way or another, no matter how the philosophers turned the problem, a *second* sphere of forces (however defined, however rationalized, however devaluated by unfavorable descriptions) had to be admitted into the system as a counter to the sphere of "That Which Truly Is." And the two had then to be co-ordinated in some kind of not quite satisfying, unrelated relationship.

The mind, for example, is part of the bodily system, though it mirrors, usually imperfectly, the light of the spirit. The mind is not uninvolved. It is not an absolutely unconcerned visitor from a higher realm. On the contrary, most of it is colored, tinged and biased, limited and supported, by the nature and material of the individual body, on and in which it grows, and which it is meant to direct and follow. The mental faculty, in all its operations, is but a function of this bodily whole, prejudiced by the peculiar quality of the gross physical substance that enwraps it, as well as by the subtle substance of which it is itself constituted. The mind is a mirror, but obscured by its own darkness; a pond ruffled by the gales of its own passions, by the winds of the transient emotions, the restlessness of "Him Who Blows." If it were only like a lovely mountain lake, sheltered against the ruffling breath by hill barriers on every side, crystal clear, unaffected by any turbid affluents to stain its clarity and give a ripple to its surface, fed by only an underground source in its own depth—then it might be capable of mirroring, without distortion, the form of truth. And yet, even then, there would remain this dualistic problem (at least so far as metaphysical arguments and explanations are concerned) of the twofold context of the mirror and the light.

The Buddhist approach to the difficulty was based on a formula of negating rather than affirming an abiding essence beyond or beneath the veiling cloud. The Buddha himself initiated this attitude with his fundmental dictum, "All is without a self," and though his followers, in spite of their Master's repeated refusal to engage in metaphysical discourse, soon enough became involved in discussion, both among themselves and with the Brāhmans, and in the end were practically back in the Hindu fold,[17] their basic tendency to negate was nevertheless carried, in the classic, culminating period of the Mahāyāna, to its own, truly wondrous, theoretical consummation in the "Doctrine of the Void." The principle of the paradox here was brought from the meditation grove into the very camp of reason, the academy of philosophical verbalization, where the mind then dismembered itself systematically in a series of thorough-going demonstrations, dissolving, one by one, its own supports and leaving the consciousness-beyond-cerebration alone in the void. And in the same spirit of trust in the transcendent, the way of the Bodhisattva was developed as an ethical application of the principle of unwavering faith in the metaphysically grounded Doctrine of the Buddha. In diametric contrast to the way of the Jaina "Crossing-Maker," whose spiritual passage to the Yonder Shore was achieved by an extreme technique of immobilization, the Bodhisattva, inspired by the immanence on this shore of the transcendency of that, established himself and his world in nondual understanding by the way of truth-revealing acts. The doctrine of the nondual void was applied courageously to the void of life. All things, Buddhas and arhats as well as "momentary particles" (dharmas), are void, even unto "nothingness" (abhāvadhātu).

---

[17] Cf. supra, pp. 529–531.

The New Man

Maurice Nicoll

Maurice Nicoll (1884–1953) was an English physician and an early pupil of Carl Jung. He later became one of the most outstanding interpreters of the teaching of G. I. Gurdjieff and P. D. Ouspensky. In addition to *The New Man*, he is the author of *Living Time* and *The Mark*.

Part One

All sacred writings contain an outer and an inner meaning. Behind the literal words lies another range of meaning, another form of knowledge. According to an old-age tradition, Man once was in touch with this inner knowledge and inner meaning. There are many stories in the Old Testament which convey another knowledge, a meaning quite different from the literal sense of the words. The story of the Ark, the story of Pharaoh's butler and baker, the story of the Tower of Babel, the story of Jacob and Esau and the mess of pottage, and many others, contain an inner *psychological* meaning far removed from their literal level of meaning. And in the Gospels the *parable* is used in a similar way.

Many parables are used in the Gospels. As they stand, taken in the literal meaning of the words, they refer apparently to vineards, to householders, to stewards, to spendthrift sons, to oil, to water and to wine, to seeds and sowers and soil, and many other things. This is their literal level of meaning. The language of parables is difficult to understand just as is, in general, the language of all sacred writings. Taken on the level of literal understanding, both the Old and New Testaments are full not only of contradictions but of cruel and repulsive meaning.

The question arises: Why are these so-called *sacred* writings cast in misleading form? Why is not what is meant explained clearly? If the story of Jacob's supplanting of Esau, or, again, of the Tower of Babel, or of the Ark constructed in three storeys riding on the flood, is not literally true but has a quite different inner meaning, why is it all not made evident? Why again should *parables* be used in the Gospels? Why not say directly what is meant? And if a person thinking in this way were to ask why the story of Creation in Genesis, which clearly cannot be taken literally, means something else, something quite different from what the literal words mean, he might very well conclude that the so-called sacred writings are nothing but a kind of fraud deliberately perpetrated on Mankind. If all these stories, allegories, myths, comparisons and parables in Sacred Scripture mean something else, why can it not be stated clearly what they mean from the starting-point so that everyone can understand? Why veil everything? Why all this mystery, this obscurity?

Source: Maurice Nicoll, *The New Man* (London, 1961), pp. 1–18. Reprinted by permission of Robinson & Watkins Books Ltd.

The idea behind all sacred writing is to convey a higher meaning than the literal words contain, the truth of which must be seen by Man *internally*. This higher, concealed, inner, or esoteric, meaning, cast in the words and sense-images of ordinary usage, can only be grasped by the understanding, and it is exactly here that the first difficulty lies in conveying higher meaning to Man. A person's literal level of understanding is not necessarily equal to grasping psychological meaning. To understand literally is one thing: to understand psychologically is another. Let us take some examples. The commandments says: "Thou shalt not kill." This is literal. But the psychological meaning is: "Thou shalt not murder in thy heart." The first meaning is literal: the second meaning is psychological, and is actually given in Leviticus. Again the commandment: "Thou shalt not commit adultery" is literal, but the psychological meaning, which is more than this, refers to mixing different doctrines, different teachings. That is why it is often said that people went *whoring* after other gods, and so on. Again, the literal meaning of the commandment: "Thou shalt not steal" is obvious, but the psychological meaning is far deeper. To steal, psychologically, means to think that you do everything *from yourself*, by your own powers, not realising that you do not know who you are or how you think or feel, or how you even move. It is, as it were, taking everything for granted and ascribing everything to yourself. It refers to an attitude. But if a man were told this directly, he would not understand. So the meaning is veiled, because if it were expressed in literal form no one would believe it, and everyone would think it mere nonsense. The idea would not be understood—and worse still, it would be taken as ridiculous. Higher knowledge, higher meaning, if it falls on the ordinary level of understanding, will either seem nonsense, or it will be wrongly understood. It will then become useless, and worse. Higher meaning can only be given to those who are close to grasping it rightly. This is one reason why all sacred writings—that is, writings that are designed to convey more than the literal sense of the words—must be concealed, as it were, by an outer wrapping. It is not a question of misleading people, but a question of preventing this higher meaning from falling in the wrong place, on lower meaning, and thereby having its finer significance destroyed. People sometimes imagine they can understand anything, once they are told it. But this is quite wrong. The development of the understanding, the seeing of differences, is a long process. Everyone knows that little children cannot be taught about life directly because their understanding is small. Again, it is realised that there are subjects in ordinary life that cannot be understood save by long preparation, such as certain branches of the sciences. It is not enough to be merely told what they are about.

The object of all *sacred* writings is to convey higher meaning and higher knowledge in terms of ordinary knowledge as a starting-point. The parables have an ordinary meaning. The object of the *parables* is to give a man higher meaning in terms of lower meaning in such a way that he can either think for himself or not. The parable is an instrument devised for this purpose. It can fall on a man literally, or it can make him think for himself. It invites him to think for himself. A man first understands on his ordinary, matter-of-fact or natural level. To lift the understanding, whatever is taught must first fall on this level to some extent, to form a starting-point. A man must get hold of what he is taught, to begin with, in a natural way. But the parable has meaning beyond its literal or natural sense. It is deliberately designed to fall first on the ordinary level of the mind and yet *to work in the mind* in the direction of lifting the natural level of comprehension to another level of meaning. From this point of view, a parable is a *transforming* instrument in regard to meaning. As we shall see later the parable is also a connecting medium between a lower and a higher level in development of the understanding.

Part Two

The Gospels speak mainly of a possible inner evolution called "re-birth." This is their *central* idea. Let us begin by taking inner evolution as meaning a development of the understanding. The Gospels teach that a man living on this earth is capable of undergoing a definite inner evolution if he comes in contact with definite teaching on this subject. For that reason, Christ said: "I am the way, and the truth, and the life" (John xiv, 6). This inner evolution is psychological. To become a more *understanding* person is a psychological development. It lies in the realm of the thoughts, the feelings, the actions, and, in short, the *understanding*. *A man is his understanding.* If you wish to see what a man *is*, and not what he is *like*, look at the level of his understanding. The Gospels speak, then, of a *real* psychology based on the teaching that Man on earth is capable of a definite inner evolution in understanding.

The Gospels are from beginning to end all about this possible self-evolution. They are psychological documents. They are about the psychology of this possible inner development—that is, about what a man must think, feel, and do in order to reach a new level of understanding. The Gospels are not about the affairs of life, save indirectly, but about this central idea—namely, that Man internally is a *seed* capable of a definite growth. Man is compared with a seed capable of a definite evolution. As he is, Man is incomplete, unfinished. A man can bring about his own evolution, his own completion, *individually*. If he does not wish to do this he need not. He is then called *grass*—that is, burned up as useless. This is the teaching of the Gospels. But this teaching can be given neither directly nor by external compulsion. A man must begin to *understand for himself* before he can receive it. You cannot make anyone understand by force, by law. But why cannot this teaching be given directly? Why come again to the question: "Why cannot higher meaning be given in plain terms? Why all this obscurity? Why these fairy-stories? Why these parables, and so on?" Everyone has an outer side that has been developed by his contact with life and an inner side which remains vague, uncertain, undeveloped. Teaching about re-birth and *inner evolution* must not fall only on the outer side of a man—the life-developed side. Some people reach a stage where they realise that life does not satisfy them, where they genuinely begin to look in other directions and seek different aims, before they can *hear* any teaching of an order similar to that of the Gospels. The outer side of a man is organised by life and its demands, and is according to his position and capacities. In a sense, it is artificial: it is acquired. But it is only the inner, *unorganised* side of a man which can *evolve* as does a seed by its own growth, *from itself*. For that reason the teaching of inner evolution must be so formed that it does not fall solely on the outer side of a man. It must fall there first, but be capable of penetrating more deeply and awakening the man himself—

the inner, unorganised man. A man evolves internally through his deeper reflection, not through his outer life-controlled side. He evolves through the spirit of his individual understanding and by inner consent to what he sees as truth. The psychological meaning of the relatively fragmentary teaching recorded in the Gospels refers to this deeper, inner side of everyone. Once one can comprehend that a man can evolve only through a growth in his own individual, and so inner, understanding, one can see that if a true teaching about the meaning of inner evolution falls solely on the outer side of a man it will be useless or will even appear to him as so much nonsense. It may, in fact, be destroyed by falling on the wrong place in him—on his business-side, his worldly side. He will then trample it underfoot. This is the meaning of Christ's remark: "Neither cast your pearls before swine, lest haply they trample them under their feet. . . ." (Matt. vii, 6). "Under" means the outer life-side of a man, the lowest side of a man's understanding, the side which only believes in what his senses show him, the side of the mind which touches the "earth" as do the feet. This side cannot receive the teaching of inner evolution because it is turned outwards and not inwards. This side therefore cannot understand about re-birth.

A man has one birth, naturally. All esoteric teaching says that he is capable of a second birth. But this re-birth or second birth belongs to the *man in himself*, the private, secret man, the internal man, not to the man as he seems to be in life and thinks himself to be, the successful man, the pretended man. All the latter belongs to the outer man, what the man appears to be, not what the man *is* inwardly. It is the inward man that is the side of re-birth.

In the psychological teaching of the Gospels, a man is not taken as what he appears to be, but as what he most deeply *is*. This is one reason why Christ attacked the Pharisees. For they were *appearances*. They appeared to be good, just, religious, and so on. In attacking the Pharisees, he was attacking that side of a man that pretends, that keeps up appearances for the sake of outer merit, fear, praise, the man who in himself is perhaps even rotten. The Pharisee, psychologically understood, is the outer side of a man who pretends to be good, virtuous, and so on. It is that side of yourself. This is the Pharisee in every man and this is the psychological meaning of Pharisee. Everything said in the Gospels, whether represented in the form of parable, miracle or discourse, has a *psychological* meaning, apart from the literal sense of the words. Therefore the psychological meaning of the *Pharisees* refers, not to certain people who lived long ago, but to oneself now—*to the Pharisee in oneself*, to the insincere person in oneself, who, of course, cannot receive any real and genuine psychological teaching without turning it into an occasion for merit, praise and award. Later on we will study the meaning of the *Pharisee in oneself* more fully.

Part Three

Since all sacred writings contain both a literal and a psychological meaning they can fall in a double way on the mind. If Man were capable of no further development this would have no sense. It is just because he is capable of a further individual evolution that parables exist. The "sacred" idea of Man—that is, the esoteric or inner idea—is that he possesses an unused higher level of understanding and that his real development consists in reaching this higher possible level. So all sacred writings, as in the form of parables, have a double meaning because they contain a literal meaning designed to fall on the level of a man as he is, and at the same time they can reach up to the higher level potentially present in him and awaiting him.

A parable is cast in the form of *ancient meaning*. A parable in the Gospels is cast in the form of an ancient language now forgotten. There was a time when the language of parables could be understood. This language—the language of the parable, allegory and miracle—is lost to the humanity of today. But sources still remain which enable us to understand something of this ancient meaning. Since the object of the parable is to connect higher and lower meanings, it can be thought of as a *bridge* between two levels, a *liaison* between literal and psychological understanding. And, as we shall see, a definite language was once well known, in which this *double rendering* was understood and certain words and terms deliberately used in an understood double sense. Through this ancient language a connexion was made between higher and lower meaning—or, which is the same—the higher and lower sides of man.

Our first birth is from the world of cells by evolution into that of Man. To be re-born or born again means to evolve up to a higher psychology, a higher possible level of understanding. This is Man's supreme aim, according to the teaching of all ancient Scriptures in which Man is regarded psychologically as an undeveloped seed. And this is esoteric teaching. This level can only be reached by new knowledge and the feeling and practice of it; and the knowledge that gives a man this possibility is sometimes called, in the Gospels, Truth, or sometimes the *Word*. But it is not ordinary truth, or ordinary knowledge. It is knowledge about this further step in development.

Let us try to gain some preliminary ideas about this ancient double language of parables. Let us begin by studying how Truth is represented. In this ancient language visible things represent psychological things. Outer life, registered by the senses, is transformed into another level of meaning.

Now Truth is not a visible object, but it was represented by means of a visible object in this language. A parable is full of visible imagery of the objects of the senses. But each visual image represents something belonging to a psychological level of meaning, distinct from the image used. In the Gospels the word *water* is often used. What does this word mean in the ancient language? In the literal sense of the word it means the physical substance called water. But psychologically, on a higher level of meaning, it has a different import. Water does not mean simply water. Christ, in speaking of re-birth to Nicodemus, says that a man must be born of *water* and the spirit: "Except a man be born of *water* and the spirit, he cannot enter into the kingdom of God" (John iii, 5). What then does water mean? It must have another meaning, a psychological or higher meaning. We might guess, perhaps, that the "spirit" means possibly the "will" or the inmost, most real part of a man. And we might understand that to be born again does not mean literally to enter the womb of the mother again, as Nicodemus thought, who stands for a man capable only of literal understanding. Whatever we may think about the meaning of "spirit," we cannot imagine, with our ordinary comprehension, what "water" means in this ancient double-sided language, in which things of the senses convey another and special meaning. There is no clue. To say that a man must be born again of physical water is sheer nonsense. What then does water mean psychologically? We can find, by means of other passages in the Bible, what this physical image represents on the psychological level of meaning. A hundred examples might be quoted. Let us take one from the Gospels. Christ spoke to the Woman of Samaria by the well-side and told her he could give her "living water." Christ says to her when she has come to draw water at the well:

> Everyone that drinketh of this water shall thirst again: but whosoever drinketh of the water that I shall give him shall never thirst; but the water that I shall give him shall become in him a well of water springing up into eternal life.
>
> (John iv, 13–14).

It is plain that "water" is being used in a special sense, belonging to this ancient forgotten language. Again in the Old Testament, in the Book of Jeremiah, it is said:

> For my people have committed two evils; they have forsaken me the fountain of living waters, and hewed them out cisterns, broken cisterns, that can hold no water.
>
> (Jeremiah ii, 13).

What then is this water, this *living water*?

In the ancient language *water* means Truth. But it means a special kind of Truth, a special form of knowledge called "living Truth." It is living Truth because it makes a man *alive in himself*, and not dead, once the knowledge of it is assented to and applied in practice. In esoteric teaching—that is, teaching about inner evolution —a man is called *dead* who knows nothing about it. It is knowledge that is true only in reference to the reaching of this higher level of inner evolution awaiting everyone. It is knowledge about this higher level of Man and leading to it. It refers to what a man must know, think, feel, understand and do to reach his next stage of development. It is not outer truth, about outer things, outer objects, but inner Truth, about the man himself. It is therefore *esoteric* Truth (esoteric meaning inner) or Truth referring to that inner development and new organisation of a man that leads to his next step in real evolution. For no one can change, no one can become different, no one can evolve and reach this higher possible level and so be re-born, unless he knows, hears and follows a teaching about it. If he thinks he knows Truth of this order by himself then he is like those mentioned above who "forsake the living waters and hew out for themselves cisterns, broken cisterns, that can hold no water." The idea is quite plain. A teaching exists—and has always existed—that can lead to a higher development. This teaching is the real psychological teaching in regard to Man and the possible development of the New Man in him. Man cannot invent it by himself. He can hew out cisterns for himself but they hold no water—that is, no Truth.

When there is no Truth of this order the state of Man is sometimes compared with thirst.

> The poor and needy seek water and there is none, and their tongue faileth for thirst.
>
> (Isiaah xli, 17).

Or when people follow wrong truth a comparison is sometimes made with drinking bitter waters, or with undrinkable or polluted water.

Let us now apply this idea of water meaning Truth, in this ancient language, to one of the sayings of Christ, and realise what psychological meaning is, in contrast to literal meaning. Christ said:

> And whosoever shall give to drink unto one of these little ones a cup of cold water only, in the name of a disciple, verily I say unto you, he shall in no wise lose his reward.
>
> (Matt. x, 42).

Here a literal-minded person will think that all that is necessary is to give a cup of cold water to a child. But if water means Truth, then the phrase refers to the handing on of Truth, however, poorly. And "little one" here does not mean a child (in the Greek) but a person small in understanding. Let us also notice that, to receive Truth, the mind must be like a cup, which receives what is poured into it. That is, a man must be ready and willing to be taught, so that his mind is like a cup to receive water. So the phrase "giving a cup of water" refers to receiving Truth and handing it on to others.

All this cannot be logically expressed, but it can be psychologically understood. And this is exactly the intention of the ancient language we have begun to study.

Part Four

Other words for Truth are used in the esoteric writings of the Old and New Testaments. *Water* is not the only image used to represent the order of Truth that we are studying. In the ancient language *stone* and *wine* are both used as images for this form of Truth, but on different scales of meaning.

Stone represents the most external and literal form of esoteric Truth. It represents esoteric Truth in its most inflexible sense. The commandments were written on tables of *stone*. It must be understood that Truth about a higher evolution must rest upon a firm basis, for those incapable of seeing any deeper meaning.

Let us take briefly the extraordinary story of the Tower of Babel recorded in Genesis. The ideas centered in this story refer to Man trying by his ordinary knowledge to reach a higher level of development. This is the meaning of the tower that was built by Man. But from what has been said so far it can be realised that to reach a higher level for a man personally or for Mankind, the teaching of the knowledge necessary for this further step must be known and be followed. Man cannot add to his stature "by taking thought"—that is, his own ideas, his own thoughts, cannot bring him up to a new level of evolution. He must submit to a teaching. His efforts must be based on this Truth that we are studying. And this special knowledge or esoteric Truth, at its lowest level of comprehending, is called *stone*. We shall see what the Tower of Babel was built of, in regard to this necessary knowledge called Truth. It was not *stone*, and it is expressly said that it was not so. That is, it did not come from a higher level of Man—from those who have become New Men.

The story of the Tower of Babel is very strange and has little meaning if we take it literally. It begins by saying that once upon a time, after the days of Noah and the Ark, all people had a common language. "And the whole earth was of one lan-guage and one speech" (Genesis xi, I). Then it is said that they journeyed "from the east" (i.e. away from Truth) and came to a plain, and began to think of building a tower to reach to heaven. Notice how the account continues: "And they had brick for stone and slime they had for mortar. And they said, Go to, let us build us a city, and a tower, whose top may reach unto heaven, and let us make us a name. . . ." Notice that they travelled from the east and they had brick—a man-made thing— and not stone. The east represents in the ancient language of parables, the source of esoteric Truth. They reached a plain—that is, came down from a higher level— and then began to think that they could of themselves *do* something, apart from what knowledge of Truth they had gained "from the east." So they began to build a tower—that is, they thought that they could, out of their own ideas and thoughts, reach to the highest level, here called "heaven" and also called similarly in the Gospel language. "Heaven " means a higher level of Man and "earth" means an ordinary man—the natural man. They began to build for themselves, but notice that it is expressly said that they not only had bricks for *stone*, but *slime* for mortar.

A higher level cannot be understood by a lower level. A man on a higher level cannot be understood by a man on a lower level. Man as he is cannot reach a higher level unless he comes into possession of the knowledge (called Truth) that can lead him to it. So the Tower was a failure. And in the strange way in which this ancient language puts things, it looks as if " God" scattered them out of jealousy. But one must look deeper to understand this language. Man was at fault, not " God." Man tried to raise himself by his own knowledge, called here "brick" and "slime"— and so was shattered.

> And the whole earth was of one language and of one speech. And it came to pass, as they journeyed from the east, that they found a plain in the land of Shinar; and they dwelt there. And they said one to another, Go to, let us make brick, and burn them throughly. And they had brick for stone, and slime they had for mortar. And they said, Go to, let us build us a city and a tower, whose top may reach unto heaven; and let us make us a name, lest we be scattered abroad upon the face of the whole earth. And the Lord came down to see the city and the tower, which the children of men builded. And the Lord said, Behold, the people is one, and they have all one language; and this they begin to do: and now nothing will be restrained from them, which they have imagined to do. Go to, let us go down and there confound their language, that they may not understand one another's speech. So the Lord scattered them abroad from thence upon the face of all the earth: and they left off to build the city. Therefore is the name of it called Babel; because the Lord did there confound the language of all the earth: and from thence did the Lord scatter them abroad upon the face of all the earth.
>
> (Genesis xi, I–9).

But it is very difficult to understand the ancient language if we take it literally. We can understand that if an engineer makes some part of an engine that is wrongly measured or of the wrong material, his engine will be no good. He may say: " It is God's fault." It is not "God" punishing: it is a wrong "request" and so the re-sponse will not be as he hoped. The response will be according to the quality of his request. And this is " God" or, if you like, the " Universe," that science studies.

A wrong request leads to a wrong response. It is not really a wrong response but an exactly right response in view of the request. The parable of the Tower of Babel is an illustration of this. Man made a tower out of brick and slime, in place of *stone* and mortar. And " God " said—that is, response to request said: " this cannot be," in so many words.

Now let us look at other examples of *stone* as a term meaning, in the ancient language, Truth about a higher development. To reach a higher state of himself a man must request rightly and for this to come about a man must *know* what to ask for. Christ says: "Ask and ye shall receive." But unless we know something about either the *stone* or the *water* of esoteric knowledge, how can we know what to ask for ? Christ is not speaking about asking for life-things, but about asking for help in inner evolution and understanding. Certain requests are made in the Lord's Prayer. They are about *right asking*. But we will study this later. Now let us take the strange incident of Christ's re-naming Simon. *Simon* means " a hearing," but Christ re-named Simon *Peter*, which in the Greek is *stone*. Christ, of course, represents this Truth of which we are speaking. He called himself " the Truth." He spoke of a high level of evolution for each individual man. He taught the means of attaining it. He taught *re-birth*. Now in re-naming Simon as Peter, he referred to the literal aspect of his teaching. Christ said to Simon: " Thou art Peter, and upon this stone I will build my church; and the gates of Hades shall not prevail against it. I will give unto thee the keys of the kingdom of heaven . . ." (Matt. vxi, 18–19). Simon Peter was given the "keys of the kingdom of heaven." Heaven means psychologically this higher level of development, intrinsically possible for man. But Christ only gave Peter, as the *stone*, the keys. The commandments, written on stone, are keys also. But, literally taken, they are not enough. They open into psychological meaning. They contain great internal meaning. Eosteric Truth in the form of *stone* is not flexible enough to lead to any real inner development. It must be *understood*, not merely followed blindly. In Genesis it is said that Jacob rolled away the stone from the well. The stone in the mouth of the well means in the ancient language that literal Truth blocks the psychological understanding of it. The stone was rolled back and the flock *watered*: for *water* is the psychological understanding of literal esoteric Truth called *stone*. In this way can the following passage be understood:

> Then Jacob went on his journey, and came to the land of the children of the east, And he looked, and behold, a well in the field, and lo, three flocks of sheep lying there by it; for out of that well they watered the flocks: and the stone upon the well's mouth was great. And thither were all the flocks gathered: and they rolled the stone from the well's mouth, and watered the sheep.
>
> (Genesis xxix, 1–3).

When a stone blocks the well, it means that people have taken esoteric Truth literally, in the sense of the words only. They prefer rituals and so on. They literally " do not kill " but see no reason why they should not murder in their hearts.

Christ himself, who represented esoteric Truth or " the Way " or the " Word," was called " the stone which the builders rejected." The Psalmist says: " The stone which the builders rejected is become the head of the corner." (Ps. 118, 22.) This is a strange phrase. Who are the builders? The builders of what? Of this world? Certainly Christ's teaching came into a world built of violence, a world in which everyone believed that violence leads to something better. But when Christ is called the *stone* it means that fundamentally he was so. His whole teaching, however, was to transform stone into water and finally water into wine. The Jews understood everything literally, as stone. Christ transformed literal into psychological meaning. This is shown in one of the "miracles," which are really psychological miracles— that is, the transformation of literal meaning into psychological understanding. A man who is bound down to the literal meaning of higher truth can destroy himself. This explains, perhaps, why some religious people seem to be destroyed by their contact with religion and made worse than life would make them. This is possibly shown in the account in the fifth chapter of Mark of the man with an unclean spirit who came out of the tombs, of whom it is said that he was always "cutting himself with stones." *Stones*—that is, taking higher Truth at a literal level—cut him, made him unclean. And since Jesus represented, let us say at present, a higher under- standing of literal Truth, the man cried out to him: "What have I to do with thee, Jesus?" And Jesus said: "Come forth, thou unclean spirit, out of the *man*." The *man* means the man's understanding which is the real man. But this is only a slight glimpse of the meaning of this miracle-parable. It refers to a certain state of a man in regard to higher teaching. The point here is that the man "cut himself with *stones*" that is, took higher truth literally and was therefore *unclean*. And his uncleanliness had to pass into the swine. But perhaps we shall be able to understand something more of what this means later on.

Jesus always represents the non-literal or non-ritualistic understanding of higher Truth. The Jews in the Gospels *represent* not actual, literal poeple, but a cer- tain literal level of taking everything belonging to higher Truth. Everyone is a *Jew* who cannot get from the sense of the letter to the psychological meaning. So the Jews are said to "stone Christ." When Christ said: "I and the Father are one" it is said that "The Jews took up stones again to stone him," because their literal minds thought his words were blasphemy. The inner meaning is that people on the level of literal and so ritualistic, external understanding throw this meaning at people who stand above its level. One can even be *stoned* by what one once understood in a literal way and now understands quite differently. And one can always *stone* a man through his actual, literal words, without allowing any existence to what he really *meant*. And literal law, of the legal courts, is and must be based on *stone*—that is, on what you actually said in words and not on what you meant.

Part Five

Let us speak for a moment about *wine* used as an image for Truth. We shall study the meaning of esoteric Truth when it has reached the stage of wine in a man's understanding later. But at present we must understand that *stone* is the literal form of esoteric Truth, and *water* refers to another way of understanding the same Truth, and *wine* to the highest form of understanding it. In the miracle recorded in the second chapter of St John's Gospel, Christ turned water into wine. In this account it is said that he asked the servants to fill the *stone*-jars with *water* and then he transformed the water into *wine*. That is, three stages of a man's relation to Truth are shown, and this means, of course, three stages in the understanding of esoteric Truth.

Part Six

The idea of wine leads naturally to the idea of *vineyards* which produce wine. Before we can continue more fully the study of the ancient language of parables, we must look at the meaning of *vineyards* and try to get some idea of their significance. It will be necessary to speak further of this Truth that refers to a man's inner development and growth of understanding. This Truth is not ordinary truth. It is sown on the earth. For example, Christ taught this particular kind of Truth. In the Sermon on the Mount he spoke quite openly about certain aspects of it. But the deeper aspects of it he concealed under the guise of parables.

Man cannot invent this Truth for himself. We have seen that this is indicated in the story of the Tower of Babel where men thought they could reach Heaven by means of "brick and slime" instead of stone and mortar. Higher Truth, which simply means Truth that leads to a higher level of self-evolution, does not arise in life, but comes from those who have already reached this higher level. Many have reached it. Some few of them are recorded in ordinary history. Let us confine ourselves to Christ. He taught this higher Truth. But he spoke many things about the establishment of this special order of Truth on earth and used the image of a *vineyard*. A school of teaching, based on Truth of this order, was called by him a vineyard, and its object was to produce fruit. If it did not, it was cut down. Christ also speaks of himself as a vine and he says to his disciples:

> I am the vine, ye are the branches: he that abideth in me, and I in him, the same beareth fruit: for apart from me ye can do nothing.
>
> (John xv, 5.)

Christ relates the following parable about a vineyard:

> A certain man had a fig-tree planted in his vineyard; and he came seeking fruit thereon, and found none. And he said unto the vinedresser, Behold, these three years I come seeking fruit on this fig-tree, and find none: cut it down: why doth it also cumber the ground? And he answering saith unto him, Lord, let it alone this year also, till I shall dig about it, and dung it; and if it bear fruit thenceforth, well; but if not, thou shalt cut it down.
>
> (Luke xiii, 6–9).

From this point of view Man was regarded as capable of a special growth, a special inner development, and "vineyards" were established to make this development possible. Of course, they were not actual vineyards. They were *schools* of teaching. What did they teach? They taught, first of all, the knowledge that could lead, *if practised*, to the higher level of development inherent in Man. What they taught a man was that he was an individual—that is, unique—who could reach this higher state of himself and that this was his real meaning and that this only could satisfy him most deeply. They began with teaching this Truth—or knowledge of this special Truth—but they led to something else. They led from Truth to a definite state of a man where he acted no longer from the Truth that brought him up to this level, but from the level itself. This was sometimes called *Good*. *All Truth must lead to some good state as its goal.* This was the idea belonging to the term "vineyard." Wine was produced. A man began to act from Good, not Truth, thus becoming a New Man.

Five

Mysticism and Spiritual Discipline

Introduction

Up until quite recently in the modern world, mysticism was generally considered a psychological phenomenon of questionable validity and significance. And the mystic was often understood as a person somewhat out of touch with reality, however inspiring his visions might be. In the past decade, however, two factors have operated to dissolve most of the old clichés about mysticism. Modern scientific psychology has grown increasingly interested in the study of varying states of human consciousness, and many investigators have found themselves drawn toward the conclusion that what we call "ordinary waking consciousness" is far short of the possibilities of human nature. Moreover, what we take to be the "real world" may be in part a construct of our consciousness and hence relative to the internal conditions which obtain in any given psychological state.

At the same time, in addition to the evidence being provided by modern psychology, there has appeared a vast body of literature, including translations of hitherto unavailable texts, which shows that the phenomenon of directly experiencing a "higher" or "divine" reality lies at the heart of every great religious system, although it is often spoken about indirectly or in symbolic form. In many, or even in most cases, such experience is understood to be the aim of religious practice, the *raison d'être* of the manifold historical forms of spiritual discipline. As we begin to perceive the interrelationship between spiritual experience and the rigorous demands of spiritual discipline, it becomes apparent that the idea of mysticism must be considerably expanded to include not only experiences of the higher being, but higher (i.e., clearer) experiences of our "lower" nature as well—the individual's own limitations and need for help.

In the opening selection, philosopher **Walter T. Stace** argues persuasively for the authenticity of mystical experience and offers a sensitive definition of it as "the apprehension of an ultimate nonsensuous unity in all things." In the end, Stace views mysticism as not necessarily linked to religious tradition and concludes by countering the conventional opinion that the mystic is isolated from the claims of morality.

The eminent historian of religion, **Gershom Scholem,** approaches the issue from an entirely different angle in his examination of the relationship between mystical experience and orthodox religious authority. After weighing each side's claims, Scholem asserts that authentic mysticism is almost always developed from within tradition. Indeed, he concludes that "it is mystical experience which conceives and gives birth to authority"; that it is the mystic who brings new life to the ideals and teachings that lie at the root of the traditions.

From Scholem's masterly historical analysis, we are then plunged into one of the most powerful expressions of mystical experience in all the religious literature of the world. The eleventh chapter of "The Bhagavad-Gita" presents a vision of the oneness of the Absolute (here named Krishna) that is both terrifyingly awesome and radiantly beautiful. Following the brilliant commentary by **Sri Krishna Prem,** we learn that such experience constitutes a stage in a disciplined path that involves the seeker in a preparatory struggle with the "lower nature" of man. And we also understand that the conventional idea of God as transcendent, all-powerful, and all-knowing may have been originally rooted in actual experience, although of a very extraordinary sort. Recognizing this possibility of the experiential root of religious ideas will enable the student of religion to be more open to the import of the philosophical proofs for the existence of God, which is the subject of Chapter Six.

After the overwhelming mystical vision of "The Bhagavad-Gita," we find ourselves in the realm of the spiritual work that is perhaps the foundation of any authentic spiritual experience. A great contemplative Christian mystic, **St. Bernard of Clairvaux,** outlines the necessity for humility, considered to be "that thorough self-examination which makes a man contemptible in his own sight," and by means of which, step by step, man can ascend to a vision of the truth.

Following this classic expression of Christian spiritual discipline, a Tibetan lama, **Chögyam Trungpa,** characterizes the practice of meditation as the art of inner self-acceptance in the midst of the relationships of life. Students of comparative religion will be interested to note the subtle ways in which even here the differences appear between the Buddhist tradition, with its emphasis on dispelling illusion, and the Christian tradition, with its emphasis on resisting the impulses of pride.

Judaism also, as Scholem has pointed out for us, has its traditions of meditation and spiritual discipline, here exemplified by the great medieval thinker, **Moses Maimonides.** These excerpts from The Guide for the Perplexed concern the practice of remembering God day by day until, as it is sometimes said, a "link within the self" is formed, a bridge between levels of reality that makes of the human being a "servant of God" in experience and not only in theory.

Our next selection, by the Jewish novelist **Chaim Potok,** dramatizes the manner in which mystical teachings have formed an integral part of the everyday lives of Hasidic Jews of Europe and America.

But to illustrate more fully the way in which a spiritual teacher works with a pupil, we have chosen the opening episode from the celebrated book, *The Teachings of Don Juan*, by **Carlos Castaneda.** We might have gone to any one of a number of familiar sources, East or West. But what is uniquely valuable about this selection is that the language is entirely fresh, and thus the educative power of the *event* that the teacher calls into being is perhaps clearer to see, stripped, as it is, of familiar theological or philosophical associations. One cannot presume to say what, exactly, a spiritual master teaches, but it is clear from this example that religious knowledge transmitted in this way is bought at an existential price. Can an example such as this, remote as it is in language, time, and setting from, say, the teaching of Jesus or Buddha, give us a glimpse of what it may have meant to be a disciple of the Master?

Finally, **John Blofeld** presents a sensitive indication of both the limitations and relevance of mysticism in the contemporary world. This excerpt from his recent book, *Beyond the Gods*, is a model of responsive thought directed from the older to the new generation.

J. N.

Subjectivity, Objectivity and the Self

Walter T. Stace

W. T. Stace (1886–1967), an Anglo-American empirical philosopher, was born in London and studied at Trinity College, Dublin. His major works include *The Concept of Morals*, *Time and Eternity*, and *Mysticism and Philosophy*.

I. Terminological

In these pages I shall often use the expressions "mysticism," "mystic," "mystical experience," "mystical consciousness," "mystical idea." "Mysticism," of course is the general name of our entire subject, and its meaning will be gradually developed. By the word "mystic" I shall always mean a person who himself has had mystical experience. Often the word is used in a much wider and looser way. Anyone who is sympathetic to mysticism is apt to be labeled a mystic. But I shall use the word always in a stricter sense. However sympathetic toward mysticism a man may be, however deeply interested, involved, enthusiastic, or learned in the subject, he will not be called a mystic unless he has, or has had, mystical experience. The phrases "mystical experience" and "mystical consciousness" will be used as synonymous with each other. But "mystical consciousness" is the better term, the word "experience" being misleading in certain respects. It will be seen that both "mysticism" and "mystic" are defined in tems of mystical experience or consciousness. This is therefore the basic thing on which we have to fasten attention and in terms of which we have to understand the whole subject. Our question "What is mysticism?" really means "What is mystical experience?"

The phrase "mystical idea" has also to be defined in terms of mystical experience. It means an idea, belief, opinion, or proposition which was originally based on mystical experience, although the connection between the experience and the opinion may have been quite forgotten. The point is that a mystical idea is a product of the conceptual intellect, whereas a mystical experience is a nonintellectual mode of consciousness. The proposition that "time is unreal" is an example of a mystical idea. It must have arisen because mystics usually feel (a) that their experience is timeless and (b) it is more "real" (in some sense) than any other experience. But many philosophers who have never had any mystical experience, nor any knowledge of how the idea originated, yet come to adopt it in their philosophies and treat it as if it were a product of a process of reasoning. A mystical idea may be either true or false, though it must have originated in a genuine mystical experience.

Source: Walter T. Stace, *The Teachings of the Mystics.* Reprinted by permission of Mrs. Walter T. Stace.

II. Experience and Interpretation

On a dark night out of doors one may see something glimmering white. One person may think it is a ghost. A second person may take it for a sheet hung out on a clothesline. A third person may suppose that it is a white-painted rock. Here we have a single experience with three different interpretations. The experience is genuine, but the interpretations may be either true or false. If we are to understand anything at all about mysticism, it is essential that we should make a similar distinction between a mystical experience and the interpretations which may be put upon it either by mystics themselves or by nonmystics. For instance, the same mystical experience may be interpreted by a Christian in terms of Christian beliefs and by a Buddhist in terms of Buddhist beliefs.

III. Some Things Which Mysticism Is Not

The word "mysticism" is popularly used in a variety of loose and inaccurate ways. Sometimes anything is called "mystical" which is misty, foggy, vague, or sloppy. It is absurd that "mysticism" should be associated with what is "misty" because of the similar sound of the words. And there is nothing misty, foggy, vague, or sloppy about mysticism.

A second absurd association is to suppose that mysticism is sort of mystery-mongering. There is, of course, an etymological connection between "mysticism" and "mystery." But mysticism is not any sort of hocus-pocus such as we commonly associate with claims to the elucidation of sensational mysteries. Mysticism is not the same as what is commonly called the "occult"—whatever that may mean. Nor has it anything to do with spiritualism, or ghosts, or table-turning. Nor does it include what are commonly called para-psychological phenomena such as telepathy, telekinesis, clairvoyance, precognition. These are not mystical phenomena. It is perhaps true that mystics may sometimes claim to possess such special powers, but even when they do so they are well aware that such powers are not part of, and are to be clearly distinguished from, their mystical experience. Such powers, if they exist—as to which I express no opinion—may be possessed by persons who are not mystics. And conversely, even the greatest mystics may be devoid of them and know nothing about them. The closest connection one can admit will be to say that it may be the case that the sort of persons who are mystics also tend to be the sort of persons who have parapsychological powers.

Finally, it is most important to realize that visions and voices are not mystical phenomena, though here again it seems to be the case that the sort of persons who are mystics may often be the sort of persons who see visions and hear voices. A few years ago it was reported that certain persons in Italy saw a vision of the Virgin Mary in the clouds. Even if we suppose that these persons really did have this vision, it must be emphatically asserted that this was not a mystical experience and had nothing to do with mysticism. Nor are the voices which certain persons in history, such as Socrates, Mohammed, and Joan of Arc, are supposed to have heard to be classed as mystical experiences. Socrates, Mohammed, and Joan of Arc may have been mystics for all I know, but they are not to be classed as such because of these voices. Returning for a moment to the subject of visions, it is well known that certain mystics saw visions but that they did not themselves regard these visions as mystical experiences. A case in point is St. Teresa of Avila. She had frequent visions, but she knew that they were not the experiences she desired. Some of them, she thought, may have been sent to her by God to comfort and encourage her in trying to attain the mystical consciousness. Others, she supposed, might have been sent by the devil in order to confuse her and distract her from the true mystic quest.

The reader may perhaps suppose that the exclusion of visions and voices from the class of mystical phenomena is a matter of arbitrary choice on the part of the present writer. Of course, one is logically entitled to define his terms as he pleases. Therefore if anyone says that he intends to use the phrase "mystical experience" so as to include visions and voices, spiritualism, telepathy, and the like, we do not say that he is wrong. But we say that his usage does not conform to that which has been usual with those who have been recognized as the great mystics of the world. The case of St. Teresa has just been mentioned. St. John of the Cross specifically warns his readers not to seek visions, not to be misled by them, and not to mistake them for the true mystical union. And there are, one must add, good reasons for this. What mystics say is that a genuine mystical experience is nonsensuous. It is formless, shapeless, colorless, odorless, soundless. But a vision is a piece of visual imagery having color and shape. A voice is an auditory image. Visions and voices are sensuous experiences.

IV. A New Kind of Consciousness

In his book *The Varieties of Religious Experience* William James suggests, as a result of his psychological researches, that "our normal consciousness, rational consciousness as we call it, is but one special type of consciousness, whilst all about it, parted from it by the filmiest of screens, there lie potential forms of consciousness entirely different." This statement exactly fits mystical consciousness. It is entirely unlike our everyday consciousness and is wholly incommensurable with it. What are the fundamental characteristics or elements of our ordinary consciousness? We may think of it as being like a building with three floors. The ground floor consists of physical sensations—sights, sounds, smells, tastes, touch sensations, and organic sensations. The second floor consists of images, which we tend to think of as mental copies of sensations. The third floor is the level of the intellect, which is the faculty of concepts. On this floor we find abstract thinking and reasoning processes. This account of the mind may be open to cavil. Some philosophers think that colors, sounds, and so on, are not properly called "sensations"; others that images are not "copies" of sensations. These fine points, however, need not seriously concern us. Our account is sufficiently clear to indicate what we are referring to when we speak of sensations, images, and concepts as being the fundamental elements of the cognitive aspects of our ordinary consciousness. Arising out of these basic cognitive elements and dependent upon them are emotions, desires, and volitions. In order to have a name for it we may call this whole structure—including sensations, images, concepts, and their attendant desires, emotions, and volitions—our *sensory-intellectual consciousness*.

Now the mystical consciousness is quite different from this. It is not merely that it involves different kinds of sensation, thought, or feeling. We are told that some insects or animals can perceive ultraviolet color and infrared color; and that some animals can hear sounds which are inaudible to us; even that some creatures may have a sixth sense quite different from any of our five senses. These are all, no doubt, kinds of sensations different from any we have. But they are still sensations. And the mystical consciousness is destitute of any sensations at all. Nor does it contain any concepts or thoughts. It is not a sensory-intellectual consciousness at all. Accordingly, it cannot be described or analyzed in terms of any of the elements of the sensory-intellectual consciousness, with which it is wholly incommensurable.

This is the reason why mystics always say that their experiences are "ineffable." All words in all languages are the products of our sensory-intellectual consciousness and express or describe its elements or some combination of them. But as these elements (with the doubtful exception of emotions) are not found in the mystical consciousness, it is felt to be impossible to describe it in any words whatever. In spite of this the mystics do describe their experiences in roundabout ways, at the same time telling us that the words they use are inadequate. This raises a serious problem for the philosophy of mysticism, but it is not possible for us to dwell on it here.

The incommensurability of the mystical with the sensory-intellectual consciousness is also the ultimate reason why we have to exclude visions and voices, telepathy, precognition, and clairvoyance from the category of the mystical. Suppose someone sees a vision of the Virgin Mary. What he sees has shape, the shape of a woman, and color—white skin, blue raiment, a golden halo, and so on. But these are all images or sensations. They are therefore composed of elements of our sensory-intellectual consciousness. The same is true of voices. Or suppose one has a precognition of a neighbor's death. The components one is aware of—a dead man, a coffin, etc.—are composed of elements of our sensory-intellectual consciousness. The only difference is that these ordinary elements are arranged in unfamiliar patterns which we have come to think cannot occur, so that if they do occur they seem supernormal. Or the fact that such elements are combined in an unusual way so as to constitute the figure of a woman up in the clouds, perhaps surrounded by other humanlike figures with wings added to them—all this does not constitute a different *kind* of consciousness at all. And just as sensory elements of any sort are excluded from the mystical consciousness, so are conceptual elements. It is not that the thoughts in the mystical consciousness are different from those we are accustomed to. It does not include any thoughts at all. The mystic, of course, expresses thoughts about his experience after that experience is over, and he remembers it when he is back again in his sensory-intellectual consciousness. But there are no thoughts *in* the experience itself.

If anyone thinks that a kind of consciousness without either sensations, images, or thoughts, because it is totally inimaginable and inconceivable to most of us, cannot exist, he is surely being very stupid. He supposes that the possibilities of this vast universe are confined to what can be imagined and understood by the brains of average human insects who crawl on a minute speck of dust floating in illimitable space.

On the other hand, there is not the least reason to suppose that the mystical consciousness is miraculous or supernatural. No doubt it has, like our ordinary consciousness, been produced by the natural processes of evolution. Its existence in a few rare men is a psychological fact of which there is abundant evidence. To deny or doubt that it exists as a psychological fact is not a reputable opinion. It is ignorance. Whether it has any value or significance beyond itself, and if so what— these, of course, are matters regarding which there can be legitimate differences of opinion. Owing to the comparative rarity of this kind of consciousness, it should no doubt be assigned to the sphere of abnormal psychology.

V. The Core of Mysticism

I shall, for the present, treat it as an hypothesis that although mystical experiences may in certain respects have different characteristics in different parts of the world, in different ages, and in different cultures, there are nevertheless a number of fundamental common characteristics. I shall also assume that the agreements are more basic and important, the differences more superficial and relatively less important. This hypothesis can only be fully justified by an elaborate empirical survey of the descriptions of their experiences given by mystics and collected from all over the world. But I believe that enough of the evidence for it will appear in the following pages to convince any reasonable person.

The most important, the central characteristic in which all *fully developed* mystical experiences agree, and which in the last analysis is definitive of them and serves to mark them off from other kinds of experiences, is that they involve the apprehension of *an ultimate nonsensuous unity in all things*, a oneness or a One to which neither the senses nor the reason can penetrate. In other words, it entirely transcends our sensory-intellectual consciousness.

It should be carefully noted that only fully developed mystical experiences are necessarily apprehensive of the One. Many experiences have been recorded, which lack this central feature but yet possess other mystical characteristics. These are borderline cases, which may be said to shade off from the central core of cases. They have to the central core the relation which some philosophers like to call "family resemblance."

We should also note that although at this stage of our exposition we speak of mystical experience as an apprehension *of* the Unity, the mystics of the Hindu and Buddhist cultures, as well as Plotinus and many others, generally insist that this is incorrect since it supposes a division between subject and object. We should rather say that the experience *is* the One. Thus Plotinus writes: "We should not speak of seeing, but instead of seen and seer, speak boldly of a simple Unity for in this seeing we neither distinguish nor are there two." But we will leave the development of this point till later. And often for convenience's sake we shall speak of the experience of the unity.

VI. Extrovertive Mysticism

There appear to be two main distinguishable types of mystical experience, both of which may be found in all the higher cultures. One may be called extrovertive mystical experience, the other introvertive mystical experience. Both are apprehensions of the One, but they reach it in different ways. The extrovertive way looks outward and through the physical senses into the external world and finds the One there. The introvertive way turns inward, introspectively, and finds the One at the bottom of the self, at the bottom of the human personality. The latter far outweighs the former in importance both in the history of mysticism and in the history of human thought generally. The introvertive way is the major strand in the history of mysticism, the extrovertive way a minor strand. I shall only briefly refer to extrovertive mysticism and then pass on, and shall take introvertive mysticism as the main subject of this book.

The extrovertive mystic with his physical senses continues to perceive the same world of trees and hills and tables and chairs as the rest of us. But he sees these objects transfigured in such manner that the Unity shines through them. Because it includes ordinary sense perceptions, it only partially realizes the description given in section (4). For the full realization of this we have to wait for the introvertive experience. I will give two brief historical instances of extrovertive experience. The great Catholic mystic Meister Eckhart (circa 1260–1329) wrote as follows: "Here [i.e., in this experience] all blades of grass, wood, and stone, all things are One. . . . When is a man in mere understanding? When he sees one thing separated from another. And when is he above mere understanding? When he sees all in all, then a man stands above mere understanding."

In this quotation we note that according to Eckhart seeing a number of things as separate and distinct, seeing the grass and the wood and the stone as three different things, is the mark of the sensory-intellectual consciousness. For Eckhart's word "understanding" means the conceptual intellect. But if one passes beyond the sensory-intellectual consciousness into the mystical consciousness, then one sees these three things as being "all one." However, it is evident that in this extrovertive experience the distinctions between things have not wholly disappeared. There is no doubt that what Eckhart means is that he sees the three things as distinct and separate and yet at the same time as not distinct but identical. The grass is identical with the stone, and the stone with the wood, although they are all different. Rudolph Otto, commenting on this, observes that it is as if one said that black is the same as white, white the same as black, although at the same time white remains white and black remains black. Of course this is a complete paradox. It is in fact contradictory. But we shall find that paradoxicality is one of the common characteristics of all mysticism. And it is no use saying that this is all logically impossible, and that no consciousness of this kind can exist, unless we wish, on these a priori grounds, to refuse to study the evidence—which is overwhelming.

What some mystics simply call the One other mystics often identify with God. Hence we find Jakob Böhme (1575–1624) saying much the same thing about the grass and the trees and the stones as Eckhart does, but saying that they are all God instead of just all One. The following is a statement of one of his experiences: "In this light my spirit saw through all things and into all creatures and I recognized God in grass and plants."

It is suggested that the extrovertive type of experience is a kind of halfway house to the introvertive. For the introvertive experience is wholly nonsensuous and nonintellectual. But the extrovertive experience is sensory-intellectual in so far as it still perceives physical objects but is nonsensuous and nonintellectual in so far as it perceives them as "all one."

We may sum up this short account of the extrovertive consciousness by saying that it is a perception of the world as transfigured and unified in one ultimate being. In some cultures the one being is identified with God; and since God is then perceived as the inner essence of all objects, this type of experience tends toward pantheism. But in some cultures—for example, Buddhism—the unity is not interpreted as God at all.

VII. Introvertive Mysticism

Suppose that one could shut all physical sensations out of one's consciousness. It may be thought that this would be easy as regards some of the senses, namely sight, hearing, taste, and smell. One can shut one's eyes, stop up one's ears, and hold one's nose. One can avoid taste sensations by keeping one's mouth empty. But one cannot shut off tactual sensations in any simple way of this kind. And it would be even more difficult to get rid of organic sensations. However, one can perhaps suppose it possible somehow to thrust tactual and organic sensations out of conscious awareness—perhaps into the unconscious. Mystics do not, as far as I know, descend to the ignominious level of holding their noses and stopping their ears. My only point is that it is possible to conceive of getting rid of all sensations, and in one way or other mystics claim that they do this.

Suppose now, after this has been done, we next try to get rid of all sensuous *images* from our minds. This is very difficult. Most people, try as they will not to picture anything at all, will find vague images floating about in consciousness. Suppose, however, that it is possible to suppress all images. And suppose finally that we manage to stop all thinking and reasoning. Having got rid of the whole empirical content of sensations, images, and thoughts, presumably all emotions and desires and volitions would also disappear, since they normally exist only as attachments to the cognitive content. What, then, would be left of consciousness? What would happen? It is natural to suppose that with all the elements of consciousness gone consciousness itself would lapse and the subject would fall asleep or become *un*conscious.

Now it happens to be the case that this total suppression of the whole empirical content of consciousness is precisely what the introvertive mystic claims to achieve. And he claims that what happens is not that all consciousness disappears but that only the ordinary sensory-intellectual consciousness disappears and is replaced by an entirely new kind of consciousness, the mystical consciousness. Naturally we now ask whether any description of this new consciousness can be given. But before trying to answer that difficult question, I propose to turn aside for a brief space to speak about the methods which mystics use to suppress sensuous images, and thinking, so as to get rid of their sensory-intellectual consciousness. There are the Yoga techniques of India: and Christian mystics in Catholic monasteries also evolved their own methods. The latter usually call their techniques "prayers," but they are not prayers in the vulgar sense of asking God for things; they are much more like the "meditation" and "concentration" of Yogis than may be commonly supposed. This is too vast a subject to be discussed in detail here. But I will give two elementary illustrations.

Everyone has heard of the breathing exercises undertaken by the yogis of India seeking samadhi—samadhi being the Indian name for mystical consciousness. What is this special method of breathing, and what is it supposed to accomplish? The theory of the matter is, I understand, something like this: It is practically impossible, or at least very difficult, to stop all sensing, imaging, and thinking by a forcible act of the will. What comes very near to it, however, is to concentrate one's attention on some single point or object so that all other mental content falls away and there is left nothing but the single point of consciousness. If this can be done, then ultimately that single point will itself disappear because contrast is necessary for our ordinary consciousness, and if there is only one point of consciousness left, there is nothing to form a contrast to it.

The question then is: On what single thing should one concentrate? A simple way is to concentrate on the stream of one's own breath. Simple instructions which I have heard given are these. One first adopts a suitable physical position with spine and neck perfectly erect. Then breathe in and out slowly, evenly, and smoothly. Concentrate your attention on this and nothing else. Some aspirants, I believe, count their breaths, 1, 2, 3, . . . up to 10, and then begin the count again. Continue this procedure till you attain the desired results.

A second method is to keep repeating in one's mind some short formula of words over and over again till the words lose all meaning. So long as they carry meaning, of course, the mind is still occupied with the thought of this meaning. But when the words become meaningless there is nothing left of consciousness except the monotonous sound image, and that too, like the consciousness of one's breath, will in the end disappear. There is an interesting connection between this method and a remark made by the poet Tennyson. From childhood up Tennyson had frequent mystical experiences. They came to him spontaneously, without effort, and unsought. But he mentions the curious fact that he could induce them at will by the odd procedure of repeating his own name over and over again to himself. I know of no evidence that he studied mysticism enough to understand the theory of his own procedure, which would presumably be that the constantly repeated sound image served as the focus of the required one-pointed attention.

This leads to another curious reflection. Mystics who follow the procedure of constantly repeating a verbal formula often, I believe, tend to choose some religious set of words, for instance a part of the Lord's Prayer or a psalm. They probably imagine that these uplifting and inspirational words will carry them upwards toward the divine. But Tennyson's procedure suggests that any nonsense words would probably do as well. And this seems to agree with the general theory of concentration. It doesn't seem to matter what is chosen as the single point of concentration, whether it be one's breathing, or the sound of one's own name, or one's navel, or anything else, provided only it serves to shut off all other mental content.

Another point on which mystics usually insist in regard to spiritual training is what they call "detachment." Emphasis on this is found just as much in Hinduism and Buddhism as in Christianity. What is sought is detachment from desire, the uprooting of desire, or at any rate of all self-centered desires. The exact psychology of the matter presents great difficulties. In Christian mysticism the idea of detachment is usually given a religious and moral twist by insisting that it means the destruction of self-will or any kind of self-assertiveness, especially the rooting out of pride and the attainment of absolute humility. In non-Christian mysticism detachment does not usually get this special slant. But in the mysticism of all cultures detachment from desires for sensations and sensory images is emphasized.

We will now return to the main question. Supposing that the sensory-intellectual consciousness has been successfully supplanted by the mystical consciousness, can we find in the literatures of the subject any descriptions of this consciousness that will give us any idea of what it is like ? The answer is that although mystics frequently say that their experiences are ineffable and indescribable, they nevertheless do often in fact describe them, and one can find plenty of such descriptive statements in the literature. They are usually extremely short—perhaps only three or four lines. And frequently they are indirect and not in the first person singular. Mystics more often than not avoid direct references to themselves.

I will give here a famous description which occurs in the Mandukya Upanishad. The Upanishads are supposed to have been the work of anonymous forest seers in India who lived between three thousand and twenty-five hundred years ago. They are among the oldest records of mysticism in the world. But they are of an unsurpassable depth of spirituality. For long ages and for countless millions of men in the East they have been, and they remain, the supreme source of the spiritual life. Of the introvertive mystical consciousness the Mandukya says that it is "beyond the senses, beyond the understanding, beyond all expression. . . . It is the pure unitary consciousness, wherein awareness of the world and of multiplicity is completely obliterated. It is ineffable peace. It is the Supreme Good. It is One without a second. It is the Self."

It will repay us, not to just slur over this passage, but to examine it carefully clause by clause. The first sentence is negative, telling us only what the experience is *not*. It is "beyond the senses, beyond the understanding." That is to say, it is beyond the sensory-intellectual consciousness; and there are in it no elements of sensation or sensuous imagery and no elements of conceptual thought. After these negatives there comes the statement that "it is the unitary consciousness, wherein all awareness of multiplicity has been obliterated." The core of the experience is thus described as an undifferentiated unity—a oneness or unity in which there is no internal division, no multiplicity.

I happen to have quoted a Hindu source. But one can find exactly the same thing in Christian mysticism. For instance the great Flemish mystic Jan van Ruysbroeck (1293–1381) says of what he calls "the God-seeing man" that "his spirit is undifferentiated and without distinction, and therefore it feels nothing but the unity." We see that the very words of the faithful Catholic are almost identical with those of the ancient Hindu, and I do not see how it can be doubted that they are describing the same experience. Not only in Christianity and Hinduism but everywhere else we find that the essence of the experience is that it is an *undifferentiated unity*, though each culture and each religion interprets this undifferentiated unity in terms of its own creeds or dogmas.

It may be objected that "undifferentiated unity" is a conceptual thought, and this is inconsistent with our statement that the experience is wholly nonintellectual.

The answer is that concepts such as "one," "unity," "undifferentiated," "God," "Nirvana," etc., are only applied to the experience *after* it has passed and when it is being *remembered*. None can be applied during the experience itself.

The passage of the Upanishad goes on to say that the undifferentiated unity "is the Self." Why is this? Why is the unity now identified with the Self? The answer is plain. We started with the full self or mind of our ordinary everyday consciousness. What was it full of? It was full of the multiplicity of sensations, thoughts, desires, and the rest. But the mind was not merely this multiplicity. These disparate elements were held together in a unity, the unity of the single mind or self. A multiplicity without a unity in which the multiple elements are together is inconceivable —e.g., many objects in one space. Now when we emptied all the multiple contents out of this unity of the self what is left, according to the Upanishad, is the unity of the self, the original unity minus its contents. And this is the self. The Upanishads go further than this. They always identify this individual self with the Universal Self, the soul of the world. For the moment we may continue to think in terms of the individual self, the pure ego of you or me. The undifferentiated unity is thought to be the pure ego.

I must draw the reader's attention to several facts about this situation. In the first place it flatly contradicts what David Hume said in a famous passage about the self. He said that when he looked introspectively into himself and searched for the I, the self, the ego, all he could ever introspect was the multiplicity of the sensations, images, thoughts, and feelings. He could never observe any I, any pure self apart from its contents, and he inferred that the I is a fiction and does not really exist. But now a vast body of empircal evidence, that of the mystics from all over the world, affirms that Hume was simply mistaken on a question of psychological fact, and that it is possible to get rid of all the mental contents and find the pure self left over and to experience this. This evidence need not mean that the self is a thing or a "substance," but can be taken as implying that it is a pure unity, the sort of being which Kant called the "transcendental unity" of the self.

The next thing to note is that the assertion of this new kind of consciousness is completely paradoxical. One way of bringing out the paradox is to point out that what we are left with here, when the contents of consciousness are gone, is a kind of consciousness which has no objects. It is not a consciousness *of* anything, but yet it is still consciousness. For the contents of our ordinary daily consciousness, the colors, sounds, wishes, thoughts are the same as the objects of consciousness, so that when the contents are gone the objects are gone. This consciousness of the mystics is not even a consciousness of consciousness, for then there would be a duality which is incompatible with the idea of an undifferentiated unity. In India it is called *pure* consciousness. The word "pure" is used in somewhat the same sense as Kant used it—meaning "without any empirical contents."

Another aspect of the paradox is that this pure consciousness is simultaneously both positive and negative, something and nothing, a fullness and an emptiness. The positive side is that it is an actual and positive consciousness. Moreover, all mystics affirm that it is pure peace, beatitude, joy, bliss, so that it has a positive affective tone. The Christians call it "the peace of God which passeth all understanding." The Buddhists call it Nirvana. But although it has this positive character, it is quite correct to say also that when we empty out all objects and contents of the mind *there is nothing whatever left*. That is the negative side of the paradox. What is left is sheer Emptiness. This is fully recognized in all mystical literature. In Mahayana Buddhism this total emptiness of the mystical consciousness is called the Void. In Christian mysticism the experience is identified with God. And this causes Eckhart and others to say that God, or the Godhead, is pure Nothingness, is a "desert," or "wilderness," and so on. Usually the two sides of the paradox are expressed in metaphors. The commonest metaphor for the positive side is light and for the negative side darkness. This is the darkness of God. It is called darkness because all distinctions disappear in it just as all distinctions disappear in a physical darkness.

We must not say that what we have here is a light *in* the darkness. For that would be no paradox. The paradox is that the light *is* the darkness, and the darkness *is* the light. This statement can be well documented from the literature of different cultures. I will give two examples, one from Christianity, one from Buddhism—and from the Buddhism of Tibet of all places in the world. Dionysius the Areopagite, a Christian, speaks of God as "the dazzling obscurity which outshines all brilliance with the intensity of its darkness." And the Tibetan Book of the Dead puts the same paradox in the words, "the clear light of the Void." In Dionysius we see that the obscurity, or the darkness, is the brilliance, and in the Tibetan book we see that the Void is a clear light.

VIII. Mysticism and Religion

Most writers on mysticism seem to take it for granted that mystical experience is a religious experience, and that mysticism is necessarily a religious phenomenon. They seem to think that mysticism and religious mysticism are one and the same thing. But this is far from being correct. It is true that there is an important connection between mysticism and religion, but it is not nearly so direct and immediate as most writers have seemed to think, nor can it be simply taken for granted as an obvious fact.

There are several grounds for insisting that intrinsically and in itself mystical experience is not a religious phenomenon at all and that its connection with religions is subsequent and even adventitious. In the first place, it seems to be clear that if we strip the mystical experience of all intellectual interpretation such as that which identifies it with God, or with the Absolute, or with the soul of the world, what is left is simply the undifferentiated unity. Now what is there that is religious about an undifferentiated unity? The answer seems to be, in the first instance, "Nothing at all." There seems to be nothing religious about an undifferentiated unity as such.

In the theistic religions of the West, in Christianity, Judaism, and Islam, the experience of the undifferentiated unity is interpreted as "union with God." But this is an interpretation and is not the experience itself. It is true that some Christian mystics, such as St. Teresa of Avila, invariably speak simply of having experienced "union with God," and do not talk about an undifferentiated unity. St. Teresa did not have a sufficiently analytical mind to distinguish between the experience and its interpretation. But other Christian mystics who are more analytically minded, such as Eckhart and Ruysbroeck, do speak of the undifferentiated unity.

These considerations are further underlined by the fact that quite different interpretations of the same experience are given in different cultures. The undifferentiated unity is interpreted by Eckhart and Ruysbroeck in terms of the Trinitarian conception of God, but by Islamic mystics as the unitarian God of Islam, and by the leading school of the Vedantists as a more impersonal Absolute. And when we come to Buddhism we find that the experience is not interpreted as any kind of God at all. For the Buddhist it becomes the Void or Nirvana. Buddha denied the existence of a Supreme Being altogether. It is often said that Buddhism is atheistic. And whether this description of Buddhism is true or not, it is certainly the case that there can exist an atheistic mysticism, a mystical experience naked and not clothed in any religious garb.

In view of these facts, we have a problem on our hands. Why is it that, in spite of exceptions, mysticism *usually* takes on some religious form and is usually found in connection with a definitely religious culture and as being a part of some definite religion? The following are, I think, the main reasons.

First, there is a very important feature of the introvertive mystical experience which I have not mentioned yet. I refer to the experience of the "melting away" into the Infinite of one's own individuality. Such phrases as "melting away," "fading away," "passing away" are found in the mystical literature of Christianity, Islam, Hinduism, and Buddhism. Among the Sufis of Islam there is a special technical term for it. It is called fanā. It must be insisted that this is not an inference or an interpretation or a theory or a speculation. It is an actual experience. The individual, as it were, directly experiences the disappearance of his own individuality, its fading away into the Infinite. To document this, one could quote from Eckhart, or from the Upanishads or the Sufis. But I believe I can bring home the point to a modern reader better by quoting a modern author. I referred earlier to the fact that Tennyson had frequent mystical experiences. His account of them is quoted by William James in his *The Varieties of Religious Experience*. Tennyson wrote, "All at once, as it were out of the intensity of the consciousness of individuality, individuality itself seemed to dissolve and fade away into boundless being. . . . the loss of personality, if such it were, seeming no extinction but the only true life." "Boundless being" seems to have the same meaning as "the Infinite." The Infinite is in most minds identified with the idea of God. We are finite beings, God is the only Infinite Being. One can see at once, therefore, how this experience of the dissolution of one's own individuality, its being merged into the Infinite, takes on a religious meaning. In theistic cultures the experience of melting away into boundless being is interpreted as union with God.

A second reason for the connection between mysticism and religion is that the undifferentiated unity is necessarily thought of by the mystics as being *beyond space and beyond time*. For it is without any internal division or multiplicity of parts, whereas the essence of time is its division into an endless multitude of successive parts, and the essence of space is its division into a multitude of parts lying side by side. Therefore the undifferentiated unity, being without any multiplicity of parts, is necessarily spaceless and timeless. Being timeless is the same as being eternal. Hence Eckhart is constantly telling us that the mystical experience transcends time and is an experience of "the Eternal Now." But in religious minds the Eternal, like the Infinite, is another name for God. Hence the mystical experience is thought of as an experience of God.

A third reason for this identification of the undifferentiated unity with God lies in the emotional side of the experience. It is the universal testimony of the mystics that their kind of consciousness brings feelings of an exalted peace, blessedness, and joy. It becomes identified with the peace of God, the gateway of the Divine, the gateway of salvation. This is also why in Buddhism, though the experience is not personified or called God, it nevertheless becomes Nirvana which is the supreme goal of the Buddhist religious life.

Thus we see that mysticism naturally, though not necessarily, becomes intimately associated with whatever is the religion of the culture in which it appears. It is, however, important to realize that it does not favor any particular religion. Mystical experience in itself does not have any tendency to make a man a Christian or a Buddhist. Into the framework of what creed he will fit his experience will tend to depend mostly on the culture in which he lives. In a Buddhist country the mystic interprets his experience as a glimpse of Nirvana, in a Christian country he may interpret it as union with God or even (as in Eckhart) as penetrating into the Godhead which is beyond God. Or if he is a highly sophisticated modern individual, who has been turned by his education into a religious skeptic, he may remain a skeptic as regards the dogmas of the different religions; he may allow his mystical experience to remain naked without any clothing of creeds or dogmas; but he is likely at the same time to feel that in that experience he has found something *sacred*. And this feeling of the sacred may quite properly be called " religious " feeling though it does not clothe itself in any dogmas. And this alone may be enough to uplift his ideals and to revolutionize his life and to give it meaning and purpose.

IX. The Ethical Aspects of Mysticism

It is sometimes asserted that mysticism is merely an escape from life and from its duties and responsibilities. The mystic, it is said, retreats into a private ecstasy of bliss, turns his back on the world, and forgets not only his own sorrows but the needs and sorrows of his fellow-men. In short, his life is essentially selfish.

It is possible that there have been mystics who deserved this kind of condemnation. To treat the bliss of the mystical consciousness as an end in itself is certainly a psychological possibility. And no doubt there have been men who have succumbed to this temptation. But this attitude is not the mystic ideal, and it is severely condemned by those who are most representative of the mystics themselves. For instance, St. John of the Cross condemns it as " spiritual gluttony." Eckhart tells us that if a man were in mystical ecstasy and knew of a poor man who needed his help, he should leave his ecstasy in order to go and serve the poor man. The Christian mystics especially have always emphasized that mystical union with God brings with it an intense and burning love of God which must needs overflow into the world in the form of love for our fellow-men; and that this must show itself in deeds of charity, mercy, and self-sacrifice, and not merely in words.

Some mystics have gone beyond this and have insisted that the mystical consciousness is the secret fountain of all love, human as well as divine; and that since love in the end is the only source of true moral activity, therefore mysticism is the source from which ethical values ultimately flow. For all selfishness and cruelty and evil result from the separateness of one human being from another. This separateness of individuals breeds egoism and the war of all against all. But in the mystical consciousness all distinctions disappear and therefore the distinction between "I" and "you" and "he" and "she." This is the mystical and metaphysical basis of love, namely the realization that my brother and I are one, and that therefore his sufferings are my sufferings and his happiness is my happiness. This reveals itself dimly in the psychological phenomena of sympathy and more positively in actual love. For one who had no touch of the mystical vision all men would be islands. And in the end it is because of mysticism that it is possible to say that "no man is an island" and that on the contrary every man is "a part of the main."

X. Alternative Interpretations of Mysticism

We have seen that the same experience may be interpreted in terms of different religious creeds. There is also another set of alternative interpretations which we ought to mention. We may believe that the mystic really is in touch, as he usually claims, with some being greater than himself, some spiritual Infinite which transcends the temporal flux of things. Or we may, on the other hand, adopt the alternative solution of the skeptic who will think that the mystical consciousness is entirely subjective and imports nothing outside itself. My own vote would be cast for the former solution. I would agree with the words of Arthur Koestler. He speaks of a higher order of reality which for us is like a text written in invisible ink. "I also liked to think," he says, "that the founders of religions, prophets, saints and seers had at moments been able to read a fragment of the invisible text; after which they had so much padded, dramatised and ornamented it, that they themselves could no longer tell what parts of it were authentic."[1]

But I wish to point out that even if one should choose the skeptical alternative and suppose that the mystical consciousness reveals no reality outside its owner's brain, one is far from having disposed of mysticism as some worthless delusion which ought to be got rid of. Even if it is wholly subjective, it still reveals something which is supremely great in human life. It is still the peace which passeth all understanding. It is still the gateway to salvation—not, I mean, in a future life, but as the highest beatitude that a man can reach in this life, and out of which the greatest deeds of love can flow. But it must be added, of course, that it belongs among those things of which Spinoza wrote in those famous words: "If the road which I have shown is very difficult, it yet can be discovered, and clearly it must be very hard if it is so rarely found. For how could it be that it is neglected by practically all, if salvation . . . could be found without difficulty. But all excellent things are as difficult as they are rare."

---

[1] See p. 235 [in *Teachings of the Mystics*. The quotation from Arthur Koestler's *The Invisible Writing* copyright 1954 by Arthur Koestler, is reproduced by permission of The Macmillan Company and A. D. Peters and Co.].

Mysticism and Religious Authority

Gershom Scholem

Gershom Scholem (1897–   ) is one of the towering figures in modern Jewish scholarship and has uniquely pioneered the study of the Judaic mystical tradition. He is the author of numerous books and articles including *Major Trends in Jewish Mysticism, Kabbalah,* and *Sabbatai Zevi.* Since 1925 he has taught at the Hebrew University in Jerusalem, where he is now professor of Jewish mysticism.

I

The problem to be dealt with in the ensuing pages is of central importance to the history of religions and can be considered under a number of aspects. We shall start from the assumption that a mystic, insofar as he participates actively in the religious life of a community, does not act in the void. It is sometimes said, to be sure, that mystics, with their personal striving for transcendence, live outside of and above the historical level, that their experience is unrelated to historical experience. Some admire this ahistorical orientation, others condemn it as a fundamental weakness of mysticism. Be that as it may, what is of interest to the history of religions is the mystic's impact on the historical world, his conflict with the religious life of his day and with his community. No historian can say—nor is it his business to answer such questions—whether a given mystic in the course of his individual religious experience actually found what he was so eagerly looking for. What concerns us here is not the mystic's inner fulfillment. But if we wish to understand the specific tension that often prevailed between mysticism and religious authority, we shall do well to recall certain basic facts concerning mysticism.

A mystic is a man who has been favored with an immediate, and to him real, experience of the divine, of ultimate reality, or who at least strives to attain such experience. His experience may come to him through sudden illumination, or it may be result of long and often elaborate preparations. From a historical point of view, the mystical quest for the divine takes place almost exclusively within a prescribed tradition—the exceptions seem to be limited to modern times, with their dissolution of all traditional ties. Where such a tradition prevails, a religious authority, established long before the mystic was born, has been recognized by the community for many generations. Grounded in the specific experience of the community, this authority has been developed through an interchange between the community and those individuals who have interpreted its fundamental experience

Source: Gershom Scholem, *Major Trends in Jewish Mysticism* (New York, 1954), pp. 5–31. Reprinted by permission of Schocken Books, Inc.

and so helped the community to express itself, who in a manner of speaking have made it articulate. There is then a scale of values that has been taken over from tradition; there is also a group of doctrines and dogmas, which are taken as authentic statements concerning the religious experience of a given community. And there is in addition a body of rites and customs, traditionally believed to transmit the values and express the mood and rhythm of religious life. Very different media can be invested with religious authority. They may be impersonal in character, a sacred book for example, or distinctly personal—in Catholicism, for example, it is the Pope who has the last word in deciding what is compatible with the Catholic tradition. There may also be mixtures and combinations of the two types, or authority may reside in the consensus of an assembly of priests or other religious persons, even where—as in Islam—these representatives of authority need not actually meet in order to formulate or lend weight to their decisions.

A mystic operates within the context of such traditional institutions and authority. If he accepts the context and makes no attempt to change the community, if he has no interests in sharing his novel experience with others and finds his peace in solitary immersion in the divine—then there is no problem, for there is nothing to bring him into conflict with others. There have assuredly been obscure mystics of this kind in all religions. The Jewish mysticism of recent centuries, in any case, has brought forth the "hidden saint" (nistar), an enormously impressive type with a profound appeal for the common people. According to a tradition that goes back to Talmudic times there are, in every generation, thirty-six righteous men who are the foundations of the world. If the anonymity, which is part of their very nature, were broken, they would be nothing. One of them is perhaps the Messiah, and he remains hidden only because the age is not worthy of him. Especially among the Hasidim of Eastern Europe, later generations spun endless legends about these most obscure of men, whose acts, because they are performed so entirely beyond the ken of the community, are free from the ambiguities inseparable from all public action. In a truly sublime sense the "hidden saint" makes religion a private affair, and because he is by definition barred from communication with other men, he is unaffected by the problems involved in all dealings with society.

But let us make no mistake. Inestimable as may be the worth of these mute, anonymous saints, the history of religions is not concerned with them. It is concerned with what happens when men attempt to enter into communcation with each other. And it is generally recognized that in the case of mystics such communication presents a problem. From a historian's point of view, the sum of religious phenomena known as mysticism consists in the attempts of mystics to communicate their "ways," their illuminations, their experience, to others. If not for such attempts it would be impossible to regard mysticism as a historical phenomenon. And it is precisely in the course of such attempts that mysticism comes to grips with religious authority.

All mysticism has two contradictory or complementary aspects: the one conservative, the other revolutionary. What does this mean?

It has been said that mystics are always striving to put new wine into old bottles —just what a famous passage in the Gospels warns us not to do. It seems to me that this formulation is strikingly apt and of the utmost relevance to our problem. How can a mystic be a conservative, a champion and interpreter of religious authority?

How is he able to do what the great mystics of Catholicism, such Sufis as Ghazzali, and most of the Jewish Kabbalists did? The answer is that these mystics seem to rediscover the sources of traditional authority. Perceiving the ancient foundations of this authority, they have no desire to change it. On the contrary, they try to preserve it in its strictest sense.

Sometimes this conservative function has been included in the very definition of mysticism—but this strikes me as questionable and one-sided. An American author, for example, has defined mysticism as "the endeavour to secure consciousness of the presence of the Agency through which (or through Whom) the conservation of socially recognized values is sought.[11]

The conservative function of mysticism is made possible by the fact that the fundamental mystical experience has two aspects. In itself it has no adequate expression; mystical experience is fundamentally amorphous. The more intensely and profoundly the contact with God is experienced, the less susceptible it is of objective definition, for by its very nature it transcends the categories of subject and object which every definition presupposes. On the other hand, such experience can be interpreted in different ways, that is, clothed in different meanings. The moment a mystic tries to clarify his experience by reflection, to formulate it, and especially when he attempts to communicate it to others, he cannot help imposing a framework of conventional symbols and ideas upon it. To be sure, there is always some part of it that he cannot adequately and fully express. But if he does try to communicate his experience—and it is only by doing so that he makes himself known to us —he is bound to interpret his experience in a language, in images amd concepts, that were created before him.

Because mystical experience as such is formless, there is in principle no limit to the forms it can assume. At the beginning of their path, mystics tend to describe their experience in forms drawn from the world of perception. At later stages, corresponding to different levels of consciousness, the world of nature recedes, and these "natural" forms are gradually replaced by specifically mystical structures. Nearly all the mystics known to us describe such structures as configurations of lights and sounds. At still later stages, as the mystic's experience progresses toward the ultimate formlessness, these structures dissolve in their turn. The symbols of the traditional religious authority play a prominent part in such structures. Only the most universal formal elements are the same in different forms of mysticism.[2] For light and sound and even the name of God are merely symbolic representations of an ultimate reality which is unformed, amorphous. But these structures which are alternately broken down and built up in the course of the mystic's development also reflect certain assumptions concerning the nature of reality, which originated in, and derived their authority from, philosophical traditions, and then surprisingly (or perhaps not so surprisingly) found confirmation in mystical experience. This applies even to assumptions that may strike us as utterly fantastic, such as certain ideas of the Kabbalists, or the Buddhist theory of the identity of the skandhas with the Buddha, no less than to the philosophico-theological hypotheses of Catholic mystics

---

[1] K. Wright, *A Student's Philosophy of Religion*, New York, 1938, p. 287.
[2] Cf. Mircea Eliade in *Eranos-Jahrbuch*, XXVI (1957), pp. 189–242.

(concerning the Trinity for example), which all seem to be confirmed by mystical experience.

In general, then, the mystic's experience tends to confirm the religious authority under which he lives; its theology and symbols are projected into his mystical experience, but do not spring from it.[3] But mysticism has another, contrasting aspect: precisely because a mystic is what he is, precisely because he stands in a direct, productive relationship to the object of his experience, he transforms the content of the tradition in which he lives. He contributes not only to the conservation of the tradition, but also to its development. Seen with new eyes, the old values acquire a new meaning, even where the mystic had no such intention or was not even aware of doing anything new. Indeed, a mystic's understanding and interpretation of his own experience may even lead him to question the religious authority he had hitherto supported.

For the same experience, which in one case makes for a conservative attitude, can in another case foster a diametrically opposite attitude. A mystic may substitute his own opinion for that prescribed by authority, precisely because his opinion seems to stem from the very same authority. This accounts for the revolutionary character of certain mystics and of the groups which accept the symbols in which mystics of this type have communicated their experience.

Occasionally a revolutionary mystic has laid claim to a prophetic gift and asserted a prophetic function in his efforts to reform his community. This brings up a question which we must briefly consider: can we and should we identify prophetic revelation and mystical experience? It is an old question, that has led to endless controversy. Personally, I reject such an identification and am convinced that it can throw no light on our problem. Nevertheless, I should like to say a few words about the paradoxical phenomenon of medieval prophetology, which is particularly instructive in this connection.

How puzzling, not to say indigestible, the phenomenon of Biblical prophecy seemed to those schooled in the systematic thinking of the Greeks may be gathered from the fact that in the medieval philosophy of both the Arabs and the Jews there developed a theory of prophecy which amounts to an identification of the prophet with the mystic. Henry Corbin's illuminating analyses show, for example, that Shiite prophetology was essentially a hierarchy of mystical experience and illumination, rising from stage to stage.[4] The Biblical or Koranic concept of the prophet as bringer of a message is so reinterpreted as to denote the ideal type of the mystic, even when he is called a prophet. Such a prophet as Amos, whom God raised up from among the dressers of sycamore trees, to make him the bearer of His message, is transformed by philosophical prophetology into something entirely different: an enlightened one, who passes through successive stages of spiritual discipline and initiation until, at the end of a long preparation, he is favored with the gift of prophecy, considered as union with the "active intellect," that is, with a divine emanation or stage of revelation. Cautiously as the authors may express themselves, this theory of prophecy as union with the "active intellect" always suggests something

---

[3] I owe this formulation to an article by G. A. Coe, "The Sources of the Mystic Revelation," *Hibbert Journal*, VI (1907–1908), p. 367.

[4] *Eranos-Jahrbuch*, XXVI (1957), pp. 57–188.

of the *unio mystica*, though not of the ultimate degree. In this respect there is no essential difference between so radically spiritualistic a doctrine as the prophetology of the Ismaili and a rationalistic theory like that of Maimonides.

But prophecy as it was originally understood is something entirely different. The prophet hears a clear message and sometimes beholds an equally plain vision, which he also remembers clearly. Undoubtedly a prophetic message of this sort lays direct claim to religious authority. In this it differs fundamentally from mystical experience. And yet, no one would think of denying the prophet's immediate experience of the divine. Plainly, we are dealing with two distant categories of experience, and I very much doubt whether a prophet can justifiably be called a mystic. For as we have said, the mystic's experience is by its very nature indistinct and inarticulate, while the prophet's message is clear and specific. Indeed, it is precisely the indefinable, incommunicable character of mystical experience that is the greatest barrier to our understanding of it. It cannot be simply and totally translated into sharp images or concepts, and often it defies any attempt to supply it—even afterward—with positive content. Though many mystics have attempted such "translation," have tried to lend their experience form and body, the center of what a mystic has to say always remains a shapeless experience, regardless of whether we choose to interpret it as *unio mystica* or as "mere" communion with the divine. But it is precisely the shapeless core of his experience which spurs the mystic to his understanding of his religious world and its values, and it is this dialectic which determines his relation to the religious authority and lends it meaning.

The most radical of the revolutionary mystics are those who not only reinterpret and transform the religious authority, but aspire to establish a new authority based on their own experience. In extreme cases, they may even claim to be above all authority, a law unto themselves. The formlessness of the original experience may even lead to a dissolution of all form, even in interpretation. It is this perspective, destructive, yet not unrelated to the original impulse of the mystic, which enables us to understand the borderline case of the nihilistic mystic as an all too natural product of inner mystical upheavals even if he was rejected with horror by all those about him. All other mystics try to find the way back to form, which is also the way to the community; he alone, because in his experience the breakdown of all form becomes a supreme value, tries to preserve this formlessness in an undialectic spirit, instead of taking it, like other mystics, as an incentive to build up new form. Here all religious authority is destroyed in the name of authority: here we have the revolutionary aspect of mysticism in its purest form.

II

In connection with this relationship between mysticism and religious authority the following point is of crucial importance: where the authority is set forth in holy scriptures, in documents bearing a character of revelation, the question rises: what is the attitude of mysticism toward such an historically constituted authority? This question in itself might well take up an entire chapter. But I shall be able to treat it briefly, because it has been amply covered in Ignaz Goldziher's work on the exegesis of the Koran (1920) and in Henry Corbin's above-mentioned paper on Ismailian Gnosis,[5] while I myself have analyzed it in detail in connection with Jewish mysticism.[6]

What happens when a mystic encounters the holy scriptures of his tradition is briefly this: the sacred text is smelted down and a new dimension is discovered in it. In other words: the sacred text loses its shape and takes on a new one for the mystic. The question of meaning becomes paramount. The mystic transforms the holy text, the crux of this metamorphosis being that the hard, clear, unmistakable word of revelation is filled with *infinite* meaning. The word which claims the highest authority is opened up, as it were, to receive the mystic's experience. It clears the way to an infinite inwardness, where ever-new layers of meaning are disclosed. Rabbi Pinhas of Koretz, a Hasidic mystic, expressed this with the utmost precision when he translated the formula *Rabbi Shim'on patah* ("Rabbi Simeon opened [his lecture with the verse of Scripture"; it is with these words that Rabbi Simeon ben Yohai's mystical exegeses and lectures are introduced in the *Zohar*) literally as "Rabbi Simeon *opened* the verse of Scripture."

The holiness of the texts resides precisely in their capacity for such metamorphosis. The word of God must be infinite, or, to put it in a different way, the absolute word is as such meaningless, but it is *pregnant* with meaning. Under human eyes it enters into significant finite embodiments which mark innumerable layers of meaning. Thus mystical exegesis, this *new* revelation imparted to the mystic, has the character of a key. The key itself may be lost, but an immense desire to look for it remains alive. In a day when such mystical impulses seem to have dwindled to the vanishing point they still retain an enormous force in the books of Franz Kafka. And the same situation prevailed seventeen centuries ago among the Talmudic mystics, one of whom left us an impressive formulation of it. In his commentary on the Psalms, Origen quotes a "Hebrew" scholar, presumably a member of the Rabbinic Academy in Caesarea, as saying that the Holy Scriptures are like a large house with many, many rooms, and that outside each door lies a key—but it is not the right one. To find the right keys that will open the doors—that is the great and arduous task.[7] This story, dating from the height of the Talmudic era, may give an idea of Kafka's deep roots in the tradition of Jewish mysticism. The rabbi whose metaphor so impressed Origen[8] still possessed the Revelation, but he knew that he no longer had the right key, and was engaged in looking for it. Another formulation of the same idea is frequent in the books of the Lurianic Kabbalah:[9] every word of the Torah has six hundred thousand "faces," that is, layers of meaning or entrances, one for each of the children of Israel who stood at the foot of Mount Sinai. Each face is turned toward only one of them; he alone can see it and decipher it. Each man has his own unique access to Revelation. Authority no longer resides in a single un-mistakable "meaning" of the divine communication, but in its infinite capacity for taking on new forms.

---

[5] Cf. Corbin's above-mentioned article.

[6] Cf. Chapter 2 of the present book.

[7] Origen, *Selecta in Psalmos* (on Psalm I), in Migne, *Patrologia Graeca*, XII, 1080. This important passage is stressed by F. I. Baer in his Hebrew article in *Zion*, XXI (1956), p. 16.

[8] Origen calls this metaphor "very ingenious."

[9] Cf. Chapter 2.

But this mystical approach to Scripture embraces two clearly discernible attitudes, the one conservative, and the other revolutionary. The conservatives recognize the eternal validity of the historical facts recorded in such books as the Torah or the Koran. Precisely because they preserve these foundations of the traditional authority for all time, they are able to treat Scripture with the almost unlimited freedom that never ceases to amaze us in the writings of the mystics, a freedom even to despair, as in our metaphor of the wrong keys. Recognition of the unaltered validity of the traditional authority is the price which these mystics pay for transforming the meanings of the texts in their exegesis. As long as the framework is kept intact, the conservative and revolutionary elements in this type of mystic preserve their balance, or perhaps it would be better to say, their creative tension. One cannot but be fascinated by the unbelievable freedom with which Meister Eckhart, the author of the *Zohar*, or the great Sufi mystics read their canonical texts, from which their own world seems to construct itself.

But even where the religious authority of the same sacred book is recognized, a revolutionary attitude is inevitable once the mystic invalidates the literal meaning. But how can he cast aside the literal meaning while still recognizing the authority of the text ? This is possible because he regards the literal meaning as simply nonexistent or as valid only for a limited time. It is *replaced* by a mystical interpretation.

The history of Judaism provides two classical examples of these two possible attitudes toward the sacred texts; both occurred after the establishment of the Biblical canon. I am referring to the attitude of the authors of the exegetic texts in the Dead Sea scrolls, probably dating from the pre-Christian era, and to that of Paul. It is not yet certain whether the Dead Sea scrolls should be regarded as mystical in the strictest sense. Our interpretation of these texts, and particularly of the personal element in them, is still so uncertain that the question will probably not be decided for some time to come.[10] But if it should turn out that the leaders of this sect were mystics (and not merely conservative reformers), this literature will provide an excellent example, indeed, the oldest known example, of a conservative attitude towards the sacred text, accompanied by the greatest freedom of exegesis. Even if the hymns which express the personal religion of this community (or perhaps even of one of its leaders) derive their ultimate inspiration from mystical illumination, the world they reflect remains entirely within the frame of the traditional authority; this exegesis is strictly conservative even when it actually transforms the authority. There can be no question of an abrogation of the authority; the aim is rather to restore it in all its harshness.

It is very different with Paul, the most outstanding example known to us of a revolutionary Jewish mystic. Paul had a mystical experience which he interpreted in such a way that it shattered the traditional authority. He could not keep it intact; but since he did not wish to forgo the authority of the Holy Scriptures as such, he was forced to declare that it was limited in time and hence abrogated. A purely

---

[10] The smoothness and expressiveness of the translations of these texts are sometimes in diametric opposition to the roughness and obscurity of the Hebrew originals. The mystical lyricism, for example, which characterizes Theodor H. Gaster's impressive translation of one of the most important of these texts in *The Dead Sea Scriptures*, New York, 1956, pp. 109–202, cannot but arouse the envy of anyone who has read the Hebrew original.

mystical exegesis of the old words replaced the original frame and provided the foundation of the new authority which he felt called upon to establish. This mystic's clash with religious authority was clear and sharp. In a manner of speaking, Paul read the Old Testament "against the grain." The incredible violence with which he did so shows not only how incompatible his experience was with the meaning of the old books, but also how determined he was to preserve, if only by purely mystical exegeses, his bond with the sacred text. The result was the paradox that never ceases to amaze us when we read the Pauline Epistles: on the one hand the Old Testament is preserved, on the other, its original meaning is completely set aside. The new authority that is set up, for which the Pauline Epistles themselves serve as a holy text, is revolutionary in nature. Having found a new source, it breaks away from the authority constituted in Judaism, but continues in part to clothe itself in the images of the old authority, which has now been reinterpreted in purely spiritual terms.

In either of these attitudes, the mystic rediscovers his own experience in the sacred text. Often it is hard to say whether the mystical meaning is actually there or whether he injects it. The genius of mystical exegeses resides in the uncanny precision with which they derive their transformation of Scripture into a *corpus symbolicum* from the exact words of the text. The literal meaning is preserved but merely as the gate through which the mystic passes, a gate, however, which he opens up to himself over and over again. The *Zohar* expresses this attitude of the mystic very succinctly in a memorable exegesis of Genesis 12:1. God's words to Abraham, *Lekh lekha*, are taken not only in their literal meaning, "Get thee out," that is, they are not interpreted as referring only to God's command to Abraham to go out into the world, but are also read with mystical literalness as "Go to thee," that is, to thine own self.

III

The conservative character so frequent in mysticism hinges largely on two elements: the mystic's own education and his spiritual guide—a matter of which I shall speak later on. As to the mystic's education, he almost always bears within him an ancient heritage. He has grown up within the framework of a recognized religious authority, and even when he begins to look at things independently and to seek his own path, all his thinking and above all his imagination are still permeated with traditional material. He cannot easily cast off this heritage of his fathers, nor does he even try to. Why does a Christian mystic always see Christian visions and not those of a Buddhist? Why does a Buddhist see the figures of his own pantheon and not, for example, Jesus or the Madonna? Why does a Kabbalist on his way of enlightenment meet the prophet Elijah and not some figure from an alien world? The answer, of course, is that the expression of their experience is immediately transposed into symbols from their own world, even if the objects of this experience are essentially the same and not, as some students of mysticism, Catholics in particular, like to suppose, fundamentally different. While recognizing different degrees and stages of mystical experience and still more numerous possibilities of interpretation, a non-Catholic tends to be extremely skeptical toward these repeated attempts which Catholics have made in line with their doctrine to demonstrate that the mystical experiences of the various religions rest on entirely different foundations.[11]

Here it may be worth our while to ask what happens when mysticism has no ties with any religious authority. This problem of the secularized interpretation of amorphous mystical experiences has been raised repeatedly since the Enlightenment. The situation is somewhat obscured by the fact that certain authors, disregarding or rejecting all traditional authority, describe their mystical experience in resolutely secular terms, yet clothe their interpretation of the same experience in traditional images. This is the case with Rimbaud and more consistently with William Blake. They regard themselves as Luciferian heretics, yet their imagination is shot through with traditional images, either of the official Catholic Church (Rimbaud) or of subterranean and esoteric, hermetic and spiritualist origin (Blake). Even in such revolutionaries, who seek their authority essentially in themselves and in a secular interpretation of their visions, tradition asserts its power. This secular mysticism takes a particularly interesting form in the Anglo-Saxon countries, where, after Blake, we encounter such figures as Walt Whitman, Richard Bucke, and Edward Carpenter, who in their interpretation of their experience recognized no authority whatsoever.

Perhaps the best example of a purely naturalistic interpretation of an overwhelming mystical experience is provided by the work, still widely read in North America, of the Canadian physician Richard Maurice Bucke, Walt Whitman's friend and the executor of his will. In 1872 Bucke experienced an overpowering mystical illumination; in the years that followed he tried to clarify its meaning and also to arrive at an undestanding of all the great mystical experiences that struck him as authentic. He recorded his findings in a book which he entitled *Cosmic Consciousness*.[12] The book makes it clear that authentic mystical experience can be interpreted, even by the "mystic" himself, in a purely immanent, naturalistic way, without the slightest reference to religious authority. But even here the scientific and philosophical theories accepted by the author play a determining role, just as the corresponding theories of the Buddhists, Neoplatonists, or Kabbalists shape their interpretations of their experience. The scientific theory which provided this late-nineteenth-century author with his basic concepts was Darwinism. In line with Darwinian theory, he regarded mystical experience as a stage in the development of human consciousness toward greater universality. Just as the coming of a new biological species is announced by mutations, which make their appearance in isolated members of the old species, the higher form of consciousness, which Bucke terms "cosmic consciousness," is today present only in a few human specimens—this heightened consciousness that will ultimately spread to all mankind is what is now termed mystical experience. Past generations put a religious interpretation on it—a historically understandable error. The mystic's claim to authority is legitimate, but

[11] Perhaps the most illuminating expression of this view—that mystical experience has not one, but several essentially different objects—is provided by R. C. Zaehner's stimulating and controversial work, *Mysticism, Sacred and Profane: An Enquiry into Some Varieties of Praeternatural Experience*, Oxford (1957). Though exceedingly useful for certain purposes, the classification of mystical phenomena as natural, praeternatural, and supernatural, which in the last thirty years has found wide currency in scholarship of Catholic inspiration, remains highly questionable.

[12] Cf. Richard Maurice Bucke, *Cosmic Consciousness: A Study in the Evolution of the Human Mind*. The book first appeared in 1901; I have used the eighteenth printing, New York, 1956.

must be interpreted in a different way: it is the authority of those whose consciousness has achieved a new stage of development. Of course Bucke's theories strike us today as naïve and scientifically untenable. Nevertheless, I find them extremely illuminating as one more indication that mystical experience is essentially amorphous and can therefore be interpreted in any number of ways.

Still, such secular mysticism is an exception. Most mystics, as we have seen, are strongly influenced by their education, which in a perfectly natural way imbues them with the traditional attitudes and symbols. But the community did not consider this a sufficient safeguard. By its very nature mysticism involves the danger of an uncontrolled and uncontrollable deviation from traditional authority. The religious training of the group still leaves room for all manner of spiritual adventures, contrary to the recognized ideas and doctrines and likely to bring about a clash between the mystic and the religious authority of his group. This is no doubt one of the many reasons for the widespread belief that a mystic requires a spiritual guide, or *guru*, as he is called in India. On the face of it the function of the *guru* is primarily psychological. He prevents the student who sets out to explore the world of mysticism from straying off into dangerous situations. For confusion or even madness lurk in wait; the path of the mystic is beset by perils. It borders on abysses of consciousness and demands a sure and measured step. The Yogis, the Sufis, and the Kabbalists, no less than the manuals of Catholic mysticism, stress the need for such a spiritual guide, without whom the mystic runs the risk of losing himself in the wilderness of mystical adventure. The guide should be capable of preserving the proper balance in the mystic's mind. He alone is familiar with the practical applications of the various doctrines, which cannot be learned from books. And he has an additional function, which has been very little discussed but is nevertheless of great importance; he represents traditional religious authority. He molds the mystic's interpretation of his experience, guiding it into channels that are acceptable to established authority. How does he accomplish this? By preparing his student for what he may expect along the way and at the goal. He provides at the outset the traditional coloration which the mystical experience, however amorphous, will assume in the consciousness of the novice.

Let us consider, for example, the *Spiritual Exercises* of Igantius of Loyola, an invaluable manual of Catholic mysticism. From the start it impregnates the consciousness of the novice with the images of Christ's Passion. It shows exactly what the novice has to expect at every step, and sets out to produce the phenomenon it promises. It is the same, to take an example from Jewish mysticism, with the Hasidic-Kabbalistic analysis of the stages of meditation and ecstasy, contained in a famous treatise emanating from the Habad school of White Russian Hasidism.[13] It informs the traveler on the path of "active" contemplation in detail of the stages through which he must pass if his mystical career is to conform to the strict Jewish conceptions of the pure fear and pure love of God, and if he is to be safeguarded against uncontrollable emotional excesses. It provides the traditional Kabbalistic symbols with which this path of the Jewish mystic toward the experience of the divine can be described or interpreted, thus making certain that the path will conform, especially at its most dangerous turning points, to the dictates of authority.

[13] *Kuntras ha-Hithpaʿaluth* by Rabbi Baer, son of Rabbi Shneʾur Zalman of Ladi, printed in the volume *Likkute Beʾurim*, Warsaw, 1868.

To keep mysticism within the framework of constituted authority, compromises were often necessary. As one might expect, they vary in the extreme, according to the requirements of the various religious groups. As a highly instructive example of such a compromise, I should like to discuss here the Kabbalistic conception of the *gilluy Eliyahu*, the "Revelation of the Prophet Elijah." It provides an example of how the conservative and the "progressive" aspects of mysticism can merge to form a single eloquent symbol.

When the first Kabbalists appeared on the scene of Jewish history, in Languedoc at the end of the twelfth century, they did not claim to have spoken directly with God. They took a compromise position. On the one hand, they wished to communicate something which obviously had not come to them through the traditional and generally accepted channels. But on the other hand, as orthodox Jews, they could not claim for their own mystical experience the same rank as for the revelation underlying the religious authority of Judaism. All monotheistic religions possess a distinct conception, one might call it a philosophy, of their own history. In this view, the first revelation expressing the fundamental contents of a religion is the greatest, the highest in rank. Each successive revelation is lower in rank and less authoritative than the last. Such a conception forbids a true believer to place a new revelation on a level with the great revelations of the past and obviously creates a serious problem for the mystic, since he imputes enormous value to his fresh, living experience. This situation necessitated compromise solutions which were inevitably reflected in the religious terminology. In Rabbinical Judaism, from which Kabbalistic mysticism developed, a number of different revelations were recognized as authentic and each in its own way authoritative, namely, the revelations of Moses, of the Prophets, of the Holy Spirit (which spoke in the authors of the Psalms and other parts of the Bible), of the receivers of the "Heavenly Voice" (*bath kol*, believed to have been audible in the Talmudic era), and finally the "revelation of the Prophet Elijah." Each of these stages represents a lesser degree of authority than the stage preceding it. The principle remained in force: each generation can claim only a certain level of experience. But mystics could still make a place for their experience within the traditional framework, provided they defined it in accordance with this descending scale of values.

This was why the Kabbalists claimed no more for themselves than the seemingly so modest rank of receivers of a "revelation of the Prophet Elijah." In this connection it should be borne in mind that in such experience the auditive factor was paramount and the visual factor only secondary, since, primarily, no doubt under the influence of the mystical theory of prophecy referred to above, the Jewish mystics accorded far more importance to the hearing of a voice than to visions of light.

Since the beginnings of Rabbinical Judaism the Prophet Elijah has been a figure profoundly identified with the central preoccupations of Jewry: it is he who carries the divine message from generation to generation, he who at the end of time will reconcile all the conflicting opinions, traditions, and doctrines manifested in Judaism.[14] Men of true piety meet him in the market place no less than in visions. Since he was conceived as the vigilant custodian of the Jewish religious ideal, the

[14] Cf. the article "Elijahu" in *Encyclopaedia Judaica*, VI (1930), pp. 487–495.

Messianic guardian and guarantor of the tradition, it was impossible to suppose that he would ever reveal or communicate anything that was in fundamental contradiction with the tradition. Thus by its very nature the interpretation of mystical experience as a revelation of the Prophet Elijah tended far more to confirm than to question the traditional authority.

It is extremely significant that the first Kabbalists said to have attained this rank were Rabbi Abraham of Posquières and his son Isaac the Blind. Abraham ben David (d. 1198) was the greatest Rabbinical authority of his generation in southern France, a man deeply rooted in Talmudic learning and culture. But at the same time he was a mystic, who formulated his experience in distinctly conservative terms.[15] He himself relates in his writings that the Holy Spirit appeared to him in his house of study; but the Kabbalists said it was the Prophet Elijah who had appeared to him. This interpretation alone could guarantee that no conflict would arise between the Rabbi's traditional knowledge and the translation of his mystical experience into new conceptions. And when his son, a pure contemplative mystic without any outstanding claim to Rabbinical authority, carried on in his father's mystical path, the same claim was raised for him. The doctrines formulated by him and his school were looked upon as a legitimate completion of Rabbinical doctrine, whose adherents were in no danger of conflict with traditional authority. Yet tremendous forces were at work in this mysticism, and the symbols in which the new revelation was communicated disclose an intense and by no means undangerous conflict with traditional authority.

This was at the very beginning of Kabbalism. The same phenomenon is to be met with in a central figure of its later development, Isaac Luria in the sixteenth century. Luria represents both aspects of mysticism in their fullest development. His whole attitude was decidedly conservative. He fully accepted the established religious authority, which indeed he undertook to reinforce by enhancing its stature and giving it deeper meaning. Nevertheless, the ideas he employed in this seemingly conservative task were utterly new and seem doubly daring in their conservative context. And yet, for all their glaring novelty, they were not regarded as a break with traditional authority. This was possible because the authority of the Prophet Elijah was claimed for them—a claim that was widely recognized thanks to Luria's impressive personality and piety. Thus Luria's source of inspiration became a new authority in its own right. But though defined in traditional categories, this new authority, once accepted, brought about profound changes in Judaism, even when its advocates claimed to be doing nothing of the sort. In line with the prevailing view that each new revelation is lower in rank than the last, Luria was reticent about the source of his inspiration. But this reticence should not mislead us. The mystical experience that was his source is still as authentic as any, and as high in rank as any earlier phenomenon in the world of Rabbinical Judaism.

IV

In connection with the conservative interpretation and function of mysticism there is another important point. I have said that a mystic's background and education

[15] Cf. the chapter on Abraham ben David in my *Reshith ha-Kabbalah* (The Beginnings of the Kabbalah), Jerusalem, 1948, pp. 66–98.

lead him to translate his experience quite spontaneously into traditional symbols. This brings us back to the problem of symbolism. Of course the question of interpreting symbols presents an abundance of aspects. To stress a single one of these aspects in the present context is not to minimize the importance of other aspects in other contexts. Symbols, by their very nature, are a means of expressing an experience that is in itself expressionless. But this psychological aspect is not the whole story. They also have a function in the human community. We may indeed go so far as to say that it is one of the main functions of religious symbols to preserve the vitality of religious experience in a traditional, conservative milieu.[16] The richness of meaning that they seem to emanate lends new life to tradition, which is always in danger of freezing into dead forms—and this process continues until the symbols themselves die or change.

The mystic who lends new symbolic meaning to his holy texts, to the doctrines and ritual of his religion—and this is just what almost all mystics have done and what accounts largely for their importance in the history of religions—discovers a new dimension, a new depth in his own tradition. In employing symbols to describe his own experience and to formulate his interpretations of it, he is actually setting out to confirm religious authority by reinterpreting it, regardless of whether he looks upon the traditional conceptions as symbols or attempts to elucidate them with the help of new symbols. But by thus opening up the symbolic dimensions, he transforms religious authority, and his symbolism is the instrument of this transformation. He bows to authority in pious veneration, but this does not prevent him from transforming it, sometimes radically. He uses old symbols and lends them new meaning, he may even use new symbols and give them an old meaning—in either case we find dialectical interrelationship between the conservative aspects and the novel, productive aspects of mysticism.

Another question arises: is it correct to distinguish these two attitudes toward authority as conscious and unconscious? Are we justified in saying that the religious authority is a conscious power in the mind of the mystic, while his conflict with it is rooted in the unconscious layers of his experience? Something can be said in favor of this view. Undoubtedly there have been mystics in whom the dividing line between conscious and unconscious coincided with the dividing line between their conservative and revolutionary tendencies. But this should not lead us to oversimplify. Usually these dividing lines are not so clear. Often enough the conflict takes place quite openly and the mystic is perfectly conscious of it. In such cases the mystic knows that he must oppose the existing authority, that he has been chosen to found a new authority or to do away with authority altogether.

This was the case with the great leaders of the Anabaptists, whose mystical inspiration is undeniable, and of the Quakers, to cite only these two striking examples from the history of Christianity. And in Judaism the same is true of the Sabbatian and Hasidic leaders. The psychological and historical categories are by no means identical. Often mystics have done their utmost to express themselves within the framework of established authority, and were driven to open conflict with it only

---

[16] For a discussion of the function of symbolism in religion, see the symposium *Religious Symbolism*, ed. F. Ernest Johnson, New York, 1955. However, I cannot by any means support the view, here put forward by Professor Abraham Heschel, that Rabbinical Judaism is a religion constituted outside the categories of symbolism.

when they met with too much opposition within their community. But if they had been free to choose, they would have avoided these conflicts which were not of their seeking. In certain cases it can be shown that the mystics began to put an increasingly radical interpretation on their ideas only after such a conflict had been forced upon them.

The *Journal* of John Wesley, founder of Methodism, provides an excellent example of such a case. Seldom has it been described so clearly how a mystic, caught up in the dialectic of his experience, struggled with all his might to avoid being drawn into conflict with the established religious authority. This conflict with the Anglican Church was forced upon Wesley, not from within but from without, but then he accepted it with full awareness and fought his battle to a finish. As far as the available documents allow us to judge, the situation of Valentinus, the outstanding Gnostic leader, seems to have been much on the same order. And we find a similar development in the history of the Hasidim, whose first leaders had no thought of clashing with the Rabbinical authority. When the conflict was forced upon them, some of them gave free rein to their spiritualist mysticism; but after a time the movement and its Rabbinical adversaries arrived at a compromise, shaky at first but gradually gaining in stability. As far as I can see, our understanding of these matters is furthered very little by a distinction between conscious and unconscious processes.

But under what circumstances does such a conflict arise? What are the decisive factors? What kind of mysticism invites conflict with authority, and what kind does not? To these questions, unfortunately, we have no satisfactory answer. Such conflicts are largely unpredictable and do not hinge essentially on the personality or doctrines of the mystic. They depend entirely on historical circumstances. But the relationship between religion and historical conditions is constantly changing and cannot be reduced to any simple common denominator. A sound answer would require a knowledge of all the historical factors and of the specific conditions under which the mystics embarked on their activites. Yet perhaps there is one exception to this statement: those mystics who may be characterized as innately radical—a specific personal quality that is by no means limited to mystics. There are plenty of men who incline by nature to the radical formulation of their ideas, who chafe at authority of any kind and have no patience whatever with the folly of their fellow men. They need not necessarily be mystics to enter into opposition to established authority. But if they do become mystics, this radical tendency becomes particularly marked, as in the case of George Fox at the inception of the English Quaker movement.

Only in the rare and extreme case of nihilistic mysticism do mystical doctrines *as such* imply conflict. Otherwise, doctrines which have been expressed with the utmost force at certain times and places without leading to any conflict whatsoever may, under other historical conditions, foment violent struggles. Of course the dialectic of symbolism, of which we have spoken, is always present; but whether it results in open conflict with authority depends on extraneous factors. Of this the history of Catholic mysticism contains famous examples, and a historian of mysticism can derive little benefit from the attempts of the apologists to prove that two doctrines, one of which has been accepted by the Church, while the other has been condemned as heretical, only appear to be similar, but are in reality fundamentally different. This is amply illustrated by the history of quietist mysticism in Christianity.[17] For it was not the doctrines of quietism as originally formulated by its representatives in the Spanish Church that had changed when Madame Guyon was condemned; what had changed was the historical situation. One of the most dramatic conflicts in the history of the Church shows how such a struggle can arise against the will of the leading participants, if a historical situation that has no bearing whatever on mystical doctrines makes it seem desirable.

We find the same situation in Hasidism. When Israel Baal-Shem, the eighteenth-century founder of Polish Hasidism, put forward the mystical thesis that communion with God (*devekuth*) is more important than the study of books, it aroused considerable opposition and was cited in all the anti-Hasidic polemics as proof of the movement's subversive and anti-Rabbinical tendencies. But the exact same theory had been advanced two hundred years before by a no lesser mystical authority, by Isaac Luria himself in Safed, without arousing the slightest antagonism. It was not the thesis that had changed, but the historical climate.

In the above we have outlined the attitude of the mystics toward authority. As to the efforts of the authorities to contain the strivings of the mystics within the traditional framework, we have shown that they usually do their best to place obstacles in the path of the mystic. They give him no encouragement, and if in the end the obstacles frighten the mystic and bring him back to the old accustomed ways— so much the better from the standpoint of authority.

All great institutional religions have shown a marked distaste for lay mystics, that is, the unlearned mystics who, fired by the intensity of their experience, believe they can dispense with the traditional and approved channels of religious life. The less educated the candidate for mystical illumination, the less he knew of theology, the greater was the danger of a conflict with authority. Quite regardless of their specific content, all manuals of mysticism written from the standpoint of traditional authority illustrate this point. The Jewish authorities, for example, tried to avoid conflicts by restricting the right to engage in mystical practice and speculation to fully trained Talmudic scholars. All Kabbalistic manuals quote Maimonides' warning: " No one is worthy to enter Paradise [the realm of mysticism] who has not first taken his fill of bread and meat,"[18] i.e., the common fare of sober Rabbinical learning.

Such warnings, it must be admitted, were none too effective. The history of the great religions abounds in lay mysticism and in movements growing out of it. In the history of Christianity lay mysticism is exemplified by such movements as the Gnostics, the Brethren of the Free Spirit, the Spanish Alumbrados, and the Protestant sects of the last four centuries. The Church, it is true, branded all such movements as heresies. But in Judaism this was not always the case. Although many of the great Kabbalists fully met the requirements of Maimonides' conservative warning, there were always Kabbalists who were not so well versed in Rabbinical knowledge or who, in any case, had no complete Talmudic schooling. A case in point is the most celebrated of all the Jewish mystics of recent centuries, Israel Baal-Shem, the founder of Polish Hasidism. His "knowledge" in the traditional

---

[17] In this connection it is interesting to compare two so different accounts as those of Heinrich Heppe, *Geschichte der quietischen Mystik in der katholischen Kirche*, Berlin, 1875, and Ronald A. Knox, *Enthusiasm: A Chapter in the History of Religion with Special Reference to the XVII and XVIII Centuries*, Oxford, 1950.

[18] Maimonides, *Mishneh Torah, Hilkhoth Yesode ha-Torah*, IV, 13.

sense of the word was very meager; he had no teacher of flesh and blood to guide him on his way—the only spiritual guide he ever alluded to was the Prophet Ahijah of Shiloh, with whom he was in constant spiritual and visionary contact. In short, he was a pure lay mystic and lay mysticism was a vital factor in the development of the movement he founded. Yet this movement (though at the price of a compromise) won the recognition of the traditional authority. Other movements, in which lay mysticism played an important part—the Sabbatians, for example—were unable to gain such recognition and were forced into open conflict with Rabbinical authority.

Especially in monotheistic religions the religious authorities had still another method of avoiding conflicts with the mystics of the community. This was to charge them with social responsibility. They put pressure on the mystics to mingle with the simple folk, to participate in their activities, instead of remaining among themselves in communities of the "enlightened." In Christianity, where since the beginnings of monasticism mystics have always been able to band together, this trend has not always been as clear as in Judaism. Since Talmudic times we find a decided disinclination to let mystics organize communities of their own. Time and time again the rabbis insisted that mystical experience, the "love of God," must be confirmed by activity in the human community, that it was not enough for an individual to pour out his soul to God. Here I shall not speak in detail of this tendency. Suffice it to say that it has been highly effective in "taming" mystics and holding them within the limits imposed by traditional authority.

In diametrical and irreconcilable opposition to all such attempts to relieve the tension between mysticism and religious authority stands the extreme case of mystical nihilism, in which all authority is rejected in the name of mystical experience or illumination. At first glance the nihilist mystic seems to be the most free, the most faithful to his central insight; for having attained the highest goal of mystical experience, namely, the dissolution of all form, he extends his mystical insight to his relation with the real world, that is to say, he rejects all values and the authority which guarantees the validity of values. Yet from the standpoint of history, he is the most constrained and unfree of mystics, for historical reality as embodied in the human community prevents him, far more than it does any other mystic, from openly proclaiming his message. This explains no doubt why the documents of nihilistic mysticism are extremely rare. Because of their subversive character the authorities suppressed and destroyed them; where they have come down to us, it is because their authors resorted to an ambiguity of expression that makes our interpretation of the texts questionable. This explains, for example, why the nihilistic character of certain mystical doctrines, such as those of the Ismailis and the Druses in particular but also of such groups as the Bektashi order of dervishes, is still a matter of discussion. On the other hand, the intentional ambiguity of such writings has caused them, time and time again, to be suspected of mystical nihilism.

For want of the original sources of second-century gnostic nihilism, which have not come down to us,[19] it seems to me that we possess no more impressive record of

[19] Valuable source material on which to base an analysis on the nihilistic possibilities of gnostic mysticism are provided by Hans Jonas in *Gnosis und spätantiker Geist*, I, Göttingen, 1933; but we are wholly dependent on quotations and reports transmitted by the Catholic adversaries of Gnosticism. Complete original texts have not been preserved. Cf. also Herbert Liboron, *Die karpokratianische Gnosis*, Leipzig, 1938.

an unmistakably nihilistic mysticism than the Polish *Book of the Words of the Lord*, in which the disciples of Jacob Frank (1726–1791) set down their master's teachings after his own spoken words.[20] I have elsewhere analyzed the circumstances which made possible this eruption of mystical nihilism within so firmly organized and authoritarian a community as Rabbinical Judaism.[21] Messianism and mysticism played equal parts in crystallizing these ideas, which sprang from the radical wing of the Sabbatian movement.[22]

What interests us here is the way in which the mystical experience of man's contact with the primal source of life could find its expression in a symbol implying the negation of all authority. An illumination concerning Messianic freedom in redemption crystallizes around the symbol of Life. In his mystical experience the mystic encounters Life. This "Life," however, is not the harmonious life of all things in bond with God, a world ordered by divine law and submissive to His authority, but something very different. Utterly free, fettered by no law or authority, this "Life" never ceases to produce forms and to destroy what it has produced. It is the anarchic promiscuity of all living things. Into this bubbling caldron, this continuum of destruction, the mystic plunges. To him it is the ultimate human experience. For Frank, anarchic destruction represented all the Luciferian radiance, all the positive tones and overtones, of the word "Life." The nihilistic mystic descends into the abyss in which the freedom of living things is born; he passes through all the embodiments and forms that come his way, committing himself to none; and not content with rejecting and abrogating all values and laws, he tramples them underfoot and desecrates them, in order to attain the elixir of Life. In this radical interpretation of a symbol, the life-giving element of mystical experience was combined with its potential destructiveness. It goes without saying that from the standpoint of the community and its institutions, such mysticism should have been regarded as demonic possession. And it is indicative of one of the enormous tensions that run through the history of Judaism that this most destructive of all visions should have been formulated in its most unrestrained form by one who rebelled against the Jewish law and broke away from Judaism.

V

It seems to me that a statement which has come down to us from Rabbi Mendel Torum of Rymanóv (d. 1814),[23] one of the great Hasidic saints, throws a striking light on this whole problem of the relationship between authority and mysticism. Let me try to interpret this statement. The revelation given to Israel on Mount Sinai is, as everyone knows, a sharply defined set of doctrines, a summons to the human

[20] Thus far extensive quotations and notes from this book are to be found solely in Alexander Kraushar's two-volume work, *Frank i Frankiści Polscy*, Cracow, 1895. The manuscripts used by Kraushar were lost during the second World War when the Polish libraries were almost entirely destroyed. An incomplete manuscript of these copious notes was found only recently in the Cracow University library.

[21] Cf. my article, "Le mouvement sabbataiste en Pologne," *Revue de l'histoire des religions*, CLIII–CLIV (1953–1954), especially the last section, CLIV, pp. 42–77.

[22] Cf. the detailed account in my two-volume Hebrew work, *Shabbetai Zevi*, Tel Aviv, 1957.

[23] Quoted by Ahron Markus, in *Der Chassidismus*, Pleschen, 1901, p. 239, from *Torath Menahem*, a collection of some sermons of the Rabbi of Rymanóv.

community; its meaning is perfectly clear, and it is certainly not a mystical formula open to infinite interpretation. But what, the question arises, is the truly divine element in this revelation? The question is already discussed in the Talmud.[24] When the children of Israel received the Ten Commandments, what could they actually hear, and what did they hear? Some maintained that all the Commandments were spoken to the children of Israel directly by the divine voice. Others said that only the first two Commandments: "I am the Lord thy God" and "Thou shalt have no other gods before me" (Exod. 20: 2–3) were communicated directly. Then the people were overwhelmed, they could no longer endure the divine voice. Thus they had been obliged to receive the remaining Commandments through Moses. Moses alone was able to withstand the divine voice, and it was he who repeated in a human voice those statements of supreme authority that are the Ten Commandments.

This conception of Moses as interpreter of the divine voice for the people was developed much more radically by Maimonides,[25] whose ideas Rabbi Mendel of Rymanóv carried to their ultimate conclusion. In Rabbi Mendel's view not even the first two Commandments were revealed directly to the whole people of Israel. All that Israel heard was the *aleph* with which in the Hebrew text the first Commandment begins, the *aleph* of the word *anokhi*, "I." This strikes me as a highly remarkable statement, providing much food for thought. For in Hebrew the consonant *aleph* represents nothing more than the position taken by the larynx when a word begins with a vowel. Thus the *aleph* may be said to denote the source of all articulate sound, and indeed the Kabbalists always regarded it as the spiritual root of all other letters, encompassing in its essence the whole alphabet and hence all other elements of human discourse.[26] To hear the *aleph* is to hear next to nothing; it is the preparation for all audible language, but in itself conveys no determinate, specific meaning. Thus, with his daring statement that the actual revelation to Israel consisted only of the *aleph*, Rabbi Mendel transformed the revelation on Mount Sinai into a mystical revelation, pregnant with infinite meaning, but without specific meaning. In order to become a foundation of religious authority, it had to be translated into human language, and that is what Moses did. In this light every statement on which authority is grounded would become a human interpretation, however valid and exalted, of something that transcends it.[27] Once in history a mystical experience was imparted to a whole nation and formed a bond between that nation and God. But the truly divine element in this revelation, the immense *aleph*, was not in itself sufficient to express the divine message, and in itself it

[24] Makkoth, 24a.

[25] Maimonides, *Guide to the Perplexed*, II, 33. Maimonides puts forward the opinion that wherever, in passages dealing with the revelation on Mount Sinai, the children of Israel are said to have heard words, it is meant that they heard the (inarticulate) sound of the voice, but that Moses heard the words (in their meaningful articulation) and communicated them.

[26] This view is expressed by Jacob Kohen of Soria at the beginning of his Kabbalistic explanation of the Hebrew alphabet, which I have published in *Madda'e ha-Yahaduth*, II (1927), especially p. 203.

[27] This opinion, as my friend Ernst Simon has called to my attention, is expressed with great precision and in a form suggesting the language of the mystics, by Franz Rosenzweig in a letter of 1925 to Martin Buber. Rosenzweig denies that the revelation on Mount Sinai gave laws. "The only immediate content of revelation ... is revelation itself; with *va-yered* [he came down, Exod. 19:20] it is essentially complete, with *va-yedabber* [he spoke, Exod. 20:1] interpretation sets in, and all the more so with *'anokhi* [the "I" at the beginning of the Ten Commandments]." Cf. Franz Rosenzweig, *Briefe*, Berlin, 1935, p. 535; English translation in F. Rosenzweig, *On Jewish Learning* ed. N. N. Glatzer, New York, 1955, p. 118.

was more than the community could bear. Only the prophet was empowered to communicate the meaning of this inarticulate voice to the community. It is mystical experience which conceives and gives birth to authority.

The Bhagavad-Gita

The Bhagavad-Gita, or Song of God, is the most popular work in all the religious literature of India, where its influence has been comparable to that of the Gospels in the West. The text occurs as part of the great epic The Mahabharata, which is dated by scholars between the fifth and second centuries before Christ. The Mahabharata relates the story of the struggle among the descendants of King Bharata, one of whom is the warrior Arjuna. The Bhagavad-Gita opens as Arjuna is about to engage in the final battle against his enemies, and is seized with fear at having to shed blood. He questions his charioteer, Krishna, an incarnation of the Absolute. The reply of Krishna to Arjuna touches on every aspect of spiritual life and cosmic law, and forms the content of the poem. The present selection constitutes the eleventh chapter of The Bhagavad-Gita.

ARJUNA

1 In thy mercy thou hast told me the secret supreme of thy Spirit, and thy words have dispelled my delusion.

2 I have heard in full from thee of the coming and going of beings, and also of thy infinite greatness.

3 I have heard thy words of truth, but my soul is yearning to see: to see thy form as God of this all.

4 If thou thinkest, O my Lord, that it can be seen by me, show me, O God of Yoga, the glory of thine own Supreme Being.

KRISHNA

5 By hundreds and then by thousands, behold, Arjuna, my manifold celestial forms of innumerable shapes and colours.

6 Behold the gods of the sun, and those of fire and light; the gods of storm and lightning, and the two luminous charioteers of heaven. Behold, descendant of Bharata, marvels never seen before.

Source: From Bhagavad-Gita, pp. 89–95, trans. Juan Mascaró. Copyright © Juan Mascaró, 1962.

7 See now the whole universe with all things that move and move not, and whatever thy soul may yearn to see. See it all as One in me.

8 But thou never canst see me with these thy mortal eyes: I will give thee divine sight. Behold my wonder and glory.

SANJAYA

9 When Krishna, the God of Yoga, had thus spoken, O king, he appeared then to Arjuna in his supreme divine form.

10 And Arjuna saw in that form countless visions of wonder: eyes from innumerable faces, numerous celestial ornaments, numberless heavenly weapons;

11 Celestial garlands and vestures, forms anointed with heavenly perfumes. The Infinite Divinity was facing all sides, all marvels in him containing.

12 If the light of a thousand suns suddenly arose in the sky, that splendour might be compared to the radiance of the Supreme Spirit.

13 And Arjuna saw in that radiance the whole universe in its variety, standing in a vast unity in the body of the God of gods.

14 Trembling with awe and wonder, Arjuna bowed his head, and joining his hands in adoration he thus spoke to his God.

ARJUNA

15 I see in thee all the gods, O my God; and the infinity of the beings of thy creation. I see god Brahma on his throne of lotus, and all the seers and serpents of light.

16 All around I behold thy Infinity: the power of thy innumerable arms, the visions from thy innumerable eyes, the words from thy innumerable mouths, and the fire of life of thy innumerable bodies. Nowhere I see a beginning or middle or end of thee, O God of all, Form Infinite!

17 I see the splendour of an infinite beauty which illumines the whole universe. It is thee! with thy crown and sceptre and circle. How difficult thou art to see! But I see thee: as fire, as the sun, blinding, incomprehensible.

18 Thou art the Imperishable, the highest End of knowledge, the support of this vast universe. Thou, the everlasting ruler of the law of righteousness, the Spirit who is and who was at the beginning.

19 I see thee without beginning, middle, or end; I behold thy infinite power, the power of thy innumerable arms. I see thine eyes as the sun and the moon. And I see thy face as a sacred fire that gives light and life to the whole universe in the splendour of a vast offering.

20 Heaven and earth and all the infinite spaces are filled with thy Spirit; and before the wonder of thy fearful majesty the three worlds tremble.

21 The hosts of the gods come to thee and, joining palms in awe and wonder, they praise and adore. Sages and saints come to thee, and praise thee with songs of glory.

22 The Rudras of destruction, the Vasus of fire, the Sadhyas of prayers, the Adityas of the sun; the lesser gods Visve-Devas, the two Asvins charioteers of heaven, the Maruts of winds and storms, the Ushmapas spirits of ancestors; the celestial choirs of Gandharvas, the Yakshas keepers of wealth, the demons of hell and the Siddhas who on earth reached perfection: they all behold thee with awe and wonder.

23 But the worlds also behold thy fearful mighty form, with many mouths and eyes, with many bellies, thighs and feet, frightening with terrible teeth: they tremble in fear, and I also tremble.

24 When I see thy vast form, reaching the sky, burning with many colours, with wide open mouths, with vast flaming eyes, my heart shakes in terror: my power is gone and gone is my peace, O Vishnu!

25 Like the fire at the end of Time which burns all in the last day, I see thy vast mouths and thy terrible teeth. Where am I? Where is my shelter? Have mercy on me, Gods of god, Refuge Supreme of the world!

26 The sons of Dhrita-rashtra, all of them, with other prin-
27 ces of this earth, and Bhishma and Drona and great Karna, and also the greatest warriors of our host, all enter rushing into thy mouths, terror-inspiring with their fearful fangs. Some are caught between them, and their heads crushed into powder.

28 As roaring torrents of waters rush forward into the ocean, so do these heroes of our mortal world rush into thy flaming mouths.

29 And as moths swiftly rushing enter a burning flame and die, so all these men rush to thy fire, rush fast to their own destruction.

30 The flames of thy mouths devour all the worlds. Thy glory fills the whole universe. But how terrible thy splendours burn!

31 Reveal thyself to me! Who art thou in this form of terror? I adore thee, O god supreme: be gracious unto me. I yearn to know thee, who are from the beginning: for I understand not thy mysterious works.

KRISHNA

32 I am all-powerful Time which destroys all things, and I have come here to slay these men. Even if thou dost not fight, all the warriors facing thee shall die.

33 Arise therefore! Win thy glory, conquer thine enemies, and enjoy thy kingdom. Through the fate of their Karma I have doomed them to die: be thou merely the means of my work.

34 Drona, Bhishma, Jayad-ratha and Karna, and other heroic warriors of this great war have already been slain by me: tremble not, fight and slay them. Thou shalt conquer thine enemies in battle.

SANJAYA

35 When Arjuna heard the words of Krishna he folded his hands trembling; and with a faltering voice, and bowing in adoration, he spoke.

ARJUNA

36 It is right O, God, that people sing thy praises, and that they are glad and rejoice in thee. All evil spirits fly away in fear; but the hosts of the saints bow down before thee.

37 How could they not bow down in love and adoration, before thee, God of gods, Spirit Supreme? Thou creator of Brahma, the god of creation, thou infinite, eternal, refuge of the world! Thou who art all that is, and all that is not, and all that is Beyond.

38 Thou God from the beginning, God in man since man was. Thou Treasure supreme of this vast universe. Thou the One to be known and the Knower, the final resting place. Thou infinite Presence in whom all things are.

39 God of the winds and the waters, of fire and death! Lord of the solitary moon, the Creator, the Ancestor of all! Adoration unto thee, a thousand adorations; and again and again unto thee adoration.

40 Adoration unto thee who art before me and behind me: adoration unto thee who art on all sides, God of all. All-powerful God of immeasurable might. Thou art the consummation of all: thou art all.

41 If in careless presumption, or even in friendliness, I said "Krishna! Son of Yadu! My friend!," this I did unconscious of thy greatness.

42 And if in irreverence I was disrespectful—when alone or with others—and made a jest of thee at games, or resting, or at a feast, forgive me in thy mercy, O thou Immeasurable!

43 Father of all. Master supreme. Power supreme in all the worlds. Who is like thee? Who is beyond thee?

44 I bow before thee, I prostrate in adoration; and I beg thy grace, O glorious Lord! As a father to his son, as a friend to his friend, as a lover to his beloved, be gracious unto me, O God.

45 In a vision I have seen what no man has seen before: I rejoice in exultation, and yet my heart trembles with fear. Have mercy upon me, Lord of gods, Refuge of the whole universe: show me again thine own human form.

46 I yearn to see thee again with thy crown and sceptre and circle. Show thyself to me again in thine own four-armed form, thou of arms infinite, Infinite Form.

KRISHNA

47 By my grace and my wondrous power I have shown to thee, Arjuna, this form supreme made of light, which is the Infinite, the All: mine own form from the beginning, never seen by man before.

48 Neither Vedas, nor sacrifices, nor studies, nor benefactions, nor rituals, nor fearful austerities can give the vision of my Form Supreme. Thou alone hast seen this Form, thou the greatest of the Kurus.

49 Thou hast seen the tremendous form of my greatness, but fear not, and be not bewildered. Free from fear and with a glad heart see my friendly form again.

SANJAYA

50 Thus spoke Vasudeva to Arjuna, and revealed himself in his human form. The God of all gave peace to his fears and showed himself in his peaceful beauty.

ARJUNA

51 When I see thy gentle human face, Krishna, I return to my own nature, and my heart has peace.

KRIJHNA

52 Thou has seen now face to face my form divine so hard to see: for even the gods in heaven ever long to see what thou hast seen.

53 Not by the Vedas, or an austere life, or gifts to the poor, or ritual offerings can I be seen as thou hast seen me.

54 Only by love can men see me, and know me, and come unto me.

55 He who works for me, who loves me, whose End Supreme I am, free from attachment to all things, and with love for all creation, he in truth comes unto me.

The Vision of the Cosmic Form

Krishna Prem

Ronald Henry Nixon was born in 1898. After service in the Royal Flying Corps, he took his M.A. at Cambridge and in 1920 went to India to pursue his interest in Buddhism and theosophy. There he met his teacher, Sri Yashoda Mai, a Bengali woman of profound mystical experience. He followed her to a remote ashram in the Himalayan foothills, took holy orders as a monk of the Hindu Vaishnava sect, and was given the name Sri Krishna Prem. After his guru's death, he was left in charge of the ashram and reluctantly accepted the task of leading the other disciples, eventually becoming one of the outstanding figures in India's spiritual life. He died in 1965.

With the opening of the eleventh chapter we find the disciple on the brink of a tremendous experience, one so great that many have thought it to be the final Goal beyond which naught remains. If that were so the Gita would have ended with this chapter; nevertheless, he who has seen this Vision has attained to the third stage, called by the Buddhists *Anāgāmin*,[1] whence but one last stage remains to tread.

The three great Secrets have been learnt so far, at least as far as *buddhi*-aided mind can grasp them. First the great Secret of the transcendental *Ātman*, the source of all that is and yet Itself unmoved for ever. Under the gaze of that unchanging One streams forth the universe of finite beings, coming and going in never-ending change; while between both, the link between the two, stands the Imperishable Greatness,[2] the Spiritual Cosmos, changeless in change, changing in changelessness.

The dawn has come, the shades of night have vanished; in a short while the Sun will rise. Eager for yet more Light, the disciple stands straining his eyes towards the East, aspiring to that Teacher in his heart who is, Himself, the Soul of all the world. Not knowing of the terror that the Vision holds for all that yet remains of self in him, he longs to look upon that Face which nothing that is mortal may behold.

"If Thou thinkest that by me it can be seen, Lord of the Cosmic *Yoga*, then show me Thine imperishable Self."

No fleshly eye can see that Sovereign Form. Only the *Ātman*'s never-closing Eye can see the *Ātman*'s self. But, for the disciple "who has made the thought in him a stranger to the world-illusion,"[3] who can pass through himself into the Life beyond, that Divine Eye is now available and flashes into dazzling, all-revealing vision.

A splendour bursts upon his gaze "as though ten thousand suns were blazing in the sky," and in that spiritual Light, which, though so brilliant, dazzles not the Eye, he sees the myriad Powers of the *Great Ātman*. There in the body of that boundless Being are all the living Powers that men have worshipped as Gods, not as if standing side by side in space, but each a facet mirroring the Whole, so interfused in being, each with each, that he who sees knows not indeed whether it is one Being that he sees or many Powers.[4]

All who have seen the Vision, for to this day, as in times past, it dawns upon the gaze of all who tread the Path, know the astonishment, the rapture mixed with terror, that fills the soul as the *Great Ātman* flashes into view.

Dead to all worldly things, standing outside himself, the disciple sees the great Expanse all blue with quivering supernal Light like lightnings massed in some world-ending cataclysm, the storm-tossed Ocean, glittering with souls, dizzily spinning in the dread Vortex Whirl, the terror of the Sound, throbbing in awful power through the vast Space like some great engine pulsing forth the Cosmic tides to ebb and flow throughout the Universe, and yet beyond the storm the changeless Peace, massively shining in a bliss beyond all words.

All this he sees and more that none can tell, sees with a vividness past all mere

---

[1] *Anāgāmin* literally means one who does not come again (to birth). The common view is that the *Anāgāmin* attains *Nirvāṇa* direct from some higher world after death. Actually the meaning is that having attained to the *Ālaya Vijñāña* (the *Mahat Ātman*) he is one with all and thinks no more "I die or I am born."

[2] The *Mahat Ātman*.

[3] Hermes, xiii, 1.

[4] Compare Plotinus, v, 8: "He who is the one God and all the gods, where each is all, blending into a unity, distinct in powers but all one god in virtue of that one divine power of many facets."

human seeing; yet all are symbols cast on the background of the Fathomless, wherein is neither Sound, nor Space, nor Sea, nor Vortex Whirl, nor any form at all.[5]

Filled with great wonder the disciple sees, and in his soul wells up the mystic Knowledge which bursts forth from his lips in an ecstatic hymn.

Within that boundless Form he sees the Gods, *Brahmā*, the great creative Power, and archetypes of all things here on earth. He sees the upward Path, the contemplative *Ṛishis*, also the Serpent's Way spiralling downwards in divinely urged desire.[6] Mouths, all-consuming, eyes of the infinite, all-seeing vision, arms wielding all things, bellies containing all; the Mace of Time's all-dominating power, the shining Discus of its evercircling flight, the Crown of sovereignty, all these are seen in a great blaze of boundless, world-consuming Light.

Perishing not throughout creation's ages, this Being stands for ever as the Treasure-House in which are stored the jewels of the Cosmos. As Cosmic Order, It maintains eternal *Dharma*, the Principle by which all things are linked to all in faultless harmony:

> *It seeth everywhere and marketh all:*
> *Do right—it recompenseth ! Do one wrong—*
> *The equal retribution must be made,*
> *Though* Dharma *tarry long.*[7]

This is the immemorial Heavenly Man, the *Adam Kadmon* of the Kabalistic wisdom; His eyes, the Sun and Moon, are life and form[8]; His mouth, a burning Fire, consumes the worlds, life feeding on itself in ceaseless sacrifice.

The consciousness that streams through three great Halls, the waking, "dreaming" and the "deep-sleep" states,[9] is agitated in its ceaseless ebb and flow by the immortal "Fourth," the Flame which all may see but none can touch.

The *Maharshis* and the *Siddhas*, mighty Teachers of the past, exist inscrutably within that radiant Being. Christ, Krishna, Buddha, all are there, and he who worships one draws near to them all.

Spanning the Void, leaping from earth to heaven, gleams the great Rainbow Bridge whose substance is composed of all the Gods. Upwards and downwards flash the waves of Light, weaving the many-coloured garment of the One. Here are the calm *Ādityas*,[10] shining in their golden Light, and there the stormy *Maruts*,[11] thrusting downwards with their flame-tipped spears.

But there is terror in the Vision too, for in that Light all forms are seen to pass. Only the Divine can live in the Divine: all that is human dies upon the threshold. All that in us which fears the so-called cruelty of nature, which trembles at the ruthless ocean waves, all that which clings to form and personality, sees Doom approaching it on flaming wings.

---

[5] This is true not only of these visions but of our ordinary experience as well. All perception is symbolic through and through. When we see a wooden door we see a symbol of a moment of the *Brahman*.
[6] See verse 5 in the Vedic Creation Hymn given in Appendix F.
[7] *Light of Asia*.
[8] See *Prashna Upanishad*, i, 5.
[9] See Appendix C.
[10] See Glossary.
[11] See Glossary.

As in an earthquake men are filled with panic terror, not so much by the actual physical dangers as by the feeling that the solid earth, unconscious symbol of stability, is rocking shudderingly beneath their feet, so in this Vision, self is seized by terror, seeing its old familiar landmarks vanish in the Void. Nowhere can self find any standing-place; all is dissolved into an ever-changing fiery flux.

The hundred sons of *Dhritarūshṭra* who are the facets of the lower self, *Bhishma* and *Droṇa*, faith and old tradition, *Karṇa*, the mighty warrior, nobly clinging to ideals but finding them in matter, all these are swallowed up in the great teeth of never-resting Time. These selves of ours, to which we cling so fiercely, are streams of psychic states linked each to each by changeless causal law; and all these streams wind through the fields of Time like rivers flowing swiftly to the sea.[12]

No forms are permanent; all come and go according to their *karma*. Even the worlds, circling around the sun, are but as moths which flutter round the lamp; their age-old rocks and "everlasting hills" melt into nothing like the down on the moth's wings. Nothing remains but *karma*'s subtle streams, flowing invisible to men, yet stronger than fine steel, linking each pattern of the universe to all that went before.

Terror unutterable fills all self in man as he beholds this world-devouring Fire. The image of a man-like, extracosmic God, Creator of the worlds, is seen to be a dream of men's weak hearts, a dream that serves to hide from human eyes the awful depths of Being's shoreless sea. "This world order, the same for all beings, neither any of the Gods hath made, nor any man; but it was always, is and shall be ever-living Fire, kindled in measure and quenched in measure.[13]

If one of unfirm heart should see this Vision he would recoil within the self of use and wont, not daring further question of the Infinite; but the strong soul of the well-tried disciple, not rooted in the self but in the *buddhi*, goes out in aspiration for yet deeper knowledge, seeking the One beyond these flaming ramparts. What is this ever-flowing Emanation, this Cosmic Fire that beats in flaming waves upon his heart?

And with the aspiration comes the answer; a Voice is heard where there is none to speak; letters of Light float on the waves of Fire. A sudden insight comes and the disciple knows that what he sees is the great flux of Time,[14] Time that is death to all things save the Soul. "Thus at the roaring loom of Time I ply, and weave for God the garment thou seest Him by."[15] All forms are seen to come and go, overmastered by the cyclic waves of Time, but this insight brings no tragic sense of loss such as inspired Villon's *Where are the Snows of Yester Year?* Rather, there comes a

---

[12] Compare the experience of the Buddha on the night of attaining the *Sambodhi*: "With the Divine eye which far surpasses human vision I saw beings in the act of passing hence and of reappearing elsewhere—beings high and low, fair or foul to view, in bliss or woe; I saw them all faring according to their pasts" (*Majjhima Nikāya*, sutta iv).
Compare also the Buddhist term for the individual self, *santāna*, meaning "continuous flow."
[13] Heracleitus, Fragment D 30.
[14] The Time here spoken of is not the same as the abstract time of mathematical physics. The latter is a mere mode of measurement of certain relations between phenomena, and no very clear reason seems to be given for the fundamental character of real time—namely, its irreversibility. The Time here referred to is the great prime mover of the universe. It has its root in Consciousness, of which, indeed, it is the active aspect. The mental construct of a four-dimensional Space-Time continuum seems to have little relevance here. To gain an understanding of real Time the best starting-point is the power of selective attention found in consciousness.
[15] Goethe.

sense of great deliverance, a sense of standing on the Eternal Rock around which the surging waves for ever beat in vain. As from a mountain height the traveller sees the road winding on towards his destination, so, from this vantage-point of insight, the disciple sees his Path and knows for certain that the obstacles will pass.

From the Goal issues forth the Path; to It the Path returns; both are within the Soul. Coming and going, bondage and liberation, all are illusions which the light of *jñāna* dispels. For ever shines the Goal, shining in golden glory; seen from another angle It itself becomes the Path. The Goal, the Path and he who treads that Path are all the same; naught is there anywhere save the One Being which, breathless, breathes eternally within Itself.

It is impossible to state in words this wondrous insight. All things remain the same yet all are changed. Time flashes bodily into Eternity; the streaming Flux itself is the Eternal, which, though It moves unceasingly, moves not at all.

This is the insight which makes the disciple what the Buddhists termed an *Anāgāmin,* one who comes to birth no more. Life and death have vanished in the Light of the Eternal, and though yet a portion of the Path remains to tread, it will be trodden with the knowledge that by Krishna Himself "already are the foes all overcome" and that no separate treader of the Path remains.

Crowned with the diadem of insight,[16] the initiated disciple gazes into the awful Mystery of Light in rapt adoration of the Eternal, clothed in Its flaming Robes, and the mystic Knowledge that now floods his soul pours forth in yet a further hymn of ecstasy.

These Hymns, parallels to which may be seen in the *Poemandres* and *Secret Sermon on the Mount* of the Hermetic books, are not to be confused with those of ordinary exoteric religion. They are the natural outflow of the mind seeking to give expression in mental terms to the great Knowledge that now streams upon it, the ferment that takes place as all the lower undergoes alchemical transmutation at the touch of the Higher. The difference between the two Hymns should be carefully noted. The first expresses chiefly awestruck terror as the disciple sees his universe dissolve into the Cosmic Fire; the second gives expression to the rapture with which he sees, within the waves of flame, the shining spiritual Cosmos.

Gazing within, he sees that all is ruled by living spiritual Law. Two mighty tidal urges rule the worlds and both of them are living spiritual Powers. One is the movement of the *Rākshasas,* fleeing as in fear to all the quarters of the Universe. This is the great outgoing Creative Breath by which not only is the universe spread forth in space, but all the inner life of thought and feeling flows outwards seeking whom it may devour.[17] This is the urge of self-assertion, self-expansion, survival of the fittest, "nature red in tooth and claw." Here is the inner cause of war and all the selfish life of competition, each for himself and devil take the hindmost, but here, as well, the force behind man's mind, wheeling in ever-widening circles to receding frontiers.

[16] Note that the disciple is now (verse 35) referred to as "the Crowned one." This is a reference to the Crown of Knowledge given to the Initiate. A parallel is to be seen in the *Atef* crown worn by *Osiris* in the Egyptian Mystic Ritual and, according to Marsham Adams, placed on the head of the Initiate after he has passed through the pylons and stands before the Throne.

[17] Compare the *Paurānik* accounts of creation in which *Brahmā* first created *Rākshasas* who promptly attempted to devour him. That is to say, the outgoing forces would, if left to themselves, dissipate the universe at once. The technical term for this outgoing is *Pravṛitti.*

The second movement, symbolised by hosts of *Siddhas*, is the *nivritti*, Home-ward-flowing Tide. By this all the rich treasures of experience, the Fruits of the World Tree, are gathered in once more to the One Life like mighty rivers flowing homewards to the sea.[18]

He sees the *Mighty Ātman*, source of both these Tides, the Primal Man of all the ancient Mysteries, the Cosmic Treasure-House, the Realm of shining Light, Knower and Known both fused in unity. Glimpsed through the robes of Cosmic Ideation stands the unmoved Eternal, poised aloof, Being, Non-being, *That* beyond them both, the Nameless One, worshipped alone by silence of the mind.

The seven great Cosmic planes, here symbolised as Gods, are all within that One, and though the disciple seeks to pour forth all his soul in utter reverence, he knows not where to turn, for now he sees that even the very earth on which he stands is holy, and that around, above, below, within, without, everywhere is the One and only One, containing all, from lowest earthy clod to that unmanifest, transcendent Self whose Light for ever shines beyond the worlds.[19]

No longer can he think that He whom he has worshipped, the Teacher in his heart, Friend of his nights and days, is any personal being, man or superman or God. Rather he sees that, be the Form what it may, it was the Light of the Eternal which, shining through loved but yet symbolic eyes, has led him on the Path and is both Path and Goal.

But yet, while he is human, there must still be Forms for him. He cannot bear for long the blaze of Light that floods upon him, shattering all his being. No human mind and body can for long endure upon the summits of eternal snow-clad peaks. He must return once more to lower levels, the dazzling Light be veiled in the fa-miliar forms of Father, Lover, Friend; for still the fourth stage of the Path remains to tread and, while he needs a body, he must see the Light in human form.[20]

Therefore he sees once more the Form of his loved Teacher in his own heart and in the hearts of all, though, as reminder of the glorious Vision, the Form is Crowned and bears the Mace and Discus, symbols of the Lord of Time. He knows that He who sits within his heart is throned beyond all Time and that, however thick the fight may press upon him, his final victory is sure, since He who rules his heart rules all the worlds.

Thus ends the Vision seen by union with the Self (*ātma yogāt*), ends as a vision though its Knowledge will remain for ever in the heart of the disciple. Henceforth that inner Knowledge must be the master-light of all his seeing, must make "the

---

[18] For further discussion of these two movements see Chapter XVI.
[19] Compare the magnificent hymn of Hermes Trismegistus:

"Whither, again, am I to turn my eyes to sing Thy praise: above, below, within, without?
There is no way, no place is there about Thee, nor any other thing of things that are.
All are in Thee; all are from Thee, O Thou who givest all and takest naught,
For Thou . . . art all and there is nothing else which Thou art not.
Hermetic Corpus, v, 10.

[20] The *chaturbhuja* form of verse 46 should be translated "*four-limbed*" (i.e. two arms and two legs) and not, as usually done, "*four-armed*." The word *bhuja* means limb as well as arm, and verses 49 and 51 clearly show that the form in question was a *human* one, four-limbed in contrast to the thousand arms and legs of the symbolic vision. The *Vishnu* form, no doubt, has four arms; but in the earliest texts, such as the *Mahābhārata*, Krishna has always the normal human two.

For this interpretation I am indebted to my friend Pandit Jagadish Chandra Chatterji, Vidyā Vāridhi.

noisy years seem moments in the being of the eternal Silence." Never may he forget what he has seen; always must he realise "the voidness of the seeming full, the fullness of the seeming void."[21] For him, not as a poet's intuition, but in sheer fact, will it be true that

> ... in a season of calm weather
> Though inland far we be,
> Our souls have sight of that immortal sea
> Which brought us hither;
> Can in a moment travel thither—
> And see the children sport upon the shore,
> And hear its mighty waters rolling evermore.[22]

Not Gods, the great impersonal waves of Light, nor men, the separate selves of mind and body, "none but thyself," the immortal soul of man, has ever or will ever see this Cosmic Form. No mystic rites, no study of philosophy, no harsh austerities, no alms or offerings, can show It, for all these are of the mind alone. Only the power of love, the Soul's own power, love that for ever seeks to give itself, straining towards Eternity, can bring about the union of the self with the One Self by which alone the Cosmic Form is seen and ultimately entered.

Therefore the chapter ends with a reiteration of the Path, a purely spiritual Path, one quite distinct from all the mystic rites and outer pieties that most men term religion:

"Giving the self in love to Me, with Me as Goal, doing all actions for Me (the One Life in all), devoid of all atachment to the forms, free from hostility to any being, man comes to Me, O Arjuna."[23]

---

[21] *The Voice of the Silence.*
[22] Wordsworth's *Ode on the Intimations of Immortality.*
[23] This verse has been described by *Shankarāchārya* as giving the quintessence of the whole Gita.

The Steps of Humility

St. Bernard of Clairvaux

St. Bernard of Clairvaux (1091–1153) was one of the great figures of Western Christendom and one of the principal shapers of the medieval epoch. By his work of reform, the Cistercian monastic order became the most important and influential in Europe. One of the greatest mystics in the history of the Church, he was also, when necessary, an extraordinarily effective man of action at the highest levels of political power. The sermons of St. Bernard are mostly mystical and allegorical, especially the famous series on the Song of Solomon. *The Steps of Humility*, from which the present selection was taken, was written for Bernard's own monks at the monastery at Clairvaux.

Author's Preface

You have asked me, Brother Godfrey, to set forth for you in more extended form that which I said to the brethren about the steps of humility. While my eagerness to grant your wish urged me on, the meagerness of my ability held me back, and, mindful of our Lord's warning, I did not dare begin until I had sat down and counted the cost, whether I had sufficient to finish it. But when love had cast out the fear of being mocked on account of an unfinished work, there arose another fear, that the fame of success might be more perilous than the shame of failure. Being thus placed in a dilemma between this fear and love, I hesitated a long time, wondering which path would be safe to follow, and fearing that a useful discourse would violate what humility I have, while humble silence would nullify what utility I have. Since I saw neither was safe, yet one or the other must be chosen, I have decided to share the fruit of my discourse with you, so far as possible, rather than seek my own safety in the haven of silence. And I am confident that, if by chance I say anything which you approve, I shall be able to keep from being proud by the help of your prayers; while if, as is more likely, I do not accomplish anything worthy of your consideration, I shall then have nothing to be proud of.

Humility, The Way to Truth

I am going to speak, therefore, about the steps of humility, which St. Benedict proposes, not to count but to mount; first I will show, if possible, whither they lead, so that knowledge of the goal may make the toil of the ascent seem less wearisome. So let the Lord tell us of the toil of the way and of the reward of that toil. He says, *I am the way, the truth, and the life.* He calls humility the way which leads to truth.

Source: Reprinted by permission of the publishers from *The Steps of Humility* by Bernard of Clairvaux, George Bosworth Burch, translator, Cambridge, Massachusetts: Harvard University Press, © 1940 by the President and Fellows of Harvard College; renewed 1968 by George B. Burch.

The former is the toil; the latter, the fruit of the toil. How am I to know, you ask, that he was speaking of humility when he said simply, *I am the way*? But hear this, which is clearer: *Learn of me, for I am meek and lowly in heart*. He offers himself as an example of humility, as the type of gentleness. If you follow him, you shall not walk in darkness, but shall have the light of life. What is the light of life but truth which lighteth every man that cometh into the world and showeth where true life is? Likewise when he said, *I am the way and the truth*, he added, *and the life*; as if to say, I am the way, leading to truth; I am the truth promising life; I am the life, and give it. *And this*, he says, *is life eternal, that they might know thee the only true God, and Jesus Christ, whom thou hast sent*. Or it is as if you should say: I know the way, humility; I want the reward, truth. But what if the toil of the way is so great that I cannot attain the desired goal? He answers, *I am the life*, that is, the means of support on the way. Thus he cries to wanderers, who have lost the way, *I am the way*; to sceptics and unbelievers, *I am the truth*; to those already mounting, but growing weary, *I am the life*. It is clear enough, I think, from the verse cited that knowledge of the truth is the fruit of humility. But hear also another: *I thank thee, O Father, Lord of heaven, and earth because thou hast hid these things*, no doubt the secrets of truth, *from the wise and prudent*, that is, from the proud, *and hast revealed them unto babes*, that is, to the humble. Here too it appears that the truth is concealed from the proud and revealed to the humble.

Humility may be defined thus: Humility is that thorough self-examination which makes a man contemptible in his own sight. It is acquired by those who set up a ladder in their hearts whereby to ascend from virtue to virtue, that is, from step to step, until they attain the summit of humility, from where, as from the Zion of speculation, they can see the truth. *For the lawgiver*, it is said, *shall give a blessing*, because he who has given the law will give a blessing too, that is, he who has commanded humility will lead to truth. Now who is this lawgiver but the gracious and righteous Lord, who teaches the abandoned in the way? For they are surely abandoned who have abandoned truth. But are they thus abandoned by the gracious Lord? Nay, for they are the very ones whom the gracious and righteous Lord commands to follow the way of humility by which they may return to knowledge of the truth. He gives an opportunity to recover salvation, because he is gracious; yet not without due discipline, because he is righteous. Gracious, because he does not allow to perish; righteous, because he does not neglect to punish.

The First Step of Truth, Knowing Yourself

If he made himself wretched who was not wretched before, in order to learn what he already knew; how much more should you. I do not say make yourself what you are not, but observe what you are, that you are wretched indeed, and so learn to be merciful, a thing you cannot know in any other way. For if you regard your neighbor's faults but do not observe your own, you are likely to be moved not to truth but to wrath, not to condole but to condemn, not to restore in the spirit of meekness but to destroy in the spirit of anger. *Ye which are spiritual*, says the apostle, *restore such an one in the spirit of meekness*. The apostle's counsel or rather command is to assist the weak brother in a gentle spirit, the spirit in which you wish to be assisted when you are weak. And that you may know how to act gently toward a trespasser, he adds, *Considering thyself, lest thou also be tempted*.

Let us see how well the disciple of Truth follows the Master's order. In the Beatitudes, which I referred to above, just as the merciful are mentioned before the pure in heart, so are the meek before the merciful. And when the apostle exhorted the spiritual to restore the carnal, he added, *In the spirit of meekness*. Restoring your brethren is the work of the merciful; the spirit is that of the meek; as if he had said, none can be considered merciful who is not meek in himself. See how the apostle clearly shows what I promised to show above, that truth is to be sought in ourselves before we seek it in our neighbors; *considering thyself*, he says, that is, how easily tempted, how liable to sin. For by considering yourself you grow meek, and thus you come to succour others in the spirit of meekness. But if you will not observe what the disciple commends, heed what the Master commands: *Thou hypocrite, first cast out the beam out of thine own eye; and then shalt thou see clearly to cast out the mote out of thy brother's eye*. The great thick beam in the eye is pride in the mind. By its great size, although empty, not sound, swollen, not solid, it dims the mind's eye and overshadows truth in such a way that when pride fills your mind, you can no longer see yourself, you can no longer feel yourself such as you are actually or potentially; but you either fancy that you are or hope you will become such as you would love to be. For what is pride but love of your own excellence, as some saint has defined it? We may say likewise, on the other hand, that humility is contempt of your own excellence. Love, like hate, is a stranger to true judgment. Will you hear a true judgment? *As I hear, I judge*; not as I hate, not as I love, not as I fear. There is a judgment of hate, for example. *We have a law, and by our law he ought to die.* Also of fear, for example, *If we let him thus alone, the Romans shall come and take away both our place and nation.* And there is a judgment of love, as David's command concerning his parricide son, *Deal gently with the young man, even with Absalom.* And I know it is a rule in human law observed in both ecclesiastical and secular cases that personal friends of the litigants cannot be admitted as judges, lest they either defraud or be defrauded by their love for their friends. Now if your love for a friend either lessens or completely conceals his guilt in your judgment, how much more will the love of yourself deceive you in judging yourself!

He therefore, who wants to know truth in himself fully must first get rid of the beam of pride, which prevents him from seeing the light, and then erect a way of ascent in his heart by which to seek himself in himself; and thus after the twelfth step of humility he will come to the first step of truth. When he has found truth in himself, or rather has found himself in truth, and is able to say, *I believed, and therefore have I spoken; but I was greatly humbled*; let him ascend to the heights of his heart, that truth may be exalted, and passing to the second step let him say in his passage, *All men are false*. Pray, did not David follow this order? Pray, did not the Prophet feel this which the Lord felt, and the apostle, and even we feel after them and through them? *I believed*, he says, in the Truth which declares, *He that followeth me shall not walk in darkness*. *I believed*, following; *and therefore have I spoken*, confessing. Confessing what? The truth which I have learned in believing. But after I both believed unto righteousness and spoke unto salvation, *I was greatly*, that is perfectly, *humbled*. As if he had said: Because I was not ashamed to confess against myself truth found in myself, I attained to perfect humility. For *greatly* can be understood to mean "perfectly," as in the phrase, *That delighteth greatly in his commandments.* If anyone should contend that *greatly* here means "extremely" rather than "perfectly," because the commentators seem to say so, that is also consistent with the prophet's meaning, and we may consider him to have said as follows: When I did not yet know truth, I thought myself to be something, whereas I was nothing; but after I learned the truth by believing in Christ, that is, imitating his humility, it was itself exalted in me by my confession; *but I was greatly humbled*, that is, I became in my own sight extremely contemptible as a result of my self-examination.

The Second Step of Truth, Knowing Your Neighbor

And so the prophet is humbled in this first step of truth, as he says in another psalm, *And in thy truth thou hast humbled me.* Let him observe himself and judge the common wretchedness from his own. And thus proceeding to the second step, let him say in his passage. *All men are false.* In what passage? In that doubtless in which, passing outside himself and cleaving to truth, he judges himself. Let him say, then, in that passage, not angrily or insolently, but pitifully and sympathetically, *All men are false.* What does this mean, *All men are false?* All men are weak, all men are wretched and impotent who can save neither themselves nor others. Just as it is said, *An horse is a vain thing for safety,* not because a horse deceives anyone, but because he deceives himself who trusts in its strength; so all men are called false, that is, frail and fickle, who can hope to achieve neither their own nor another's salvation. Rather does he incur a curse that trusteth in man. And so the prophet humbly advances under the leadership of truth, seeing in others what he deplores in himself; *and he that increaseth knowledge increaseth sorrow,* so as to say, broadly but truthfully, *All men are false.*

See how differently the proud Pharisee felt about himself. What did he exclaim in his passage? *God, I thank thee that I am not as other men are.* He exults in himself exceedingly; he insults all others arrogantly. David is otherwise. For he says, *All men are false.* He excludes none, and so deludes none, knowing that all have sinned and come short of the glory of God. The Pharisee deludes only himself when he excludes only himself and condemns all others. The prophet does not exclude himself from the common passion, lest he be excluded from the compassion; the Pharisee disdains mercy when he disclaims misery. The prophet maintains of all, as of himself, *All men are false;* the Pharisee complains of all, except himself, saying, *I am not as other men are.* And he gives thanks, not that he is good, but that he is different; not so much because of his own virtues as because of the vices which he sees in others. He has not yet cast out the beam out of his own eye, yet he points out the motes in his brother's eyes. For he adds, *Unjust, extortioners.* This digressing passage is not in vain, I think, if you have learned to distinguish the different kinds of passage.

Now to return to the thesis. Those whom truth has caused to know, and so condemn themselves must now find distasteful those things they used to love, even their own selves. Standing before themselves, they are forced to see that they are such as they blush to appear, even to themselves. Displeased with what they are, they aspire to what they are not and have no hope of becoming through themselves. Loudly mourning their lot, they find only this comfort, that, severe judges of themselves, who love truth and hunger and thirst after justice, contemptuous even of themselves, they require of themselves the strictest expiation and, what is more, emendation. But when they see that they are not sufficient for this (for when they have done all those things which are commanded them, say they, We are unprofitable servants), they flee from justice to mercy. In order to obtain this they follow the precept of Truth: *Blessed are the merciful, for they shall obtain mercy.* And this is the second step of truth, when they seek it in their neighbors, when they learn others' wants from their own, when they know from their own miseries how to commiserate with others who are miserable.

The Third Step of Truth, Knowing God

Those who persevere, therefore, in these three things, the remorse of repentance, desire of justice, and works of mercy, may then pass through contemplation to the third step, having purged the spiritual vision of the three obstacles arising from ignorance and weakness and willfulness. For these are the ways which seem good to men, to those at least *who rejoice to do evil and delight in the forwardness of the wicked,* and cover themselves with weakness or ignorance to plead as excuses in sinning. But they plead weakness or ignorance without avail who choose to be ignorant or weak in order to sin more freely. Do you suppose it availed the first man or was it allowed that he did not sin willingly, because he pleaded his wife, that is, the weakness of the flesh, in defence? Or will the stoners of the first martyr, because they stopped their ears, be excusable through ignorance? Those who feel themselves alienated from truth by delight and gladness in sinning and overcome by weakness and ignorance, must change their delight to despite, their gladness to sadness, conquer the weakness of the flesh with the zeal of justice, and resist ignorance with philanthropy. Otherwise, if they do not know truth needy, naked, and weak as it is now; they may shamefacedly recognize it too late when it comes with great power and strength, terrifying and accusing, and may in vain answer tremblingly, *When saw we thee in need and did not minister unto thee? The Lord shall be known when he executeth judgments,* if he is not known now when he seeketh mercy. Then *they shall look on him whom they pierced,* and likewise the avaricious on him whom they despised. From every blemish, therefore, arising from weakness or ignorance or willfulness the eye of the heart is purified by weeping, hungering for justice, and devotion to works of mercy. To such a heart Truth promises to appear in his splendor: *Blessed are the pure in heart: for they shall see God.* Since there are therefore three steps or states of truth, we ascend to the first by the toil of humility, to the second by the emotion of compassion, to the third by the ecstasy of contemplation. In the first, truth is found harsh: in the second, loving; in the third, pure. Reason, by which we examine ourselves, leads us to the first; love, by which we sympathize with others, entices us to the second; purity, by which we are lifted to invisible heights, snatches us up to the third. . . .

The Steps of Humility

There is a way down and a way up, a way to the good and a way to evil. Shun the evil one, choose the good one. If you cannot do so of yourself, pray with the prophet and say, *Remove from me the way of lying*. How? *And grant me thy law graciously*; that law namely which thou hast given to the abandoned in the way, who have abandoned truth, and one of whom am I, surely fallen from truth. But shall not he who falls endeavour to rise again? This is why *I have chosen the way of truth*, by which I shall go up in humility thither whence I came down in pride. I shall go up, I say, singing, *It is good for me, O Lord, that I have been humbled. The law of thy mouth is better unto me than thousands of gold and silver*. David seems to have offered you two ways, but you know there is only one. Yet it is distinguished from itself and is called by different names, either *the way of lying* for those going down, or *the way of truth* for those going up. The same steps lead up to the throne and down; the same road leads to the city and from it; one door is the entrance of the house and the exit; Jacob saw the angels ascending and descending on the same ladder. What does all this mean? Simply that if you desire to return to truth, you do not have to seek a new way which you know not, but the known way by which you descended. Retracing your own path, you may ascend in humility by the same steps which you descended in pride, so that what was the twelfth step of pride going down is the first step of humility going up; the eleventh is found second; the tenth, third; the ninth, fourth; the eighth, fifth; the seventh, sixth; the sixth, seventh; the fifth, eighth; the fourth, ninth; the third, tenth; the second, eleventh; and the first, twelfth. When these steps of pride are discovered or rather remembered in yourself, there is no difficulty in finding the way of humility.

The First Step of Pride, Curiosity

The first step of pride, then, is curiosity, and you may recognize it by these marks. If you shall see a monk, whom you formerly trusted confidently, beginning to roam with his eyes, hold his head erect, prick up his ears, wherever he is standing, walking, sitting; you may know the changed inner man from the movements of the outer. For a wicked man *winketh with his eyes, speaketh with his feet, teacheth with his fingers*; and the strange movement of the body reveals a new disease in the soul which has tired of introspection and which neglect of self makes curious toward others. For, as it knows not itself, it is sent forth to feed its kids. I shall rightly have called the eyes and ears kids, which signify sin; for just as death enters into the world by sin, so by these windows it enters into the mind. The curious man, therefore, occupies himself with feeding these, no longer curious to know how he has left himself within. And it would be strange indeed, O man, if while watchfully attending thyself thou shouldst likewise be extending thyself to aught else. Hearken to Solomon, thou curious fellow; hearken to the wise man, thou fool. *Keep thy heart,* he says, *with all diligence*; let all thy senses be alert for keeping that out of which *are the issues of life*. For whither wilt thou withdraw from thyself, thou curious fellow? To whom wilt thou commit thyself meanwhile? How dost thou dare lift thy eyes to heaven, when thou has sinned against heaven? Look at the earth in order to know thyself. Only it will show thee an image of thyself, *for dust thou art, and unto dust shalt thou return.*

There are two reasons, however, for which you may lift up your eyes without reproach, namely, to seek help or to offer it. David lifted up his eyes unto the hills, to seek it; and the Lord lifted up his over the multitude, to offer it. The one pitiably, the other pitifully, both blamelessly. If you also, considering the time, place, and cause, lift up your eyes because of your own or your brother's necessity, not only I do not condemn but I highly approve. For affliction excuses the one, while affection commends the other. But if for any other reason, then I will call you an imitator not of the prophet or the Lord but of Dinah or Eve or even Satan. For when Dinah goes out to feed her kids, her father loses his maid and she her maidenhood. O Dinah, why must thou go out to see the daughters of the land? What is the need? What is the use? Mere curiosity? Though thou seest them idly, thou art not idly seen. Thou lookest curiously, but art looked at more curiously. Who would then suppose that this curious idleness or idle curiosity would prove to be not idle but suicidal for thee, thy friends, and thy foes?

[*At this point Bernard lists and discusses, in addition to curiosity, the following as the steps of pride:*
The second step of pride, frivolity.
The third step of pride, foolish mirth.
The fourth step of pride, boastfulness.
The fifth step of pride, singularity (i.e., thinking that "I am not as other men are").
The sixth step of pride, conceit.
The seventh step of pride, audacity.
The eighth step of pride, excusing sins.
The ninth step of pride, hypocritical confession.
The tenth step of pride, defiance.
The eleventh step of pride, freedom to sin (i.e., "allured into satisfying [one's] own desires with the confidence of freedom").
The twelfth step of pride, habitual sinning.]

Conclusion

You may say, Brother Godfrey, that I have set forth something other than what you requested and I promised, as I seem to have described the steps of pride instead of the steps of humility. I reply, I could only teach what I had learned. I who know more about going down than going up did not think it would be proper for me to describe the way up. Let St. Benedict tell you about the steps of humility, which he first set up in his own heart; I have nothing to tell you about except the order of my own descent. Yet if this is carefully examined, the way up may be found in it. For if when going to Rome you should meet a man coming from there and ask him the way, what way could he tell better than that which he had come? In naming the castles, towns and cities, rivers and mountains, along which he has passed, he describes his own road and prescribes yours, so that you may recognize the same places in going which he has passed along in coming. Similarly in this descent of mine you will find, perhaps, the steps leading up, and ascending will read them in your own heart better than in my book.

Meditation

Chögyam Trungpa

Chögyam Trungpa (1939–   ) was born in Tibet as an incarnate lama of high rank. During the takeover of Tibet by the Chinese in 1959, he escaped to India in a dramatic flight described in his first book, *Born in Tibet*. He emigrated to Great Britain, attended Oxford University, and went on to establish a Buddhist center in Scotland. He now lives and teaches in America, principally at his center in Boulder, Colorado, although groups connected to his teachings are now located in many American cities. His recent books include *Cutting Through Spiritual Materialism* and *The Myth of Freedom*.

Meditation is a vast subject and there have been many developments throughout the ages and many variations among the different religious traditions. But broadly speaking the basic character of meditation takes on one of two forms. The first stems from the teachings which are concerned with the discovery of the nature of existence; the second concerns communication with the external or universal concept of God. In either case meditation is the only way to put the teachings into practice.

Where there is the concept of an external, "higher" Being, there is also internal personality—which is known as "I" or the Ego. In this case meditation practice becomes a way of developing communication with an external Being. This means that one feels oneself to be inferior and one is trying to contact something higher, greater. Such meditation is based on devotion. This is basically an inward, or introvert practice of meditation, which is well known in the Hindu teachings, where the emphasis is on going into the inward state of samadhi, into the depths of the heart. One finds a similar technique practised in the Orthodox teachings of Christianity, where the prayer of the heart is used and concentration on the heart is emphasised. This is a means of identifying oneself with an external Being and necessitates purifying oneself. The basic belief is that one is separate from God, but there is still a link, one is still part of God. This confusion sometimes arises, and in order to clarify it one has to work inwards and try to raise the standard of individuality to the level of a higher consciousness. This approach makes use of

Source: Chögyam Trungpa, *Meditation in Action* (Berkeley, Calif., 1969), pp. 51–64. Used by permission from the publisher, Shambala Publications, 1409 5th St., Berkeley, Calif. 94710.

emotions and devotional practices which are aimed at making contact with God or gods or some particular saint. These devotional practices may also include the recitation of mantra.

The other principal form of meditation is almost entirely opposite in its approach, though finally it might lead to the same results. Here there is no belief in higher and lower; the idea of different levels, or of being in an under-developed state, does not arise. One does not feel inferior, and what one is trying to achieve is not something higher than oneself. Therefore the practice of meditation does not require an inward concentration on the heart. There is no centralising concept at all. Even such practices as concentrating on the chakras, or psychic centres of the body, are approached in a different way. Although in certain teachings of Buddhism the concept of chakras is mentioned, the practices connected with them are not based on the development of an inward centre. So this basic form of meditation is concerned with trying to see what *is*. There are many variations on this form of meditation, but they are generally based on various techniques for opening oneself. The achievement of this kind of meditation is not, therefore, the result of some long-term, arduous practise through which we build ourselves up into a "higher" state, not does it necessitate going into any kind of inner trance state. It is rather what one might call "working meditation" or extrovert meditation, where skilful means and wisdom must be combined like the two wings of a bird. This is not a question of trying to retreat from the world. In fact without the external world, the world of apparent phenomena, meditation would be almost impossible to practise, for the individual and the external world are not separate, but merely co-exist together. Therefore the concept of trying to communicate and trying to become one with some higher Being does not arise.

In this kind of meditation practise the concept of *nowness* plays a very important part. In fact, it is the essence of meditation. Whatever one does, whatever one tries to practise, is not aimed at achieving a higher state or at following some theory or ideal, but simply, without any object or ambition, trying to see what is here and now. One has to become aware of the present moment through such means as concentrating on the breathing, a practise which has been developed in the Buddhist tradition. This is based on developing the knowledge of nowness, for each respiration is unique, it is an expression of *now*. Each breath is separate from the next and is fully seen and fully felt, not in a visualised form, nor simply as an aid to concentration, but it should be fully and properly dealt with. Just as a very hungry man, when he is eating, is not even conscious that he is eating food. He is so engrossed in the food that he completely identifies himself with what he is doing and almost becomes one with the taste and enjoyment of it. Similarly with the breathing, the whole idea is to try and see through that very moment in time. So in this case the concept of trying to become something higher does not arise at all, and opinions do not have much importance. In a sense opinions provide a way to escape; they create a kind of slothfulness and obscure one's clarity of vision. The clarity of our consciousness is veiled by prefabricated concepts and whatever we see we try to fit into some pigeon-hole or in some way make it fit in with our preconceived ideas. So concepts and theories—and, for that matter, theology—can become obstacles. One might ask, therefore, what is the point of studying Buddhist philosophy? Since there are Scriptures and texts and there is surely some philosophy to believe in, wouldn't that also be a concept? Well, that depends on the individual, but basically it is not so. From the start one tries to transcend concepts, and one tries, perhaps in a very critical way, to find out what *is*. One has to develop a critical mind which will stimulate intelligence. This may at first cause one to reject what is said by teachers or what is written in books, but then gradually one begins to feel something and to find something for oneself. That is what is known as the meeting of imagination and reality, where the feeling of certain words and concepts meets with intuitive knowledge, perhaps in a rather vague and imprecise way. One may be uncertain whether what one is learning is right or not, but there is a general feeling that one is about to discover something. One cannot really start by being perfect, but one must start with something. And if one cultivates this intelligent, intuitive insight, then gradually, stage by stage, the real intuitive feeling develops and the imaginary or hallucinatory element is gradually clarified and eventually dies out. Finally that vague feeling of discovery becomes very clear, so that almost no doubt remains. Even at this stage it is possible that one may be unable to explain one's discovery verbally or write it down exactly on paper, and in fact if one tried to do so it would be limiting one's scope and would be rather dangerous. Nevertheless, as this feeling grows and develops one finally attains direct knowledge, rather than achieving something which is separate from oneself. As in the analogy of the hungry man, you become one with the subject. This can only be achieved through the practice of meditation. Therefore meditation is very much a matter of exercise—it is a working practice. It is not a question of going into some inward depth, but of widening and expanding outwards.

These are the basic differences between the two types of meditation practice. The first may be more suitable for some people and the second may be more suitable for others. It is not a question of one being superior or more accurate than the other. But for any form of meditation one must first overcome that great feeling of demand and ambition which acts as a major obstacle. Making demands on a person, such as a Guru, or having the ambition to achieve something out of what one is doing, arises out of a built-up desire or wantingness; and that wanting-ness is a centralized notion. This centralized notion is basically blind. It is like having one eye, and that one eye being situated in the chest. When you try to walk you cannot turn your head round and you can only see a limited area. Because you can see in only one direction the intelligence of turning the head is lacking. Therefore there is a great danger of falling. This wantingness acts as a veil and becomes an obstacle to the discovery of the moment of nowness, because the wanting is based either on the future or on trying to continue something which existed in the past, so the nowness is completely forgotten. There may be a certain effort to focus on the nowness, but perhaps only twenty per cent of the conscious-ness is based on the present and the rest is scattered into the past or the future. Therefore there is not enough force to see directly what is there.

Here, too, the teaching of selflessness plays a very important part. This is not merely a question of denying the existence of Ego, for Ego is something relative. Where there is an external person, a higher Being, or the concept of something which is separate from oneself, then we tend to think that because there is some-thing outside there must be something here as well. The external phenomenon sometimes becomes such an overwhelming thing and seems to have all sorts of seductive or aggressive qualities, so we erect a kind of defense mechanism against it, failing to see that that is itself a continuity of the external thing. We try to segregate ourselves from the external, and this creates a kind of gigantic bubble in us which consists of nothing but air and water or, in this case, fear and the reflection of the external thing. So this huge bubble prevents any fresh air from coming in, and that is "I"—the Ego. So in that sense there is the existence of Ego, but it is in fact illusory. Having established that, one generally wants to create some external idol or refuge. Subconsciously one knows that this "I" is only a bubble and it could burst at any moment, so one tries to protect it as much as one can—either consciously or subconsciously. In fact we have achieved such skill at protecting this Ego that we have managed to preserve it for hundreds of years. It is as though a person has a very precious pair of spectacles which he puts in a box or various containers in order to keep it safe, so that even if other things are broken this would be preserved. He may feel that other things could bear hardship, but he knows that this could not, so this would last longer. In the same way, Ego lasts longer just because one feels it could burst at any time. There is fear of it being destroyed because that would be too much, one would feel too exposed. And there is such character, such a fascinating pattern established outside us, although it is in fact our own reflection. That is why the concept of Egolessness is not really a question of whether there is a Self or not, or, for that matter, whether there is the existence of God or not; it is rather the taking away of that concept of the bubble. Having done so, one doesn't have to deliberately destroy the Ego or deliberately condemn God. And when that barrier is removed one can expand and swim through straight away. But this can only be achieved through the practice of meditation which must be approached in a very practical and simple way. Then the mystical experience of joy or Grace, or whatever it might be, can be found in every object. That is what one tries to achieve through Vipassana, or "Insight" meditation practice. Once we have established a basic pattern of discipline and we have developed a regular way of dealing with the situation—whether it is breathing or walking or what-have-you—then at some stage the technique gradually dies out. Reality gradually expands so that we do not have to use the technique at all. And in this case one does not have to concentrate inwards, but one can expand outwards more and more. And the more one expands, the closer one gets to the realisation of centreless existence.

That is the basic pattern of this kind of meditation, which is based on three fundamental factors: firstly, not centralising inwards: secondly, not having any longing to become higher; and thirdly, becoming completely identified with here and now. These three elements run right through the practice of meditation, from the beginning up to the moment of realisation.

Q. You mentioned nowness in your talk, and I was wondering how it is possible to become aware of the absolute through awareness of a relative moment in time?

A. Well, we have to start by working through the relative aspect, until finally this nowness takes on such a living quality that it is no longer dependent on a relative way of expressing nowness. One might say that *now* exists all the time, beyond the concept of relativity. But since all concepts are based on the idea of relativity, it is impossible to find any words which go beyond that. So nowness is the only way to see directly. First it is between the past and the future— now. Then gradually one discovers that nowness is not dependent on relativity at all. One discovers that the past does not exist, the future does not exist, and everything happens now. Similarly, in order to express space one might have first to create a vase, and then one has to break it, and then one sees that the emptiness in the vase is the same as the emptiness outside. That is the whole meaning of technique. At first that nowness is, in a sense, not perfect. Or one might even say that the meditation is not perfect, it is a purely man-made practice. One sits and tries to be still and concentrates on the breathing, and so on. But then, having started in that way, one gradually discovers something more than that. So the effort one has put into it—into the discovery of nowness, for example—would not be wasted, though at the same time one might see that it was rather foolish. But that is the only way to start.

Q. For meditation, would a student have to rid himself of Ego before he started, or would this come naturally as he is studying?

A. This comes naturally, because you can't start without Ego. And basically Ego isn't bad. Good and bad doesn't really exist anywhere, it is only a secondary thing. Ego is, in a sense, a false thing, but it isn't necessarily bad. You have to start with Ego, and use Ego, and from there it gradually wears out, like a pair of shoes. But you have to use it and wear it out thoroughly, so it is not preserved. Otherwise, if you try to push Ego aside and start perfect, you may become more and more perfect in a rather one-sided way, but the same amount of imperfection is building up on the other side, just as creating intense light creates intense darkness as well.

Q. You mentioned that there are two basic forms of meditation—devotional practise, or trying to communicate with something higher, and the other one, which is simply awareness of what is—but this devotional practice still plays a part in Buddhism as well, and you have devotional chants and so on, but I am not quite sure how this comes in. I mean, the two appear to be different, so can they in fact be combined?

A. Yes, but the kind of devotional practice which is found in Buddhism is merely a process of opening, of surrendering the Ego. It is a process of creating a container. I don't mean to condemn the other kind of devotion, but if one looks at it from the point of view of a person who has an unskilful way of using that technique, then devotion becomes a longing to free oneself. One sees oneself as being very separate, and as being imprisoned and imperfect. One regards oneself as basically bad, and one is trying to break out. In other words the imperfection part of oneself is identified with "I" and anything perfect is identified with some external being, so all that is left is trying to get through the imprisonment. This kind of devotion is an overemphasised awareness of Ego, the negative aspect of Ego. Although there are hundreds of variations of devotional practice in Buddhism and there are many accounts of devotion to Gurus, or being able to communicate with the Guru, and of achieving the Awakened State of mind through devotion. But in these cases devotion is always begun without centralising on the Ego. In any chants or ceremonies, for example, which make use of symbolism, or the visualisation of Buddhas, before any visualisation is created there is first a formless meditation, which creates an entirely open space. And at the end one always recites what is known as the Threefold Wheel: "I do not exist; the external visualisation does not exist; and the act of visualising does not exist"—the idea being that any feeling of achievement is thrown back to the openness, so one doesn't feel that one is collecting anything. I think that is the basic point. One may feel a great deal of devotion, but that devotion is a kind of abstract form of devotion, which does not centralise inwardly. One simply identifies with that feeling of devotion, and that's all. This is perhaps a different concept of devotion, where no centre exists, but only devotion exists. Whereas, in the other case devotion contains a demand. There is an expectation of getting something out of it in return.

Q. Is there not a great fear generated when we get to this point of opening up and surrendering?

A. Fear is one of the weapons of Ego. It protects the Ego. If one reaches the stage where one begins to see the folly of Ego, then there is fear of losing the Ego, and fear is one of its last weapons. Beyond that point fear no longer exists, because the object of fear is to frighten somebody, and when that somebody is not there, then fear loses its function. You see, fear is continually given life by your response, and when there is no one to respond to the fear—which is Ego loss—then fear ceases to exist.

Q. You are talking about the Ego as an object?

A. In what sense?

Q. In the sense that it is part of the external environment.

A. Ego is, as I have already said, like a bubble. It is an object up to a point, because although it does not really exist—it is an impermanent thing—it in fact shows itself as an object more than actually being one. That is another way of protecting oneself, of trying to maintain Ego.

Q. This is an aspect of the Ego?

A. Yes.

Q. Then you can't destroy the Ego, or you would lose the power to recognise, the power to cognate.

A. No, not necessarily. Because Ego does not contain understanding, it does not contain any insight at all. Ego exists in a false way all the time and can only create confusion, whereas insight is something more than that.

Q. Would you say that Ego is a secondary phenomenon rather than a primary phenomenon?

A. Yes, very much so. In a sense Ego is wisdom, but Ego happens to be ignorant as well. You see, when you realise that you are ignorant, that is the beginning of the discovery of wisdom—it is wisdom itself.

Q. How does one decide in oneself whether Ego is ignorance or wisdom?

A. It is not really a question of deciding. It is simply that one sees in that way. You see, basically there is no solid substance, although we talk about Ego existing as a solid thing having various aspects. But in fact it merely lives through time as a continual process of creation. It is continually dying and being reborn all the time. Therefore Ego doesn't really exist. But Ego also acts as a kind of wisdom: when Ego dies, that is wisdom itself, and when Ego is first formulated that is the beginning of ignorance itself. So wisdom and Ego are not really separate at all. It seems rather difficult to define, and in a way one would be happier if there was clear-cut black and white, but somehow that is not the natural pattern of existence. There is no clear-cut black and white at all, and all things are interdependent. Darkness is an aspect of light, and light is an aspect of darkness, so one can't really condemn one side and build up everything on the other. It is left entirely to the individual to find his own way, and it is possible to do so. It is the same for a dog who has never swum— if he was suddenly thrown in the water he could swim. Similarly, we have a kind of spiritual instinct in us and if we are willing to open ourselves then somehow we find our way directly. It is only a question of opening up and one doesn't have to have a clear-cut definition at all.

Q. Would you care to sum up the purpose of meditation?

A. Well, meditation is dealing with purpose itself. It is not that meditation is for something, but it is dealing with the aim. Generally we have a purpose for whatever we do: something is going to happen in the future, therefore what I am doing now is important—everything is related to that. But the whole idea of meditation is to develop an entirely different way of dealing with things, where you have no purpose at all. In fact meditation is dealing with the question of whether nor not there is such a thing as purpose. And when one learns a different way of dealing with the situation, one no longer has to have a purpose. One is not on the way to somewhere. Or rather, one is on the way and one is also at the destination at the same time. That is really what meditation is for.

Q. Would you say, then, that it would be a merging with reality?

A. Yes, because reality is there all the time. Reality is not a separate entity, so it is a question of becoming one with reality, or of being in reality—not *achieving* oneness, but becoming identified with it. One is already a part of that reality, so all that remains is to take away the doubt. Then one discovers that one has been there all the time.

Q. Would it be correct to describe it as the realisation that the visible is not reality?

A. The visible? Can you define a bit more?

Q. I am thinking of Willian Blake's theory of the merging of the observer with the observed, and the visible not being the reality at all.

A. Visible things in this sense are reality. There is nothing beyond nowness, therefore what we see is reality. But because of our usual way of seeing things, we do not see them exactly as they are.

Q. Would you say, then, that each person is an individual and must find an individual way towards that?

A. Well, I think that brings us back to the question of Ego, which we have been talking about. You see, there is such a thing as personality, in a way, but we are not really individuals as separate from the environment, or as separate from external phenomena. That is why a different approach is necessary. Whereas, if we were individuals and had no connection with the rest of things, then there would be no need for a different technique which would lead to oneness. The point is that there is appearance of individuality, but this individuality is based on relativity. If there is individuality, there must also be oneness as well.

Q. Yes, but it is the individuality that makes for oneness. If we weren't individuals we couldn't be one. Is that so?

A. Well, the word "individual" is rather ambiguous. At the beginning individuality may be overemphasised, because there are various individual aspects.

Even when we reach the stage of realisation there is perhaps an element of compassion, an element of wisdom, an element of energy and all sorts of different variations. But what we describe as an individual is something more than that. We tend to see it as one character with many things built onto it, which is a way of trying to find some sort of security. When there is wisdom, we try to load everything onto it, and it then becomes an entirely separate entity, a separate person—which is not so. But still there are individual aspects, there is individual character. So in Hinduism one finds different aspects of God, different deities and different symbols. When one attains oneness with reality, that reality is not just one single thing, but one can see from a very wide angle.

Q. If a student has a receptive mind and wishes to make himself at one with Nature, can he be taught how to meditate, or does he have to develop his own form?

A. Nature? How do you mean?

Q. If he wishes to study, can he accept other people's teaching, or can he develop them himself?

A. In fact it is necessary to receive oral instruction, oral teaching. Though he must learn to give before he can accept anything, he must learn to surrender. Secondly, he finds that the whole idea of learning stimulates his understanding. Also this avoids building up a great feeling of achievement, as though everything is "my own work"—the concept of the self-made man.

Q. Surely that is not sufficient reason for going to receive instruction from a teacher, just to avoid the feeling that otherwise everything is self-made. I mean, in the case of someone like Ramana Maharshi, who attained realisation without an external teacher, surely he shouldn't go and find a Guru just in case he might become big-headed?

A. No. But he is exceptional, that is the whole point. There is a way, it is possible. And basically no one can transmit or impart anything to anybody. One has to discover within oneself. So perhaps in certain cases people could do that. But building up on oneself is somehow similar to Ego's character, isn't it? One is on rather dangerous ground. It could easily become Ego's activity, because there is already the concept of "I" and then one wants to build up more on that side. I think—and this may sound simple, but it is really the whole thing—that one learns to surrender gradually, and that surrendering of the Ego is a very big subject. Also, the teacher acts as a kind of mirror, the teacher gives back one's own reflection. Then for the first time you are able to see how beautiful you are, or how ugly you are.

Perhaps I should mention here one or two small points about meditation, although we have already discussed the general background of the subject.

Generally, meditation instruction cannot be given in a class. There has to be a personal relationship between teacher and pupil. Also there are certain variations within each basic technique, such as awareness of breathing. But perhaps I should briefly mention the basic way of meditating, and then, if you want to go further, I am sure you could do so and receive further instruction from a meditation teacher.

As we have mentioned already, this meditation is not concerned with trying to develop concentration. Although many books on Buddhism speak of such practices as *Samatha* as being the development of concentration, I think this term is misleading in a way. One might get the idea that the practice of meditation could be put to commercial use, and that one would be able to concentrate on counting money or something like that. But meditation is not just for commercial uses, it is a different concept of concentration. You see, generally one cannot really concentrate. If one tries very hard to concentrate, then one needs the thought that is concentrating on the subject and also something which makes that accelerate further. Thus there are two processes involved and the second process is a kind of watchman, which makes sure that you are doing it properly. That part of it must be taken away, otherwise one ends up being more self-conscious and merely aware that one is concentrating, rather than actually being in a state of concentration. This becomes a vicious circle. Therefore one cannot develop concentration alone, without taking away the centralised watchfulness, the trying to be careful—which is Ego. So the *Samatha* practice, the awareness of breathing, is not concerned with concentrating on the breathing.

The cross-legged posture is the one generally adopted in the East, and if one can sit in that position, it is preferable to do so. Then one can train oneself to sit down and meditate anywhere, even in the middle of a field, and one need not feel conscious of having a seat or of trying to find something to sit on. Also, the physical posture does have a certain importance. For instance, if one lies down this might inspire one to sleep; if one stands one might be inclined to walk. But for those who find it difficult to sit cross-legged, sitting on a chair is quite good, and, in fact, in Buddhist iconography the posture of sitting on a chair is known as the *Maitreya asana*, so it is quite acceptable. The important thing is to keep the back straight so that there is no strain on the breathing. And for the breathing itself it is not a matter of concentrating, as we have already said, but of trying to become one with the feeling of breath. At the beginning some effort is needed, but after practising for a while the awareness is simply kept on the verge of the movement of breath; it just follows it quite naturally and one is not trying particularly to bind the mind to breathing. One tries to feel the breath—outbreathing, inbreathing, outbreathing, inbreathing—and it usually happens that the outbreathing is longer than the inbreathing, which helps one become aware of space and the expansion of breathing outwards.

It is also very important to avoid becoming solemn and to avoid the feeling that one is taking part in some special ritual. One should feel quite natural and spontaneous, and simply try to identify oneself with the breath. That is all there is to it, and there are no ideas or analysing involved. Whenever thoughts arise, just observe them *as thoughts*, rather than as being a subject. What usually happens when we have thoughts is that we are not aware that they are thoughts at all. Supposing one is planning one's next holiday trip: one is so engrossed in the thoughts that it is almost as though one were already on the trip and one is not even aware that these are thoughts. Whereas, if one sees that this is merely thought creating such a picture, one begins to discover that it has a less real quality. One should not try to suppress thoughts in meditation, but one should just try to see the transitory nature, the translucent nature of thoughts. One should not become involved in them, nor reject them, but simply observe them and then come back to the awareness of breathing. The whole point is to cultivate the acceptance of everything, so one should not discriminate or become involved in any kind of struggle. That is the basic meditation technique, and it is quite simple and direct. There should be no deliberate effort, no attempt to control and no attempt to be peaceful. This is why breathing is used. It is easy to feel the breathing, and one has no need to be self-conscious or to try and do anything. The breathing is simply available and one should just feel that. That is the reason why technique is important to start with. This is the primary way of starting, but it generally continues and develops in its own way. One sometimes finds oneself doing it slightly differently from when one first started, quite spontaneously. This is not classified as an advanced technique or a beginner's technique. It simply grows and develops gradually.

The Practice of the Presence of God

Maimonides

Maimonides (Moses ben Maimon, 1135–1204), rabbi, physician, and philosopher, was the most significant Jewish thinker of the Middle Ages. Among his many famous writings are *The Guide for the Perplexed* and the *Mishnah Torah*.

I will begin the subject of this chapter with a simile. A king is in his palace, and all his subjects are partly in the country, and partly abroad. Of the former, some have their backs turned towards the king's palace, and their faces in another direction; and some are desirous and zealous to go to the palace, seeking "to inquire in his temple," and to minister before him, but have not yet seen even the face of the wall of the house. Of those that desire to go to the palace, some reach it, and go round about in search of the entrance gate; others have passed through the gate, and walk about in the ante-chamber; and others have succeeded in entering into the inner part of the palace, and being in the same room with the king in the royal palace. But even the latter do not immediately on entering the palace see the king, or speak to him; for, after having entered the inner part of the palace, another effort is required before they can stand before the king—at a distance, or close by—hear his words, or speak to him. I will now explain the simile which I have made. The people who are abroad are all those that have no religion, neither one based on speculation nor one received by tradition. Such are the extreme Turks

Source: Moses Maimonides, *The Guide for the Perplexed*, translated by M. Friedländer, Second Edition, (New York: Dover Publications, Inc., 1956), pp. 384–392.

that wander about in the north, the Kushites who live in the south, and those in our country who are like these. I consider these as irrational beings, and not as human beings; they are below mankind, but above monkeys, since they have the form and shape of man, and a mental faculty above that of the monkey.

Those who are in the country, but have their backs turned towards the king's palace, are those who possess religion, belief, and thought, but happen to hold false doctrines, which they either adopted in consequence of great mistakes made in their own speculations, or received from others who misled them. Because of these doctrines they recede more and more from the royal palace the more they seem to proceed. These are worse than the first class, and under certain circumstances it may become necessary to slay them, and to extirpate their doctrines, in order that others should not be misled.

Those who desire to arrive at the palace, and to enter it, but have never yet seen it, are the mass of religious people; the multitude that observe the divine commandments, but are ignorant. Those who arrive at the palace, but go round about it, are those who devote themselves exclusively to the study of the practical law; they believe traditionally in true principles of faith, and learn the practical worship of God, but are not trained in philosophical treatment of the principles of the Law, and do not endeavour to establish the truth of their faith by proof. Those who undertake to investigate the principles of religion, have come into the ante-chamber; and there is no doubt that these can also be divided into different grades. But those who have succeeded in finding a proof for everything that can be proved, who have a true knowledge of God, so far as a true knowledge can be attained, and are near the truth, wherever an approach to the truth is possible, they have reached the goal, and are in the palace in which the king lives.

My son, so long as you are engaged in studying the Mathematical Sciences and Logic, you belong to those who go round about the palace in search of the gate. Thus our Sages figuratively use the phrase: "Ben-zoma is still outside." When you understand Physics, you have entered the hall; and when, after completing the study of Natural Philosophy, you master Metaphysics, you have entered the innermost court, and are with the king in the same palace. You have attained the degree of the wise men, who include men of different grades of perfection. There are some who direct all their mind toward the attainment of perfection in Metaphysics, devote themselves entirely to God, exclude from their thought every other thing, and employ all their intellectual faculties in the study of the Universe, in order to derive therefrom a proof for the existence of God, and to learn in every possible way how God rules all things; they form the class of those who have entered the palace, namely, the class of prophets. One of these has attained so much knowledge, and has concentrated his thoughts to such an extent in the idea of God, that it could be said of him, "And he was with the Lord forty days," etc. (Exod. xxxiv. 28); during that holy communion he could ask Him, answer Him, speak to Him, and be addressed by Him, enjoying beatitude in that which he had obtained to such a degree that "he did neither eat bread nor drink water" (ibid.); his intellectual energy was so predominant that all coarser functions of the body, especially those connected with the sense of touch, were in abeyance. Some prophets are only able to see, and of these some approach near and see, whilst others see from a distance: comp. "The Lord hath appeared from far unto me" (Jer. xxxi. 3). We have already spoken of the various degrees of prophets; we will therefore return to the subject of this chapter, and exhort those who have attained a knowledge of God, to concentrate all their thoughts in God. This is the worship peculiar to those who have acquired a knowledge of the highest truths; and the more they reflect on Him, and think of Him, the more are they engaged in His worship. Those, however, who think of God, and frequently mention His name, without any correct notion of Him, but merely following some imagination, or some theory received from another person, are, in my opinion, like those who remain outside the palace and distant from it. They do not mention the name of God in truth, nor do they reflect on it. That which they imagine and mention does not correspond to any being in existence; it is a thing invented by their imagination, as has been shown by us in our discussion on the Divine Attributes (Part I. chap. 1). The true worship of God is only possible when correct notions of Him have previously been conceived. When you have arrived by way of intellectual research at a knowledge of God and His works, then commence to devote yourselves to Him, try to approach Him and strengthen the intellect, which is the link that joins you to Him. Thus Scripture says, "Unto these it was showed, that thou mightest know that the Lord He is God" (Deut. iv. 35); "Know therefore this day, and consider it in thine heart, that the Lord He is God" (ibid. 36); "Know ye that the Lord is God" (Ps. c. 3). Thus the Law distinctly states that the highest kind of worship to which we refer in this chapter, is only possible after the acquisition of the knowledge of God. For it is said, "To love the Lord your God, and to serve Him with all your heart and with all your soul" (Deut. xi. 13), and, as we have shown several times, man's love of God is identical with His knowledge of Him. The Divine service enjoined in these words must, accordingly, be preceded by the love of God. Our Sages have pointed out to us that it is a service in the heart, which explanation I understand to mean this: man concentrates all his thoughts on the First Intellect, and is absorbed in these thoughts as much as possible. David therefore commands his son Solomon these two things, and exhorts him earnestly to do them: to acquire a true knowledge of God, and to be earnest in His service after that knowledge has been acquired. For he says, "And thou, Solomon my son, know thou the God of thy father, and serve him with a perfect heart . . . if thou seek him, he will be found of thee; but if thou forsake him, he will cast thee off for ever" (1 Chron. xxviii. 9). The exhortation refers to the intellectual conceptions, not to the imaginations; for the latter are not called "knowledge," but "that which cometh into your mind" (Ezek. xx. 32). It has thus been shown that it must be man's aim, after having acquired the knowledge of God, to deliver himself up to Him, and to have his heart constantly filled with longing after Him. He accomplishes this generally by seclusion and retirement. Every pious man should therefore seek retirement and seclusion, and should only in case of necessity associate with others.

Note.—I have shown you that the intellect which emanates from God unto us is the link that joins us to God. You have it in your power to strengthen that bond, if you choose to do so, or to weaken it gradually till it breaks, if you prefer this. It will only become strong when you employ it in the love of God, and seek that love; it will be weakened when you direct your thoughts to other things. You must know that even if you were the wisest man in respect to the true knowledge of God, you break the bond between you and God whenever you turn entirely your thoughts to the necessary food or any necessary business; you are then not with God, and He is not with you; for that relation between you and Him is actually interrupted in those moments. The pious were therefore particular to restrict the time in which they could not meditate upon the name of God, and cautioned others about it, saying, "Let not your minds be vacant from reflections upon God." In the same sense did David say, "I have set the Lord always before me; because he is at my right hand, I shall not be moved" (Ps. xvi. 8); i.e., I do not turn my thoughts away from God; He is like my right hand, which I do not forget even for a moment on account of the ease of its motions, and therefore I shall not be moved, I shall not fall.

We must bear in mind that all such religious acts as reading the Law, praying, and the performance of other precepts, serve exclusively as the means of causing us to occupy and fill our mind with the precepts of God, and free it from worldly business; for we are thus, as it were, in communication with God, and undisturbed by any other thing. If we, however, pray with the motion of our lips, and our face toward the wall, but at the same time think of our business; if we read the Law with our tongue, whilst our heart is occupied with the building of our house, and we do not think of what we are reading; if we perform the commandments only with our limbs, we are like those who are engaged in digging in the ground, or hewing wood in the forest, without reflecting on the nature of those acts, or by whom they are commanded, or what is their object. We must not imagine that [in this way] we attain the highest perfection; on the contrary, we are then like those in reference to whom Scripture says, "Thou art near in their mouth, and far from their reins" (Jer. xii. 2).

I will now commence to show you the way how to educate and train yourselves in order to attain that great perfection.

The first thing you must do is this: Turn your thoughts away from everything while you read *Shema'* or during the *Tefillah*, and do not content yourself with being devout when you read the first verse of Shema, or the first paragraph of the prayer. When you have successfully practised this for many years, try in reading the Law or listening to it, to have all your heart and all your thought occupied with understanding what you read or hear. After some time when you have mastered this, accustom yourself to have your mind free from all other thoughts when you read any portion of the other books of the prophets, or when you say any blessing; and to have your attention directed exclusively to the perception and the understanding of what you utter. When you have succeeded in properly performing these acts of divine service, and you have your thought, during their performance, entirely abstracted from worldly affairs, take then care that your thought be not disturbed by thinking of your wants or of superfluous things. In short, think of worldly matters when you eat, drink, bathe, talk with your wife and little children, or when you converse with other people. These times, which are frequent and long, I think, must suffice to you for reflecting on everything that is necessary as regards business, household, and health. But when you are engaged in the performance of religious duties, have your mind exclusively directed to what you are doing.

When you are alone by yourself, when you are awake on your couch, be careful to meditate in such precious moments on nothing but the intellectual worship of God, viz., to approach Him and to minister before Him in the true manner which I have described to you—not in hollow emotions. This I consider as the highest perfection wise men can attain by the above training.

When we have acquired a true knowledge of God, and rejoice in that knowledge in such a manner, that whilst speaking with others, or attending to our bodily wants, our mind is all that time with God; when we are with our heart constantly near God, even whilst our body is in the society of men; when we are in that state which the Song on the relation between God and man poetically describes in the following words: "I sleep, but my heart waketh; it is the voice of my beloved that knocketh" (Song v. 2):—then we have attained not only the height of ordinary prophets, but of Moses, our Teacher, of whom Scripture relates: "And Moses alone shall come near before the Lord" (ibid. xxxiv. 28); "But as for thee, stand thou here by me" (Deut. v. 28). The meaning of these verses has been explained by us.

The Patriarchs likewise attained this degree of perfection; they approached God in such a manner that with them the name of God became known in the world. Thus we read in Scripture: "The God of Abraham, the God of Isaac, and the God of Jacob. . . . This is My name for ever" (Exod. iii. 15). Their mind was so identified with the knowledge of God, that He made a lasting covenant with each of them: "Then will I remember my covenant with Jacob," etc. (Lev. xxvi. 42). For it is known from statements made in Scripture that these four, viz., the Patriarchs and Moses, had their minds exclusively filled with the name of God, that is, with His knowledge and love; and that in the same measure was Divine Providence attached to them and their descendants. When we therefore find them also, engaged in ruling others, in increasing their property, and endeavouring to obtain possession of wealth and honour, we see in this fact a proof that when they were occupied in these things, only their bodily limbs were at work, whilst their heart and mind never moved away from the name of God. I think these four reached that high degree of perfection in their relation to God, and enjoyed the continual presence of Divine Providence, even in their endeavours to increase their property, feeding the flock, toiling in the field, or managing the house, only because in all these things their end and aim was to approach God as much as possible. It was the chief aim of their whole life to create a people that should know and worship God. Comp. "For I know him, that he will command his children and his household after him" (Gen. xviii. 19). The object of all their labours was to publish the Unity of God in the world, and to induce people to love Him; and it was on this account that they succeeded in reaching that high degree; for even those [worldly] affairs were for them a perfect worship of God. But a person like myself must not imagine that he is able to lead men up to this degree of perfection. It is only the next degree to it that can be attained by means of the above-mentioned training. And let us pray to God and beseech Him that He clear and remove from our way everything that forms an obstruction and a partition between us and Him, although most of these obstacles are our own creation, as has several times been shown in this treatise. Comp. "Your iniquities have separated between you and your God" (Isa. lix. 2).

An excellent idea presents itself here to me, which may serve to remove many doubts, and may help to solve many difficult problems in metaphysics. We have already stated in the chapters which treat of Divine Providence, that Providence watches over every rational being according to the amount of intellect which that being possesses. Those who are perfect in their perception of God, whose mind is never separated from Him, enjoy always the influence of Providence. But those who, perfect in their knowledge of God, turn their mind sometimes away from God, enjoy the presence of Divine Providence only when they meditate on God; when their thoughts are engaged in other matters, divine Providence departs from them. The absence of Providence in this case is not like its absence in the case of those who do not reflect on God at all; it is in this case less intense, because when a person perfect in his knowledge [of God] is busy with worldly matters, he has not knowledge in actuality, but only knowledge in potentiality [though ready to become actual]. This person is then like a trained scribe when he is not writing. Those who have no knowledge of God are like those who are in constant darkness and have never seen light. We have explained in this sense the words: "The wicked shall be silent in darkness" (1 Sam. ii. 9), whilst those who possess the knowledge of God, and have their thoughts entirely directed to that knowledge, are, as it were, always in bright sunshine; and those who have the knowledge, but are at times engaged in other themes, have then as it were a cloudy day: the sun does not shine for them on account of the cloud that intervenes between them and God.

Hence it appears to me that it is only in times of such neglect that some of the ordinary evils befall a prophet or a perfect and pious man; and the intensity of the evil is proportional to the duration of those moments, or to the character of the things that thus occupy their mind. Such being the case, the great difficulty is removed that led philosophers to assert that Providence does not extend to every individual, and that man is like any other living being in this respect, viz., the argument based on the fact that good and pious men are afflicted with great evils. We have thus explained this difficult question even in accordance with the philosophers' own principles. Divine Providence is constantly watching over those who have obtained that blessing which is prepared for those who endeavour to obtain it. If man frees his thoughts from worldly matters, obtains a knowledge of God in the right way, and rejoices in that knowledge, it is impossible that any kind of evil should befall him while he is with God, and God with him. When he does not meditate on God, when he is separated from God, then God is also separated from him; then he is exposed to any evil that might befall him; for it is only that intellectual link with God that secures the presence of Providence and protection from evil accidents. Hence it may occur that the perfect man is at times not happy, whilst no evil befalls those who are imperfect; in these cases what happens to them is due to chance. This principle I find also expressed in the Law. Comp. "And I will hide my face from them, and they shall be devoured, and many evils and troubles shall befall them; so that they will say in that day, Are not these evils come upon us, because our God is not among us?" (Deut. xxxi. 17). It is clear that we ourselves are the cause of this hiding of the face, and that the screen that separates us from God is of our own creation. This is the meaning of the words: "And I will surely hide my face in that day, for all the evils which they shall have wrought" (ibid. ver. 18). There is undoubtedly no difference in this regard between one single person and a whole community. It is now clearly established that the cause of our being exposed to chance, and abandoned to destruction like cattle, is to be found in our separation from God. Those who have their God dwelling in their hearts, are not touched by any evil whatever. For God says: "Fear thou not, for I am with thee; be not dismayed, for I am thy God" (Isa. xli. 10). "When thou passest through the waters, I will be with thee; and through the rivers, they shall not overflow thee" (ibid, xliii. 2). For if we prepare ourselves, and attain the influence of the Divine Intellect, Providence is joined to us, and we are guarded against all evils. Comp. "The Lord is on my side; I will not fear; what can man do unto me?" (Ps. cxviii. 6). "Acquaint now thyself with him, and be at peace" (Job xxii. 21); i.e., turn unto Him, and you will be safe from all evil.

Consider the Psalm on mishaps, and see how the author describes that great Providence, the protection and defense from all mishaps that concern the body, both from those that are common to all people, and those that concern only one certain individual; from those that are due to the laws of Nature, and those that are caused by our fellow-men. The Psalmist says: "Surely he will deliver thee from the snare of the fowler, and from the noisome pestilence. He shall cover thee with his feathers, and under his wings shalt thou trust: His truth shall be thy shield and buckler. Thou shalt not be afraid for the terror by night; nor for the arrow that flieth by day" (Ps. xci. 3–5). The author then relates how God protects us from the troubles caused by men, saying, If you happen to meet on your way with an army fighting with drawn swords, killing thousands at your left hand and myriads at your right hand, you will not suffer any harm; you will behold and see how God judges and punishes the wicked that are being slain, whilst you remain unhurt. "A thousand shall fall at thy side, and ten thousand at thy right hand; but it shall not come nigh thee. Only with thine eyes shalt thou behold and see the reward of the wicked" (ibid. vers. 7, 8). The author then continues his description of the divine defence and shelter, and shows the cause of this great protection, saying that such a man is well guarded "Because he hath set his love upon me, therefore will I deliver him: I will set him on high, because he hath known my name" (ibid. ver. 14). We have shown in previous chapters that by the "knowledge of God's name," the knowledge of God is meant. The above passage may therefore be paraphrased as follows: "This man is well guarded, because he hath known me, and then (bi chashak) loved me." You know the difference between the two Hebrew terms that signify "to love," ahab and ḥashak. When a man's love is so intense that his thought is exclusively engaged with the object of his love, it is expressed in Hebrew by the term ḥashak.

The philosophers have already explained how the bodily forces of man in his youth prevent the development of moral principles. In a greater measure this is the case as regards the purity of thought which man attains through the perfection of those ideas that lead him to an intense love of God. Man can by no means attain this so long as his bodily humours are hot. The more the forces of his body are weakened, and the fire of passion quenched, in the same measure does man's intellect increase in strength and light; his knowledge becomes purer, and he is happy with his knowledge. When this perfect man is stricken in age and is near death, his knowledge mightily increases, his joy in that knowledge grows greater, and his love for the object of his knowledge more intense, and it is in this great delight that the soul separates from the body. To this state our Sages referred, when in reference to the death of Moses, Aaron, and Miriam, they said that death was in these three cases nothing but a kiss. They say thus: We learn from the words, "And Moses the servant of the Lord died there in the land of Moab by the mouth of the Lord" (Deut. xxxiv. 5), that his death was a kiss. The same expression is used of Aaron: "And Aaron the priest went up into Mount Hor . . . by the mouth of the Lord, and died there" (Num. xxxiii. 38). Our Sages said that the same was the case with Miriam; but the phrase "by the mouth of the Lord" is not employed, because it was not considered appropriate to use these words in the description of her death as she was a female. The meaning of this saying is that these three died in the midst of the pleasure derived from the knowledge of God and their great love for Him. When our Sages figuratively call the knowledge of God united with intense love for Him a kiss, they follow the well-known poetical diction, "Let him kiss me with the kisses of his mouth" (Song i. 2). This kind of death, which in truth is deliverance from death, has been ascribed by our Sages to none but to Moses, Aaron, and Miriam. The other prophets and pious men are beneath that degree; but their knowledge of God is strengthened when death approaches. Of them Scripture says, "Thy righteousness shall go before thee; the glory of the Lord shall be thy reward" (Isa. lviii. 8). The intellect of these men remains then constantly in the same condition, since the obstacle is removed that at times has intervened between the intellect and the object of its action; it continues for ever in that great delight, which is not like bodily pleasure. We have explained this in our work, and others have explained it before us.

Try to understand this chapter, endeavour with all your might to spend more and more time in communion with God, or in the attempt to approach Him; and to reduce the hours which you spend in other occupations, and during which you are striving to come nearer unto Him. This instruction suffices for the object of this treatise.

Chapter LII

We do not sit, move, and occupy ourselves when we are alone and at home, in the same manner as we do in the presence of a great king; we speak and open our mouth as we please when we are with the people of our own household and with our relatives, but not so when we are in a royal assembly. If we therefore desire to attain human perfection, and to be truly men of God, we must awake from our sleep, and bear in mind that the great king that is over us, and is always joined to us, is greater than any earthly king, greater than David and Solomon. The king that cleaves to us and embraces us is the Intellect that influences us, and forms the link between us and God. We perceive God by means of that light that He sends down unto us, wherefore the Psalmist says, "In Thy light shall we see light" (Ps. xxxvi. 9): so God looks down upon us through that same light, and is always with us beholding and watching us on account of this light. "Can any hide himself in secret places that I shall not see him?" (Jer. xxiii. 24). Note this particularly.

When the perfect bear this in mind, they will be filled with fear of God, humility, and piety, with true, not apparent, reverence and respect of God, in such a manner that their conduct, even when alone with their wives or in the bath, will be as modest as they are in public intercourse with other people. Thus it is related of our renowned Sages that even in their sexual intercourse with their wives they behaved with great modesty. They also said, "Who is modest? He whose conduct in the dark night is the same as in the day." You know also how much they warned us not to walk proudly, since "the fulness of the whole earth is His glory" (Isa. vi. 3). They thought that by these rules the above-mentioned idea will be firmly established in the hearts of men, viz., that we are always before God, and it is in the presence of His glory that we go to and fro. The great men among our Sages would not uncover their heads because they believed that God's glory was round them and over them; for the same reason they spoke little. In our Commentary on the Sayings of the Fathers (chap. i. 17) we have fully explained how we have to restrict our speech. Comp. "For God is in heaven and thou upon earth, therefore let thy words be few" (Eccles. v. 1).

What I have here pointed out to you is the object of all our religious acts. For by [carrying out] all the details of the prescribed practices, and repeating them continually, some few pious men may attain human perfection. They will be filled with respect and reverence towards God; and bearing in mind who is with them, they will perform their duty. God declares in plain words that it is the object of all religious acts to produce in man fear of God and obedience to His word—the state of mind which we have demonstrated in this chapter for those who desire to know the truth, as being our duty to seek. Comp. "If thou wilt not observe to do all the words of this law that are written in this book, that thou mayest fear this glorious and fearful name, the Lord thy God" (Deut. xxviii. 58). Consider how clearly it is stated here that the only object and aim of "all the words of this law" is to [make man] fear "the glorious and fearful name." That this end is attained by certain acts we learn likewise from the phrase employed in this verse: "If thou wilt not observe *to do* . . . that thou mayest fear." For this phrase clearly shows that fear of God is inculcated [into our hearts] when we act in accordance with the positive and the negative precepts. But the truths which the Law teaches us— the knowledge of God's Existence and Unity—create in us love of God, as we have shown repeatedly. You know how frequently the Law exhorts us to love God. Comp. "And thou shalt love the Lord thy God with all thine heart, and with all thy soul, and with all thy might" (Deut. vi. 5). The two objects, love and fear of God, are acquired by two different means. The love is the result of the truths taught in the Law, including the true knowledge of the Existence of God; whilst fear of God is produced by the practices prescribed in the Law. Note this explanation.

Reb Saunders

Chaim Potok

Chaim Potok (1929–   ) was ordained as a rabbi in 1954. From a career as a theologian, he turned to the art of the novel in 1967 with his enormously popular *The Chosen*. He has since published *The Promise*, *My Name is Asher Levi*, and, most recently, *In the Beginning*.

Everyone waited, and no one moved, no one coughed, no one even took a deep breath. The silence became unreal and seemed suddenly filled with a noise of its own, the noise of a too long silence. Even the child was staring now at his father, his eyes like black stones against the naked whiteness of his veined face.

And then Reb Saunders began to speak.

He swayed back and forth in the leather chair, his eyes closed, his left hand in the crook of his right elbow, the fingers of his right hand stroking his black beard, and I could see everyone at the tables lean forward, eyes staring, mouths slightly open, some of the older men cupping their hands behind their ears to catch his words. He began in a low voice, the words coming out slowly in a singsong kind of chant.

"The great and holy Rabban Gamaliel," he said, "taught us the following: 'Do His will as if it were thy will, that He may do thy will as if it were His will. Nullify thy will before His will that He may nullify the will of others before thy will.' What does this mean? It means that if we do as the Master of the Universe wishes, then He will do as we wish. A question immediately presents itself. What does it mean to say that the Master of the Universe will do what we wish? He is after all the Master of the Universe, the Creator of heaven and earth, the King of kings. And what are we? Do we not say every day, 'Are not all the mighty as naught before Thee, the men of renown as though they had not been, the wise as if without knowledge, and the men of understanding as if without discernment'? What are we that the Master of the Universe should do our will?"

Reb Saunders paused, and I saw two of the old men who were sitting at our table look at each other and nod. He swayed back and forth in his leather chair, his fingers stroking his beard, and continued to speak in a quiet, singsong voice.

"All men come into the world in the same way. We are born in pain, for it is written, 'In pain shall ye bring forth children.' We are born naked and without strength. Like dust are we born. Like dust can the child be blown about, like dust is his life, like dust is his strength. And like dust do many remain all their lives, until they are put away in dust, in a place of worms and maggots. Will the Master of the Universe obey the will of a man whose life is dust? What is the great and holy Rabban Gamaliel teaching us?" His voice was beginning to rise now. "What is he telling us? What does it mean to say the Master of the Universe will

Source: From Chaim Potok, *The Chosen.* Copyright © 1967 by Chaim Potok. Reprinted by permission of Simon & Schuster, Inc.

do our will? The will of men who remain dust? Impossible! The will of what men, then? We must say, the will of men who do *not* remain dust. But how can we raise ourselves above dust? Listen, listen to me, for this is a mighty thing the rabbis teach us."

He paused again, and I saw Danny glance at him, then stare down again at his paper plate.

"Rabbi Halafta son of Dosa teaches us, 'When ten people sit together and occupy themselves with the Torah, the Presence of God abides among them, as it is said, "God standeth in the congregation of the godly." And whence can it be shown that the same applies to five? Because it is said, "He had founded his band upon the earth." And whence can it be shown that the same applies to three? Because it is said, "He judgeth among the judges." And whence can it be shown that the same applies to two? Because it is said, "Then they that feared the Lord spake one With the other, and the Lord gave heed and heard." And whence can it be shown that the same applies even to one? Because it is said, "In every place where I cause my name to be remembered I will come into thee and I will bless thee."' Listen, listen to this great teaching. A congregation is ten. It is nothing new that the holy Presence resides among ten. A band five. It is also nothing new that the holy Presence resides among five. Judges are three. If the holy Presence did not reside among judges there would be no justice in the world. So this, too, is not new. That the Presence can reside even among two is also not impossible to understand. But that the Presence can reside in one! In one! Even in one! That already is a mighty thing. Even in one! If one man studies Torah, the Presence is with him. If one man studies Torah, the Master of the Universe is already in the world. A mighty thing! And to bring the Master of the World *into* the world is also to raise oneself up from the dust. Torah raises us from the dust! Torah gives us strength! Torah clothes us! Torah brings the Presence!"

The singsong chant had died away. He was talking in a straight, loud voice that rang through the terrible silence in the synagogue.

"But to study Torah is not such a simple thing. Torah is a task for all day and all night. It is a task filled with danger. Does not Rabbi Meir teach us, 'He who is walking by the way and studying, and breaks off his study and says, "How fine is that tree, how fine is that field," him the Scripture regards as if he had forfeited his life'?"

I saw Danny glance quickly at his father, then lower his eyes. His body sagged a little, a smile played on his lips, and I thought I even heard him sigh quietly.

"He had forfeited his life! His life! So great is the study of Torah. And now listen, listen to this word. Whose task is it to study Torah? Of whom does the Master of the Universe demand 'Ye shall meditate over it day and night'? Of the world? No! What does the world know of Torah? The world is Esav! The world is Amalek! The world is Cossacks! The world is Hitler, may his name and memory be erased! Of whom, then? Of the people of Israel! *We* are commanded to study His Torah! *We* are commanded to sit in the light of the Presence! It is for this that we were created! Does not the great and holy Rabbi Yochanan son of Zakkai teach us, 'If thou hast learnt much Torah, ascribe not any merit to thyself, for thereunto wast thou created'? Not the world, but the people of Israel! The people of Israel must study His Torah!"

His voice stormed the silence. I found myself holding my breath, my heart thumping in my ears. I could not take my eyes off his face, which was alive now, or his eyes, which were open and filled with dark fire. He struck the table with his hand, and I felt myself go cold with fright. Danny was watching him now, too, and his little brother stared at him as though in a trance, his mouth open, his eyes glazed.

"The world kills us! The world flays our skin from our bodies and throws us to the flames! The world laughs at Torah! And if it does not kill us, it tempts us! It misleads us! It contaminates us! It asks us to join in its ugliness, its impurities, its abominations! The world is Amalek! It is not the world that is commanded to study Torah, but the people of Israel! Listen, listen to this mighty teaching." His voice was suddenly lower, quieter, intimate. "It is written, 'This world is like a vestibule before the world-to-come; prepare thyself in the vestibule, that thou mayest enter into the hall.' The meaning is clear: The vestibule is this world, and the hall is the world-to-come. Listen. In gematriya, the words 'this world' come out one hundred sixty-three, and the words 'the world-to-come' come out one hundred and fifty-four. The difference between 'this world' and 'the world-to-come' comes out to nine. Nine is half of eighteen. Eighteen is chai, life. In this world there is only half of chai. We are only half alive in this world! Only half alive!"

A whisper went through the crowd at the tables, and I could see heads nod and lips smile. They had been waiting for this apparently, the gematriya, and they strained forward to listen. One of my teachers in school had told me about gematriya. Each letter of the Hebrew alphabet is also a number, so that every Hebrew word has a numerical value. The word for "this world" in Hebrew is "olam hazeh," and by adding the numerical value of each letter, the total numerical value of the word becomes one hundred and sixty-three. I had heard others do this before, and I enjoyed listening because sometimes they were quite clever and ingenious. I was beginning to feel relaxed again, and I listened carefully.

"Hear me now. Listen. How can we make our lives full? How can we fill our lives so that we are eighteen, chai, and not nine, not half chai? Rabbi Joshua son of Levi teaches us, 'Whoever does not labor in the Torah is said to be under the divine censure.' He is a nozuf, a person whom the Master of the Universe hates! A righteous man, a tzaddik, studies Torah, for it is written, 'For his delight is in the Torah of God, and over His Torah doth he meditate day and night.' In gematriya, 'nozuf' comes out one hundred forty-three, and 'tzaddik' comes out two hundred and four. What is the difference between 'nozuf' and 'tzaddik'? Sixty-one. To whom does a tzaddik dedicate his life? To the Master of the Universe! La-el, to God! The word, 'La-el' in gematriya is sixty-one! It is a life dedicated to God that makes the difference between the nozuf and the tzaddik!"

Another murmur of approval went through the crowd. Reb Saunders was very good at gematriya, I thought. I was really enjoying myself now.

"And now listen to me further. In gematriya, the letters of the word 'traklin,' hall, the hall that refers to the world-to-come, come out three hundred ninety-nine, and 'prozdor,' the vestibule, the vestibule that is this world, comes out five hundred thirteen. Take 'traklin' from 'prozdor,' and we have one hundred fourteen. Now listen to me. A righteous man, we said, is two hundred four. A righteous man lives by Torah. Torah is mayim, water; the great and holy rabbis always compare Torah to water. The word 'mayim' in gematriya is ninety. Take 'mayim' from 'tzaddik' and we also have one hundred fourteen. From this we learn that the righteous man who removes himself from Torah also removes himself from the world-to-come!"

The whisper of delight was loud this time, and men nodded their heads and smiled. Some of them were even poking each other with their elbows to indicate their pleasure. That one had really been clever. I started to go over it again in my mind.

"We see that without Torah there is only half a life. We see that without Torah we are dust. We see that without Torah we are abominations." He was saying this quietly, almost as if it were a litany. His eyes were still open, and he was looking directly at Danny now. "When we study Torah, *then* the Master of the Universe listens. *Then* He hears our words. *Then* He will fulfill our wishes. For the Master of the Universe promises strength to those who preoccupy themselves in Torah, as it is written, 'So ye may be strong,' and He promises length of days, as it is written. 'So that your days may be lengthened.' May Torah be a fountain of waters to all who drink from it, and may it bring to us the Messiah speedily and in our day. Amen!"

A chorus of loud and scattered amens answered.

I sat in my seat and saw Reb Saunders looking at Danny, then at me. I felt completely at ease, and I somewhat brazenly smiled and nodded, as if to indicate that I had enjoyed his words, or at least the gematriya part of his words. I didn't agree at all with his notions of the world as being contaminated. Albert Einstein is part of the world, I told myself. President Roosevelt is part of the world. The millions of soldiers fighting Hitler are part of the world.

I thought that the meal was ended now and we would start the Evening Service, and I almost began to get out of my seat when I realized that another silence had settled upon the men at the tables. I sat still and looked around. They seemed all to be staring at Danny. He was sitting quietly, smiling a little, his fingers playing with the edge of his paper plate.

Reb Saunders sat back in his leather chair and folded his arms across his chest. The little boy was poking at the tomato again and glancing at Danny from the tops of his dark eyes. He twirled a side curl round one of his fingers, and I saw his tongue dart out of his mouth, run over his lips, then dart back in. I wondered what was going on.

Reb Saunders sighed loudly and nodded at Danny, "Nu, Daniel, you have something to say?" His voice was quiet, almost gentle.

I saw Danny nod his head.

"Nu, what is it?"

"It is written in the name of Rabbi Yaakov, not Rabbi Meir," Danny said quietly, in Yiddish.

A whisper of approval came from the crowd. I glanced around quickly. Everyone sat staring at Danny.

Reb Saunders almost smiled. He nodded, and the long black beard went back and forth against his chest. Then I saw the thick black eyebrows arch upward and the lids go about halfway down across the eyes. He leaned forward slightly, his arms still folded across his chest.

"And nothing more?" he asked very quietly.

Danny shook his head—a little hesitantly, I thought.

"So," Reb Saunders said, sitting back in the leather chair, "there is nothing more."

I looked at the two of them, wondering what was happening. What was this about Rabbi Yaakov and Rabbi Meir?

"The words were said by Rabbi Yaakov, not by Rabbi Meir," Danny repeated. "Rabbi Yaakov, not Rabbi Meir, said, 'He who is walking by the way and studying, and breaks off his study and—"

"Good," Reb Saunders broke in quietly. "The words were said by Rav Yaakov. Good. You saw it. Very good. And where is it found?"

"In *Pirkei Avos*," Danny said. He was giving the Talmudic source for the quote. Many of the quotes Reb Saunders had used had been from *Pirkei Avos*—or *Avot*, as my father had taught me to pronounce it, with the Sephardic rather than the Ashkenazic rendering of the Hebrew letter "tof." I had recognized the quotes easily. *Pirkei Avot* is a collection of Rabbinic maxims, and a chapter of it is studied by many Jews every Shabbat between Passover and the Jewish New Year.

"Nu," Reb Saunders said, smiling, "how should you not know that? Of course. Good. Very good. Now, tell me—"

As I sat there listening to what then took place between Danny and his father, I slowly realized what I was witnessing. In many Jewish homes, especially homes where there are yeshiva students and where the father is learned, there is a tradition which takes place on Shabbat afternoon: The father quizzes the son on what he has learned in school during the past week. I was witnessing a kind of public quiz, but a strange, almost bizarre quiz, more a contest than a quiz, because Reb Saunders was not confining his questions only to what Danny had learned during the week but was ranging over most of the major tractates of the Talmud and Danny was obviously required to provide the answers. Reb Saunders asked where else there was a statement about one who interrupts his studies, and Danny coolly, quietly, answered. He asked what a certain medieval commentator had remarked about that statement, and Danny answered. He chose a minute aspect of the answer and asked who had dealt with it in an altogether different way, and Danny answered. He asked whether Danny agreed with this interpretation, and Danny said he did not, he agreed with another medieval commentator, who had given another interpretation. His father asked how could the commentator have offered such an interpretation when in another passage in the Talmud he had said exactly the opposite, and Danny, very quietly, calmly, his fingers still playing with the rim of the paper plate, found a difference between the contradictory statements by quoting two other sources where one of the statements appeared in a somewhat different context, thereby nullifying the contradiction. One of the two sources Danny had quoted contained a biblical verse, and his father asked him who else had based a law upon this verse. Danny repeated a short passage from the tractate *Sanhedrin*, and then his father quoted another passage from *Yoma* which contradicted the passage in *Sanhedrin*, and Danny answered with a passage from *Gittin* which dissolved the contradiction. His father questioned the validity of his interpretation of the passage in *Gittin* by citing a commentary on the passage that disagreed with his interpretation, and Danny said it was difficult to understand this commentary— he did not say the commentary was wrong, he said it was difficult to understand it —because a parallel passage in *Nedarin* clearly confirmed his own interpretation.

This went on and on, until I lost track of the thread that held it all together and sat and listened in amazement to the feat of memory I was witnessing. Both Danny and his father spoke quietly, his father nodding his approval each time Danny responded. Danny's brother sat staring at them with his mouth open, finally lost interest, and began to eat some of the food that was still on his plate. Once he started picking his nose, but stopped immediately. The men around the tables were watching as if in ecstasy, their faces glowing with pride. This was almost like the pilpul my father had told me about, except that it wasn't really pilpul, they weren't twisting the texts out of shape, they seemed more interested in b'kiut, in straightforward knowledge and simple explanations of the Talmudic passages and commentaries they were discussing. It went on like that for a long time. Then Reb Saunders sat back and was silent.

The contest, or quiz, had apparently ended, and Reb Saunders was smiling at his son. He said, very quietly, "Good. Very good. There is no contradiction. But tell me, you have nothing more to say about what I said earlier?"

Danny was suddenly sitting very straight.

"Nothing more?" Reb Saunders asked again. "You have nothing more to say?"

Danny shook his head, hesitantly.

"Absolutely nothing more to say?" Reb Saunders insisted, his voice flat, cold, distant. He was no longer smiling.

I saw Danny's body go rigid again, as it had done before his father began to speak. The ease and certainty he had worn during the Talmud quiz had disappeared.

"So," Reb Saunders said. "There is nothing more. Nu, What should I say?"

"I did not hear—"

"You did not hear, you did not hear. You heard the first mistake, and you stopped listening. Of course you did not hear. How could you hear when you were not listening?" He said it quietly and without anger.

Danny's face was rigid. The crowd sat silent. I looked at Danny. For a long moment he sat very still—and then I saw his lips part, move, curve slowly upward, and freeze into a grin. I felt the skin on the back of my neck begin to crawl, and I almost cried out. I stared at him, then looked quickly away.

Reb Saunders sat looking at his son. Then he turned his eyes upon me. I felt his eyes looking at me. There was a long, dark silence, during which Danny sat very still, staring fixedly at his plate and grinning. Reb Saunders began to play with the earlock along the right side of his face. He caressed it with the fingers of his right hand, wound it around the index finger, released it, then caressed it again, all the time looking at me. Finally, he sighed loudly, shook his head, and put his hands on the table.

"Nu," he said, "it is possible I am not right. After all, my son is not a mathematician. He has a good head on him, but it is not a head for mathematics. But we have a mathematician with us. The son of David Malter is with us. He is a mathematician." He was looking straight at me, and I felt my heart pound and the blood drain from my face. "Reuven," Reb Saunders was saying, looking straight at me, "you have nothing to say?"

I found I couldn't open my mouth. Say about what? I hadn't the faintest idea what he and Danny had been talking about.

"You heard my little talk?" Reb Saunders asked me quietly.

I felt my head nod.

"And you have nothing to say?"

I felt his eyes on me and found myself staring down at the table. The eyes were like flames on my face.

"Reuven, you liked the gematriya?" Reb Saunders asked softly.

I looked up and nodded. Danny hadn't moved at all. He just sat there, grinning. His little brother was playing with the tomato again. And the men at the tables were silent, staring at *me* now.

"I am very happy," Reb Saunders said gently. "You liked the gematriya. Which gematriya did you like?"

I heard myself say, lamely and hoarsely, "They were all very good."

Reb Saunders' eyebrows went up. "All?" he said. "A very nice thing. They were all very good. Reuven, were they *all* very good?"

I felt Danny stir and saw him turn his head, the grin gone now from his lips. He glanced at me quickly, then looked down again at his paper plate.

I looked at Reb Saunders. "No," I heard myself say hoarsely. "They were not all good."

There was a stir from the men at the tables. Reb Saunders sat back in his leather chair.

"Nu, Reuven," he said quietly, tell me, which one was not good?"

"One of the gematriyot was wrong," I said. I thought the world would fall in on me after I said that. I was a fifteen-year-old boy, and there I was, telling Reb Saunders he had been wrong! But nothing happened. There was another stir from the crowd, but nothing happened. Instead, Reb Saunders broke into a warm broad smile.

"And which one was it?" he asked me quietly.

"The gematriya for 'prozdor' is five hundred and three, not five hundred and thirteen," I answered.

"Good. Very good," Reb Saunders said, smiling and nodding his head, the black beard going back and forth against his chest, the earlocks swaying. "Very good, Reuven. The gematriya for 'prozdor' comes out five hundred three. Very good." He looked at me, smiling broadly, his teeth showing white through the beard, and I almost thought I saw his eyes mist over. There was a loud murmur from the crowd, and Danny's body sagged as the tension went out of him. He glanced at me, his face a mixture of surprise and relief, and I realized with astonishment that I, too, had just passed some kind of test.

"Nu," Reb Saunders said loudly to the men around the tables, "say Kaddish!"

An old man stood up and recited the Scholar's Kaddish. Then the congregants broke to go back to the front section of the synagogue for the Evening Service.

Danny and I said nothing to each other throughout the service, and though I prayed the words, I did not know what I was saying. I kept going over what had happened at the table. I couldn't believe it. I just couldn't get it through my head that Danny had to go through something like that every week, and that I myself had gone through it tonight.

The followers of Reb Saunders obviously had been pleased with my performance, because I could see they were no longer staring questions at me but were glancing at me admiringly. One of them, an old man with a white beard who was sitting in my row, even nodded at me and smiled, the corners of his eyes crinkling. I had clearly passed the test.

Instruction in Self-Discovery: An Example

Carlos Castaneda

Carlos Castaneda (1931–   ) teaches in the department of anthropology at UCLA. While doing graduate work in anthropology, he spent several years in Mexico as a student of a Yaqui Indian teacher and has written four celebrated books about his experiences with don Juan: *The Teachings of Don Juan, A Separate Reality, Journey to Ixtlan,* and *Tales of Power.*

Sunday, June 25, 1961

I stayed with don Juan all afternoon on Friday. I was going to leave about 7 P.M. We were sitting on the porch in front of his house and I decided to ask him once more about the teaching. It was almost a routine question and I expected him to refuse again. I asked him if there was a way in which he could accept just my desire to learn, as if I were an Indian. He took a long time to answer. I was compelled to stay because he seemed to be trying to decide something.

Finally he told me that there was a way, and proceeded to delineate a problem. He pointed out that I was very tired sitting on the floor, and that the proper thing to do was to find a "spot" (*sitio*) on the floor where I could sit without fatigue. I had been sitting with my knees up against my chest and my arms locked around my calves. When he said I was tired, I realized that my back ached and that I was quite exhausted.

I waited for him to explain what he meant by a "spot," but he made no overt attempt to elucidate the point. I thought that perhaps he meant that I should change positions, so I got up and sat closer to him. He protested my movement and clearly emphasized that a spot meant a place where a man could feel naturally happy and strong. He patted the place where he sat and said it was his own spot, adding that he had posed a riddle I had to solve by myself without any further deliberation.

Source: Carlos Castaneda, *The Teachings of Don Juan: A Yaqui Way of Knowledge* (Berkeley, Calif., 1968), pp. 14–34. Originally published by the University of California Press; reprinted by permission of The Regents of the University of California.

What he had posed as a problem to be solved was certainly a riddle. I had no idea how to begin or even what he had in mind. Several times I asked for a clue, or at least a hint, as to how to proceed in locating a point where I felt happy and strong. I insisted and argued that I had no idea what he really meant because I couldn't conceive the problem. He suggested I walk around the porch until I found the spot.

I got up and began to pace the floor. I felt silly and sat down in front of him.

He became very annoyed with me and accused me of not listening, saying that perhaps I did not want to learn. After a while he calmed down and explained to me that not every place was good to sit or be on, and that within the confines of the porch there was one spot that was unique, a spot where I could be at my very best. It was my task to distinguish it from all the other places. The general pattern was that I had to "feel" all the possible spots that were accessible until I could determine without a doubt which was the right one.

I argued that although the porch was not too large (12×8 feet), the number of possible spots was overwhelming, and it would take me a very long time to check all of them, and that since he had not specified the size of the spot, the possibilities might be infinite. My arguments were futile. He got up and very sternly warned me that it might take me days to figure it out, but that if I did not solve the problem, I might as well leave because he would have nothing to say to me. He emphasized that he knew where my spot was, and that therefore I could not lie to him; he said this was the only way he could accept my desire to learn about Mescalito as a valid reason. He added that nothing in his world was a gift, that whatever there was to learn had to be learned the hard way.

He went around the house to the chaparral to urinate. He returned directly into his house through the back.

I thought the assignment to find the alleged spot of happiness was his own way of dismissing me, but I got up and started to pace back and forth. The sky was clear. I could see everything on and near the porch. I must have paced for an hour or more, but nothing happened to reveal the location of the spot. I got tired of walking and sat down; after a few minutes I sat somewhere else, and then at another place, until I had covered the whole floor in a semisystematic fashion. I deliberately tried to "feel" differences between places, but I lacked the criteria for differentiation. I felt I was wasting my time, but I stayed. My rationalization was that I had come a long way just to see don Juan, and I really had nothing else to do.

I lay down on my back and put my hands under my head like a pillow. Then I rolled over and lay on my stomach for a while. I repeated this rolling process over the entire floor. For the first time I thought I had stumbled upon a vague criterion. I felt warmer when I lay on my back.

I rolled again, this time in the opposite direction, and again covered the length of the floor, lying face down on all the places where I had lain face up during my first rolling tour. I experienced the same warm and cold sensations, depending on my position, but there was no difference between spots.

Then an idea occurred to me which I thought to be brilliant: don Juan's spot! I sat there, and then lay, face down at first, and later on my back, but the place was just like all the others. I stood up. I had had enough. I wanted to say good-bye to don Juan, but I was embarrassed to wake him up. I looked at my watch. It was two o'clock in the morning! I had been rolling for six hours.

At that moment don Juan came out and went around the house to the chaparral. He came back and stood at the door. I felt utterly dejected, and I wanted to say something nasty to him and leave. But I realized that it was not his fault; that it was my own choice to go through all that nonsense. I told him I had failed; I had been rolling on his floor like an idiot all night and still couldn't make any sense of his riddle.

He laughed and said that it did not surprise him because I had not proceeded correctly. I had not been using my eyes. That was true, yet I was very sure he had said to feel the difference. I brought that point up, but he argued that one can feel with the eyes, when the eyes are not looking right into things. As far as I was concerned, he said, I had no other means to solve this problem but to use all I had—my eyes.

He went inside. I was certain that he had been watching me. I thought there was no other way for him to know that I had not been using my eyes.

I began to roll again, because that was the most comfortable procedure. This time, however, I rested my chin on my hands and looked at every detail.

After an interval the darkness around me changed. When I focused on the point directly in front of me, the whole peripheral area of my field of vision became brilliantly colored with a homogeneous greenish yellow. The effect was startling. I kept my eyes fixed on the point in front of me and began to crawl sideways on my stomach, one foot at a time.

Suddenly, at a point near the middle of the floor, I became aware of another change in hue. At a place to my right, still in the periphery of my field of vision, the greenish yellow became intensely purple. I concentrated my attention on it. The purple faded into a pale, but still brilliant, color which remained steady for the time I kept my attention on it.

I marked the place with my jacket, and called don Juan. He came out to the porch. I was truly excited; I had actually seen the change in hues. He seemed unimpressed, but told me to sit on the spot and report to him what kind of feeling I had.

I sat down and then lay on my back. He stood by me and asked me repeatedly how I felt; but I did not feel anything different. For about fifteen minutes I tried to feel or to see a difference, while don Juan stood by me patiently. I felt disgusted. I had a metallic taste in my mouth. Suddenly I had developed a headache. I was about to get sick. The thought of my nonsensical endeavours irritated me to a point of fury. I got up.

Don Juan must have noticed my profound frustration. He did not laugh, but very seriously stated that I had to be inflexible with myself if I wanted to learn. Only two choices were open to me, he said: either to quit and go home, in which case I would never learn, or to solve the riddle.

He went inside again. I wanted to leave immediately, but I was too tired to drive; besides, perceiving the hues had been so startling that I was sure it was a criterion of some sort, and perhaps there were other changes to be detected. Anyway, it was too late to leave. So I sat down, stretched my legs back, and began all over again.

During this round I moved rapidly through each place, passing don Juan's spot, to the end of the floor, and then turned around to cover the outer edge. When I reached the center, I realized that another change in coloration was taking place, again on the edge of my field of vision. The uniform chartreuse I was seeing all over the area turned, at one spot to my right, into a sharp verdigris. It remained for a moment and then abruptly metamorphosed into another steady hue, different from the other one I had detected earlier. I took off one of my shoes and marked the point, and kept on rolling until I had covered the floor in all possible directions. No other change of coloration took place.

I came back to the point marked with my shoe, and examined it. It was located five to six feet away from the spot marked by my jacket, in a south-easterly direction. There was a large rock next to it. I lay down there for quite some time trying to find clues, looking at every detail, but I did not feel anything different.

I decided to try the other spot. I quickly pivoted on my knees and was about to lie down on my jacket when I felt an unusual apprehension. It was more like a physical sensation of something actually pushing on my stomach. I jumped up and retreated in one movement. The hair on my neck pricked up. My legs had arched slightly, my truck was bent forward, and my arms stuck out in front of me rigidly with my fingers contracted like a claw. I took notice of my strange posture and my fright increased.

I walked back involuntarily and sat down on the rock next to my shoe. From the rock, I slumped to the floor. I tried to figure out what had happened to cause me such a fright. I thought it must have been the fatigue I was experiencing. It was nearly daytime. I felt silly and embarrassed. Yet I had no way to explain what had frightened me, nor had I figured out what don Juan wanted.

I decided to give it one last try. I got up and slowly approached the place marked by my jacket, and again I felt the same apprehension. This time I made a strong effort to control myself. I sat down, and then knelt in order to lie face down, but I could not lie in spite of my will. I put my hands on the floor in front of me. My breathing accelerated; my stomach was upset. I had a clear sensation of panic, and fought not to run away. I thought don Juan was perhaps watching me. Slowly I crawled back to the other spot and propped my back against the rock. I wanted to rest for a while to organize my thoughts, but I fell asleep.

I heard don Juan talking and laughing above my head. I woke up.

"You have found the spot," he said.

I did not understand him at first, but he assured me again that the place where I had fallen asleep was the spot in question. He again asked me how I felt lying there. I told him I really did not notice any difference.

He asked me to compare my feelings at that moment with what I had felt while lying on the other spot. For the first time it occurred to me that I could not possibly explain my apprehension of the preceding night. He urged me in a kind of challenging way to sit on the other spot. For some inexplicable reason I was actually afraid of the other place, and did not sit on it. He asserted that only a fool could fail to see the difference.

I asked him if each of the two spots had a special name. He said that the good one was called the *sitio* and the bad one the enemy: he said these two places were the key to a man's well-being, especially for a man who was pursuing knowledge.

The sheer act of sitting on one's spot created superior strength; on the other hand, the enemy weakened a man and could even cause his death. He said I had replenished my energy, which I had spent lavishly the night before, by taking a nap on my spot.

He also said that the colors I had seen in association with each specific spot had the same overall effect either of giving strength or of curtailing it.

I asked him if there were other spots for me like the two I had found, and how I should go about finding them. He said that many places in the world would be comparable to those two, and that the best way to find them was by detecting their respective colors.

It was not clear to me whether or not I had solved the problem, and in fact I was not even convinced that there had been a problem; I could not avoid feeling that the whole experience was forced and arbitrary. I was certain that don Juan had watched me all night and then proceeded to humor me by saying that wherever I had fallen asleep *was* the place I was looking for. Yet I failed to see a logical reason for such an act, and when he challenged me to sit on the other spot I could not do it. There was a strange cleavage between my pragmatic experience of fearing the "other spot" and my rational deliberations about the total event.

Don Juan, on the other hand, was very sure I had succeeded, and, acting in accordance with my success, let me know he was going to teach me about peyote.

"You asked me to teach you about Mescalito," he said, "I wanted to find out if you had enough backbone to meet him face to face. Mescalito is not something to make fun of. You must have command over your resources. Now I know I can take your desire alone as a good reason to learn."

"You really are going to teach me about peyote?"

"I prefer to call him Mescalito. Do the same."

"When are you going to start?"

"It is not so simple as that. You must be ready first."

"I think I am ready."

"This is not a joke. You must wait until there is no doubt, and then you will meet him."

"Do I have to prepare myself?"

"No. You simply have to wait. You may give up the whole idea after a while. You get tired easily. Last night you were ready to quit as soon as it got difficult. Mescalito requires a very serious intent."

Monday, August 7, 1961

I arrived at don Juan's house in Arizona about seven o'clock on Friday night. Five other Indians were sitting with him on the porch of his house. I greeted him and sat waiting for them to say something. After a formal silence one of the men got up, walked over to me, and said, "Buenas noches." I stood up and answered, "Buenas noches." Then all the other men got up and came to me and we all mumbled "buenas noches" and shook hands either by barely touching one another's fingertips or by holding the hand for an instant and then dropping it quite abruptly.

We all sat down again. They seemed to be rather shy—at a loss for words, although they all spoke Spanish.

It must have been about half past seven when suddenly they all got up and walked toward the back of the house. Nobody had said a word for a long time. Don Juan signaled me to follow and we all got inside an old pickup truck parked there. I sat in the back with don Juan and two younger men. There were no cushions or benches and the metal floor was painfully hard, especially when we left the highway and got onto a dirt road. Don Juan whispered that we were going to the house of one of his friends who had seven Mescalitos for me.

I asked him, "Don't you have any of them yourself, don Juan?"

"I do, but I couldn't offer them to you. You see, someone else has to do this."

"Can you tell me why?"

"Perhaps you are not agreeable to 'him' and 'he' won't like you, and then you will never be able to know 'him' with affection, as one should; and our friendship will be broken."

"Why wouldn't he like me? I have never done anything to him."

"You don't have to *do* anything to be liked or disliked. He either takes you, or throws you away."

"But, if he doesn't take me, isn't there anything I can do to make him like me?"

The other two men seemed to have overheard my question and laughed.

"No! I can't think of anything one can do," don Juan said.

He turned half away from me and I could not talk to him anymore.

We must have driven for at least an hour before we stopped in front of a small house. It was quite dark, and after the driver had turned off the headlights I could make out only the vague contour of the building.

A young woman, a Mexican, judging by her speech inflection, was yelling at a dog to make him stop barking. We got out of the truck and walked into the house. The men mumbled "Buenas noches" as they went by her. She answered back and went on yelling at the dog.

The room was large and was stacked up with a multitude of objects. A dim light from a very small electric bulb rendered the scene quite gloomy. There were quite a few chairs with broken legs and sagging seats leaning against the walls. Three of the men sat down on a couch, which was the largest single piece of furniture in the room. It was very old and had sagged down all the way to the floor; in the dim light it seemed to be red and dirty. The rest of us sat in chairs. We sat in silence for a long time.

One of the men suddenly got up and went into another room. He was perhaps in his fifties, dark, tall, and husky. He came back a moment later with a coffee jar. He opened the lid and handed the jar to me; inside there were seven odd-looking items. They varied in size and consistency. Some of them were almost round, others were elongated. They felt to the touch like the pulp of walnuts, or the surface of cork. Their brownish color made them look like hard, dry nutshells. I handled them, rubbing their surfaces for quite some time.

"This to be chewed [*esto se masca*]" don Juan said in a whisper.

I had not realized that he had sat next to me until he spoke. I looked at the other men, but no one was looking at me; they were talking among themselves in very low voices. This was a moment of acute indecision and fear. I felt almost unable to control myself.

"I have to go the bathroom," I said to him. "I'll go outside and take a walk."

He handed me the coffee jar and I put the peyote buttons in it. I was leaving the room when the man who had given me the jar stood up, came to me, and said he had a toilet bowl in the other room.

The toilet was almost against the door. Next to it, nearly touching the toilet, was a large bed which occupied more than half of the room. The woman was sleeping there. I stood motionless at the door for a while, then I came back to the room where the other men were.

The man who owned the house spoke to me in English: "Don Juan says you're from South America. Is there any mescal there?" I told him that I had never even heard of it.

They seemed to be interested in South America and we talked about the Indians for a while. Then one of the men asked me why I wanted to eat peyote. I told him that I wanted to know what it was like. They all laughed shyly.

Don Juan urged me softly. "Chew it, chew it [Masca, masca]."

My hands were wet and my stomach contracted. The jar with the peyote buttons was on the floor by the chair. I bent over, took one at random, and put it in my mouth. It had a stale taste. I bit it in two and started to chew one of the pieces. I felt a strong, pungent bitterness; in a moment my whole mouth was numb. The bitterness increased as I kept on chewing, forcing an incredible flow of saliva. My gums and the inside of my mouth felt as if I had eaten salty dry meat or fish, which seems to force one to chew more. After a while I chewed the other piece and my mouth was so numb I couldn't feel the bitterness anymore. The peyote button was a bunch of shreds, like the fibrous part of an orange or like sugarcane, and I didn't know whether to swallow it or spit it out. At that moment the owner of the house got up and invited everybody to go out to the porch.

We went out and sat in the darkness. It was quite comfortable outside, and the host brought out a bottle of tequila.

The men were seated in a row with their backs to the wall. I was at the extreme right of the line. Don Juan, who was next to me, placed the jar with the peyote buttons between my legs. Then he handed me the bottle, which was passed down the line, and told me to take some of the tequila to wash away the bitterness.

I spat out the shreds of the first button and took a sip. He told me not to swallow it, but to just rinse out my mouth with it to stop the saliva. It did not help much with the saliva, but it certainly helped to wash away some of the bitterness.

Don Juan gave me a piece of dried apricot, or perhaps it was a dried fig—I couldn't see it in the dark, nor could I taste it—and told me to chew it thoroughly and slowly, without rushing. I had difficulty swallowing it; it felt as if it would not go down.

After a short pause the bottle went around again. Don Juan handed me a piece of crispy dried meat. I told him I did not feel like eating.

"This is not eating," he said firmly.

The pattern was repeated six times. I remember having chewed six peyote buttons when the conversation became very lively; although I could not distinguish what language was spoken, the topic of the conversation, in which everybody participated, was very interesting, and I attempted to listen carefully so that I could take part. But when I tried to speak I realized I couldn't; the words shifted aimlessly about in my mind.

I sat with my back propped against the wall and listened to what the men were saying. They were talking in Italian, and repeated over and over one phrase about the stupidity of sharks. I thought it was a logical, coherent topic. I had told don Juan earlier that the Colorado River in Arizona was called by the early Spaniards "el rio de los tizones [the river of charred wood]"; and someone misspelled or misread "tizones," and the river was called "el rio de los tiburones [the river of the sharks]." I was sure they were discussing that story, yet it never occurred to me to think that none of them could speak Italian.

I had a very strong desire to throw up, but I don't recall the actual act. I asked if somebody would get me some water. I was experiencing an unbearable thirst.

Don Juan brought me a large saucepan. He placed it on the ground next to the wall. He also brought a little cup or can. He dipped it into the pan and handed it to me, and said I could not drink but should just freshen my mouth with it.

The water looked strangely shiny, glossy, like a thick varnish. I wanted to ask don Juan about it and laboriously I tried to voice my thoughts in English, but then I realized he did not speak English. I experienced a very confusing moment, and became aware of the fact that although there was a clear thought in my mind, I could not speak. I wanted to comment on the strange quality of the water, but what followed next was not speech; it was the feeling of my unvoiced thoughts coming out of my mouth in a sort of liquid form. It was an effortless sensation of vomiting without the contractions of the diaphragm. It was a pleasant flow of liquid words.

I drank. And the feeling that I was vomiting disappeared. By that time all noises had vanished and I found I had difficulty focusing my eyes. I looked for don Juan and as I turned my head I noticed that my field of vision had diminished to a circular area in front of my eyes. This feeling was neither frightening nor discomforting, but, quite to the contrary, it was a novelty; I could literally sweep the ground by focusing on one spot and then moving my head slowly in any direction. When I had first come out to the porch I had noticed it was all dark except for the distant glare of the city lights. Yet within the circular area of my vision everything was clear. I forgot about my concern with don Juan and the other men, and gave myself entirely to exploring the ground with my pinpoint vision.

I saw the juncture of the porch floor and the wall. I turned my head slowly to the right, following the wall, and saw don Juan sitting against it. I shifted my head to the left in order to focus on the water. I found the bottom of the pan; I raised my head slightly and saw a medium-size black dog approaching. I saw him coming toward the water. The dog began to drink. I raised my hand to push him away from my water; I focused my pinpoint vision on the dog to carry on the movement, and suddenly I saw him become transparent. The water was a shiny viscous liquid. I saw it going down the dog's throat into his body. I saw it flowing evenly through his entire length and then shooting out through each one of the hairs. I saw the iridescent fluid traveling along the length of each individual hair and then projecting out of the hairs to form a long, white, silky mane.

At that moment I had the sensation of intense convulsions, and in a matter of instants a tunnel formed around me, very low and narrow, hard and strangely cold.

It felt to the touch like a wall of solid tinfoil. I found I was sitting on the tunnel floor. I tried to stand up, but hit my head on the metal roof, and the tunnel compressed itself until it was suffocating me. I remember having to crawl toward a sort of round point where the tunnel ended; when I finally arrived, if I did, I had forgotten all about the dog, don Juan, and myself. I was exhausted. My clothes were soaked in a cold, sticky liquid. I rolled back and forth trying to find a position in which to rest, a position where my heart would not pound so hard. In one of those shifts I saw the dog again.

Every memory came back to me at once, and suddenly all was clear in my mind. I turned around to look for don Juan, but I could not distinguish anything or anyone. All I was capable of seeing was the dog becoming iridescent; an intense light radiated from his body. I saw again the water flowing through him, kindling him like a bonfire. I got to the water, sank my face in the pan, and drank with him. My hands were in front of me on the ground and, as I drank, I saw the fluid running through my veins setting up hues of red and yellow and green. I drank more and more. I drank until I was all afire; I was all aglow. I drank until the fluid went out of my body through each pore, and projected out like fibers of silk, and I too acquired a long, lustrous, iridescent mane. I looked at the dog and his mane was like mine. A supreme happiness filled my whole body, and we ran together toward a sort of yellow warmth that came from some indefinite place. And there we played. We played and wrestled until I knew his wishes and he knew mine. We took turns manipulating each other in the fashion of a puppet show. I could make him move his legs by twisting my toes, and every time he nodded his head I felt an irresistable impulse to jump. But his most impish act was to make me scratch my head with my foot while I sat; he did it by flapping his ears from side to side. This action was to me utterly, unbearably funny. Such a touch of grace and irony; such mastery, I thought. The euphoria that possessed me was indescribable. I laughed until it was almost impossible to breathe.

I had the clear sensation of not being able to open my eyes; I was looking through a tank of water. It was a long and very painful state filled with the anxiety of not being able to wake up and yet being awake. Then slowly the world became clear and in focus. My field of vision became again very round and ample, and with it came an ordinary conscious act, which was to turn around and look for that marvelous being. At this point I encountered the most difficult transition. The passage from my normal state had taken place almost without my realizing it: I was aware; my thoughts and feelings were a corollary of that awareness; and the passing was smooth and clear. But this second change, the awakening to serious, sober consciousness, was genuinely shocking. I had forgotten I was a man! The sadness of such an irreconcilable situation was so intense that I wept.

Saturday, August 5, 1961

Later that morning, after breakfast, the owner of the house, don Juan, and I drove back to don Juan's place. I was very tired, but I couldn't go to sleep in the truck. Only after the man had left did I fall asleep on the porch of don Juan's house.

When I woke up it was dark; don Juan had covered me up with a blanket. I looked for him, but he was not in the house. He came later with a pot of fried beans and a stack of tortillas. I was extremely hungry.

After we had finished eating and were resting he asked me to tell him all that had happened to me that night before. I related my experience in great detail and as accurately as possible.

When I finished he nodded his head and said, "I think you are fine. It is difficult for me to explain how and why. But I think it went all right for you. You see, sometimes he is playful, like a child; at other times he is terrible, fearsome. He either frolics, or he is dead serious. It is impossible to know beforehand what he will be like with another person. Yet, when one knows him well—sometimes. You played with him tonight. You are the only person I know who has had such an encounter."

"In what way does my experience differ from that of others?"

"You're not an Indian; therefore it is hard for me to figure out what is what. Yet he either takes people or rejects them, regardless of whether they are Indians or not. That I know. I have seen numbers of them. I also know that he frolics, he makes some people laugh, but never have I seen him play with anyone."

"Can you tell me now, don Juan, how does peyote protect . . ."

He did not let me finish. Vigorously he touched me on the shoulder.

"Don't you ever name him that way. You haven't seen enough of him yet to know him."

"How does Mescalito protect people?"

"He advises. He answers whatever questions you ask."

"Then Mescalito is real? I mean he is something you can see?"

He seemed to be baffled by my question. He looked at me with a sort of blank expression.

"What I meant to say, is that Mescalito . . ."

"I heard what you said. Didn't you see him last night?"

I wanted to say that I saw only a dog, but I noticed his bewildered look.

"Then you think what I saw last night was him?"

He looked at me with contempt. He chuckled, shook his head as though he couldn't believe it, and in a very belligerent tone he added, "A poco crees que era tu—mamá [Don't tell me you believe it was your—mama]?" He paused before saying "mamá" because what he meant to say was "tu chingada madre," an idiom used as a disrespectful allusion to the other party's mother. The word "mamá" was so incongruous that we both laughed for a long time.

Then I realized he had fallen asleep and had not answered my question.

Sunday, August 6, 1961

I drove don Juan to the house where I had taken peyote. On the way he told me the name of the man who had "offered me to Mescalito" was John. When we got to the house we found John sitting on his porch with two young men. All of them were extremely jovial. They laughed and talked with great ease. The three of them spoke English perfectly. I told John that I had come to thank him for having helped me.

I wanted to get their views on my behavior during the hallucinogenic experience, and told them I had been trying to think of what I had done that night and that I couldn't remember. They laughed and were reluctant to talk about it. They seemed to be holding back on account of don Juan. They all glanced at him as though waiting for an affirmative cue to go on. Don Juan must have cued them, although I did not notice anything, because suddenly John began to tell me what I had done that night.

He said he knew I had been "taken" when he heard me puking. He estimated that I must have puked thirty times. Don Juan corrected him and said it was only ten times.

John continued: "Then we all moved next to you. You were stiff, and were having convulsions. For a very long time, while lying on your back, you moved your mouth as though talking. Then you began to bump your head on the floor, and don Juan put an old hat on your head and you stopped it. You shivered and whined for hours, lying on the floor. I think everybody fell asleep then; but I heard you puffing and groaning in my sleep. Then I heard you scream and I woke up. I saw you leaping up in the air, screaming. You made a dash for the water, knocked the pan over, and began to swim in the puddle.

"Don Juan brought you more water. You sat quietly in front of the pan. Then you jumped up and took off all your clothes. You were kneeling in front of the water, drinking in big gulps. Then you just sat there and stared into space. We thought you were going to be there forever. Nearly everybody was asleep, including don Juan, when suddenly you jumped up again, howling, and took after the dog. The dog got scared and howled too, and ran to the back of the house. Then everybody woke up.

"We all got up. You came back from the other side still chasing the dog. The dog was running ahead of you barking and howling. I think you must have gone twenty times around the house, running in circles, barking like a dog. I was afraid people were going to be curious. There are no neighbors close, but your howling was so loud it could have been heard for miles."

One of the young men added, "You caught up with the dog and brought it to the porch in your arms."

John continued: "Then you began to play with the dog. You wrestled with him, and the dog and you bit each other and played. That, I thought, was funny. My dog does not play usually. But this time you and the dog were rolling on each other."

"Then you ran to the water and the dog drank with you," the young man said. "You ran five or six times to the water with the dog."

"How long did this go on?" I asked.

"Hours," John said. "At one time we lost sight of you two. I think you must have run to the back. We just heard you barking and groaning. You sounded so much like a dog that we couldn't tell you two apart."

"Maybe it was just the dog alone," I said.

They laughed, and John said, "You were barking there, boy!"

"What happened next?"

The three men looked at one another and seemed to have a hard time deciding what happened next. Finally the young man who had not yet said anything spoke up.

"He choked," he said, looking at John.

"Yes, you certainly choked. You began to cry very strangely, and then you fell to the floor. We thought you were biting your tongue; don Juan opened your jaws and poured water on your face. Then you started shivering and having convulsions all over again. Then you stayed motionless for a long time. Don Juan said it was all over. By then it was morning, so we covered you with a blanket and left you to sleep on the porch."

He stopped there and looked at the other men who were obviously trying not to laugh. He turned to don Juan and asked him something. Don Juan smiled and answered the question. John turned to me and said, "We left you here on the porch because we were afraid you were going to piss all over the rooms."

They all laughed very loudly.

"What was the matter with me?" I asked. "Did I . . ."

"Did you?" John sort of mimicked me. "We were not going to mention it, but don Juan says it is all right. You pissed all over my dog!"

"What did I do?"

"You don't think the dog was running because he was afraid of you, do you? The dog was running because you were pissing on him."

There was general laughter at this point. I tried to question one of the young men, but they were all laughing and he didn't hear me.

John went on: "My dog got even though: he pissed on you too!"

This statement was apparently utterly funny because they all roared with laughter, including don Juan. When they had quieted down, I asked in all earnestness, "Is it really true? This really happened?"

Still laughing, John replied: "I swear my dog really pissed on you."

Driving back to don Juan's place I asked him: "Did all that really happen, don Juan?"

"Yes," he said, "but they don't know what you saw. They don't realize you were playing with 'him.' That is why I did not disturb you."

"But is this business of the dog and me pissing on each other true?"

"It was not a dog! How many times do I have to tell you that? This is the only way to understand it. It's the only way! It was 'he' who played with you."

"Did you know all this was happening before I told you about it?"

He vacillated for an instant before answering.

"No, I remembered, after you told me about it, the strange way you looked. I just suspected you were doing fine because you didn't seem scared."

"Did the dog really play with me as they say?"

"Goddammit! It was not a dog!"

Thursday, August 17, 1961

I told don Juan how I felt about my experience. From the point of view of my intended work it had been a disastrous event. I said I did not care for another similar "encounter" with Mescalito. I agreed that everything that had happened to me had been more than interesting, but added that nothing in it could really move me toward seeking it again. I seriously believed that I was not constructed for that type of endeavor. Peyote had produced in me, as a postreaction, a strange kind of physical discomfort. It was an indefinite fear or unhappiness; a melancholy of some sort, which I could not define exactly. And I did not find that state noble in any way.

Don Juan laughed and said, "You were beginning to learn."

"This type of learning is not for me. I am not made for it, don Juan."

"You always exaggerate."

"This is not exaggeration."

"It is. The only trouble is that you exaggerate the bad points only."

"There are no good points so far as I am concerned. All I know is that it makes me afraid."

"There is nothing wrong with being afraid. When you fear, you see things in a different way."

"But I don't care about seeing things in a different way, don Juan. I think I am going to leave the learning about Mescalito alone. I can't handle it, don Juan. This is really a bad situation for me."

"Of course it is bad— even for me. You are not the only one who is baffled."

"Why should you be baffled, don Juan?"

"I have been thinking about what I saw the other night. Mescalito actually played with you. That baffled me, because it was an indication [omen]."

"What kind of an indication, don Juan?"

"Mescalito was pointing you out to me."

"What for?"

"It wasn't clear to me then, but now it is. He meant you were the 'chosen man' [escogido]. Mescalito pointed you out to me and by doing that he told me you were the chosen man."

"Do you mean I was chosen among others for some task, or something of the sort?"

"No. What I mean is, Mescalito told me you could be the man I am looking for."

"When did he tell you that, don Juan?"

"By playing with you, he told me that. This makes you the chosen man for me."

"What does it mean to be the chosen man?"

"There are some secrets I know [Tengo secretos]. I have secrets I won't be able to reveal to anyone unless I find my chosen man. The other night when I saw you playing with Mescalito it was clear to me you were that man. But you are not an Indian. How baffling!"

"But what does it mean to me, don Juan? What do I have to do?"

"I've made up my mind and I am going to teach you the secrets that make up the lot of a man of knowledge."

"Do you mean the secrets about Mescalito?"

"Yes, but those are not all the secrets I know. There are others, of a different kind, which I would like to give to someone. I had a teacher myself, my benefactor, and I also became his chosen man upon performing a certain feat. He taught me all I know."

I asked him again what this new role would require of me; he said learning was the only thing involved, learning in the sense of what I had experienced in the two sessions with him.

The way in which the situation had evolved was quite strange. I had made up my mind to tell him I was going to give up the idea of learning about peyote, and then before I could really make my point, he offered to teach me his "knowlege." I did not know what he meant by that, but I felt that this sudden turn was very serious. I argued I had no qualifications for such a task, as it required a rare kind of courage which I did not have. I told him that my bent of character was to talk about acts others performed. I wanted to hear his views and opinions about everything. I told him I could be happy if I could sit there and listen to him talk for days. To me, *that* would be learning.

He listened without interrupting me. I talked for a long time. Then he said:

"All this is very easy to understand. Fear is the first natural enemy a man must overcome on his path to knowledge. Besides, you are curious. That evens up the score. And you will learn in spite of yourself; that's the rule."

I protested for a while longer, trying to dissuade him. But he seemed to be convinced there was nothing else I could do but learn.

"You are not thinking in the proper order," he said. "Mescalito actually played with you. That's the point to think about. Why don't you dwell on that instead of on your fear?"

"Was it so unusual?"

"You are the only person I have ever seen playing with him. You are not used to this kind of life; therefore the indications [omens] bypass you. Yet you are a serious person, but your seriousness is attached to what you do, not to what goes on outside you. You dwell upon yourself too much. That's the trouble. And that produces a terrible fatigue."

"But what else can anyone do, don Juan?"

"Seek and see the marvels all around you. You will get tired of looking at yourself alone, and that fatigue will make you deaf and blind to everything else."

'You have a point, don Juan, but how can I change?"

"Think about the wonder of Mescalito playing with you. Think about nothing else: The rest will come to you of itself."

Sunday, August 20, 1961

Last night don Juan proceeded to usher me into the realm of his knowledge. We sat in front of his house in the dark. Suddenly, after a long silence, he began to talk. He said he was going to advise me with the same words his own benefactor had used the first day he took him as his apprentice. Don Juan had apparently memorized the words, for he repeated them several times, to make sure I did not miss any:

"A man goes to knowledge as he goes to war, wide-awake, with fear, with respect, and with absolute assurance. Going to knowledge or going to war in any other manner is a mistake, and whoever makes it will live to regret his steps."

I asked him why was it so and he said that when a man has fulfilled those four requisites there are no mistakes for which he will have to account; under such conditions his acts lose the blundering quality of a fool's acts. If such a man fails, or suffers a defeat, he will have lost only a battle, and there will be no pitiful regrets over that.

Then he said he intended to teach me about an "ally" in the very same way his own benefactor had taught him. He put strong emphasis on the words "very same way," repeating the phrase several times.

An "ally," he said, is a power a man can bring into his life to help him, advise him, and give him the strength necessary to perform acts, whether big or small, right or wrong. This ally is necessary to enhance a man's life, guide his acts, and further his knowledge. In fact, an ally is the indispensable aid to knowing. Don Juan said this with great conviction and force. He seemed to choose his words carefully. He repeated the following sentence four times:

"An ally will make you see and understand things about which no human being could possibly enlighten you."

"Is an ally something like a guardian spirit?"

"It is neither a guardian nor a spirit. It is an aid."

"Is Mescalito your ally?"

"No! Mescalito is another kind of power. A unique power! A protector, a teacher."

"What makes Mescalito different from an ally?"

"He can't be tamed and used as an ally is tamed and used. Mescalito is outside oneself. He chooses to show himself in many forms to whoever stands in front of him, regardless of whether that person is a brujo or a farm boy."

Don Juan spoke with deep fervor about Mescalito's being the teacher of the proper way to live. I asked him how Mescalito taught the "proper way of life," and don Juan replied that Mescalito *showed* how to live.

"How does he show it?" I asked.

"He has many ways of showing it. Sometimes he shows it on his hand, or on the rocks, or the trees, or just in front of you."

"Is it like a picture in front of you?"

"No. It is a teaching in front of you."

"Does Mescalito talk to the person?"

"Yes. But not in words."

"How does he talk, then?"

"He talks differently to every man."

I felt my questions were annoying him. I did not ask any more. He went on explaining that there were no exact steps to knowing Mescalito; therefore no one could teach about him except Mescalito himself. This quality made him a unique power; he was not the same for every man.

On the other hand, the acquiring of an ally required, don Juan said, the most precise teaching and the following of stages or steps without a single deviation. There are many such ally powers in the world, he said, but he was familiar with only two of them. And he was going to lead me to them and their secrets, but it was up to me to choose *one* of them, for I could have only one. His benefactor's ally was in *la yerba del diablo* (devil's weed), he said, but he personally did not like it, even though his benefactor had taught him its secrets. His own ally was in the *humito* (the little smoke), he said, but he did not elaborate on the nature of the smoke.

I asked him about it. He remained quiet. After a long pause I asked him:

"What kind of a power is an ally?"

"It is an aid. I have already told you."

"How does it aid?"

"An ally is a power capable of carrying a man beyond the boundaries of himself. This is how an ally can reveal matters no human being could."

"But Mescalito also takes you out of the boundaries of yourself. Doesn't that make him an ally?"

"No. Mescalito takes you out of yourself to teach you. An ally takes you out to give you power."

I asked him to explain this point to me in more detail, or to describe the difference in effect between the two. He looked at me for a long time and laughed. He said that learning through conversation was not only a waste, but stupidity, because learning was the most difficult task a man could undertake. He asked me to remember the time I had tried to find my spot, and how I wanted to find it without doing any work because I had expected him to hand out all the information. If he had done so, he said, I would never have learned. But, knowing how difficult it was to find my spot, and, above all, knowing that it existed, would give me a unique sense of confidence. He said that while I remained rooted to my "good spot" nothing could cause me bodily harm, because I had the assurance that at that particular spot I was at my very best. I had the power to shove off anything that might be harmful to me. If, however, he had *told* me where it was, I would never have had the confidence needed to claim it as true knowledge. Thus, knowledge was indeed power.

Don Juan said then that every time a man sets himself to learn he has to labor as hard as I did to find that spot, and the limits of his learning are determined by his own nature. Thus he saw no point in talking about knowledge. He said that certain kinds of knowledge were too powerful for the strength I had, and to talk about them would only bring harm to me. He apparently felt there was nothing else he wanted to say. He got up and walked toward his house. I told him the situation overwhelmed me. It was not what I had conceived or wanted it to be.

He said that fears are natural; that all of us experience them and there is nothing we can do about it. But on the other hand, no matter how frightening learning is, it is more terrible to think of a man without an ally, or without knowledge.

Words for My Son

John Blofeld

John Blofeld (1913–   ) has spent 40 years living and traveling in the Far East. He was Cultural Attaché to the British Embassy in wartime China and later worked for the U.N. He now lives and teaches in Bangkok. He is the author of numerous distinguished books and translations related to the living Eastern traditions. Among his more recent works are *The Wheel of Life*, *The Secret and Sublime*, and *The Book of Changes*, a new translation of the *I Ching*.

Not long ago my twenty-five-year-old son voiced an urgent longing to "break away from it all." Asked whether he were unhappy, he replied: "Happiness? For my generation the pay's alright. It covers food, clothes and rent, leaving enough over for running an old car and occasionally whooping things up. But mostly we work at depressingly routine jobs, go home to supper, watch TV a bit or maybe pop out for a drink with friends, then tumble into bed and that's about all. Growing older brings no real change besides more pay and more responsibilities. True, there are no hardships in this sort of life, no struggle for survival—but is slaving to timetables and machines the good life we hoped for as kids? Is that all there is?"

Well, mysticism offers no broad remedies for modern ills. Poverty of the tragic kind found, say, in India or Bangladesh demands vast-scale collective action and so does the terrifyingly rapid deterioration of the environment; but boredom and discontent in the midst of plenty are a problem for the individual and it is here that the ancient mystical traditions may be looked to for an answer. Only, before going further, I should like to stress two points: first, that I am innocent of missionary intention and do not for one moment advocate wholesale conversion to traditions that are still largely alien to the West; second, that what remedies occur to me are strictly for a certain kind of individual, being so intensely personal that whoever accepts them is obliged to do something drastic for himself that neither God nor man can do on his behalf.

The First Step

To enquirers like my son, I would say: "Remember that mind is the king. Of mind is frustration born; by mind is life endowed with happiness and meaning." Since not many such enquirers are likely to be potential mystics, I would begin by suggesting cultivation of a mental attitude that could, not too fancifully, be called Taoistic; this much could be achieved without the austerities demanded of Short Path adepts whose thirst for the bliss that arises from within makes them ready

Source: John Blofeld, *Beyond the Gods* (New York, 1974), pp. 152–161. Reprinted by permission of E. P. Dutton & Co., Inc.

for great sacrifices. Indeed, the achievement would be almost effortless, being carried out in the spirit of *wu-wei*.

Forced slavery is rare these days; rather, servitude is willingly embraced by those eager for wealth and status, though the eagerness may arise less from greed than from the assumption that what most people seem to want so much must be supremely worth having. For the sake of wealth, people already well above the poverty line slave all their lives, not realising that withdrawal from the rat-race would immediately increase rather than diminish their wealth. Obviously anyone who finds the full satisfaction of all his material desires well within his means can be said to be wealthy; it follows that, except by the truly poor, wealth can be achieved overnight by a change of mental attitude that will set bounds to desires. As Laotzû put it, "He who is contented always has enough." This is a principle completely lost sight of by present-day society. Like helpless birds mesmerised by serpents, we allow self-appointed arbiters of fashion to dictate length of skirt and width of trousers, thus gulling us into unnecessarily replenishing our wardrobes every year, instead of being satisfied with what is comfortable and pleasing to ourselves. This is slavery indeed—voluntary slavery to manufacturers and advertisers whose cynical purpose is to seduce us into buying what is entirely unnecessary to our wellbeing. For those unfortunates who suffer actual want, a very different remedy is needed; as to the rest, the act of withdrawing the mind from the race for wealth and status and making freedom to be oneself the goal would enrich them at one bound—mentally, spiritually and, in an important sense, materially. All the energy and time expended on keeping up with the Changs and the Joneses would be freed for constructive use. Incidentally, status, the second object of the rat-race, is an even more illusory benefit than wealth, the pleasure it confers being purely relative; however high one climbs, there are always others higher—and, as Laotzû said: "He who stands on tiptoe, totters." On the other hand, caring nothing for prestige and public opinion confers a relaxation that knows no bounds.

How wonderful were the ancient Taoist sages! Calling them cloud-riding immortals was not wholly a figure of speech, for the sense of freedom that comes from renouncing ambition, being true to one's own principles without the least concern about what others think and learning to accept with equanimity all that life or death may bring, is a draught so heady that those who have quaffed it feel as exultant as if sun, moon and stars were their playthings. Absolved of anxiety, they revel in a weightlessness of spirit closely comparable to the lightness of body needed for riding upon clouds.

The achievement of joyous tranquillity should prove a satisfying remedy for discontent. As to those who wish to go further, they should begin by taking this same step, for the freedom of spirit won by frugality is indispensible to success in attaining the much more difficult goal of intuitive wisdom.

The Second Step

The essence of tantric practice is that the adept learn how to harness the energy of everything whatsoever—good, bad and indifferent—to the task of self-realisation. When, almost twenty years ago, I began to study tantric Buddhism seriously, I went first to a Mongolian Geshé (highly qualified exponent of the Dharma) who began by expounding the inner meaning of the passage: "See all beings as the Buddha! Hear all sounds as mantra! Recognise all places as Nirvana!" These are much more than pious injunctions rooted in Mahayana doctrine, for they inculcate a tantric attitude to life whereby many marvels can be wrought. It is this that I would next recommend to enquirers like my son, regardless of whether or not they are Buddhist. In part, the practice for attaining this attitude of mind may seem at the early stages like a system of make-believe; that is to say, while still at the level of relative truth and as yet unable to experience the divine perception whereby all dualism (e.g. between Buddhas and ordinary beings, between sounds pleasing and discordant, between sights beautiful and ugly) is negated, one tries to behave *as if* in the light of that perception. The purpose is to discipline the mind in such a manner as to make the experience much easier to attain. If in the fairy-tale, Beauty had known the hideous Beast for a handsome young prince temporarily transformed and had learnt to visualise him as he really was, her love would have blossomed more readily and the kiss that revealed him in his original form been given the sooner.

"See all beings as the Buddha" refers doctrinally both to the potentiality for Enlightenment (Buddhahood) with which every being is endowed (cf. the Christian term, "the Christ within") and, what is more important in this context, to the state of absolute truth wherein exists no distinction between mind and Mind, delusion and Wisdom. In practice, revering all beings as supremely holy, no matter how gross or monstrous some may appear to be, just as one esteems the wish-fulfilling gem whether housed in an ivory casket or hidden in a dung-heap, means discarding every grain of scorn, malice, hatred, cruelty. No one sincerely dedicated to this practice would wilfully harm others, discriminate among them or withhold sympathy, compassion and whatever aid lay within his power. Of course attaining such an attitude is easier said than done—lifelong habits and prejudices are hard to set aside—but the very aspiration to see all beings as holy makes one kinder and more tolerant. Carrying the practice further revolutionises one's character; ugly and perverse qualities decrease by leaps and bounds.

"Hear all sounds as mantra," that is to say as holy, also relates to the doctrine that phenomena in their absolute state are beyond duality, from which it follows that "raucous" and "melodious" are illusory distinctions. The practice is comparatively easy; one learns to hear "raucous" as "melodious" by a process similar to playing the children's game of seeing pictures in the fire. Soon one can mentally convert the din of midnight traffic into something just as noisy but pleasant, such as the roar of ocean waves dashing against a rocky shore. The immediate consequence is to eliminate what, for city-dwellers especially constitutes one of the greatest sources of disturbance in modern life. The further consequence and true purpose is to win increasing perception of the holiness inherent in all things.

"Recognise all places as Nirvana" is an injunction to perceive things as they really are. Since the myriad transient forms comprise an aspect of the undifferentiated Void, there can be no *leaving* the realm of form, no *entering* Nirvana, but simply a cleansing of the mind that results in direct perception of what has always been from the first. "Going to" resolves itself into awakening to "what is here." In practice, this task is the easiest of the three, being (at the earliest stage) analogous to conjuring delightful figures from the patterns formed by frost on glass or the grain of a flat wooden surface, or willing one's eyes to discern glimpses of sea amidst a vista of blue hills, or viewing clouds as peaks and peaks as clouds. Presently one comes to see beauty in the most unpromising surrounding—bleak concrete yards or grimy brick walls. Dung takes on the loveliness of amber; spittle is recognised as partaking of the holy essence of the Void. It is not a matter of learning to perceive falsely, but of teaching mind and senses to recognise the beauty and holiness of all that is. Once, when driving, I came upon what seemed to be a mass of lovely scarlet blossom clothing distant trees, only to find on drawing nearer some ordinary trees fenced by corrugated zinc with a coating of red lead. What I had seen as exquisitely beautiful now struck me as intensely ugly, yet nothing in the scene had changed, only the manner of my viewing. The experience brought home to me that beauty and ugliness are but the creations of our own minds.

Acquiring a tantric attitude, though still far removed from the attainment of intuitive wisdom, creates a lively awareness of the perfection transfusing the world of form. Were someone like my son to get thus far, he might be content to rest in that joyful state, but it is likely he would need no urging to go further. Those who sense imminent reality envision it sometimes as a divine being, sometimes as a divine state. What matters is not whether one thinks of it as God or Tao, but the certainty of its existence. This certainty is what in Mahayana terminology is called "faith"; but faith in an ultimate perfection not conceptually defined differs greatly from faith centred upon a particular concept and name, whether Allah or Jehova, and no other. Buddhists are discouraged from attempting to conceptualise what is intuitively apprehended; to all attempts to define it, the Buddhist answer is "Not so, not so, not so." Similarly Taoists hold that whatever can be conveyed in words is not the Eternal Tao.

The Third Step

For those who desire to go still further, acquiring such an attitude of mind must be accompanied by contemplative practice. The sense of something infinitely holy transfusing all that is perceived arouses a thirst for clear, direct perception of that sublime reality. To attain it, ego-consciousness must be progressively purged; wherever a sense of "I" and "IT" ("HIM") and of "I" and "others" persists, duality—that king of demons—continues to deceive. The finite mind must address itself to realising its unity with Mind. This is a hard task, for the seeming "ego," albeit no more than the illusory creation of dualistic thought, is powerful enough to fight tenaciously for continued recognition as "the real me." To frugal living and the containment of inordinate desires must now be added firm discipline. It is a dangerous error to suppose that, at this stage, the adept is ready to discard all rules of conduct on the grounds that good and evil, being a dual concept, cannot in reality exist, or that passion must be given free rein to destroy passion; though both these doctrines are valid, they pertain to the realm of absolute truth and are suited only to adepts who having successfully practised rigorous austerity for many years, have transcended the stage of responding to ego-prompted desire; were people of less than great attainment to renounce self-discipline, contemplative practice would be attended by certain failure. The stress placed by Buddhist meditation teachers on the need for restraint may discourage beginners, who are likely to react to it by exclaiming: "What you preach is positively calvinistic in its joylessness!" But that is a confused and superficial view. Enjoyment that causes no hurt is not held to be sinful; when adepts on the Short Path renounce certain pleasures, the restrictions are analogous to those governing an athlete's training; those who undertake a valorous task voluntarily accept a mode of life not required of ordinary people; moreover, the joys they renounce are as nothing compared with those they expect to attain.

Just as intensive meditation unaccompanied by a special discipline would surely prove a waste of effort, so, too, it would be folly to practise it without simultaneously cultivating compassion—the surest antidote to discrimination between "self" and "other." Such qualities as frugality, restraint and overflowing compassion are contrary to what is often said to be human nature, but they are fully consonant with one's *real* nature which, as the meditator presently discovers, is not "his" at all. As to the method of meditation and whether certain physical yogas should accompany it, or whether some other method such as concentration upon a sacred formula should replace it—these depend on individual aptitudes. For some, an overtly devotional approach is best; for some, the Ch'an (Zen) methods; for others, a more nearly intellectual approach like that of the Pure Consciousness Sect. Only an able meditation teacher familiar with his pupil's character and capabilities is in a position to give advice on this matter. In all cases, to attain that direct perception of reality which is the crown of mystical experience requires an unswerving dedication that makes great demands upon the adept.

I have observed that Westerners generally are prone to a danger that scarcely arises among Asians. Whether because of over-dependence upon intellect or because they fight shy of attitudes reminiscent of the religion of their childhood, they tend to disdain devotional practices. Nevertheless, a profound sense of reverence, awe, devotion is essential. Though it is from Ch'an (Zen) texts that a concept of non-devotional Buddhism derives, I doubt if there are Ch'an (Zen) temples anywhere in the East where offerings are not made before statues of the Buddhas and of the Wisdom Bodhisattva, Manjusri. No matter what provisional concept one may hold (whether of a divine being, divine state or divine state of being), reverence cannot be dispensed with; for then the meditator must surely fall into the error of reflecting "*I* have progressed thus far," "*I* have attained such and such a state"—thoughts which instantly negate all progress by giving new life to that pertinacious delusion, "I." For all that Ch'an (Zen) meditation stresses "self-power," Chinese and Japanese adepts seldom question the identity of "self-power" and "other-power," since "inside" and "outside" are meaningless in connection with space-transcending mind.

I particularly treasure the advice of one of my Tibetan teachers who, speaking of levels of practice suited to varying degrees of understanding and attainment, said: "Some start by worshipping an external object as though it were a self-existent deity; next they are taught to visualise the object of devotion as residing in their hearts, then to perceive that self and object are identical; and finally all concepts are abandoned. But, at whichever level you practise, learn to embrace them all; for each expresses an aspect of truth that it would be unwise to discard."

Similarly, in temples of the Ch'an Sect, though meditation is of the "self-power" kind, devotional rites are daily performed, lest the meditators lose perspective with dangerous consequences. Although it is clearly recognised that the celestial Buddhas and Bodhisattvas are personifications of various attributes of the Wisdom streaming from Pure Mind (apart from which neither they nor any other beings or objects can be said to exist), during devotional rites they are treated *as though* they were actual deities. To regard them as separate from one's own mind (which is also Mind) would be delusion, yet they cannot be dismissed like characters in an unfounded legend (Father Christmas, for example); at the level of relative truth, the entities they personify exist. The objection that worshipping celestial beings involves an element of make-believe can also be met in another way. In a universe where naught but Mind exists, all concepts, all objects are ultimately void (and therefore make-believe) what is thought or dreamed or visualised is no less real than what is objectively perceived.

In my view, when a Christian mystic deep in prayer or meditation experiences a divine response, when a Pure Land devotee feels the presence of Amitabha or Kuanyin, and when a Ch'an meditator feels Mind respond to mind, all three are visited by an identical experience; yet it might not do for them to interchange their methods, since each has been conditioned to conceive of the Inconceivable in his own way. With the dawning of intuitive wisdom in their minds, they will be able to laugh together at their former differences.

The reason why "other-power" methods are more effective in some cases appears to me simple, though it may not be simple to convey. With the "self-power" method taught in Ch'an monasteries, a degree of effort is involved. Well, in a sense, all meditation involves effort in that one pursues a certain course in order to achieve a goal; but, in another sense, it must be effortless; there must be no straining of the mind. When engaged in "other-power" meditation, it is easier to dispense with effort. The adept says to himself: "Stop striving! There is nothing you can do of yourself. Just be still and attentive." With stillness, something, as it were, "enters in," but not until, besides abandoning effort, one has abandoned also the desire for attainment; for such desire (or its converse, fear of failure) creates a stir that mars mind's perfect stillness. If I have not made my point, I am sorry I have no better way of expressing it. One thing is sure: what is apprehended by some as a particular and exclusive being (God), by others as a celestial "being" of their own or their teacher's choosing, and by yet others as no being at all is in all three cases identical.

Where the mystic's path is concerned, I doubt that any real importance attaches to whether the adept subscribes to one religion or another (although Buddhism and Taosim do have the advantage that, besides *openly* proclaiming the supremacy of mystical experience, they have evolved very effective methods of attaining it). I hope that this rather personal account of some aspects of Chinese and Tibetan mysticism will be of interest to people of many faiths; for it should not be difficult to adapt contemplative methods to any sort of doctrine—the more so as, beyond a certain point, doctrinal differences cease to matter one iota.

Though the Way is arduous and those who follow it are sometimes beset by fiends—boredom, frustration, sensuous longing, discouragement, despair—the goal is unutterably sublime. One glimpse of its splendour is enough to rout those fiends for long enough to gain new courage to defy them. Of the many names given to the

Nameless, I love best the Taoist term, Tao or Way, just because it has no flavour of a special creed or concept. May there be followers of the Way for as long as the universe endures and may they be happy in the knowledge that they belong to a band of men whose compassion has leavened with sweetness this strife-torn earth since the beginning of recorded history!

Six

The Existence
of God

Introduction

What is the real meaning of the question, "Does God exist?" Of course, it is
for each person to answer this for himself, but for many people in the modern
world, shaped as it has been by rationalistic and scientific thinking, the question
as to the existence of God has led to the search for intellectual proof. Is it
possible to *know* that God exists, independently of any personal commitment
or direct experience of God? Can the intellect, by itself, lead us to a definite
conclusion about the reality or unreality of a supreme being?

The great Christian thinkers of the Middle Ages, here represented by
St. Anselm of Canterbury and St. Thomas Aquinas, while themselves men of
faith, sought to demonstrate that even the isolated intellect, without faith, can
be brought to the conviction that a supreme being must exist. **St. Anselm's**
"Ontological Argument" is an extraordinarily ingenious example of such a
proof. The reader may wish to sit down quietly with this proof and follow it
with care before turning to the objection that was made by Anselm's contemporary, **Gaunilo,** and the reply which Anselm made to Gaunilo. If the
reader is like countless other students of religion throughout the centuries,
he will find the ontological argument as difficult to deny as it is to accept, and
he will understand why the question of its validity continues to challenge
philosophers and theologians up to the present day.

In the next selection, the greatest of all medieval Catholic philosophers,
St. Thomas Aquinas, neatly summarizes the arguments for the existence of
God that have been grouped under the label "the cosmological proofs." The
method here is to examine nature, and through principles observed to be in
operation in nature to infer logically the necessary existence of a supreme
being. Anyone who has ever looked at the world that surrounds him and
wondered about a first cause of all that exists will appreciate why these
arguments in one form or another have always been part of religious thinking.

Equally "native" to the questioning religious mind is the proof of the existence of God known as "the teleological argument," here expressed with exemplary clarity by the eighteenth-century philosopher, **William Paley.** Just as the existence of a watch implies the existence of a watchmaker, Paley argues, so the purposefully ordered universe with all its elements harmoniously designed to work together implies the existence of a creator. This proof has also been called "the argument from design," but it might as well have been named "the argument from wonder," being the logical formulation of the sense of awe one feels when contemplating the construction of even the most insignificant element in the world of nature.

One of the most intriguing modern responses to this question, one which has captured the imagination of many people who find no other proofs acceptable, was offered in the seventeenth century by the French scientist and philosopher, **Blaise Pascal.** Known as "Pascal's Wager," it says, to put it simply, that just by being alive a human being is inextricably involved in a "game" in which he must "bet" with his reason whether or not to believe in God. No intellectual certainty is possible in advance, but since what he has to gain (infinite happiness and immortality) far exceeds what he has to risk (his finite life), belief in the existence of God is an overwhelmingly sensible wager. In examining this proof, it is important to note that Pascal also offers counsel to those who may be intellectually convinced, but who still cannot feel an emotional commitment to believe. He offers what is in effect a general form of spiritual discipline—the struggle to master one's passions. This latter aspect of "Pascal's Wager" is often overlooked in many contemporary presentations.

But perhaps the whole enterprise of proving the existence of God is mistaken. Many philosophers, notably David Hume and Immanuel Kant, offered important refutations of the arguments on logical grounds. It remained, however, for the great nineteenth-century Danish thinker, **Søren Kierkegaard,** to argue that it was also a *spiritual* mistake to attempt to prove God's existence. In this brief excerpt from his *Philosophical Fragments*, Kierkegaard attempts to show how reason, when separated from the leap of faith, obscures the main element in our relationship to God, and instead of proving the existence of a transcendent deity actually only reduces the idea of God to its own limited understanding.

Our final selection is by the contemporary religious thinker, **Frithjof Schuon.** This essay is not easy reading, but it forms a unique contribution to this whole issue. Speaking from a vast conception of the reach of spiritual tradition, Schuon places the arguments for the existence of God in such a way as to cast doubt not on their validity, but on the way they have been treated by most modern philosophers and theologians. After reading Schuon's essay, the reader may well find himself pondering whether the very aim of passing independent judgment on the existence of God is itself a misunderstanding of the function of logical thought in the total spiritual life of mankind, and an underestimation of the variety of ways by which the traditions have offered to help man in search of God.

J. N.

The Ontological Argument

St. Anselm

St. Anselm of Canterbury was born in Acosta in 1033. In 1093 he was made Archbishop of Canterbury. During his years in the abbey he wrote the works for which he is best known, *The Monologium*, *The Proslogium* (which contains the famous ontological argument for the existence of God), and *Cur Deus Homo?*, a demonstration of the necessity of the Incarnation to atone for human sin. St. Anselm died in 1109.

Truly there is a God, although the fool hath said in his heart, There is no God.

And so, Lord, do thou, who dost give understanding to faith, give me, so far as thou knowest it to be profitable, to understand that thou art as we believe; and that thou art that which we believe. And, indeed, we believe that thou art a being than which nothing greater can be conceived. Or is there no such nature, since the fool hath said in his heart, there is no God? (Psalms xiv. i). But, at any rate, this very fool, when he hears of this being of which I speak—a being than which nothing greater can be conceived—understands what he hears, and what he understands is in his understanding; although he does not understand it to exist.

For, it is one thing for an object to be in the understanding, and another to understand that the object exists. When a painter first conceives of what he will afterwards perform, he has it in his understanding, but he does not yet understand it to be, because he has not yet performed it. But after he has made the painting, he both has it in his understanding and he understands that it exists, because he has made it.

Hence, even the fool is convinced that something exists in the understanding, at least, than which nothing greater can be conceived. For, when he hears of this, he understands it. And whatever is understood, exists in the understanding. And assuredly that, than which nothing greater can be conceived, cannot exist in the understanding alone. For, suppose it exists in the understanding alone: then it can be conceived to exist in reality; which is greater.

Therefore, if that, than which nothing greater can be conceived, exists in the understanding alone, the very being, than which nothing greater can be conceived, is one, than which a greater can be conceived. But obviously this is impossible. Hence, there is no doubt that there exists a being, than that which nothing greater can be conceived, and it exists both in the understanding and in reality.

Source: "The Proslogium" and Gaunilo, "In Behalf of the Fool," in *St. Anselm: Basic Writings*, 2nd ed., trans. by S. N. Deane, intro. by Charles Hartshorne (La Salle, Ill., 1962). Reprinted by permission of Open Court Publishing Company.

God cannot be conceived not to exist—God is that, than which nothing greater can be conceived.—That which can be conceived not to exist is not God.

And it assuredly exists so truly, that it cannot be conceived not to exist. For, it is possible to conceive of a being which cannot be conceived not to exist; and this is greater than one which can be conceived not to exist. Hence, if that, than which nothing greater can be conceived, can be conceived not to exist, it is not that, than which nothing greater can be conceived. But this is an irreconcilable contradiction. There is, then, so truly a being than which nothing greater can be conceived to exist, that it cannot even be conceived not to exist; and this being thou art, O Lord, our God.

So truly, therefore, dost thou exist, O Lord, my God, that thou canst not be conceived not to exist; and rightly. For, if a mind could conceive of a being better than thee, the creature would rise above the Creator; and this is most absurd. And, indeed, whatever else there is, except thee alone, can be conceived not to exist. To thee alone, therefore, it belongs to exist more truly than all other beings, and hence in a higher degree than all others. For, whatever else exists does not exist so truly, and hence in a less degree it belongs to it to exist. Why, then, has the fool said in his heart, there is no God (Psalms xiv. 1), since it is so evident, to a rational mind, that thou dost exist in the highest degree of all? Why, except that he is dull and a fool?

How the fool has said in his heart what cannot be conceived.—A thing may be conceived in two ways: (1) when the word signifying it is conceived; (2) when the thing itself is understood; As far as the word goes, God can be conceived not to exist; in reality he cannot.

But how has the fool said in his heart what he could not conceive; or how is it that he could not conceive what he said in his heart? since it is the same to say in the heart, and to conceive.

But, if really, nay, since really, he both conceived, because he said in his heart; and did not say in his heart, because he could not conceive; there is more than one way in which a thing is said in the heart or conceived. For, in one sense, an object is conceived, when the word signifying it is conceived; and in another, when the very entity, which the object is, is understood.

In the former sense, then, God can be conceived not to exist; but in the latter, not at all. For no one who understands what fire and water are can conceive fire to be water, in accordance with the nature of the facts themselves, although this is possible according to the words. So, then, no one who understands what God is can conceive that God does not exist; although he says these words in his heart, either without any, or with some foreign signification. For God is that than which a greater cannot be conceived. And he who thoroughly understands this, assuredly understands that this being so truly exists, that not even in concept can it be non-existent. Therefore, he who understands that God so exists, cannot conceive that he does not exist.

I thank thee, gracious Lord, I thank thee; because what I formerly believed by thy bounty, I now so understand by thine illumination, that if I were unwilling to believe that thou dost exist, I should not be able not to understand this to be true.

Gaunilo's Reply to St. Anselm

Gaunilo, a contemporary of St. Anselm, was a monk who is remembered for his critique of St. Anselm's argument for the existence of God.

> "*For if it [an island more excellent than all other countries] does not exist, any land which really exists will be more excellent than it; and so the island already understood by you to be more excellent will not be more excellent.*" *If a man should try to prove to me by such reasoning that this island truly exists, . . . either I should believe that he was jesting, or I know not which I ought to regard as the greater fool: myself, . . . or him.*

The fool might make this reply:

This being is said to be in my understanding already, only because I understand what is said. Now could it not with equal justice be said that I have in my understanding all manner of unreal objects, having absolutely no existence in themselves, because I understand these things if one speaks of them, whatever they may be?

Unless indeed it is shown that this being is of such a character that it cannot be held in concept like all unreal objects, or objects whose existence is uncertain: and hence I am not able to conceive of it when I hear of it, or to hold it in concept; but I must understand it and have it in my understanding; because, it seems, I cannot conceive of it in any other way than by understanding it, that is, by comprehending in my knowledge its existence in reality.

But if this is the case, in the first place there will be no distinction between what has precedence in time—namely, the having of an object in the understanding—and what is subsequent in time—namely, the understanding that an object exists; as in the example of the picture, which exists first in the mind of the painter, and afterwards in his work.

Moreover, the following assertion can hardly be accepted: that this being, when it is spoken of and heard of, cannot be conceived not to exist in the way in which even God can be conceived not to exist. For if this is impossible, what was the object of this argument against one who doubts or denies the existence of such a being?

Finally, that this being so exists that it cannot be perceived by an understanding convinced of its own indubitable existence, unless this being is afterwards conceived of—this should be proved to me by an indisputable argument, but not by that which you have advanced: namely, that what I understand, when I hear it, already is in my understanding. For thus in my understanding, as I still think, could be all sorts of things whose existence is uncertain, or which do not exist at all, if some one whose words I should understand mentioned them. And so much the more if I should be deceived, as often happens, and believe in them: though I do not yet believe in the being whose existence you would prove. . . .

But that this being must exist, not only in the understanding but also in reality, is thus proved to me:

If it did not so exist, whatever exists in reality would be greater than it. And so the being which has been already proved to exist in my understanding, will not be greater than all other beings.

I still answer: if it should be said that a being which cannot be even conceived in terms of any fact, is in the understanding, I do not deny that this being is, accordingly, in my understanding. But since through this fact it can in no wise attain to real existence also, I do not yet concede to it that existence at all, until some certain proof of it shall be given.

For he who says that this being exists, because otherwise the being which is greater than all will not be greater than all, does not attend strictly enough to what he is saying. For I do not yet say, no, I even deny or doubt that this being is greater than any real object. Nor do I concede to it any other existence than this (if it should be called existence) which it has when the mind, according to a word merely heard, tries to form the image of an object absolutely unknown to it.

How, then, is the veritable existence of that being proved to me from the assumption, by hypothesis, that it is greater than all other beings? For I should still deny this, or doubt your demonstration of it, to this extent, that I should not admit that this being is in my understanding and concept even in the way in which many objects whose real existence is uncertain and doubtful, are in my understanding and concept. For it should be proved first that this being itself really exists somewhere; and then, from the fact that it is greater than all, we shall not hesitate to infer that it also subsists in itself.

For example: it is said that somewhere in the ocean is an island, which, because of the difficulty, or rather the impossibility, of discovering what does not exist, is called the lost island. And they say that this island has an inestimable wealth of all manner of riches and delicacies in greater abundance than is told of the Islands of the Blest; and that having no owner or inhabitant, it is more excellent than all other countries, which are inhabited by mankind, in the abundance with which it is stored.

Now if some one should tell me that there is such an island, I should easily understand his words, in which there is no difficulty. But suppose that he went on to say, as if by a logical inference: "You can no longer doubt that this island which is more excellent than all lands exists somewhere, since you have no doubt that it is in your understanding. And since it is more excellent not to be in the understanding alone, but to exist both in the understanding and in reality, for this reason it must exist. For if it does not exist, any land which really exists will be more excellent than it; and so the island already understood by you to be more excellent will not be more excellent."

If a man should try to prove to me by such reasoning that this island truly exists, and that its existence should no longer be doubted, either I should believe that he was jesting, or I know not which I ought to regard as the greater fool: myself, supposing that I should allow this proof; or him, if he should suppose that he had established with any certainty the existence of this island. For he ought to show first that the hypothetical excellence of this island exists as a real and indubitable fact, and in no wise as any unreal object, or one whose existence is uncertain, in my understanding.

St. Anselm's Reply to the Criticisms of Gaunilo

But, you say, suppose that someone imagined an island in the ocean, surpassing all lands in its fertility. Because of the difficulty, or rather the impossibility, of finding something that does not exist, it might well be called "Lost Island." By reasoning like yours, he might then say that we cannot doubt that it truly exists in reality, because anyone can easily conceive it from a verbal description.[1] I state confidently that if anyone discovers something for me, other than that "than which a greater cannot be thought," existing either in reality or in thought alone, to which the logic of my argument can be applied, I shall find his lost island and give it to him, never to be lost again. But it now seems obvious that this being than which a greater cannot be thought cannot be thought of as nonexistent, because it exists by such a sure reason of truth. For otherwise it would not exist at all. In short, if anyone says that he thinks it does not exist, I say that when he thinks this, he either thinks of something than which a greater cannot be thought or he does not think. If he does not think, he does not think of what he is not thinking of as nonexistent. But if he does think, then he thinks of something which cannot be thought of as non-existent. For if it could be thought of as nonexistent, it could be thought of as having a beginning and an end. But this is impossible. Therefore, if anyone thinks of it, he thinks of something that cannot even be thought of as nonexistent. But he who thinks of this does not think that it does not exist; if he did, he would think what cannot be thought. Therefore, that than which a greater cannot be thought cannot be thought of as nonexistent.

You say, moreover, that when it is said that the highest reality cannot be *thought of* as nonexistent, it would perhaps be better to say that it cannot be *understood* as nonexistent, or even as possibly nonexistent. But it is more correct to say, as I said, that it cannot be thought. For if I had said that the reality itself cannot be understood not to exist, perhaps you yourself, who say that according to the very definition of the term what is false cannot be understood, would object that nothing that is can be understood as nonexistent. For it is false to say that what exists does not exist. Therefore it would not be peculiar to God to be unable to be understood as nonexistent. But if some one of the things that most certainly are can be understood as nonexistent, other certain things can similarly be understood as nonexistent. But this objection cannot be applied to "thinking," if it is rightly considered. For although none of the things that exist can be understood not to exist, still they can all be thought of as nonexistent, except that which most fully is. For all those things—and only those—which have a beginning or end or are composed of parts can be thought of as nonexistent, along with anything that does not exist as a whole anywhere or at any time (as I have already said). But the only being that cannot be thought of as nonexistent is that in which no thought finds beginning or end or composition of parts, but which any thought finds as a whole, always and everywhere.

You must realize, then, that you can think of yourself as nonexistent, even while you know most certainly that you exist. I am surprised that you said you did not know this. For we think of many things as nonexistent when we know that they exist, and of many things as existent when we know that they do not exist—all this not by a real judgment, but by imagining that what we think is so. And indeed, we can think of something as nonexistent, even while we know that it exists, because we are able at the same time to think the one and know the other. And yet we cannot

[1] Cf. Gaunilo, *Pro insipiente*, 6.

think of it as nonexistent, while we know that it exists, because we cannot think of something as at once existent and nonexistent. Therefore, if anyone distinguishes these two senses of the statement in this way, he will understand that nothing, as long as it is known to exist, can be thought of as nonexistent, and that whatever exists, except that than which a greater cannot be thought, can be thought of as nonexistent, even when it is known to exist. So, then, it is peculiar to God to be unable to be thought of as nonexistent, and nevertheless many things, as long as they exist, cannot be thought of as nonexistent. I think that the way in which it can still be said that God is thought of as nonexistent is stated adequately in the little book itself.[2]

[2] Cf. *Proslogion*, Chapter IV.

Five Proofs of the Existence of God

St. Thomas Aquinas

St. Thomas Aquinas (1225–1274), born in Roccasicca (lower Italy), received his education at the Monte Cassino Abbey and in Naples, Cologne, and Paris. He taught theology in Paris (1256–1272) and for several years in Rome and other cities. He is generally regarded as the greatest of the scholastic theologians. His major works are *Summa Theologica* and *Summa Contra Gentiles*, which respectively synthesized Aristotelian and Christian doctrines and attempted to answer the objections against Catholicism.

Whether God Exists?

Objection 1. It seems that God does not exist; because if one of two contraries be infinite, the other would be altogether destroyed. But the name *God* means that He is infinite goodness. If, therefore, God existed, there would be no evil discoverable; but there is evil in the world. Therefore God does not exist.

Obj. 2. Further, it is superfluous to suppose that what can be accounted for by a few principles has been produced by many. But it seems that everything we see in the world can be accounted for by other principles, supposing God did not exist. For all natural things can be reduced to one principle, which is nature; and all

Source: Anton C. Pegis (ed.), *Basic Writings of St. Thomas Aquinas*, Vol. 1 (New York, 1945), Copyright © 1945 by Random House, Inc., and Burns & Oates. Reprinted by permission.

voluntary things can be reduced to one principle, which is human reason, or will. Therefore there is no need to suppose God's existence.

On the contrary, It is said in the person of God: *I am who am* (Exod. iii. 14).

I answer that, The existence of God can be proved in five ways.

The first and more manifest way is the argument from motion. It is certain, and evident to our senses, that in the world some things are in motion. Now whatever is moved is moved by another, for nothing can be moved except it is in potentiality to that towards which it is moved; whereas a thing moves inasmuch as it is in act. For motion is nothing else than the reduction of something from potentiality to actuality. But nothing can be reduced from potentiality to actuality, except by something in a state of actuality. Thus that which is actually hot, as fire, makes wood, which is potentially hot, to be actually hot, and thereby moves and changes it. Now it is not possible that the same thing should be at once in actuality and potentiality in the same respect, but only in different respects. For what is actually hot cannot simultaneously be potentially hot; but it is simultaneously potentially cold. It is therefore impossible that in the same respect and in the same way a thing should be both mover and moved, *i.e.,* that it should move itself. Therefore, whatever is moved must be moved by another. If that by which it is moved be itself moved, then this also must needs be moved by another, and that by another again. But this cannot go on to infinity, because then there would be no first mover, and, consequently, no other mover, seeing that subsequent movers move only inasmuch as they are moved by the first mover; as the staff moves only because it is moved by the hand. Therefore it is necessary to arrive at a first mover, moved by no other; and this everyone understands to be God.

The second way is from the nature of efficient cause. In the world of sensible things we find there is an order of efficient causes. There is no case known (neither is it, indeed, possible) in which a thing is found to be the efficient cause of itself; for so it would be prior to itself, which is impossible. Now in efficient causes it is not possible to go to infinity, because in all efficient causes following in order, the first is the cause of the intermediate cause, and the intermediate is the cause of the ultimate cause, whether the intermediate cause be several, or one only. Now to take away the cause is to take away the effect. Therefore, if there be no first cause among efficient causes, there will be no ultimate, nor any intermediate, cause. But if in efficient causes it is possible to go on to infinity, there will be no first efficient cause, neither will there be an ultimate effect, nor any intermediate efficient causes; all of which is plainly false. Therefore it is necessary to admit a first efficient cause, to which everyone gives the name of God.

The third way is taken from possibility and necessity, and runs thus. We find in nature things that are possible to be and not to be, since they are found to be generated, and to be corrupted, and consequently, it is possible for them to be and not to be. But it is impossible for these always to exist, for that which can not-be at some time is not. Therefore, if everything can not-be, then at one time there was nothing in existence. Now if this were true, even now there would be nothing in existence, because that which does not exist begins to exist only through something already existing. Therefore, if at one time nothing was in existence, it would have been impossible for anything to have begun to exist; and thus even now nothing would be in existence—which is absurd. Therefore, not all beings are merely possible, but there must exist something the existence of which is necessary. But every necessary thing either has its necessity caused by another, or not. Now it is impossible to go on to infinity in necessary things which have their necessity caused by another, as has been already proved in regard to efficient causes. Therefore we cannot but admit the existence of some being having of itself its own necessity, and not receiving it from another, but rather causing in others their necessity. This all men speak of as God.

The fourth way is taken from the gradation to be found in things. Among beings there are some more and some less good, true, noble, and the like. But *more* and *less* are predicated of different things according as they resemble in their different ways something which is the maximum, as a thing is said to be hotter according as it more nearly resembles that which is hottest; so that there is something which is truest, something best, something noblest, and, consequently, something which is most being, for those things that are greatest in truth are greatest in being, as it is written in [Aristotle's] *Metaphysics* ii. Now the maximum in any genus is the cause of all in that genus, as fire, which is the maximum of heat, is the cause of all hot things, as is said in the same book. Therefore there must also be something which is to all beings the cause of their being, goodness, and every other perfection; and this we call God.

The fifth way is taken from the governance of the world. We see that things which lack knowledge, such as natural bodies, act for an end, and this is evident from their acting always, or nearly always, in the same way, so as to obtain the best result. Hence it is plain that they achieve their end, not fortuitously, but designedly. Now whatever lacks knowledge cannot move towards an end, unless it be directed by some being endowed with knowledge and intelligence; as the arrow is directed by the archer. Therefore some intelligent being exists by whom all natural things are directed to their end: and this being we call God.

Reply Obj. 1 As Augustine says: *Since God is the highest good, He would not allow any evil to exist in His works; unless His omnipotence and goodness were such as to bring good even out of evil.* This is part of the infinite goodness of God, that He should allow evil to exist, and out of it produce good.

Reply Obj. 2. Since nature works for a determinate end under the direction o a higher agent, whatever is done by nature must be traced back to God as to its first cause. So likewise whatever is done voluntarily must be traced back to some higher cause other than human reason and will, since these can change and fail; for all things that are changeable and capable of defect must be traced back to an immovable and self-necessary first principle, as has been shown.

The Teleological Argument

William Paley

William Paley (1743–1805), Archdeacon of Carlisle, wrote a number of apologetic works, of which the two most famous are his *Evidences of Christianity* and *Natural Theology, or Evidences of the Existences and Attributes of the Deity Collected from the Appearances of Nature.*

Statement of the Argument

In crossing a heath, suppose I pitched my foot against a *stone*, and were asked how the stone came to be there, I might possibly answer, that, for anything I knew to the contrary, it had lain there forever; nor would it, perhaps be very easy to show the absurdity of this answer. But suppose I found a *watch* upon the ground, and it should be inquired how the watch happened to be in that place, I should hardly think of the answer which I had before given—that, for anything I knew, the watch might have always been there. Yet why should not this answer serve for the watch as well as for the stone? Why is it not as admissible in the second case as in the first? For this reason, and for no other, viz., that, when we come to inspect the watch, we perceive (what we could not discover in the stone) that its several parts are framed and put together for a purpose, e.g. that they are so formed and adjusted as to produce motion, and that motion so regulated as to point out the hour of the day; that, if the different parts had been differently shaped from what they are, if a different size from what they are, or placed after any other manner, or in any other order than that in which they are placed, either no motion at all would have been carried on in the machine, or none which would have answered the use that is now served by it. To reckon up a few of the plainest of these parts, and of their offices, all tending to one result:—We see a cylindrical box containing a coiled elastic spring, which, by its endeavor to relax itself, turns round the box. We next observe a flexible chain (artificially wrought for the sake of flexure) communicating the action of the spring from the box to the fusee. We then find a series of wheels, the teeth of which catch in, and apply to, each other, conducting the motion from the fusee to the balance, and from the balance to the pointer, and at the same time, by the size and shape of those wheels, so regulating that motion as to terminate in causing an index, by an equable and measured progression, to pass over a given space in a given time. We take notice that the wheels are made of brass, in order to keep them from rust; the springs of steel, no other metal being so elastic; that over the face of the watch there is placed a glass, a material employed in no other part of

Source: William Paley, *Natural Theology* (1802).

the work, but in the room of which, of there had been any other than a transparent substance, the hour could not be seen without opening the case. This mechanism being observed (it requires indeed an examination of the instrument, and perhaps some previous knowledge of the subject, to perceive and understand it; but being once, as we have said, observed and understood), the inference, we think, is inevitable, that the watch must have had a maker; that there must have existed, at some time, and at some place or other, an artificer or artificers who formed it for the purpose which we find it actually to answer; who comprehended its construction, and designed its use.

I. Nor would it, I apprehend, weaken the conclusion, that we had never seen a watch made; that we had never known an artist capable of making one; that we were altogether incapable of executing such a piece of workmanship ourselves, or of understanding in what manner it was performed; all this being no more than what is true of some exquisite remains of ancient art, of some lost arts, and, to the generality of mankind, of the more curious productions of modern manufacture. Does one man in a million know how oval frames are turned? Ignorance of this kind exalts our opinion of the unseen and unknown artist's skill, if he be unseen and unknown, but raises no doubt in our minds of the existence and agency of such an artist, at some former time, and in some place or other. Nor can I perceive that it varies at all the inference, whether the question arise concerning a human agent, or concerning an agent of a different species, or an agent possessing, in some respect, a different nature.

II. Neither, secondly, would it invalidate our conclusion, that the watch sometimes went wrong, or that it seldom went exactly right. The purpose of the machinery, the design, and the designer, might be evident, and, in the case supposed, would be evident, in whatever way we accounted for the irregularity of the movement, or whether we could account for it or not. It is not necessary that a machine be perfect, in order to show with what design it was made; still less necessary, where the only question is, whether it were made with any design at all.

III. Nor, thirdly, would it bring any uncertainty into the argument, if there were a few parts of the watch, concerning which we could not discover, or had not yet discovered, in what manner they conduced to the general effect; or even some parts, concerning which we could not ascertain whether they conduced to that effect in any manner whatever. For, as to the first branch of the case, if by the loss, or disorder, or decay of the parts in question, the movement of the watch were found in fact to be stopped, or disturbed, or retarded, no doubt would remain in our minds as to the utility or intention of these parts, although we should be unable to investigate the manner according to which, or the connection by which, the ultimate effect depended upon their action or assistance; and the more complex is the machine, the more likely is this obscurity to arise. Then, as to the second thing supposed, namely, that there were parts which might be spared without prejudice to the movement of the watch, and that he had proved this by experiment, these superfluous parts, even if we were completely assured that they were such, would not vacate the reasoning which we had instituted concerning other parts. The indication of contrivance remained, with respect to them, nearly as it was before.

IV. Nor, fourthly, would any man in his senses think the existence of the watch, with its various machinery, accounted for, by being told that it was one out of possible combinations of material forms; that whatever he had found in the place where he found the watch, must have contained some internal configuration or other; and that this configuration might be the structure now exhibited, viz., of the works of a watch, as well as a different structure.

V. Nor, fifthly, would it yield his inquiry more satisfaction, to be answered, that there existed in things a principle of order, which had disposed the parts of the watch into their present form and situation. He never knew a watch made by the principle of order; nor can he even form to himself an idea of what is meant by a principle of order, distinct from the intelligence of the watchmaker.

VI. Sixthly, he would be surprised to hear that the mechanism of the watch was no proof of contrivance, only a motive to induce the mind to think so:

VII. And not less surprised to be informed, that the watch in his hand was nothing more than the result of the laws of *metallic* nature. It is a perversion of language to assign any law as the efficient, operative cause of anything. A law presupposes an agent; for it is only the mode according to which an agent proceeds; it implies a power; for it is the order according to which that power acts. Without this agent, without this power, which are both distinct from itself, the *law* does nothing, is nothing. The expression, "the law of metallic nature," may sound strange and harsh to a philosophic ear; but it seems quite as justifiable as some others which are more familiar to him such as "the law of vegetable nature," "the law of animal nature," or, indeed, as "the law of nature" in general, when assigned as the cause of phenomena in exclusion of agency and power, or when it is substituted into the place of these.

VIII. Neither, lastly, would our observer be driven out of his conclusion, or from his confidence in its truth, by being told that he knew nothing at all about the matter. He knows enough for his argument: he knows the utility of the end: he knows the subserviency and adaptation of the means to the end. These points being known, his ignorance of other points, his doubts concerning other points, affect not the certainty of his reasoning. The consciousness of knowing little need not beget a distrust of that which he does know. . . .

Application of the Argument

Every indication of contrivance, every manifestation of design, which existed in the watch, exist in the works of nature; with the difference, on the side of nature, of being greater and more, and that in a degree which exceeds all computation. I mean that the contrivances of nature surpass the contrivances of art, in the complexity, subtilty, and curiosity of the mechanism; and still more, if possible, do they go beyond them in number and variety; yet in a multitude of cases, are not less evidently mechanical, not less evidently contrivances, not less evidently accommodated to their end, or suited to their office, than are the most perfect productions of human ingenuity. . . .

The Wager

Blaise Pascal

Blaise Pascal (1623–1662). Philosopher, scientist and mystic, Pascal was already making important contributions to mathematics and physics by the time of his conversion to Jansenist Christianity in 1653. He is regarded as the founder of modern probability theory and he significantly advanced the study of differential calculus. His religious writings were published posthumously in 1670 under the title *Pensées de M. Pascal sur la religion et sur quelques autres subjets.*

. . .

Let us speak now according to natural lights.

If there is a God, He is infinitely incomprehensible, since, having neither parts nor limits, He has no affinity with us. We are incapable, therefore, of knowing either *what* He is or *if* He is. That being so, who will dare undertake to decide this question? Not we, who have no affinity with Him.

Who then can blame the Christians for not being able to give reasons for their belief, professing as they do a religion which they cannot explain by reason. They declare, when expounding it to the world, that it is foolishness, *stultitiam*;[1] and then you complain that they do not prove it! If they proved it they would give the lie to their own words; it is in lacking proof that they do not lack sense.

"Yes; but while this is an excuse for those who offer it as such, and frees them from blame for not basing their belief upon reason, it does not excuse those who accept what they say."

Let us examine this point and declare: "Either God exists, or He does not." To which view shall we incline? Reason cannot decide for us one way or the other: we are separated by an infinite gulf. At the extremity of this infinite distance a game is in progress, where either heads or tails may turn up. What will you wager? According to reason you cannot bet either way; according to reason you can defend neither proposition.

So do not attribute error to those who have made a choice; for you know nothing about it.

"No; I will not blame them for having made *this* choice, but for having made one at all; for since he who calls heads and he who calls tails are equally at fault, both are in the wrong. The right thing is not to wager at all." Yes; but a bet must be laid. There is no option: you have joined the game. Which will you choose, then? Since a choice has to be made, let us see which is of least moment to you. You have two things to lose, the true and the good; and two things to wager, your reason

Source: From *Pensées* by Blaise Pascal, translated by John Warrington. Copyright © 1960 by J. M. Dent & Sons Ltd. An Everyman's Library Edition. Published in the United States by E. P. Dutton & Co., Inc., and reprinted with their permission.

[1] I Cor. i. 18.

and your will, your knowledge and your happiness; and your nature has two things to shun, error and unhappiness. Your reason suffers no more violence in choosing one rather than the other, since you must of necessity make a choice. That is one point cleared up. But what about your happiness? Let us weigh the gain and the loss involved by wagering that God exists. Let us estimate these two possibilities: if you win, you win all; if you lose, you lose nothing. Wager then, without hesitation, that He does exist.

"That is all very fine. Yes, I must wager, but maybe I am wagering too much."

Let us see. Since there is an equal risk of winning and of losing, if you had only two lives to win you might still wager; but if there were three lives to win, you would still have to play (since you are under the necessity of playing); and being thus obliged to play, you would be imprudent not to risk your life to win three in a game where there is an equal chance of winning and of losing. But there is an eternity of life and happiness. That being so, if there were an infinity of chances of which only one was in your favour, you would still do right to stake one to win two, and you would act unwisely in refusing to play one life against three, in a game where you had only one chance out of an infinite number, if there were an infinity of an infinitely happy life to win. But here there *is* an infinity of infinitely happy life to win, one chance of winning against a finite number of chances of losing, and what you stake is finite. That removes all doubt as to choice; wherever the infinite is, and there is not an infinity of chances of loss against the chance of winning, there are no two ways about it, all must be given. And so, when a man is obliged to play, he must renounce reason to preserve his life, rather than risk it for infinite gain which is just as likely to occur as loss of nothing.

For it is no use alleging the uncertainty of winning and the certainty of risk, or to say that the infinite distance between the certainty of what one risks and the uncertainty of what one will win equals that between the finite good, which one certainly risks, and the infinite, which is uncertain. This is not so; every player risks a certainty to win an uncertainty, and yet he risks a finite certainty to win a finite uncertainty, without offending reason. There is no infinite distance between the certainty risked and the uncertainty of the gain; it is not true. There is, indeed, infinity between the certainty of winning and the certainty of losing, but the uncertainty of winning is proportionate to the certainty of what is risked, according to the proportion of the chances of gain and loss. Hence, if there are as many risks on one side as on the other, the right course is to play even; and then the certainty of the risk is equal to the uncertainty of the gain, so far are they from being infinitely distant. Thus our proposition is of infinite force, when there is the infinite at stake in a game where there are equal chances of winning and losing, but the infinite to gain. This is conclusive, and if men are capable of truth at all, there it is.

"I agree, I admit it; but is there yet no way of getting a look behind the scenes?" Yes, Scripture and the rest, etc.

"Quite; but my hands are tied and my mouth is gagged; I am forced to wager, and am not free; no one frees me from these bonds, and I am so made that I cannot believe. What then do you wish me to do?"

That is true. But understand at least that your inability to believe is the result of your passions; for, although reason inclines you to believe, you cannot do so. Try therefore to convince yourself, not by piling up proofs of God, but by subduing your passions. You desire to attain faith, but you do not know the way. You would like to cure yourself of unbelief, and you ask for remedies. Learn of those who were once bound and gagged like you, and who now stake all that they possess. They are men who know the road that you desire to follow, and who have been cured of a sickness of which you desire to be cured. Follow the way by which they set out, acting as if they already believed, taking holy water, having masses said, etc. Even this will naturally cause you to believe and blunt your cleverness.

"But that is what I fear." Why? what have you to lose?

But to show you that such practices lead you to belief, it is those things which will curtail your passions which are your main obstacles.

End of this discourse. Now, to what harm will you come by making this choice? You will be faithful, honest, humble, grateful, generous, a sincere friend, truthful. Certainly you will not enjoy those pernicious delights—glory and luxury; but will you not experience others?

I tell you, you will thereby profit in this life; and at every step you take along this road you will see so great an assurance of gain, and so little in what you risk, that you will come to recognize your stake to have been laid for something certain, infinite, which has cost you nothing.

"Oh, your discourse delights me, carries me away!"

If it pleases you and appears convincing, know that it has been uttered by a man who has knelt, both before and after its delivery, in prayer to that Being, infinite and without parts, before whom he submits all that is his, begging Him to subject to Himself all that is *yours*, for your own good and for His glory; and that thus strength is made consistent with lowliness.

God Cannot Be Proven

Søren Kierkegaard

Søren Kierkegaard (1813–1855) is now generally recognized as the greatest religious thinker of the nineteenth century. He brilliantly, wittily, and mercilessly attacked all attempts, implicit or explicit, to mitigate the demand for total self-questioning which he saw as the essence of the Christian message. The modern school of existentialism took much inspiration from his writings, but he is now also being seen as a unique interpreter of the inward-contemplative dimension of the Christian teaching. Among his many works are *Concluding Unscientific Postscript*, *Fear and Trembling*, and *The Concept of Dread*.

But what is this unknown something with which the Reason collides when inspired by its paradoxical passion, with the result of unsettling even man's knowledge of himself? It is the Unknown. It is not a human being, insofar as we know what man is; nor is it any other known thing. So let us call this unknown something: *God*. It is nothing more than a name we assign to it. The idea of demonstrating that this unknown something (God) exists could scarcely suggest itself to the Reason. For if God does not exist it would of course be impossible to prove it; and if he does exist it would be folly to attempt it. For at the very outset, in beginning my proof, I will have presupposed it, not as doubtful but as certain (a presupposition is never doubtful, for the very reason that it is a presupposition), since otherwise I would not begin, readily understanding that the whole would be impossible if he did not exist. But if when I speak of proving God's existence I mean that I propose to prove that the Unknown, which exists, is God, then I express myself unfortunately. For in that case I do not prove anything, least of all an existence, but merely develop the content of a conception. Generally speaking, it is a difficult matter to prove that anything exists; and what is still worse for the intrepid souls who undertake the venture, the difficulty is such that fame scarcely awaits those who concern themselves with it. The entire demonstration always turns into something very different from what it assumes to be, and becomes an additional development of the consequences that flow from [our] having assumed that the object in question exists. Thus I always reason from existence, not toward existence, whether I move in the sphere of palpable sensible fact or in the realm of thought. I do not, for example, prove that a stone exists, but that some existing thing is a stone. The procedure in a court of justice does not prove that a criminal exists, but that the accused, whose existence is given, is a criminal. Whether we call existence an *accessorium* or the eternal *prius*, it is never subject to demonstration. Let us take ample time for con-

Source: Søren Kierkegaard, *Philosophical Fragments*, 2nd ed., original translation by David Swenson, new introduction and commentary by Niels Thulstrup, translation revised and commentary translated by Howard V. Hong (Princeton, N.J., 1962), pp. 49–57. Copyright © 1936, 1962 by Princeton University Press; Princeton Paperback, 1967. Reprinted by permission.

sideration. We have no such reason for haste as have those who from concern for themselves or for God or for some other thing, must make haste to get its existence demonstrated. Under such circumstances there may indeed be need for haste, especially if the prover sincerely seeks to appreciate the danger that he himself, or the thing in question, may be non-existent unless the proof is finished; and does not surreptitiously entertain the thought that it exists whether he succeeds in proving it or not.

If it were proposed to prove Napoleon's existence from Napoleon's deeds, would it not be a most curious proceeding? His existence does indeed explain his deeds, but the deeds do not prove his existence, unless I have already understood the word "his" so as thereby to have assumed his existence. But Napoleon is only an individual, and insofar there exists no absolute relationship between him and his deeds; some other person might have performed the same deeds. Perhaps this is the reason why I cannot pass from the deeds to existence. If I call these deeds the deeds of Napoleon, the proof becomes superfluous, since I have already named him; if I ignore this, I can never prove from the deeds that they are Napoleon's, but only in a purely ideal manner that such deeds are the deeds of a great general, and so forth. But between God and his works there exists an absolute relationship; God is not a name but a concept. Is this perhaps the reason that his *essentia involvit existentiam* [essence involves existence]? The works of God are such that only God can perform them. Just so, but where then are the works of God? The works from which I would deduce his existence are not immediately given. The wisdom of God in nature, his goodness, his wisdom in the governance of the world—are all these manifest, perhaps, upon the very face of things? Are we not here confronted with the most terrible temptations to doubt, and is it not impossible finally to dispose of all these doubts? But from such an order of things I will surely not attempt to prove God's existence; and even if I began I would never finish, and would in addition have to live constantly in suspense, lest something so terrible should suddenly happen that my bit of proof would be demolished. From what works then do I propose to derive the proof? From the works as apprehended through an ideal interpretation, i.e., such as they do not immediately reveal themselves. But in that case it is not from the works that I prove God's existence. I merely develop the ideality I have presupposed, and because of my confidence in *this* I make so bold as to defy all objections, even those that have not yet been made. In beginning my proof I presuppose the ideal interpretation, and also that I will be successful in carrying it through; but what else is this but to presuppose that God exists, so that I really begin by virtue of confidence in him?

And how does God's existence emerge from the proof? Does it follow straightway, without any breach of continuity? Or have we not here an analogy to the behaviour of these toys, the little Cartesian dolls? As soon as I let go of the doll it stands on its head. As soon as I let it go—I must therefore let it go. So also with the proof for God's existence. As long as I keep my hold on the proof, i.e., continue to demonstrate, the existence does not come out, if for no other reason than that I am engaged in proving it; but when I let the proof go, the existence is there. But this act of letting go is surely also something; it is indeed a contribution of mine. Must not this also be taken into the account, this little moment, brief as it may be— it need not be long, for it is a *leap*. However brief this moment, if only an instantaneous now, this "now" must be included in the reckoning. If anyone wishes to have it ignored, I will use it to tell a little anecdote, in order to show that it really does exist. Chrysippus was experimenting with a sorites to see if he could not bring about a break in its quality, either progressively or retrogressively. But Carneades could not get it in his head when the new quality actually emerged. Then Chrysippus told him to try making a little pause in the reckoning, and so—so it would be easier to understand. Carneades replied: "With the greatest pleasure, please do not hesitate on my account; you may not only pause, but even lie down to sleep, and it will help you just as little; for when you awake we will begin again where you left off. Just so; it boots as little to try to get rid of something by sleeping as to try to come into the possession of something in the same manner."

Whoever therefore attempts to demonstrate the existence of God (except in the sense of clarifying the concept, and without the *reservatio finalis* noted above, that the existence emerges from the demonstration by a leap) proves in lieu thereof something else, something which at times perhaps does not need a proof, and in any case needs none better; for the fool says in his heart that there is no God, but whoever says in his heart or to men: "Wait just a little and I will prove it"—what a rare man of wisdom is he![1] If in the moment of beginning his proof it is not absolutely undetermined whether God exists or not, he does not prove it; and if it is thus undetermined in the beginning he will never come to begin, partly from fear of failure, since God perhaps does not exist, and partly because he has nothing with which to begin. A project of this kind would scarcely have been undertaken by the ancients. Socrates at least, who is credited with having put forth the physico-teleological proof for God's existence, did not go about it in any such manner. He always presupposes God's existence, and under this presupposition seeks to inter-penetrate nature with the idea of purpose. Had he been asked why he pursued this method, he would doubtless have explained that he lacked the courage to venture out upon so perilous a voyage of discovery without having made sure of God's existence behind him. At the word of God he casts his net as if to catch the idea of purpose; for nature herself finds many means of frightening the inquirer, and distracts him by many a digression.

The paradoxical passion of the Reason thus comes repeatedly into collision with the Unknown, which does indeed exist, but is unknown, and insofar does not exist. The Reason cannot advance beyond this point, and yet it cannot refrain in its paradoxicalness from arriving at this limit and occupying itself therewith. It will not serve to dismiss its relation to it simply by asserting that the Unknown does not exist, since this itself involves a relationship. But what then is the Unknown, since the designation of it as God merely signifies for us that it is unknown? To say that it is the Unknown because it cannot be known, and even if it were capable of being known, it could not be expressed, does not satisfy the demands of passion, though it correctly interprets the Unknown as a limit; but a limit is precisely a torment for passion, though it also serves as an incitement. And yet the Reason can come no further, whether it risks an issue *via negationis* or *via eminentia*.[2]

---

[1] What an excellent subject for a comedy of the higher lunacy!

[2] I.e., by the method of making negative statements about God or by the method of attributing known qualities to God in a higher degree (ED.).

What then is the Unknown? It is the limit to which the Reason repeatedly comes, and insofar, substituting a static form of conception for the dynamic, it is the different, the absolutely different. But because it is absolutely different, there is no mark by which it could be distinguished. When qualified as absolutely different it seems on the verge of disclosure, but this is not the case; for the Reason cannot even conceive an absolute unlikeness. The Reason cannot negate itself absolutely, but uses itself for the purpose, and thus conceives only such an unlikeness within itself as it can conceive by means of itself; it cannot absolutely transcend itself, and hence conceives only such a superiority over itself as it can conceive by means of itself. Unless the Unknown (God) remains a mere limiting conception, the single idea of difference will be thrown into a state of confusion, and become many ideas of many differences. The Unknown is then in a condition of dispersion διασπορά and the Reason may choose at pleasure from what is at hand and the imagination may suggest (the monstrous, the ludicrous, etc.).

But it is impossible to hold fast to a difference of this nature. Every time this is done it is essentially an arbitrary act, and deepest down in the heart of piety lurks the mad caprice which knows that it has itself produced its God. If no specific determination of difference can be held fast, because there is no distinguishing mark, like and unlike finally become identified with one another, thus sharing the fate of all such dialectical opposites. The unlikeness clings to the Reason and confounds it, so that the Reason no longer knows itself and quite consistently confuses itself with the unlikeness. On this point paganism has been sufficiently prolific in fantastic inventions. As for the last-named supposition, the self-irony of the Reason, I shall attempt to delineate it merely by a stroke or two, without raising any question of its being historical. There lives an individual whose appearance is precisely like that of other men; he grows up to manhood like others, he marries, he has an occupation by which he earns his livelihood, and he makes provision for the future as befits a man. For though it may be beautiful to live like the birds of the air, it is not lawful, and may lead to the sorriest of consequences: either starvation if one has enough persistence, or dependence on the bounty of others. This man is also God. How do I know? I cannot know it, for in order to know it I would have to know God, and the nature of the difference between God and man; and this I cannot know, because the Reason has reduced it to likeness with that from which it was unlike. Thus God becomes the most terrible of deceivers, because the Reason has deceived itself. The Reason has brought God as near as possible, and yet he is as far away as ever.

Concerning the Proofs of God

Frithjof Schuon

Frithjof Schuon was born in Switzerland in 1907 of German parents. His many books on religious subjects—from gnosis to the symbolism of American Indian ritual—reflect the range and authority of his spiritual insight. His essays are published regularly in the British journal, *Studies in Comparative Religion*, and he is the author of many books, including *Understanding Islam*, *Logic and Transcendence*, and *The Transcendent Unity of Religions*.

The classical proofs of God are as it were suspended between two extremes that lie beyond their reach—the one in an upward and the other in a downward direction, or the one through its plenitude and the other through its indigence—and these are, on the one hand, direct Intellection and, on the other, materialistic rationalism. There remains nonetheless a sufficiently wide area between these two positions to justify the existence of arguments which aim at establishing the evidence of the Divine Being in terms of logic. No doubt one can accept the supernatural straight away and have no need of such proofs, *Deo juvante;* nevertheless it shows a lack of sense of proportion and a certain temerity, hardly compatible, moreover, with true certitude and somewhat uncharitable with regard to the needs of others, to despise these proofs as though they were valueless in themselves and could have no possible usefulness. Such an attitude would indeed be strangely presumptuous, all the more so as a logical demonstration in favor of the Eternal and of our final ends always offers some illumination and some "consolation,"[1] even for those who possess certitude either through intellection or through grace. In any case, a man's spiritual behaviour does not depend only upon his conviction but also upon its perspicacity and depth.

Assuredly, there can be no question of underestimating the possibility of a spontaneous intuition which, if it is authentic, necessarily contains in an infused manner the certitude transmitted by the proofs of God or of the supernatural; but what is under no circumstances admissible is when lukewarm people claim to place themselves *de jure* above syllogisms, seeing that there are so many who have lost their faith while laboring under the belief that they could do without any sort of "scholasticism." This shows that below a certain spiritual level, which it would be most imprudent to attribute to oneself *a priori*, one should beware, not exactly of

---

Source: Frithjof Schuon, *Logic and Transcendence* (Bedfont, Middlesex, England, Harper Torchbooks, New York, 1975), pp. 56–74. Reprinted by permission of Perennial Books, Ltd.

[1] Or some "appeasement" (*itmi'nān*), as Moslems would say. The latter bestow a canonical importance on the proofs of God, and in the opinion of some, a knowledge of them is even obligatory. Thus Fudālī declares that "one is a believer (*mu'min*) only if one knows each of the fifty dogmas (nine of which concern the Prophet) with its particular proof"—which is exaggerated, but not altogether meaningless.

intuitive faith as such, but of its seeming imperviousness to every test, for there is a faith which may be effective only insofar as it is sheltered *de facto* from temptations. Doctrinal arguments obviously do not constitute a complete safeguard for every intelligence or every will, but this is not the question at issue, for neither do religions save those who reject them. What matters is that these arguments have their own value and constitute by their own nature a possible support, infallible moreover from the intellectual or purely logical point of view; and *pax hominibus bonae voluntatis*.

In order to clarify the function of metaphysical proof, one must start from the idea that human intelligence coincides in its essence with certainty of the Absolute. If this does not appear as self-evident to the majority of our contemporaries, that is because for them awareness of "accidents" has stifled the intuitive awareness of "Substance"; hence an intelligence that is systematically superficial, fixed upon a fragmentary reality. Should anyone object that the innateness of metaphysical ideas—assuming this is admitted—does not prove the reality of the content of these ideas, it may be replied that such an opinion is equivalent to the destruction of the very notion of intelligence and that, were it true, our intelligence could never prove anything at all. To speak of intelligence is to speak of innateness, for the latter is at the root of every intellectual and mental operation, man being obviously incapable of "starting from zero" since this "zero" is nonexistent. One cannot replace the optical nerve with some external light, and, with all the more reason, one cannot have a substitute for the Self, or God, from whom are derived the notions inherent in the human spirit.

It is in the light of these data that one should approach the question of the proofs of God; such proofs, far from being merely apologetical, can serve as keys helping to restore to intelligence its characteristic and integral nature. First of all, however, an answer should be made to a curious objection put forward by rationalists, even though it has already been mentioned elsewhere in this book. The objection is as follows: whoever affirms that "God exists" is under the obligation to prove it, whereas the skeptic is in no way obliged to prove the contrary, since, so it seems, only he who makes an affirmation owes his critics a proof, he who denies it being under no such obligation. Consequently, the skeptic has the right to reject the "existence" of God without being required in his turn to prove the "non-existence" of God. Now this kind of reasoning is arbitrary, and for the following reason: a man who finds himself unable to verify a statement has undoubtedly the right not to accept it as certain or as probable, but he has by no means the logical right to reject it without providing valid reasons for doing so. It is not difficult to discover the basis of the objection in question: it starts from the preconceived notion that the affirmation of God is something "extraordinary," whereas the denial of God is "normal." The skeptic starts, of course, from the idea that the normal man is the atheist, and from this he deduces a kind of one-way jurisprudence.

In the spiritual order a proof is of assistance only to the man who wishes to understand and who, by virtue of this wish, has already in some measure understood; it is of no practical use to one who, deep in his heart, does not want to change his position, and whose philosophy merely expresses this desire. It has been claimed that it is up to religion to prove itself in the face of the utmost ill-will, that "religion is made for man,"[2] that it must therefore adapt itself to his needs, and that through its failure to do so it has become bankrupt. One might as well say that the alphabet has become bankrupt in a class where the pupils are determined not to learn it; with this kind of "infralogic" one might declare that the law is made for the honest people who are pleased to conform to it and that a new law is required for the others, a law "adapted" to the needs of their maliciousness and "rejuvenated" in conformity with their propensity for crime.

To be able to accept the ontological proof of God, which deduces from the existence of an innate concept the existence of the objective reality corresponding thereto, one must begin by realizing that the truth does not depend on reasoning—obviously it is not reason that has created it[3]—but that it reveals itself or becomes explicit with the help of the key provided by the mental operation. In every act of assent by the intellect there is an element which escapes the thinking process, rather as light and color elude the grasp of geometry, which can, none the less, symbolize them indirectly and remotely. There is no such thing as "pure proof"; every proof presupposes the knowledge of certain data. The ontological proof, formulated by Saint Augustine and Saint Anselm,[4] carries weight for the person who already has at his disposal some initial certainties, but it has no effect upon the willfully and systematically superficial mind. Such a mind no longer possesses any conception of the profound nature of causality; it regards intelligence as proceeding not from the outward toward the inward, but vice versa, until the very *raison d'être* of human understanding is forgotten.

As we know, those who belittle the ontological argument will assert that the existence of a notion does not necessarily involve the objective existence of the content of that notion. The answer to this is that it all depends on the nature of the notion in question, since what is plausible in the case of a notion relating to a fact is by no means so in the case of a notion relating to a principle. Some people will no doubt point out that Buddhism proves that the notion of God has nothing fundamental about it, and that one can very well dispense with it both in metaphysics and spirituality. They would be right if the Buddhists did not possess the idea of the Absolute or that of transcendence, or that of immanent Justice with its complement, Mercy; this is all that is needed to show that Buddhism, if it does not possess the word for God, or if it does not possess our word, in any case possesses the reality itself.

The cosmological proof of God, which is found in both Aristotle and Plato,[5] and which consists in inferring from the existence of the world that of a transcendent, positive and infinite Cause,[6] finds no greater favor in the eyes of those who deny the supernatural. According to these people the notion of God merely com-

---

[2] Which is false if one does not immediately add that man exists for religion; the falsity is in the isolation of the proposition. Religion is made for man in so far as it must be accessible to him according to the measure of his goodwill, and not regardless of it, since man is free; and man is made for religion in so far as it represents the sufficient reason for human existence.

[3] "Only thought can produce that which has the right to be acknowledged as Being," one of the pioneers of post-Kantian integral rationalism has dared to say.

[4] Some of the Scholastic philosophers were too Aristotelian to be able to accept the usefulness of the ontological proof; reason was considered by them as leading to a certainty that was in some way new, rather than to Platonic "reminiscence."

[5] In Islam all the proofs of God which, according to certain authorities, form a part of faith (*imān*), are to a greater or lesser extent developments of the cosmological argument.

[6] The word "exist," when applied either explicitly or implicitly to the Divine Principle, has only a provisional logical function and means "to be real."

pensates, in this case, for our ignorance of causes, a gratuitous argument, if ever there was one, for the cosmological proof implies, not a purely logical and abstract supposition, but a profound knowledge of causality. If we know what total causality is, namely the "vertical" and "descending" projection of a possibility through different degrees of existence, then we can conceive the First Cause; otherwise we cannot do so. Here again we observe that the objection arises from ignoring what is implicit: rationalists forget that "proof," on the level in question, is a key or a symbol, a means of drawing back a veil rather than of providing actual illumination; it is not by itself a leap out of ignorance and into knowledge. The principal argument "indicates" rather than "proves"; it cannot be anything more than a guideline or an *aide-mémoire*, since it is impossible to prove the Absolute outside itself. If "to prove" means to know something by virtue of a particular mental stratagem— but for which one would perforce remain in ignorance—then there are no possible "proofs of God"; and this, moreover, explains why one can do without them in symbolist and contemplative metaphysics.

Divine causality has so to speak two dimensions, one relating to the static nature of things, the other to their destinies: God is at once the cause of perfections and the cause of their ultimate limit. He makes the sun to shine, but also causes it to set; both phenomena are proofs of God.

This Divine causality implies the homogeneity of the Universe, which brings us back to Substance, that Divine fabric wherein things are in God and God is in things, with a kind of discontinuous continuity (if such a paradoxical ellipsis be permissible). This notion of Substance furnishes the key to eschatological mysteries such as the Last Judgment and the resurrection of the flesh: formal Existence, both material and animic, is like a desiccated, overcompacted substance, and the final coming of God is comparable to rain which causes seeds to germinate.[7] Essence returns toward form, Substance toward accident, the Center toward the periphery, Life returns towards death; the Inward vivifies the outward and resuscitates the nuclei of which we consist, products, on the one hand, of creation and, on the other, but secondarily, of our attitudes and actions. But one could also say, in a metaphysically more adequate manner although in terms that are further removed from the terrestrial aspect of things, that the outward flows back toward the Inward: *Ātmā* "breathes," creation is renewed and dilates,[8] the Divine proximity causes bodies to be reborn and gives them the forms that belong to them according to the measures of heaven; universal desiccation calls down the "blessed rain"; there can be no resurrection "unless the seed dies." All the apparently senseless enigmas of the traditional eschatologies are explained in part—for nothing belonging to this order ever gives up its whole secret—by the homogeneity of Substance, the Divine *Māyā* or *Prakriti*, and by the rhythms proper to it, rhythms prefigured in the very nature of the relations between the Principle and its manifestation. Human norms are broken, the Divine norms endure.

According to the Koran, all natural processes such as the growth of creatures or the alternation of day and night are "signs" or proofs of God "for those endowed

[7] On this subject the Koran says: "And we send down from the sky rain charged with blessing, and we produce thereby gardens and the grain of the harvest. . . . And we give life thereby to a land that is dead; so will be the resurrection" (Sura *Qāf*, 9-11).

[8] "We will bring them together," says the Koran: or "to Us is the returning," indicating the flowing back of the periphery toward the Center.

with understanding." The cosmological proof is combined with the teleological proof, the latter being founded not simply upon the existence of things but upon the inner order of creation, and so upon the immanent prescience governing it.

No proof can be founded on a void. Those who look down upon the teleological proof of Socrates, and the moral proof related to it, should begin by finding out what universal harmony really implies and what human virtue is in its deepest meaning; knowing nothing of this either from lack of doctrinal knowledge or lack of intellectual intuition,[9] the proofs founded upon universal order and upon the virtues remain inaccessible to them; yet this ignorance is not an excuse since it springs from a willful perversion of the spirit. Skepticism and bitterness have nothing spontaneous about them, they are products of a civilization that is supersaturated and aberrant, of a "culture" that sets itself up as "art for art's sake," and they presuppose, in consequence, a whole jungle of detours placed between man and the Real.

The teleological proof of God is furnished, for example, by the amazing combination of conditions which makes life on earth possible; another proof is provided by the biological homogeneity of the organic world and by the equilibrium between species, an equilibrium derived, precisely, from this homogeneity. And this takes us to the Hindu myth of the primordial sacrifice of *Purusha*: all living beings issue from the sacrificed members of the celestial and "prematerial" body; hence, on the one hand, the difference between creatures and, on the other, the equilibrium of creation. *Purusha* contains all possibilities, the luminous and the obscure, the fiery and the cold, the destructive and the peaceful; from these are derived the opposed species found in the world, species whose opposition—that between carnivores and ruminants, for example—corresponds nonetheless to a biological equilibrium which could not be explained apart from the existence of an underlying unity. Man can upset this balance, abnormally at least, and this he does by means of his machines and serums, in short by all those inroads into nature which follow upon the acquisitions and misdeeds of modern civilization. This proves, not that the teleological proofs lack validity, but on the contrary that man has something of the Divine about him, and this something, which in the above example is affirmed in an evil form, shows in reality that man is a being "apart," that his position is central because he is situated beneath the Divine axis, and that consequently his end can only be found beyond the material world. Man is made for what he is able to conceive; the very ideas of absoluteness and transcendence prove both his spiritual nature and the supraterrestrial character of his destiny.

The teleological proof does not save believers who are not metaphysically minded from the difficulty which awareness of the sufferings of this world poses for them. The weakness is not in the proof, which is perfect in its order and which no believer can take exception to; it is due to superficiality of understanding, which arises all too often from simple negligence or mental laziness. It is quite without justification that in these circumstances some people resort to an appeal to mystery and assert that our reason is inadequate to explain the imperfections present in creation, for there is nothing incomprehensible or indescribable here; the fissures of this world cannot but exist, seeing that the world is not God and that this difference or

[9] As is proved *ad nauseam* by the pessimism, or the "dysteleology," of a Schopenhauer, of a Haeckel, and, in our day, of the existentialists.

this remoteness cannot fail to be manifested in varying degrees in the very flesh of creation, even Paradise could not be without the serpent. To the religious argument invoking the insufficiency of the reason, atheistic rationalists reply that if this were true it would simply prove that our reason is absurd no less than the world, since it falls short of its goal. Now, setting aside the fact that *ratio*, if truly inspired, can reach much further than some theologians suppose, it is in no wise its object to storm the true mysteries, so that the rationalist objection in any case misses the mark; reason indeed, has no more than a provisional function, at least so far as the supernatural is concerned; it is far from being the whole of intelligence. In order to activate intellectual "reminiscence," man, who bears the mark of the fall, needs to proceed circuitously and to come to the inward by way of the outward; to become wholly what it is, or to become aware of its innate content, intelligence has to make detours through more outward modalities.

The teleological proof also embraces the "aesthetic" proof, in the profoundest sense of that term. Under this aspect it is perhaps even less accessible than under the cosmological or moral aspects; for to be sensitive to the metaphysical transparency of beauty, to the radiation of forms and sounds, is already to possess—in common, with a Rūmī or a Ramakrishna—a visual and auditive intuition capable of ascending through phenomena right up to the essences and the eternal melodies.

In the context of this particular aspect of the teleological proof, one cannot fail to observe how the modern world has been unique among civilizations in creating (on Greek foundations!) a world in which ugliness and triviality are the order of the day and in which they are presented shamelessly as the "genuine" and the "real." Beauty, along with outward dignity, is consigned to the sphere of dreams, luxuries, and playthings, whence the reproach associated with the words "poetic," "picturesque," "romantic," and "exotic." There is no such thing as chance, and the significance of this strange phenomenon is that it eliminates a natural argument in favor of God, while at the same time eliminating the human capacity to be responsive to this argument. One may note, in the same order of ideas, the sharp distinction that is made between the "romantic" side of traditional civilizations and their "real" side, their misery that is to say. That such misery exists we would not dream of denying—in any case it is impossible that it should not exist—but to attribute "reality" to it, and to it alone, is quite simply diabolical. The devil indeed sees creation as in a shattered or distorting mirror, and he always reduces the essential, which is the positive symbolic content and which has the quality of beauty, to the level of some accidental infirmity. For the devil, man is the body under its aspect of misery and the world is impure, cruel, and absurd; beyond that there there is nothing else, proportions and compensations do not count, nothing has any sense in it, everything is a kind of senseless play of chance and only he who believes this to be true is accounted intelligent and honest. This manner of seeing and feeling things is at the opposite pole to the nobility of soul presupposed by the teleological argument, and once again this shows that every proof calls for a subjective qualification, not of an exceptional kind but one that is normal according to the criteria of Heaven.

There remains the experimental or mystical proof of God. While admitting that logically and in the absence of a doctrine, it proves nothing to anyone who has not undergone the unitive experience, nonetheless there is no justification for concluding that because it is incommunicable it must be false; this was the error of Kant, who moreover gave the name of "theurgy" to this direct experience of the Divine Substance. The mystical proof of the Divinity belongs to the order of extrinsic arguments and carries the weight of the latter; the unanimous witness of the sages and the saints, over the whole surface of the globe and throughout the ages, is a sign or a criterion which no man of good faith can despise, short of asserting that the human species has neither intelligence nor dignity; and if it possess neither the one nor the other, if truth has never been within its grasp, then neither can it hope to discover truth when *in extremis*. The idea of the absurdity both of the world and of man, supposing this to be true, would remain inaccessible to us; in other words, if modern man is so intelligent, ancient man cannot have been so stupid. Much more is implied in this simple reflection than might appear at first sight.

Consequently, before putting aside the mystical or experimental proof as unacceptable from the outset, one should not forget to ask oneself what kind of men have invoked it. There can be no common measure between the intellectual and moral worth of the greatest of the contemplatives and the absurdity that their illusion would imply, were it nothing but that. If we have to choose between some encyclopedist or other and Jesus, it is Jesus whom we choose; we would also of course choose some infinitely lesser figure, but we cannot fail to choose the side where Jesus is to be found.

In connection with the questions raised by the mystical proof and, at the other extreme, by the assurance displayed by negators of the supernatural—who deny others any right to a similar assurance without having access to their elements of certainty—we would say that the fact that the contemplative may find it impossible to furnish proof of his knowledge in no wise proves the nonexistence of that knowledge, any more than the spiritual unawareness of the rationalist does away with the falseness of his denials. As we have already remarked, the fact that a madman does not know that he is mad is obviously no proof to the contrary, just as, inversely, the fact that a man of sound mind cannot prove to a madman that his mind is sound in no way proves it to be unsound. These are almost truisms, but their sense is too often missed by philosophers as well as by men of lesser pretensions.

It has been asserted that there is no possible proof available to a Prophet of the authenticity and truth of the revelations he receives. This shows ignorance of the criteria which the gift of prophecy itself implies, and amounts in practice to saying that no proof is possible for anything whatever, since every argument can be invalidated verbally by recourse to some sort of sophistry. Those who maintain that nothing can confer absolute certainty on a celestial Messenger do not, however, demand proof for their own conviction that they are not dreaming when they are awake and when their own interests are at stake; obviously one can admit in theory that strictly speaking no such proof exists, but one cannot deny that the conviction exists and that no one questions it in his own case.

Modern science, with its denial in practice or in principle of all that is really fundamental, and its subsequent rejection of the "one thing needful,"[10] is like a

---

[10] "Scientific" atheism is affirmed indirectly by the postulate of empty space and therefore of discontinuity, which, however, cannot be maintained with complete consistency. Now, to deny plenitude and continuity, including rhythm and necessity, or the providential element, is to deny Universal Substance with all its implications of homogeneity and transcendence.

planimetry that has no notion of the other directions. It shuts itself up entirely in physical reality or unreality, and there it accumulates an enormous mass of information, while at the same time committing itself to ever more complex conjectures. Starting out from the illusion that nature will end by yielding its ultimate secret and will allow itself to be reduced to some mathematical formula or other, this Promethean science everywhere runs up against enigmas which give the lie to its postulates and which appear as unforeseen fissures in this laboriously erected system. These fissures get plastered over with fresh hypotheses and the vicious circle goes on unchecked, with all the threats we are aware of. Some of its hypotheses, such as the theory of evolution, in practice become dogmas by reason of their usefulness, if not of their plausibility; this usefulness is not only scientific, it can just as well be philosophical or even political, according to circumstances.

In reality, the evolutionary theory, to stress this point once again, is a substitute for the traditional theory of emanation and consists in denying the periphery-center relationship.[11] Thus the very existence of the Center, source of emanation, and of the radii leading to it is denied, and an attempt is made to situate every hierarchical relationship on the curve marking the periphery. Instead of proceeding upward, starting from the corporeal level and passing through the animic sphere, then mounting toward realities at first supraformal and finally principal or metacosmic, an evolving hierarchy is imagined, advancing from matter, through vegetable and animal life, to human consciousness, itself considered as some kind of transitory accident. With a thoughtlessness that is infinitely culpable when they call themselves believers some people imagine a superman who is destined to take man's place, and who consequently would also render Christ's humanity contemptible;[12] and a certain "genius" imagines at the end of the evolutionist and progressivist chain something he is not ashamed to call "God" and which is no more than a pseudoabsolute decked out in a pseudotranscendence; for the Eternal will always be Alpha and has always been Omega. Creatures are crystallized in the corporeal zone emanating, in a manner at once continuous and discontinuous, from the Center and from on high, they do not "evolve" by coming from matter and so from the periphery and from below. But at the same time, and beyond reach of our human point of view, creatures are all "contained" in God and do not really come out from Him; the whole play of relationships between God and the world is but a monologue of relativity.

The mystical proof of God is always, in some degree, a participation in the profound nature of things, and consequently it excludes and discredits all speculations which tend to falsify within us the image of the Real and to transfer the Divine Ideas of the Immutable on to the plane of becoming. Modern man wants to conquer space, but the least of contemplative states, or the least of intellections bearing on

[11] This must not, of course, be confused with the emanationist heresy, which has nothing metaphysical about it and which reduces the Principle to the level of manifestation, or Substance to the level of accidents.

[12] For God manifests himself directly in a support which by definition marks the presence of the Absolute in relativity and is for this reason "relatively absolute." This "relative absoluteness" is the justification of the possibility homo sapiens. Man might disappear, if God so wished, but he could not change into another species; the Platonic ideas are precise possibilities and not just misty vagueness: every possibility is what it is and what it ought to be.

metaphysical realities, carries us to heights from which the nebula of Andromeda appears scarcely more than a terrestrial accident.

These considerations permit us to underline certain points that have already been touched on. Promethean minds believe themselves to be creatures of chance moving freely in a vacuum and capable of "self-creation," all within the framework of an existence devoid of meaning; the world, so it seems, is absurd, but no notice is taken—and this is typical—of the absurdity of admitting the appearance within an absurd world of a being regarded as capable of remarking that absurdity. Modern man is fundamentally ignorant of what the most childish of catechisms reveals, doubtless in a language that is pictorial and sentimental, yet adequate for its purpose; namely, that we are inwardly connected with a Substance which is Being, Consciousness, and Life, and of which we are contingent and transitory modalities. He is consequently unaware of being involved in a titanic drama in terms of which this world, seemingly so solid, is as tenuous as a spider's web. Existence, invisible and underlying, is concrete, not abstract; it "sleeps" and "awakes," it "breathes" and can make worlds collapse; space, time, and man are no more than minute fragments of a Being and a Movement which escapes all our measurements and all that we can imagine. The Divine Substance, however, cannot have the limiting properties of matter, nor those of an animic fluid. Its homogeneity implies a trans cending discontinuity the traces of which are indeed apparent around us and within us (the body is not life and life is not intelligence), but which we cannot grasp adequately with the help of our terrestrial categories alone.

The great misconception, then, is to believe that the basis of our existence is space and that the factors which make up our individual destinies are contained in it, whereas in reality this basis—at one and the same time immutable and in movement according to the relationship envisaged—is situated in a "supraspace" which we can perceive only through the heart-intellect and about which those explosions of total Consciousness, the Revelations, speak to us symbolically. The error is to believe that the causes which determine human history or which carry it to its conclusion belong to the same order as our matter or as "natural laws," whereas in fact the whole visible cosmos is resting upon an invisible volcano—but also, at a deeper ontological level, upon a formless ocean of bliss. Men imagine that this earth, these mountains, or bodies can only be destroyed by forces on their own level, by masses or energies belonging to our physical universe. What they do not see, however, is that this world in appearance so compact, can collapse *ab intra*, that matter can flow back "inward" by a process of transmutation, and that the whole of space can shrink like a balloon emptied of air; in short, that fragility and impermanence not only affect things within a space naively supposed to be stable, they also affect existence itself with all its categories. Our nature consists precisely in the ability to escape, in our innermost core and in the "unchanging Center," from the break-up of a macrocosm that has become oversolidified, and to become reintegrated in the Immutable whence we came forth. What proves this possibility is our capacity to conceive this Immutability; it is also proved, in a concordant manner, by the fact (at once unique and multiple) of Revelation.

To be shocked by the anthropomorphic character of the God of the Bible amounts, logically speaking, to being surprised by man's existence as such; that is to say, the Reality which we call "God" necessarily assumes a certain human demeanor on contact with the human being, which cannot, however, be taken to imply that it is human in its own nature.[13] The source of our knowledge of God is at one and the same time the Intellect and Revelation. In principle the Intellect knows everything because all possible knowledge is inscribed in its very substance, and it promises absolute certainty because its knowledge is a "being," or a participation in being, and not merely a "seeing." In fact, however, man is a fallen being who has lost access to his own transpersonal kernel, so that nothing remains to him but that faint light which is reason and, beyond this quite indirect and discursive mode of intelligence, an intuition of the Intellect that is purely virtual and fragmentary. If one were to leave an infant to grow up among wild animals his knowledge of God would be no greater than his knowledge of language, which shows that man cannot draw everything out of himself, at least not under ordinary conditions. It is Revelation that confers spiritual knowledge at its different levels, transmitting to men truths of which they were unaware and awakening in some an Intellection that had hitherto remained latent. The most decisive truths concerning existence, truths referring to the invisible Reality which determines us and to the destinies that await us *post mortem*, are not simply and solely imposed on us from without; they slumber within us and, with a clarity that is at once adamantine and dazzlingly brilliant, form part of our very being.

For primordial man, Revelation and Intellection coincided: contingency was still transparent so that there were as yet neither "points of view" nor "perspectives." Whereas in later times Revelation is multiple because, geometrically speaking, the circumference implies many radii, the "point of view" of primordial man corresponded to the whole circle; the center was everywhere. Likewise, the unavoidably limiting aspect of expressions, forms, or symbols did not yet imprison human minds; there could be no question, therefore, of a diversity of forms, each expressing the same Truth in the name of the impersonal Self while being mutually exclusive in the name of this or that particular manifestation of the personal God. Now that these diverse manifestations exist, what matters is to know that intrinsically they speak in absolute mode, since it is the Absolute which is speaking, but that extrinsically they are clothed in the language of a particular mental coloring and a particular system of contingencies, since they are addressed to man. The man to whom they are addressed in this manner is already cut off from that inward Revelation which is direct and "supernaturally natural" Intellection.

Of quite a different order from the intellectual proofs of God and of the beyond is a type of proof which in the first place is purely phenomenal, namely the miracle. Quite contrary to what most people suppose, miracles, without being in the least degree contrary to reason, do not carry conviction in the manner of physical effects which may prove such and such causes, for then the certainty offered would be only an approximation, miraculous causation being unverifiable;[14] this, moreover, is

---

[13] If the Scriptures describe creation, as they do, in a simple, synthetic and pictorial language and not in the style of a scientific analysis, this shows, not that they are mistaken, but that we have no need of anything else on this level. All Promethean and profane science, even though neutral in principle as a source of exact information, is in fact harmful so far as its human effects are concerned. This is the real significance of the trial of Galileo which was the trial (in anticipation) of scientific euphoria, of the machine and of the atom bomb. The theories of astronomy matter little in themselves, but the fruit of the forbidden tree poisons humanity *de facto*.

[14] There are indeed magical phenomena which have every appearance of being miracles without, of course, having any connection with the causality of the latter.

the objection most commonly raised against the conviction in question, quite apart from the habitual denial of the phenomenon as such. What a miracle seeks to produce, and what it does indeed produce, is the rending of a veil; it operates like a surgical intervention which, far from consisting merely of an abstract discussion, removes the obstacle in a concrete way. A miracle breaks down the wall separating outward and fallible consciousness from inward and infallible consciousness, which is omniscient and blissful. By means of a "therapeutic shock" it delivers the soul from its shell of ignorance, but it would amount to nothing if it sought to convince merely by a demonstration of phenomena, for then as we have seen, many doubts might be permissible as to the level and significance of the prodigy.

The miraculous phenomenon cannot help but exist given that one has the supernatural, on the one hand, and the natural, on the other. The supernatural, moreover, is not the contra-natural; it is itself "natural" on the universal scale. If the Divine Principle is transcendent in relation to the world while at the same time embracing it within its unique substance, then miracles must occur; the celestial must sometimes break through into the terrestrial, the Center must appear like a flash of lightning on the periphery. To take an example in the physical realm, inert matter is of little worth, but gold and diamonds cannot fail to appear therein. Metaphysically the miracle is a possiblity which, as such, must necessarily be manifested in view of the hierarchical structure of the whole Universe.

This brings us back to the teleological argument, in the sense that harmony or beauty, whether inward or outward, possesses something that convinces *ab intra* and which brings deliverance. Like miracles, beauty only possesses this "alchemical" and liberating capacity when linked with truth and the sacred, and only for those who are called to understand this language which may truly be described as angelic. The *Avatāra* does not convince by his words and his marvels alone, he transmits certainty to an equal extent by the visible harmony of his being, which allows us to glimpse the shores of the Infinite and revives the deepest yearnings while also appeasing them. This superhuman harmony is perpetuated in sacred art and, without need of proofs, has the power to seize hold of souls at their center, by penetrating the encrustations which separate them from Heaven and make them strangers to themselves.

Seven

The Interpretation
of Death

Introduction

Many of the most terrifying depictions of the fact of death are to be found in
the writings of the great religious teachers. Such writings are particularly
shocking to those of us who have come to associate religiosity with some
candy-coated view of life after death. As our first selection shows, the religious
interpretation of death may be very far from the sort of wishful thinking which
has brought the whole question of immortality into disrepute in the modern
world. In the songs of the great Tibetan saint, **Milarepa**, we are told that
death as destruction and as the disappearance of myself is a fact that needs to
be faced directly without any compromise whatever. Does that mean there is
no hope? That life is inherently meaningless? As far as Buddhism is concerned—
at least the Buddhism that stands behind this brief, but powerful song about
dying—the answer is "between the lines" of the song and involves an entirely
transformed sense of the human self which can only be experienced through
the practice of the teaching, the *dharma*.

The next selection would seem on the surface diametrically opposed to the
teaching of Milarepa. "The Martyrdom of Saint Polycarp" is the oldest known
account of the martyrdom of a Christian for his faith and presents an extraordinarily moving account of belief in immortality. We have chosen this
particular selection even though one aspect may be unacceptable to the
contemporary reader—namely, the author's statements about the malice of
the Jews. No doubt such statements require a historical perspective to prevent
our linking them automatically with the forces of antisemitism and religious
oppression. In any case, there is a question of overriding importance raised
specifically by the actions of a great martyr that needs to be asked as impartially
as possible, a question that is almost never treated with sufficient depth in the
growing contemporary psychological literature about death: when is a religious
teaching a help and when is it an obstacle in a human being's relationship to
the fact of death? When is it an escape, a crutch, and when is it an ally against

the egoistic emotions that, according to all traditions, make human life infinitely less than it was meant to be? If the issue is put that way, particularly with respect to the question of death, then the contents of one teaching, even though they verbally contradict another, may be equivalently true in the larger sense of being a force against egoistic fear and rationalization.

The next selection about death is by a scientist. Writing with a deceptively light touch, **Lewis Thomas** completely turns around the conceptions about death and dying that are the general legacy of the modern world view. Speculating strictly within the fold of medical and biological science, his train of thought leads him directly to ideas that have been part of the psychological and metaphysical teachings of many ancient traditions, Eastern and Western.

In the final selection, the great modern theologian **Paul Tillich** argues that the enemy of a valid human life is not death but anxiety in the face of the unknown. This anxiety clouds man's understanding of his own possibilities, the greatest of which is to affirm oneself in spite of the threat against the individual self. For Tillich, man comes into real relationship to God only if he has the courage to be in the face of the possible loss of everything that men ordinarily take as a support for their sense of self. Death is precisely this loss and therefore precisely the fact that man must face with help from nowhere. Only then does help from God appear.

J. N.

The Story of Shindormo and Lesebum

Milarepa

The greatest poet-saint of the Buddhist tradition, Milarepa lived in Tibet during the eleventh century. The story of his life as recorded by his disciple Retchung and soon to be published by E. P. Dutton in a new translation reveals a man of extraordinary compassion and spiritual force, able to speak directly across the barriers of time and cultural setting. The present selection is from *The Hundred Thousand Songs of Milarepa* in the pioneering translation of Garma C. C. Chang (1962).

Obeisance to All Gurus

Shindormo and Lese were a [married] couple who had had great faith in the Jetsun from early days. At one time they invited him to Tsar Ma. As soon as Shindormo saw him coming, she [went to him] at once and held his hands, saying, "Now that we are growing old and death is approaching, we are afraid, and sorry that we have not been able to practice the Dharma with you." Saying this, she cried mournfully for a long time. Milarepa said to her, "My dear patroness, except for advanced Dharma practitioners, the pains of birth, decay, illness, and death descend upon everyone. It is good to think about and fear them, because this enables one to practice the Dharma when death is approaching." Whereupon he sang:

> In the river of birth, decay, illness,
> And death we worldly beings are submerged;
> Who can escape these pains on earth?
> We drift on with the tide. Amidst
> Waves of misery and darkness
> We flow on and on. Seldom in
> Saṃsāra can one find joy.
>
> More miseries come by trying to avoid them;
> Through pursuing pleasures one's sins increase.
> To be free from pain, wrong
> Deeds should be shunned.
>
> When death draws near, the wise
> Always practice Dharma.

"I do not know how to observe the suffering of birth," said Shindormo, "Please instruct me how to meditate upon it." In answer, the Jetsun sang:

Source: *The 100,000 Songs of Milarepa*, trans. by Garma C. C. Chang (Secaucus, N.J.), pp. 552–557. Published by permission of University Books.

My faithful patroness, I will
Explain the suffering of birth.

The wanderer in the Bardo plane
Is the Ālaya Consciousness.
Driven by lust and hatred
It enters a mother's womb.

Therein it feels like a fish
In a rock's crevice caught.
Sleeping in blood and yellow fluid,
It is pillowed in discharges;
Crammed in filth, it suffers pain.
A bad body from bad Karma's born.

Though remembering past lives,
It cannot say a single word.
Now scorched by heat,
Now frozen by the cold,
In nine months it emerges
From the womb in pain
Excruciating, as if
Pulled out gripped by pliers.
When from the womb its head is squeezed, the pain
Is like being thrown into a bramble pit.
The tiny body on the mother's lap,
Feels like a sparrow grappled by a hawk.
When from the baby's tender body
The blood and filth are being cleansed,
The pain is like being flayed alive.
When the umbilical cord is cut,
It feels as though the spine were severed.
When wrapped in the cradle it feels bound
By chains, imprisoned in a dungeon.

He who realizes not the truth of No-arising,
Never can escape from the dread pangs of birth.

There is no time to postpone devotion:
When one dies one's greatest need
Is the divine Dharma.
You should then exert yourself
To practice Buddha's teaching.

Shindormo asked again, "Please preach for us the sufferings of old age." In response, the Jetsun sang:

Listen, my good patrons, listen
To the sufferings of old age.

Painful is it to see one's body
Becoming frail and quite worn out.
Who can help but feel dismayed
At the threat of growing old?

When old age descends upon one,
His straight body becomes bent;
When he tries to step firmly,
He staggers against his will;
His black hairs turn white,
His clear eyes grow dim;
His head shakes with dizziness,
And his keen ears turn deaf;
His ruddy cheeks grow pale,
And his blood dries up.

His nose—the pillar of his face—sinks in;
His teeth—the essence of his bones—protrude.
Losing control of tongue, he stammers.
On the approach of death, his anguish and debts grow.
He gathers food and friends,
But he cannot keep them;
Trying not to suffer,
He only suffers more;
When he tells the truth to people,
Seldom is he believed;
The sons and nephews he has raised
And cherished, oft become his foes.
He gives away his savings,
But wins no gratitude.

Unless you realize the truth of Non-decay,
You will suffer misery in old age.
He who when old neglects the Dharma,
Should know that he is bound by Karma.
It is good to practice the Divine
Dharma while you still can breathe.

Shindormo then said, "What you have just told us is very true; I have experienced these things myself. Now please preach for us the sufferings of sickness." In reply, Milarepa sang:

Dear patrons, you who know grief and sorrow,
Listen to the miseries of sickness.

This frail body is subject e'er to sickness,
So that one suffers excruciating pain.
The illness of Prāṇa, mind, gall, and phlegm
Constantly invade this frail human body,
Causing its blood and matter to be heated;
The organs are thus gripped by pain.
In a safe and easy bed
The sick man feels no comfort,
But turns and tosses, groaning in lament.
Through the Karma of [past] meanness,
Though with best of food you feed him,
He vomits all that he can take,
When you lay him in the cool,
He still feels hot and burning;
When you wrap him in warm cloth,

He feels cold as though soaked in sleet.
Though friends and kinsmen gather round,
None can relieve or share his pains.
Though warlocks and physicians are proficient,
They cannot help cases caused by Ripening Karma.
He who has not realized the truth of No-illness,
Much suffering must undergo.

Since we know not when sicknesses will strike,
It is wise to practice Holy Dharma—
The sure conqueror of illness!

" I hope to practice [more] Dharma when death draws near," said Shindormo. "Now please preach for me the suffering of death." In answer, Milarepa sang:

Listen, my disheartened patroness:
Like the pain of repaying compound debts,
One must undergo the suffering of death.
Yama's guards catch and carry one
When the time of death arrives.
The rich man cannot buy it off with money.
With his sword the hero cannot conquer it.
Nor can the clever woman outwit it by a trick.
Even the learned scholar cannot
Postpone it with his eloquence.
Here, no coward like a fox can sneak away;
Here, the unlucky cannot make appeal.
Nor can a brave man here display his valor.

When all the Nāḍīs converge in the body,
One is crushed as if between two mountains—
All vision and sensation become dim.
When Bon priests and diviners become useless,
The trusted physician yields to his despair.
None can communicate with the dying man,
Protecting guards and Devas vanish into nought.
Though the breath has not completely stopped,
One can all but smell the stale odor of dead flesh.
Like a lump of coal in chilly ashes
One approaches to the brink of death.

When dying, some still count the dates and stars;
Others cry and shout and groan;
Some think of worldly goods;
Some that their hard-earned wealth
Will be enjoyed by others.

However deep one's love or great one's sympathy,
He can but depart and journey on alone.
His good friend and consort
Can only leave him there;
In a bundle his beloved body
Will be folded and carried off,
Then thrown in water, burned in fire,
Or simply cast off in a desolate land.

Faithful patrons, what in the end can we retain?
Must we sit idly by and let all things go?
When your breath stops tomorrow
No wealth on earth can help you.
Why, then, should one be mean?

Kind kinsmen circle round
The bed of the dying,
But none can help him for a moment.
Knowing that all must be left behind,
One realizes that all great love
And attachment must be futile.
When that final moment comes,
Only Holy Dharma helps.

You should strive, dear patroness.
For a readiness to die!
Be certain and ready; when the time
Comes, you will have no fear and no regret.

Whereupon, Shindormo besought the Jetsun for instructions. Practicing them [for some time, she gained such great progress that] at the time of her death she entered the initial stage of the Path.

The Martyrdom of Saint Polycarp, Bishop of Smyrna, as Told in a Letter of the Church of Smyrna to the Church of Philomelium

The date of St. Polycarp's martyrdom has been fixed with reasonable certainty at the year 155 or 156 and he is thought to have been born in the year 69 or 70. His life thus spans a crucial period in the development of the early Christian Church—the death of the first apostles and the menacing growth of Roman persecution.

The Text

The church of God that sojourns at Smyrna to the church of God that sojourns at Philomelium, and to all those of the holy and Catholic Church who sojourn in every place: may mercy, peace, and love be multiplied from God the Father and our Lord Jesus Christ.[1]

We write you, brethren, the things concerning those who suffered martyrdom, especially the blessed Polycarp, who put an end to the persecution by sealing it, so to speak, through his own witness. For almost everything that led up to it happened in order that the Lord might show once again a martyrdom conformable to the gospel.[2] For he waited to be betrayed, just as the Lord did, to the end that we also might be imitators of him, "not looking only to that which concerns ourselves, but also to that which concerns our neighbors."[3] For it is a mark of true and steadfast love for one not only to desire to be saved oneself, but all the brethren also.

Blessed and noble, indeed, are all the martyrdoms that have taken place according to God's will; for we ought to be very reverent in ascribing to God power over all things. For who would not admire their nobility and patient endurance and love

Source: Cyril C. Richardson (ed.), *The Early Christian Fathers* (New York, 1970), pp. 149–157. Reprinted by permission of The Westminster Press.

[1] I Peter 1:1, 2; Jude 2; I Clem., pref.; Polycarp, Phil., pref.
[2] John 18:37; cf. Rev. 1:5; 3:14. The Passion of Christ is the pattern of that of his martyrs. Cf. Polycarp, Phil. 8:2.
[3] Phil. 2:4.

of their Master? Some of them, so torn by scourging that the anatomy of their flesh was visible as far as the inner veins and arteries, endured with such patience that even the bystanders took pity and wept; others achieved such heroism that not one of them uttered a cry or a groan, thus showing all of us that at the very hour of their tortures the most noble martyrs of Christ were no longer in the flesh, but rather that the Lord stood by them and conversed with them. And giving themselves over to the grace of Christ they despised the tortures of this world, purchasing for themselves in the space of one hour the life eternal. To them the fire of their inhuman tortures was cold; for they set before their eyes escape from the fire that is everlasting and never quenched,[4] while with the eyes of their heart they gazed upon the good things reserved for those that endure patiently, "which things neither ear has heard nor eye has seen, nor has there entered into the heart of man."[5] But they were shown to them by the Lord, for they were no longer men, but were already angels. Similarly, those condemned to the wild beasts endured fearful punishments, being made to lie on sharp shells and punished with other forms of various torments, in order that [the devil][6] might bring them, if possible, by means of the prolonged punishment, to a denial of their faith.

Many, indeed, were the machinations of the devil against them. But, thanks be to God, he did not prevail against them all. For the most noble Germanicus encouraged their timidity through his own patient endurance—who also fought with the beasts in a distinguished way. For when the proconsul, wishing to persuade him, bade him have pity on his youth, he forcibly dragged the wild beast toward himself, wishing to obtain more quickly a release from their wicked and lawless life. From this circumstance, all the crowd, marveling at the heroism of the God-loving and God-fearing race of the Christians, shouted: "Away with the atheists![8] Make search for Polycarp!"

But a Phrygian,[9] named Quintus, lately arrived from Phrygia, took fright when he saw the wild beasts. In fact, he was the one who had forced himself and some others to come forward voluntarily. The proconsul by much entreaty persuaded him to take the oath and to offer the sacrifice. For this reason, therefore, brethren, we do not praise those who come forward of their own accord, since the gospel does not teach us so to do.[10]

The most admirable Polycarp, when he first heard of it, was not perturbed, but desired to remain in the city. But the majority induced him to withdraw, so he retired to a farm not far from the city and there stayed with a few friends, doing nothing else night and day but pray for all men and for the churches throughout the world, as was his constant habit.[11] And while he was praying, it so happened, three days before his arrest, that he had a vision and saw his pillow blazing with fire, and turning to those who were with him he said, "I must be burned alive."

---

[4] Matt. 3:12; Mark 9:43; Ignatius, Eph. 16:2.
[5] I Cor. 2:9; Isa. 64:4; 65:16.
[6] The subject is supplied from ch. 3:1.
[7] Cf. Ignatius, Rom. 5:2.
[8] Cf. Justin, Apol. I, chs. 6; 13; Athenagoras, Leg., chs. 3 ff.
[9] The name "Phrygian" was often given to an adherent of the Montanist sect. See the Introduction.
[10] Cf. Matt 10:23; John 7:1; 8:59; 10:39; Acts 13:51; 17:14; 19:30, 31.
[11] Cf. Polycarp, Phil. 12:3.

And while those who were searching for him continued their quest, he moved to another farm, and forthwith those searching for him arrived. And when they did not find him, they seized two young slaves, one of whom confessed under torture. For it was really impossible to conceal him, since the very ones who betrayed him were of his own household.[12] And the chief of the police, who chanced to have the same name as Herod, was zealous to bring him into the arena in order that he might fulfill his own appointed lot of being made a partaker with Christ; while those who betrayed him should suffer the punishment of Judas himself.

Taking, therefore, the young slave on Friday about suppertime, the police, mounted and with their customary arms, set out as though "hasting after a robber."[13] And late in the evening they came up with him and found him in bed in the upper room of a small cottage. Even so he could have escaped to another farm, but he did not wish to do so, saying, "God's will be done."[14] Thus, when he heard of their arrival, he went downstairs and talked with them, while those who looked on marveled at his age and constancy, and at how there should be such zeal over the arrest of so old a man. Straightway he ordered food and drink, as much as they wished, to be set before them at that hour, and he asked them to give him an hour so that he might pray undisturbed. And when they consented, he stood and prayed—being so filled with the grace of God that for two hours he could not hold his peace, to the amazement of those who heard. And many repented that they had come to get such a devout old man.

When at last he had finished his prayer, in which he remembered all who had met with him at any time, both small and great, both those with and those without renown, and the whole Catholic Church throughout the world, the hour of departure having come, they mounted him on an ass and brought him into the city. It was a great Sabbath.[15] And there the chief of the police, Herod, and his father, Nicetas, met him and transferred him to their carriage, and tried to persuade him, as they sat beside him, saying, "What harm is there to say 'Lord Caesar,' and to offer incense and all that sort of thing, and to save yourself?"

At first he did not answer them.[16] But when they persisted, he said, "I am not going to do what you advise me."

Then when they failed to persuade him, they uttered dire threats and made him get out with such speed that in dismounting from the carriage he bruised his shin. But without turning around, as though nothing had happened, he proceeded swiftly, and was led into the arena, there being such a tumult in the arena that no one could be heard. But as Polycarp was entering the arena, a voice from heaven[17] came to him, saying, "Be strong, Polycarp, and play the man,"[18] No one saw the one speaking, but those of our people who were present heard the voice.[19]

And when finally he was brought up, there was a great tumult on hearing that Polycarp had been arrested. Therefore, when he was brought before him, the pro-

---

[12] Cf. Matt. 10:36.
[13] Matt. 26:55.
[14] Matt. 6:10; Acts 21:14.
[15] Cf. John 19:31.
[16] Cf. Mark 14:61; John 19:9, 10.
[17] Cf. John 12:28.
[18] Josh. 1:6; 7, 9; cf. Deut. 31:7, 23; Ps. 27:14; 31:24.
[19] Acts 9:7.

consul asked him if he were Polycarp. And when he confessed that he was, he tried to persuade him to deny [the faith], saying, "Have respect to your age"—and other things that customarily follow this, such as, "Swear by the fortune of Caesar; change your mind; say, 'Away with the atheists!'"

But Polycarp looked with earnest face at the whole crowd of lawless heathen in the arena, and motioned to them with his hand. Then, groaning and looking up to heaven, he said, "Away with the atheists!"

But the proconsul was insistent and said: "Take the oath and I shall release you. Curse Christ."

Polycarp said: "Eighty-six years I have served him, and he never did me any wrong. How can I blaspheme my King who saved me?"

And upon his persisting still and saying, "Swear by the fortune of Caesar," he answered, "If you vainly suppose that I shall swear by the fortune of Caesar, as you say, and pretend that you do not know who I am, listen plainly: I am a Christian. But if you desire to learn the teaching of Christianity, appoint a day and give me a hearing."

The proconsul said, "Try to persuade the people."

But Polycarp said, "You, I should deem worthy of an account; for we have been taught to render honor, as is befitting, to rulers and authorities appointed by God[20] so far as it does us no harm; but as for these, I do not consider them worthy that I should make defense to them."

But the proconsul said: "I have wild beasts. I shall throw you to them, if you do not change your mind."

But he said: "Call them. For repentance from the better to the worse is not permitted us; but it is noble to change from what is evil to what is righteous."

And again [he said] to him, "I shall have you consumed with fire, if you despise the wild beasts, unless you change your mind."

But Polycarp said: "The fire you threaten burns but an hour and is quenched after a little; for you do not know the fire of the coming judgment and everlasting punishment that is laid up for the impious. But why do you delay? Come, do what you will."

And when he had said these things and many more besides he was inspired with courage and joy, and his face was full of grace, so that not only did it not fall with dismay at the things said to him, but on the contrary, the proconsul was astonished, and sent his own herald into the midst of the arena to proclaim three times: "Polycarp has confessed himself to be a Christian."

When this was said by the herald, the entire crowd of heathen and Jews who lived in Smyrna[21] shouted with uncontrollable anger and a great cry: "This one is the teacher of Asia, the father of the Christians, the destroyer of our gods, who teaches many not to sacrifice nor to worship."[22]

Such things they shouted and asked the Asiarch Philip[23] that he let loose a lion on Polycarp. But he said it was not possible for him to do so, since he had brought

---

[20] Rom. 13:1, 7; I Peter 2:13 ff.; I Clem., ch. 61.

[21] Cf. Rev. 2:9.

[22] Cf. Acts 16:20, 21.

[23] See note 40. The Asiarchs were officials who maintained the cult of Rome and the emperor in the province of Asia. Cf. Acts 19:31.

the wild-beast sports to a close. Then they decided to shout with one accord that he burn Polycarp alive. For it was necessary that the vision which had appeared to him about his pillow should be fulfilled, when he saw it burning while he was praying, and turning around had said prophetically to the faithful who were with him, "I must be burned alive."[24]

Then these things happened with such dispatch, quicker than can be told—the crowds in so great a hurry to gather wood and faggots from the workshops and the baths, the Jews being especially zealous, as usual, to assist with this. When the fire was ready, and he had divested himself of all his clothes and unfastened his belt, he tried to take off his shoes, though he was not heretofore in the habit of doing this because [each of] the faithful always vied with one another as to which of them would be first to touch his body. For he had always been honored, even before his martyrdom, for his holy life. Straightway then, they set about him the material prepared for the pyre. And when they were about to nail him also, he said: "Leave me as I am. For he who grants me to endure the fire will enable me also to remain on the pyre unmoved, without the security you desire from the nails."

So they did not nail him, but tied him. And with his hands put behind him and tied, like a noble ram out of a great flock ready for sacrifice, a burnt offering ready and acceptable to God, he looked up to heaven and said:

"Lord God Almighty,[25] Father of thy beloved and blessed Servant Jesus Christ, through whom we have received full knowledge of thee, 'the God of angels and powers and all creation'[26] and of the whole race of the righteous who live in thy presence: I bless thee, because thou hast deemed me worthy of this day and hour,[27] to take my part in the number of the martyrs, in the cup of thy Christ,[28] for 'resurrection to eternal life'[29] of soul and body in the immortality of the Holy Spirit; among whom may I be received in thy presence this day as a rich and acceptable sacrifice, just as thou hast prepared and revealed beforehand and fulfilled, thou that art the true God without any falsehood. For this and for everything I praise thee, I bless thee I glorify thee, through the eternal and heavenly High Priest, Jesus Christ, thy beloved Servant, through whom be glory to thee with him and Holy Spirit both now and unto the ages to come. Amen."

And when he had concluded the Amen and finished his prayer, the men attending to the fire lighted it. And when the flame flashed forth, we saw a miracle, we to whom it was given to see. And we are preserved in order to relate to the rest what happened. For the fire made the shape of a vaulted chamber, like a ship's sail filled by the wind, and made a wall around the body of the martyr. And he was in the midst, not as burning flesh, but as bread baking or as gold and silver refined in a furnace. And we perceived such a sweet aroma as the breath of incense or some other precious spice.

At length, when the lawless men saw that his body could not be consumed by the fire, they commanded an executioner to go to him and stab him with a dagger.

[24] Cf. ch. 5:2.
[25] Rev. 4:8; 11:17; 15:3; 16:7; 21:22.
[26] Ps. 58:6, LXX; Judith 9:12, 14.
[27] Cf. John 12:27.
[28] Cf. Mark 10:38, 39; Matt. 20:22; 23; 26:39.
[29] Cf. John 5:29.

And when he did this [a dove and][30] a great quantity of blood came forth, so that the fire was quenched and the whole crowd marveled that there should be such a difference between the unbelievers and the elect. And certainly the most admirable Polycarp was one of these [elect], in whose times among us he showed himself an apostolic and prophetic teacher and bishop of the Catholic Church in Smyrna.[31] Indeed, every utterance that came from his mouth was accomplished and will be accomplished.

But the jealous and malicious evil one, the adversary of the race of the righteous, seeing the greatness of his martyrdom and his blameless life from the beginning, and how he was crowned with the wreath of immortality and had borne away an incontestable reward, so contrived it that his corpse should not be taken away by us, although many desired to do this and to have fellowship with his holy flesh. He instigated Nicetas, the father of Herod and brother of Alce,[32] to plead with the magistrate not to give up his body, "else," said he, "they will abandon the Crucified and begin worshiping this one." This was done at the instigation and insistence of the Jews, who also watched when we were going to take him from the fire, being ignorant that we can never forsake Christ, who suffered for the salvation of the whole world of those who are saved, the faultless for the sinners,[33] nor can we ever worship any other. For we worship this One as Son of God, but we love the martyrs as disciples and imitators of the Lord, deservedly so, because of their unsurpassable devotion to their own King and Teacher. May it be also our lot to be their companions and fellow disciples!

The captain of the Jews, when he saw their contentiousness, set it [i.e., his body] in the midst and burned it, as was their custom. So we later took up his bones, more precious than costly stones and more valuable than gold, and laid them away in a suitable place. There the Lord will permit us, so far as possible, to gather together in joy and gladness to celebrate the day of his martyrdom as a birthday, in memory of those athletes who have gone before, and to train and make ready those who are to come hereafter.

Such are the things concerning the blessed Polycarp, who, martyred at Smyrna along with twelve others from Philadelphia is alone remembered so much the more by everyone, that he is even spoken of by the heathen in every place. He was not only a noble teacher, but also a distinguished martyr, whose martyrdom all desire to imitate as one according to the gospel of Christ. By his patient endurance he overcame the wicked magistrate and so received the crown of immortality; and he rejoices with the apostles and all the righteous to glorify God the Father Almighty and to bless our Lord Jesus Christ, the Saviour of our souls and Helmsman of our bodies and Shepherd[34] of the Catholic Church throughout the world.

You requested, indeed, that these things be related to you more fully, but for the present we have briefly reported them through our brother Marcion. When you have informed yourselves of these things, send his letter to the brethren elsewhere, in order that they too might glorify the Lord, who makes his choices from his own

[30] This is probably a late interpolation in the text.
[31] See Smyr. 8:2.
[32] Cf. the Alce mentioned in Smyr., ch. 13; Poly., ch. 8.
[33] Cf. I Peter 3:18.
[34] I Peter 2:25.

servants. To him who is able[35] by his grace and bounty to bring us to his everlasting Kingdom, through his Servant, the only-begotten Jesus Christ, be glory, honor, might, majesty, throughout the ages. Greet all the saints. Those with us greet you and also Evarestus, who wrote this, with his whole household.

The blessed Polycarp was martyred on the second day of the first part of the month Xanthicus, the seventh day before the kalends of March, a great Sabbath, at two o'clock P.M.[36] He was arrested by Herod, when Philip of Tralles was high priest,[37] and Statius Quadratus was proconsul,[38] but in the everlasting reign of our Lord Jesus Christ. To him be glory, honor, majesty, and the eternal throne, from generation to generation. Amen.

We bid you farewell, brethren, as you live by the word of Jesus Christ according to the gospel, with whom be glory to God the Father and Holy Spirit, unto the salvation of his holy elect; just as the blessed Polycarp suffered martyrdom, in whose footsteps may it be our lot to be found in the Kingdom of Jesus Christ.

These things Gaius[39] copied from the papers of Irenaeus, a disciple of Polycarp; he also lived with Irenaeus. And Isocrates, wrote it in Corinth from the copy of Gaius. Grace be with all.

I, Pionius,[40] again wrote it from the aforementioned copy, having searched for it according to a revelation of the blessed Polycarp, who appeared to me, as I shall explain in the sequel. I gathered it together when it was almost worn out with age, in order that the Lord Jesus Christ might bring me also with his elect unto his heavenly Kingdom. To him be glory with the Father and Holy Spirit unto the ages of ages. Amen.

[35] Cf. Jude 24, 25; I Clem., ch. 64.
[36] In the year 156 (a leap year) the Sabbath of Purim was on February 22. The Syriac Martyrology commemorates Polycarp, however, on February 23. See the Introduction.
[37] Gaius Julius Philippus was appointed high priest and Asiarch sometime between 149 and 153. The term of office was four years. See Lightfoot's edition, I, 628–635, 666 f.; II, 241, 383–385.
[38] Lucius Statius Quadratus was consul in 142, but the date of his proconsulship of Asia is unknown. It could have been c. 154–156. See Lightfoot's *The Apostolic Fathers*, I, 646–677; II, 368, 369, 635–637.
[39] This may be the Gaius in Eusebius, *Hist. eccl.* II. 25:6.
[40] On the identity of this Pionius, see the Introduction.

The Long Habit

Lewis Thomas

Lewis Thomas (1913–   ) is president of the Memorial Sloan-Kettering Cancer Center in New York. Before assuming his present post, he served as professor of pediatric research at the University of Minnesota, as chairman of the departments of pathology and medicine and also dean at the New York University-Bellevue Medical Center, and as chairman of pathology and dean at Yale Medical School.

We continue to share with our remotest ancestors the most tangled and evasive attitudes about death, despite the great distance we have come in understanding some of the profound aspects of biology. We have as much distaste for talking about personal death as for thinking about it; it is an indelicacy, like talking in mixed company about venereal disease or abortion in the old days. Death on a grand scale does not bother us in the same special way: we can sit around a dinner table and discuss war, involving 60 million volatilized human deaths, as though we were talking about bad weather; we can watch abrupt bloody death every day, in color, on films and television, without blinking back a tear. It is when the numbers of dead are very small, and very close, that we begin to think in scurrying circles. At the very center of the problem is the naked cold deadness of one's own self, the only reality in nature of which we can have absolute certainty, and it is unmentionable, unthinkable. We may be even less willing to face the issue at first hand than our predecessors because of a secret new hope that maybe it will go away. We like to think, hiding the thought, that with all the marvelous ways in which we seem now to lead nature around by the nose, perhaps we can avoid the central problem if we just become, next year, say, a bit smarter.

"The long habit of living," said Thomas Browne, "indisposeth us to dying." These days, the habit has become an addiction: we are hooked on living; the tenacity of its grip on us, and ours on it, grows in intensity. We cannot think of giving it up, even when living loses its zest—even when we have lost the zest for zest.

We have come a long way in our technologic capacity to put death off, and it is imaginable that we might learn to stall it for even longer periods, perhaps matching the life-spans of the Abkhasian Russians, who are said to go on, springily, for a century and a half. If we can rid ourselves of some of our chronic, degenerative diseases, and cancer, strokes, and coronaries, we might so on and on. It sounds attractive and reasonable, but it is no certainty. If we became free of disease, we would make a much better run of it for the last decade or so, but might still terminate on about the same schedule as now. We may be like the genetically different lines of mice, or like Hayflick's different tissue-culture lines, programmed to die after

Source: From The Lives of a Cell by Lewis Thomas. Copyright © 1974 by Lewis Thomas. Reprinted by permission of Viking Penguin, Inc.

a predetermined number of days, clocked by their genomes. If this is the way it is, some of us will continue to wear out and come unhinged in the sixth decade, and some much later, depending on genetic timetables.

If we ever do achieve freedom from most of today's diseases, or even complete freedom from disease, we will perhaps terminate by drying out and blowing away on a light breeze, but we will still die.

Most of my friends do not like this way of looking at it. They prefer to take it for granted that we only die because we get sick, with one lethal ailment or another, and if we did not have our diseases we might go on indefinitely. Even biologists choose to think this about themselves, despite the evidences of the absolute inevitability of death that surround their professional lives. Everything dies, all around, trees, plankton, lichens, mice, whales, flies, mitochondria. In the simplest creatures it is sometimes difficult to see it as death, since the strands of replicating DNA they leave behind are more conspicuously the living parts of themselves than with us (not that it is fundamentally any different, but it seems so). Flies do not develop a ward round of diseases that carry them off, one by one. They simply age, and die, like flies.

We hanker to go on, even in the face of plain evidence that long, long lives are not necessarily pleasurable in the kind of society we have arranged thus far. We will be lucky if we can postpone the search for new technologies for a while, until we have discovered some satisfactory things to do with the extra time. Something will surely have to be found to take the place of sitting on the porch re-examining one's watch.

Perhaps we would not be so anxious to prolong life if we did not detest so much the sickness of withdrawal. It is astonishing how little information we have about this universal process, with all the other dazzling advances in biology. It is almost as though we wanted not to know about it. Even if we could imagine the act of death in isolation, without any preliminary stage of being struck down by disease, we would be fearful of it.

There are signs that medicine may be taking a new interest in the process, partly from curiosity, partly from an embarrassed realization that we have not been handling this aspect of disease with as much skill as physicians once displayed, back in the days before they became convinced that disease was their solitary and sometimes defeatable enemy. It used to be the hardest and most important of all the services of a good doctor to be on hand at the time of death and to provide comfort, usually in the home. Now it is done in hospitals, in secrecy (one of the reasons for the increased fear of death these days may be that so many people are totally unfamiliar with it; they never actually see it happen in real life). Some of our technology permits us to deny its existence, and we maintain flickers of life for long stretches in one community of cells or another, as though we were keeping a flag flying. Death is not a sudden-all-at-once-affair, cells go down in sequence, one by one. You can, if you like, recover great numbers of them many hours after the lights have gone out, and grow them out in cultures. It takes hours, even days, before the irreversible word finally gets around to all the provinces.

We may be about to rediscover that dying is not such a bad thing to do after all. Sir Willian Osler took this view: he disapproved of people who spoke of the agony of death, maintaining that there was no such thing.

In a nineteenth-century memoir on an expedition in Africa, there is a story by David Livingstone about his own experience of near-death. He was caught by a lion, crushed across the chest in the animal's great jaws, and saved in the instant by a lucky shot from a friend. Later, he remembered the episode in clear detail. He was so amazed by the extraordinary sense of peace, calm, and total painlessness associated with being killed that he constructed a theory that all creatures are provided with a protective physiologic mechanism, switched on at the verge of death, carrying them through in a haze of tranquillity.

I have seen agony in death only once, in a patient with rabies; he remained acutely aware of every stage in the process of his own disintegration over a twenty-four-hour period, right up to his final moment. It was as though, in the special neuropathology of rabies, the switch had been prevented from turning.

We will be having new opportunities to learn more about the physiology of death at first hand, from the increasing numbers of cardiac patients who have been through the whole process and then back again. Judging from what has been found out thus far, from the first generation of people resuscitated from cardiac standstill (already termed the Lazarus syndrome), Osler seems to have been right. Those who remember parts or all of their espisodes do not recall any fear, or anguish. Several people who remained conscious throughout, while appearing to have been quite dead, could only describe a remarkable sensation of detachment. One man underwent coronary occlusion with cessation of the heart and dropped for all practical purposes dead, in front of a hospital; within a few minutes his heart had been restarted by electrodes and he breathed his way back into life. According to his account, the strangest thing was that there were so many people around him, moving so urgently, handling his body with such excitement, while all his awareness was of quietude.

In a recent study of the reaction to dying in patients with obstructive disease of the lungs, it was concluded that the process was considerably more shattering for the professional observers than the observed. Most of the patients appeared to be preparing themselves with equanimity for death, as though intuitively familiar with the business. One elderly woman reported that the only painful and distressing part of the process was in being interrupted; on several occasions she was provided with conventional therapeutic measures to maintain oxygenation or restore fluids and electrolytes, and each time she found the experience of coming back harrowing; she deeply resented the interference with her dying.

I find myself surprised by the thought that dying is an all-right thing to do, but perhaps it should not surprise. It is, after all, the most ancient and fundamental of biologic functions, with its mechanisms worked out with the same attention to detail, the same provision for the advantage of the organism, the same abundance of genetic information for guidance through the stages, that we have long since become accustomed to finding in all the crucial acts of living.

Very well. But even so, if the transformation is a coordinated, integrated physiologic processs in its initial, local stages, there is still that permanent vanishing of consciousness to be accounted for. Are we to be stuck forever with this problem? Where on earth does it go? Is it simply stopped dead in its tracks, lost in humus, wasted? Considering the tendency of nature to find uses for complex and intricate mechanisms, this seems to me unnatural. I prefer to think of it as somehow separated off at the filaments of its attachment, and then drawn like an easy breath back into the membrane of its origin, a fresh memory for a biospherical nervous system, but I have no data on the matter.

This is for another science, another day. It may turn out, as some scientists suggest, that we are forever precluded from investigating consciousness by a sort of indeterminacy principle that stipulates that the very act of looking will make it twitch and blur out of sight. If this is true, we will never learn. I envy some of my friends who are convinced about telepathy; oddly enough, it is my European scientist acquaintances who believe it most freely and take it most lightly. All their aunts have received Communications, and there they sit, with proof of the motility of consciousness at their fingertips, and the making of a new science. It is discouraging to have had the wrong aunts, and never the ghost of a message.

The Courage To Be

Paul Tillich

Paul Tillich (1886–1965), one of the most influential Christian thinkers of the twentieth century, was born in Germany. In 1933, he immigrated to America, where he taught at Union Theological Seminary, Harvard, and the University of Chicago. His major work is the three-volume *Systematic Theology*, but he is author of many other important books, including *Dynamics of Faith*, *The Courage To Be*, and *Theology of Culture*.

The Interdependence of Fear and Anxiety

Anxiety and fear have the same ontological root but they are not the same in actuality. This is common knowledge, but it has been emphasized and overemphasized to such a degree that a reaction against it may occur and wipe out not only the exaggerations but also the truth of the distinction. Fear, as opposed to anxiety, has a definite object (as most authors agree), which can be faced, analyzed, attacked, endured. One can act upon it, and in acting upon it participate in it—even if in the form of struggle. In this way one can take it into one's self-affirmation. Courage can meet every object of fear, because it is an object and makes participation possible. Courage can take the fear produced by a definite object into itself, because this object, however frightful it may be, has a side with which it participates in us and we in it. One could say that as long as there is an *object* of fear love in the sense of participation can conquer fear.

Source: Paul Tillich, *The Courage To Be* (New Haven, Conn., 1952), pp. 36–54, 182–190. Copyright © 1952 by Yale University Press. Reprinted by permission.

But this is not so with anxiety, because anxiety has no object, or rather, in a paradoxical phrase, its object is the negation of every object. Therefore participation, struggle, and love with respect to it are impossible. He who is in anxiety is, insofar as it is mere anxiety, delivered to it without help. Helplessness in the state of anxiety can be observed in animals and humans alike. It expresses itself in loss of direction, inadequate reactions, lack of "intentionality" (the being related to meaningful contents of knowledge or will). The reason for this sometimes striking behavior is the lack of an object on which the subject (in the state of anxiety) can concentrate. The only object is the threat itself, but not the source of the threat, because the source of the threat is "nothingness."

One might ask whether this threatening "nothing" is not the unknown, the indefinite possibility of an actual threat? Does not anxiety cease in the moment in which a known object of fear appears? Anxiety then would be fear of the unknown. But this is an insufficient explanation of anxiety. For there are innumerable realms of the unknown, different for each subject, and faced without any anxiety. It is the unknown of a special type which is met with anxiety. It is the unknown which by its very nature cannot be known, because it is nonbeing.

Fear and anxiety are distinguished but not separated. They are immanent within each other: The sting of fear is anxiety, and anxiety strives toward fear. Fear is being afraid of something, a pain, the rejection by a person or a group, the loss of something or somebody, the moment of dying. But in the anticipation of the threat originating in these things, it is not the negativity itself which they will bring upon the subject that is frightening but the anxiety about the possible implications of this negativity. The outstanding example—and more than an example—is the fear of dying. Insofar as it is *fear* its object is the anticipated event of being killed by sickness or an accident and thereby suffering agony and the loss of everything. Insofar as it is *anxiety* its object is the absolutely unknown "after death," the nonbeing which remains nonbeing even if it is filled with images of our present experience. The dreams in Hamlet's soliloquy, "to be or not to be," which we may have after death and which make cowards of us all are frightful not because of their manifest content but because of their power to symbolize the threat of nothingness, in religious terms of "eternal death." The symbols of hell created by Dante produce anxiety not because of their objective imagery but because they express the "nothingness" whose power is experienced in the anxiety of guilt. Each of the situations described in the *Inferno* could be met by courage on the basis of participation and love. But of course the meaning is that this is impossible; in other words they are not real situations but symbols of the objectless, of nonbeing.

The fear of death determines the element of anxiety in every fear. Anxiety, if not modified by the fear of an object, anxiety in its nakedness, is always the anxiety of ultimate nonbeing. Immediately seen, anxiety is the painful feeling of not being able to deal with the threat of a special situation. But a more exact analysis shows that in the anxiety about any special situation anxiety about the human situation as such is implied. It is the anxiety of not being able to preserve one's own being which underlies every fear and is the frightening element in it. In the moment, therefore, in which "naked anxiety" lays hold of the mind, the previous objects of fear cease to be definite objects. They appear as what they always were in part, symptoms of man's basic anxiety. As such they are beyond the reach of even the most courageous attack upon them.

This situation drives the anxious subject to establish objects of fear. Anxiety strives to become fear, because fear can be met by courage. It is impossible for a finite being to stand naked anxiety for more than a flash of time. People who have experienced these moments, as for instance some mystics in their visions of the "night of the soul," or Luther under the despair of the demonic assaults, or Nietzsche-Zarathustra in the experience of the "great disgust," have told of the unimaginable horror of it. This horror is ordinarily avoided by the transformation of anxiety into fear of something, no matter what. The human mind is not only, as Calvin has said, a permanent factory of idols, it is also a permanent factory of fears—the first in order to escape God, the second in order to escape anxiety; and there is a relation between the two. For facing the God who is really God means facing also the absolute threat of nonbeing. The "naked absolute" (to use a phrase of Luther's) produces "naked anxiety"; for it is the extinction of every finite self-affirmation, and not a possible object of fear and courage. . . . But ultimately the attempts to transform anxiety into fear are vain. The basic anxiety, the anxiety of a finite being about the threat of nonbeing, cannot be eliminated. It belongs to existence itself.

Types of Anxiety

The Three Types of Anxiety and the Nature of Man. Nonbeing is dependent on the being it negates. "Dependent" means two things. It points first of all to the ontological priority of being over nonbeing. The term nonbeing itself indicates this, and it is logically necessary. There could be no negation if there were no preceding affirmation to be negated. Certainly one can describe being in terms of non-nonbeing; and one can justify such a description by pointing to the astonishing prerational fact that there is something and not nothing. One could say that "being is the negation of the primordial night of nothingness." But in doing so one must realize that such an aboriginal nothing would be neither nothing nor something, that it becomes nothing only in contrast to something; in other words, that the ontological status of nonbeing as nonbeing is dependent on being. Secondly, nonbeing is dependent on the special qualities of being. In itself nonbeing has no quality and no difference of qualities. But it gets them in relation to being. The character of the negation of being is determined by that in being which is negated. This makes it possible to speak of qualities of nonbeing and, consequently, of types of anxiety.

Up to now we have used the term nonbeing without differentiation, while in the discussion of courage several forms of self-affirmation were mentioned. They correspond to different forms of anxiety and are understandable only in correlation with them. I suggest that we distinguish three types of anxiety according to the three directions in which nonbeing threatens being. Nonbeing threatens man's ontic self-affirmation, relatively in terms of fate, absolutely in terms of death. It threatens man's spiritual self-affirmation, relatively in terms of emptiness, absolutely in terms of meaninglessness. It threatens man's moral self-affirmation, relatively in terms of guilt, absolutely in terms of condemnation. The awareness of this threefold threat is anxiety appearing in three forms, that of fate and death (briefly, the anxiety of death), that of emptiness and loss of meaning (briefly, the anxiety of meaninglessness), that of guilt and condemnation (briefly, the anxiety of condemnation). In all three forms anxiety is existential in the sense that it belongs to existence as such and not to an abnormal state of mind as in neurotic (and psychotic) anxiety. . . .

The Anxiety of Fate and Death. Fate and death are the way in which our ontic self-affirmation is threatened by nonbeing. "Ontic," from the Greek *on*, "being," means here the basic self-affirmation of a being in its simple existence. (Onto-logical designates the philosophical analysis of the nature of being.) The anxiety of fate and death is most basic, most universal, and inescapable. All attempts to argue it away are futile. Even if the so-called arguments for the "immortality of the soul" had argumentative power (which they do not have) they would not convince existentially. For existentially everybody is aware of the complete loss of self which biological extinction implies. The unsophisticated mind knows instinctively what sophisticated ontology formulates: that reality has the basic structure of self-world correlation and that with the disappearance of the one side, the world, the other side, the self, also disappears, and what remains is their common ground but not their structural correlation. It has been observed that the anxiety of death increases with the increase of individualization and that people in collectivistic cultures are less open to this type of anxiety. The observation is correct yet the explanation that there is no basic anxiety about death in collectivist cultures is wrong. The reason for the difference from more individualized civilizations is that the special type of courage which characterizes collectivism . . . , as long as it is unshaken, allays the anxiety of death. But the very fact that courage has to be created through many internal and external (psychological and ritual) activities and symbols shows that basic anxiety has to be overcome even in collectivism. Without its at least potential presence neither war nor the criminal law in these societies would be understandable. If there were no fear of death, the threat of the law or of a superior enemy would be without effect—which it obviously is not. Man as man in every civilization is anxiously aware of the threat of nonbeing and needs the courage to affirm himself in spite of it.

The anxiety of death is the permanent horizon within which the anxiety of fate is at work. For the threat against man's ontic self-affirmation is not only the absolute threat of death but also the relative threat of fate. Certainly the anxiety of death overshadows all concrete anxieties and gives them their ultimate seriousness. They have, however, a certain independence and, ordinarily, a more immediate impact than the anxiety of death. The term "fate" for this whole group of anxieties stresses one element which is common to all of them: their contingent character, their unpredictability, the impossibility of showing their meaning and purpose. One can describe this in terms of the categorical structure of our experience. One can show the contingency of our temporal being, the fact that we exist in this and no other period of time, beginning in a contingent moment, ending in a contingent moment, filled with experiences which are contingent themselves with respect to quality and quantity. One can show the contingency of our spatial being (our finding ourselves in this and no other place, and the strangeness of this place in spite of its familiarity); the contingent character of ourselves and the place from which we look at our world; and the contingent character of the reality at which we look, that is, our world. Both could be different: this is their contingency and this produces the anxiety about our spatial existence. One can show the contingency of the causal interdependence of which one is a part, both with respect to the past and to the present, the vicissitudes coming from our world and the hidden forces in the depths of our own self. Contingent does not mean causally undetermined but it means that the determining causes of our existence have no ultimate necessity. They are given, and they cannot be logically derived. Contingently we are put into the whole web of causal relations. Contingently we are determined by them in every moment and thrown out by them in the last moment.

Fate is the rule of contingency, and the anxiety about fate is based on the finite being's awareness of being contingent in every respect, of having no ultimate necessity. Fate is usually identified with necessity in the sense of an inescapable causal determination. Yet it is not causal necessity that makes fate a matter of anxiety but the lack of ultimate necessity, the irrationality, the impenetrable darkness of fate.

The threat of nonbeing to man's ontic self-affirmation is absolute in the threat of death, relative in the threat of fate. But the relative threat is a threat only because in its background stands the absolute threat. Fate would not produce inescapable anxiety without death behind it. And death stands behind fate and its contingencies not only in the last moment when one is thrown out of existence but in every moment within existence. Nonbeing is omnipresent and produces anxiety even where an immediate threat of death is absent. It stands behind the experience that we are driven, together with everything else, from the past toward the future without a moment of time which does not vanish immediately. It stands behind the insecurity and homelessness of our social and individual existence. It stands behind the attacks on our power of being in body and soul by weakness, disease, and accidents. In all these forms fate actualizes itself, and through them the anxiety of nonbeing takes hold of us. We try to transform the anxiety into fear and to meet courageously the objects in which the threat is embodied. We succeed partly, but somehow we are aware of the fact that it is not these objects with which we struggle that produce the anxiety but the human situation as such. Out of this the question arises: Is there a courage to be, a courage to affirm oneself in spite of the threat against man's ontic self-affirmation?

The Anxiety of Emptiness and Meaninglessness. Nonbeing threatens man as a whole, and therefore threatens his spiritual as well as his ontic self-affirmation. Spiritual self-affirmation occurs in every moment in which man lives creatively in the various spheres of meaning. Creative, in this context, has the sense not of original creativity as performed by the genius but of living spontaneously, in action and reaction, with the contents of one's cultural life. In order to be spiritually creative one need not be what is called a creative artist or scientist or statesman, but one must be able to participate meaningfully in their original creations. Such a participation is creative insofar as it changes that in which one participates, even if in very small ways. The creative transformation of a language by the interdependence of the creative poet or writer and the many who are influenced by him directly or indirectly and react spontaneously to him is an outstanding example. Everyone who lives creatively in meanings affirms himself as a participant in these meanings. He affirms himself as receiving and transforming reality creatively. He loves himself as participating in the spiritual life and as loving its contents. He loves them because they are his own fulfillment and because they are actualized through him. The scientist loves both the truth he discovers and himself insofar as he discovers it. He is held by the content of his discovery. This is what one can call "spiritual self-affirmation." And if he has not discovered but only participates in the discovery, it is equally spiritual self-affirmation.

Such an experience presupposes that the spiritual life is taken seriously, that it is a matter of ultimate concern. And this again presupposes that in it and through it ultimate reality becomes manifest. A spiritual life in which this is not experienced is threatened by nonbeing in the two forms in which it attacks spiritual self-affirmation: emptiness and meaninglessness.

We use the term meaninglessness for the absolute threat of nonbeing to spiritual self-affirmation, and the term emptiness for the relative threat to it. They are no more identical than are the threat of death and fate. But in the background of emptiness lies meaninglessness as death lies in the background of the vicissitudes of fate.

The anxiety of meaninglessness is anxiety about the loss of an ultimate concern, of a meaning which gives meaning to all meanings. This anxiety is aroused by the loss of a spiritual center, of an answer, however symbolic and indirect, to the question of the meaning of existence.

The anxiety of emptiness is aroused by the threat of nonbeing to the special contents of the spiritual life. A belief breaks down through external events or inner processes: one is cut off from creative participation in a sphere of culture, one feels frustrated about something which one had passionately affirmed, one is driven from devotion to one object to devotion to another and again on to another, because the meaning of each of them vanishes and the creative eros is transformed into indifference or aversion. Everything is tried and nothing satisfies. The contents of the tradition, however excellent, however praised, however loved once, lose their power to give content *today*. And present culture is even less able to provide the content. Anxiously one turns away from all concrete contents and looks for an ultimate meaning, only to discover that it was precisely the loss of a spiritual center which took away the meaning from the special contents of the spiritual life. But a spiritual center cannot be produced intentionally, and the attempt to produce it only produces deeper anxiety. The anxiety of emptiness drives us to the abyss of meaninglessness.

Emptiness and loss of meaning are expressions of the threat of nonbeing to the spiritual life. This threat is implied in man's finitude and actualized by man's estrangement. It can be described in terms of doubt, its creative and its destructive function in man's spiritual life. Man is able to ask because he is separated *from*, while participating *in*, what he is asking about. In every question an element of doubt, the awareness of not having, is implied. In systematic questioning systematic doubt is effective; e.g. of the Cartesian type. This element of doubt is a condition of all spiritual life. The threat to spiritual life is not doubt as an element but the total doubt. If the awareness of not having has swallowed the awareness of having, doubt has ceased to be methodological asking and has become existential despair. On the way to this situation the spiritual life tries to maintain itself as long as possible by clinging to affirmations which are not yet undercut, be they traditions, autonomous convictions, or emotional preferences. And if it is impossible to remove the doubt, one courageously accepts it without surrendering one's convictions. One takes the risk of going astray and the anxiety of this risk upon oneself. In this way one avoids the extreme situation—till it becomes unavoidable and the despair of truth becomes complete.

Then man tries another way out: Doubt is based on man's separation from the whole of reality, on his lack of universal participation, on the isolation of his individual self. So he tries to break out of this situation, to identify himself with something transindividual, to surrender his separation and self-relatedness. He flees from his freedom of asking and answering for himself to a situation in which no further questions can be asked and the answers to previous questions are im-imposed on him authoritatively. In order to avoid the risk of asking and doubting he surrenders the right to ask and to doubt. He surrenders himself in order to save his spiritual life. He "escapes from his freedom" (Fromm) in order to escape the anxiety of meaninglessness. Now he is no longer lonely, not in existential doubt, not in despair. He "participates" and affirms by participation the contents of his spiritual life. Meaning is saved, but the self is sacrificed. And since the conquest of doubt was a matter of sacrifice, the sacrifice of the freedom of the self, it leaves a mark on the regained certitude: a fanatical self-assertiveness. Fanaticism is the correlate to spiritual self-surrender: it shows the anxiety which it was supposed to conquer, by attacking with disproportionate violence those who disagree and who demonstrate by their disagreement elements in the spiritual life of the fanatic which he must suppress in himself. Because he must suppress them in himself he must suppress them in others. His anxiety forces him to persecute dissenters. The weakness of the fanatic is that those whom he fights have a secret hold upon him; and to this weakness he and his group finally succumb.

It is not always personal doubt that undermines and empties a system of ideas and values. It can be the fact that they are no longer understood in their original power of expressing the human situation and of answering existential human questions. (This is largely the case with the doctrinal symbols of Christianity.) Or they lose their meaning because the actual conditions of the present period are so different from those in which the spiritual contents were created that new creations are needed. (This was largely the case with artistic expression before the industrial revolution.) In such circumstances a slow process of waste of the spiritual contents occurs, unnoticeable in the beginning, realized with a shock as it progresses, producing the anxiety of meaninglessness at its end.

Ontic and spiritual self-affirmation must be distinguished but they cannot be separated. Man's being includes his relation to meanings. He is human only by understanding and shaping reality, both his world and himself, according to meanings and values. His being is spiritual even in the most primitive expressions of the most primitive human being. In the "first" meaningful sentence all the richness of man's spiritual life is potentially present. Therefore the threat to his spiritual being is a threat to his whole being. The most revealing expression of this fact is the desire to throw away one's ontic existence rather than stand the despair of emptiness and meaninglessness. The death instinct is not an ontic but a spiritual phenomenon. Freud identified this reason to the meaninglessness of the never-ceasing and never-satisfied libido with man's essential nature. But it is only an expression of his existential self-estrangement and of the disintegration of his spiritual life into meaninglessness. If, on the other hand, the ontic self-affirmation is weakened by nonbeing, spiritual indifference and emptiness can be the consequence, producing a circle of ontic and spiritual negativity. Nonbeing threatens from both sides, the ontic and the spiritual; if it threatens the one side it also threatens the other.

The Anxiety of Guilt and Condemnation. Nonbeing threatens from a third side; it threatens man's moral self-affirmation. Man's being, ontic as well as spiritual, is not only given to him but also demanded of him. He is responsible for it; literally, he is required to answer, if he is asked, what he has made of himself. He who asks him is his judge, namely he himself, who, at the same time, stands against him. This situation produces the anxiety which, in relative terms, is the anxiety of guilt; in absolute terms, the anxiety of self-rejection or condemnation. Man is essentially "finite freedom"; freedom not in the sense of indeterminacy but in the sense of being able to determine himself through decisions in the center of his being. Man, as finite freedom, is free within the contingencies of his finitude. But within these limits he is asked to make of himself what he is supposed to become, to fulfill his destiny. In every act of moral self-affirmation man contributes to the fulfillment of his destiny, to the actualization of what he potentially is. It is the task of ethics to describe the nature of this fulfillment, in philosophical or theological terms. But however the norm is formulated man has the power of acting against it, of contradicting his essential being, of losing his destiny. And under the conditions of man's estrangement from himself this is an actuality. Even in what he considers his best deed nonbeing is present and prevents it from being perfect. A profound ambiguity between good and evil permeates everything he does, because it permeates his personal being as such. Nonbeing is mixed with being in his moral self-affirmation as it is in his spiritual and ontic self-affirmation. The awareness of this ambiguity is the feeling of guilt. The judge who is oneself and who stands against oneself, he who "knows with" (conscience) everything we do and are gives a negative judgment, experienced by us as guilt. The anxiety of guilt shows the same complex characteristics as the anxiety about ontic and spiritual nonbeing. It is present in every moment of moral self-awareness and can drive us toward complete self-rejection, to the feeling of being condemned—not to an external punishment but to the despair of having lost our destiny.

To avoid this extreme situation man tries to transform the anxiety of guilt into moral action regardless of its imperfection and ambiguity. Courageously he takes nonbeing into his moral self-affirmation. This can happen in two ways, according to the duality of the tragic and the personal in man's situation, the first based on the contingencies of fate, the second on the responsibility of freedom. The first way can lead to a defiance of negative judgments and the moral demands on which they are based; the second way can lead to a moral rigor and the self-satisfaction derived from it. In both of them—usually called anonism and legalism

—the anxiety of guilt lies in the background and breaks again and again into the open, producing the extreme situation of moral despair.

Nonbeing in a moral respect must be distinguished but cannot be separated from ontic and spiritual nonbeing. The anxiety of the one type is immanent in the anxieties of the other types. The famous words of Paul about "sin as the sting of death" point to the immanence of the anxiety of guilt within the fear of death. And the threat of fate and death has always awakened and increased the consciousness of guilt. The threat of moral nonbeing was experienced in and through the threat of ontic nonbeing. The contingencies of fate received moral interpretation: fate executes the negative moral judgment by attacking and perhaps destroying the ontic foundation of the morally rejected personality. The two forms of anxiety provoke and augment each other. In the same way spiritual and moral nonbeing are interdependent. Obedience to the moral norm, i.e. to one's own essential being, excludes emptiness and meaninglessness in their radical forms. If the spiritual contents have lost their power the self-affirmation of the moral personality is a way in which meaning can be rediscovered. The simple call to duty can save from emptiness, while the disintegration of the moral consciousness is an almost irresistible basis for the attack of spiritual nonbeing. On the other hand, existential doubt can undermine moral self-affirmation by throwing into the abyss of skepticism not only every moral principle but the meaning of moral self-affirmation as such. In this case the doubt is felt as guilt, while at the same time guilt is undermined by doubt.

Theism Transcended

The courage to take meaninglessness into itself presupposes a relation to the ground of being which we have called "absolute faith." It is without a *special* content, yet it is not without content. The content of absolute faith is the "God above God." Absolute faith and its consequences, the courage that takes the radical doubt, the doubt about God, into itself, transcends the theistic idea of God.

Theism can mean the unspecified affirmation of God. Theism in this sense does not say what it means if it uses the name of God. Because of the traditional and psychological connotations of the word God such an empty theism can produce a reverent mood if it speaks of God. Politicians, dictators, and other people who wish to use rhetoric to make an impression on their audience like to use the word God in this sense. It produces the feeling in their listeners that the speaker is serious and morally trustworthy. This is especially successful if they can brand their foes as atheistic. On a higher level people without a definite religious commitment like to call themselves theistic, not for special purposes but because they cannot stand a world without God, whatever this God may be. They need some of the connotations of the word God and they are afraid of what they call atheism. On the highest level of this kind of theism the name of God is used as a poetic or practical symbol, expressing a profound emotional state or the highest ethical idea. It is a theism which stands on the boundary line between the second type of theism and what we call "theism transcended." But it is still too indefinite to cross this boundary line. The atheistic negation of this whole type of theism is as vague as the theism itself. It may produce an irreverent mood and angry reaction of those who take their theistic affirmation seriously. It may even be felt as justified against the rhetorical-political abuse of the name God, but it is ultimately as irrelevant as the theism which it negates. It cannot reach the state of despair any more than the theism against which it fights can reach the state of faith.

Theism can have another meaning, quite contrary to the first one: it can be the name of what we have called the divine-human encounter. In this case it points to those elements in the Jewish-Christian tradition which emphasize the person-to-person relationship with God. Theism in this sense emphasizes the personalistic passages in the Bible and the Protestant creeds, the personalistic image of God, the word as the tool of creation and revelation, the ethical and social character of the kingdom of God, the personal nature of human faith and divine forgiveness, the historical vision of the universe, the idea of a divine purpose, the infinite distance between creator and creature, the absolute separation between God and the world, the conflict between holy God and sinful man, the person-to-person character of prayer and practical devotion. Theism in this sense is the nonmystical side of biblical religion and historical Christianity. Atheism from the point of view of this theism is the human attempt to escape the divine-human encounter. It is an existential—not a theoretical—problem.

Theism has a third meaning, a strictly theological one. Theological theism is, like every theology, dependent on the religious substance which it conceptualizes. It is dependent on theism in the first sense insofar as it tries to prove the necessity of affirming God in some way; it usually develops the so-called arguments for the "existence" of God. But it is more dependent on theism in the second sense insofar as it tries to establish a doctine of God which transforms the person-to-person encounter with God into a doctrine about two persons who may or may not meet but who have a reality independent of each other.

Now theism in the first sense must be transcended because it is irrelevant, and theism in the second sense must be transcended because it is one-sided. But theism in the third sense must be transcended because it is wrong. It is bad theology. This can be shown by a more penetrating analysis. The God of theological theism is a being beside others and as such a part of the whole of reality. He certainly is considered its most important part, but as a part and therefore as subjected to the structure of the whole. He is supposed to be beyond the ontological elements and categories which constitute reality. But every statement subjects him to them. He is seen as a self which has a world, as an ego which is related to a thou, as a cause which is separated from its effect, as having a definite space and an endless time. He is a being, not being-itself. As such he is bound to the subject-object structure of reality, he is an object for us as subjects. At the same time we are objects for him as a subject. And this is decisive for the necessity of transcending theological theism. For God as a subject makes me into an object which is nothing more than an object. He deprives me of my subjectivity because he is all-powerful and all-knowing. I revolt and try to make *him* into an object, but the revolt fails and becomes desperate. God appears as the invincible tyrant, the being in contrast with whom all other beings are without freedom and subjectivity. He is equated with the recent tyrants who with the help of terror try to transform everything into a mere object, a thing among things, a cog in the machine they control. He becomes the model of everything against which Existentialism revolted. This is the God Nietzsche said had to be killed because nobody can tolerate being made into a mere object of absolute knowledge and absolute control. This is the deepest root of atheism. It is an atheism which is justified as the reaction against theological theism and its disturbing implications. It is also the deepest root of the Existentialist despair and the widespread anxiety of meaninglessness in our period.

Theism in all its forms is transcended in the experience we have called absolute faith. It is the accepting of the acceptance without somebody or something that accepts. It is the power of being-itself that accepts and gives the courage to be. This is the highest point to which our analysis has brought us. It cannot be described in the way the God of all forms of theism can be described. It cannot be described in mystical terms either. It transcends both mysticism and personal encounter, as it transcends both the courage to be as a part and the courage to be as oneself.

The God Above God and the Courage To Be

The ultimate source of the courage to be is the "God above God"; this is the result of our demand to transcend theism. Only if the God of theism is transcended can the anxiety of doubt and meaninglessness be taken into the courage to be. The God above God is the object of all mystical longing, but mysticism also must be transcended in order to reach him. Mysticism does not take seriously the concrete and the doubt concerning the concrete. It plunges directly into the ground of being and meaning, and leaves the concrete, the world of finite values and meanings, behind. Therefore it does not solve the problem of meaninglessness. In terms of the present religious situation this means that Eastern mysticism is not the solution of the problems of Western Existentialism, although many people attempt this solution. The God above the God of theism is not the devaluation of the meanings which doubt has thrown into the abyss of meaninglessness; he is their potential restitution. Nevertheless absolute faith agrees with the faith implied in mysticism in that both transcend the theistic objectivation of a God who is a being. For mysticism such a God is not more real than any finite being, for the courage to be such a God has disappeared in the abyss of meaninglessness with every other value and meaning.

The God above the God of theism is present, although hidden, in every divine-human encounter. Biblical religion as well as Protestant theology are aware of the paradoxical character of this encounter. They are aware that if God encounters man God is neither object nor subject and is therefore above the scheme into which theism has forced him. They are aware that personalism with respect to God is balanced by a transpersonal presence of the divine. They are aware that forgiveness can be accepted only if the power of acceptance is effective in man— biblically speaking, if the power of grace is effective in man. They are aware of the paradoxical character of every prayer, of speaking to somebody to whom you cannot speak because he is not "somebody," of asking somebody of whom you cannot ask anything because he gives or gives not before you ask, of saying "thou" to somebody who is nearer to the I than the I is to itself. Each of these paradoxes drives the religious consciousness toward a God above the God of theism.

The courage to be which is rooted in the experience of the God above the God of theism unites and transcends the courage to be as a part and the courage to be as oneself. It avoids both the loss of oneself by participation and the loss of one's world by individualization. The acceptance of the God above the God of theism makes us a part of that which is not also a part but is the ground of the whole. Therefore our self is not lost in a larger whole, which submerges it in the life of a limited group. If the self participates in the power of being-itself it receives itself back. For the power of being acts through the power of the individual selves. It does not swallow them as every limited whole, every collectivism, and every conformism does. This is why the Church, which stands for the power of being-itself or for the God who transcends the God of the religions, claims to be the meditator of the courage to be. A church which is based on the authority of the God of theism cannot make such a claim. It inescapably develops into a collectivist or semicollectivist system itself.

But a church which raises itself in its message and its devotion to the God above the God of theism without sacrificing its concrete symbols can mediate a courage which takes doubt and meaninglessness into itself. It is the Church under the Cross which alone can do this, the Church which preaches the Crucified who cried to God who remained his God after the God of confidence had left him in the darkness of doubt and meaninglessness. To be as a part in such a church is to receive a courage to be in which one cannot lose one's self and in which one receives one's world.

Absolute faith, or the state of being grasped by the God beyond God, is not a state which appears beside other states of the mind. It never is something separated and definite, an event which could be isolated and described. It is always a movement in, with, and under other states of the mind. It is the situation on the boundary of man's possibilities. It *is* this boundary. Therefore it is both the courage of despair and the courage in and above every courage. It is not a place where one can live, it is without the safety of words and concepts, it is without a name, a church, a cult, a theology. But it is moving in the depth of all of them. It is the power of being, in which they participate and of which they are fragmentary expressions.

One can become aware of it in the anxiety of fate and death when the traditional symbols, which enable men to stand the vicissitudes of fate and the horror of death, have lost their power. When "providence" has become a superstition and "immortality" something imaginary that which once was the power in these symbols can still be present and create the courage to be in spite of the experience of a chaotic world and a finite existence. The Stoic courage returns but not as the faith in universal reason. It returns as the absolute faith which says Yes to being without seeing anything concrete which could conquer the nonbeing in fate and death.

And one can become aware of the God above the God of theism in the anxiety of guilt and condemnation when the traditional symbols that enable men to withstand the anxiety of guilt and condemnation have lost their power. When "divine judgment" is interpreted as a psychological complex and forgiveness as a remnant of the "father-image," what once was the power in those symbols can still be present and create the courage to be in spite of the experience of an infinite gap between what we are and what we ought to be. The Lutheran courage returns but not supported by the faith in a judging and forgiving God. It returns in terms of the absolute faith, which says Yes although there is no special power that conquers guilt. The courage to take the anxiety of meaninglessness upon oneself is the boundary line up to which the courage to be can go. Beyond it is mere nonbeing. Within it all forms of courage are re-established in the power of the God above the God of theism. *The courage to be is rooted in the God who appears when God has disappeared in the anxiety of doubt.*